THE PENGUIN BOOK OF

# Victorian Verse

# THE PENGUIN BOOK OF
# Victorian Verse

*Edited with an introduction and notes by*

## DANIEL KARLIN

## ALLEN LANE
## THE PENGUIN PRESS

ALLEN LANE
THE PENGUIN PRESS

Published by the Penguin Group
Penguin Books Ltd, 27 Wrights Lane, London W8 5TZ, England
Penguin Books USA Inc., 375 Hudson Street, New York, New York 10014, USA
Penguin Books Australia Ltd, Ringwood, Victoria, Australia
Penguin Books Canada Ltd, 10 Alcorn Avenue, Toronto, Ontario, Canada M4V 3B2
Penguin Books (NZ) Ltd, 182–190 Wairau Road, Auckland 10, New Zealand

Penguin Books Ltd, Registered Offices: Harmondsworth, Middlesex, England

First published 1997

1 3 5 7 9 10 8 6 4 2

Set in 10.75/13.5pt Postscript Monotype Sabon
Typeset by Cambridge Photosetting Services
Printed in Great Britain by Clays Ltd, St Ives plc

A CIP catalogue record for this book is available from the British Library

ISBN 0-713-99049-X

*In memory of my beloved stepfather,*
*Dr John Anthony Henderson, CBE*
*1915–92*

# Contents

# Preface

I take the term 'Victorian poetry' to mean poetry written and published in Britain and Ireland in the years of Queen Victoria's reign, that is 1837 to 1901. Most of the poems in this anthology conform to this definition, and the exceptions (such as Tennyson's 'The Lady of Shalott', some unpublished poems by, among others, Emily Brontë and Robert Louis Stevenson, and the poetry of Hopkins) are, I hope, not controversial. The use of chronological and geographical boundaries is neutral in intention and of practical, as opposed to theoretical, value. The term 'Victorian' still has currency: what it means is debatable, but it means something different from 'Romantic', 'nineteenth-century' or 'modern'. I have preferred this negative way of drawing boundaries to others which seem to me to raise more problems than they solve.

Apart from the Prelude (a kind of textual frontispiece) the anthology is structured by author, and the sequence by date of birth.[1] There is no point in engaging here in a detailed defence of this system as against others. All are flawed; this one stems from my belief that the work of the major poets in the anthology ought to be kept together, and that ordering by date of birth yields a more intuitive sequence than by date of first publication. I hope that readers will still be able to gain a sense of the ways in which older and younger poets overlapped and responded to each other. I have also provided a reasonably detailed index so that poems can be grouped by theme. Authors' names are given in preference to pseudonyms, except where the pseudonym has displaced the name in popular use (e.g. Lewis Carroll, George Eliot; but B. W. Procter, not 'Barry Cornwall', James Thomson, not 'B. V.'). With this exception,

---

1. In cases where the date of birth is not known, I have assigned an arbitrary date twenty-five years before the date of the poet's earliest known publication. These writers are marked by a symbol ✳ in the table of contents.

names follow title-pages; in cases where this principle does not apply I have retained familiar forms: Gerard Manley Hopkins, Emily Brontë.

In general I have included only complete poems, but I have not adhered slavishly to this practice. Most period anthologies, mine included, are unavoidably biased towards shorter works, because more of them take up less room. On the other hand I have included a number of works in their entirety which have usually only been given in extracts, notably sequences such as *Sonnets from the Portuguese*, *Modern Love*, and *The City of Dreadful Night*. I regret not being able to include in its entirety the greatest sequence-poem of the period, *In Memoriam*, but too much other Tennyson, or too much else of other poets, would have to have been left out.

The texts of the poems are taken where possible from collected editions published within the period, otherwise from the original volumes or other form of publication. Obvious misprints have been silently corrected. In a few cases (FitzGerald's *Rubáiyát of Omar Khayyám* is the obvious example) I have preferred the text of an early edition. Hardy and Yeats appear here in 'Victorian' dress, which seems proper given the late dates of their final collected editions. Several poets present unusual textual difficulties, and these have been dealt with on an individual basis. The texts of some of the Brontës' poems, for example, have been taken from modern editions, because the contemporary texts are defective. The poems of John Clare are taken from a modern edition which transcribes them directly from the manuscripts; I have normalized them to a very small extent, by regularizing initial capitals, replacing ampersands with 'and' and supplying a few apostrophes for words such as 'I've' and 'o'er', but leaving other punctuation and spelling untouched.

I have translated all foreign and dialect words where familiarity or context did not give a sufficient clue; otherwise the poems are not annotated. Victorian poetry can be wide-rangingly learned and allusive, its vocabulary rich and often playfully odd, its syntax far from transparent. The question of where to stop was the main bar to starting; that, and the belief that readers of an anthology would prefer poems to notes. For the same reason I have kept biographical information about each poet to a minimum. Concision sometimes produces odd effects, but I hope readers will find even a brief notation of dates and places useful and suggestive.

# Acknowledgements

Many people made suggestions for what should go in, or be left out; I am grateful to all of them, especially those who wrote to me in response to requests in the *TLS* and elsewhere: Alan Brownjohn, Stephen Collins, Philip Davis, Donald Hickling, Linda K. Hughes, Charlotte Mitchell, Kenneth Muir, Perry Pontac and Warren Keith Wright. Naturally I take responsibility for all my decisions.

Part of the Introduction was given as a paper to the graduate seminar at the University of Birmingham, and I am grateful to those who attended for their comments and suggestions. I have discussed the anthology with many colleagues at University College London, always with profit: Philip Horne, Samantha Matthews, Peter Swaab and Henry Woudhuysen have been especially patient in listening and responding. I could not have compiled the subject index without Joe Britton's help and advice. I would also like to thank Tim Scott for lending the publisher his copy of *A Book of Nonsense* by Edward Lear from which the illustrations on pages 275–80 have been taken.

To Pat O'Shea, Sylvia Adamson and John Woolford I owe a continuing and inestimable debt of friendly and forthright criticism.

I have benefited from every anthology of Victorian verse which I have consulted, and I have consulted many. I single out my predecessor George MacBeth's selection for Penguin Classics, first published in 1969, and Angela Leighton and Margaret Reynolds's *Victorian Women Poets* (Blackwell, 1995): both are original, strong-minded volumes in content and comment, and I have been helped and prompted by them even in disagreement; both drew my attention to many excellent and unfamiliar poems. As for Christopher Ricks's *New Oxford Book of Victorian Verse* (1987), it is as 'crumpled, dogs-eared and defaced' as any anthologist could wish, from much and envious use. I take this opportunity of saying how much my knowledge and love of poetry owe to his teaching and example.

# Introduction

## 1. BAD DREAMS

Ripple, tinkle, ripple, tinkle,
  Gladly-babbling gentle sea,
Stop and sprinkle drops that twinkle
  Wavelet crystal, wavelet free.
    Ripple, tinkle;
    Babble, sea;
    Twinkle, sprinkle
    Melody.

Yes, some Victorian poetry really is like that. This particular example comes from a poem called 'Sunium' by 'Caerleon', a pseudonym which time has – mercifully, perhaps – refused to uncover.[1] 'Sunium' bears some, if not all, of the stigmas of Victorian poetry. A poetry of sentiment, as opposed to feeling; of dreaminess and retreat from the world, abandoning the 'hard' topics of writing for those of idealization and fantasy. 'Are you the poet?' Mr Snodgrass is asked in chapter 3 of *Pickwick Papers*. 'I – I do a little in that way,' confesses Mr Snodgrass (the word *little* combines his modesty with Dickens's belittlement).[2] 'Ah!' his interlocutor says, 'poetry makes life what lights and music do the stage – strip the one of its false embellishments and the other of its illusions,

1. The poem appeared in *Waifs and Strays*, London: Provost & Co., 1876; I cannot find 'Caerleon' in any dictionary of literary pseudonyms, and he seems to have published nothing else. (I am assuming it is a 'he'; the internal evidence suggests so, but I can't be conclusive.) A very different poem by 'Caerleon' is included in this anthology, and discussed at the end of the Introduction.
2. In chapter 15, just before the description of Mrs Leo Hunter (see below, p. lvi), Mr Snodgrass is again referred to as the author of 'some beautiful little poems'. To be fair, Jingle offers a rival version of poetry in chapter 2: 'Epic poem, – ten thousand lines – revolution of July – composed it on the spot – Mars by day, Apollo by night, – bang the field-piece, twang the lyre.' But we hear no more of Jingle's muse.

and what is there real in either to live or care for?' 'Very true,' replies Mr Snodgrass, who hasn't read the small print on this agreement. Victorian poets struggled constantly to escape the imputation of 'false embellishment' and 'illusion' which still clings to their collective achievement. A related accusation is of emptiness, or at best generality: Walt Whitman found a warning in even the 'finest verbalism' of Tennyson – 'such a latent charm in mere words, cunning collocutions, and in the voice ringing them'.[3] And last, self-indulgence: Victorian poets arguably suffered in comparison with novelists and dramatists from a lack of interference with their work. Robert Browning boasted that 'for fifty years [I] have stipulated that my publishers should never read a line of the work they were to publish until it was in *corrected* proofs',[4] but such immunity carries a price. Browning himself gently criticized Elizabeth Barrett for going on too much, and she confessed: 'I do *not say everything I think* ... but I *take every means to say what I think*.'[5] She was able to do this because there was no inherent reason why her 'means' should be restricted. When Jane Austen wrote, in the final chapter of *Northanger Abbey*, that her readers 'will see in the tell-tale compression of the pages before them, that we are all hastening together to perfect felicity', she was playfully exploiting a constraint, both economic and generic, from which Victorian poets were dubiously free.

We associate the Victorian period with profusion, with outpourings of energy, with uncontrolled expansion: all this is true of its poetry. More volumes of poetry appeared in the nineteenth century than in the two preceding ones combined, and the poets who published these volumes were themselves a fraction of a vast, shadowy population in the hinterland of Victorian literary culture – magazine and newspaper poets (local and regional especially), contributors to gatherings and garlands and posies and nosegays, the hundreds of fugitives from poetic justice. Not that the publication of a volume of one's own brought much distinction. The following batch, bound together in the University Library in Cambridge (catalogue ref. Q.26.68) is a typical sample from the mid-century:

3. 'A Word about Tennyson', *The Critic*, vol. 7 (1 January 1887), pp. 1–2.
4. Letter of 17 February 1884, in W. S. Petersen (ed.), *Browning's Trumpeter: The Correspondence of Robert Browning and Frederick J. Furnivall, 1872–1889* (Washington, D.C.: Decatur House Press, 1979), p. 93.
5. Browning's letter of 10 January 1845, and Elizabeth Barrett's reply of 15 January, in P. Kelley and S. Lewis (eds.), *The Brownings' Correspondence*, vol. 10 (Winfield, Kansas: Wedgestone Press, 1992), pp. 21–2, 26.

Poems. By Ellen C—. London: Charles Westerton, 1855

Sonnets on Various Subjects. By R. W. Elliot, B.A., of Corpus Christi College, Cambridge. London: Longman, Green, 1854

Christmas Dawn 1854 and New Year's Eve 1855. By H. R. F. Cambridge: Macmillan & Co., 1855

The Only Real Ode to Cologne; a Legend Concerning the Invention of Eau de Cologne. By [symbol]. London: Hope & Co., 1855

The Londoniad: (Complete.) Giving a Full Description of the Principal Establishments, Together with the Most Honourable and Substantial Business Men, in the Capital of England &c., &c. By James Torrington Spencer Lidstone, of Toronto, Upper Canada. Author of the 'Conquest of Canada,' 'Ancient America,' 'Pictorial Description of the British Provinces in North America,' &c. London: Published under Universal Patronage, 1856

Ceci Morinel: A Tale. Edited by R. W. Essington. London: John W. Parker and Son, 1853

Summer Sketches, and Other Poems. By Bessie Rayner Parkes. London: John Chapman, 1854

Thoughts, in Verse, on a Plurality of Worlds. By the Rev. John Peat, M.A. of St. Peter's College, Cambridge, Incumbent of the Weald, Sevenoaks, Kent. Second Edition, Enlarged. London: Rivingtons, 1856

The Ballad of Sir Rupert, a Ghost Story. By E. H. R. Monmouth: Printed by T. Farror [n.d.]

Fugitive Poems. By Tristram. London: R. Hardwicke, 1855

It is worth pausing for a moment over this strange pedlar's pack, in which there is only one joker, namely Bessie Rayner Parkes, who has real accomplishments to her name (and also gave birth to Hilaire Belloc). Ellen C— writes poems of watery orientalism ('The Eastern Love Letter') and gesturing sentiment ('Go! I scorn thee!'), and also landscape poems and poems about the seasons ('The Wishes of the Spring', 'The Good Greenwood', 'The Banks of the Wye'); one poem, 'The Mystery of Love', opens 'Shall I weave a ditty / Telling how Love comes?' and hurries on before anyone can say 'No, thanks.' At the other end of the volume, Tristram's fugitives include three poems of mourning – one for a 'favourite bloodhound', one for a young woman, and one for a child – in which, harsh though it seems to say this, the tiny measure of convincing feeling and avoidance of utter banality belong wholly to the dog. The two tales in the volume – 'Sir Rupert' and 'Ceci Morinel' – offer conventional renderings of the supernatural and the chivalric idyll. The

Rev. John Peat has mastered the art of sinking: 'Stupendous Universe! gigantic plan! / Wast thou conceiv'd alone for earth-born man?' H. R. F. sees signs of Christian social regeneration in the response of the nation to the Crimean War: 'Art takes the patriot's tone, and Science lends / Her vast appliances to aid the toil / Of Mercy'. The symbolic author of the Ode to Cologne is grindingly facetious, and R. W. Elliot, B.A., with sonnets on York Cathedral and Tintern Abbey, on the piety of agricultural labourers, on the sky-lark and the death of Wellington, demonstrates how Romanticism could be purified and piped into every home for domestic consumption. As for *The Londoniad*, this is a truly bizarre item, a kind of verse gazetteer of astounding vulgarity and incompetence, driven by an unstable mixture of colonial anxiety and vanity, and itself colonizing for poetry whole provinces of social and commercial life as foreign to the other poets of the volume as the far side of the moon.

I dwell on such poetry not just because it is enjoyably bad, but because it raises questions about what a period anthology should set out to do. The general notion that an anthology should be 'representative' usually conceals a set of particular assumptions about the constituency being represented, and, in the case of Victorian poetry, may come down to the issue of whether Arnold should be given more space than Swinburne, or whether Elizabeth Barrett Browning merits as much attention as her husband. The idea that a truly representative anthology of Victorian poetry might be interpreted as meaning the poems of Ellen C— and Tristram simply doesn't figure. Yet it is arguable that such poetry – the poetry of the commonplace, of received ideas and derivative language, of conventional religious and ethical sentiment, of false consciousness about the past and inadequate understanding of the present (ignorance, or disregard, of the complex material and psychological pressures upon the lived experience of men and women) – is indeed *representative* of what the Victorians wrote and read, just as it would be, *mutatis mutandis*, of the writing and reading of other periods, including our own.

Furthermore, the issue is not merely one of bad writing in the technical or stylistic sense. It affects the subject-matter of poetry, the characteristic preoccupations of poets and readers. A composite Victorian poem, uniting some of the most common themes found in reading for this anthology, might run as follows:

The purple shades of evening
    Flit o'er the Angel child
Whose woeful mother's weeping
    Resounds across the wild.
He joined the gallant Navy
    And found a watery grave.
Ah, better far than being
    An orphan factory slave!
Or worse, in evil city
    A village lass to sink
And fall a prey to Mammon
    And bestial vice, and drink.
She hears the thrush's singing
    And cooing of the dove
And blesses the dispenser
    Of goodness, peace, and love.
So back she goes contented
    Towards her humble home
And curtseys to the Parson
    Who's on his way to Rome.
And as the Squire passes
    Like Lancelot of yore
She shrieks, swoons and expires
    And is never heard of more.

Of course there are good Victorian poems about the death of children, good patriotic poems, good poems about rural landscapes, fallen women, the age of chivalry, and so on. Readers of this anthology will find examples of each, but they will also find many poems which are included despite – or because of – their *un*representativeness – poems which are deviant, eccentric, dissenting, abnormal, which resist their own time and place, or at least our notions of their time and place.

Nevertheless the Cambridge University Library volume does suggest something of the scope of Victorian poetry, the wide and sometimes eccentric spreading of its net. Any consideration of the collective achievement of Victorian poetry must have thoughts, like those of the Rev. John Peat, on a plurality of worlds. Victorian poetry responds to rapid expansions and transformations of the physical and social environment, and of the categories and boundaries of knowledge: the phenomena of modern life – railways, factories, parliamentary reform, women's rights, the theory of evolution – multiply the topics which poetry might (if it dared) address. The category of those who could legitimately claim to be poets also expanded, though national, or metropolitan, literary culture remained (with rare exceptions) the preserve of an educated and economically powerful middle class. There were working-class poets who were taken up and discarded by patrons and subscribers (such as William Thom, the 'Hand-Loom Weaver': see no. 38), but this does not tell the whole story; many 'self-taught' poets sought their legitimacy from their own audience, whether constituted by political affiliation or by local and regional identity.[6] Women wrote and published poetry in greater numbers, and with greater success in terms of reputation and sales, than in any previous period, though the call for a female Laureate went unheeded and no Victorian female poet gained – or, more accurately, retained – an unchallenged critical rank.

It might be thought that the variety of the material makes any categorical generalization about it invalid: that the very term 'Victorian poetry' suggests a uniformity of self-conception, if not of sensibility, which plainly did not exist. The heterogeneous poems in Q.26.68 are yoked by bibliographical violence together, but have no other bond than the stitching; we should think, not of Victorian poetry, but of Victorian poetries, assuming even that we want to retain the historical designation at all. Yet these poetries would be no less artificially 'constructed' than the general category; it makes more sense, in my view, to think of Victorian poetry as rather like Victorian Christianity, an originating term which authorized a diverse set of beliefs and practices, some orthodox and some decidedly eccentric or schismatic.

Diversification was helped by a sustained attempt on the part of all the major poets of the period to redirect the energies of traditional forms, so that poetry could participate in modern intellectual movements and debates. I am thinking of the transformation of elegy in *In Memoriam*, of dramatic soliloquy in 'Caliban upon Setebos', of the sonnet-sequence in *Sonnets from the Portuguese* and *Modern Love*, of

6. See Brian Maidment's introduction to his excellent anthology, *The Poorhouse Fugitives: Self-taught poets and poetry in Victorian Britain* (Carcanet, 1987), for a survey of the 'three traditions' which Maidment identifies: Chartist and Radical; 'Parnassian'; and 'homely rhymers'. Of these, only 'Parnassian' poetry made 'a conscious cultural attempt to join in literary discourse at the highest possible level' (p. 15).

the epistolary form in *Amours de Voyage*, of the devotional lyric in 'The Heart Knoweth Its Own Bitterness' (among many others of Christina Rossetti's poems). A more profound or inward adaptation can be seen in the 'voicing' of figures from the past, and from different kinds of past (history, the Bible, literature, classical and oriental myth), which is so pervasive a feature of Victorian poetry. Like an imperial power, Victorian poetry rules over the past and exploits it with a combination of nobility and unscrupulous self-interest. History matters to Victorian poetry, as it did to Victorian fiction, because of its narrative and ideological fertility; but the particular quality which poetry could bring to historical writing is perhaps best illustrated in this anthology by Charles Turner's sonnet 'Welsh Lucy' (no. 68), whose moral gaze – 'Victorian' perhaps, but tender and grave – sweeps outward in the last line to encompass 'the headsman's world below', history's recurring scene of violence and suffering.

The breadth of interest of Victorian poetry is, in Darwinian terms, a creative adaptation by which the genre survived and flourished. It faced increased competition from some literary forms, especially those of narrative fiction, and decreased competition from others, such as the drama.[7] The weakness of new writing for the 'legitimate' theatre in the period allowed poetry to appropriate some of the techniques and language of the stage: the continuing influence of Elizabethan writing in Victorian literature is to be found in the poets rather than the playwrights. At the same time the energy and high colour of the popular theatre (melodrama, burlesque, music hall) found its way into poetry and especially into the multiple voices of literary comedy and parody. The only literary ground which poetry lost was that of the discursive essay: Wordsworth's *Sonnets upon the Punishment of Death*, published in 1841 in the *Quarterly Review*, were a belated flowering (if that is the right word, for they're a grim bunch) of an eighteenth-century genre; Matthew Arnold was the only major poet of the period who might even have wanted to emulate Carlyle, or Mill, or George Eliot, or Ruskin, and he chose not to do so in verse. Poetry was, perhaps surprisingly, more open to the popular press, which offered new means of dissemination and a model of vivid reportage. 'New Year's Day' (no. 345), one of John Davidson's *Fleet*

---

7. The novel is often cited as the main challenger to poetry, but we should not forget the short story, whose flowering at the end of the century is clearly indebted to the economy, psychological subtlety and mastery of point of view of the dramatic monologue in verse.

*Street Eclogues*, says everything that can be said against the 'pestilent reeking stye' of the press, yet concludes with a euphoric toast to the profession, delivered, with a typically Victorian flourish of facetiousness, in cod Anglo-Saxon. At any rate the impact of the medium is palpable enough: 'The Charge of the Light Brigade' (no. 83) came from a newspaper report, was published in a newspaper, and combines the urgency of a dispatch with the authority of a leading article; another Crimean War poem, Sydney Dobell's 'The Wounded' (no. 176), is if anything more like the report of a television journalist with a hand-held camera than that of a print journalist. Coventry Patmore's 'A London Fête' (no. 168) is a columnist's piece, its polemic fired by indignant observation.

The heterogeneity of the newspaper, its juxtaposition of different kinds of 'story' (different in length, provenance, character, tone), the medley of its voices – these are features of urban modernity, which poetry tracks through the period with alternate fascination and repulsion. The city is already a strong presence in the poetry of the eighteenth century and in Romanticism, but it becomes of central importance in Victorian poetry, and the values that were invested in other landscapes are self-consciously relocated, as in Alexander Smith's 'Glasgow' (no. 192). The association of love-poetry with pastoral is broken: Elizabeth Barrett Browning, though she begins *Sonnets from the Portuguese* (no. 59) with an allusion to Theocritus, wrestles with desire and belief in a place which is recognizably Wimpole Street. Christina Rossetti's metaphysical and devotional solitude is urban, despite the pastoral setting of many of her lyrics; she is not a figure in a landscape, but lost in a crowd. Only Emily Brontë, of the major poets of the period, goes against the urban grain.

If the city – and by association the condition of modernity – is a place of nightmare and negation, perhaps poetry might take flight from it – in dream, in fantasy, in nonsense, or in regression to childhood. Such poetry is strong in the period, so strong that it enabled F. R. Leavis to state what seemed the obvious: 'Nineteenth-century poetry, we realize, was characteristically preoccupied with the creation of a dreamworld.'[8] But Victorian dreaming is a more complex matter than Leavis allows, and fantasy may serve other purposes than flight. Victor Plarr's

8. *New Bearings in English Poetry* (1932). I have commented on this judgement in my introduction to the printed bibliography of the *English Poetry Full-Text Database* (Chadwyck-Healey, 1995), pp. v–vi.

'Twilight-Piece' (no. 382) consists of four four-line stanzas, the first two of which depict a 'golden river-reach' reflecting 'golden skies of even', while the 'river murmurs' and the 'amorous west wind soughs'. But the last two stanzas complete the picture in an unexpected way:

> And here on the slim arch that spans
> The rippling stream, in dark outline,
> You see the poor old fisherman's
> Bowed form and patient rod and line.
>
> A picture better than all art,
> Since none could catch that sunset stain,
> Or set in the soft twilight's heart
> This small strange touch of human pain!

The turn in the poem is marked by a syntax which 'spans' and bends across the lines, and by the pun on 'catch': signs of a quickened and reflexive intelligence, which has certainly 'created a dream-world' of erotic reflections but has placed at its 'heart' the figure of a solitary and suffering desire. In Robert Browning's 'Dubiety' (no. 109), the indulgence of dreaming is rejected with Leavisian sternness, but there are many Victorian poems which welcome the escape from reality; yet even in these the escape has often been earned by a greater labour of imagination than we are willing to credit, as it has in Alice Meynell's sonnet 'Renouncement' (no. 307). The 'plot' of this poem is simple and conventional: the speaker has renounced her beloved and avoids thinking of him all day long, but dreams of him at night; we may, if we wish, thicken this stock motif with a spoonful of biography (the unattainable beloved is the young priest who instructed Meynell during her conversion to Roman Catholicism). 'I must not think of thee', the poem begins; this is the first in a chain of imperatives. The thought of her beloved 'must never, never come in sight; / I must stop short of thee the whole day long.' (The idiomatic play on 'short' and 'long' is a grace-note, an extra gift.) These 'musts' are to do with self-control: *I must not* does not mean *I may not* but *I should not, and I won't let myself*. The speaker's syntax mimes her control: the dangerous phrase 'The thought of thee' in the first quatrain, for example, is held within a parenthesis as though to prevent it from breaking out. But then, in the transition from waking to sleep, the nature of the imperatives changes:

> But when sleep comes to close each difficult day,
>   When night gives pause to the long watch I keep,
>   And all my bonds I needs must loose apart,

>   Must doff my will as raiment laid away, –
>   With the first dream that comes with the first sleep
>   I run, I run, I am gathered to thy heart.

These 'musts' are truly commands, they enforce themselves. I am bound to sleep, yet sleep unbinds me. In contrast to the syntax of willed containment in the octave, the syntax of the sestet flows forward and gathers itself to a release of energy, a surge of active desire ('I run, I run') which is immediately met and fulfilled ('I am gathered to thy heart'). Like Caliban, I cry to dream again.

As for regression, there is a fine example in May Kendall's 'Lay of the Trilobite' (no. 372), which yearns with satiric wistfulness for the fate of the crustacean (or arachnid) hero. A different kind of playfulness, serious-minded if not serious-faced, governs the nonsense poetry of both Edward Lear and Lewis Carroll, but especially that of Lear, whose emotional and conceptual range is wider than is usually allowed. In the limericks the elements of the absurd, the whimsical, and the eccentric do not evade feeling, or disguise it, but fuse with it in new and strange compounds. His control of rhythm and cadence is astonishing, and belongs to him even in parody ('The Courtship of the Yonghy-Bonghy-Bò' [no. 122], for its own delight, takes off *from* Tennyson as much as it takes him off). If there is a lovelier ending to a Victorian love-poem than the last five lines of 'The Owl and the Pussy-Cat' (no. 121), I will go to sea in a sieve.

Lear was the only great poet who wrote from the beginning to please children; poets such as William Brighty Rands, the 'Laureate of the Nursery', are forgotten today, though the subversive fantasy of 'Lilliput Levee' (no. 169) suggests that Rands himself is worth another look. This poem is notable, too, for its ending, in which the poet applies for the post of 'Lilliput Laureate', a joke which is also a recognition that children formed a real and distinct audience for poetry. They were often treated (the wrong word) to facile sweetness and dull whimsy, but both Christina Rossetti and, to a lesser extent, Robert Louis Stevenson wrote poems that 'realize' and speak to children while speaking to adults about them. Certainly the poems of *Sing-Song* (no. 219) are childlike, but they are not childish, and they do not belong on a poetic scale at whose other end are poems which treat adults like children.

## 2. GIVING A LIFE TO THE WORDS

The industrial quantity of Victorian poetry was a focus of anxiety for Victorian poets themselves. 'Our shelves groan with little books over which their readers groan less metaphorically,' wrote Elizabeth Barrett in 1842; 'there is a plague of poems in the land apart from poetry.'[9] The groaning took metrical form, too, in many poems about how many poems there were. As early as 1827, in the prefatory poem to *Poems by Two Brothers*, Charles Tennyson (later Turner) was worried that 'in this age' there were 'too many' poets: 'And they who now would fain awake the lyre, / May swell this supernumerary choir'. Ebenezer Elliott, the 'Corn Law Rhymer', put it less genteelly: 'In these days, every mother's son or daughter / Writes verse, which no one reads except the writer'; and, he went on, with a reflexive turn wholly characteristic of the period,

> Hundreds of unstaunch'd Shelleys daily water
> Unanswering dust; a thousand Wordsworths scribble;
> And twice a thousand Cornlaw Rhymers dribble
> Rhymed prose, unread.                                   (ll. 5–8)[10]

Sir Francis Doyle, in 'The Poetaster's Plea', offers a witty and charming defence of the scribblers and dribblers, and a sardonic comment on their perennial hardiness:

---

9. Review of Wordsworth's *Poems, chiefly of Early and Late Years* in the *Athenaeum* of 27 August 1842 (p. 759).

10. Compare Tennyson's castigation of his imitators in 'The Flower', published in 1864: 'Read my little fable: / He that runs may read. / Most can raise the flowers now, / For all have got the seed' (ll. 16–20). In this poem, too, quantity is linked to decline in quality, as it is in Browning's 'Popularity', where Keats is the poet whose original genius is pillaged by a multitude of inferior imitators.

> In self-conceit invulnerably mailed,
> We stand, however savagely assailed,
> And pour into the drowsy ear of time
> Our never ebbing tides of blank and rhyme.[11]

But others were not so tolerant. Ebenezer Jones's strange and savage 'The Poet's Death' (no. 147) concludes with an image of gross and mass oblivion:

> In the churchyard lies the Poet, and his scent the air depraves;
> And ten thousand thousand like him, stuff the earth with such like graves.

The tragedy of an unfulfilled talent is multiplied into farce and futility; Jones's scorn looks fearfully self-directed here. James Rhoades (1841–1923, not otherwise represented in this anthology) wrote a poem in 1893 called 'The Public and the Poet' in which the 'Public' expresses its scorn for poetry:

> Time was when a poet was deemed *rara avis*;
> Now they babble on bough like the merle or the mavis.
> One or two in a lifetime was all very well;
> But who's to keep pace when some sixty break shell?     (ll. 9–12)

Rhoades gives us an additional context for this worry about the 'supernumerary choir'. First, there is competition – not between poets, but between poetry and other kinds of writing or other arts altogether. As the 'Public' cheerfully confesses:

> we squander our shillings to swill
> At the rubble-fed bookstall's perennial rill,
> And trample each other to pounce on the prize,
> When the flesh-prophet caters for prurient eyes.     (ll. 5–8)

I assume that the allusion here is to low fiction, especially the sensation novel; and Rhoades goes on to disparage painting, which 'craves no thinking, yields something to show, / Has an air so aesthetic' (ll. 15–16)

---

11. Publ. in *The Return of the Guards, and other poems*, 1883. Doyle (1810–88) was a friend of Gladstone and Professor of Poetry at Oxford, 1867–77.

and music, which 'tickles our ears / With a tender shampooing', so that 'our approval we clap / When some brave singer turns on the tremolo-tap' (ll. 19–20, 23–4). All these inferior arts 'wade ankle-deep in our money' (l. 25), but poetry is rejected; and this is because, as Rhoades's imagery suggests, the competition between poetry and other arts is also a contrast between low and high culture. Poetry, according to Rhoades, is the vehicle of high thought and spiritual refinement, and that is why the 'Public' won't tolerate it:

> you, who would have us look inward, give ear
> Unto vague spirit-voices the flesh cannot hear,
> Purge sense of its grossness, strip wealth of its lure,
> In the soul and in Nature seek charms that endure;
> To the old mythic virtues look backward, and scan
> How woman's love wakens the God in a man;
> Through the roar of life's labour find silence and ease
> In the thought of high mountains, and heaven over these;
> Catch anon the far music of stars in their spheres,
> Dive to life's hidden meaning through laughter and tears –
> Oh, it's all very splendid, and high, and sublime,
> But, to put the thing plainly, we can't spare the time ...
>
> (ll. 27–38)

It's appropriate that the only two good lines in this passage are the last, which show that poetry can be robust and plain, rather than clichéd and metrically incompetent, and certainly give a better impression of its scope than the 'vague spirit-voices', 'charms that endure', and 'old mythic virtues'. Many Victorian poets, who were as anxious about poetry's cultural standing as Rhoades, were wary of giving the hostages to fortune which he offers here. They feared that poetry would be *relegated* to Nature and the soul, stranded out of earshot of 'the roar of life's labour', seen as archaic and out of touch. Addressing 'the Poets of the New Generation' in 1856, Eliza Ogilvy accused them of being hermits and 'minstrel-monks': 'With introverted gaze / In self obser-vances ye waste your days,' she wrote,[12] alluding specifically to the Crimean War and the obligation of poets, like war reporters, to cover the story:

12. 'To the Poets of the New Generation', ll. 45–6, in *Poems of Ten Years* (1856).

The troops are trampling in the streets,
Down, poets, from your still retreats,
Where each with analytic knife
Traces the nerves of spirit-life;
The world is in its throes,
    Can ye but sing poetic pains?
Amid the writhe of orphaned woes
    Can ye but note the birth of some fantastic strain?    (ll. 54–61)

Not everyone agreed that the alternative to singing 'poetic pains' was to write directly about 'orphaned woes'; a poem such as Arnold's 'Resignation' (no. 154) offers a quite different solution. Arnold agrees that poetry should not be autobiographical or confessional:

The poet, to whose mighty heart
Heaven doth a quicker pulse impart,
Subdues that energy to scan
Not his own course, but that of man.        (ll. 144–7)

But this activity is still one of *scanning*, and Arnold insists that poetry must remain disengaged from the contemporary, attentive to the 'murmur of a thousand years' (l. 188) and to the 'general life' (l. 191) of nature and of the human race. The poet's 'sad lucidity of soul' (l. 198) differentiates him, in Arnold's eyes, from the self-regard criticized by Ogilvy, but she would argue that his outlook constituted simply another way of talking about 'poetic pains'.

Ogilvy was a friend of Elizabeth Barrett Browning, and her poem was published in the same year as *Aurora Leigh*, in which the challenge to poetry's ability to deal with the 'throes' of the modern world is vigorously taken up. Elizabeth Barrett Browning had planned *Aurora Leigh*, from the beginning, as

a sort of novel-poem – a poem as completely modern as 'Geraldine's Courtship,' running into the midst of our conventions, & rushing into drawingrooms and the like 'where angels fear to tread'; – & so, meeting face to face & without mask, the Humanity of the age, & speaking the truth as I conceive of it, out plainly.[13]

13. Letter to Robert Browning of 27 February 1845, in P. Kelley and S. Lewis (eds.), *The Brownings' Correspondence*, vol. 10 (Winfield, Kansas: Wedgestone Press, 1992), p. 103.

In another letter she expressed herself even more forcibly on the need to be 'completely modern', this time in renouncing the classics:

I am inclined to think that we want new *forms* ... as well as thoughts – The old gods are dethroned. Why should we go back to the antique moulds ... classical moulds, as they are so improperly called. If it is a necessity of Art to do so, why then those critics are right who hold that Art is exhausted & the world too worn out for poetry. I do not, for my part, believe this: & I believe the so called necessity of Art, to be the mere feebleness of the artist – Let us all rather aspire to *Life* – & let the dead bury their dead. If we have but courage to face these conventions, to touch this low ground, we shall take strength from it instead of losing it; & of that, I am intimately persuaded.[14]

This isn't a facile gesture: Elizabeth Barrett Browning knew and loved the Greek and Latin classics as common reader, erudite scholar, and translator; indeed, her knowledge is wittily deployed in this very passage, since taking strength from the 'low ground' alludes to the myth of Antaeus, the son of Earth who wrestled with Hercules and got stronger every time he fell. Nevertheless something else is going on besides the desire to emulate the novel, strong and urgent though that desire is. The novel has the advantage over poetry in its ability to move in the modern social world (and not just drawing-rooms, of course), so poetry must challenge the novel on this ground; but the task of 'meeting face to face & without mask, the Humanity of the age' and of 'speaking the truth ... out plainly' still belongs, in Elizabeth Barrett Browning's belief, to the poet, and in this her belief turns out not to be so far from Rhoades's after all.

In *Aurora Leigh* itself, published over ten years after these letters were written, the poet-heroine certainly engages with 'the Humanity of the age' in its drawing-rooms and urban slums, yet simultaneously makes claims for poetry which explicitly set it above the arts of realism or reportage. Indeed a major part of the poem is taken up with the 'poetic pains' from which Ogilvy urged poets to avert their 'introverted gaze'. When Aurora, as a child, 'chanced upon the poets' in her dead father's

*Footnote continued*

She alludes to 'Lady Geraldine's Courtship', a poem with a contemporary setting and subject (aristocratic lady crosses social divide to marry lower-class poet) recently published in her two-volume *Poems* (1844).

14. Letter to Robert Browning of 20 March 1845, *Correspondence* (see note 13), p. 135.

library, she experienced an earthquake of feeling which opened her soul to 'elemental freedom' (I. 845–50). Then the older Aurora, who is narrating the story, interrupts herself:

> What's this, Aurora Leigh,
> You write so of the poets, and not laugh?
> Those virtuous liars, dreamers after dark,
> Exaggerators of the sun and moon,
> And soothsayers in a tea-cup?
>             I write so
> Of the only truth-tellers now left to God,
> The only speakers of essential truth,
> Opposed to relative, comparative,
> And temporal truths; the only holders by
> His sun-skirts, through conventional gray glooms;
> The only teachers who instruct mankind
> From just a shadow on a charnel-wall
> To find man's veritable stature out
> Erect, sublime, – the measure of a man,
> And that's the measure of an angel, says
> The apostle. Ay, and while your common men
> Lay telegraphs, gauge railroads, reign, reap, dine,
> And dust the flaunty carpets of the world
> For kings to walk on, or our president,
> The poet suddenly will catch them up
> With his voice like a thunder, – 'This is soul,
> This is life, this word is being said in heaven,
> Here's God down on us! what are you about?'
> How all those workers start amid their work,
> Look round, look up, and feel, a moment's space,
> That carpet-dusting, though a pretty trade
> Is not the imperative labour after all.
>                             (ll. 854–80)

It is not unkind, I hope, to hear a creak in these lines – the creak which comes from straining to have it both ways. *Aurora Leigh* certainly claims to represent the plural 'temporal truths' of contemporary life as effectively as the novel or the newspaper, but Elizabeth Barrett Browning will not relinquish her unique access as a poet to a singular 'essential truth'. Yet the poet's intervention in the social world and the world of work is represented as radical and polemical, and, so to speak, vertical: he comes down on 'common men' from a great height, or calls God down on them, and they in turn 'look up' from their horizontal labours of laying down railroads and carpets.[15] The poet himself is neither an engineer nor a courtier, he is estranged both from labour and from the rituals of power, and he judges the world from an alien perspective.

The attempt to preserve for poetry what was felt to be an age-old privilege inevitably conflicted with the worry that 'age-old' in this context meant no more than *archaic* and outmoded. The last poem to reflect this worry which I have found within the dates of this anthology is Sir Walter Alexander Raleigh's jolly 'Ode to the Glasgow Ballad Club', recited at a meeting of the club on 21 December 1901. Poetry is a diminished art, Raleigh confesses: 'our songs / Cannot vanquish ancient wrongs', and 'our cage / Is this narrow Iron Age'. The poem ends on a note of jaunty defiance, but it acknowledges a serious predicament:

> Some are foes
> To whatever is not prose;
> Verse, they say, is merely fact
>     Cracked.
>
> You may meet
> Daily in the public street
> Men who call a sonnet clap-
>     Trap.
>
> Here's a health!
> To the poets wine and wealth;
> Let the critics go to – well –
>     Hell!

Raleigh is cocking a snook at an old enemy. The tone of much Victorian scorn for poetry was set by Thomas Love Peacock's brilliant satire *The Four Ages of Poetry*, written in 1821, in which Peacock characterized poetry as a primitive and barbaric art, an art of superstition and the irrational, redundant in an enlightened and rational civilization. Poetry

15. Alexander Anderson's 'Railway Dreamings' (no. 291) makes an interesting comment on this image.

told lies about the past in comparison with history, was ignorant of the nature of the physical world in comparison with science, and was incompetent to think clearly about moral or social questions in comparison with modern philosophy. It was, indeed, 'fact / Cracked'.[16]

Shelley's answer to Peacock, in *A Defence of Poetry*, though written in the same year, was actually first published in 1840, and so, like Wordsworth's *Prelude*, is an honorary Victorian work. But Shelley's arguments proved in some ways more of a hindrance than a help to his Victorian disciples. For if Peacock's strictures seem in tune with the future – with the rational, scientific, progressive, and utilitarian tendencies of nineteenth-century thought – Shelley's defence is rather the consummate expression of a Romantic ideology whose historical moment had already passed. Shelley's formula, 'A poem is the very image of life expressed in its eternal truth', is uneasily echoed throughout the period by poets who are accused by others, and who suspect themselves, of not being able to back it up. Elizabeth Barrett Browning's insistence on the primacy of 'essential truth' over 'temporal truths' has its roots in the distinction which Shelley draws between a *story* ('a catalogue of detached facts, which have no other connexion than time, place, circumstance, cause, and effect') and a *poem* ('the creation of actions according to the unchangeable forms of human nature'), but *Aurora Leigh* also bears witness to a desire to heal the gap so trenchantly opened up. For Elizabeth Barrett Browning the attempt to make poetry engage with modern life was at least an answer to the anxiety that 'Art is exhausted', that poetry had nothing left to say. This anxiety is expressed in its clearest and simplest form in a short poem by Dollie Radford, published in 1891:

16. Peacock's influence is discernible in, for example, W. H. Mallock's pamphlet 'Every Man His Own Poet; or, the Inspired Singer's Recipe Book' (1872), in which Mallock declares that poetry has followed three stages of development: 'first a work of inspiration, secondly of science, and lastly now of trick'. Poetry has become 'the art of expressing what is too foolish, too profane, or too indecent to be expressed in any other way'; and the art of poetic cookery consists in concocting a 'popular poem from the weakest emotions, and the most tiresome platitudes'. Mallock goes on to give the 'recipes' for some of these poems. 'How to make an ordinary love poem', for example: 'Take two large and tender human hearts, which match one another perfectly. Arrange these close together, but preserve them from actual contact by placing between them some cruel barrier. Wound them both in several places, and insert through the openings thus made a fine stuffing of wild yearnings, hopeless tenderness, and a general admiration for stars. Then completely cover up one heart with a sufficient quantity of chill churchyard mould, which may be garnished according to taste with dank waving weeds or tender violets: and promptly break over it the other heart.'

> There is no unawakened string,
> No untried note for me to ring,
> No new-found song for me to sing.
>
> . . .
>
> The songs I strive to sing have rolled
> Through times and ages manifold,
> A mighty chorus fully told.[17]

The defeatism of these lines is tempered by a sense almost of pleasure at being subsumed into the 'mighty chorus'; but others felt differently, and were prepared to make Shelley's case with dogmatic assurance. Here, for example, is Cosmo Monkhouse, in the 'Proem' to his volume *A Dream of Idleness* in 1865:

> Alas, and thrice alas, for him who said
> That Poetry, sweet Poetry, is dead,
> Fair daughter of the everlasting Truth,
> Who knows no taint of Time, but lives in changeless youth.
>
> Of Truth divine hath she her matchless birth,
> Not that sad Fact, the child of fallen Earth;
> There was no need before the falsehood came,
> Of that unlovely, mean, and melancholy name.          (ll. 1–8)

Monkhouse represents a whole militant tendency of Victorian poetry, according to which it is not the duty of poetry to reflect the modern world to its readers, but the duty of those readers to repent and follow the poetic gospel:

> It is not yet too late; release thine ear
> From the world's deafening din, and thou shalt hear.
> Forsake thy gold, thy lust, – whate'er they be,
> Tear off thy selfish scales and thou again shalt see.
>
> Behold her rosy on the morning heights,
> See how she flashes in the noonday lights,
> How trembles in the mistiness of eve,
> And in her starry crown behold her and believe.          (ll. 29–36)

17. 'My Songs', ll. 1–3, 13–15, in *A Light Load* (1891).

Those alexandrines at the end of each stanza are, as so often in Victorian poetry, the sign of a disabling sonority and self-importance, encouraging the poet to issue orders that have no authority behind them.

But if the attempt to adapt poetry to the modern world while continuing to assert its cultural primacy was too strained, and the pure Romantic affirmation of the power of poetry no longer carried conviction, perhaps the solution was to re-state the terms of the problem. The most extreme example of this which I have found is a poem called 'Crescent?' by H. Cholmondeley-Pennell (1836–1915), a civil servant and occasional contributor to *Punch*. The question implied in the title of 'Crescent?' is whether poetry is growing or declining in power and scope, and Cholmondeley-Pennell argues vigorously that it is growing. The opening stanzas of the poem belong to two dramatized speakers who voice the conventional wisdom that 'The Age of Poetry is past', that it 'died / On chivalry's splintered spear', and that there are no more great poets: 'The king-roll of the bards is sealed; / The thrones are filled, up to the end of time ... The harp those masters smote is now unstrung'. 'A LIE!' thunders Cholmondeley-Pennell; 'A lie that poetry is dead!' The conditions of life have indeed changed, and with them the way in which poets are regarded, but all this means is that the poets of today must look for their subject-matter and reputation in these changed conditions, where they will find poetry already before them. For example, poetry has been associated with war, but war is only the expression of 'Incarnate Force, embodied Power'; the same force, today, is incarnated in 'half a million roaring factory tow'rs' and in the 'brazen throats' of steamships. 'Shout for the age of Iron – proclaim your day', the poet urges.

Furthermore, the change in social and material conditions is an improvement: historically, Victorian England is an advance on earlier times, and poetry, Cholmondeley-Pennell argues, has a share in this improvement. The past we admire so much was primitive, barbaric, a 'green waste' compared to the 'cultured Eden' of the modern world. In this part of his argument Cholmondeley-Pennell entirely accepts Peacock's association between poetry and a reactionary social order, but he believes that poetry can evolve in parallel with the social order itself. If beauty is the inspiration for poetry, then the poetry of our age has nothing to worry about:

Ours is the beauty INTELLECT implants,
Graft on a perfect stem of loveliest earth;
A beauty blossoming in gracious deeds,
Hopes deeper set, and aims of larger girth.
A beauty lighted up by gentle thoughts,
By modest truth and sweet domestic grace;
By every beaming star Refinement sets
In the soft heaven of a woman's face.
By freer love; by pure speech, doubly free;
By true ambitions purged of civil broil;
By faith broad-based, with loftier temples crown'd
By fairer office and a nobler toil.

Fairer our forms, from nature's latest touch, –
From delicate growth, – finer each moulded limb;
Red lips as red, more white the etherial brow,
More mind to flash beneath its cloudy rim:
Less beauty then, or more, to wake the inspired hymn?

Every day and in every way we are getting better and better: this is a text-book example of Victorian evolutionary optimism, in which everything from the social and political system to the sexual characteristics of men and women (but mainly women, of course) benefits from the march of mind. The sexuality of the past was fleshly and coarse, ours is 'lighted up by gentle thoughts'; they had bawdy sensuality, we have 'pure speech'; we have purged the 'civil broil' of the past, and its sectarian religious strife, and have a political and economic order characterized by 'fairer office' and 'nobler toil'. The term 'fair' functions as a punning bridge from politics to the body, from 'fairer office' to 'fairer forms'. Poets, faced with these expanded opportunities to 'wake inspired hymns', have only themselves to blame if they don't get up and get on with it.

Cholmondeley-Pennell's ideas about poetry and society might be easier to swallow if 'Crescent?' were itself a better poem. But how could it be? It is truly the poem of those ideas: conventional, self-blinded, banal, bathetic. The social and political complacencies of which it is so pure a product articulate themselves in flabby declamation and cliché. To be told that there was hope for poetry in verse so stultified and regressive would be enough to make you want to drink the contents of your inkwell rather than dip a quill in it.

The profound message of Cholmondeley-Pennell's poem is not about poetry, but about conformity. In this sense the question-mark in the title is a fake, for the poem is not in the least interrogative, and its challenge is rigged. Poetry is offered as the ideological accomplice of a boastful materialism, resting on a caricature of historical and scientific evolutionary theory, unbounded by scepticism or irony (those philosophical and rhetorical checks on the power of the executive). Above all what is lacking in Cholmondeley-Pennell's formula for poetry is a concept of *difference*, a sense of what it is that makes poetry unlike other forms of art, other modes of language, other 'discourses' (in the modern sense of the term). Elizabeth Barrett Browning has such a concept, that of poetry as the visionary apprehension of the real: poetry partakes of (if it does not emulate or displace) the way God sees, and more important moves within, the world of humanity and nature. The trouble with this idea is that it makes poetry, in the end, instrumental to a purpose whose origin lies elsewhere: poems are guided missiles, not free in flight. If *Aurora Leigh* is a good poem, it is despite, and not because of, the truth of its author's heart-sinking announcement that this was the work 'into which my highest convictions upon Life and Art have entered'.[18]

Elizabeth Barrett Browning's use of the word 'work' to describe her poem is itself a significant fact. It accompanies her belief that being a poet was, so to speak, a proper job, as well as a divinely ordained vocation – that poets need not be ashamed of being poets and nothing else. She wrote of Wordsworth's career as exemplary in this respect, as presenting 'a high moral to his generation' in terms of 'what a true poet is, what his work is, and what his patience and successes must be'. But the example was not being followed:

'Art,' it was said long ago, 'requires the whole man,' and 'Nobody,' it was said later, 'can be a poet who is anything else;' but the present idea of Art requires the segment of a man, and everybody who is anything at all is a poet in a parenthesis. And our shelves groan with little books over which their readers groan less metaphorically; there is a plague of poems in the land apart from poetry; and many poets who live and are true do not live by their truth, but hold back their full strength from Art because they do not *reverence* it fully; and all booksellers cry aloud and do not spare, that poetry will not sell . . .[19]

18. From the dedication to John Kenyon.
19. For the reference, see note 9 above.

Certainly there were many poets who did not *live by their truth*, for the very good reason that they couldn't make a living by it. As the biographical notes in this volume indicate, most poets in the period, if they did not have a private income, long-suffering parents, or a Government pension, had to support themselves either by other, more remunerative kinds of writing, or by doing something else in the way of a profession. But if poetry was a part-time occupation, it could also be insinuated that it was a pastime, a frivolous leisure activity; perhaps (dread thought) it was not quite manly. Gossip reached Elizabeth Barrett (as she was then) about the fact that her future husband Robert Browning lived at home and didn't have any employment; she defended him against Mary Russell Mitford's charge of effeminacy, and rebutted the view of Anne Procter (wife of the lawyer and minor poet B. W. Procter, who wrote under the pseudonym 'Barry Cornwall') 'that it was a pity he [Browning] had not seven or eight hours a day of occupation'.[20] Browning was one of those who, like Wordsworth, had committed himself to poetry, who was not 'a poet in a parenthesis' – she linked him with Tennyson in this respect, praising him for a dedication to his *work* which (it was exasperating to be reminded) was actually funded by someone else's.

As for herself, Elizabeth Barrett insisted in her preface to her *Poems* of 1844 that poetry took up, not just all of her time, but all of her self as well:

If it must be said of me that I have contributed immemorable verses to the many rejected by the age, it cannot at least be said that I have done so in a light and irresponsible spirit. Poetry has been as serious a thing to me as life itself ... I never mistook pleasure for the final cause of poetry; nor leisure, for the hour of the poet. I have done my work, so far, as work, – not as mere hand and head work, apart from the personal being, – but as the completest expression of that being to which I could attain, – and as work I offer it to the public ...

The problem with this is that it begs the question of whether the 'being' is worth expressing. Lyric utterance seems to authorize itself, and Elizabeth Barrett's whole-heartedness could easily be travestied as Romantic – or worse, pseudo-Romantic – presumption. Her solemn affirmation of seriousness was also vulnerable, if it could be implied

---

20. See D. Karlin, *The Courtship of Robert Browning and Elizabeth Barrett* (Oxford: Clarendon Press, 1985), pp. 120–21.

that the inner life, the terrain of poetry, was actually limited to vague impressions and sensations, easily translated into ridicule. Put this alongside the notion of poetry as a pastime, and the figure of the 'poetess' takes shape, and of the feminized male poet; they are already present in *Pickwick Papers* in the characters of Mr Snodgrass and, in a brilliant cameo appearance, Mrs Leo Hunter. Mrs Hunter is fervently described to Mr Pickwick by her husband in chapter 15:

'She doats on poetry, sir. She adores it; I may say that her whole soul and mind are wound up, and entwined with it. She has produced some delightful pieces, herself, sir. You may have met with her "Ode to an Expiring Frog," sir.'

'I don't think I have,' said Mr Pickwick.

'You astonish me, sir,' said Mr Leo Hunter. 'It created an immense sensation. It was signed with an "L" and eight stars, and appeared originally in a Lady's Magazine. It commenced

> "Can I view thee panting, lying
> On thy stomach, without sighing;
> Can I unmoved see thee dying
>> On a log,
>> Expiring frog!"'

'Beautiful!' said Mr Pickwick.

'Fine,' said Mr Leo Hunter, 'so simple.'

'Very,' said Mr Pickwick.

Mrs Leo Hunter's devotion to poetry is too close for comfort to what Elizabeth Barrett advocates: it preoccupies 'her whole soul and mind', yet its product is not work but idleness, whose emblem is the 'Lady's Magazine'. To Dickens it was axiomatic that nothing serious could make its appearance in such a form, and the frog expires accordingly. Even the rhymes ('lying', 'sighing', 'dying') which exude false and inflated sentiment are 'feminine'. Poetry is simple, all right; it is the product and the preserve of the simple-minded.[21]

21. For a very different view of the opportunities opened to women writers by the magazines, albums, and annuals of the period, see Margaret Reynolds's introduction to her and Angela Leighton's anthology, *Victorian Women Poets* (Blackwell, 1995). For another novelist's assault on feminine poetry, see chapter 2 of Thackeray's *The Fitz-Boodle Papers* (1842–3), in which the lovely Ottilia founds her own literary journal in the little German town of Kalbsbraten-Pumpernickel. The journal is printed 'upon light-blue or primrose paper', and Ottilia writes melancholy ballads; she 'never would willingly let off the

The answer to such mockery was to insist that poetry was, indeed, masculine work, and to inculcate poetic values which matched that view. As early as 1835, in a review of Browning's *Paracelsus*, W. J. Fox, editor of the Radical and Unitarian *Monthly Repository*, was eager to stress the poem's credentials:

This poem is what few modern publications either are, or affect to be; it is A WORK. It is the result of thought, skill, and toil. Defects and irregularities there may be, but they are those of a building which the architect has erected for posterity, and not the capricious anomalies of the wattled pleasure house, which has served its turn when the summer day's amusement is over, and may be blown about by the next breeze, or washed away by the next torrent, to be replaced by another as fantastic and as transient.

Dignity, solidity, permanence: the poem-as-building is figured explicitly as *product* (a 'work', the 'result ... of toil') and implicitly as *producer*: it transmits (and will continue to transmit) the values by which it was made. Fox's materialism has a metaphysical dimension, and, by the same token, an aesthetic one: 'thought, skill, and toil' are opposed to 'amusement' and to the 'fantastic' and 'transient' life of the passions.

Fox's praise for *Paracelsus* differentiates it from most 'modern publications', but only by assimilating it to something else. 'A lasting poem,' Fox declares, 'must have a great purpose, moral, political, or philosophical.' The *purpose* of poetry in this sense is like that of political action, or advances in science, or moral philosophy: progress, reform, enlightenment. To be sure, poetry uses peculiar means to accomplish its purpose – at one point in his review Fox refers admiringly to Browning's 'varied and most poetical illustration' of one of Paracelsus's arguments. But it is fundamentally on the same side as politics, science, and moral philosophy, and this is the true answer to Peacock's attempt (as, indeed, of Plato's) to expel poetry from the city of modern culture.

Victorian poets were influenced by this work ethic, but most of the

*Footnote continued*
heroines without a suicide or a consumption', having 'an appetite for grief quite amazing in so young a person'. One of these ballads, 'The Willow-Tree', is cited and then parodied. Still another example comes in chapter 17 of Mark Twain's *Huckleberry Finn*, which contains the 'Ode to Stephen Dowling Bots, Dec'd' (by a young lady herself deceased): 'No whooping-cough did rack his frame, / Nor measles drear, with spots; / Not these impaired the sacred name / Of Stephen Dowling Bots.'

greatest Victorian poetry, and Browning's is exemplary in this respect, was written by transgressing it. Confronted by Fox's earnest opposition between the grand building and the 'wattled pleasure house', poets might hesitate, but eventually they voted with their metrical feet. I do not mean to be frivolous here, unless pleasure is to be stigmatized as frivolity. Wordsworth was responsible for some of the worst excesses of Victorian poetic earnestness, but it was Wordsworth who argued, in the preface to *Lyrical Ballads* (still the greatest and most potent defence of poetry ever written, a Jupiter to Shelley's belt of asteroids) that it was 'the necessity of giving immediate pleasure to a Human Being' which distinguished poetry from every other kind of writing, and that this necessity, far from being 'a degradation of the Poet's art', was 'a homage paid to the native and naked dignity of man, to the grand elementary principle of pleasure, by which he knows, and feels, and lives, and moves'.[22] Elizabeth Barrett's pride in never having mistaken pleasure for the final cause of poetry is, in this light, utterly misplaced. And Wordsworth located the pleasure of poetry where you might think it was most apparent, but where it has often been least regarded: in rhythm, in the constitutive and elemental principle of poetic form.

What kind of pleasure does metrical language give us? It is, says Wordsworth, 'the pleasure which the mind derives from the perception of similitude in dissimilitude', and it has a wide scope:

This principle is the great spring of the activity of our minds, and their chief feeder. From this principle the direction of the sexual appetite, and all the passions connected with it, take their origin: it is the life of our ordinary conversation; and upon the accuracy with which similitude in dissimilitude, and dissimilitude in similitude are perceived, depend our taste and our moral feelings.

Poetry, then, is connected at the most fundamental level with the way our minds work, with their 'chief feeder' – the pleasure we take in poetry is nourished from the same source as that which we take in our sexual life, poetry being as much of the body as sex is of the mind.

This principle of pleasure is the more vital because it is so often left out of account in discussions of Victorian poetry, except with regard to

22. The text is that of the 1802 version, in M. Mason (ed.), *Lyrical Ballads*, Longman, 1992, pp. 73–4. Mason's note on p. 74 helpfully elucidates Wordsworth's idea of poetic pleasure in relation to its sources in eighteenth-century aesthetic and psychological theories.

the 'aesthetic' movement in the later part of the period. But the poetry of aestheticism or decadence was no more intrinsically a poetry of pleasure than the poetry of Arthurian romance or of the domestic idyll, just as such poetry could not command attention simply because of its subject matter or ideology.[23] It could not then, and it cannot now: to exhort people to read Victorian poetry because of its engagement in the production of Victorian culture is as sterile as it was to exhort them to read it because it provided moral teaching or spiritual uplift. Or rather: if we are to read Victorian poetry as the product of its time, then the issue of pleasure is immaterial, and the issue of cultural engagement is all that matters. This anthology would look very different if its contents were selected according to the latter criterion. It is not that the poems here are disengaged from their context, floating in some timeless dimension of value; context is inescapable. Any poem can be situated and studied in relation to its historical moment; poems are recognizably 'authored' by circumstance, social as well as personal, their design is shaped by the atmospheric pressure in which they are made to live. But many of the poems in this anthology could be replaced by others which would function equally well as carriers of Victorian culture, assuming that was the main purpose. Many believe it should be; as William Allingham puts it, 'Many for Poems care much, for Poesie little or nothing.' We might wince a little at the word 'poesie', but Allingham means nothing coy or twee by it:

> Many for Poems care much, for Poesie little or nothing;
> Story, character, reasoning, subtlety, eloquence, wit,
> They find; the verse at most is merely taken as clothing
> And decoration, – 'tis well if they be not 'bored' with it;
> But the fine, the mystical, magical influence, all-involving,
> Lifting, dissolving, reshaping, into music revolving,
> Giving a life to the words, putting an atmosphere round them,
> Of this no sense have they, and Poesie leaves where it found them.[24]

23. Anyone who believes that the subject of a poem determines our pleasure in reading it should compare Shelley's 'Ozymandias' with Horace Smith's sonnet 'On a Stupendous Leg of Granite, discovered standing by itself in the Deserts of Egypt, with the Inscription inserted below', and which opens: 'In Egypt's sandy silence, all alone, / Stands a gigantic Leg...'
24. In *Blackberries* (1890); the complete poem.

Allingham leads by example here: his own handling of the hexameter is beautifully and appositely varied within the poem's short space, from the crisp balance of the opening line, through the ungainly awkwardness of line 4, the surge in lines 5–7, to the downbeat ending, monosyllabic except for the word 'Poesie' which is itself a parting gesture. I have gathered the poems in this anthology with his priority in mind. 'Story, character, reasoning, subtlety, eloquence, wit': readers will find all these, but they will also, I hope, find what gives life to these words.

## 3. I THAT WAS I

Victorian verse is polymorphous, but in metrical terms it is not polymorphously perverse. No major British poet 'broke the pentameter' as Whitman did, or saw any need to free poetic language from its traditional shackles. Indeed there is little in Victorian poetry as radical in this respect as Blake, let alone T. S. Eliot. Hopkins might appear the exception, but Hopkins himself saw his metrical technique not as revolutionary but as (creatively) regressive, a return to an older accentual tradition; and in fact he never wrote free verse, never departed either from strict (if eccentric) metrical structure or from rhyme. He is less a proto-Modernist in his metre than the Tennyson of certain parts of *Maud* (so clearly an influence on *The Waste Land*). Yet even where verse in the period is 'free' in terms of metrical pattern, it is almost never unrhymed.[25] Traditional forms and metres – the sonnet, the ode, the ballad; blank verse, the heroic couplet, the hexameter – were endlessly discussed, polished, varied, and experimented with, but were all as fixed at the end of Victoria's reign as at its beginning. The sonnet, in particular, attracted an enormous amount of reflexive interest – almost everyone who wrote one seems to have written a sonnet on the subject of sonnet-writing – and there was a prolonged debate about the possibility

25. Examples of unpatterned rhymed verse would be Christina Rossetti's *Goblin Market* (no. 195) and Coventry Patmore's poems in *The Unknown Eros* (nos. 165–7); some of T. E. Brown's poems in the *Roman Women* sequence (not included in this anthology) are also of this kind. There are rare examples of true 'free verse' in W. E. Henley's *In Hospital* sequence (e.g. the final poem, 'Discharged', no. 313); other examples include the second section of R. L. Stevenson's 'The Light-Keeper' (no. 321) and his 'The Cruel Mistress' (not in this anthology). Matthew Arnold's 'Philomela' (no. 158) comes close to free verse, though it makes intermittent use of rhyme and half-rhyme.

or desirability of using classical (i.e. quantitative) metres in English. But a poet from the end of the eighteenth century – Cowper, say – would have had no trouble in recognizing as verse a poem from the end of the nineteenth (whatever else he might have thought of it); he would be in difficulties today.

The traditionalism of Victorian metre was enforced by a weight of precedent which proved very hard to shake off. But the will to shake it off was not in any case very strong; there were patriotic reasons for regarding the burden of the past as an inheritance, an estate to be culti-vated. If Hopkins looks back to pre-Elizabethan verse for the sources of 'sprung rhythm', James Smetham (the painter and friend of D. G. Rossetti) characterizes blank verse as quintessentially English, 'like a lane / In the deep rural regions'. His poem, called 'Blank Verse', con-cludes with an explicitly patriotic invocation:

> Come then, dear English muse, whoe'er thou art,
> Come like a mild, dear daughter of the land,
> The land and language that I always love.
> Come like an English matron, pure and bright,
> Or like an English maiden, frank and fair;
> Come with the honeysuckle breath of eve;
> Come with the simple wild-rose flush of morn;
> Come with no Greek pretension – Russian cold –
> Or Persian fever. Come just as thou art,
> Clasped by the loving Present; teach to me
> The long, mellifluous, voluntary lay,
> Unvexed by hard necessities of sound,
> Yet always sensibly subordinate
> To one clear music and unshackled law.[26]

The influence of Wordsworth and Tennyson is evident here, and behind them that of Cowper and other eighteenth-century practitioners of the meditative idyll; like the English countryside itself, blank verse is a product of cultivation over so long a period that it seems natural, native to 'the land and language'. There is a political dimension, too, in the rejection of foreign forms and in the 'English' compromise by which verse is 'sensibly subordinate' to an 'unshackled law'. Though this is an

26. *Literary Works of James Smetham*, ed. W. Davies, 1893, pp. 279–80.

extreme example, it suggests how problematic the notion of metrical rebellion would have seemed to most Victorian poets, and helps to account for the virtual absence of such a rebellion throughout the period.

The persistence of traditional metre is not, however, the whole story. The radicalism of Victorian poetry lies elsewhere, not in the forms of poetry but in its voice and tone. Each of these aspects of poetry, voice and tone, is governed by opposing forces – for Victorian poetry, like Victorian politics, sees the emergence and consolidation of a two-party system. In voice: speech and song; in tone: light and dark. The greatest achievements of Victorian poetry belong to these divisions.

## Light and Dark

I confess to an indiscriminate taste for Victorian light verse, but some discrimination is appropriate here. To begin with, 'light' is not necessarily the equivalent of 'comic'. Quentin Blake dismisses 'the mixture of high spirits and dogged verbal effort' in comic writing before Lear;[27] perhaps this is too sweeping, but the facetiousness of *Punch* and its like can certainly be wearying, and sometimes worse than wearying. Most Victorian racial humour is so offensive that it cannot be reprinted; modern taboos are real enough, as those of the Victorians were to them. (But we caricature theirs, on matters of sex and religion; ours are different, because, after all, we are right and they were wrong.) Still, there is excellent comic writing in the period, particularly in the form of literary parody, a genre in which Victorian poets take unerring aim at 'Victorian' poetry. Good though such poems are, however, there is 'light verse' which is better, and more distinctive, and whose effect is not to make you laugh but to make you see.

Christopher Ricks praises Victorian light verse for offering 'unique combinations of acumen and pathos'.[28] He cites Swinburne's reading – not less generous than just – of the last stanza of Browning's 'Youth and Art' (no. 103), whose 'quiet note of commonplace resignation is more bitter and more impressive in the self-scornful sadness of its retrospect than any shriek of rebellion or any imprecation of appeal'. Certainly Swinburne could speak with authority from the other side of the com-

27. Introduction to *Edward Lear's Complete Nonsense* (Folio Society, 1996), p. 10.
28. *The New Oxford Book of Victorian Verse* (1987), p. xxix.

parison, and I intend to return his compliment with, I hope, equal conviction. But it should also be said that much Victorian light verse has acumen without pathos, and is admirable for that reason. The trigger for such poetry is often a scepticism about the conventional triggers of poetic feeling. Hartley Coleridge's 'The Larch Grove' (no. 33) moves from delicate and true description to a flat conclusion: the first stanza is beautifully observed, the second is a bit pretty, the third is frankly soppy, with the larches hoping 'to soothe the pensive woe, / Or hide the joy of stealthy tripping lover'; but *no such luck*, the final stanza tells us:

> Ah, larches! that shall never be your lot;
> Nought shall you have to do with amorous weepers,
> Nor shall ye prop the roof of cozy cot,
> But rumble out your days as railway sleepers.

As this poem progresses it loses faith in 'poetic' language, especially the pathetic fallacy; it also resists the tendency of lyric towards a point of rest, the 'sleepers' at the end being anything but quiet. It's a reflexive poem, perhaps too knowing about poetic convention; other such 'unpoetic' poems have the same flaw, for example Mary Montgomerie Lamb's '"For One Man's Pleasure"' (no. 278), yet the excellence of this poem is inseparable from its self-conscious fluttering of the Victorian dovecot.

These poems are 'light' not simply in being humorous, but in eschewing a 'great purpose, moral, political, or philosophical' for poetry. This is a poetry both of 'commonplace resignation' and of commonplace rejoicing, but in either case poised in that feeling itself (which is a different thing, or can be at its best, from the false poise of complacency). It is a poetry of image but not of symbol. I am thinking of poems such as W. E. Henley's 'Back-View' (no. 314), or William Canton's 'The Crow' (no. 295), or C. S. Calverley's 'Peace' (no. 226); the last lines of Henley's poem, in particular, epitomize this mode, as the 'outline' of the woman's body stays in the mind of the observer, poignantly evocative and inconsequential:

> Your grace was quick my sense to seize:
> The quaint looped hat, the twisted tresses,
> The close-drawn scarf, and under these
> The flowing, flapping draperies –
> My thought an outline still caresses,
> Enchanting, comic, Japanese!

'Flowing, flapping' is daring and original in its unpoetic lilt, as the whole poem is; but these effects are not confined to whole poems, or to poets who work primarily at creating them. Shreds and patches may be woven into any Victorian poet's Sunday best. Not loss of dignity, but change of focus is involved, a change which allows Swinburne, for the tiniest and briefest of moments, to shrug something off:

> A live thing maybe; who shall know?
> The summer knows and suffers it . . .
>
> ('The Sundew' [no. 251], ll. 6–7)

'Suffers' means 'tolerates'; this is a glimpse of a world without suffering, in which something is known, and may be alive, without the pain which Swinburne habitually attaches to these states.

Light verse, in this sense, is committed to observation, and lets the thing seen (or the thought that occurs) shape the poem's design. The observer's standpoint barely matters: it 'motivates' the observation only in the sense of setting it in motion. The poet's subjectivity may be in play, but is not at stake. 'Michael Field's' 'A curling thread' (no. 298) exemplifies this quality, in contrast to their poem 'L'Indifférent' (no. 297), which is not light verse but verse about lightness, a work of art which ponders a work of art whose central figure denies interpretation and desire. The poets' curious, passionate, baffled gaze at Watteau's painting is central to 'L'Indifférent', whose rhythm represents their enchantment as much as it does the dancer's charm. 'A curling thread' has no such centre of gravity. By a cunning variation of end-stopped and run-on lines, the poem curls and wavers like the trail of smoke it describes, and the two longer lines imitate the broadening and thickening of the smoke as it rises. There are glances, intimations of 'higher' meaning in the poem's language (might it be about human breath and evanescence?) but the form is like a smile and a shake of the head. 'Upward flight' turns to 'upward float', and effacement comes in a drifting time of 'by-and-bye'.

The 'lightness' of this poem is a matter of balance and self-possession: the poets do not contemplate the dance of 'L'Indifférent', they perform it. But Victorian poetry is wonderful, too, at losing its balance, at letting go – especially at letting go in the dark – and then setting that vertiginous fall to music. We tend to think that an excess of emotion makes for bad art, but there are times when, emotionally speaking, you can't have too much of a bad thing. The Great Exhibition of Victorian poetic gloom is rightly excessive, opulent and self-indulgent. I come back to Swinburne's praise of 'Youth and Art'. Yes, the lightness and ironic restraint of Browning's poem are powerfully affecting, but Swinburne too easily caricatures the 'shriek of rebellion'. There are times when you don't feel like this –

> And nobody calls you a dunce,
>   And people suppose me clever:
> This could but have happened once,
>   And we missed it, lost it for ever.

but like this –

> Let Love clasp Grief lest both be drown'd,
>   Let darkness keep her raven gloss:
> Ah, sweeter to be drunk with loss,
> To dance with death, to beat the ground . . .

Tennyson says *sweeter*, not just *better*: he's talking about being drunk, about dancing, about physical abandonment; the rhyme of 'loss' with 'gloss' is like a secretion. If grief were not a pleasure we wouldn't (to use Swinburne's word) suffer it. *In Memoriam* devotes itself to getting out of this state of mind, but it takes time (and the poem takes its time). James Thomson's approach is not temporal, but spatial, as the metaphor of *The City of Dreadful Night* indicates: he is not a pilgrim, or a mourner, but a sojourner, a citizen and inhabitant; and he is imbued with civic pride. Thomson's imagination, which creates the symbolic landscapes and architecture of the city, presents itself to us as a profound and unscrupulous *curiosity*, a determination to explore every part of his city (central squares and outlying suburbs, bridges and temples, public and private spaces), to take every view of it from the panoramic to the claus-trophobic, to eavesdrop on all its voices: a madman declaiming in an empty square, intimate conversations overheard by the riverbank, a sermon from a 'dark pulpit'.[29] It is a long poem not because the 'work of mourning', as Freud calls it, is lengthy, but because, as the tourist brochures say, there is so much to enjoy in the city's night-life.

Thomson's poem differs from Tennyson's in another respect, in that

---

29. There are only two encounters between the poet-narrator and another figure (sec-tions II and XVIII); everywhere else he is an observer or listener.

the anguish he evokes is not to do with lost love, but with impotence and infertility; he is suffering not from the absence of a beloved, but from the loss of libido, realized in multiple images of stagnation, emptiness, and disconnection. It is a different suffering, too, from that described by Hopkins in 'No worst, there is none' (no. 287), where the figure of a known and desired redeemer shapes the utterance as firmly as the form of the sonnet; or from that in Christina Rossetti's 'Introspective' (no. 209), in which an indomitable rhythmic energy affirms the potency of the self to resist 'terrible pain'. Among the inhabitants of Thomson's city, the desire for death is as little like a sexual urge as it can be, but in many other poets the reverse is true. Swinburne's 'The Garden of Proserpine' (no. 252) is a dance in which Death is swept off its feet: though describing a state of exhaustion and indifference to life (including its erotic profit or loss), the verse is unmisgivingly sensual and inventive, and cheats the poem of the idea it is supposed to manifest.

The quality of excess is vital to these poems: Hopkins ('No worst, there is none') and Christina Rossetti ('No sap in my uttermost root') reach for extremes that press against the limits of language and suggest both the desire to transcend it and the terror of that desire. Language, like the mirror in D. G. Rossetti's 'A Superscription' (no. 190), is 'Of ultimate things unuttered the frail screen'. But it is also a matter of concentration: where light verse specializes in mixing modes and registers, 'dark' verse is single-minded and strives for clarity and intensity, even when what it describes is an extravagance of feeling. Swinburne's poetry, at its best, has this unwavering focus and the shapeliness which springs from it, even in the wealth of negation displayed and catalogued in 'Ilicet' (no. 254). A poem like Ernest Dowson's 'Non Sum Qualis Eram Bonae Sub Regno Cynarae' (no. 405) couldn't afford a less splendid costume than it wears, or to economize by a single flourish on its gestures: it would be really absurd instead of truthful to its mood. But nor could it afford a less stringent metrical pattern; it may be melodramatic and self-absorbed, but it is staged with utter concentration and precision.

## Speech and Song

Consider these two passages, the opening lines of 'Bishop Blougram's Apology' by Robert Browning (not, alas, included in this anthology, for reasons of length), and Tennyson's 'Tithonus' (no. 76):

No more wine? then we'll push back chairs and talk.
A final glass for me, though: cool, i' faith!
We ought to have our Abbey back, you see.
It's different, preaching in basilicas,
And doing duty in some masterpiece
Like this of brother Pugin's, bless his heart!
I doubt if they're half-baked, those chalk rosettes,
Ciphers and stucco-twiddlings everywhere;
It's just like breathing in a lime-kiln: eh?
These long hot ceremonies of our church
Cost us a little – oh, they pay the price,
You take me – amply pay it! Now, we'll talk.

---

The woods decay, the woods decay and fall,
The vapours weep their burthen to the ground,
Man comes and tills the field and lies beneath,
And after many a summer dies the swan.
Me only cruel immortality
Consumes: I wither slowly in thine arms,
Here at the quiet limit of the world,
A white-hair'd shadow roaming like a dream
The ever-silent spaces of the East,
Far-folded mists, and gleaming halls of morn.

Both of these poems are dramatic monologues, in which a speaker addresses a silent partner, and both are in blank verse. But the verse sounds very different. Bishop Blougram is unaware of being in a poem, whereas Tithonus could be nowhere else. Browning tries to foster the illusion that the Bishop is simply talking to his dinner-guest, as he would do in real life, with all the little touches and turns of phrase that characterize ordinary conversational speech; the Bishop helps by twice using the word *talk* himself, but it's mainly done by prosaic syntax and cadence, 'prosaic' in the sense of not departing from normal word-order and inflexion. Browning takes especial care with line-endings: line 5 runs on into line 6 with barely a tremor, and the strong stresses on 'Ciphers' (line 8) and 'Cost' (line 10) come where the speaker would 'naturally' put them. The poem, 'Bishop Blougram's Apology', is disguised as Bishop Blougram's speech; but it is a poem, and not 'somebody talking', and our appreciation (and penetration) of the disguise is the key to the pleasure we take in it.[30]

In Tennyson's poem, the 'speaker' is notional; no one talks like that (to say that the speech is in character for a mythological personage addressing the goddess Aurora is simply to rephrase this point). The speech dramatizes a mood, an internal state of consciousness, and what represents the movement of consciousness is the verse itself, and especially its rhythm. The first four lines, though they speak of ending, seem never to end, whereas the line which speaks of immortality hurries on, precipitated by that tremendous syntactical inversion 'Me only', and runs over into the next as though eternity were a speedier process than mortal decay: by this paradox Tennyson suggests the acuteness (and acute pain) with which Tithonus grasps the predicament of duration. Death truly means you have all the time in the world; without it, time becomes abstract and immaterial, an architecture of empty 'spaces'.

These two poems are emblems of an aesthetic conflict, which had been gathering momentum over the previous two centuries (at least), and which is still active today, the conflict between speech and song as the foundation of poetic language.[31] The Victorians inherited this conflict from Romanticism (though they did so with a complication which I shall come to further on) and in particular from the dispute between Wordsworth and Coleridge about poetic diction. In the preface to *Lyrical Ballads*, Wordsworth stated that his intention had been to write poems 'in a selection of language really used by men',[32] and by 'used' he means primarily 'used in conversation'. The poet is 'a man speaking to men'[33] – speaking, not chanting, and speaking to his fellows; man, not bard. In chapter 18 of *Biographia Literaria*, Coleridge ridiculed this idea, and cited Wordsworth's own verse to disprove it; and he 'reflect[ed] with delight how little a mere theory, though of his own workmanship, interferes with the processes of genuine imagination in a man of true poetic

30. A pleasure which contrasts with the reaction of the hapless journalist Gigadibs, Blougram's silent (and silenced) interlocutor within the poem, 'Who played with spoons, explored his plate's design, / And ranged the olive-stones about its edge ...' (ll. 976–7).
31. I have discussed this conflict within Browning's own poetry, and its origins in Romantic debates about poetic language, in chapter 2 of J. Woolford and D. Karlin, *Robert Browning* (Longman, 1996). Some of the material from this chapter is repeated here in a modified and abbreviated form.
32. Reference as in n. 22 above, p. 59.
33. As above, p. 71.

genius'.[34] For Coleridge, the poet is emphatically not 'a man speaking to men', but someone who is endowed with (again he turns Wordsworth's own phrase against him) 'the vision and the faculty divine'.[35]

Needless to say this conflict is not resolvable; equally obviously, both parties to it are divided against themselves, at least if they have any sense; for good poetry almost always comes from taking the line of most resistance. Still, the primary allegiance matters, and can be traced in this anthology in the form of an answer (given with however much reluctance and qualification) to Wordsworth's question: 'What is a Poet? To whom does he address himself? And what language is to be expected of him?'[36]

The speaking voice is closely identified with the dramatic monologue, as Browning developed the form, where its idiom is colloquial and knowingly unpoetic. The speaker of 'How It Strikes a Contemporary' (*Men and Women*, 1855) begins: 'I only knew one poet in my life: / And this, or something like it, was his way.' He ends on the same note: 'Well, I could never write a verse, – could you?' (l. 114). The joke is a bit obvious here, but it flags up a principle which animates every dramatic monologue of its type. Nor is it necessary that the speakers of such monologues should be 'contemporaries' – Fra Lippo Lippi from the fifteenth century speaks as colloquially as Bishop Blougram from the nineteenth. Browning was especially good at 'hearing' cadences of ordinary speech which haven't dated at all, but there are plenty of examples from other poets: Victorian poetry, if it did not invent such effects, is the first to exploit them as part of a recognizable aesthetic design.

Dramatic monologue is the focus of this design because of the strong historical association in literary language between the dramatic and the colloquial. Common speech also entered the meditative lyric, as it did narrative and descriptive verse, but it did so dramatically, in the sense of borrowing from dramatic monologue its assumption of a listener who occupies the same ground as the speaker. This listener becomes, in the lyric, the reader; and the reader's participation in the *mise-en-scène* of the poem marks a striking difference from the bardic or Romantic mode which forms the other great stream of Victorian lyric verse.

34. *Biographia Literaria*, ed. G. Watson (Dent, 1975), p. 201.
35. Reference as above; Coleridge also uses this phrase in chapter 12 (p. 139). It comes from *The Excursion*, I, 79; the passage as a whole is actually about poets who have this 'faculty' but lack 'the accomplishment of verse', so Coleridge's use of it in an argument about poetic language is double-edged.
36. Preface to *Lyrical Ballads*, reference as above (n. 22), pp. 70–71.

I can best trace this difference by comparing two poems from the beginning and end of the Victorian period, Wordsworth's 'Hark! 'tis the Thrush' (no. 1), written in 1838, and Hardy's 'The Darkling Thrush' (no. 268), written in 1899 or 1900. Though Wordsworth's poetics are the foundation of the 'spoken lyric', this poem is the reverse of such a lyric in that it implicitly excludes or ignores the presence of a reader. The reader is a spectator, from outside the poem's frame, of the communion which takes place between the poet and the bird – a communion which is created by the poet with an unselfconscious authority from the very first word, 'Hark!', an exclamation addressed by the speaker to himself and not to us. When, in line 6, the poet addresses the bird, he speaks of it as though it had purposefully 'snapped a fire-side Prisoner's chain', but the purpose is all the poet's: there is a 'plot' in the poem (of an old man's recapturing of poetic and erotic power) but it is the plot of a monodrama. Poet and bird are joined by having 'mute' female partners to whom and for whom they sing; one effect of hearing the bird's song is to get the poet on his feet and out of the house, no longer cosseting himself in old age and vile weather, but restoring his youth and potency by 'front[ing] the blast'. The bird prompts this renewal: it turns out that the poet has been the bird's surrogate partner, though not a mute one. The silent female will be 'thrilled' by the poet's 'social Lay' (including this poem) but her apprehension of it, like ours, is projected beyond the space of the poem itself.

In Hardy's poem the reader is differently placed; the poet does not need direct address to imply the reader as witness to the drama of his encounter with the thrush (which is also an encounter with Wordsworth's poem, and with many other poems on this theme from the nineteenth century and before).[37] The reader is addressed precisely because the thrush is not; the poet and the thrush are not at one, but at odds, and the object of the poem is to communicate this at-oddsness to someone else – to us. Hardy does not need to be tempted away from his 'household fire' – he is already out there, while everyone else has taken shelter – yet 'all mankind' is emblematically with him. Although Hardy's vocabulary and syntax are quirky and complicated, they are those of a speaker, and the poem is (in the most un-trivial sense) anecdotal. Its story – of the poet's perception of suffering baffled by an enigmatic bliss – belongs to us and to our fellowship with Hardy's voice.

37. Further sources for 'perhaps Hardy's most allusive poem' are suggested by Tim Armstrong: see *Thomas Hardy: Selected Poems*, Longman, 1993, p. 89.

Wordsworth perhaps can't avoid appearing selfish, or at least self-regarding, when compared with Hardy in this way. It's nice for him to have his cares charmed to rest, but it does rather put the 'exulting Warbler' at his service, and it puts the reader in the shade. Keats called this aspect of Wordsworth's poetic character the 'egotistical sublime',[38] but he was giving both terms their due weight, and so should we. The 'undaunted' singer in Wordsworth's poem is admirable, and repays our admiration, in the measure of his sincerity. If he were to catch our eye the effect would be dissipated. The sincerity need not be authentic (true to a real-life event or feeling), but its rhetoric must be convincing, for that is what invites us into the poem. (As the cannibal chief advises his son in the old Flanders and Swann sketch: 'Always be sincere – whether you mean it or not.') The 'I' of the poem is a complex phenomenon. The pronoun itself appears first in line 9, the first line of the sestet and thus, traditionally, the turning point of the sonnet. Before that we have an implied consciousness (the mind which receives sense-impressions and forms ideas about them) in lines 1–5 and then, in lines 6–8, the creation of a self in the shift from third to first person:

> Thanks; thou hast snapped a fire-side Prisoner's chain,
> Exulting Warbler! eased a fretted brain,
> And in a moment charmed my cares to rest.
> Yes, I will forth . . .

Strictly speaking, 'my' in line 8 should be 'his', but the poet stops talking about himself in the third person and grammatically (and dramatically) re-possesses himself. It is this figure who commands our attention, not that of the 'real' Wordsworth whose egotism outside his poetry so exasperated Keats and others.

The comparison between Wordsworth and Hardy draws attention to a division in the lyric voice of Victorian poetry between the 'egotistical sublime', the poetry of 'song', whose supreme exponents are Tennyson and Christina Rossetti, and the dramatic and humanist 'speaking' of Browning and Hardy. But these examples from different ends of the period illustrate a complicating difficulty for both sides of this divide. What is striking about Wordsworth's poem is its confidence: it has an authority, self-conscious but not self-doubting, which is also traceable in

38. Letter to Richard Woodhouse, 27 October 1818.

his other late poems. Arguments about whether Wordsworth should figure in an anthology of Victorian poetry miss the point if they focus on chronological propriety: a much stronger case might be made for saying that Wordsworth shouldn't be included because he represents everything which Victorian poets know they have lost, and lost for ever. Browning saw Wordsworth as the 'Lost Leader' (see no. 96) because of his political apostasy, but he is also lost, and mourned, because his greatness cannot be truly inherited. 'Never glad confident morning again!' is a cry from the heart of Victorian poetry which echoes down to Hardy's contemplation of the 'weakening eye of day' and a sky which is itself an emblem of broken music. But Wordsworth had been there before them. In the last poem of his which I have included, and which is one of the last he wrote, the sonnet 'To an Octogenarian' (no. 7), he depicts a condition of utter bleakness and desolation in order to deny its hold over him: 'fear not such a dearth'. Lear-like he may be in destitution and 'utmost solitude of age', but he is his own Cordelia, too: the heart's capacity for love accomplishes his salvation, and rescues him from the condition of being a 'sole survivor'. He bequeaths this condition with ruthless economy to others – to his heirs, or rather non-heirs. Victorian poetry is Wordsworth's decrepit orphan, which can 'never hope to reach a second birth'. Browning's phrase 'Never glad confident morning again', which suggests that he can never think of Wordsworth with the love and respect he once felt for him, should also be set alongside these lines from a poem which explicitly invokes Wordsworth's 'Hark! 'tis the Thrush':

> Hark, where my blossomed pear-tree in the hedge
> Leans to the field and scatters on the clover
> Blossoms and dewdrops – at the bent spray's edge –
> That's the wise thrush; he sings each song twice over
> Lest you should think he never could recapture
> The first fine careless rapture!
>
>     ('Home-Thoughts, from Abroad' [no. 95], ll. 11–16)

Wordsworth may be this 'wise thrush', but it is a position which the speaker of Browning's poem can only conjure 'from abroad', which he can dramatize but not possess.

    Why should Victorian poets have felt collectively that they were orphans of Romanticism? Some, like Arnold and Hardy, see the problem as, in part at least, a product of larger social developments, by which poetry is discountenanced: materialism, Philistinism, the expansion and disaggregation of communities, the failure of ideas of revolution or, on the contrary, their alarming success. Poets such as Elizabeth Barrett Browning, however, as we have seen, did not accept that poetry could not flourish in modern conditions; their difficulty was with the poetics of Romanticism itself, the primacy it placed on a self-affirming energy which was also self-consuming, which denied the possibility of succession. In her 1842 review-essay in the *Athenaeum* which I mentioned above, Barrett Browning quotes from the 'Prelude' to Wordsworth's volume, *Poems, chiefly of Early and Late Years*:

> Go, single – yet aspiring to be joined
> With thy Forerunners that through many a year
> Have faithfully prepared each other's way ... [39]

Each of Wordsworth's volumes plays a dual role: John the Baptist in relation to the volume to follow, Christ in relation to the one which came before.[40] The exceptions, obviously, would be the first and the last. What a masterstroke, then, to issue *Poems, chiefly of Early and Late Years* as the final individual volume of his career! This is to be alpha and omega with a vengeance; and indeed the 'Prelude' to the volume announces the redemptive influence of Wordsworth's 'sapient Art' on a cosmic scale,

> Softening the toils and pains that have not ceased
> To cast their shadows on our mother Earth
> Since the primeval doom.                                    (ll. 26–8)

39. This poem opens with the same image of the thrush 'urged rather than restrained / By gusts of vernal storm' (ll. 3–4) as in 'Hark! 'tis the Thrush', which had been published four years earlier. The thrush sings 'above showers of blossom swept / From tossing boughs' (ll. 7–8), an image which Browning adapts in 'Home-Thoughts, from Abroad' where the pear-tree 'scatters / Blossoms and dewdrops'; I'd guess that Browning knew both of Wordsworth's poems and might really have thought of him as singing his song twice over.

40. The image is from the synoptic gospels (Matthew, Mark, Luke) in which John the Baptist comes to 'prepare the way of the Lord' and announces that 'he that cometh after me is mightier than I'. The term 'forerunner' itself, however, occurs not in the gospels but in one of St Paul's epistles, where it is applied not to John but to Jesus (Hebrews 6: 20), and means that Jesus has gone before us, and on our behalf, 'within the veil'.

This influence is the 'grace' which 'fails not to descend / With heavenly inspiration' on the chosen poet (ll. 29–31), and Wordsworth anticipates that it will operate both in 'private life' as a healing and comforting 'Voice' (ll. 33–42), and on public opinion in days of political turmoil, 'Among a People mournfully cast down, / Or into anger roused by venal words', as a force 'tending to console / And reconcile' (ll. 42–52).[41]

Victorian poets who attempt to imitate Wordsworth's sublime presumption often sound merely presumptuous, or, worse, impertinent, as Cosmo Monkhouse does in the poem I quoted earlier. Only Tennyson, and then only in a handful of poems ('In the Valley of Cauteretz' [no. 85] is the clearest example) can take on this persona. Whether 'speakers' or 'singers', Victorian poets had to negotiate a less determinate authority. Christina Rossetti's 'Spring Quiet', for example (no. 199), is governed grammatically by a conditional clause in the first stanza which is never fulfilled – and even if it could be, the last stanza tells us, you would catch no more than an 'echo' of the 'far sea'. In the first of Elizabeth Barrett Browning's Sonnets from the Portuguese (no. 59), the poet is empowered by being overcome: the voice which speaks to her 'in mastery' asks her a question whose answer she gets wrong, and so she wins the prize. A last example: 'Aeschylus Homer and Shakespeare' (no. 329), by 'Caerleon', my easy opening target. A poem of despairing self-abnegation? Yes and no: the pressure of the great poetry of the past creates in the poem which records this pressure an answering resilience. The poet's formal control is notable: he thinks thematically in threes (three poets, three mountain ranges, three other forms of nature, three violent actions, three forms of suffering) and rhythmically in twos (the alternation of long and short lines). The sense of order in the poem is also grammatical. The first stanza is without a main verb, the poets are simply there, like the mountains. In the second stanza the scale changes from the vertical to the horizontal and from one concept of immensity

41. It was somewhat disingenuous of Wordsworth to pretend that this salutary influence lay in an unspecified future; in the note to the poem which he dictated to Isabella Fenwick he admits that he intended a specific allusion to the thoroughly contemporary 'agitators of the Anti-Corn-Law League', whose 'venal words' are opposed by the words of his poems. He excused himself for doing so: 'the particular causes of such troubles are transitory, but disposition to excite and liability to be excited are nevertheless permanent, and therefore proper objects for the Poet's regard'. It is comforting, in a way which Wordsworth did not intend, to know that the agitators, as well as the poor, will always be with us. But O! if only Hazlitt had survived to write the review of the Poetical Works in which this note appeared!

to another; and this excites the first response ('Vain to compass you') and the first indication of why this inability should be tragic: against the great 'souls' of the past '*The* soul must yield' (it should be 'My soul', but generalizing the point shields him from its impact a little longer). This yielding does not yet seem mortal to the soul; it might be a question of giving in gracefully, accepting the posture of worship: but surrender is followed by annihilation.[42] In the last stanza, names and nouns are gathered into a personal 'Ye' and the verbs are all in all: the stasis of the first stanza converts itself into terrible movement, from mountain to avalanche. The movement is also one of time, from the great poets' frozen eternity of fame to an apparently irreversible process in which the lesser poet's self is lost: 'I *am* crushed . . . I that *was* I.' 'Apparently' – yet the last line paradoxically regenerates this lost self. 'I that was I' is a redundant phrase: the 'action' of the poem finishes in the previous line, which is grammatically self-contained.[43] But this redundant expression is *rhythmically* necessary for the poem to end, and this is a figure of its power. The two strong beats in the line fall on the 'I' that has been erased, and the poet's 'soul' is reborn. Self-pity? Well, there is a way to true pathos, even from the gates of self-pity.

Many of the finest Victorian poems are founded on such inter- and contradictions, on thwarted energies which force themselves through unexpected channels, on impulses of restlessness and misgiving. But the misgivings of Victorian poetry were truly a gift to Modernism, a treas-ure which funded its experiments and which the ungrateful pirates claimed to have dug up themselves. The contest between 'speech' and 'song', which is carried on by Eliot and Pound among others, and which animates English poetry up to Larkin and beyond, suggests something of the intelligence of Victorian poetry and of its enduring vitality.

---

42. Compare another short poem on the same subject, Digby Mackworth Dolben's 'After Reading Aeschylus', which opens with the line 'I will not sing my little puny songs', and ends: 'Therefore in passiveness I will lie still, / And let the multitudinous music of the Greek / Pass into me, till I am musical.' Dolben wrote a similar, though less intemperate, poem called 'After Reading Homer'.

43. In grammatical terms the last line is a descriptive modifier, giving you extra information about the 'I' in the penultimate line. It could be differently placed: 'I – I that was I – am crushed', etc., but the placing is all-important here.

# PRELUDE: TO VICTORIA

(i)

## Anonymous

### Queen Victoria (1837)

Welcome now, VICTORIA!
Welcome to the throne!
May all the trades begin to stir,
    Now you are Queen of England;
For your most gracious Majesty,
May see what wretched poverty,
Is to be found on England's ground,
    Now you are Queen of England.

While o'er the country you preside,
Providence will be your guide,
The people then will never chide
    Victoria, Queen of England.
She doth declare it her intent
To extend reform in Parliament,
On doing good she's firmly bent,
    While she is Queen of England.

Says she, I'll try my utmost skill,
That the poor may have their fill;
Forsake them! – no, I never will,
    When I am Queen of England.
For oft my mother said to me,
Let this your study always be,
To see the people blest and free,
    Should you be Queen of England.

And now, my daughter, you do reign,
Much opposition to sustain,
You'll surely have, before you gain
    The blessings of Old England.

O yes, dear mother, that is true,
I know my sorrows won't be few,
Poor people shall have work to do,
    When I am Queen of England.

I will encourage every trade,
For their labour must be paid,
In this free country then she said,
    Victoria, Queen of England;
The poor-law bill, with many more,
Shall be trampled on the floor –
The rich must keep the helpless poor,
    While I am Queen of England.

The Royal Queen of Britain's isle
Soon will make the people smile,
Her heart none can the least defile,
    Victoria, Queen of England.
Although she is of early years,
She is possess'd of tender cares,
To wipe away the orphan's tears,
    While she is Queen of England.

With joy each Briton doth exclaim,
Both far and near across the main,
Victoria we now proclaim
    The Royal Queen of England;
Long may she live, and happy be,
Adorn'd with robes of Royalty,
With blessings from her subjects free,
    While she is Queen of England.

In every town and village gay,
The bells shall ring, and music play,
Upon her Coronation-day,
    Victoria, Queen of England.

While her affections we do win,
And every day fresh blessings bring,
Ladies, help me for to sing,
    Victoria, Queen of England.

(ii)                    Elizabeth Barrett Browning

            *from* Crowned and Wedded (1840)

But now before her people's face she bendeth hers anew,
And calls them, while she vows, to be her witness thereunto.
She vowed to rule, and in that oath her childhood put away:
She doth maintain her womanhood, in vowing love to-day.
O lovely lady! let her vow! such lips become such vows,
And fairer goeth bridal wreath than crown with vernal brows.
O lovely lady! let her vow! yea, let her vow to love!
And though she be no less a queen, with purples hung above,
The pageant of a court behind, the royal kin around,
And woven gold to catch her looks turned maidenly to ground,
Yet may the bride-veil hide from her a little of that state,
While loving hopes for retinues about her sweetness wait.
SHE vows to love who vowed to rule – (the chosen at her side)
Let none say, God preserve the queen! but rather, Bless the bride!
None blow the trump, none bend the knee, none violate the dream
Wherein no monarch but a wife she to herself may seem.
Or if ye say, Preserve the queen! oh, breathe it inward low –
She is a *woman*, and *beloved!* and 'tis enough but so.
Count it enough, thou noble prince who tak'st her by the hand
And claimest for thy lady-love our lady of the land!
And since, Prince Albert, men have called thy spirit high and rare,
And true to truth and brave for truth as some at Augsburg were,
We charge thee by thy lofty thoughts and by thy poet-mind
Which not by glory and degree takes measure of mankind,
Esteem that wedded hand less dear for sceptre than for ring,
And hold her uncrowned womanhood to be the royal thing.

And now, upon our queen's last vow what blessings shall we pray?
None straitened to a shallow crown will suit our lips to-day:
Behold, they must be free as love, they must be broad as free,
Even to the borders of heaven's light and earth's humanity.
Long live she! – send up loyal shouts, and true hearts pray between, –
'The blessings happy PEASANTS have, be thine, O crownèd queen!'


(iii)                    Thomas Cooper

*from* The Purgatory of Suicides (1845)

*Book 7, stanzas 7–9*

I saw thee on the day thou wast a bride,
And shouted, 'mid my joy-tears, with the crowd:
Thou wert a woman, and thou sattst beside
Thy bosom's choice, while happiness o'erflowed
Thy heart, and in thy fair young countenance glowed.
Beholding thine, what could I less than feel
A sympathetic joy? Ay, though a proud
Worship of England's stern old Commonweal
Was mine, – for thee, that day, I breathed devotion leal.

And many a heart, yielding, that festive day,
To Nature's impulses of hope and joy,
Confiding, blessed thee! Queen! if thou delay
To help thy Poor – if thou, thyself, destroy
The promise of that time, and harsh alloy
Of blame with memory of our joy now blend –
What marvel? Hopes, that do the heart upbuoy,
Turned to despair by sufferings slighted, rend
All gentle feelings in their way to some dire end.

When next thou passest by Whitehall, look up,
I pray thee, and remember who felt there
The fatal axe! Ay, – look! – nor be the dupe
Of tinselled traitors who would thee ensnare

To ease and grandeur, till – thy People's prayer
For justice all too long delayed – they rise
With that old heart the Stuart to despair
Drove, first, – and, then, to vengeance! Hunger cries
Throughout thy realm – 'Queen! from the fearful Past –
    be wise!'


(iv)              Alfred Tennyson

## To the Queen (1851)

Revered, beloved – O you that hold
   A nobler office upon earth
   Than arms, or power of brain, or birth
Could give the warrior kings of old,

Victoria, – since your Royal grace
   To one of less desert allows
   This laurel greener from the brows
Of him that utter'd nothing base;

And should your greatness, and the care
   That yokes with empire, yield you time
   To make demand of modern rhyme
If aught of ancient worth be there;

Then – while a sweeter music wakes,
   And thro' wild March the throstle calls,
   Where all about your palace-walls
The sun-lit almond-blossom shakes –

Take, Madam, this poor book of song;
   For tho' the faults were thick as dust
   In vacant chambers, I could trust
Your kindness. May you rule us long,

And leave us rulers of your blood
　　As noble till the latest day!
　　May children of our children say,
'She wrought her people lasting good;

'Her court was pure; her life serene;
　　God gave her peace; her land reposed;
　　A thousand claims to reverence closed
In her as Mother, Wife, and Queen;

'And statesmen at her council met
　　Who knew the seasons when to take
　　Occasion by the hand, and make
The bounds of freedom wider yet

'By shaping some august decree,
　　Which kept her throne unshaken still,
　　Broad-based upon her people's will,
And compass'd by the inviolate sea.'

(v)                    A. E. Housman

## 1887

From Clee to heaven the beacon burns,
　　The shires have seen it plain,
From north and south the sign returns
　　And beacons burn again.

Look left, look right, the hills are bright,
　　The dales are light between,
Because 'tis fifty years to-night
　　That God has saved the Queen.

Now, when the flame they watch not towers
    About the soil they trod,
Lads, we'll remember friends of ours
    Who shared the work with God.

To skies that knit their heartstrings right,
    To fields that bred them brave,
The saviours come not home to-night:
    Themselves they could not save.

It dawns in Asia, tombstones show
    And Shropshire names are read;
And the Nile spills his overflow
    Beside the Severn's dead.

We pledge in peace by farm and town
    The Queen they served in war,
And fire the beacons up and down
    The land they perished for.

'God save the Queen' we living sing,
    From height to height 'tis heard;
And with the rest your voices ring,
    Lads of the Fifty-third.

Oh, God will save her, fear you not:
    Be you the men you've been,
Get you the sons your fathers got,
    And God will save the Queen.

(vi)                  Mary Montgomerie Lamb

Victoria

*21st June 1887*

Queen of so many nations that the sun
   Sets not upon the boundaries of thy sway, –
   Whom men of varied clime and creed obey, –
Mother of many Princes, – wife of one
Who, – now these fleet-foot fifty years are run
   Whereof the festival is held to-day, –
   Sees not thy golden tresses turn'd to grey,
But, – in eternal slumber, slumbers on; –
How many glorious images unite
   'Round thine illustrious name! – The Dragon's head
Beneath St. George's heel: – the Lion's might: –
   Britannia: – India's Empress, – robed in red,
Crown'd and enthroned! – Then lo! thou com'st in sight, –
   A lonely woman, – sable garmented.


(vii)                      Thomas Hardy

V. R. 1819–1901

A REVERIE

Moments the mightiest pass uncalendared,
   And when the Absolute
In backward Time outgave the deedful word
   Whereby all life is stirred:
'Let one be born and throned whose mould shall
      constitute
The norm of every royal-reckoned attribute,'
   No mortal knew or heard.

But in due days the purposed Life outshone –
   Serene, sagacious, free;
– Her waxing seasons bloomed with deeds well done,
   And the world's heart was won . . .
Yet may the deed of hers most bright in eyes to be
Lie hid from ours – as in the All-One's thought lay she –
   Till ripening years have run.

*Sunday Night, 27th January 1901*

# WILLIAM WORDSWORTH

## 1770–1850

1
    Hark! 'tis the Thrush, undaunted, undeprest,
    By twilight premature of cloud and rain;
    Nor does that roaring wind deaden his strain
    Who carols thinking of his Love and nest,
    And seems, as more incited, still more blest.
    Thanks; thou hast snapped a fire-side Prisoner's chain,
    Exulting Warbler! eased a fretted brain,
    And in a moment charmed my cares to rest.
    Yes, I will forth, bold Bird! and front the blast,
    That we may sing together, if thou wilt,
    So loud, so clear, my Partner through life's day,
    Mute in her nest love-chosen, if not love-built
    Like thine, shall gladden, as in seasons past,
    Thrilled by loose snatches of the social Lay.

*Rydal Mount, 1838*

2   Upon the Sight of the Portrait of a Female Friend

    Upon those lips, those placid lips, I look
    Nor grieve that they are still and mute as death;
    I gaze – I read as in an Angel's Book,
    And ask not speech from them, but long for breath.

3
    Near Anio's stream, I spied a gentle Dove
    Perched on an olive branch, and heard her cooing
    'Mid new-born blossoms that soft airs were wooing,
    While all things present told of joy and love.

But restless Fancy left that olive grove
To hail the exploratory Bird renewing
Hope for the few, who, at the world's undoing,
On the great flood were spared to live and move.
O bounteous Heaven! signs true as dove and bough
Brought to the ark are coming evermore,
Given though we seek them not, but, while we plough
This sea of life without a visible shore,
Do neither promise ask nor grace implore
In what alone is ours, the living Now.


4       So fair, so sweet, withal so sensitive,
        Would that the little Flowers were born to live,
        Conscious of half the pleasure which they give;

        That to this mountain-daisy's self were known
        The beauty of its star-shaped shadow, thrown
        On the smooth surface of this naked stone!

        And what if hence a bold desire should mount
        High as the Sun, that he could take account
        Of all that issues from his glorious fount!

        So might he ken how by his sovereign aid
        These delicate companionships are made;
        And how he rules the pomp of light and shade;

        And were the Sister-power that shines by night
        So privileged, what a countenance of delight
        Would through the clouds break forth on human sight!

        Fond fancies! wheresoe'er shall turn thine eye
        On earth, air, ocean, or the starry sky,
        Converse with Nature in pure sympathy;

All vain desires, all lawless wishes quelled,
Be Thou to love and praise alike impelled,
Whatever boon is granted or withheld.


5   On the Projected Kendal and Windermere Railway

Is then no nook of English ground secure
From rash assault? Schemes of retirement sown
In youth, and mid the busy world kept pure
As when their earliest flowers of hope were blown,
Must perish; – how can they this blight endure?
And must he too the ruthless change bemoan
Who scorns a false utilitarian lure
Mid his paternal fields at random thrown?
Baffle the threat, bright Scene, from Orrest-head
Given to the pausing traveller's rapturous glance:
Plead for thy peace, thou beautiful romance
Of nature; and, if human hearts be dead,
Speak, passing winds; ye torrents, with your strong
And constant voice, protest against the wrong.

*October 12th, 1844*

The degree and kind of attachment which many of the yeomanry feel to their small inheritances can scarcely be overrated. Near the house of one of them stands a magnificent tree, which a neighbour of the owner advised him to fell for profit's sake. 'Fell it!' exclaimed the yeoman, 'I had rather fall on my knees and worship it.' It happens, I believe, that the intended railway would pass through this little property, and I hope that an apology for the answer will not be thought necessary by one who enters into the strength of the feeling.


6        The unremitting voice of nightly streams
That wastes so oft, we think, its tuneful powers,
If neither soothing to the worm that gleams
Through dewy grass, nor small birds hushed in bowers,

Nor unto silent leaves and drowsy flowers, –
That voice of unpretending harmony
(For who what is shall measure by what seems
To be, or not to be,
Or tax high Heaven with prodigality?)
Wants not a healing influence that can creep
Into the human breast, and mix with sleep
To regulate the motion of our dreams
For kindly issues – as through every clime
Was felt near murmuring brooks in earliest time;
As at this day, the rudest swains who dwell
Where torrents roar, or hear the tinkling knell
Of water-breaks, with grateful heart could tell.

7            Sonnet (To an Octogenarian)

Affections lose their object; Time brings forth
No successors; and, lodged in memory,
If love exist no longer, it must die, –
Wanting accustomed food must pass from earth,
Or never hope to reach a second birth.
This sad belief, the happiest that is left
To thousands, share not Thou; howe'er bereft,
Scorned, or neglected, fear not such a dearth.
Though poor and destitute of friends thou art,
Perhaps the sole survivor of thy race,
One to whom Heaven assigns that mournful part
The utmost solitude of age to face,
Still shall be left some corner of the heart
Where Love for living Thing can find a place.

# WALTER SAVAGE LANDOR

## 1775–1864

8    Along this coast I led the vacant Hours
      To the lone sunshine on the uneven strand,
And nipt the stubborn grass and juicier flowers
      With one unconscious inobservant hand,
While crept the other by degrees more near
      Until it rose the cherisht form around,
And prest it closer, only that the ear
      Might lean, and deeper drink some half-heard sound.


9    Where alders rise up dark and dense
But just behind the wayside fence,
A stone there is in yonder nook
Which once I borrow'd of the brook:
You sate beside me on that stone,
Rather (not much) too wide for one.
Untoward stone! and never quite
(Tho' often very near it) right,
And putting to sore shifts my wit
To roll it out, then steady it,
And then to prove that it must be
Too hard for anyone but me.
Ianthe, haste! ere June declines
We'll write upon it all these lines.


10    The leaves are falling; so am I;
The few late flowers have moisture in the eye;
      So have I too.

Scarcely on any bough is heard
Joyous, or even unjoyous, bird
The whole wood through.
Winter may come: he brings but nigher
His circle (yearly narrowing) to the fire
Where old friends meet:
Let him; now heaven is overcast,
And spring and summer both are past,
And all things sweet.


11                 To a Cyclamen

I come to visit thee again,
My little flowerless cyclamen!
To touch the hands, almost to press,
That cheer'd thee in thy loneliness.
What could those lovely sisters find,
Of thee in form, of me in mind,
What is there in us rich or rare,
To make us worth a moment's care?
Unworthy to be so carest,
We are but wither'd leaves at best.


12                    Plays

How soon, alas, the hours are over,
Counted us out to play the lover!
And how much narrower is the stage,
Allotted us to play the sage!
But when we play the fool, how wide
The theatre expands; beside,
How long the audience sits before us!
How many prompters! what a chorus!

13          Cottage Left for London

The covert walk, the mossy apple-trees,
    And the long grass that darkens underneath,
I leave for narrow streets and gnats and fleas,
    Water unfit to drink and air to breathe.

14               Malvolio

Thou hast been very tender to the moon,
Malvolio! and on many a daffodil
And many a daisy hast thou yearn'd, until
The nether jaw quiver'd with thy good heart.
But tell me now, Malvolio, tell me true,
Hast thou not sometimes driven from their play
The village children, when they came too near
Thy study, if hit ball rais'd shouts around,
Or if delusive trap shook off thy muse,
Pregnant with wonders for another age?
Hast thou sat still and patient (tho' sore prest
Hearthward to stoop and warm thy blue-nail'd hand)
Lest thou shouldst frighten from a frosty fare
The speckled thrush, raising his bill aloft
To swallow the red berry on the ash
By thy white window, three short paces off?
If *this* thou hast not done, and hast done *that*,
I do exile thee from the moon twelve whole
Calendar months, debarring thee from use
Of rose, bud, blossom, odour, simile,
And furthermore I do hereby pronounce
Divorce between the nightingale and thee.

15        The Duke of York's Statue

> Enduring is the bust of bronze,
> And thine, O flower of George's sons,
> Stands high above all laws and duns.
>
> As honest men as ever cart
> Convey'd to Tyburn took thy part
> And raised thee up to where thou art.

16        I strove with none, for none was worth my strife;
>   Nature I loved, and, next to Nature, Art;
> I warmed both hands before the fire of life;
>   It sinks, and I am ready to depart.

# WILLIAM STEWART ROSE

## 1775–1843

17         Sonnet

*Occasioned by a visit to Torzelo, one of the*
*Venetian Isles, and formerly the Villeggiatura,*
*or summer resort of the Venetian nobility*

On a December's morn, nor dim nor dark,
   I, while a bright and brilliant sun outshone,
   (Such as in southern climate beams alone)
From Venice to Torzelo loosed my barque:
Cottage I saw 'mid palace overthrown,
   And wasted vineyard, garden close, or park; –
   And viewed an older fane than thine, St. Mark,
With door and window-shutters framed of stone:
While I considered fane and fallen bower,
   And standing hut, 'mid these well pleased to range,
A clock tolled twenty from a neighbouring tower:
   Time, changing all, himself had known no change;
But taught, as to another age, the hour,
   Warning his little world in language strange.

# EBENEZER ELLIOTT
## 1781–1849

18    British Rural Cottages in 1842

The scentless rose, train'd by the poor,
May sometimes grace the peasant's door;
But when will comfort enter there?
Beauty without, hides death within,
Like flowers upon the shroud of sin:
For ev'n the poor man's marriage-joys,
His wife, his sad-lipp'd girls and boys,
In mercy or in mockery given,
But brighten, with their 'hour of heav'n,'
A life of ghastly toil and care:
His pay is pain, his hope despair,
Although the cottage-rose is fair!
Out of his weekly pittance small,
Three crowns, for children, wife, and all,
Poor British Slave! how can he save
A pittance for his evening's close?
No roses deck the workhouse-grave!
Where is the aged pauper's rose!

19     Will It Rain?

'Bread!' the starver faintly sigheth;
'I have none!' the robb'd replieth;
Doall loseth, Starveall winneth;
Cheatall laugheth, while he sinneth;
Work grim-gaspeth o'er spare diet;
And the Million-Tongued is quiet.

When the forest breatheth deeply,
Darkèd sun down shining steeply;
When the noon-night scarcely shifteth;
And the windy cloud uplifteth
Not a leaf the mute heav'ns under;
Then, the thoughtful look for thunder!


20    Not die? Who saith that Nature cannot die?
Everywhere spreadeth, all things covereth
Echoless, motionless, unbounded snow.
The vagrant's footfall waketh no reply:
Starved wretch! he pauseth – Whither would he go?
He listeneth finger-lipp'd, and nothing saith
Of all the thoughts that fill'd his soul with woe,
But, freezing into stiffness, lacketh breath.
Dumb deadness pilloweth day on every hill.
Earth has no sound, no motion the dead sky;
No current, sensible to ear or eye,
The muffled stream's unconquerable will.
The pulse of Being seemeth standing still;
And January is the King of Death.

## The Fish, the Man, and the Spirit

*To Fish*

You strange, astonish'd-looking, angle-faced,
　　Dreary-mouth'd, gaping wretches of the sea,
　　Gulping salt-water everlastingly,
Cold-blooded, though with red your blood be graced,
And mute, though dwellers in the roaring waste;
　　And you, all shapes beside, that fishy be, –
　　Some round, some flat, some long, all devilry,
Legless, unloving, infamously chaste: –

O scaly, slippery, wet, swift, staring wights,
　　What is't ye do? what life lead? eh, dull goggles?
How do ye vary your vile days and nights?
　　How pass your Sundays? Are ye still but joggles
In ceaseless wash? Still nought but gapes and bites,
　　And drinks, and stares, diversified with boggles?

*A Fish Answers*

Amazing monster! that, for aught I know,
　　With the first sight of thee didst make our race
　　Forever stare! O flat and shocking face,
Grimly divided from the breast below!
Thou that on dry land horribly dost go
　　With a split body and most ridiculous pace,
　　Prong after prong, disgracer of all grace,
Long-useless-finned, hair'd, upright, unwet, slow!

O breather of unbreathable, sword-sharp air,
   How canst exist? How bear thyself, thou dry
And dreary sloth? What particle canst share
   Of the only blessed life, the watery?
I sometimes see of ye an actual *pair*
   Go by! link'd fin by fin! most odiously.

*The Fish turns into a Man, and then into a Spirit,*
*and again speaks*

Indulge thy smiling scorn, if smiling still,
   O man! and loathe, but with a sort of love:
   For difference must its use by difference prove,
And, in sweet clang, the spheres with music fill.
One of the spirits am I, that at his will
   Live in whate'er has life – fish, eagle, dove –
   No hate, no pride, beneath nought, nor above,
A visitor of the rounds of God's sweet skill.

Man's life is warm, glad, sad, 'twixt loves and graves,
   Boundless in hope, honour'd with pangs austere,
Heaven-gazing; and his angel-wings he craves:
   The fish is swift, small-needing, vague yet clear,
A cold, sweet, silver life, wrapp'd in round waves,
   Quicken'd with touches of transporting fear.

## 22         Rondeau

Jenny kiss'd me when we met,
   Jumping from the chair she sat in;
Time, you thief, who love to get
   Sweets into your list, put that in:
Say I'm weary, say I'm sad,
   Say that health and wealth have miss'd me,
Say I'm growing old, but add,
   Jenny kiss'd me.

# BRYAN WALLER PROCTER
1787–1874

23                    The Sexes

As the man beholds the woman,
As the woman sees the man,
Curiously they note each other,
As each other only can.

Never can the man divest her
Of that wondrous charm of sex;
Ever must she, dreaming of him,
The same mystic charm annex.

Strange, inborn, profound attraction!
Not the Poet's range of soul,
Learning, Science, sexless Virtue,
Can the gazer's thought control.

But, thro' every nerve and fancy
Which the inmost heart reveals,
Twined, ingrained, the Sense of difference,
Like the subtle serpent, steals.

# JOHN CLARE
## 1793–1864

24             ## The Gipsy Camp

The snow falls deep; the Forest lies alone:
The boy goes hasty for his load of brakes,
Then thinks upon the fire and hurries back;
The Gipsy knocks his hands and tucks them up,
And seeks his squalid camp, half hid in snow,
Beneath the oak, which breaks away the wind,
And bushes close, with snow like hovel warm:
There stinking mutton roasts upon the coals,
And the half-roasted dog squats close and rubs,
Then feels the heat too strong and goes aloof;
He watches well, but none a bit can spare,
And vainly waits the morsel thrown away:
'Tis thus they live – a picture to the place;
A quiet, pilfering, unprotected race.


25

The red bagged bee on never weary wing
Pipes his small trumpet round the early flowers
And the white nettles by the hedge in spring
Hears his low music all the sunny hours
Till clouds come on and leaves the falling showers
Herald of spring and music of wild blooms
It seems the minstrel of spring's early flowers
On banks where the red nettle flowers it comes
And there all the long sunny morning hums

26       The thunder mutters louder and more loud
With quicker motion hay folks ply the rake
Ready to burst slow sails the pitch black cloud
And all the gang a bigger haycock make
To sit beneath – the woodland winds awake
The drops so large wet all thro' in an hour
A tiney flood runs down the leaning rake
In the sweet hay yet dry the hay folks cower
And some beneath the waggon shun the shower


27       Look through the naked bramble and black thorn
And see the arum show its vivid green
Glossy and rich and some ink spotted like the morn
Ing sky with clouds – in sweetest neuks I've been
And seen the arum sprout its happy green
Full of spring visions and green thoughts o' may
Dead leaves a' litter where its leaves are seen
Broader and brighter green from day to day
Beneath the hedges in their leafless spray


28       I am – yet what I am, none cares or knows;
My friends forsake me like a memory lost: –
I am the self-consumer of my woes; –
They rise and vanish in oblivion's host,
Like shadows in love's frenzied stifled throes: –
And yet I am, and live – like vapours tost

Into the nothingness of scorn and noise, –
Into the living sea of waking dreams,
Where there is neither sense of life or joys,
But the vast shipwreck of my life's esteems;
Even the dearest, that I love the best
Are strange – nay, rather stranger than the rest.

I long for scenes, where man hath never trod
A place where woman never smiled or wept
There to abide with my Creator, God;
And sleep as I in childhood, sweetly slept,
Untroubling, and untroubled where I lie,
The grass below – above the vaulted sky.

29                          An Invite to Eternity

Wilt thou go with me sweet maid
Say maiden wilt thou go with me
Through the valley depths of shade
Of night and dark obscurity
Where the path hath lost its way
Where the sun forgets the day
Where there's nor life nor light to see
Sweet maiden wilt thou go with me

Where stones will turn to flooding streams
Where plains will rise like ocean waves
Where life will fade like visioned dreams
And mountains darken into caves
Say maiden wilt thou go with me
Through this sad non-identity
Where parents live and are forgot
And sisters live and know us not

Say maiden wilt thou go with me
In this strange death of life to be
To live in death and be the same
Without this life, or home, or name
At once to be, and not to be
That was, and is not – yet to see
Things pass like shadows – and the sky
Above, below, around us lie

The land of shadows wilt thou trace
And look – nor know each other's face
The present mixed with reasons gone
And past, and present all as one
Say maiden can thy life be led
To join the living with the dead
Then trace thy footsteps on with me
We're wed to one eternity


30                    The Shepherd Boy

The fly or beetle on their track
Are things that know no sin
And when they whemble on their back
What terror they seem in
The shepherd boy wi' bits o' bents
Will turn them up again
And start them where they nimbly went
Along the grassy plain
And such the shepherd boy is found
While lying on the sun crackt ground

The lady-bird that seldom stops
From climbing all the day
Climbs up the rushes' tassle tops
Spreads wings and flies away
He sees them – lying on the grass
Musing the whole day long
And clears the way to let them pass
And sings a nameless song
He watches pismires on the hill
Always busy never still

He sees the traveller beetle run
Where thick the grass wood weaves
To hide the black-snail from the sun
He props up plantain leaves

The lady-cows have got a house
Within the cowslip pip
The spider weaving for his spouse
On threads will often slip
So looks and lyes the shepherd boy
The summer long his whole employ –

# HENRY FRANCIS LYTE
## 1793–1847

31                    Abide with Me

*'Abide with us: for it is towards evening, and the*
*day is far spent.' St. Luke xxiv. 29*

Abide with me! Fast falls the eventide;
The darkness deepens: Lord, with me abide!
When other helpers fail, and comforts flee,
Help of the helpless, O abide with me!

Swift to its close ebbs out life's little day;
Earth's joys grow dim; its glories pass away:
Change and decay in all around I see;
O Thou, who changest not, abide with me!

Not a brief glance I beg, a passing word,
But as Thou dwell'st with Thy disciples, Lord,
Familiar, condescending, patient, free,
Come, not to sojourn, but abide, with me!

Come not in terrors, as the King of kings;
But kind and good, with healing in Thy wings:
Tears for all woes, a heart for every plea.
Come, Friend of sinners, and thus abide with me!

Thou on my head in early youth didst smile,
And, though rebellious and perverse meanwhile,
Thou hast not left me, oft as I left Thee.
On to the close, O Lord, abide with me!

I need Thy presence every passing hour.
What but Thy grace can foil the Tempter's power?
Who like Thyself my guide and stay can be?
Through cloud and sunshine, O abide with me!

I fear no foe with Thee at hand to bless:
Ills have no weight, and tears no bitterness.
Where is death's sting? where, grave, thy victory?
I triumph still, if Thou abide with me.

Hold then Thy cross before my closing eyes;
Shine through the gloom, and point me to the skies:
Heaven's morning breaks, and earth's vain shadows flee.
In life and death, O Lord, abide with me!

*Berryhead, September, 1847*

# HARTLEY COLERIDGE

## 1796–1849

32      Think upon Death, 'tis good to think of Death,
But better far to think upon the Dead.
Death is a spectre with a bony head,
Or the mere mortal body without breath,
The state foredoom'd of every son of Seth,
Decomposition – dust, or dreamless sleep.
But the dear Dead are they for whom we weep,
For whom I credit all the Bible saith.
Dead is my father, dead is my good mother,
And what on earth have I to do but die?
But if by grace I reach the blessed sky,
I fain would see the same, and not another;
The very father that I used to see,
The mother that has nursed me on her knee.


33              The Larch Grove

Line above line the nursling larches planted,
   Still as they climb with interspace more wide,
Let in and out the sunny beams that slanted,
   And shot and crankled down the mountain's side.

The larches grew, and darker grew the shade;
   And sweeter aye the fragrance of the Spring;
Pink pencils all the spiky boughs arrayed,
   And small green needles called the birds to sing.

They grew apace as fast as they could grow,
   As fain the tawny fell to deck and cover,
They haply thought to soothe the pensive woe,
   Or hide the joy of stealthy tripping lover.

Ah, larches! that shall never be your lot;
 Nought shall you have to do with amorous weepers,
Nor shall ye prop the roof of cozy cot,
 But rumble out your days as railway sleepers.

# JAMES HENRY

## 1798–1876

34      Breáthe not a murmur thou of querulous
Dissatisfaction at the inscrutably
Dárk and mysterious ways of Providence,
Íf in thy fortune's ruin thou 'st preserved
A pair of easy, wool-lined, velvet slippers,
About the color, whether black or brown
Or green or scarlet, be not too fastidious;
Bút, if stern destiny allows a choice,
Choose yellow, as the prettiest and most Turkish.
I like the Turks because they 're Mussulmen,
Not preaching, praying, money-loving Christians;
I like the Turks because they hate the Russians
And will, I doubt not, give them a sound drubbing;
I like the Turks because they 've a fine city,
Cónstantinople on the Bosphorus,
Where one can plainly see the sun at midday;
But most I like the Turks because they never
Wear boóts at home, but always yellow slippers.
I won't suppose thou hast on either foot
A hard or soft corn, as the Earl of Mayo
Advertises he had before he got them
Extracted by that notable chirúrgeon,
Chiropodist and boot-and-shoe-maker,
Válentine Prendergast in Sackville street,
Right opposite the General Post Office,
And next door to the general breeches-maker,
Quáker, and gentleman, Friend Richard Allen –
I wón't suppose thou hast on each great toe
A bunion large and round as a small apple;
I wón't suppose it, though I might since bunions
Are never out of fashion with high gentry –
Bút I 'll suppose thou 'st half the day been walking
(A lady on each arm) in the genteelest

Least desert part of our once florishing city,
Deáth and the Doctors' side of Merrion Square,
In that same pair of boots thou now hast ón thee,
Shórter by two full inches than thy foot
And full three inches narrower, and hast cóme home,
Ánd with the aid of twó maids and a boótjack
Fórced, with convulsive struggles desperate,
The polished instruments of torture off,
And set the crippled joints at liberty –
Góds! thy contentment as thou 'dst slip first one
And then the other quivering, lame, and wounded
Extremity into the refuge safe
Of a large, wool-lined, velvet pair of slippers.
Then if thou wert not thankful, didst not bless
High Heaven's beneficence to wretched sinners,
Thou 'dst merit, not Saint Patrick's Purgatory
Or Hell's sulphureous fires unquenchable,
Bút to be doomed on Heaven's hard sapphire pavement
To promenade for ever in those sáme boots,
And find, to all eternity, no boótjack,
No pitying angel's hand, to rid thee óf them.

*Trompeter-Schlösschen, Dresden, Febr. 6, 1854*

## 35   Man's Universal Hymn

The Lord 's my God and still shall be,
Fór a kind God he is to me,
And gives me a carte-blanche to rob
His óther creatures, and to fob
Fór my own use their property,
So good and kind he is to me.
He bids me pluck the goose and take
Her sóft warm down my bed to make,
Then turn her out with raw skin bare
To shiver in the cold, night air;

Her néw-laid eggs he bids me steal
To make me a delicious meal,
And, when she has no more to lay,
Commands me cram her every day
With oaten meal 'till she 's so plump
The fat 's an inch deep on her rump,
Then cut her throat and roast and eat
And thank him for the luscious treat.

The Lord 's my God and still shall be,
Fór a kind God he is to me;
He makes the bee construct his cell
Of yellow wax and fill it well
With honey for his winter store,
And, when it 's so fúll 'twill hold no more,
Cómes and points out the hive to me,
And says: – 'I give it all to thee;
Small need 's for winter store the bee
Who never a winter is to see;
Kill him and eat his honey thou,
Í 'm the bee's God, and thee allow.'

I lóve the Lord my God, for he
Loves all his creatures tenderly,
But more than all his creatures, me.
He bids me from the dam's side tear
The tender lambkin and not spare: –
'Piteous though bleat the orphan'd dam,
Túrn a deaf ear and dine on lamb.'

I love the Lord my God, for he
Loves áll his creatures tenderly,
But more than all his creatures, me.
He bids the gallant horse live free
And more than life love liberty;
Then says to me: – 'The horse is thine;
Thou shalt in slavery make him pine;
Confine him in a dungeon dim,
Fétter him every joint and limb,

Maím him, cut off his tail and ears –
Thou know'st the use of knife and shears –
A réd-hot brand the bleeding sears;
Don't mind his quivering or his groans,
I 'd have men's hearts as hard as stones.
So far so good, but much remains
Stíll to be done ere fór thy pains
Thou hast a willing, servile brute,
Who shall not dare the will dispute
Of his taskmaster; a bold, free
And noble spirit he has from me,
And worse than death hates slavery;
This noble spirit how to quell
I 'll teach thee now – remember well
Í am the God and friend of both
The horse and thee, and would be loth
Either to one or tó the other
Aught íll should happen; thou 'st a brother
In every creature great or small;
The same Lord God has made ye all –
So when thou 'st cropped him ears and tail,
And maimed him so he 's neither male
Nor female more, fasten a strong
Stout bar of iron with a thong
Between his jaws; then through a ring
Ín the bar's neár end run a string
Of twisted hemp, and hold it tight
Ín thy left hand, while with thy right
Thou scourgest him with a long lash so
That, will-he nill-he, he must go –
Not onward, for thou hast him bound
Fást by the jaw, but round and round,
Thoú in the middle standing still
And plying the lash with right good will;
At first, no doubt, he 'll fume and fret
And fáll perhaps into a sweat
Of agony, and upward rear,
And spurn the ground, and paw the air –

What is 't to thee? lash thoú the more;
When tired behind, begin before,
Still holding him by the muzzle fast;
Pain breaks the stoutest heart at last;
Ere a short month he 'll do thy will,
Gallop, trot, canter or stand still
At thy least bidding, carry, draw,
And labour for thee until raw
And galled his flesh and blind his eyes
And lame his feet, and so he dies,
If thou so little know'st of thrift
Ánd of the right use of my gift
Of all my creatures unto thee
Both great and small whate'er they be,
Ás to allow thine old worn-out
And battered slave to go about
Consuming goód food every day
And standing awkward in the way,
Whén for the fee of his shoes and hide
Thou might'st have all his wants supplied
By the knacker's knife; be merciful
And when he can no longer pull,
Nor carry thee upon his back,
Tó the knacker send thy hack.'

Ye little birds, in God rejoice,
And praise him with melodious voice:
Small though ye are, he minds ye all,
And 'never to the ground shall fall
A sparrow without his consent,'
By which beyond all doubt is meant –
Mán, take thy victim; clip his wing;
Put out his eyes that he may sing
As sweet in winter as in spring;
Confine him in close prison-house
Where scarcely could turn round a mouse;
What though I made him wild and free
In the woód to range from tree to tree
And more than life love liberty,

Lét it not fret thee, he is thine
By virtue of a writ divine –
Cáge him, if he sings soft and sweet;
If bad his voice, kill him and eat.

Indwellers of the deep, blue sea,
To praise the Lord unite with me;
Ye grampuses and mighty whales
That lash the water with your tails
Ínto a foam, and spirt it high
Úp through your nostrils to the sky,
Rejoice with me; the Lord of heaven
Ínto my hands your lives has given,
And taught me how best to pursue
And hunt ye through the waters blue
With barbed harpoon, till far and wide
The ocean with your life's blood 's dyed.

Ye salmon, herring, wide-mouthed cod,
Praise in your hearts the Lord your God,
Who has made you of the ocean free,
Then whispered in the ear to me: –
'Gó, take thy nets and trawl for fish;
On fast-days they 're an excellent dish
With vinegar, mustard and cayenne' –
Praise ye the Lord; I 'll say Amen.

Come hither every living thing,
And in full chorus with me sing
The praise of him who reigns above,
The God of justice, and of love,
Who for my use has made ye all,
Bird, beast, fish, insect; great and small.
For me ye build, for me ye breed;
For me ye work, for me ye bleed;
I fatten on ye; ye are mine;
Come praise with me the work divine
Ánd its great author, just and good,
Who has given ye all to me for food,

Clothing or pleasure, or mere sport;
His praise to all the ends report
Óf the wide earth: sing, ever sing
The all-righteous maker, father, king.

*Begun near Augst during a foot tour in*
*Switzerland, Octob. 22; finished on the*
*Neckar near Heidelberg, Nov. 24, 1853*

36    The húman skull is of deceit
As fúll as any egg of meat;
Fúll of deceít 's the human skull
As ány egg of meat is full.
Some eggs are addled, some are sweet,
But évery egg 's chokefúl of meat;
Cléver some skúlls, some skulls are dull,
Bút of deceít each skull 's chokeful.
Lét your egg áddled be or sweet,
To háve your éggshell clean and neat
The first step is: scoop out the meat;
And cléver let it be or dull,
If you would háve an honest skull,
Oút you must scrape to the last grain
The vile, false, lýing, pérjured brain.

*Verona, August 19, 1854*

37   The són 's a poor, wrétched, unfórtunate creáture,
With a náme no less wrétched: I-WOULD-IF-I-COULD;
But the fáther 's rich, glórious and háppy and míghty
And his térrible náme is I-COULD-IF-I-WOULD.

*Dalkey Lodge, Dalkey, April 12, 1855*

# WILLIAM THOM

?1798–1848


38        Whisperings for the Unwashed

*'Tyrants make not slaves – slaves make tyrants.'*

*Scene – A Town in the North. Time – Six o'clock morning.*
*Enter Town Drummer.*

| | |
|---|---|
| Rubadub, rubadub, row-dow-dow! | |
| The sun is glinting on hill and knowe, | *knoll* |
| An' saft the pillow to the fat man's pow – | *poll, head* |
| Sae fleecy an' warm the guid '*hame-made*,' | |
| An' cozie the happin o' the farmer's bed. | *covering* |
| The feast o' yestreen how it oozes through, | |
| In bell an' blab on his burly brow. | *bubble and droplet* |
| Nought recks he o' drum an' bell, | *(of sweat)* |
| The girnal's fou an' sure the 'sale;' | *granary's full* |
| The laird an' he can crap an keep – | *(gather the) crop* |
| Weel, weel may he laugh in his gowden sleep. | |
| His dream abounds in stots, or full | *bullocks* |
| Of cow an' corn, calf an' bull; | |
| Of cattle shows, of dinner speaks – | |
| Toom, torn, and patch'd like weavers' breeks; | *Thin* |
| An' sic like meaning hae, I trow, | |
| As rubadub, rubadub, row-dow-dow. | |
| | |
| Rubadub, rubadub, row dow-dow! | |
| Hark, how he waukens the Weavers now! | |
| Wha lie belair'd in a dreamy steep – | *stuck fast; tub* |
| A mental swither 'tween death an' sleep – | *doubt* |
| Wi' hungry wame and hopeless breast, | *belly* |
| Their food no feeding, their sleep no rest. | |
| Arouse ye, ye sunken, unravel your rags, | |
| No coin in your coffers, no meal in your bags; | |

Yet cart, barge, and waggon, with load after load,
Creak mockfully, passing your breadless abode.
The stately stalk of Ceres bears,
But not for you, the bursting ears;
In vain to you the lark's lov'd note,
For you no summer breezes float,
Grim winter through your hovel pours –
Dull, din, and healthless vapour yours.
The nobler Spider weaves alone,
And feels the little web his *own*,
His hame, his fortress, foul or fair,
Nor factory whipper swaggers there.
Should ruffian wasp, or flaunting fly
Touch his lov'd lair, 'TIS TOUCH AND DIE!
Supreme in rags, ye weave, in tears,
The shining robe your murderer wears;
Till worn, at last, to very '*waste*,'
A hole to die in, at the best;
And, dead, the session saints begrudge ye          *church elders*
The twa-three deals in death to lodge ye;      *planks (for coffin)*
They grudge the grave wherein to drap ye,
An' grudge the very *muck* to hap ye.                      *cover you*

\* \* \*

Rubadub, rubadub, row-dow-dow!
The drunkard clasps his aching brow;
And there be they, in their squalor laid,
The supperless brood on loathsome bed;
Where the pallid mother croons to rest,
The withering babe at her milkless breast.
She, wakeful, views the risen day
Break gladless o'er her home's decay,
And God's blest light a ghastly glare
Of grey and deathy dimness there.
In all things near, or sight or sounds,
Sepulchral rottenness abounds;
Yet he, the sovereign filth, will prate,
In stilted terms, of Church and State,

As things that *he* would mould anew –
Could all but his brute self subdue.
Ye vilest of the crawling things,
Lo! how well the fetter clings
To recreant collar! Oh, may all
The self-twined lash unbroken fall,
Nor hold until our land is free'd
Of craven, crouching slugs, that breed
In fetid holes, and, day by day,
Yawn their unliving life away!
But die they will not, cannot – why?
They live not – therefore, cannot die.
In soul's dark deadness dead are they,
Entomb'd in thick corkswollen clay.
What tho' they yield their fulsome breath,
The change but mocks the name of death!
Existence, skulking from the sun,
In misery many, in meanness one.
When brave hearts would the fight renew,
Hope, weeping, withering points to you!

   Arouse ye, but neither with bludgeon nor blow,
Let *mind* be your armour, *darkness* your foe;
'Tis not in the ramping of demagogue rage,
Nor yet in the mountebank patriot's page,
In sounding palaver, nor pageant, I ween,
In blasting of trumpet, nor vile tambourine;
For these are but mockful and treacherous things –
The thorns that 'crackle' to sharpen their stings.
When fair Science gleams over city and plain,
When Truth walks abroad all unfetter'd again,
When the breast glows to Love and the brow beams
   in Light –
Oh! hasten it Heaven! MAN LONGS FOR HIS RIGHT.

# THOMAS HOOD
## 1799–1845

39          The Song of the Shirt

With fingers weary and worn,
    With eyelids heavy and red,
A Woman sat, in unwomanly rags,
    Plying her needle and thread –
      Stitch! stitch! stitch!
In poverty, hunger, and dirt,
    And still with a voice of dolorous pitch
She sang the 'Song of the Shirt.'

    'Work! work! work!
While the cock is crowing aloof!
    And work – work – work,
Till the stars shine through the roof!
It's O! to be a slave
    Along with the barbarous Turk,
Where woman has never a soul to save,
    If this is Christian work!

'Work – work – work
Till the brain begins to swim;
    Work – work – work
Till the eyes are heavy and dim!
Seam, and gusset, and band,
    Band, and gusset, and seam,
      Till over the buttons I fall asleep,
And sew them on in a dream!

'O! Men, with Sisters dear!
    O! Men! with Mothers and Wives!
It is not linen you're wearing out,
    But human creatures' lives!

Stitch – stitch – stitch,
　In poverty, hunger and dirt,
Sewing at once, with a double thread,
　A Shroud as well as a Shirt.

'But why do I talk of Death?
　That Phantom of grisly bone,
I hardly fear his terrible shape,
　It seems so like my own –
　It seems so like my own,
　Because of the fasts I keep,
Oh! God! that bread should be so dear,
　And flesh and blood so cheap!

'Work – work – work!
　My labour never flags;
And what are its wages? A bed of straw,
　A crust of bread – and rags.
That shatter'd roof – and this naked floor –
　A table – a broken chair –
And a wall so blank, my shadow I thank
　For sometimes falling there!

　'Work – work – work!
From weary chime to chime,
　Work – work – work –
As prisoners work for crime!
　Band, and gusset, and seam,
　Seam, and gusset, and band,
Till the heart is sick, and the brain benumb'd,
　As well as the weary hand.

　'Work – work – work,
In the dull December light,
　And work – work – work,
When the weather is warm and bright –

While underneath the eaves
  The brooding swallows cling
As if to show me their sunny backs
  And twit me with the spring.

'Oh! but to breathe the breath
Of the cowslip and primrose sweet –
  With the sky above my head,
And the grass beneath my feet,
For only one short hour
  To feel as I used to feel,
Before I knew the woes of want
  And the walk that costs a meal!

'Oh but for one short hour!
  A respite however brief!
No blessed leisure for Love or Hope,
  But only time for Grief!
A little weeping would ease my heart,
  But in their briny bed
My tears must stop, for every drop
  Hinders needle and thread!'

With fingers weary and worn,
  With eyelids heavy and red,
A Woman sate in unwomanly rags,
  Plying her needle and thread –
    Stitch! stitch! stitch!
  In poverty, hunger, and dirt,
And still with a voice of dolorous pitch,
Would that its tone could reach the Rich!
  She sang this 'Song of the Shirt!'

# MARY HOWITT

1799–1888

## 40

The Dor-Hawk

Fern-owl, Churn-owl, or Goat-sucker,
  Night-jar, Dor-hawk, or whate'er
Be thy name among a dozen, –
Whip-poor-Will's and Who-are-you's cousin,
Chuck-Will's-widow's near relation,
Thou art at thy night vocation,
  Thrilling the still evening air!

In the dark brown wood beyond us,
  Where the night lies dusk and deep;
Where the fox his burrow maketh,
Where the tawny owl awaketh
  Nightly from his day-long sleep;

There Dor-hawk is thy abiding,
  Meadow green is not for thee;
While the aspen branches shiver,
'Mid the roaring of the river,
  Comes thy chirring voice to me.

Bird, thy form I never looked on,
  And to see it do not care;
Thou hast been, and thou art only
As a voice of forests lonely,
  Heard and dwelling only there.

Bringing thoughts of dusk and shadow;
  Trees huge-branched in ceaseless change;
Pallid night-moths, spectre-seeming;
All a silent land of dreaming,
  Indistinct and large and strange.

Be thou thus, and thus I prize thee
    More than knowing thee face to face,
Head and beak and leg and feather,
Kept from harm of touch and weather,
    Underneath a fine glass-case.

I can read of thee, and find out
    How thou fliest, fast or slow;
Of thee in the north and south too,
Of thy great moustachioed mouth too,
    And thy Latin name also.

But, Dor-hawk, I love thee better
    While thy voice unto me seems
Coming o'er the evening meadows,
From a dark brown land of shadows,
    Like a pleasant voice of dreams!

# SIR HENRY TAYLOR
## 1800–1886

## 41

## To the Author's Wife

Dear Alice, through much mockery of yours
  (Impatient of my labours long and slow
  And small results that I made haste to show
From time to time), you scornfullest of reviewers,
  These verses work'd their way: 'Get on, get on,'
Was mostly my encouragement: But I
  Dead to all spurring kept my pace foregone
And long had learnt all laughter to defy.
I thought, moreover, that your laugh (for hard
Would be the portion of the hapless Bard
Who found not in each comment, grave or gay,
Some flattering unction) ... In your laugh, I say,
A subtle something glimmer'd; 'twas a laugh,
If half of mockery, yet of pleasure half.
And since, on looking round, I know not who
  Will greet my offering with as good a grace
  And in their favour give it half a place,
These flights, for fault of better, short and few,
Dear Alice, I must dedicate to you.

                    *Mortlake, Nov., 1847*

# WILLIAM BARNES
## 1801–86


42                    Evenen in the Village

Now the light o' the west is a-turn'd to gloom,
  An' the men be at hwome vrom ground;                    *field*
An' the bells be a-zendèn all down the Coombe    (i.e. *field-work*)
  From tower, their mwoansome sound.
      An' the wind is still,
      An' the house-dogs do bark,
An' the rooks be a-vled to the elems high an' dark,
    An' the water do roar at mill.


An' the flickerèn light drough the window-peäne
  Vrom the candle's dull fleäme do shoot,
An' young Jemmy the smith is a-gone down leäne,
  A-playèn his shrill-vaïced flute.
      An' the miller's man
    Do zit down at his ease
On the seat that is under the cluster o' trees,
    Wi' his pipe an' his cider can.


43                         To Me

At night, as drough the meäd I took my waÿ,
In aïr a-sweeten'd by the new-meäde haÿ,
A stream a-vallèn down a rock did sound,
Though out o' zight wer foam an' stwone to me.

Behind the knap, above the gloomy copse,                    *hillock*
The wind did russle in the trees' high tops,
Though evenèn darkness, an' the risèn hill,
Kept all the quiv'rèn leaves unshown to me.

Within the copse, below the zunless sky,
I heärd a nightèngeäle, a-warblèn high
Her lwoansome zong, a-hidden vrom my zight,
An' showèn nothèn but her mwoan to me.

An' by a house, where rwoses hung avore
The thatch-brow'd window, an' the oben door,
I heärd the merry words, an' hearty laugh,
O' zome feäir maïd, as eet unknown to me.     *yet*

High over head the white-rimm'd clouds went on,
Wi' woone a-comèn up, vor woone a-gone;
An' feäir they floated in their sky-back'd flight,
But still they never meäde a sound to me.

An' there the miller, down the stream did float
Wi' all his childern, in his white-saïl'd bwoat,
Vur off, beyond the stragglèn cows in meäd,
But zent noo vaïce, athirt the ground, to me.   *athwart, across*

An' then a buttervlee, in zultry light,
A-wheelèn on about me, vier-bright,
Did show the gaÿest colors to my eye,
But still did bring noo vaïce around to me.

I met the merry laugher on the down,
Bezide her mother, on the path to town,
An' oh! her sheäpe wer comely to the zight,
But wordless then wer she a-vound to me.

Zoo, sweet ov unzeen things mid be the sound,
An' feäir to zight mid soundless things be vound,
But I've the laugh to hear, an' feäce to zee,
Vor they be now my own, a-bound to me.

# RICHARD HILL SANDYS

## 1801–92

44         The Schoolboy at Home

The pony's lamed, the cat is dead,
The pigs are in the tulip bed;
The flue with rubbish has been filled,
And all my lady's plants are killed;
A strange wet cur of low degree
Is planted on the rich settee;
The grave mackaw has lost his tail,
And slowly tears a Brussels veil;
The pistol's cleaned with sister's shawl,
For midday practice in the hall;
And little Jane, so prim and good,
Is scampering wild about the wood;
The maids are whimpering with affright,
Because a ghost was seen last night;
The linen's burnt, the roller's split,
The tangled chain won't turn the spit;
The ale is running all about,
And in the urn's a ragged clout;
And all around, at every pass,
Is smash and clash and broken glass;
And here's a neighbour come to fret,
And, mercy! there's a hive upset!

# LETITIA ELIZABETH LANDON
## 1802–38

45                                Gossipping

These are the spiders of society;
They weave their petty webs of lies and sneers,
And lie themselves in ambush for the spoil.
The web seems fair, and glitters in the sun,
And the poor victim winds him in the toil
Before he dreams of danger, or of death.
Alas, the misery that such inflict!
A word, a look, have power to wring the heart,
And leave it struggling hopeless in the net
Spread by the false and cruel, who delight
In the ingenious torment they contrive.


46                              The Marriage Vow

The altar, 'tis of death! for there are laid
The sacrifice of all youth's sweetest hopes.
It is a dreadful thing for woman's lip
To swear the heart away; yet know that heart
Annuls the vow while speaking, and shrinks back
From the dark future that it dares not face.
The service read above the open grave
Is far less terrible than that which seals
The vow that binds the victim, not the will:
For in the grave is rest.

47              The Power of Words

'Tis a strange mystery, the power of words!
Life is in them, and death. A word can send
The crimson colour hurrying to the cheek,
Hurrying with many meanings; or can turn
The current cold and deadly to the heart.
Anger and fear are in them; grief and joy
Are on their sound; yet slight, impalpable: –
A word is but a breath of passing air.

# THOMAS LOVELL BEDDOES
## 1803–49

Dream-Pedlary

### I

If there were dreams to sell,
  What would you buy?
Some cost a passing bell;
  Some a light sigh,
That shakes from Life's fresh crown
Only a rose-leaf down.
If there were dreams to sell,
Merry and sad to tell,
And the crier rung the bell,
  What would you buy?

### II

A cottage lone and still,
  With bowers nigh,
Shadowy, my woes to still,
  Until I die.
Such pearl from Life's fresh crown
Fain would I shake me down.
Were dreams to have at will,
This would best heal my ill,
  This would I buy.

### III

But there were dreams to sell,
  Ill didst thou buy;
Life is a dream, they tell,
  Waking, to die.

Dreaming a dream to prize,
Is wishing ghosts to rise;
And, if I had the spell
To call the buried well,
   Which one would I?

IV

If there are ghosts to raise,
   What shall I call,
Out of hell's murky haze,
   Heaven's blue pall?
Raise my loved long-lost boy
To lead me to his joy. –
There are no ghosts to raise;
Out of death lead no ways;
   Vain is the call.

V

Know'st thou not ghosts to sue?
   No love thou hast.
Else lie, as I will do,
   And breathe thy last.
So out of Life's fresh crown
Fall like a rose leaf down.
Thus are the ghosts to woo;
Thus are all dreams made true,
   Ever to last!

49               A Night-Scene

The lake, like her, heaves gently
Its breast of waves under a heaven of sleep,
And pictures in its soothed, transparent being
The depth of worlds o'erhanging: o'er the pillow,
Washed by the overflowing, flowery locks,
A silver promise of the moon is breathed:

And the light veil of hieroglyphic clouds
The curious wind rends ever and anon,
Revealing the deep dream of Alpine heights,
Which fill the distance of its wondering spirit,
And on its hectic cheeks the prophecies
Do fearfully reflect, that flicker up
Out of the sun's grave underneath the world.


50                    The Phantom-Wooer

A ghost, that loved a lady fair,
Ever in the starry air
   Of midnight at her pillow stood;
And, with a sweetness skies above
The luring words of human love,
   Her soul the phantom wooed.
Sweet and sweet is their poisoned note,
The little snakes' of silver throat,
In mossy skulls that nest and lie,
Ever singing 'die, oh! die.'

Young soul, put off your flesh, and come
With me into the quiet tomb,
   Our bed is lovely, dark, and sweet;
The earth will swing us, as she goes,
Beneath our coverlid of snows,
   And the warm leaden sheet.
Dear and dear is their poisoned note,
The little snakes' of silver throat,
In mossy skulls that nest and lie,
Ever singing 'die, oh! die.'

51 ## Song on the Water

> As mad sexton's bell, tolling
>> For earth's loveliest daughter,
> Night's dumbness breaks rolling
>> Ghostily:
>> So our boat breaks the water
>> Witchingly.

> As her look the dream troubles
>> Of her tearful-eyed lover,
> So our sails in the bubbles
>> Ghostily
>> Are mirrored, and hover
>> Moonily.

52 ## The Slight and Degenerate Nature of Man

### *Antediluvianus loquitur*

Pitiful post-diluvians! from whose hearts
The print of passions by the tide of hours
Is washed away for ever and for ever,
As lions' footmark on the ocean sands;
While we, Adam's coevals, carry in us
The words indelible of buried feelings,
Like the millennial trees, whose hoary barks
Grow o'er the secrets cut into their core.

52. *Antediluvianus loquitur*   An antediluvian man speaks

# ROBERT STEPHEN HAWKER
## 1803–75

53        The Cornish Emigrant's Song

Oh! the eastern winds are blowing;
  The breezes seem to say,
'We are going, we are going,
  To North Americay.

'There the merry bees are humming
  Around the poor man's hive;
Parson Kingdon is not coming
  To take away their tithe.

'There the yellow corn is growing
  Free as the king's highway;
So, we're going, we are going,
  To North Americay.

'Uncle Rab shall be churchwarden,
  And Dick shall be the squire,
And Jem, that lived at Norton,
  Shall be leader of the quire;

'And I will be the preacher,
  And preach three times a day
To every living creature
  In North Americay.'

# JAMES CLARENCE MANGAN
## 1803–49

54                              Siberia

In Siberia's wastes
   The Ice-wind's breath
Woundeth like the toothèd steel;
Lost Siberia doth reveal
   Only blight and death.

Blight and death alone.
   No Summer shines.
Night is interblent with Day.
In Siberia's wastes alway
   The blood blackens, the heart pines.

In Siberia's wastes
   No tears are shed,
For they freeze within the brain.
Nought is felt but dullest pain,
   Pain acute, yet dead;

Pain as in a dream,
   When years go by
Funeral-paced, yet fugitive,
When man lives, and doth not live,
   Doth not live – nor die.

In Siberia's wastes
   Are sands and rocks.
Nothing blooms of green or soft,
But the snow-peaks rise aloft
   And the gaunt ice-blocks.

And the exile there
  Is one with those;
They are part, and he is part,
For the sands are in his heart,
  And the killing snows.

Therefore, in those wastes
  None curse the Czar.
Each man's tongue is cloven by
The North Blast, that heweth nigh
  With sharp scymitar.

And such doom each drees,
  Till, hunger-gnawn,
And cold-slain, he at length sinks there,
Yet scarce more a corpse than ere
  His last breath was drawn.

# SAMUEL LAMAN BLANCHARD
## 1804–45

55           A Song of Contradictions

*'I am not what I am.' – Iago*

The Passions, in festival meeting,
I saw seated round, in a dream;
And vow, by my hatred of cheating,
The Passions are not what they seem.
There's mirth under faces the gravest,
There's woe under visages droll;
There's fear in the breast of the bravest,
And light in the desolate soul.

Thus Joy, in my singular vision,
Sat sobbing and gnashing his teeth;
While Gentleness scoffed in derision,
And Hope picked the buds from his wreath.
Despair, her tight bodice unlacing,
With Laughter seemed ready to die;
And Hate, her companions embracing,
Won each with a smile or a sigh.

There Peace bellowed louder and louder,
For Freedom, sent off to the hulks;
Fear sat on a barrel of powder,
And Pleasure stood by in the sulks.
Here Dignity shoots like a rocket
Past Grace, who is rolling in fat;
There Probity's picking a pocket,
Here Pity sits skinning a cat.

Then Temperance reeling off, quite full,
Charged Friendship with drugging her draught;
She vowed it was Love that was spiteful,
While Charity, blaming all, laught;
When Rage, with the blandest expression,
And Vengeance, low-voiced like a child,
Cried, 'Mercy, forgive the transgression!'
But Mercy look'd horribly wild.

Old Wisdom was worshipping Fashion,
And Jollity dozing in gloom;
While Meekness was foaming with passion,
And Misery danced round the room.
Sweet Envy tripped off to her garret,
Bright Malice smiled worthy of trust,
Gay Want was enjoying his claret,
And Luxury gnawed a dry crust.

At Pride, as she served up the dinner,
Humility turned up her nose;
Suspicion shook hands with each sinner,
While Candour shunned all as her foes.
There's mirth under faces the gravest,
There's woe under visages droll,
There's fear in the breast of the bravest,
And light in the desolate soul!

# R. E. EGERTON-WARBURTON
## 1804–91

56              Past and Present

On four-horse coach, whose luggage pierced the sky,
   Perch'd on back seat, like clerk on office-stool,
   While wintry winds my dangling heels kept cool,
   In Whitney white envelop'd and blue tie,
Unpillow'd slumber from my half-closed eye
   Scared by the shrill tin horn; when welcome Yule
   Brought holiday season, it was thus from school
   I homeward came some forty years gone by.
Thus two long days and one long night I rode,
   Stage after stage, till the last change of team
   Stopp'd, splash'd and panting, at my fire's abode.
How nowaday from school comes home my son?
   Through duct and tunnel by a puff of steam,
   Shot like a pellet from his own pop-gun.

# CHARLES WHITEHEAD
1804–62

57     A type of human life this forest old;
All leafy, wither'd, blooming, teeming, blasted;
Bloom that the reign of summer hath outlasted,
And early sere, and blight that flaunts in gold;
And grass, like sorrow, springing from the mould,
Choking the wholesome tree; and verdure wasted,
Like peace; and berries, like our bliss, untasted;
And thorns, like adverse chances, uncontroll'd.
These flowers are joy that ne'er shall form a wreath;
These lilies are unsure affection crown'd
Above neglect, the water; underneath,
Reeds, which are hope, still sadly standing, drown'd.
This hoary sedge is age of noteless years,
This pool, epitome of human tears!

# GEORGE OUTRAM

1805–56

58                              The Annuity

*Air – 'Duncan Davidson'*

I gaed to spend a week in Fife –
An unco week it proved to be –
For there I met a waesome wife
Lamentin' her viduity.
Her grief brak out sae fierce and fell,
I thought her heart wad burst the shell,
And – I was sae left to mysel' –
I sell't her an annuity.

The bargain lookit fair eneugh –
She just was turned o' saxty-three;
I couldna guessed she'd prove sae teugh,
By human ingenuity.
But years have come, and years have gane,    *as unyielding*
An' there she's yet as stieve's a stane      *as a stone*
The limmer's growin' young again,            *jade, hussy*
Since she got her annuity.

She's crined awa' to bane an' skin,          *withered*
But that it seems is naught to me;
She's like to live – although she's in
The last stage o' tenuity.
She munches wi' her wizened gums,
An' stumps about on legs o' thrums,          *threads*
But comes – as sure as Christmas comes –
To ca' for her annuity.

She jokes her joke, an' cracks her crack,
    As spunkie as a growin' flea –
An' there she sits upon my back,
    A livin' perpetuity.
She hurkles by her ingle side,                    *huddles*
An' toasts an' tans her wrunkled hide –
Lord kens how lang she yet may bide
    To ca' for her annuity.

I read the tables drawn wi' care
    For an Insurance Company;
Her chance o' life was stated there,
    Wi' perfect perspicuity.
But tables here or tables there,
She's lived ten years beyond her share,
An's like to live a dozen mair,
    To ca' for her annuity.

I gat the loon that drew the deed –
    We spelled it o'er right carefully; –
In vain he yerked his souple head,
    To find an ambiguity:
It's dated – tested – a' complete –
The proper stamp – nae word delete –
And diligence, as on decreet,                    *as by decree*
    May pass for her annuity.

Last Yule she had a fearfu' hoast –              *cough*
    I thought a kink might set me free;      *coughing-fit*
I led her out, 'mang snaw and frost,
    Wi' constant assiduity.
But Deil ma' care – the blast gaed by,
An' missed the auld anatomy;
It just cost me a tooth, forbye
    Discharging her annuity.

I thought that grief might gar her quit –
Her only son was lost at sea –
But aff her wits behuved to flit,
An' leave her in fatuity!
She threeps, an' threeps, he's livin' yet,
For a' the tellin' she can get;
But catch the doited runt forget          *doddering old hag*
     To ca' for her annuity!


If there's a sough o' cholera
Or typhus – wha sae gleg as she?          *sprightly*
She buys up baths, an' drugs, an' a',
     In siccan superfluity!
She doesna need – she's fever proof –
The pest gaed o'er her very roof;
She tauld me sae – an' then her loof      *palm (of the hand)*
     Held out for her annuity.


Ae day she fell – her arm she brak, –
A compound fracture as could be;
Nae Leech the cure wad undertak,
     Whate'er was the gratuity.
It's cured! – She handles't like a flail –
It does as weel in bits as hale;
But I'm a broken man mysel'
     Wi' her and her annuity.


Her broozled flesh an' broken banes,
Are weel as flesh an' banes can be.
She beats the taeds that live in stanes,          *toads*
     An' fatten in vacuity!
They die when they're exposed to air –
They canna thole the atmosphere;          *endure*
But her! – expose her onywhere, –
     She lives for her annuity.

If mortal means could nick her thread,
  Sma' crime it wad appear to me;
  Ca't murder – or ca't homicide –
  I'd justify't – an' do it tae.
But how to fell a withered wife
That's carved out o' the tree o' life –
The timmer limmer daurs the knife       *timber*
  To settle her annuity.

  I'd try a shot. – But whar's the mark? –
  Her vital parts are hid frae me;
  Her backbane wanders through her sark     *garment*
  In an unkenn'd corkscrewity.
She's palsified – and shakes her head
Sae fast about, ye scarce can see't;
It's past the power o' steel or lead
  To settle her annuity.

  She might be drowned; but go she'll not
  Within a mile o' loch or sea; –
  Or hanged – if cord could grip a throat
  O' siccan exiguity.
It's fitter far to hang the rope –
It draws out like a telescope;
'Twad tak a dreadfu' length o' drop
  To settle her annuity.

  Will puzion do't? – It has been tried;
  But, be't in hash or fricassee,
  That's just the dish she can't abide,
  Whatever kind o' *goût* it hae.
It's needless to assail her doubts, –
She gangs by instinct – like the brutes –
An' only eats an' drinks what suits
  Hersel' an' her annuity.

The Bible says the age o' man
Threescore an' ten perchance may be;
She's ninety-four; – let them wha can
Explain the incongruity.
She should hae lived afore the Flood –
She's come o' Patriarchal blood –
She's some auld Pagan, mummified
Alive for her annuity.

She's been embalmed inside and out –
She's sauted to the last degree –                    *salted*
There's pickle in her very snout
Sae caper-like an' cruety;
Lot's wife was fresh compared to her;
They've Kayanized the useless knir –        *preserved the*
She canna decompose – nae mair                 *useless witch*
Than her accursed annuity.

The water-drap wears out the rock
As this eternal jaud wears me;                            *jade*
I could withstand the single shock,
But no the continuity.
It's pay me here – an' pay me there –
An' pay me, pay me, evermair;
I'll gang demented wi' despair –
I'm *charged* for her annuity!

# ELIZABETH BARRETT BROWNING
## 1806–61

59         Sonnets from the Portuguese

### I

I thought once how Theocritus had sung
Of the sweet years, the dear and wished-for years,
Who each one in a gracious hand appears
To bear a gift for mortals, old or young:
And, as I mused it in his antique tongue,
I saw, in gradual vision through my tears,
The sweet, sad years, the melancholy years,
Those of my own life, who by turns had flung
A shadow across me. Straightway I was 'ware,
So weeping, how a mystic Shape did move
Behind me, and drew me backward by the hair;
And a voice said in mastery, while I strove, –
'Guess now who holds thee?' – 'Death,' I said. But, there,
The silver answer rang, – 'Not Death, but Love.'

## II

But only three in all God's universe
Have heard this word thou hast said, – Himself, beside
Thee speaking, and me listening! and replied
One of us ... *that* was God, ... and laid the curse
So darkly on my eyelids, as to amerce
My sight from seeing thee, – that if I had died,
The deathweights, placed there, would have signified
Less absolute exclusion. 'Nay' is worse
From God than from all others, O my friend!
Men could not part us with their worldly jars,
Nor the seas change us, nor the tempests bend;
Our hands would touch for all the mountain-bars:
And, heaven being rolled between us at the end,
We should but vow the faster for the stars.

## III

Unlike are we, unlike, O princely Heart!
Unlike our uses and our destinies.
Our ministering two angels look surprise
On one another, as they strike athwart
Their wings in passing. Thou, bethink thee, art
A guest for queens to social pageantries,
With gages from a hundred brighter eyes
Than tears even can make mine, to play thy part
Of chief musician. What hast *thou* to do
With looking from the lattice-lights at me,
A poor, tired, wandering singer, singing through
The dark, and leaning up a cypress tree?
The chrism is on thine head, – on mine, the dew, –
And Death must dig the level where these agree.

## IV

Thou hast thy calling to some palace-floor,
Most gracious singer of high poems! where
The dancers will break footing, from the care
Of watching up thy pregnant lips for more.
And dost thou lift this house's latch too poor
For hand of thine? and canst thou think and bear
To let thy music drop here unaware
In folds of golden fulness at my door?
Look up and see the casement broken in,
The bats and owlets builders in the roof!
My cricket chirps against thy mandolin.
Hush, call no echo up in further proof
Of desolation! there's a voice within
That weeps ... as thou must sing ... alone, aloof.

## V

I lift my heavy heart up solemnly,
As once Electra her sepulchral urn,
And, looking in thine eyes, I overturn
The ashes at thy feet. Behold and see
What a great heap of grief lay hid in me,
And how the red wild sparkles dimly burn
Through the ashen greyness. If thy foot in scorn
Could tread them out to darkness utterly,
It might be well perhaps. But if instead
Thou wait beside me for the wind to blow
The grey dust up, ... those laurels on thine head,
O my Belovèd, will not shield thee so,
That none of all the fires shall scorch and shred
The hair beneath. Stand farther off then! go.

## VI

Go from me. Yet I feel that I shall stand
Henceforward in thy shadow. Nevermore
Alone upon the threshold of my door
Of individual life, I shall command
The uses of my soul, nor lift my hand
Serenely in the sunshine as before,
Without the sense of that which I forbore –
Thy touch upon the palm. The widest land
Doom takes to part us, leaves thy heart in mine
With pulses that beat double. What I do
And what I dream include thee, as the wine
Must taste of its own grapes. And when I sue
God for myself, He hears that name of thine,
And sees within my eyes the tears of two.

## VII

The face of all the world is changed, I think,
Since first I heard the footsteps of thy soul
Move still, oh, still, beside me, as they stole
Betwixt me and the dreadful outer brink
Of obvious death, where I, who thought to sink,
Was caught up into love, and taught the whole
Of life in a new rhythm. The cup of dole
God gave for baptism, I am fain to drink,
And praise its sweetness, Sweet, with thee anear.
The names of country, heaven, are changed away
For where thou art or shalt be, there or here;
And this . . . this lute and song . . . loved yesterday,
(The singing angels know) are only dear
Because thy name moves right in what they say.

## VIII

What can I give thee back, O liberal
And princely giver, who hast brought the gold
And purple of thine heart, unstained, untold,
And laid them on the outside of the wall
For such as I to take or leave withal,
In unexpected largesse? am I cold,
Ungrateful, that for these most manifold
High gifts, I render nothing back at all?
Not so; not cold, – but very poor instead.
Ask God who knows. For frequent tears have run
The colours from my life, and left so dead
And pale a stuff, it were not fitly done
To give the same as pillow to thy head.
Go farther! let it serve to trample on.

## IX

Can it be right to give what I can give?
To let thee sit beneath the fall of tears
As salt as mine, and hear the sighing years
Re-sighing on my lips renunciative
Through those infrequent smiles which fail to live
For all thy adjurations? O my fears,
That this can scarce be right! We are not peers,
So to be lovers; and I own, and grieve,
That givers of such gifts as mine are, must
Be counted with the ungenerous. Out, alas!
I will not soil thy purple with my dust,
Nor breathe my poison on thy Venice-glass,
Nor give thee any love – which were unjust.
Beloved, I only love thee! let it pass.

## X

Yet, love, mere love, is beautiful indeed
And worthy of acceptation. Fire is bright,
Let temple burn, or flax; an equal light
Leaps in the flame from cedar-plank or weed:
And love is fire. And when I say at need
*I love thee* ... mark! ... *I love thee* – in thy sight
I stand transfigured, glorified aright,
With conscience of the new rays that proceed
Out of my face toward thine. There's nothing low
In love, when love the lowest: meanest creatures
Who love God, God accepts while loving so.
And what I *feel*, across the inferior features
Of what I *am*, doth flash itself, and show
How that great work of Love enhances Nature's.

## XI

And therefore if to love can be desert,
I am not all unworthy. Cheeks as pale
As these you see, and trembling knees that fail
To bear the burden of a heavy heart, –
This weary minstrel-life that once was girt
To climb Aornus, and can scarce avail
To pipe now 'gainst the valley nightingale
A melancholy music, – why advert
To these things? O Belovèd, it is plain
I am not of thy worth nor for thy place!
And yet, because I love thee, I obtain
From that same love this vindicating grace,
To live on still in love, and yet in vain, –
To bless thee, yet renounce thee to thy face.

## XII

Indeed this very love which is my boast,
And which, when rising up from breast to brow,
Doth crown me with a ruby large enow
To draw men's eyes and prove the inner cost, –
This love even, all my worth, to the uttermost,
I should not love withal, unless that thou
Hadst set me an example, shown me how,
When first thine earnest eyes with mine were crossed,
And love called love. And thus, I cannot speak
Of love even, as a good thing of my own:
Thy soul hath snatched up mine all faint and weak,
And placed it by thee on a golden throne, –
And that I love (O soul, we must be meek!)
Is by thee only, whom I love alone.

## XIII

And wilt thou have me fashion into speech
The love I bear thee, finding words enough,
And hold the torch out, while the winds are rough,
Between our faces, to cast light on each? –
I drop it at thy feet. I cannot teach
My hand to hold my spirit so far off
From myself – me – that I should bring thee proof
In words, of love hid in me out of reach.
Nay, let the silence of my womanhood
Commend my woman-love to thy belief, –
Seeing that I stand unwon, however wooed,
And rend the garment of my life, in brief,
By a most dauntless, voiceless fortitude,
Lest one touch of this heart convey its grief.

## XIV

If thou must love me, let it be for nought
Except for love's sake only. Do not say
'I love her for her smile – her look – her way
Of speaking gently, – for a trick of thought
That falls in well with mine, and certes brought
A sense of pleasant ease on such a day' –
For these things in themselves, Belovèd, may
Be changed, or change for thee, – and love, so
    wrought,
May be unwrought so. Neither love me for
Thine own dear pity's wiping my cheeks dry, –
A creature might forget to weep, who bore
Thy comfort long, and lose thy love thereby!
But love me for love's sake, that evermore
Thou mayst love on, through love's eternity.

## XV

Accuse me not, beseech thee, that I wear
Too calm and sad a face in front of thine;
For we two look two ways, and cannot shine
With the same sunlight on our brow and hair.
On me thou lookest with no doubting care,
As on a bee shut in a crystalline;
Since sorrow hath shut me safe in love's divine,
And to spread wing and fly in the outer air
Were most impossible failure, if I strove
To fail so. But I look on thee – on thee –
Beholding, besides love, the end of love,
Hearing oblivion beyond memory;
As one who sits and gazes from above,
Over the rivers to the bitter sea.

## XVI

And yet, because thou overcomest so,
Because thou art more noble and like a king,
Thou canst prevail against my fears and fling
Thy purple round me, till my heart shall grow
Too close against thine heart henceforth to know
How it shook when alone. Why, conquering
May prove as lordly and complete a thing
In lifting upward, as in crushing low!
And as a vanquished soldier yields his sword
To one who lifts him from the bloody earth,
Even so, Belovèd, I at last record,
Here ends my strife. If *thou* invite me forth,
I rise above abasement at the word.
Make thy love larger to enlarge my worth.

## XVII

My poet, thou canst touch on all the notes
God set between His After and Before,
And strike up and strike off the general roar
Of the rushing worlds a melody that floats
In a serene air purely. Antidotes
Of medicated music, answering for
Mankind's forlornest uses, thou canst pour
From thence into their ears. God's will devotes
Thine to such ends, and mine to wait on thine.
How, Dearest, wilt thou have me for most use?
A hope, to sing by gladly? or a fine
Sad memory, with thy songs to interfuse?
A shade, in which to sing – of palm or pine?
A grave, on which to rest from singing? Choose.

## XVIII

I never gave a lock of hair away
To a man, Dearest, except this to thee,
Which now upon my fingers thoughtfully,
I ring out to the full brown length and say
'Take it.' My day of youth went yesterday;
My hair no longer bounds to my foot's glee,
Nor plant I it from rose or myrtle-tree,
As girls do, any more: it only may
Now shade on two pale cheeks the mark of tears,
Taught drooping from the head that hangs aside
Through sorrow's trick. I thought the funeral-shears
Would take this first, but Love is justified, –
Take it thou, – finding pure, from all those years,
The kiss my mother left here when she died.

## XIX

The soul's Rialto hath its merchandise;
I barter curl for curl upon that mart,
And from my poet's forehead to my heart
Receive this lock which outweighs argosies, –
As purply black, as erst to Pindar's eyes
The dim purpureal tresses gloomed athwart
The nine white Muse-brows. For this counterpart, ...
The bay-crown's shade, Belovèd, I surmise,
Still lingers on thy curl, it is so black!
Thus, with a fillet of smooth-kissing breath,
I tie the shadows safe from gliding back,
And lay the gift where nothing hindereth;
Here on my heart, as on thy brow, to lack
No natural heat till mine grows cold in death.

## XX

Beloved, my Belovèd, when I think
That thou wast in the world a year ago,
What time I sat alone here in the snow
And saw no footprint, heard the silence sink
No moment at thy voice, but, link by link,
Went counting all my chains as if that so
They never could fall off at any blow
Struck by thy possible hand, – why, thus I drink
Of life's great cup of wonder! Wonderful,
Never to feel thee thrill the day or night
With personal act or speech, – nor ever cull
Some prescience of thee with the blossoms white
Thou sawest growing! Atheists are as dull,
Who cannot guess God's presence out of sight.

## XXI

Say over again, and yet once over again,
That thou dost love me. Though the word repeated
Should seem 'a cuckoo-song,' as thou dost treat it,
Remember, never to the hill or plain,
Valley and wood, without her cuckoo-strain
Comes the fresh Spring in all her green completed.
Belovèd, I, amid the darkness greeted
By a doubtful spirit-voice, in that doubt's pain
Cry, 'Speak once more – thou lovest!' Who can fear
Too many stars, though each in heaven shall roll,
Too many flowers, though each shall crown the year?
Say thou dost love me, love me, love me – toll
The silver iterance! – only minding, Dear,
To love me also in silence with thy soul.

## XXII

When our two souls stand up erect and strong,
Face to face, silent, drawing nigh and nigher,
Until the lengthening wings break into fire
At either curvèd point, – what bitter wrong
Can the earth do to us, that we should not long
Be here contented? Think. In mounting higher,
The angels would press on us and aspire
To drop some golden orb of perfect song
Into our deep, dear silence. Let us stay
Rather on earth, Belovèd, – where the unfit
Contrarious moods of men recoil away
And isolate pure spirits, and permit
A place to stand and love in for a day,
With darkness and the death-hour rounding it.

## XXIII

Is it indeed so? If I lay here dead,
Wouldst thou miss any life in losing mine?
And would the sun for thee more coldly shine
Because of grave-damps falling round my head?
I marvelled, my Belovèd, when I read
Thy thought so in the letter. I am thine –
But ... *so* much to thee? Can I pour thy wine
While my hands tremble? Then my soul, instead
Of dreams of death, resumes life's lower range.
Then, love me, Love! look on me – breathe on me!
As brighter ladies do not count it strange,
For love, to give up acres and degree,
I yield the grave for thy sake, and exchange
My near sweet view of Heaven, for earth with thee!

## XXIV

Let the world's sharpness, like a clasping knife,
Shut in upon itself and do no harm
In this close hand of Love, now soft and warm,
And let us hear no sound of human strife
After the click of the shutting. Life to life –
I lean upon thee, Dear, without alarm,
And feel as safe as guarded by a charm
Against the stab of worldlings, who if rife
Are weak to injure. Very whitely still
The lilies of our lives may reassure
Their blossoms from their roots, accessible
Alone to heavenly dews that drop not fewer,
Growing straight, out of man's reach, on the hill.
God only, who made us rich, can make us poor.

## XXV

A heavy heart, Belovèd, have I borne
From year to year until I saw thy face,
And sorrow after sorrow took the place
Of all those natural joys as lightly worn
As the stringed pearls, each lifted in its turn
By a beating heart at dance-time. Hopes apace
Were changed to long despairs, till God's own grace
Could scarcely lift above the world forlorn
My heavy heart. Then *thou* didst bid me bring
And let it drop adown thy calmly great
Deep being! Fast it sinketh, as a thing
Which its own nature doth precipitate,
While thine doth close above it, mediating
Betwixt the stars and the unaccomplished fate.

## XXVI

I lived with visions for my company
Instead of men and women, years ago,
And found them gentle mates, nor thought to know
A sweeter music than they played to me.
But soon their trailing purple was not free
Of this world's dust, their lutes did silent grow,
And I myself grew faint and blind below
Their vanishing eyes. Then THOU didst come – to be,
Belovèd, what they seemed. Their shining fronts,
Their songs, their splendours (better, yet the same,
As river-water hallowed into fonts),
Met in thee, and from out thee overcame
My soul with satisfaction of all wants:
Because God's gifts put man's best dreams to shame.

## XXVII

My own Belovèd, who hast lifted me
From this drear flat of earth where I was thrown,
And, in betwixt the languid ringlets, blown
A life-breath, till the forehead hopefully
Shines out again, as all the angels see,
Before thy saving kiss! My own, my own,
Who camest to me when the world was gone,
And I who looked for only God, found *thee*!
I find thee; I am safe, and strong, and glad.
As one who stands in dewless asphodel
Looks backward on the tedious time he had
In the upper life, – so I, with bosom-swell,
Make witness, here, between the good and bad,
That Love, as strong as Death, retrieves as well.

## XXVIII

My letters! all dead paper, mute and white!
And yet they seem alive and quivering
Against my tremulous hands which loose the string
And let them drop down on my knee to-night.
This said, – he wished to have me in his sight
Once, as a friend: this fixed a day in spring
To come and touch my hand ... a simple thing,
Yet I wept for it! – this, ... the paper's light ...
Said, *Dear, I love thee*; and I sank and quailed
As if God's future thundered on my past.
This said, *I am thine* – and so its ink has paled
With lying at my heart that beat too fast.
And this ... O love, thy words have ill availed
If, what this said, I dared repeat at last!

## XXIX

I think of thee! – my thoughts do twine and bud
About thee, as wild vines, about a tree,
Put out broad leaves, and soon there's nought to see
Except the straggling green which hides the wood.
Yet, O my palm-tree, be it understood
I will not have my thoughts instead of thee
Who art dearer, better! Rather, instantly
Renew thy presence; as a strong tree should,
Rustle thy boughs and set thy trunk all bare,
And let these bands of greenery which insphere thee
Drop heavily down, – burst, shattered, everywhere!
Because, in this deep joy to see and hear thee
And breathe within thy shadow a new air,
I do not think of thee – I am too near thee.

## XXX

I see thine image through my tears to-night,
And yet to-day I saw thee smiling. How
Refer the cause? – Belovèd, is it thou
Or I, who makes me sad? The acolyte
Amid the chanted joy and thankful rite
May so fall flat, with pale insensate brow,
On the altar-stair. I hear thy voice and vow,
Perplexed, uncertain, since thou art out of sight,
As he, in his swooning ears, the choir's Amen.
Belovèd, dost thou love? or did I see all
The glory as I dreamed, and fainted when
Too vehement light dilated my ideal,
For my soul's eyes? Will that light come again,
As now these tears come – falling hot and real?

## XXXI

Thou comest! all is said without a word.
I sit beneath thy looks, as children do
In the noon-sun, with souls that tremble through
Their happy eyelids from an unaverred
Yet prodigal inward joy. Behold, I erred
In that last doubt! and yet I cannot rue
The sin most, but the occasion – that we two
Should for a moment stand unministered
By a mutual presence. Ah, keep near and close,
Thou dovelike help! and, when my fears would rise,
With thy broad heart serenely interpose:
Brood down with thy divine sufficiencies
These thoughts which tremble when bereft of those,
Like callow birds left desert to the skies.

## XXXII

The first time that the sun rose on thine oath
To love me, I looked forward to the moon
To slacken all those bonds which seemed too soon
And quickly tied to make a lasting troth.
Quick-loving hearts, I thought, may quickly loathe;
And, looking on myself, I seemed not one
For such man's love! – more like an out-of-tune
Worn viol, a good singer would be wroth
To spoil his song with, and which, snatched in haste,
Is laid down at the first ill-sounding note.
I did not wrong myself so, but I placed
A wrong on *thee*. For perfect strains may float
'Neath master-hands, from instruments defaced, –
And great souls, at one stroke, may do and doat.

## XXXIII

Yes, call me by my pet-name! let me hear
The name I used to run at, when a child,
From innocent play, and leave the cowslips piled,
To glance up in some face that proved me dear
With the look of its eyes. I miss the clear
Fond voices which, being drawn and reconciled
Into the music of Heaven's undefiled,
Call me no longer. Silence on the bier,
While I call God – call God! – So let thy mouth
Be heir to those who are now exanimate.
Gather the north flowers to complete the south,
And catch the early love up in the late.
Yes, call me by that name, – and I, in truth,
With the same heart, will answer and not wait.

## XXXIV

With the same heart, I said, I'll answer thee
As those, when thou shalt call me by my name –
Lo, the vain promise! is the same, the same,
Perplexed and ruffled by life's strategy?
When called before, I told how hastily
I dropped my flowers or brake off from a game,
To run and answer with the smile that came
At play last moment, and went on with me
Through my obedience. When I answer now,
I drop a grave thought, break from solitude;
Yet still my heart goes to thee – ponder how –
Not as to a single good, but all my good!
Lay thy hand on it, best one, and allow
That no child's foot could run fast as this blood.

## XXXV

If I leave all for thee, wilt thou exchange
And be all to me? Shall I never miss
Home-talk and blessing and the common kiss
That comes to each in turn, nor count it strange,
When I look up, to drop on a new range
Of walls and floors, another home than this?
Nay, wilt thou fill that place by me which is
Filled by dead eyes too tender to know change?
That's hardest. If to conquer love, has tried,
To conquer grief, tries more, as all things prove;
For grief indeed is love and grief beside.
Alas, I have grieved so I am hard to love.
Yet love me – wilt thou? Open thine heart wide,
And fold within the wet wings of thy dove.

## XXXVI

When we met first and loved, I did not build
Upon the event with marble. Could it mean
To last, a love set pendulous between
Sorrow and sorrow? Nay, I rather thrilled,
Distrusting every light that seemed to gild
The onward path, and feared to overlean
A finger even. And, though I have grown serene
And strong since then, I think that God has willed
A still renewable fear ... O love, O troth ...
Lest these enclaspèd hands should never hold,
This mutual kiss drop down between us both
As an unowned thing, once the lips being cold.
And Love, be false! if *he*, to keep one oath,
Must lose one joy, by his life's star foretold.

## XXXVII

Pardon, oh, pardon, that my soul should make,
Of all that strong divineness which I know
For thine and thee, an image only so
Formed of the sand, and fit to shift and break.
It is that distant years which did not take
Thy sovranty, recoiling with a blow,
Have forced my swimming brain to undergo
Their doubt and dread, and blindly to forsake
Thy purity of likeness and distort
Thy worthiest love to a worthless counterfeit:
As if a shipwrecked Pagan, safe in port,
His guardian sea-god to commemorate,
Should set a sculptured porpoise, gills a-snort
And vibrant tail, within the temple-gate.

## XXXVIII

First time he kissed me, he but only kissed
The fingers of this hand wherewith I write;
And ever since, it grew more clean and white,
Slow to world-greetings, quick with its 'Oh, list,'
When the angels speak. A ring of amethyst
I could not wear here, plainer to my sight,
Than that first kiss. The second passed in height
The first, and sought the forehead, and half missed,
Half falling on the hair. O beyond meed!
That was the chrism of love, which love's own crown,
With sanctifying sweetness, did precede.
The third upon my lips was folded down
In perfect, purple state; since when, indeed,
I have been proud and said, 'My love, my own.'

## XXXIX

Because thou hast the power and own'st the grace
To look through and behind this mask of me
(Against which years have beat thus blanchingly
With their rains), and behold my soul's true face,
The dim and weary witness of life's race, –
Because thou hast the faith and love to see,
Through that same soul's distracting lethargy,
The patient angel waiting for a place
In the new Heavens, – because nor sin nor woe,
Nor God's infliction, nor death's neighbourhood,
Nor all which others viewing, turn to go,
Nor all which makes me tired of all, self-viewed, –
Nothing repels thee, ... Dearest, teach me so
To pour out gratitude, as thou dost, good!

## XL

Oh, yes! they love through all this world of ours!
I will not gainsay love, called love forsooth.
I have heard love talked in my early youth,
And since, not so long back but that the flowers
Then gathered, smell still. Mussulmans and Giaours
Throw kerchiefs at a smile, and have no ruth
For any weeping. Polypheme's white tooth
Slips on the nut if, after frequent showers,
The shell is over-smooth, – and not so much
Will turn the thing called love, aside to hate
Or else to oblivion. But thou art not such
A lover, my Belovèd! thou canst wait
Through sorrow and sickness, to bring souls to touch,
And think it soon when others cry 'Too late.'

## XLI

I thank all who have loved me in their hearts,
With thanks and love from mine. Deep thanks to all
Who paused a little near the prison-wall
To hear my music in its louder parts
Ere they went onward, each one to the mart's
Or temple's occupation, beyond call.
But thou, who, in my voice's sink and fall
When the sob took it, thy divinest Art's
Own instrument didst drop down at thy foot
To hearken what I said between my tears, ...
Instruct me how to thank thee! Oh, to shoot
My soul's full meaning into future years,
That *they* should lend it utterance, and salute
Love that endures, from Life that disappears!

## XLII

'*My future will not copy fair my past*' –
I wrote that once; and thinking at my side
My ministering life-angel justified
The word by his appealing look upcast
To the white throne of God, I turned at last,
And there, instead, saw thee, not unallied
To angels in thy soul! Then I, long tried
By natural ills, received the comfort fast,
While budding, at thy sight, my pilgrim's staff
Gave out green leaves with morning dews impearled.
I seek no copy now of life's first half:
Leave here the pages with long musing curled,
And write me new my future's epigraph,
New angel mine, unhoped for in the world!

## XLIII

How do I love thee? Let me count the ways.
I love thee to the depth and breadth and height
My soul can reach, when feeling out of sight
For the ends of Being and ideal Grace.
I love thee to the level of everyday's
Most quiet need, by sun and candle-light.
I love thee freely, as men strive for Right;
I love thee purely, as they turn from Praise.
I love thee with the passion put to use
In my old griefs, and with my childhood's faith.
I love thee with a love I seemed to lose
With my lost saints, – I love thee with the breath,
Smiles, tears, of all my life! – and, if God choose,
I shall but love thee better after death.

## XLIV

Belovèd, thou hast brought me many flowers
Plucked in the garden, all the summer through
And winter, and it seemed as if they grew
In this close room, nor missed the sun and showers.
So, in the like name of that love of ours,
Take back these thoughts which here unfolded too,
And which on warm and cold days I withdrew
From my heart's ground. Indeed, those beds and bowers
Be overgrown with bitter weeds and rue,
And wait thy weeding; yet here's eglantine,
Here's ivy! – take them, as I used to do
Thy flowers, and keep them where they shall not pine.
Instruct thine eyes to keep their colours true,
And tell thy soul their roots are left in mine.


60       The Runaway Slave at Pilgrim's Point

### I

I stand on the mark beside the shore
   Of the first white pilgrim's bended knee,
Where exile turned to ancestor,
   And God was thanked for liberty.
I have run through the night, my skin is as dark,
I bend my knee down on this mark:
   I look on the sky and the sea.

### II

O pilgrim-souls, I speak to you!
   I see you come proud and slow
From the land of the spirits pale as dew
   And round me and round me ye go.
O pilgrims, I have gasped and run
All night long from the whips of one
   Who in your names works sin and woe!

### III

And thus I thought that I would come
   And kneel here where ye knelt before,
And feel your souls around me hum
   In undertone to the ocean's roar;
And lift my black face, my black hand,
Here, in your names, to curse this land
   Ye blessed in freedom's, evermore.

### IV

I am black, I am black,
   And yet God made me, they say:
But if He did so, smiling back
   He must have cast His work away
Under the feet of His white creatures,
With a look of scorn, that the dusky features
   Might be trodden again to clay.

### V

And yet He has made dark things
   To be glad and merry as light:
There's a little dark bird sits and sings,
   There's a dark stream ripples out of sight,
And the dark frogs chant in the safe morass,
And the sweetest stars are made to pass
   O'er the face of the darkest night.

### VI

But *we* who are dark, we are dark!
   Ah God, we have no stars!
About our souls in care and cark
   Our blackness shuts like prison-bars:
The poor souls crouch so far behind
That never a comfort can they find
   By reaching through the prison-bars.

### VII

Indeed we live beneath the sky,
   That great smooth Hand of God stretched out
On all His children fatherly,
   To save them from the dread and doubt
Which would be if, from this low place,
All opened straight up to His face
   Into the grand eternity.

### VIII

And still God's sunshine and His frost,
   They make us hot, they make us cold,
As if we were not black and lost;
   And the beasts and birds, in wood and fold,
Do fear and take us for very men:
Could the whip-poor-will or the cat of the glen
   Look into my eyes and be bold?

### IX

I am black, I am black!
   But, once, I laughed in girlish glee,
For one of my colour stood in the track
   Where the drivers drove, and looked at me,
And tender and full was the look he gave –
Could a slave look *so* at another slave? –
   I look at the sky and the sea.

### X

And from that hour our spirits grew
   As free as if unsold, unbought:
Oh, strong enough, since we were two,
   To conquer the world, we thought.
The drivers drove us day by day;
We did not mind, we went one way,
   And no better a freedom sought.

### XI

In the sunny ground between the canes,
　　He said 'I love you' as he passed;
When the shingle-roof rang sharp with the rains,
　　I heard how he vowed it fast:
While others shook he smiled in the hut,
As he carved me a bowl of the cocoa-nut
　　Through the roar of the hurricanes.

### XII

I sang his name instead of a song,
　　Over and over I sang his name,
Upward and downward I drew it along
　　My various notes, – the same, the same!
I sang it low, that the slave-girls near
Might never guess, from aught they could hear,
　　It was only a name – a name.

### XIII

I look on the sky and the sea.
　　We were two to love, and two to pray:
Yes, two, O God, who cried to Thee,
　　Though nothing didst Thou say!
Coldly Thou sat'st behind the sun:
And now I cry who am but one,
　　Thou wilt not speak to-day.

### XIV

We were black, we were black,
　　We had no claim to love and bliss,
What marvel if each went to wrack?
　　They wrung my cold hands out of his,
They dragged him – where? I crawled to touch
His blood's mark in the dust ... not much,
　　Ye pilgrim-souls, though plain as *this*!

### XV

Wrong, followed by a deeper wrong!
   Mere grief's too good for such as I:
So the white men brought the shame ere long
   To strangle the sob of my agony.
They would not leave me for my dull
Wet eyes! – it was too merciful
   To let me weep pure tears and die.

### XVI

I am black, I am black!
   I wore a child upon my breast,
An amulet that hung too slack,
   And, in my unrest, could not rest:
Thus we went moaning, child and mother,
One to another, one to another,
   Until all ended for the best.

### XVII

For hark! I will tell you low, low,
   I am black, you see, –
And the babe who lay on my bosom so,
   Was far too white, too white for me;
As white as the ladies who scorned to pray
Beside me at church but yesterday,
   Though my tears had washed a place for my knee.

### XVIII

My own, own child! I could not bear
   To look in his face, it was so white;
I covered him up with a kerchief there,
   I covered his face in close and tight:
And he moaned and struggled, as well might be,
For the white child wanted his liberty –
   Ha, ha! he wanted the master-right.

### XIX

He moaned and beat with his head and feet,
　His little feet that never grew;
He struck them out, as it was meet,
　Against my heart to break it through:
I might have sung and made him mild,
But I dared not sing to the white-faced child
　The only song I knew.

### XX

I pulled the kerchief very close:
　He could not see the sun, I swear,
More, then, alive, than now he does
　From between the roots of the mango ... where?
I know where. Close! A child and mother
Do wrong to look at one another
　When one is black and one is fair.

### XXI

Why, in that single glance I had
　Of my child's face, ... I tell you all,
I saw a look that made me mad!
　The *master's* look, that used to fall
On my soul like his lash ... or worse!
And so, to save it from my curse,
　I twisted it round in my shawl.

### XXII

And he moaned and trembled from foot to head,
　He shivered from head to foot;
Till after a time, he lay instead
　Too suddenly still and mute.
I felt, beside, a stiffening cold:
I dared to lift up just a fold,
　As in lifting a leaf of the mango-fruit.

### XXIII

But *my* fruit ... ha, ha! – there, had been
   (I laugh to think on't at this hour!)
Your fine white angels (who have seen
   Nearest the secret of God's power)
And plucked my fruit to make them wine,
And sucked the soul of that child of mine
   As the humming-bird sucks the soul of the
      flower.

### XXIV

Ha, ha, the trick of the angels white!
   They freed the white child's spirit so.
I said not a word, but day and night
   I carried the body to and fro,
And it lay on my heart like a stone, as chill.
– The sun may shine out as much as he will:
   I am cold, though it happened a month ago.

### XXV

From the white man's house, and the black
      man's hut,
   I carried the little body on;
The forest's arms did round us shut,
   And silence through the trees did run:
They asked no question as I went,
They stood too high for astonishment,
   They could see God sit on His throne.

### XXVI

My little body, kerchiefed fast,
   I bore it on through the forest, on;
And when I felt it was tired at last,
   I scooped a hole beneath the moon:
Through the forest-tops the angels far,
With a white sharp finger from every star,
   Did point and mock at what was done.

### XXVII

Yet when it was all done aright, –
   Earth, 'twixt me and my baby, strewed, –
All, changed to black earth, – nothing white, –
   A dark child in the dark! – ensued
Some comfort, and my heart grew young;
I sate down smiling there and sung
   The song I learnt in my maidenhood.

### XXVIII

And thus we two were reconciled,
   The white child and black mother, thus;
For as I sang it soft and wild,
   The same song, more melodious,
Rose from the grave whereon I sate:
It was the dead child singing that,
   To join the souls of both of us.

### XXIX

I look on the sea and the sky.
   Where the pilgrims' ships first anchored lay
The free sun rideth gloriously,
   But the pilgrim-ghosts have slid away
Through the earliest streaks of the morn:
My face is black, but it glares with a scorn
   Which they dare not meet by day.

### XXX

Ha! – in their stead, their hunter sons!
   Ha, ha! they are on me – they hunt in a ring!
Keep off! I brave you all at once,
   I throw off your eyes like snakes that sting!
You have killed the black eagle at nest, I think:
Did you ever stand still in your triumph, and shrink
   From the stroke of her wounded wing?

### XXXI

(Man, drop that stone you dared to lift! – )
   I wish you who stand there five abreast,
Each, for his own wife's joy and gift,
   A little corpse as safely at rest
As mine in the mangoes! Yes, but *she*
May keep live babies on her knee,
   And sing the song she likes the best.

### XXXII

I am not mad: I am black.
   I see you staring in my face –
I know you staring, shrinking back,
   Ye are born of the Washington-race,
And this land is the free America,
And this mark on my wrist – (I prove what I say)
   Ropes tied me up here to the flogging-place.

### XXXIII

You think I shrieked then? Not a sound!
   I hung, as a gourd hangs in the sun;
I only cursed them all around
   As softly as I might have done
My very own child: from these sands
Up to the mountains, lift your hands,
   O slaves, and end what I begun!

### XXXIV

Whips, curses; these must answer those!
   For in this Union you have set
Two kinds of men in adverse rows,
   Each loathing each; and all forget
The seven wounds in Christ's body fair,
While He sees gaping everywhere
   Our countless wounds that pay no debt.

### XXXV

Our wounds are different. Your white men
      Are, after all, not gods indeed,
Nor able to make Christs again
      Do good with bleeding. *We* who bleed
(Stand off!) we help not in our loss!
*We* are too heavy for our cross,
      And fall and crush you and your seed.

### XXXVI

I fall, I swoon! I look at the sky.
      The clouds are breaking on my brain;
I am floated along, as if I should die
      Of liberty's exquisite pain.
In the name of the white child waiting for me
In the death-dark where we may kiss and agree,
White men, I leave you all curse-free
      In my broken heart's disdain!

## 61       Mother and Poet

*(Turin, after news from Gaeta, 1861)*

### I

Dead! One of them shot by the sea in the east,
      And one of them shot in the west by the sea.
Dead! both my boys! When you sit at the feast
      And are wanting a great song for Italy free,
      Let none look at *me*!

### II

Yet I was a poetess only last year,
      And good at my art, for a woman, men said;
But *this* woman, *this*, who is agonised here,
      – The east sea and west sea rhyme on in her head
      For ever instead.

### III

What art can a woman be good at? Oh, vain!
　　What art *is* she good at, but hurting her breast
With the milk-teeth of babes, and a smile at the pain?
　　Ah boys, how you hurt! you were strong as you pressed,
　　　　And I proud, by that test.

### IV

What art's for a woman? To hold on her knees
　　Both darlings! to feel all their arms round her throat,
Cling, strangle a little! to sew by degrees
　　And 'broider the long-clothes and neat little coat;
　　　　To dream and to doat.

### V

To teach them ... It stings there! *I* made them indeed
　　Speak plain the word *country*. *I* taught them, no doubt,
That a country's a thing men should die for at need.
　　*I* prated of liberty, rights, and about
　　　　The tyrant cast out.

### VI

And when their eyes flashed ... O my beautiful eyes! ...
　　*I* exulted; nay, let them go forth at the wheels
Of the guns, and denied not. But then the surprise
　　When one sits quite alone! Then one weeps, then one
　　　　　kneels!
　　　　God, how the house feels!

### VII

At first, happy news came, in gay letters moiled
　　With my kisses, – of camp-life and glory, and how
They both loved me; and, soon coming home to be spoiled
　　In return would fan off every fly from my brow
　　　　With their green laurel-bough.

### VIII

Then was triumph at Turin: 'Ancona was free!'
  And some one came out of the cheers in the street,
With a face pale as stone, to say something to me.
  My Guido was dead! I fell down at his feet,
    While they cheered in the street.

### IX

I bore it; friends soothed me; my grief looked sublime
  As the ransom of Italy. One boy remained
To be leant on and walked with, recalling the time
  When the first grew immortal, while both of us strained
    To the height he had gained.

### X

And letters still came, shorter, sadder, more strong,
  Writ now but in one hand, 'I was not to faint, –
One loved me for two – would be with me ere long:
  And *Viva l'Italia! – he* died for, our saint,
    Who forbids our complaint.'

### XI

My Nanni would add, 'he was safe, and aware
  Of a presence that turned off the balls, – was imprest
It was Guido himself, who knew what I could bear,
  And how 'twas impossible, quite dispossessed
    To live on for the rest.'

### XII

On which, without pause, up the telegraph-line
  Swept smoothly the next news from Gaeta: – *Shot.*
*Tell his mother.* Ah, ah, 'his,' 'their' mother, – not 'mine,'
  No voice says '*My* mother' again to me. What!
    You think Guido forgot?

### XIII

Are souls straight so happy that, dizzy with Heaven,
　　They drop earth's affections, conceive not of woe?
I think not. Themselves were too lately forgiven
　　Through THAT Love and Sorrow which reconciled so
　　　　The Above and Below.

### XIV

O Christ of the five wounds, who look'dst through the dark
　　To the face of Thy mother! consider, I pray,
How we common mothers stand desolate, mark,
　　Whose sons, not being Christs, die with eyes turned away,
　　　　And no last word to say!

### XV

Both boys dead? but that's out of nature. We all
　　Have been patriots, yet each house must always keep one.
'Twere imbecile, hewing out roads to a wall;
　　And, when Italy's made, for what end is it done
　　　　If we have not a son?

### XVI

Ah, ah, ah! when Gaeta's taken, what then?
　　When the fair wicked queen sits no more at her sport
Of the fire-balls of death crashing souls out of men?
　　When the guns of Cavalli with final retort
　　　　Have cut the game short?

### XVII

When Venice and Rome keep their new jubilee,
　　When your flag takes all heaven for its white, green,
　　　　and red,
When *you* have your country from mountain to sea,
　　When King Victor has Italy's crown on his head,
　　　　(And *I* have my Dead) –

### XVIII

What then? Do not mock me. Ah, ring your bells low,
    And burn your lights faintly! *My* country is *there*,
Above the star pricked by the last peak of snow:
    My Italy's THERE, with my brave civic Pair,
        To disfranchise despair!

### XIX

Forgive me. Some women bear children in strength,
    And bite back the cry of their pain in self-scorn;
But the birth-pangs of nations will wring us at length
    Into wail such as this – and we sit on forlorn
        When the man-child is born.

### XX

Dead! One of them shot by the sea in the east,
    And one of them shot in the west by the sea.
Both! both my boys! If in keeping the feast
    You want a great song for your Italy free,
        Let none look at *me*!

## 62        My Heart and I

### I

Enough! we're tired, my heart and I.
    We sit beside the headstone thus,
    And wish that name were carved for us.
The moss reprints more tenderly
    The hard types of the mason's knife,
    As heaven's sweet life renews earth's life
With which we're tired, my heart and I.

### II

You see we're tired, my heart and I.
    We dealt with books, we trusted men,
    And in our own blood drenched the pen,
As if such colours could not fly.

We walked too straight for fortune's end,
    We loved too true to keep a friend;
At last we're tired, my heart and I.


### III

How tired we feel, my heart and I!
    We seem of no use in the world;
    Our fancies hang grey and uncurled
About men's eyes indifferently;
    Our voice which thrilled you so, will let
    You sleep; our tears are only wet:
What do we here, my heart and I?


### IV

So tired, so tired, my heart and I!
    It was not thus in that old time
    When Ralph sat with me 'neath the lime
To watch the sunset from the sky.
    'Dear love, you're looking tired,' he said;
    I, smiling at him, shook my head:
'Tis now we're tired, my heart and I.


### V

So tired, so tired, my heart and I!
    Though now none takes me on his arm
    To fold me close and kiss me warm
Till each quick breath end in a sigh
    Of happy languor. Now, alone,
    We lean upon this graveyard stone,
Uncheered, unkissed, my heart and I.


### VI

Tired out we are, my heart and I.
    Suppose the world brought diadems
    To tempt us, crusted with loose gems
Of powers and pleasures? Let it try.
    We scarcely care to look at even
    A pretty child, or God's blue heaven,
We feel so tired, my heart and I.

### VII

Yet who complains? My heart and I?
    In this abundant earth no doubt
    Is little room for things worn out:
Disdain them, break them, throw them by!
    And if before the days grew rough
    We once were loved, used, – well enough,
I think, we've fared, my heart and I.

# THOMAS MILLER
1807–74

63                    The Ant-Lion

By digging a hole in the sand
I live – and catch what comes to hand;
Hard work it is when there are stones,
And often tries my poor old bones.
I get a stone upon my back,
Just as a pedlar does his pack;
But mine is loose and his is fast.
Out of my pit I must it cast,
And many times I have to try
Before I get it up so high;
Many a heavy tug and strain,
I reach the top, it's down again.
Then I must descend my pit
And once more have a tug at it;
Neither cord nor strap to bind it,
And no one behind to mind it.
Hard work it is, and so you'd say
If you but tried it for a day.
If you can but spare the time,
Up a steep embankment climb,
On your back a large loose stone,
And what it is will then be known.
I have no doubt you would own,
If like me you earned your bread,
You'd need no rocking when in bed.

Out of this hole a head you'll see,
And two crooked paws – that is me,
At least all I care to show;
My body's in the hole below.

An insect near the top now crawls;
The sand is loose, and down he falls.
Then into my hole I go,
And eat him up as you would do
If you had nothing else to eat,
Ah! and consider it a treat.
Sometimes he bigger is than I,
Then showers of sand I at him shy,
And happen hit him in the eye;
Then he can't see his way at all,
But hits his head against the wall;
And while he in his anger hums,
Another shower at him comes,
And then he says, 'Well, hit or miss,
I must try and get out of this.'
We go at it hammer and tongs;
He tries to stab me with his prongs,
But tries in vain, he can't get out,
So quick I kick the sand about,
So thick it comes, he cannot see
Even the slightest bit of me,
But wonders who's his enemy;
And so at random makes a thrust,
While I keep kicking up a dust.
If he's a wasp and got a sting,
Then I lay fast hold of one wing,
And turn as he turns round for hours,
Still throwing up the sand in showers;
Nor ever all the time leave go –
A trick worth two of that I know.
He bends, he twists, while round I dodge,
Lest he his sting should in me lodge,
For that I know would be my death.
We never once stop to take breath,
But still continue the fierce strife –
We know we fight for very life;
For he would not go away,
Till with his sting he did me slay,

Even if I would let him go,
(You ask him and he'll tell you so).
I knowing this, go in again –
I pull, I haul, I kick, I strain;
Then get into the sand his head,
Give it a bite, and he is dead:
And say, as I sit down to dine,
'What a hard life this is of mine!'
I only wish I could eat sand,
For that in plenty lies at hand;
But an ant-lion must lead a lion-like life,
And both of us live by slaughter and strife.

# CHARLES TURNER
## 1808–79

64              A Brilliant Day

O keen pellucid air! nothing can lurk
Or disavow itself on this bright day;
The small rain-plashes shine from far away,
The tiny emmet glitters at his work;
The bee looks blithe and gay, and as she plies
Her task, and moves and sidles round the cup
Of this spring flower, to drink its honey up,
Her glassy wings, like oars that dip and rise,
Gleam momently. Pure-bosomed, clear of fog,
The long lake glistens, while the glorious beam
Bespangles the wet joints and floating leaves
Of water-plants, whose every point receives
His light; and jellies of the spawning frog,
Unmarked before, like piles of jewels seem!


65              A Photograph on the Red Gold

*Jersey, 1867*

About the knoll the airs blew fresh and brisk,
And, musing as I sat, I held my watch
Upon my open palm; its smooth bright disk
Was uppermost, and so it came to catch,
And dwarf, the figure of a waving tree,
Backed by the West. A tiny sunshine peeped
About a tiny elm, – and both were steeped
In royal metal, flaming ruddily:
How lovely was that vision to behold!

How passing sweet that fairy miniature,
That streamed and flickered o'er the burning gold!
God of small things and great! do Thou ensure
Thy gift of sight, till all my days are told,
Bless all its bliss, and keep its pleasures pure!

66　　　　　　　Joy Came from Heaven

Joy came from heaven, for men were mad with pain,
And sought a mansion on this earth below;
He could not settle on the wrinkled brow,
Close-gathered to repel him; and, again,
Upon the cheek he sought repose in vain;
He found that pillow all too chill and cold,
Where sorrow's streams might float him from his hold,
Caught sleeping in their channel. Th' eye would fain
Receive the stranger on her slippery sphere,
Where life had purer effluence than elsewhere,
But where no barrier might forbid the tear
To sweep it, when it listed. So not there
He staid, nor could the lips his couch prepare,
Shifting untenably from smile to sneer.

67　　　　　　　Wind on the Corn

Full often as I rove by path or style,
To watch the harvest ripening in the vale,
Slowly and sweetly, like a growing smile –
A smile that ends in laughter – the quick gale
Upon the breadths of gold-green wheat descends;
While still the swallow, with unbaffled grace,
About his viewless quarry dips and bends –
And all the fine excitement of the chase

Lies in the hunter's beauty: in the eclipse
Of that brief shadow, how the barley's beard
Tilts at the passing gloom, and wild-rose dips
Among the white-tops in the ditches reared:
And hedgerow's flowery breast of lacework stirs
Faintly in that full wind that rocks th' outstanding firs.

68                     Welsh Lucy

OR, THE DUKE OF MONMOUTH'S
MOTHER

Poor Lucy Walters! who remembers thee?
Thy name is lost, though on thy native hill
Perchance they know it, yea, and see thee still;
But, in the outer world, how few there be
To speak of Monmouth's mother! To thy door
The tempter came, and thy young heart beguil'd;
Then came the birth of that half-royal child,
Who, when his feeble battle-shout was o'er,
Crept into lone Shag's Heath from lost Sedgemoor;
Then fell his kinsman's axe, whose triple blow
Thy spirit still hears! sore penance for that tryst
Of shame, which brought thy motherhood of woe –
Or sighs, at breaking of the mountain-mist,
To view, each morn, the headsman's world below.

# EDWARD FITZGERALD

## 1809–83

69        Rubáiyát of Omar Khayyám

### I

Awake! for Morning in the Bowl of Night
Has flung the Stone that puts the Stars to Flight:
   And Lo! the Hunter of the East has caught
The Sultán's Turret in a Noose of Light.

### II

Dreaming when Dawn's Left Hand was in the Sky
I heard a Voice within the Tavern cry,
   'Awake, my Little ones, and fill the Cup
Before Life's Liquor in its Cup be dry.'

### III

And, as the Cock crew, those who stood before
The Tavern shouted – 'Open then the Door!
   You know how little while we have to stay,
And, once departed, may return no more.'

### IV

Now the New Year reviving old Desires,
The thoughtful Soul to Solitude retires,
   Where the WHITE HAND OF MOSES on the
      Bough
Puts out, and Jesus from the Ground suspires.

## V

Irám indeed is gone with all its Rose,
And Jamshýd's Sev'n-ring'd Cup where no one knows;
   But still the Vine her ancient Ruby yields,
And still a Garden by the Water blows.

## VI

And David's Lips are lock't; but in divine
High piping Péhleví, with 'Wine! Wine! Wine!
   *Red* Wine!' – the Nightingale cries to the Rose
That yellow Cheek of her's to'incarnadine.

## VII

Come, fill the Cup, and in the Fire of Spring
The Winter Garment of Repentance fling:
   The Bird of Time has but a little way
To fly – and Lo! the Bird is on the Wing.

## VIII

And look – a thousand Blossoms with the Day
Woke – and a thousand scatter'd into Clay:
   And this first Summer Month that brings the Rose
Shall take Jamshýd and Kaikobád away.

## IX

But come with old Khayyám, and leave the Lot
Of Kaikobád and Kaikhosrú forgot:
   Let Rustum lay about him as he will,
Or Hátim Tai cry Supper – heed them not.

### X

With me along some Strip of Herbage strown
That just divides the desert from the sown,
  Where name of Slave and Sultán scarce is known,
And pity Sultán Máhmúd on his Throne.

### XI

Here with a Loaf of Bread beneath the Bough,
A Flask of Wine, a Book of Verse – and Thou
  Beside me singing in the Wilderness –
And Wilderness is Paradise enow.

### XII

'How sweet is mortal Sovranty!' – think some:
Others – 'How blest the Paradise to come!'
  Ah, take the Cash in hand and waive the Rest;
Oh, the brave Music of a *distant* Drum!

### XIII

Look to the Rose that blows about us – 'Lo,
Laughing,' she says, 'into the World I blow:
  At once the silken Tassel of my Purse
Tear, and its Treasure on the Garden throw.'

### XIV

The Worldly Hope men set their Hearts upon
Turns Ashes – or it prospers; and anon,
  Like Snow upon the Desert's dusty Face
Lighting a little Hour or two – is gone.

## XV

And those who husbanded the Golden Grain,
And those who flung it to the Winds like Rain,
    Alike to no such aureate Earth are turn'd
As, buried once, Men want dug up again.

## XVI

Think, in this batter'd Caravanserai
Whose Doorways are alternate Night and Day,
    How Sultán after Sultán with his Pomp
Abode his Hour or two, and went his way.

## XVII

They say the Lion and the Lizard keep
The Courts where Jamshýd gloried and drank deep:
    And Bahrám, that great Hunter – the Wild Ass
Stamps o'er his Head, and he lies fast asleep.

## XVIII

I sometimes think that never blows so red
The Rose as where some buried Cæsar bled;
    That every Hyacinth the Garden wears
Dropt in its Lap from some once lovely Head.

## XIX

And this delightful Herb whose tender Green
Fledges the River's Lip on which we lean –
    Ah, lean upon it lightly! for who knows
From what once lovely Lip it springs unseen!

## XX

Ah, my Belovéd, fill the Cup that clears
To-DAY of past Regrets and future Fears –
    To-morrow? – Why, To-morrow I may be
Myself with Yesterday's Sev'n Thousand Years.

## XXI

Lo! some we loved, the loveliest and best
That Time and Fate of all their Vintage prest,
    Have drunk their Cup a Round or two before,
And one by one crept silently to Rest.

## XXII

And we, that now make merry in the Room
They left, and Summer dresses in new Bloom,
    Ourselves must we beneath the Couch of Earth
Descend, ourselves to make a Couch – for whom?

## XXIII

Ah, make the most of what we yet may spend,
Before we too into the Dust descend;
    Dust into Dust, and under Dust, to lie,
Sans Wine, sans Song, sans Singer, and – sans End!

## XXIV

Alike for those who for To-DAY prepare,
And those that after a To-MORROW stare,
    A Muezzín from the Tower of Darkness cries
'Fools! your Reward is neither Here nor There!'

## XXV

Why, all the Saints and Sages who discuss'd
Of the Two Worlds so learnedly, are thrust
   Like foolish Prophets forth; their Words to Scorn
Are scatter'd, and their Mouths are stopt with Dust.

## XXVI

Oh, come with the old Khayyám, and leave the Wise
To talk; one thing is certain, that Life flies;
   One thing is certain, and the Rest is Lies;
The Flower that once has blown for ever dies.

## XXVII

Myself when young did eagerly frequent
Doctor and Saint, and heard great Argument
   About it and about: but evermore
Came out by the same Door as in I went.

## XXVIII

With them the Seed of Wisdom did I sow,
And with my own hand labour'd it to grow:
   And this was all the Harvest that I reap'd –
'I came like Water, and like Wind I go.'

## XXIX

Into this Universe, and *why* not knowing,
Nor *whence*, like Water willy-nilly flowing:
   And out of it, as Wind along the Waste,
I know not *whither*, willy-nilly blowing.

### XXX

What, without asking, hither hurried *whence*?
And, without asking, *whither* hurried hence!
    Another and another Cup to drown
The Memory of this Impertinence!

### XXXI

Up from Earth's Centre through the Seventh Gate
I rose, and on the Throne of Saturn sate,
    And many Knots unravel'd by the Road;
But not the Knot of Human Death and Fate.

### XXXII

There was a Door to which I found no Key:
There was a Veil past which I could not see:
    Some little Talk awhile of ME and THEE
There seemed – and then no more of THEE and ME.

### XXXIII

Then to the rolling Heav'n itself I cried,
Asking, 'What Lamp had Destiny to guide
    Her little Children stumbling in the Dark?'
And – 'A blind Understanding!' Heav'n replied.

### XXXIV

Then to this earthen Bowl did I adjourn
My Lip the secret Well of Life to learn:
    And Lip to Lip it murmur'd – 'While you live
Drink! – for once dead you never shall return.'

### XXXV

I think the Vessel, that with fugitive
Articulation answer'd, once did live,
    And merry-make; and the cold Lip I kiss'd
How many Kisses might it take – and give!

### XXXVI

For in the Market-place, one Dusk of Day,
I watch'd the Potter thumping his wet Clay:
    And with its all obliterated Tongue
It murmur'd – 'Gently, Brother, gently, pray!'

### XXXVII

Ah, fill the Cup: – what boots it to repeat
How Time is slipping underneath our Feet:
    Unborn TO-MORROW, and dead YESTERDAY,
Why fret about them if TO-DAY be sweet!

### XXXVIII

One Moment in Annihilation's Waste,
One Moment, of the Well of Life to taste –
    The Stars are setting and the Caravan
Starts for the Dawn of Nothing – Oh, make haste!

### XXXIX

How long, how long, in infinite Pursuit
Of This and That endeavour and dispute?
    Better be merry with the fruitful Grape
Than sadden after none, or bitter, Fruit.

### XL

You know, my Friends, how long since in my House
For a new Marriage I did make Carouse:
  Divorced old barren Reason from my Bed,
And took the Daughter of the Vine to Spouse.

### XLI

For 'Is' and 'Is-not' though *with* Rule and Line,
And 'Up-and-down' *without*, I could define,
  I yet in all I only cared to know,
Was never deep in anything but – Wine.

### XLII

And lately, by the Tavern Door agape,
Came stealing through the Dusk an Angel Shape
  Bearing a Vessel on his Shoulder; and
He bid me taste of it; and 'twas – the Grape!

### XLIII

The Grape that can with Logic absolute
The Two-and-Seventy jarring Sects confute:
  The subtle Alchemist that in a Trice
Life's leaden Metal into Gold transmute.

### XLIV

The mighty Mahmúd, the victorious Lord,
That all the misbelieving and black Horde
  Of Fears and Sorrows that infest the Soul
Scatters and slays with his enchanted Sword.

### XLV

But leave the Wise to wrangle, and with me
The Quarrel of the Universe let be:
   And, in some corner of the Hubbub coucht,
Make Game of that which makes as much of Thee.

### XLVI

For in and out, above, about, below,
'Tis nothing but a Magic Shadow-show,
   Play'd in a Box whose Candle is the Sun,
Round which we Phantom Figures come and go.

### XLVII

And if the Wine you drink, the Lip you press,
End in the Nothing all Things end in – Yes –
   Then fancy while Thou art, Thou art but what
Thou shalt be – Nothing – Thou shalt not be less.

### XLVIII

While the Rose blows along the River Brink,
With old Khayyám the Ruby Vintage drink:
   And when the Angel with his darker Draught
Draws up to Thee – take that, and do not shrink.

### XLIX

'Tis all a Chequer-board of Nights and Days
Where Destiny with Men for Pieces plays:
   Hither and thither moves, and mates, and slays,
And one by one back in the Closet lays.

L

The Ball no Question makes of Ayes and Noes,
But Right or Left as strikes the Player goes;
   And He that toss'd Thee down into the Field,
*He* knows about it all – HE knows – HE knows!

LI

The Moving Finger writes; and, having writ,
Moves on: nor all thy Piety nor Wit
   Shall lure it back to cancel half a Line,
Nor all thy Tears wash out a Word of it.

LII

And that inverted Bowl we call The Sky,
Whereunder crawling coop't we live and die,
   Lift not thy hands to *It* for help – for It
Rolls impotently on as Thou or I.

LIII

With Earth's first Clay They did the Last Man's knead,
And then of the Last Harvest sow'd the Seed:
   Yea, the first Morning of Creation wrote
What the Last Dawn of Reckoning shall read.

LIV

I tell Thee this – When, starting from the Goal,
Over the shoulders of the flaming Foal
   Of Heav'n Parwín and Mushtara they flung,
In my predestin'd Plot of Dust and Soul

## LV

The Vine had struck a Fibre; which about
If clings my Being – let the Súfi flout;
    Of my Base Metal may be filed a Key,
That shall unlock the Door he howls without.

## LVI

And this I know: whether the one True Light,
Kindle to Love, or Wrathconsume me quite,
    One Glimpse of It within the Tavern caught
Better than in the Temple lost outright.

## LVII

Oh Thou, who didst with Pitfall and with Gin
Beset the Road I was to wander in,
    Thou wilt not with Predestination round
Enmesh me, and impute my Fall to Sin?

## LVIII

Oh, Thou, who Man of baser Earth didst make,
And who with Eden didst devise the Snake;
    For all the Sin wherewith the Face of Man
Is blacken'd, Man's Forgiveness give – and take!

\* \* \*

## KÚZA-NÁMA.

## LIX

Listen again. One Evening at the Close
Of Ramazán, ere the better Moon arose,
    In that old Potter's Shop I stood alone
With the clay Population round in Rows.

## LX

And, strange to tell, among that Earthen Lot
Some could articulate, while others not:
   And suddenly one more impatient cried –
'Who *is* the Potter, pray, and who the Pot?'

## LXI

Then said another – 'Surely not in vain
My Substance from the common Earth was ta'en,
   That He who subtly wrought me into Shape
Should stamp me back to common Earth again.'

## LXII

Another said – 'Why, ne'er a peevish Boy,
Would break the Bowl from which he drank in Joy;
   Shall He that *made* the Vessel in pure Love
And Fancy, in an after Rage destroy!'

## LXIII

None answer'd this; but after Silence spake
A Vessel of a more ungainly Make:
   'They sneer at me for leaning all awry;
What! did the Hand then of the Potter shake?'

## LXIV

Said one – 'Folks of a surly Tapster tell,
And daub his Visage with the Smoke of Hell;
   They talk of some strict Testing of us – Pish!
He's a Good Fellow, and 'twill all be well.'

### LXV

Then said another with a long-drawn Sigh,
'My Clay with long oblivion is gone dry:
   But, fill me with the old familiar Juice,
Methinks I might recover by-and-bye!'

### LXVI

So while the Vessels one by one were speaking,
One spied the little Crescent all were seeking:
   And then they jogg'd each other, 'Brother! Brother!
Hark to the Porter's Shoulder-knot a-creaking!'

\* \* \*

### LXVII

Ah, with the Grape my fading Life provide,
And wash my Body whence the Life has died,
   And in a Windingsheet of Vine-leaf wrapt,
So bury me by some sweet Garden-side.

### LXVIII

That ev'n my buried Ashes such a Snare
Of Perfume shall fling up into the Air,
   As not a True Believer passing by
But shall be overtaken unaware.

### LXIX

Indeed the Idols I have loved so long
Have done my Credit in Men's Eye much wrong:
   Have drown'd my Honour in a shallow Cup,
And sold my Reputation for a Song.

## LXX

Indeed, indeed, Repentance oft before
I swore – but was I sober when I swore?
  And then and then came Spring, and Rose-in-hand
My thread-bare Penitence apieces tore.

## LXXI

And much as Wine has play'd the Infidel,
And robb'd me of my Robe of Honour – well,
  I often wonder what the Vintners buy
One half so precious as the Goods they sell.

## LXXII

Alas, that Spring should vanish with the Rose!
That Youth's sweet-scented Manuscript should close!
  The Nightingale that in the Branches sang,
Ah, whence, and whither flown again, who knows!

## LXXIII

Ah Love! could thou and I with Fate conspire
To grasp this sorry Scheme of Things entire,
  Would not we shatter it to bits – and then
Re-mould it nearer to the Heart's Desire!

## LXXIV

Ah, Moon of my Delight who know'st no wane,
The Moon of Heav'n is rising once again:
  How oft hereafter rising shall she look
Through this same Garden after me – in vain!

## LXXV

And when Thyself with shining Foot shall pass
Among the Guests Star-scatter'd on the Grass,
　And in thy joyous Errand reach the Spot
Where I made one – turn down an empty Glass!

## TAMÁM SHUD

# THOMAS GORDON HAKE
## 1809–95

70

### Unrest

Is this a remnant of old Paradise
   Where now a shivering, dimpled river creeps,
   Driven out from bliss, between these desert steeps,
Pine-armed and bristling to the loveless skies,
No heaven above but where the wild flocks rise,
   No world below but where the torrent leaps
   And down green steps of dripping foliage sweeps
The writhing gulph that ever rest denies
   To those lost waters? Rather here were driven
From Paradise the once offending pair,
   To find a peaceful sky by rough winds riven,
And look above through the mist-threaded air,
   That wanders 'twixt the mountain-tops and Heaven
To weave for evermore a world's despair.

# SIR JOHN HANMER
## 1809–81

71                          To an Eagle

Wild bird, they say that who like thee
Would soar, must single-minded be,
Nor love life's light variety;
Over seas and mountains blue
Ever with the sun in view,
If it shine not in the sky,
Seeing still with inner eye;
   And so in famous story
   Shall they have after glory.

But the supple snake below,
With his winding courses slow,
Uttereth in his heart, 'Ho, Ho!
For one spirit of the air
There are thousands of the earth;
Cautiously with me they fare,
Through the depths I lead them forth:
   And so in famous story
   Have they the surer glory.'

The while comes Winter with his frosts behind
And stayeth either course, and killeth all the kind.

72 Poetry by the Way-Side

Wandering along the vision-haunted way,
One did I meet, whom straight my heart did know;
But in strange seeming he was pleased to go,
And quaint, as by the forest-brook the jay;
The leaf-hid brook, with one particular ray
That the sun gilds, and of his orbèd glow
Gives thence suggestion to the sense; e'en so
On mine the quick poetic spirit did play,
From a feather in the head of one who followed
A trade associate with the tortoise-shell,
Client of Mercury, through the towns and shires,
A rude Autolycus with hat rain-hollowed;
And still, as droopt fantastically it fell,
The shows of things conformed to his desires.

# ALFRED TENNYSON

## 1809–92

73        The Lady of Shalott

### PART I

On either side the river lie
Long fields of barley and of rye,
That clothe the wold and meet the sky;
And thro' the field the road runs by
      To many-tower'd Camelot;
And up and down the people go,
Gazing where the lilies blow
Round an island there below,
      The island of Shalott.

Willows whiten, aspens quiver,
Little breezes dusk and shiver
Thro' the wave that runs for ever
By the island in the river
      Flowing down to Camelot.
Four gray walls, and four gray towers,
Overlook a space of flowers,
And the silent isle imbowers
      The Lady of Shalott.

By the margin, willow-veil'd,
Slide the heavy barges trail'd
By slow horses; and unhail'd
The shallop flitteth silken-sail'd
      Skimming down to Camelot:
But who hath seen her wave her hand?
Or at the casement seen her stand?
Or is she known in all the land,
      The Lady of Shalott?

Only reapers, reaping early
In among the bearded barley,
Hear a song that echoes cheerly
From the river winding clearly,
  Down to tower'd Camelot:
And by the moon the reaper weary,
Piling sheaves in uplands airy,
Listening, whispers ''Tis the fairy
  Lady of Shalott.'

### PART II

There she weaves by night and day
A magic web with colours gay.
She has heard a whisper say,
A curse is on her if she stay
  To look down to Camelot.
She knows not what the curse may be,
And so she weaveth steadily,
And little other care hath she,
  The Lady of Shalott.

And moving thro' a mirror clear
That hangs before her all the year,
Shadows of the world appear.
There she sees the highway near
  Winding down to Camelot:
There the river eddy whirls,
And there the surly village-churls,
And the red cloaks of market girls,
  Pass onward from Shalott.

Sometimes a troop of damsels glad,
An abbot on an ambling pad,
Sometimes a curly shepherd-lad,
Or long-hair'd page in crimson clad,
  Goes by to tower'd Camelot;

And sometimes thro' the mirror blue
The knights come riding two and two:
She hath no loyal knight and true,
    The Lady of Shalott.

But in her web she still delights
To weave the mirror's magic sights,
For often thro' the silent nights
A funeral, with plumes and lights
    And music, went to Camelot:
Or when the moon was overhead,
Came two young lovers lately wed;
'I am half sick of shadows,' said
    The Lady of Shalott.

## PART III

A bow-shot from her bower-eaves,
He rode between the barley-sheaves,
The sun came dazzling thro' the leaves,
And flamed upon the brazen greaves
    Of bold Sir Lancelot.
A red-cross knight for ever kneel'd
To a lady in his shield,
That sparkled on the yellow field,
    Beside remote Shalott.

The gemmy bridle glitter'd free,
Like to some branch of stars we see
Hung in the golden Galaxy.
The bridle bells rang merrily
    As he rode down to Camelot:
And from his blazon'd baldric slung
A mighty silver bugle hung,
And as he rode his armour rung,
    Beside remote Shalott.

All in the blue unclouded weather
Thick-jewell'd shone the saddle-leather,
The helmet and the helmet-feather
Burn'd like one burning flame together,
    As he rode down to Camelot.
As often thro' the purple night,
Below the starry clusters bright,
Some bearded meteor, trailing light,
    Moves over still Shalott.

His broad clear brow in sunlight glow'd;
On burnish'd hooves his war-horse trode;
From underneath his helmet flow'd
His coal-black curls as on he rode,
    As he rode down to Camelot.
From the bank and from the river
He flash'd into the crystal mirror,
'Tirra lirra,' by the river
    Sang Sir Lancelot.

She left the web, she left the loom,
She made three paces thro' the room,
She saw the water-lily bloom,
She saw the helmet and the plume,
    She look'd down to Camelot.
Out flew the web and floated wide;
The mirror crack'd from side to side;
'The curse is come upon me,' cried
    The Lady of Shalott.

## PART IV

In the stormy east-wind straining,
The palé yellow woods were waning,
The broad stream in his banks complaining,
Heavily the low sky raining
    Over tower'd Camelot;

Down she came and found a boat
Beneath a willow left afloat,
And round about the prow she wrote
*The Lady of Shalott.*

And down the river's dim expanse
Like some bold seër in a trance,
Seeing all his own mischance –
With a glassy countenance
  Did she look to Camelot.
And at the closing of the day
She loosed the chain, and down she lay;
The broad stream bore her far away,
  The Lady of Shalott.

Lying, robed in snowy white
That loosely flew to left and right –
The leaves upon her falling light –
Thro' the noises of the night
  She floated down to Camelot:
And as the boat-head wound along
The willowy hills and fields among,
They heard her singing her last song,
  The Lady of Shalott.

Heard a carol, mournful, holy,
Chanted loudly, chanted lowly,
Till her blood was frozen slowly,
And her eyes were darken'd wholly,
  Turn'd to tower'd Camelot.
For ere she reach'd upon the tide
The first house by the water-side,
Singing in her song she died,
  The Lady of Shalott.

Under tower and balcony,
By garden-wall and gallery,
A gleaming shape she floated by,
Dead-pale between the houses high,
    Silent into Camelot.
Out upon the wharfs they came,
Knight and burgher, lord and dame,
And round the prow they read her name,
    *The Lady of Shalott.*

Who is this? and what is here?
And in the lighted palace near
Died the sound of royal cheer;
And they cross'd themselves for fear,
    All the knights at Camelot:
But Lancelot mused a little space;
He said, 'She has a lovely face;
God in his mercy lend her grace,
    The Lady of Shalott.'

74        Break, break, break,
    On thy cold gray stones, O Sea!
And I would that my tongue could utter
    The thoughts that arise in me.

O well for the fisherman's boy,
    That he shouts with his sister at play!
O well for the sailor lad,
    That he sings in his boat on the bay!

And the stately ships go on
    To their haven under the hill;
But O for the touch of a vanish'd hand,
    And the sound of a voice that is still!

Break, break, break
At the foot of thy crags, O Sea!
But the tender grace of a day that is dead
Will never come back to me.

75                            Ulysses

It little profits that an idle king,
By this still hearth, among these barren crags,
Match'd with an aged wife, I mete and dole
Unequal laws unto a savage race,
That hoard, and sleep, and feed, and know not me.

I cannot rest from travel: I will drink
Life to the lees: all times I have enjoy'd
Greatly, have suffer'd greatly, both with those
That loved me, and alone; on shore, and when
Thro' scudding drifts the rainy Hyades
Vext the dim sea: I am become a name;
For always roaming with a hungry heart
Much have I seen and known; cities of men
And manners, climates, councils, governments,
Myself not least, but honour'd of them all;
And drunk delight of battle with my peers,
Far on the ringing plains of windy Troy.
I am a part of all that I have met;
Yet all experience is an arch wherethro'
Gleams that untravell'd world, whose margin fades
For ever and for ever when I move.
How dull it is to pause, to make an end,
To rust unburnish'd, not to shine in use!
As tho' to breathe were life. Life piled on life
Were all too little, and of one to me
Little remains: but every hour is saved
From that eternal silence, something more,
A bringer of new things; and vile it were
For some three suns to store and hoard myself,

And this gray spirit yearning in desire
To follow knowledge like a sinking star,
Beyond the utmost bound of human thought.

   This is my son, mine own Telemachus,
To whom I leave the sceptre and the isle –
Well-loved of me, discerning to fulfil
This labour, by slow prudence to make mild
A rugged people, and thro' soft degrees
Subdue them to the useful and the good.
Most blameless is he, centred in the sphere
Of common duties, decent not to fail
In offices of tenderness, and pay
Meet adoration to my household gods,
When I am gone. He works his work, I mine.

   There lies the port; the vessel puffs her sail:
There gloom the dark broad seas. My mariners,
Souls that have toil'd, and wrought, and thought
      with me –
That ever with a frolic welcome took
The thunder and the sunshine, and opposed
Free hearts, free foreheads – you and I are old;
Old age hath yet his honour and his toil;
Death closes all: but something ere the end,
Some work of noble note, may yet be done,
Not unbecoming men that strove with Gods.
The lights begin to twinkle from the rocks:
The long day wanes: the slow moon climbs: the deep
Moans round with many voices. Come, my friends,
'Tis not too late to seek a newer world.
Push off, and sitting well in order smite
The sounding furrows; for my purpose holds
To sail beyond the sunset, and the baths
Of all the western stars, until I die.
It may be that the gulfs will wash us down:
It may be we shall touch the Happy Isles,
And see the great Achilles, whom we knew.
Tho' much is taken, much abides; and tho'

We are not now that strength which in old days
Moved earth and heaven; that which we are, we are;
One equal temper of heroic hearts,
Made weak by time and fate, but strong in will
To strive, to seek, to find, and not to yield.

## 76                   Tithonus

The woods decay, the woods decay and fall,
The vapours weep their burthen to the ground,
Man comes and tills the field and lies beneath,
And after many a summer dies the swan.
Me only cruel immortality
Consumes: I wither slowly in thine arms,
Here at the quiet limit of the world,
A white-hair'd shadow roaming like a dream
The ever-silent spaces of the East,
Far-folded mists, and gleaming halls of morn.

Alas! for this gray shadow, once a man –
So glorious in his beauty and thy choice,
Who madest him thy chosen, that he seem'd
To his great heart none other than a God!
I ask'd thee, 'Give me immortality.'
Then didst thou grant mine asking with a smile,
Like wealthy men who care not how they give.
But thy strong Hours indignant work'd their wills,
And beat me down and marr'd and wasted me.
And tho' they could not end me, left me maim'd
To dwell in presence of immortal youth,
Immortal age beside immortal youth,
And all I was, in ashes. Can thy love,
Thy beauty, make amends, tho' even now,
Close over us, the silver star, thy guide,
Shines in those tremulous eyes that fill with tears
To hear me? Let me go: take back thy gift:
Why should a man desire in any way

To vary from the kindly race of men,
Or pass beyond the goal of ordinance
Where all should pause, as is most meet for all?

A soft air fans the cloud apart; there comes
A glimpse of that dark world where I was born.
Once more the old mysterious glimmer steals
From thy pure brows, and from thy shoulders pure,
And bosom beating with a heart renew'd.
Thy cheek begins to redden thro' the gloom,
Thy sweet eyes brighten slowly close to mine,
Ere yet they blind the stars, and the wild team
Which love thee, yearning for thy yoke, arise,
And shake the darkness from their loosen'd manes,
And beat the twilight into flakes of fire.

Lo! ever thus thou growest beautiful
In silence, then before thine answer given
Departest, and thy tears are on my cheek.

Why wilt thou ever scare me with thy tears,
And make me tremble lest a saying learnt,
In days far-off, on that dark earth, be true?
'The Gods themselves cannot recall their gifts.'

Ay me! ay me! with what another heart
In days far-off, and with what other eyes
I used to watch – if I be he that watch'd –
The lucid outline forming round thee; saw
The dim curls kindle into sunny rings;
Changed with thy mystic change, and felt my blood
Glow with the glow that slowly crimson'd all
Thy presence and thy portals, while I lay,
Mouth, forehead, eyelids, growing dewy-warm
With kisses balmier than half-opening buds
Of April, and could hear the lips that kiss'd
Whispering I knew not what of wild and sweet,
Like that strange song I heard Apollo sing,
While Ilion like a mist rose into towers.

Yet hold me not for ever in thine East:
How can my nature longer mix with thine?
Coldly thy rosy shadows bathe me, cold
Are all thy lights, and cold my wrinkled feet
Upon thy glimmering thresholds, when the steam
Floats up from those dim fields about the homes
Of happy men that have the power to die,
And grassy barrows of the happier dead.
Release me, and restore me to the ground;
Thou seëst all things, thou wilt see my grave:
Thou wilt renew thy beauty morn by morn;
I earth in earth forget these empty courts,
And thee returning on thy silver wheels.


77          Audley Court

'The Bull, the Fleece are cramm'd, and not a room
For love or money. Let us picnic there
At Audley Court.'

               I spoke, while Audley feast
Humm'd like a hive all round the narrow quay,
To Francis, with a basket on his arm,
To Francis just alighted from the boat,
And breathing of the sea. 'With all my heart,'
Said Francis. Then we shoulder'd thro' the swarm,
And rounded by the stillness of the beach
To where the bay runs up its latest horn.

   We left the dying ebb that faintly lipp'd
The flat red granite; so by many a sweep
Of meadow smooth from aftermath we reach'd
The griffin-guarded gates, and pass'd thro' all
The pillar'd dusk of sounding sycamores,
And cross'd the garden to the gardener's lodge,
With all its casements bedded, and its walls
And chimneys muffled in the leafy vine.

There, on a slope of orchard, Francis laid
A damask napkin wrought with horse and hound,
Brought out a dusky loaf that smelt of home,
And, half-cut-down, a pasty costly-made,
Where quail and pigeon, lark and leveret lay,
Like fossils of the rock, with golden yolks
Imbedded and injellied; last, with these,
A flask of cider from his father's vats,
Prime, which I knew; and so we sat and eat
And talk'd old matters over; who was dead,
Who married, who was like to be, and how
The races went, and who would rent the hall:
Then touch'd upon the game, how scarce it was
This season; glancing thence, discuss'd the farm,
The four-field system, and the price of grain;
And struck upon the corn-laws, where we split,
And came again together on the king
With heated faces; till he laugh'd aloud;
And, while the blackbird on the pippin hung
To hear him, clapt his hand in mine and sang –

  'Oh! who would fight and march and countermarch,
Be shot for sixpence in a battle-field,
And shovell'd up into some bloody trench
Where no one knows? but let me live my life.
  'Oh! who would cast and balance at a desk,
Perch'd like a crow upon a three-legg'd stool,
Till all his juice is dried, and all his joints
Are full of chalk? but let me live my life.
  'Who'd serve the state? for if I carved my name
Upon the cliffs that guard my native land,
I might as well have traced it in the sands;
The sea wastes all: but let me live my life.
  'Oh! who would love? I woo'd a woman once,
But she was sharper than an eastern wind,
And all my heart turn'd from her, as a thorn
Turns from the sea; but let me live my life.'

He sang his song, and I replied with mine:
I found it in a volume, all of songs,
Knock'd down to me when old Sir Robert's pride,
His books – the more the pity, so I said –
Came to the hammer here in March – and this –
I set the words, and added names I knew.

'Sleep, Ellen Aubrey, sleep, and dream of me:
Sleep, Ellen, folded in thy sister's arm,
And sleeping, haply dream her arm is mine.
'Sleep, Ellen, folded in Emilia's arm;
Emilia, fairer than all else but thou,
For thou art fairer than all else that is.
'Sleep, breathing health and peace upon her breast:
Sleep, breathing love and trust against her lip:
I go to-night: I come to-morrow morn.
'I go, but I return: I would I were
The pilot of the darkness and the dream.
Sleep, Ellen Aubrey, love, and dream of me.'

So sang we each to either, Francis Hale,
The farmer's son, who lived across the bay,
My friend; and I, that having wherewithal,
And in the fallow leisure of my life
A rolling stone of here and everywhere,
Did what I would; but ere the night we rose
And saunter'd home beneath a moon, that, just
In crescent, dimly rain'd about the leaf
Twilights of airy silver, till we reach'd
The limit of the hills; and as we sank
From rock to rock upon the glooming quay,
The town was hush'd beneath us: lower down
The bay was oily calm; the harbour-buoy,
Sole star of phosphorescence in the calm,
With one green sparkle ever and anon
Dipt by itself, and we were glad at heart.

78          Morte d'Arthur

So all day long the noise of battle roll'd
Among the mountains by the winter sea;
Until King Arthur's table, man by man,
Had fallen in Lyonesse about their Lord,
King Arthur: then, because his wound was deep,
The bold Sir Bedivere uplifted him,
Sir Bedivere, the last of all his knights,
And bore him to a chapel nigh the field,
A broken chancel with a broken cross,
That stood on a dark strait of barren land.
On one side lay the Ocean, and on one
Lay a great water, and the moon was full.

   Then spake King Arthur to Sir Bedivere:
'The sequel of to-day unsolders all
The goodliest fellowship of famous knights
Whereof this world holds record. Such a sleep
They sleep – the men I loved. I think that we
Shall never more, at any future time,
Delight our souls with talk of knightly deeds,
Walking about the gardens and the halls
Of Camelot, as in the days that were.
I perish by this people which I made, –
Tho' Merlin sware that I should come again
To rule once more – but let what will be, be,
I am so deeply smitten thro' the helm
That without help I cannot last till morn.
Thou therefore take my brand Excalibur,
Which was my pride: for thou rememberest how
In those old days, one summer noon, an arm
Rose up from out the bosom of the lake,
Clothed in white samite, mystic, wonderful,
Holding the sword – and how I row'd across
And took it, and have worn it, like a king:
And, wheresoever I am sung or told
In aftertime, this also shall be known:

But now delay not: take Excalibur,
And fling him far into the middle mere:
Watch what thou seëst, and lightly bring me word.'

   To him replied the bold Sir Bedivere:
'It is not meet, Sir King, to leave thee thus,
Aidless, alone, and smitten thro' the helm.
A little thing may harm a wounded man.
Yet I thy hest will all perform at full,
Watch what I see, and lightly bring thee word.'

   So saying, from the ruin'd shrine he stept
And in the moon athwart the place of tombs,
Where lay the mighty bones of ancient men,
Old knights, and over them the sea-wind sang
Shrill, chill, with flakes of foam. He, stepping down
By zig-zag paths, and juts of pointed rock,
Came on the shining levels of the lake.

   There drew he forth the brand Excalibur,
And o'er him, drawing it, the winter moon,
Brightening the skirts of a long cloud, ran forth
And sparkled keen with frost against the hilt:
For all the haft twinkled with diamond sparks,
Myriads of topaz-lights, and jacinth-work
Of subtlest jewellery. He gazed so long
That both his eyes were dazzled, as he stood,
This way and that dividing the swift mind,
In act to throw: but at the last it seem'd
Better to leave Excalibur conceal'd
There in the many-knotted waterflags,
That whistled stiff and dry about the marge.
So strode he back slow to the wounded King.

   Then spake King Arthur to Sir Bedivere:
'Hast thou perform'd my mission which I gave?
What is it thou hast seen? or what hast heard?'

And answer made the bold Sir Bedivere:
'I heard the ripple washing in the reeds,
And the wild water lapping on the crag.'

To whom replied King Arthur, faint and pale:
'Thou hast betray'd thy nature and thy name,
Not rendering true answer, as beseem'd
Thy fëalty, nor like a noble knight:
For surer sign had follow'd, either hand,
Or voice, or else a motion of the mere.
This is a shameful thing for men to lie.
Yet now, I charge thee, quickly go again
As thou art lief and dear, and do the thing
I bad thee, watch, and lightly bring me word.'

Then went Sir Bedivere the second time
Across the ridge, and paced beside the mere,
Counting the dewy pebbles, fix'd in thought;
But when he saw the wonder of the hilt,
How curiously and strangely chased, he smote
His palms together, and he cried aloud,

'And if indeed I cast the brand away,
Surely a precious thing, one worthy note,
Should thus be lost for ever from the earth,
Which might have pleased the eyes of many men.
What good should follow this, if this were done?
What harm, undone? deep harm to disobey,
Seeing obedience is the bond of rule.
Were it well to obey then, if a king demand
An act unprofitable, against himself?
The King is sick, and knows not what he does.
What record, or what relic of my lord
Should be to aftertime, but empty breath
And rumours of a doubt? but were this kept,
Stored in some treasure-house of mighty kings,
Some one might show it at a joust of arms,
Saying, "King Arthur's sword, Excalibur,
Wrought by the lonely maiden of the Lake.

Nine years she wrought it, sitting in the deeps
Upon the hidden bases of the hills."
So might some old man speak in the aftertime
To all the people, winning reverence.
But now much honour and much fame were lost.'

So spake he, clouded with his own conceit,
And hid Excalibur the second time,
And so strode back slow to the wounded King.

Then spoke King Arthur, breathing heavily:
'What is it thou hast seen? or what hast heard?'

And answer made the bold Sir Bedivere:
'I heard the water lapping on the crag,
And the long ripple washing in the reeds.'

To whom replied King Arthur, much in wrath:
'Ah, miserable and unkind, untrue,
Unknightly, traitor-hearted! Woe is me!
Authority forgets a dying king,
Laid widow'd of the power in his eye
That bow'd the will. I see thee what thou art,
For thou, the latest-left of all my knights,
In whom should meet the offices of all,
Thou wouldst betray me for the precious hilt;
Either from lust of gold, or like a girl
Valuing the giddy pleasure of the eyes.
Yet, for a man may fail in duty twice,
And the third time may prosper, get thee hence:
But, if thou spare to fling Excalibur,
I will arise and slay thee with my hands.'

Then quickly rose Sir Bedivere, and ran,
And, leaping down the ridges lightly, plunged
Among the bulrush-beds, and clutch'd the sword,
And strongly wheel'd and threw it. The great brand
Made lightnings in the splendour of the moon,

And flashing round and round, and whirl'd in an arch,
Shot like a streamer of the northern morn.
Seen where the moving isles of winter shock
By night, with noises of the northern sea.
So flash'd and fell the brand Excalibur:
But ere he dipt the surface, rose an arm
Clothed in white samite, mystic, wonderful,
And caught him by the hilt, and brandish'd him
Three times, and drew him under in the mere.
And lightly went the other to the King.

　　Then spoke King Arthur, drawing thicker breath:
'Now see I by thine eyes that this is done.
Speak out: what is it thou hast heard, or seen?'

　　And answer made the bold Sir Bedivere:
'Sir King, I closed mine eyelids, lest the gems
Should blind my purpose, for I never saw,
Nor shall see, here or elsewhere, till I die,
Not tho' I live three lives of mortal men,
So great a miracle as yonder hilt.
Then with both hands I flung him, wheeling him;
But when I look'd again, behold an arm,
Clothed in white samite, mystic, wonderful,
That caught him by the hilt, and brandish'd him
Three times, and drew him under in the mere.'

　　And answer made King Arthur, breathing hard:
'My end draws nigh; 'tis time that I were gone.
Make broad thy shoulders to receive my weight,
And bear me to the margin; yet I fear
My wound hath taken cold, and I shall die.'

　　So saying, from the pavement he half rose,
Slowly, with pain, reclining on his arm,
And looking wistfully with wide blue eyes
As in a picture. Him Sir Bedivere
Remorsefully regarded thro' his tears,
And would have spoken, but he found not words,

Then took with care, and kneeling on one knee,
O'er both his shoulders drew the languid hands,
And rising bore him thro' the place of tombs.

But, as he walk'd, King Arthur panted hard,
Like one that feels a nightmare on his bed
When all the house is mute. So sigh'd the King,
Muttering and murmuring at his ear, 'Quick, quick!
I fear it is too late, and I shall die.'
But the other swiftly strode from ridge to ridge,
Clothed with his breath, and looking, as he walk'd,
Larger than human on the frozen hills.
He heard the deep behind him, and a cry
Before. His own thought drove him, like a goad.
Dry clash'd his harness in the icy caves
And barren chasms, and all to left and right
The bare black cliff clang'd round him, as he based
His feet on juts of slippery crag that rang
Sharp-smitten with the dint of armed heels –
And on a sudden, lo! the level lake,
And the long glories of the winter moon.

Then saw they how there hove a dusky barge,
Dark as a funeral scarf from stem to stern,
Beneath them; and descending they were ware
That all the decks were dense with stately forms
Black-stoled, black-hooded, like a dream – by these
Three Queens with crowns of gold – and from them rose
A cry that shiver'd to the tingling stars,
And, as it were one voice, an agony
Of lamentation, like a wind, that shrills
All night in a waste land, where no one comes,
Or hath come, since the making of the world.

Then murmur'd Arthur, 'Place me in the barge,'
And to the barge they came. There those three Queens
Put forth their hands, and took the King, and wept.
But she, that rose the tallest of them all
And fairest, laid his head upon her lap,

And loosed the shatter'd casque, and chafed his hands,
And call'd him by his name, complaining loud,
And dropping bitter tears against his brow
Striped with dark blood: for all his face was white
And colourless, and like the wither'd moon
Smote by the fresh beam of the springing east;
And all his greaves and cuisses dash'd with drops
Of onset; and the light and lustrous curls –
That made his forehead like a rising sun
High from the daïs-throne – were parch'd with dust;
Or, clotted into points and hanging loose,
Mix'd with the knightly growth that fringed his lips.
So like a shatter'd column lay the King;
Not like that Arthur who, with lance in rest,
From spur to plume a star of tournament,
Shot thro' the lists at Camelot, and charged
Before the eyes of ladies and of kings.

Then loudly cried the bold Sir Bedivere,
'Ah! my Lord Arthur, whither shall I go?
Where shall I hide my forehead and my eyes?
For now I see the true old times are dead.
When every morning brought a noble chance,
And every chance brought out a noble knight.
Such times have been not since the light that led
The holy Elders with the gift of myrrh.
But now the whole ROUND TABLE is dissolved
Which was an image of the mighty world;
And I, the last, go forth companionless,
And the days darken round me, and the years,
Among new men, strange faces, other minds.'

And slowly answered Arthur from the barge:
'The old order changeth, yielding place to new,
And God fulfils Himself in many ways,
Lest one good custom should corrupt the world.
Comfort thyself: what comfort is in me?
I have lived my life, and that which I have done
May He within Himself make pure! but thou,

If thou shouldst never see my face again,
Pray for my soul. More things are wrought by prayer
Than this world dreams of. Wherefore, let thy voice
Rise like a fountain for me night and day.
For what are men better than sheep or goats
That nourish a blind life within the brain,
If, knowing God, they lift not hands of prayer
Both for themselves and those who call them friend?
For so the whole round earth is every way
Bound by gold chains about the feet of God.
But now farewell. I am going a long way
With these thou seëst – if indeed I go –
(For all my mind is clouded with a doubt)
To the island-valley of Avilion;
Where falls not hail, or rain, or any snow,
Nor ever wind blows loudly; but it lies
Deep-meadow'd, happy, fair with orchard-lawns
And bowery hollows crown'd with summer sea,
Where I will heal me of my grievous wound.'

So said he, and the barge with oar and sail
Moved from the brink, like some full-breasted swan
That, fluting a wild carol ere her death,
Ruffles her pure cold plume, and takes the flood
With swarthy webs. Long stood Sir Bedivere
Revolving many memories, till the hull
Look'd one black dot against the verge of dawn,
And on the mere the wailing died away.

79 ## The Eagle

### FRAGMENT

He clasps the crag with crooked hands;
Close to the sun in lonely lands,
Ring'd with the azure world, he stands.

The wrinkled sea beneath him crawls;
He watches from his mountain walls,
And like a thunderbolt he falls.

## SONGS FROM THE PRINCESS

80     Tears, idle tears, I know not what they mean,
Tears from the depth of some divine despair
Rise in the heart, and gather to the eyes,
In looking on the happy Autumn-fields,
And thinking of the days that are no more.

Fresh as the first beam glittering on a sail,
That brings our friends up from the underworld,
Sad as the last which reddens over one
That sinks with all we love below the verge;
So sad, so fresh, the days that are no more.

Ah, sad and strange as in dark summer dawns
The earliest pipe of half-awaken'd birds
To dying ears, when unto dying eyes
The casement slowly grows a glimmering square;
So sad, so strange, the days that are no more.

Dear as remember'd kisses after death,
And sweet as those by hopeless fancy feign'd
On lips that are for others; deep as love,
Deep as first love, and wild with all regret;
O Death in Life, the days that are no more.


81    Now sleeps the crimson petal, now the white;
Nor waves the cypress in the palace walk;
Nor winks the gold fin in the porphyry font:
The fire-fly wakens: waken thou with me.

Now droops the milkwhite peacock like a ghost,
And like a ghost she glimmers on to me.

Now lies the Earth all Danaë to the stars,
And all thy heart lies open unto me.

Now slides the silent meteor on, and leaves
A shining furrow, as thy thoughts in me.

Now folds the lily all her sweetness up,
And slips into the bosom of the lake:
So fold thyself, my dearest, thou, and slip
Into my bosom and be lost in me.

––––––––––

82     *from* In Memoriam A. H. H.

OBIIT MDCCCXXXIII

I

I held it truth, with him who sings
    To one clear harp in divers tones,
    That men may rise on stepping-stones
Of their dead selves to higher things.

But who shall so forecast the years
    And find in loss a gain to match?
    Or reach a hand thro' time to catch
The far-off interest of tears?

Let Love clasp Grief lest both be drown'd,
    Let darkness keep her raven gloss:
    Ah, sweeter to be drunk with loss,
To dance with death, to beat the ground,

Than that the victor Hours should scorn
    The long result of love, and boast,
    'Behold the man that loved and lost,
But all he was is overworn.'

II

Old Yew, which graspest at the stones
    That name the under-lying dead,
    Thy fibres net the dreamless head,
Thy roots are wrapt about the bones.

The seasons bring the flower again,
    And bring the firstling to the flock;
    And in the dusk of thee, the clock
Beats out the little lives of men.

O not for thee the glow, the bloom,
   Who changest not in any gale,
   Nor branding summer suns avail
To touch thy thousand years of gloom:

And gazing on thee, sullen tree,
   Sick for thy stubborn hardihood,
   I seem to fail from out my blood
And grow incorporate into thee.

### III

O Sorrow, cruel fellowship,
   O Priestess in the vaults of Death,
   O sweet and bitter in a breath,
What whispers from thy lying lip?

'The stars,' she whispers, 'blindly run;
   A web is wov'n across the sky;
   From out waste places comes a cry,
And murmurs from the dying sun:

'And all the phantom, Nature, stands –
   With all the music in her tone,
   A hollow echo of my own, –
A hollow form with empty hands.'

And shall I take a thing so blind,
   Embrace her as my natural good;
   Or crush her, like a vice of blood,
Upon the threshold of the mind?

### IV

To Sleep I give my powers away;
   My will is bondsman to the dark;
   I sit within a helmless bark,
And with my heart I muse and say:

O heart, how fares it with thee now,
   That thou should'st fail from thy desire,
   Who scarcely darest to inquire,
'What is it makes me beat so low?'

Something it is which thou hast lost,
   Some pleasure from thine early years.
   Break, thou deep vase of chilling tears,
That grief hath shaken into frost!

Such clouds of nameless trouble cross
   All night below the darken'd eyes;
   With morning wakes the will, and cries,
'Thou shalt not be the fool of loss.'

## V

I sometimes hold it half a sin
   To put in words the grief I feel;
   For words, like Nature, half reveal
And half conceal the Soul within.

But, for the unquiet heart and brain,
   A use in measured language lies;
   The sad mechanic exercise,
Like dull narcotics, numbing pain.

In words, like weeds, I'll wrap me o'er,
   Like coarsest clothes against the cold:
   But that large grief which these enfold
Is given in outline and no more.

## VI

One writes, that 'Other friends remain,'
   That 'Loss is common to the race' –
   And common is the commonplace,
And vacant chaff well meant for grain.

That loss is common would not make
  My own less bitter, rather more:
  Too common! Never morning wore
To evening, but some heart did break.

O father, wheresoe'er thou be,
  Who pledgest now thy gallant son;
  A shot, ere half thy draught be done,
Hath still'd the life that beat from thee.

O mother, praying God will save
  Thy sailor, – while thy head is bow'd,
  His heavy-shotted hammock-shroud
Drops in his vast and wandering grave.

Ye know no more than I who wrought
  At that last hour to please him well;
  Who mused on all I had to tell,
And something written, something thought;

Expecting still his advent home;
  And ever met him on his way
  With wishes, thinking, 'here to-day,'
Or 'here to-morrow will he come.'

O somewhere, meek, unconscious dove,
  That sittest ranging golden hair;
  And glad to find thyself so fair,
Poor child, that waitest for thy love!

For now her father's chimney glows
  In expectation of a guest;
  And thinking 'this will please him best,'
She takes a riband or a rose;

For he will see them on to-night;
  And with the thought her colour burns;
  And, having left the glass, she turns
Once more to set a ringlet right;

And, even when she turn'd, the curse
   Had fallen, and her future Lord
   Was drown'd in passing thro' the ford,
Or kill'd in falling from his horse.

O what to her shall be the end?
   And what to me remains of good?
   To her, perpetual maidenhood,
And unto me no second friend.

## VII

Dark house, by which once more I stand
   Here in the long unlovely street,
   Doors, where my heart was used to beat
So quickly, waiting for a hand,

A hand that can be clasp'd no more –
   Behold me, for I cannot sleep,
   And like a guilty thing I creep
At earliest morning to the door.

He is not here; but far away
   The noise of life begins again,
   And ghastly thro' the drizzling rain
On the bald street breaks the blank day.

## VIII

A happy lover who has come
   To look on her that loves him well,
   Who 'lights and rings the gateway bell,
And learns her gone and far from home;

He saddens, all the magic light
   Dies off at once from bower and hall,
   And all the place is dark, and all
The chambers emptied of delight:

So find I every pleasant spot
   In which we two were wont to meet,
   The field, the chamber and the street,
For all is dark where thou art not.

Yet as that other, wandering there
   In those deserted walks, may find
   A flower beat with rain and wind,
Which once she foster'd up with care;

So seems it in my deep regret,
   O my forsaken heart, with thee
   And this poor flower of poesy
Which little cared for fades not yet.

But since it pleased a vanish'd eye,
   I go to plant it on his tomb,
   That if it can it there may bloom,
Or dying, there at least may die.

## IX

Fair ship, that from the Italian shore
   Sailest the placid ocean-plains
   With my lost Arthur's loved remains,
Spread thy full wings, and waft him o'er.

So draw him home to those that mourn
   In vain; a favourable speed
   Ruffle thy mirror'd mast, and lead
Thro' prosperous floods his holy urn.

All night no ruder air perplex
   Thy sliding keel, till Phosphor, bright
   As our pure love, thro' early light
Shall glimmer on the dewy decks.

Sphere all your lights around, above;
  Sleep, gentle heavens, before the prow;
  Sleep, gentle winds, as he sleeps now,
My friend, the brother of my love;

My Arthur, whom I shall not see
  Till all my widow'd race be run;
  Dear as the mother to the son,
More than my brothers are to me.

### X

I hear the noise about thy keel;
  I hear the bell struck in the night:
  I see the cabin-window bright;
I see the sailor at the wheel.

Thou bring'st the sailor to his wife,
  And travell'd men from foreign lands;
  And letters unto trembling hands;
And, thy dark freight, a vanish'd life.

So bring him: we have idle dreams:
  This look of quiet flatters thus
  Our home-bred fancies: O to us,
The fools of habit, sweeter seems

To rest beneath the clover sod,
  That takes the sunshine and the rains,
  Or where the kneeling hamlet drains
The chalice of the grapes of God;

Than if with thee the roaring wells
  Should gulf him fathom-deep in brine;
  And hands so often clasp'd in mine,
Should toss with tangle and with shells.

## XI

Calm is the morn without a sound,
   Calm as to suit a calmer grief,
   And only thro' the faded leaf
The chestnut pattering to the ground:

Calm and deep peace on this high wold,
   And on these dews that drench the furze,
   And all the silvery gossamers
That twinkle into green and gold:

Calm and still light on yon great plain
   That sweeps with all its autumn bowers,
   And crowded farms and lessening towers,
To mingle with the bounding main:

Calm and deep peace in this wide air,
   These leaves that redden to the fall;
   And in my heart, if calm at all,
If any calm, a calm despair:

Calm on the seas, and silver sleep,
   And waves that sway themselves in rest,
   And dead calm in that noble breast
Which heaves but with the heaving deep.

## XII

Lo, as a dove when up she springs
   To bear thro' Heaven a tale of woe,
   Some dolorous message knit below
The wild pulsation of her wings;

Like her I go; I cannot stay;
   I leave this mortal ark behind,
   A weight of nerves without a mind,
And leave the cliffs, and haste away

O'er ocean-mirrors rounded large,
   And reach the glow of southern skies,
   And see the sails at distance rise,
And linger weeping on the marge,

And saying; 'Comes he thus, my friend?
   Is this the end of all my care?'
   And circle moaning in the air:
'Is this the end? Is this the end?'

And forward dart again, and play
   About the prow, and back return
   To where the body sits, and learn
That I have been an hour away.

## XIII

Tears of the widower, when he sees
   A late-lost form that sleep reveals,
   And moves his doubtful arms, and feels
Her place is empty, fall like these;

Which weep a loss for ever new,
   A void where heart on heart reposed;
   And, where warm hands have prest and closed,
Silence, till I be silent too.

Which weep the comrade of my choice,
   An awful thought, a life removed,
   The human-hearted man I loved,
A Spirit, not a breathing voice.

Come Time, and teach me, many years,
   I do not suffer in a dream;
   For now so strange do these things seem,
Mine eyes have leisure for their tears;

My fancies time to rise on wing,
    And glance about the approaching sails,
    As tho' they brought but merchants' bales,
And not the burthen that they bring.


## XIV

If one should bring me this report,
    That thou hadst touch'd the land to-day,
    And I went down unto the quay,
And found thee lying in the port;

And standing, muffled round with woe,
    Should see thy passengers in rank
    Come stepping lightly down the plank,
And beckoning unto those they know;

And if along with these should come
    The man I held as half-divine;
    Should strike a sudden hand in mine,
And ask a thousand things of home;

And I should tell him all my pain,
    And how my life had droop'd of late,
    And he should sorrow o'er my state
And marvel what possess'd my brain;

And I perceived no touch of change,
    No hint of death in all his frame,
    But found him all in all the same,
I should not feel it to be strange.


## XV

To-night the winds begin to rise
    And roar from yonder dropping day:
    The last red leaf is whirl'd away,
The rooks are blown about the skies;

The forest crack'd, the waters curl'd,
   The cattle huddled on the lea;
   And wildly dash'd on tower and tree
The sunbeam strikes along the world:

And but for fancies, which aver
   That all thy motions gently pass
   Athwart a plane of molten glass,
I scarce could brook the strain and stir

That makes the barren branches loud;
   And but for fear it is not so,
   The wild unrest that lives in woe
Would dote and pore on yonder cloud

That rises upward always higher,
   And onward drags a labouring breast,
   And topples round the dreary west,
A looming bastion fringed with fire.

## XVI

What words are these have fall'n from me?
   Can calm despair and wild unrest
   Be tenants of a single breast,
Or sorrow such a changeling be?

Or doth she only seem to take
   The touch of change in calm or storm;
   But knows no more of transient form
In her deep self, than some dead lake

That holds the shadow of a lark
   Hung in the shadow of a heaven?
   Or has the shock, so harshly given,
Confused me like the unhappy bark

That strikes by night a craggy shelf,
　　And staggers blindly ere she sink?
　　And stunn'd me from my power to think
And all my knowledge of myself;

And made me that delirious man
　　Whose fancy fuses old and new,
　　And flashes into false and true,
And mingles all without a plan?

### XVII

Thou comest, much wept for: such a breeze
　　Compell'd thy canvas, and my prayer
　　Was as the whisper of an air
To breathe thee over lonely seas.

For I in spirit saw thee move
　　Thro' circles of the bounding sky,
　　Week after week: the days go by:
Come quick, thou bringest all I love.

Henceforth, wherever thou may'st roam,
　　My blessing, like a line of light,
　　Is on the waters day and night,
And like a beacon guards thee home.

So may whatever tempest mars
　　Mid-ocean, spare thee, sacred bark;
　　And balmy drops in summer dark
Slide from the bosom of the stars.

So kind an office hath been done,
　　Such precious relics brought by thee;
　　The dust of him I shall not see
Till all my widow'd race be run.

## XVIII

'Tis well; 'tis something; we may stand
　　Where he in English earth is laid,
　　And from his ashes may be made
The violet of his native land.

'Tis little; but it looks in truth
　　As if the quiet bones were blest
　　Among familiar names to rest
And in the places of his youth.

Come then, pure hands, and bear the head
　　That sleeps or wears the mask of sleep,
　　And come, whatever loves to weep,
And hear the ritual of the dead.

Ah yet, ev'n yet, if this might be,
　　I, falling on his faithful heart,
　　Would breathing thro' his lips impart
The life that almost dies in me;

That dies not, but endures with pain,
　　And slowly forms the firmer mind,
　　Treasuring the look it cannot find,
The words that are not heard again.

## XIX

The Danube to the Severn gave
　　The darken'd heart that beat no more;
　　They laid him by the pleasant shore,
And in the hearing of the wave.

There twice a day the Severn fills;
　　The salt sea-water passes by,
　　And hushes half the babbling Wye,
And makes a silence in the hills.

The Wye is hush'd nor moved along,
    And hush'd my deepest grief of all,
    When fill'd with tears that cannot fall.
I brim with sorrow drowning song.

The tide flows down, the wave again
    Is vocal in its wooded walls;
    My deeper anguish also falls,
And I can speak a little then.

## XX

The lesser griefs that may be said,
    That breathe a thousand tender vows,
    Are but as servants in a house
Where lies the master newly dead;

Who speak their feeling as it is,
    And weep the fulness from the mind:
    'It will be hard,' they say, 'to find
Another service such as this.'

My lighter moods are like to these,
    That out of words a comfort win;
    But there are other griefs within,
And tears that at their fountain freeze;

For by the hearth the children sit
    Cold in that atmosphere of Death,
    And scarce endure to draw the breath,
Or like to noiseless phantoms flit:

But open converse is there none,
    So much the vital spirits sink
    To see the vacant chair, and think,
'How good! how kind! and he is gone.'

## XXI

I sing to him that rests below,
    And, since the grasses round me wave,
    I take the grasses of the grave,
And make them pipes whereon to blow.

The traveller hears me now and then,
    And sometimes harshly will he speak:
    'This fellow would make weakness weak,
And melt the waxen hearts of men.'

Another answers, 'Let him be,
    He loves to make parade of pain
    That with his piping he may gain
The praise that comes to constancy.'

A third is wroth: 'Is this an hour
    For private sorrow's barren song,
    When more and more the people throng
The chairs and thrones of civil power?

'A time to sicken and to swoon,
    When Science reaches forth her arms
    To feel from world to world, and charms
Her secret from the latest moon?'

Behold, ye speak an idle thing:
    Ye never knew the sacred dust:
    I do but sing because I must,
And pipe but as the linnets sing:

And one is glad; her note is gay,
    For now her little ones have ranged;
    And one is sad; her note is changed,
Because her brood is stol'n away.

## XXII

The path by which we twain did go,
    Which led by tracts that pleased us well,
    Thro' four sweet years arose and fell,
From flower to flower, from snow to snow:

And we with singing cheer'd the way,
    And, crown'd with all the season lent,
    From April on to April went,
And glad at heart from May to May:

But where the path we walk'd began
    To slant the fifth autumnal slope,
    As we descended following Hope,
There sat the Shadow fear'd of man;

Who broke our fair companionship,
    And spread his mantle dark and cold,
    And wrapt thee formless in the fold,
And dull'd the murmur on thy lip,

And bore thee where I could not see
    Nor follow, tho' I walk in haste,
    And think, that somewhere in the waste
The Shadow sits and waits for me.

## XXIII

Now, sometimes in my sorrow shut,
    Or breaking into song by fits,
    Alone, alone, to where he sits,
The Shadow cloak'd from head to foot,

Who keeps the keys of all the creeds,
    I wander, often falling lame,
    And looking back to whence I came,
Or on to where the pathway leads;

And crying, How changed from where it ran
   Thro' lands where not a leaf was dumb;
   But all the lavish hills would hum
The murmur of a happy Pan:

When each by turns was guide to each,
   And Fancy light from Fancy caught,
   And Thought leapt out to wed with Thought
Ere Thought could wed itself with Speech;

And all we met was fair and good,
   And all was good that Time could bring,
   And all the secret of the Spring
Moved in the chambers of the blood;

And many an old philosophy
   On Argive heights divinely sang,
   And round us all the thicket rang
To many a flute of Arcady.

## XXIV

And was the day of my delight
   As pure and perfect as I say?
   The very source and fount of Day
Is dash'd with wandering isles of night.

If all was good and fair we met,
   This earth had been the Paradise
   It never look'd to human eyes
Since our first Sun arose and set.

And is it that the haze of grief
   Makes former gladness loom so great?
   The lowness of the present state,
That sets the past in this relief?

Or that the past will always win
  A glory from its being far;
  And orb into the perfect star
We saw not, when we moved therein?

### XXV

I know that this was Life, – the track
  Whereon with equal feet we fared;
  And then, as now, the day prepared
The daily burden for the back.

But this it was that made me move
  As light as carrier-birds in air;
  I loved the weight I had to bear,
Because it needed help of Love:

Nor could I weary, heart or limb,
  When mighty Love would cleave in twain
  The lading of a single pain,
And part it, giving half to him.

### XXVI

Still onward winds the dreary way,
  I with it; for I long to prove
  No lapse of moons can canker Love,
Whatever fickle tongues may say.

And if that eye which watches guilt
  And goodness, and hath power to see
  Within the green the moulder'd tree,
And towers fall'n as soon as built –

Oh, if indeed that eye foresee
  Or see (in Him is no before)
  In more of life true life no more
And Love the indifference to be,

Then might I find, ere yet the morn
　　Breaks hither over Indian seas,
　　That Shadow waiting with the keys,
To shroud me from my proper scorn.

## XXVII

I envy not in any moods
　　The captive void of noble rage,
　　The linnet born within the cage,
That never knew the summer woods:

I envy not the beast that takes
　　His license in the field of time,
　　Unfetter'd by the sense of crime,
To whom a conscience never wakes;

Nor, what may count itself as blest,
　　The heart that never plighted troth
　　But stagnates in the weeds of sloth;
Nor any want-begotten rest.

I hold it true, whate'er befall;
　　I feel it, when I sorrow most;
　　'Tis better to have loved and lost
Than never to have loved at all.

## XXVIII

The time draws near the birth of Christ:
　　The moon is hid; the night is still;
　　The Christmas bells from hill to hill
Answer each other in the mist.

Four voices of four hamlets round,
　　From far and near, on mead and moor,
　　Swell out and fail, as if a door
Were shut between me and the sound:

Each voice four changes on the wind,
  That now dilate, and now decrease,
  Peace and goodwill, goodwill and peace,
Peace and goodwill, to all mankind.

This year I slept and woke with pain,
  I almost wish'd no more to wake,
  And that my hold on life would break
Before I heard those bells again:

But they my troubled spirit rule,
  For they controll'd me when a boy;
  They bring me sorrow touch'd with joy,
The merry merry bells of Yule.

### XXIX

With such compelling cause to grieve
  As daily vexes household peace,
  And chains regret to his decease,
How dare we keep our Christmas-eve;

Which brings no more a welcome guest
  To enrich the threshold of the night
  With shower'd largess of delight
In dance and song and game and jest?

Yet go, and while the holly boughs
  Entwine the cold baptismal font,
  Make one wreath more for Use and Wont,
That guard the portals of the house;

Old sisters of a day gone by,
  Gray nurses, loving nothing new;
  Why should they miss their yearly due
Before their time? They too will die.

## XXX

With trembling fingers did we weave
   The holly round the Christmas hearth;
   A rainy cloud possess'd the earth,
And sadly fell our Christmas-eve.

At our old pastimes in the hall
   We gambol'd, making vain pretence
   Of gladness, with an awful sense
Of one mute Shadow watching all.

We paused: the winds were in the beech:
   We heard them sweep the winter land;
   And in a circle hand-in-hand
Sat silent, looking each at each.

Then echo-like our voices rang;
   We sung, tho' every eye was dim,
   A merry song we sang with him
Last year: impetuously we sang:

We ceased: a gentler feeling crept
   Upon us: surely rest is meet:
   'They rest,' we said, 'their sleep is sweet,'
And silence follow'd, and we wept.

Our voices took a higher range;
   Once more we sang: 'They do not die
   Nor lose their mortal sympathy,
Nor change to us, although they change;

'Rapt from the fickle and the frail
   With gather'd power, yet the same,
   Pierces the keen seraphic flame
From orb to orb, from veil to veil.'

Rise, happy morn, rise, holy morn,      .
   Draw forth the cheerful day from night:
   O Father, touch the east, and light
The light that shone when Hope was born.

## XLVIII

If these brief lays, of Sorrow born,
   Were taken to be such as closed
   Grave doubts and answers here proposed,
Then these were such as men might scorn:

Her care is not to part and prove;
   She takes, when harsher moods remit,
   What slender shade of doubt may flit,
And makes it vassal unto love:

And hence, indeed, she sports with words,
   But better serves a wholesome law,
   And holds it sin and shame to draw
The deepest measure from the chords:

Nor dare she trust a larger lay,
   But rather loosens from the lip
   Short swallow-flights of song, that dip
Their wings in tears, and skim away.

## L

Be near me when my light is low,
   When the blood creeps, and the nerves prick
   And tingle; and the heart is sick,
And all the wheels of Being slow.

Be near me when the sensuous frame
   Is rack'd with pangs that conquer trust;
   And Time, a maniac scattering dust,
And Life, a Fury slinging flame.

Be near me when my faith is dry,
   And men the flies of latter spring,
   That lay their eggs, and sting and sing
And weave their petty cells and die.

Be near me when I fade away,
   To point the term of human strife,
   And on the low dark verge of life
The twilight of eternal day.

## LIV

Oh yet we trust that somehow good
   Will be the final goal of ill,
   To pangs of nature, sins of will,
Defects of doubt, and taints of blood;

That nothing walks with aimless feet;
   That not one life shall be destroy'd,
   Or cast as rubbish to the void,
When God hath made the pile complete;

That not a worm is cloven in vain;
   That not a moth with vain desire
   Is shrivell'd in a fruitless fire,
Or but subserves another's gain.

Behold, we know not anything;
   I can but trust that good shall fall
   At last – far off – at last, to all,
And every winter change to spring.

So runs my dream: but what am I?
   An infant crying in the night:
   An infant crying for the light:
And with no language but a cry.

## LV

The wish, that of the living whole
 No life may fail beyond the grave,
 Derives it not from what we have
The likest God within the soul?

Are God and Nature then at strife,
 That Nature lends such evil dreams?
 So careful of the type she seems,
So careless of the single life;

That I, considering everywhere
 Her secret meaning in her deeds,
 And finding that of fifty seeds
She often brings but one to bear,

I falter where I firmly trod,
 And falling with my weight of cares
 Upon the great world's altar-stairs
That slope thro' darkness up to God,

I stretch lame hands of faith, and grope,
 And gather dust and chaff, and call
 To what I feel is Lord of all,
And faintly trust the larger hope.

## LVI

'So careful of the type?' but no.
 From scarpèd cliff and quarried stone
 She cries, 'A thousand types are gone:
I care for nothing, all shall go.

'Thou makest thine appeal to me:
 I bring to life, I bring to death:
 The spirit does but mean the breath:
I know no more.' And he, shall he,

Man, her last work, who seem'd so fair,
　　Such splendid purpose in his eyes,
　　Who roll'd the psalm to wintry skies,
Who built him fanes of fruitless prayer,

Who trusted God was love indeed
　　And love Creation's final law –
　　Tho' Nature, red in tooth and claw
With ravine, shriek'd against his creed –

Who loved, who suffer'd countless ills,
　　Who battled for the True, the Just,
　　Be blown about the desert dust,
Or seal'd within the iron hills?

No more? A monster then, a dream,
　　A discord. Dragons of the prime,
　　That tare each other in their slime,
Were mellow music match'd with him.

O life as futile, then, as frail!
　　O for thy voice to soothe and bless!
　　What hope of answer, or redress?
Behind the veil, behind the veil.

### LXXVII

What hope is here for modern rhyme
　　To him, who turns a musing eye
　　On songs, and deeds, and lives, that lie
Foreshorten'd in the tract of time?

These mortal lullabies of pain
　　May bind a book, may line a box,
　　May serve to curl a maiden's locks;
Or when a thousand moons shall wane

A man upon a stall may find,
  And, passing, turn the page that tells
  A grief, then changed to something else,
Sung by a long-forgotten mind.

But what of that? My darken'd ways
  Shall ring with music all the same;
  To breathe my loss is more than fame,
To utter love more sweet than praise.

## LXXXVI

Sweet after showers, ambrosial air,
  That rollest from the gorgeous gloom
  Of evening over brake and bloom
And meadow, slowly breathing bare

The round of space, and rapt below
  Thro' all the dewy-tassell'd wood,
  And shadowing down the hornèd flood
In ripples, fan my brows and blow

The fever from my cheek, and sigh
  The full new life that feeds thy breath
  Throughout my frame, till Doubt and Death,
Ill brethren, let the fancy fly

From belt to belt of crimson seas
  On leagues of odour streaming far,
  To where in yonder orient star
A hundred spirits whisper 'Peace.'

## LXXXVIII

Wild bird, whose warble, liquid sweet,
  Rings Eden thro' the budded quicks,
  O tell me where the senses mix,
O tell me where the passions meet,

Whence radiate: fierce extremes employ
   Thy spirits in the darkening leaf,
   And in the midmost heart of grief
Thy passion clasps a secret joy:

And I – my harp would prelude woe –
   I cannot all command the strings;
   The glory of the sum of things
Will flash along the chords and go.

### XCIII

I shall not see thee. Dare I say
   No spirit ever brake the band
   That stays him from the native land
Where first he walk'd when claspt in clay?

No visual shade of some one lost,
   But he, the Spirit himself, may come
   Where all the nerve of sense is numb;
Spirit to Spirit, Ghost to Ghost.

O, therefore from thy sightless range
   With gods in unconjectured bliss,
   O, from the distance of the abyss
Of tenfold-complicated change,

Descend, and touch, and enter; hear
   The wish too strong for words to name;
   That in this blindness of the frame
My Ghost may feel that thine is near.

### CVI

Ring out, wild bells, to the wild sky,
   The flying cloud, the frosty light:
   The year is dying in the night;
Ring out, wild bells, and let him die.

Ring out the old, ring in the new,
   Ring, happy bells, across the snow:
   The year is going, let him go;
Ring out the false, ring in the true.

Ring out the grief that saps the mind,
   For those that here we see no more;
   Ring out the feud of rich and poor,
Ring in redress to all mankind.

Ring out a slowly dying cause,
   And ancient forms of party strife;
   Ring in the nobler modes of life,
With sweeter manners, purer laws.

Ring out the want, the care, the sin,
   The faithless coldness of the times;
   Ring out, ring out my mournful rhymes,
But ring the fuller minstrel in.

Ring out false pride in place and blood,
   The civic slander and the spite;
   Ring in the love of truth and right,
Ring in the common love of good.

Ring out old shapes of foul disease;
   Ring out the narrowing lust of gold;
   Ring out the thousand wars of old,
Ring in the thousand years of peace.

Ring in the valiant man and free,
   The larger heart, the kindlier hand;
   Ring out the darkness of the land,
Ring in the Christ that is to be.

## CXIX

Doors, where my heart was used to beat
   So quickly, not as one that weeps
   I come once more; the city sleeps;
I smell the meadow in the street;

I hear a chirp of birds; I see
   Betwixt the black fronts long-withdrawn
   A light-blue lane of early dawn,
And think of early days and thee,

And bless thee, for thy lips are bland,
   And bright the friendship of thine eye;
   And in my thoughts with scarce a sigh
I take the pressure of thine hand.

## CXXX

Thy voice is on the rolling air;
   I hear thee where the waters run;
   Thou standest in the rising sun,
And in the setting thou art fair.

What art thou then? I cannot guess;
   But tho' I seem in star and flower
   To feel thee some diffusive power,
I do not therefore love thee less:

My love involves the love before;
   My love is vaster passion now;
   Tho' mix'd with God and Nature thou,
I seem to love thee more and more.

Far off thou art, but ever nigh;
   I have thee still, and I rejoice;
   I prosper, circled with thy voice;
I shall not lose thee tho' I die.

## CXXXI

O living will that shalt endure
  When all that seems shall suffer shock,
  Rise in the spiritual rock,
Flow thro' our deeds and make them pure,

That we may lift from out of dust
  A voice as unto him that hears,
  A cry above the conquer'd years
To one that with us works, and trust,

With faith that comes of self-control,
  The truths that never can be proved
  Until we close with all we loved,
And all we flow from, soul in soul.


83      The Charge of the Light Brigade

### I

Half a league, half a league,
  Half a league onward,
All in the valley of Death
  Rode the six hundred.
'Forward, the Light Brigade!
Charge for the guns!' he said:
Into the valley of Death
  Rode the six hundred.

### II

'Forward, the Light Brigade!'
Was there a man dismay'd?
Not tho' the soldier knew
  Some one had blunder'd:

Their's not to make reply,
Their's not to reason why,
Their's but to do and die:
Into the valley of Death
  Rode the six hundred.

### III

Cannon to right of them,
Cannon to left of them,
Cannon in front of them
  Volley'd and thunder'd;
Storm'd at with shot and shell,
Boldly they rode and well,
Into the jaws of Death,
Into the mouth of Hell
  Rode the six hundred.

### IV

Flash'd all their sabres bare,
Flash'd as they turn'd in air
Sabring the gunners there,
Charging an army, while
  All the world wonder'd:
Plunged in the battery-smoke
Right thro' the line they broke;
Cossack and Russian
Reel'd from the sabre-stroke
  Shatter'd and sunder'd.
Then they rode back, but not
  Not the six hundred.

### V

Cannon to right of them,
Cannon to left of them,
Cannon behind them
  Volley'd and thunder'd;
Storm'd at with shot and shell,
While horse and hero fell,
They that had fought so well

Came thro' the jaws of Death,
Back from the mouth of Hell,
All that was left of them,
    Left of six hundred.


VI

When can their glory fade?
O the wild charge they made!
    All the world wonder'd.
Honour the charge they made!
Honour the Light Brigade,
    Noble six hundred!


84                *from* Maud


[PART ONE]


XXII


I

Come into the garden, Maud,
    For the black bat, night, has flown,
Come into the garden, Maud,
    I am here at the gate alone;
And the woodbine spices are wafted abroad,
    And the musk of the rose is blown.


II

For a breeze of morning moves,
    And the planet of Love is on high,
Beginning to faint in the light that she loves
    On a bed of daffodil sky,
To faint in the light of the sun she loves,
    To faint in his light, and to die.

### III

All night have the roses heard
  The flute, violin, bassoon;
All night has the casement jessamine stirr'd
  To the dancers dancing in tune;
Till a silence fell with the waking bird,
  And a hush with the setting moon.

### IV

I said to the lily, 'There is but one
  With whom she has heart to be gay.
When will the dancers leave her alone?
  She is weary of dance and play.'
Now half to the setting moon are gone,
  And half to the rising day;
Low on the sand and loud on the stone
  The last wheel echoes away.

### V

I said to the rose, 'The brief night goes
  In babble and revel and wine.
O young lord-lover, what sighs are those,
  For one that will never be thine?
But mine, but mine,' so I sware to the rose,
  'For ever and ever, mine.'

### VI

And the soul of the rose went into my blood,
  As the music clash'd in the hall;
And long by the garden lake I stood,
  For I heard your rivulet fall
From the lake to the meadow and on to the wood,
  Our wood, that is dearer than all;

### VII

From the meadow your walks have left so sweet
    That whenever a March-wind sighs
He sets the jewel-print of your feet
    In violets blue as your eyes,
To the woody hollows in which we meet
    And the valleys of Paradise.

### VIII

The slender acacia would not shake
    One long milk-bloom on the tree;
The white lake-blossom fell into the lake
    As the pimpernel dozed on the lea;
But the rose was awake all night for your sake,
    Knowing your promise to me;
The lilies and roses were all awake,
    They sigh'd for the dawn and thee.

### IX

Queen rose of the rosebud garden of girls,
    Come hither, the dances are done,
In gloss of satin and glimmer of pearls,
    Queen lily and rose in one;
Shine out, little head, sunning over with curls,
    To the flowers, and be their sun.

### X

There has fallen a splendid tear
    From the passion-flower at the gate.
She is coming, my dove, my dear;
    She is coming, my life, my fate;
The red rose cries, 'She is near, she is near;'
    And the white rose weeps, 'She is late;'
The larkspur listens, 'I hear, I hear;'
    And the lily whispers, 'I wait.'

XI

She is coming, my own, my sweet;
    Were it ever so airy a tread,
My heart would hear her and beat,
    Were it earth in an earthy bed;
My dust would hear her and beat,
    Had I lain for a century dead;
Would start and tremble under her feet,
    And blossom in purple and red.


85          In the Valley of Cauteretz

All along the valley, stream that flashest white,
Deepening thy voice with the deepening of the night,
All along the valley, where thy waters flow,
I walk'd with one I loved two and thirty years ago.
All along the valley, while I walk'd to-day,
The two and thirty years were a mist that rolls away;
For all along the valley, down thy rocky bed,
Thy living voice to me was as the voice of the dead,
And all along the valley, by rock and cave and tree,
The voice of the dead was a living voice to me.


86          The Voyage of Maeldune

(FOUNDED ON AN IRISH LEGEND. A.D. 700)

I

I was the chief of the race – he had stricken my father dead –
But I gather'd my fellows together, I swore I would strike off his head.
Each of them look'd like a king, and was noble in birth as in worth,
And each of them boasted he sprang from the oldest race upon earth.

Each was as brave in the fight as the bravest hero of song,
And each of them liefer had died than have done one another a wrong.
*He* lived on an isle in the ocean – we sail'd on a Friday morn –
He that had slain my father the day before I was born.

II

And we came to the isle in the ocean, and there on the shore was he.
But a sudden blast blew us out and away thro' a boundless sea.

III

And we came to the Silent Isle that we never had touch'd at before,
Where a silent ocean always broke on a silent shore,
And the brooks glitter'd on in the light without sound, and the long
    waterfalls
Pour'd in a thunderless plunge to the base of the mountain walls,
And the poplar and cypress unshaken by storm flourish'd up beyond
    sight,
And the pine shot aloft from the crag to an unbelievable height,
And high in the heaven above it there flicker'd a songless lark,
And the cock couldn't crow, and the bull couldn't low, and the dog
    couldn't bark.
And round it we went, and thro' it, but never a murmur, a breath –
It was all of it fair as life, it was all of it quiet as death,
And we hated the beautiful Isle, for whenever we strove to speak
Our voices were thinner and fainter than any flittermouse-shriek;
And the men that were mighty of tongue and could raise such a
    battle-cry
That a hundred who heard it would rush on a thousand lances and
    die –
O they to be dumb'd by the charm! – so fluster'd with anger were they
They almost fell on each other; but after we sail'd away.

IV

And we came to the Isle of Shouting, we landed, a score of wild birds
Cried from the topmost summit with human voices and words;
Once in an hour they cried, and whenever their voices peal'd
The steer fell down at the plow and the harvest died from the field,
And the men dropt dead in the valleys and half of the cattle went lame,
And the roof sank in on the hearth, and the dwelling broke into flame;

And the shouting of these wild birds ran into the hearts of my crew,
Till they shouted along with the shouting and seized one another and
    slew;
But I drew them the one from the other; I saw that we could not stay,
And we left the dead to the birds and we sail'd with our wounded
    away.

V

And we came to the Isle of Flowers: their breath met us out on the seas,
For the Spring and the middle Summer sat each on the lap of the
    breeze;
And the red passion-flower to the cliffs, and the dark-blue clematis,
    clung,
And starr'd with a myriad blossom the long convolvulus hung;
And the topmost spire of the mountain was lilies in lieu of snow,
And the lilies like glaciers winded down, running out below
Thro' the fire of the tulip and poppy, the blaze of gorse, and the blush
Of millions of roses that sprang without leaf or a thorn from the bush;
And the whole isle-side flashing down from the peak without ever a
    tree
Swept like a torrent of gems from the sky to the blue of the sea;
And we roll'd upon capes of crocus and vaunted our kith and our kin,
And we wallow'd in beds of lilies, and chanted the triumph of Finn,
Till each like a golden image was pollen'd from head to feet
And each was as dry as a cricket, with thirst in the middle-day heat.
Blossom and blossom, and promise of blossom, but never a fruit!
And we hated the Flowering Isle, as we hated the isle that was mute,
And we tore up the flowers by the million and flung them in bight and
    bay,
And we left but a naked rock, and in anger we sail'd away.

VI

And we came to the Isle of Fruits: all round from the cliffs and the
    capes,
Purple or amber, dangled a hundred fathom of grapes,
And the warm melon lay like a little sun on the tawny sand,
And the fig ran up from the beach and rioted over the land,
And the mountain arose like a jewell'd throne thro' the fragrant air,
Glowing with all-colour'd plums and with golden masses of pear,

And the crimson and scarlet of berries that flamed upon bine and vine,
But in every berry and fruit was the poisonous pleasure of wine;
And the peak of the mountain was apples, the hugest that ever were
    seen,
And they prest, as they grew, on each other, with hardly a leaflet
    between,
And all of them redder than rosiest health or than utterest shame,
And setting, when Even descended, the very sunset aflame;
And we stay'd three days, and we gorged and we madden'd, till every
    one drew
His sword on his fellow to slay him, and ever they struck and they
    slew;
And myself, I had eaten but sparely, and fought till I sunder'd the fray,
Then I bad them remember my father's death, and we sail'd away.

### VII

And we came to the Isle of Fire: we were lured by the light from afar,
For the peak sent up one league of fire to the Northern Star;
Lured by the glare and the blare, but scarcely could stand upright,
For the whole isle shudder'd and shook like a man in a mortal affright;
We were giddy besides with the fruits we had gorged, and so crazed
    that at last
There were some leap'd into the fire; and away we sail'd, and we past
Over that undersea isle, where the water is clearer than air:
Down we look'd: what a garden! O bliss, what a Paradise there!
Towers of a happier time, low down in a rainbow deep
Silent palaces, quiet fields of eternal sleep!
And three of the gentlest and best of my people, whate'er I could say,
Plunged head down in the sea, and the Paradise trembled away.

### VIII

And we came to the Bounteous Isle, where the heavens lean low on the
    land,
And ever at dawn from the cloud glitter'd o'er us a sunbright hand,
Then it open'd and dropt at the side of each man, as he rose from his
    rest,
Bread enough for his need till the labourless day dipt under the West;
And we wander'd about it and thro' it. O never was time so good!
And we sang of the triumphs of Finn, and the boast of our ancient blood,

And we gazed at the wandering wave as we sat by the gurgle of springs,
And we chanted the songs of the Bards and the glories of fairy kings;
But at length we began to be weary, to sigh, and to stretch and yawn,
Till we hated the Bounteous Isle and the sunbright hand of the dawn,
For there was not an enemy near, but the whole green Isle was our own,
And we took to playing at ball, and we took to throwing the stone,
And we took to playing at battle, but that was a perilous play,
For the passion of battle was in us, we slew and we sail'd away.

IX

And we past to the Isle of Witches and heard their musical cry –
'Come to us, O come, come' in the stormy red of a sky
Dashing the fires and the shadows of dawn on the beautiful shapes,
For a wild witch naked as heaven stood on each of the loftiest capes,
And a hundred ranged on the rock like white sea-birds in a row,
And a hundred gamboll'd and pranced on the wrecks in the sand
        below,
And a hundred splash'd from the ledges, and bosom'd the burst of the
        spray,
But I knew we should fall on each other, and hastily sail'd away.

X

And we came in an evil time to the Isle of the Double Towers,
One was of smooth-cut stone, one carved all over with flowers,
But an earthquake always moved in the hollows under the dells,
And they shock'd on each other and butted each other with clashing of
        bells,
And the daws flew out of the Towers and jangled and wrangled in
        vain,
And the clash and boom of the bells rang into the heart and the brain,
Till the passion of battle was on us, and all took sides with the
        Towers,
There were some for the clean-cut stone, there were more for the
        carven flowers,
And the wrathful thunder of God peal'd over us all the day,
For the one half slew the other, and after we sail'd away.

### XI

And we came to the Isle of a Saint who had sail'd with St. Brendan of
  yore,
He had lived ever since on the Isle and his winters were fifteen score,
And his voice was low as from other worlds, and his eyes were sweet,
And his white hair sank to his heels and his white beard fell to his feet,
And he spake to me, 'O Maeldune, let be this purpose of thine!
Remember the words of the Lord when he told us "Vengeance is mine!"
His fathers have slain thy fathers in war or in single strife,
Thy fathers have slain his fathers, each taken a life for a life,
Thy father had slain his father, how long shall the murder last?
Go back to the Isle of Finn and suffer the Past to be Past.'
And we kiss'd the fringe of his beard and we pray'd as we heard him
  pray,
And the Holy man he assoil'd us, and sadly we sail'd away.

### XII

And we came to the Isle we were blown from, and there on the shore
  was he,
The man that had slain my father. I saw him and let him be.
O weary was I of the travel, the trouble, the strife and the sin,
When I landed again, with a tithe of my men, on the Isle of Finn.

## 87          Crossing the Bar

Sunset and evening star,
  And one clear call for me!
And may there be no moaning of the bar,
  When I put out to sea,

But such a tide as moving seems asleep,
  Too full for sound and foam,
When that which drew from out the boundless deep
  Turns again home.

Twilight and evening bell,
 And after that the dark!
And may there be no sadness of farewell,
 When I embark;

For tho' from out our bourne of Time and Place
 The flood may bear me far,
I hope to see my Pilot face to face
 When I have crost the bar.

# ALFRED DOMETT

1811–87

88                    Invisible Sights

'So far away so long – and now
    Returned to England? – Come with me!
Some of our great "celebrities"
    You will be glad to see!'


. . . . . .


Carlyle – the Laureate – Browning – *these*!
    These walking bipeds – Nay, you joke! –
Each wondrous power for thirty years
    O'er us head-downward folk

Wrapt skylike, at the Antipodes, –
    Those common limbs – that common trunk!
'Tis the Arab-Jinn who reached the clouds,
    Into his bottle shrunk.

The flashing Mind – the boundless Soul
    We felt ubiquitous, that mash
Medullary or cortical –
    That six inch brain-cube! – Trash!

# WILLIAM BELL SCOTT

## 1811–90

89          The Witch's Ballad

O, I hae come from far away,
   From a warm land far away,
A southern land across the sea,
With sailor-lads about the mast,
Merry and canny, and kind to me.

And I hae been to yon town,
   To try my luck in yon town;
Nort, and Mysie, Elspie too.
Right braw we were to pass the gate,
Wi' gowden clasps on girdles blue.

Mysie smiled wi' miminy mouth,
   Innocent mouth, miminy mouth;
Elspie wore her scarlet gown,
Nort's grey eyes were unco' gleg,       *quick, sharp*
My Castile comb was like a crown.

We walked abreast all up the street,
   Into the market up the street;
Our hair with marygolds was wound,
Our bodices with love-knots laced,
Our merchandise with tansy bound.

Nort had chickens, I had cocks,
   Gamesome cocks, loud-crowing cocks;
Mysie ducks, and Elspie drakes, –
For a wee groat or a pound:
We lost nae time wi' gives and takes.

Lost nae time, for well we knew,
  In our sleeves full well we knew,
When the gloaming came that night,
Duck nor drake nor hen nor cock
Would be found by candle-light.

And when our chaffering all was done,
  All was paid for, sold and done,
We drew a glove on ilka hand,
We sweetly curtsied each to each,
And deftly danced a saraband.

The market lasses looked and laughed,
  Left their gear and looked and laughed;
They made as they would join the game,
But soon their mithers, wild and wud,          *enraged*
With whack and screech they stopped the same.

Sae loud the tongues o' randies grew,          *scolds, viragos*
  The flitin' and the skirlin' grew,           *scolding and*
At all the windows in the place,               *shrill crying*
Wi' spoons or knives, wi' needle or awl,
Was thrust out every hand and face.

And down each stair they thronged anon,
  Gentle, semple, thronged anon;
Souter and tailor, frowsy Nan,                 *shoemaker*
The ancient widow young again,
Simpering behind her fan.

Without a choice, against their will,
  Doited, dazed, against their will,
The market lassie and her mither,
The farmer and his husbandman,
Hand in hand dance a' thegether.

Slow at first, but faster soon,
  Still increasing wild and fast,
Hoods and mantles, hats and hose,
Blindly doffed and cast away,
Left them naked, heads and toes.

They would have torn us limb from limb,
  Dainty limb from dainty limb;
But never one of them could win
Across the line that I had drawn
With bleeding thumb a-widdershin.

But there was Jeff the provost's son,
  Jeff the provost's only son;
There was Father Auld himsel',
The Lombard frae the hostelry,
And the lawyer Peter Fell.

All goodly men we singled out,
  Waled them well, and singled out,     *chose*
And drew them by the left hand in;
Mysie the priest, and Elspie won
The Lombard, Nort the lawyer carle,
I mysel' the provost's son.

Then, with cantrip kisses seven,     *spell-binding*
  Three times round with kisses seven,
Warped and woven there spun we,
Arms and legs and flaming hair,
Like a whirlwind on the sea.

Like the wind that sucks the sea,
  Over and in and on the sea,
Good sooth it was a mad delight;
And every man of all the four
Shut his eyes and laughed outright.

Laughed as long as they had breath,
   Laughed while they had sense or breath;
And close about us coiled a mist
Of gnats and midges, wasps and flies,
Like the whirlwind shaft it rist.

Drawn up I was right off my feet,
   Into the mist and off my feet;
And, dancing on each chimney-top,
I saw a thousand darling imps
Keeping time with skip and hop.

And on the provost's brave ridge-tile,
   On the provost's grand ridge-tile,
The Blackamoor first to master me
I saw, – I saw that winsome smile,
The mouth that did my heart beguile,
And spoke the great Word over me,
In the land beyond the sea.

I called his name, I called aloud,
   Alas! I called on him aloud;
And then he filled his hand with stour,       *dust*
And threw it towards me in the air;
My mouse flew out, I lost my pow'r!

My lusty strength, my power, were gone;
   Power was gone, and all was gone.
He will not let me love him more!
Of bell and whip and horse's tail
He cares not if I find a store.

But I am proud if he is fierce!
   I am as proud as he is fierce;
I'll turn about and backward go,
If I meet again that Blackamoor,
And he'll help us then, for he shall know
I seek another paramour.

And we'll gang once more to yon town,
  Wi' better luck to yon town;
We'll walk in silk and cramoisie,
And I shall wed the provost's son;
My-lady of the town I'll be!

For I was born a crowned king's child,
  Born and nursed a king's child,
King o' a land ayont the sea,
Where the Blackamoor kissed me first,
And taught me art and glamourie.

Each one in her wame shall hide                   *womb, belly*
  Her hairy mouse, her wary mouse,
Fed on madwort and agramie, –
Wear amber beads between her breasts,
And blind-worm's skin about her knee.

The Lombard shall be Elspie's man,
  Elspie's gowden husband-man;
Nort shall take the lawyer's hand;
The priest shall swear another vow:
We'll dance again the saraband!

90             Silence

Speech is silver, silence gold:
   Speech goes out,
   Speech roams about,
To market flies, is bought and sold:
Silence at home spins fold on fold,
   Folds thick or thin
   To wrap her in,
   Thoughts strong or weak,
Spins she round her body bare,
Having nothing else to wear:
But speech is silver, silence gold!
   Why should we speak?

# WILLIAM MAKEPEACE THACKERAY
## 1811–63

91      The Three Sailors [Little Billee]

There were three sailors in Bristol city,
Who took a boat and went to sea.

But first with beef and captain's biscuit,
And pickled pork they loaded she.

There was guzzling Jack and gorging Jimmy,
And the youngest he was little Bill-*ly*.

Now very soon they were so greedy,
They didn't leave not one split pea.

Says guzzling Jack to gorging Jimmy,
'I am confounded hung-*ery*.'

Says gorging Jim to guzzling Jacky,
'We have no wittles, so we must eat *we*.'

Says guzzling Jack to gorging Jimmy,
'Oh! gorging Jim, what a fool you be!'

'There's little Bill as is young and tender,
We're old and tough – so let's eat *he*.'

'Oh! Bill, we're going to kill and eat you,
So undo the collar of your chemie.'

When Bill he heard this information,
He used his pocket-handkerchie.

'Oh! let me say my catechism,
As my poor mammy taught to me.'

'Make haste, make haste,' says guzzling Jacky,
Whilst Jim pulled out his snicker-snee.

So Bill went up the maintop-gallant mast,
When down he fell on his bended knee.

He scarce had said his catechism,
When up he jumps; 'There's land I see:

'There's Jerusalem and Madagascar,
And North and South Ameri-*key*.

'There's the British fleet a-riding at anchor,
With Admiral Napier, K.C.B.'

So when they came to the Admiral's vessel,
He hanged fat Jack, and flogged Jim-*my*.

But as for little Bill, he made him
The Captain of a Seventy-three.

# ROBERT BROWNING

## 1812–89

## My Last Duchess

### *Ferrara*

That's my last Duchess painted on the wall,
Looking as if she were alive. I call
That piece a wonder, now: Frà Pandolf's hands
Worked busily a day, and there she stands.
Will't please you sit and look at her? I said
'Frà Pandolf' by design, for never read
Strangers like you that pictured countenance,
The depth and passion of its earnest glance,
But to myself they turned (since none puts by
The curtain I have drawn for you, but I)
And seemed as they would ask me, if they durst,
How such a glance came there; so, not the first
Are you to turn and ask thus. Sir, 't was not
Her husband's presence only, called that spot
Of joy into the Duchess' cheek: perhaps
Frà Pandolf chanced to say 'Her mantle laps
'Over my lady's wrist too much,' or 'Paint
'Must never hope to reproduce the faint
'Half-flush that dies along her throat:' such stuff
Was courtesy, she thought, and cause enough
For calling up that spot of joy. She had
A heart – how shall I say? – too soon made glad,
Too easily impressed; she liked whate'er
She looked on, and her looks went everywhere.
Sir, 't was all one! My favour at her breast,
The dropping of the daylight in the West,
The bough of cherries some officious fool
Broke in the orchard for her, the white mule

She rode with round the terrace – all and each
Would draw from her alike the approving speech,
Or blush, at least. She thanked men, – good! but thanked
Somehow – I know not how – as if she ranked
My gift of a nine-hundred-years-old name
With anybody's gift. Who'd stoop to blame
This sort of trifling? Even had you skill
In speech – (which I have not) – to make your will
Quite clear to such an one, and say, 'Just this
'Or that in you disgusts me; here you miss,
'Or there exceed the mark' – and if she let
Herself be lessoned so, nor plainly set
Her wits to yours, forsooth, and made excuse,
– E'en then would be some stooping; and I choose
Never to stoop. Oh sir, she smiled, no doubt,
When'er I passed her; but who passed without
Much the same smile? This grew; I gave commands;
Then all smiles stopped together. There she stands
As if alive. Will't please you rise? We'll meet
The company below, then. I repeat,
The Count your master's known munificence
Is ample warrant that no just pretence
Of mine for dowry will be disallowed;
Though his fair daughter's self, as I avowed
At starting, is my object. Nay, we'll go
Together down, sir. Notice Neptune, though,
Taming a sea-horse, thought a rarity,
Which Claus of Innsbruck cast in bronze for me!

## 93 Waring

### I

#### 1

What's become of Waring
Since he gave us all the slip,
Chose land-travel or seafaring,
Boots and chest or staff and scrip,
Rather than pace up and down
Any longer London town?

#### II

Who'd have guessed it from his lip
Or his brow's accustomed bearing,
On the night he thus took ship
Or started landward? – little caring
For us, it seems, who supped together
(Friends of his too, I remember)
And walked home thro' the merry weather,
The snowiest in all December.
I left his arm that night myself
For what's-his-name's, the new prose-poet
Who wrote the book there, on the shelf –
How, forsooth, was I to know it
If Waring meant to glide away
Like a ghost at break of day?
Never looked he half so gay!

#### III

He was prouder than the devil:
How he must have cursed our revel!
Ay and many other meetings,
Indoor visits, outdoor greetings,
As up and down he paced this London,
With no work done, but great works undone,

Where scarce twenty knew his name.
Why not, then, have earlier spoken,
Written, bustled? Who's to blame
If your silence kept unbroken?
'True, but there were sundry jottings,
'Stray-leaves, fragments, blurrs and blottings,
'Certain first steps were achieved
'Already which' – (is that your meaning?)
'Had well borne out whoe'er believed
'In more to come!' But who goes gleaning
Hedgeside chance-blades, while full-sheaved
Stand cornfields by him? Pride, o'erweening
Pride alone, puts forth such claims
O'er the day's distinguished names.

IV

Meantime, how much I loved him,
I find out now I've lost him.
I who cared not if I moved him,
Who could so carelessly accost him,
Henceforth never shall get free
Of his ghostly company,
His eyes that just a little wink
As deep I go into the merit
Of this and that distinguished spirit –
His cheeks' raised colour, soon to sink,
As long I dwell on some stupendous
And tremendous (Heaven defend us!)
Monstr'-inform'-ingens-horrend-ous
Demoniaco-seraphic
Penman's latest piece of graphic.
Nay, my very wrist grows warm
With his dragging weight of arm.
E'en so, swimmingly appears,
Through one's after-supper musings,
Some lost lady of old years
With her beauteous vain endeavour
And goodness unrepaid as ever;
The face, accustomed to refusings,

We, puppies that we were ... Oh never
Surely, nice of conscience, scrupled
Being aught like false, forsooth, to?
Telling aught but honest truth to?
What a sin, had we centupled
Its possessor's grace and sweetness!
No! she heard in its completeness
Truth, for truth's a weighty matter,
And, truth at issue, we can't flatter!
Well, 't is done with; she's exempt
From damning us thro' such a sally;
And so she glides, as down a valley,
Taking up with her contempt,
Past our reach; and in, the flowers
Shut her unregarded hours.

V

Oh, could I have him back once more,
This Waring, but one half-day more!
Back, with the quiet face of yore,
So hungry for acknowledgment
Like mine! I'd fool him to his bent.
Feed, should not he, to heart's content?
I'd say, 'to only have conceived,
'Planned your great works, apart from progress,
'Surpasses little works achieved!'
I'd lie so, I should be believed.
I'd make such havoc of the claims
Of the day's distinguished names
To feast him with, as feasts an ogress
Her feverish sharp-toothed gold-crowned child!
Or as one feasts a creature rarely
Captured here, unreconciled
To capture; and completely gives
Its pettish humours license, barely
Requiring that it lives.

## VI

Ichabod, Ichabod,
The glory is departed!
Travels Waring East away?
Who, of knowledge, by hearsay,
Reports a man upstarted
Somewhere as a god,
Hordes grown European-hearted,
Millions of the wild made tame
On a sudden at his fame?
In Vishnu-land what Avatar?
Or who in Moscow, toward the Czar,
With the demurest of footfalls
Over the Kremlin's pavement bright
With serpentine and syenite,
Steps, with five other Generals
That simultaneously take snuff,
For each to have pretext enough
And kerchiefwise unfold his sash
Which, softness' self, is yet the stuff
To hold fast where a steel chain snaps,
And leave the grand white neck no gash?
Waring in Moscow, to those rough
Cold northern natures borne perhaps,
Like the lambwhite maiden dear
From the circle of mute kings
Unable to repress the tear,
Each as his sceptre down he flings,
To Dian's fane at Taurica,
Where now a captive priestess, she alway
Mingles her tender grave Hellenic speech
With theirs, tuned to the hailstone-beaten beach
As pours some pigeon, from the myrrhy lands
Rapt by the whirlblast to fierce Scythian strands
Where breed the swallows, her melodious cry
Amid their barbarous twitter!
In Russia? Never! Spain were fitter!

Ay, most likely 't is in Spain
That we and Waring meet again
Now, while he turns down that cool narrow lane
Into the blackness, out of grave Madrid
All fire and shine, abrupt as when there's slid
Its stiff gold blazing pall
From some black coffin-lid.
Or, best of all,
I love to think
The leaving us was just a feint;
Back here to London did he slink,
And now works on without a wink
Of sleep, and we are on the brink
Of something great in fresco-paint:
Some garret's ceiling, walls and floor,
Up and down and o'er and o'er
He splashes, as none splashed before
Since great Caldara Polidore.
Or Music means this land of ours
Some favour yet, to pity won
By Purcell from his Rosy Bowers, –
'Give me my so-long promised son,
'Let Waring end what I begun!'
Then down he creeps and out he steals
Only when the night conceals
His face; in Kent 't is cherry-time,
Or hops are picking: or at prime
Of March he wanders as, too happy,
Years ago when he was young,
Some mild eve when woods grew sappy
And the early moths had sprung
To life from many a trembling sheath
Woven the warm boughs beneath;
While small birds said to themselves
What should soon be actual song,
And young gnats, by tens and twelves,
Made as if they were the throng

That crowd around and carry aloft
The sound they have nursed, so sweet and pure,
Out of a myriad noises soft,
Into a tone that can endure
Amid the noise of a July noon
When all God's creatures crave their boon,
All at once and all in tune,
And get it, happy as Waring then,
Having first within his ken
What a man might do with men:
And far too glad, in the even-glow,
To mix with the world he meant to take
Into his hand, he told you, so –
And out of it his world to make,
To contract and to expand
As he shut or oped his hand.
Oh Waring, what's to really be?
A clear stage and a crowd to see!
Some Garrick, say, out shall not he
The heart of Hamlet's mystery pluck?
Or, where most unclean beasts are rife,
Some Junius – am I right? – shall tuck
His sleeve, and forth with flaying-knife!
Some Chatterton shall have the luck
Of calling Rowley into life!
Some one shall somehow run a muck
With this old world for want of strife
Sound asleep. Contrive, contrive
To rouse us, Waring! Who's alive?
Our men scarce seem in earnest now.
Distinguished names! – but 't is, somehow,
As if they played at being names
Still more distinguished, like the games
Of children. Turn our sport to earnest
With a visage of the sternest!
Bring the real times back, confessed
Still better than our very best!

## II

### I

'When I last saw Waring ...'
(How all turned to him who spoke!
You saw Waring? Truth or joke?
In land-travel or sea-faring?)

### II

'We were sailing by Triest
'Where a day or two we harboured:
'A sunset was in the West,
'When, looking over the vessel's side,
'One of our company espied
'A sudden speck to larboard.
'And as a sea-duck flies and swims
'At once, so came the light craft up,
'With its sole lateen sail that trims
'And turns (the water round its rims
'Dancing, as round a sinking cup)
'And by us like a fish it curled,
'And drew itself up close beside,
'Its great sail on the instant furled,
'And o'er its thwarts a shrill voice cried,
'(A neck as bronzed as a Lascar's)
'"Buy wine of us, you English Brig?
'"Or fruit, tobacco and cigars?
'"A pilot for you to Triest?
'"Without one, look you ne'er so big,
'"They'll never let you up the bay!
'"We natives should know best."
'I turned, and "just those fellows' way,"
'Our captain said, "The 'long-shore thieves
'"Are laughing at us in their sleeves."

III

'In truth, the boy leaned laughing back;
'And one, half-hidden by his side
'Under the furled sail, soon I spied,
'With great grass hat and kerchief black,
'Who looked up with his kingly throat,
'Said somewhat, while the other shook
'His hair back from his eyes to look
'Their longest at us; then the boat,
'I know not how, turned sharply round,
'Laying her whole side on the sea
'As a leaping fish does; from the lee
'Into the weather, cut somehow
'Her sparkling path beneath our bow
'And so went off, as with a bound,
'Into the rosy and golden half
'O' the sky, to overtake the sun
'And reach the shore, like the sea-calf
'Its singing cave; yet I caught one
'Glance ere away the boat quite passed,
'And neither time nor toil could mar
'Those features: so I saw the last
'Of Waring!' – You? Oh, never star
Was lost here but it rose afar!
Look East, where whole new thousands are!
In Vishnu-land what Avatar?

94    The Bishop Orders His Tomb
      at Saint Praxed's Church

*Rome, 15—*

Vanity, saith the preacher, vanity!
Draw round my bed: is Anselm keeping back?
Nephews – sons mine ... ah God, I know not! Well –
She, men would have to be your mother once,
Old Gandolf envied me, so fair she was!

What's done is done, and she is dead beside,
Dead long ago, and I am Bishop since,
And as she died so must we die ourselves,
And thence ye may perceive the world's a dream.
Life, how and what is it? As here I lie
In this state-chamber, dying by degrees,
Hours and long hours in the dead night, I ask
'Do I live, am I dead?' Peace, peace seems all.
Saint Praxed's ever was the church for peace;
And so, about this tomb of mine. I fought
With tooth and nail to save my niche, ye know:
– Old Gandolf cozened me, despite my care;
Shrewd was that snatch from out the corner South
He graced his carrion with, God curse the same!
Yet still my niche is not so cramped but thence
One sees the pulpit o' the epistle-side,
And somewhat of the choir, those silent seats,
And up into the aery dome where live
The angels, and a sunbeam's sure to lurk:
And I shall fill my slab of basalt there,
And 'neath my tabernacle take my rest,
With those nine columns round me, two and two,
The odd one at my feet where Anselm stands:
Peach-blossom marble all, the rare, the ripe
As fresh-poured red wine of a mighty pulse.
– Old Gandolf with his paltry onion-stone,
Put me where I may look at him! True peach,
Rosy and flawless: how I earned the prize!
Draw close: that conflagration of my church
– What then? So much was saved if aught were missed!
My sons, ye would not be my death? Go dig
The white-grape vineyard where the oil-press stood,
Drop water gently till the surface sink,
And if ye find ... Ah God, I know not, I! ...
Bedded in store of rotten fig-leaves soft,
And corded up in a tight olive-frail,
Some lump, ah God, of *lapis lazuli*,
Big as a Jew's head cut off at the nape,
Blue as a vein o'er the Madonna's breast ...

Sons, all have I bequeathed you, villas, all,
That brave Frascati villa with its bath,
So, let the blue lump poise between my knees,
Like God the Father's globe on both his hands
Ye worship in the Jesu Church so gay,
For Gandolf shall not choose but see and burst!
Swift as a weaver's shuttle fleet our years:
Man goeth to the grave, and where is he?
Did I say basalt for my slab, sons? Black –
'T was ever antique-black I meant! How else
Shall ye contrast my frieze to come beneath?
The bas-relief in bronze ye promised me,
Those Pans and Nymphs ye wot of, and perchance
Some tripod, thyrsus, with a vase or so,
The Saviour at his sermon on the mount,
Saint Praxed in a glory, and one Pan
Ready to twitch the Nymph's last garment off,
And Moses with the tables . . . but I know
Ye mark me not! What do they whisper thee,
Child of my bowels, Anselm? Ah, ye hope
To revel down my villas while I gasp
Bricked o'er with beggar's mouldy travertine
Which Gandolf from his tomb-top chuckles at!
Nay, boys, ye love me – all of jasper, then!
'T is jasper ye stand pledged to, lest I grieve
My bath must needs be left behind, alas!
One block, pure green as a pistachio-nut,
There's plenty jasper somewhere in the world –
And have I not Saint Praxed's ear to pray
Horses for ye, and brown Greek manuscripts,
And mistresses with great smooth marbly limbs?
– That's if ye carve my epitaph aright,
Choice Latin, picked phrase, Tully's every word,
No gaudy ware like Gandolf's second line –
Tully, my masters? Ulpian serves his need!
And then how I shall lie through centuries,
And hear the blessed mutter of the mass,
And see God made and eaten all day long,
And feel the steady candle-flame, and taste

Good strong thick stupefying incense-smoke!
For as I lie here, hours of the dead night,
Dying in state and by such slow degrees,
I fold my arms as if they clasped a crook,
And stretch my feet forth straight as stone can point,
And let the bedclothes, for a mortcloth, drop
Into great laps and folds of sculptor's-work:
And as yon tapers dwindle, and strange thoughts
Grow, with a certain humming in my ears,
About the life before I lived this life,
And this life too, popes, cardinals and priests,
Saint Praxed at his sermon on the mount,
Your tall pale mother with her talking eyes,
And new-found agate urns as fresh as day,
And marble's language, Latin pure, discreet,
– Aha, ELUCESCEBAT quoth our friend?
No Tully, said I, Ulpian at the best!
Evil and brief hath been my pilgrimage.
All *lapis*, all, sons! Else I give the Pope
My villas! Will ye ever eat my heart?
Ever your eyes were as a lizard's quick,
They glitter like your mother's for my soul,
Or ye would heighten my impoverished frieze,
Piece out its starved design, and fill my vase
With grapes, and add a vizor and a Term,
And to the tripod ye would tie a lynx
That in his struggle throws the thyrsus down,
To comfort me on my entablature
Whereon I am to lie till I must ask
'Do I live, am I dead?' There, leave me, there!
For ye have stabbed me with ingratitude
To death – ye wish it – God, ye wish it! Stone –
Gritstone, a-crumble! Clammy squares which sweat
As if the corpse they keep were oozing through –
And no more *lapis* to delight the world!
Well go! I bless ye. Fewer tapers there,
But in a row: and, going, turn your backs

94. ELUCESCEBAT  He shone, was notable (fifth-century Latin, not classical)

– Ay, like departing altar-ministrants,
And leave me in my church, the church for peace,
That I may watch at leisure if he leers –
Old Gandolf, at me, from his onion-stone,
As still he envied me, so fair she was!

## 95        Home-Thoughts, from Abroad

I

Oh, to be in England
Now that April's there,
And whoever wakes in England
Sees, some morning, unaware,
That the lowest boughs and the brushwood sheaf
Round the elm-tree bole are in tiny leaf,
While the chaffinch sings on the orchard bough
In England – now!

II

And after April, when May follows,
And the whitethroat builds, and all the swallows!
Hark, where my blossomed pear-tree in the hedge
Leans to the field and scatters on the clover
Blossoms and dewdrops – at the bent spray's edge –
That's the wise thrush; he sings each song twice over,
Lest you should think he never could recapture
The first fine careless rapture!
And though the fields look rough with hoary dew
All will be gay when noontide wakes anew
The buttercups, the little children's dower
– Far brighter than this gaudy melon-flower!

96 ## The Lost Leader

### I

Just for a handful of silver he left us,
    Just for a riband to stick in his coat –
Found the one gift of which fortune bereft us,
    Lost all the others she lets us devote;
They, with the gold to give, doled him out silver,
    So much was theirs who so little allowed:
How all our copper had gone for his service!
    Rags – were they purple, his heart had been proud!
We that had loved him so, followed him, honoured him,
    Lived in his mild and magnificent eye,
Learned his great language, caught his clear accents,
    Made him our pattern to live and to die!
Shakespeare was of us, Milton was for us,
    Burns, Shelley, were with us, – they watch from their
        graves!
He alone breaks from the van and the freemen,
    – He alone sinks to the rear and the slaves!

### II

We shall march prospering, – not thro' his presence;
    Songs may inspirit us, – not from his lyre;
Deeds will be done, – while he boasts his quiescence,
    Still bidding crouch whom the rest bade aspire:
Blot out his name, then, record one lost soul more,
    One task more declined, one more footpath untrod,
One more devils'-triumph and sorrow for angels,
    One wrong more to man, one more insult to God!
Life's night begins: let him never come back to us!
    There would be doubt, hesitation and pain,
Forced praise on our part – the glimmer of twilight,
    Never glad confident morning again!
Best fight on well, for we taught him – strike gallantly,
    Menace our heart ere we master his own;
Then let him receive the new knowledge and wait us,
    Pardoned in heaven, the first by the throne!

97                          Fra Lippo Lippi

I am poor brother Lippo, by your leave!
You need not clap your torches to my face.
Zooks, what 's to blame? you think you see a monk!
What, 't is past midnight, and you go the rounds,
And here you catch me at an alley's end
Where sportive ladies leave their doors ajar?
The Carmine's my cloister: hunt it up,
Do, – harry out, if you must show your zeal,
Whatever rat, there, haps on his wrong hole,
And nip each softling of a wee white mouse,
Weke, *weke*, that 's crept to keep him company!
Aha, you know your betters! Then, you'll take
Your hand away that's fiddling on my throat,
And please to know me likewise. Who am I?
Why, one, sir, who is lodging with a friend
Three streets off – he's a certain ... how d' ye call?
Master – a ... Cosimo of the Medici,
I' the house that caps the corner. Boh! you were best!
Remember and tell me, the day you're hanged,
How you affected such a gullet's-gripe!
But you, sir, it concerns you that your knaves
Pick up a manner nor discredit you:
Zooks, are we pilchards, that they sweep the streets
And count fair prize what comes into their net?
He's Judas to a tittle, that man is!
Just such a face! Why, sir, you make amends.
Lord, I'm not angry! Bid your hangdogs go
Drink out this quarter-florin to the health
Of the munificent House that harbours me
(And many more beside, lads! more beside!)
And all's come square again. I'd like his face –
His, elbowing on his comrade in the door
With the pike and lantern, – for the slave that holds
John Baptist's head a-dangle by the hair
With one hand ('Look you, now,' as who should say)
And his weapon in the other, yet unwiped!

It's not your chance to have a bit of chalk,
A wood-coal or the like? or you should see!
Yes, I'm the painter, since you style me so.
What, brother Lippo's doings, up and down,
You know them and they take you? like enough!
I saw the proper twinkle in your eye –
'Tell you, I liked your looks at very first.
Let's sit and set things straight now, hip to haunch.
Here's spring come, and the nights one makes up bands
To roam the town and sing out carnival,
And I've been three weeks shut within my mew,
A-painting for the great man, saints and saints
And saints again. I could not paint all night –
Ouf! I leaned out of window for fresh air.
There came a hurry of feet and little feet,
A sweep of lute-strings, laughs, and whifts of song, –
*Flower o' the broom,*
*Take away love, and our earth is a tomb!*
*Flower o' the quince,*
*I let Lisa go, and what good in life since?*
*Flower o' the thyme* – and so on. Round they went.
Scarce had they turned the corner when a titter
Like the skipping of rabbits by moonlight, – three slim
    shapes,
And a face that looked up ... zooks, sir, flesh and blood,
That's all I'm made of! Into shreds it went,
Curtain and counterpane and coverlet,
All the bed-furniture – a dozen knots,
There was a ladder! Down I let myself,
Hands and feet, scrambling somehow, and so dropped,
And after them. I came up with the fun
Hard by Saint Laurence, hail fellow, well met, –
*Flower o' the rose,*
*If I've been merry, what matter who knows?*
And so as I was stealing back again
To get to bed and have a bit of sleep
Ere I rise up to-morrow and go work
On Jerome knocking at his poor old breast
With his great round stone to subdue the flesh,

You snap me of the sudden. Ah, I see!
Though your eye twinkles still, you shake your head –
Mine's shaved – a monk, you say – the sting's in that!
If Master Cosimo announced himself,
Mum's the word naturally; but a monk!
Come, what am I a beast for? tell us, now!
I was a baby when my mother died
And father died and left me in the street.
I starved there, God knows how, a year or two
On fig-skins, melon-parings, rinds and shucks,
Refuse and rubbish. One fine frosty day,
My stomach being empty as your hat,
The wind doubled me up and down I went.
Old Aunt Lapaccia trussed me with one hand,
(Its fellow was a stinger as I knew)
And so along the wall, over the bridge,
By the straight cut to the convent. Six words there,
While I stood munching my first bread that month:
'So, boy, you're minded,' quoth the good fat father
Wiping his own mouth, 't was refection-time, –
'To quit this very miserable world?
'Will you renounce' ... 'the mouthful of bread?' thought I;
By no means! Brief, they made a monk of me;
I did renounce the world, its pride and greed,
Palace, farm, villa, shop and banking-house,
Trash, such as these poor devils of Medici
Have given their hearts to – all at eight years old.
Well, sir, I found in time, you may be sure,
'T was not for nothing – the good bellyful,
The warm serge and the rope that goes all round,
And day-long blessed idleness beside!
'Let's see what the urchin's fit for' – that came next.
Not overmuch their way, I must confess.
Such a to-do! They tried me with their books:
Lord, they'd have taught me Latin in pure waste!
*Flower o' the clove,*
*All the Latin I construe is, 'amo' I love!*
But, mind you, when a boy starves in the streets
Eight years together, as my fortune was,

Watching folk's faces to know who will fling
The bit of half-stripped grape-bunch he desires,
And who will curse or kick him for his pains, –
Which gentleman processional and fine,
Holding a candle to the Sacrament,
Will wink and let him lift a plate and catch
The droppings of the wax to sell again,
Or holla for the Eight and have him whipped, –
How say I? – nay, which dog bites, which lets drop
His bone from the heap of offal in the street, –
Why, soul and sense of him grow sharp alike,
He learns the look of things, and none the less
For admonition from the hunger-pinch.
I had a store of such remarks, be sure,
Which, after I found leisure, turned to use.
I drew men's faces on my copy-books,
Scrawled them within the antiphonary's marge,
Joined legs and arms to the long music-notes,
Found eyes and nose and chin for A's and B's,
And made a string of pictures of the world
Betwixt the ins and outs of verb and noun,
On the wall, the bench, the door. The monks looked black.
'Nay,' quoth the Prior, 'turn him out, d' ye say?
'In no wise. Lose a crow and catch a lark.
'What if at last we get our man of parts,
'We Carmelites, like those Camaldolese
'And Preaching Friars, to do our church up fine
'And put the front on it that ought to be!'
And hereupon he bade me daub away.
Thank you! my head being crammed, the walls a blank,
Never was such prompt disemburdening.
First, every sort of monk, the black and white,
I drew them, fat and lean: then, folk at church,
From good old gossips waiting to confess
Their cribs of barrel-droppings, candle-ends, –
To the breathless fellow at the altar-foot,
Fresh from his murder, safe and sitting there
With the little children round him in a row
Of admiration, half for his beard and half

For that white anger of his victim's son
Shaking a fist at him with one fierce arm,
Signing himself with the other because of Christ
(Whose sad face on the cross sees only this
After the passion of a thousand years)
Till some poor girl, her apron o'er her head,
(Which the intense eyes looked through) came at eve
On tiptoe, said a word, dropped in a loaf,
Her pair of earrings and a bunch of flowers
(The brute took growling), prayed, and so was gone.
I painted all, then cried "T is ask and have;
'Choose, for more 's ready!' – laid the ladder flat,
And showed my covered bit of cloister-wall
The monks closed in a circle and praised loud
Till checked, taught what to see and not to see,
Being simple bodies, – 'That 's the very man!
'Look at the boy who stoops to pat the dog!
'That woman's like the Prior's niece who comes
'To care about his asthma: it's the life!'
But there my triumph's straw-fire flared and funked;
Their betters took their turn to see and say:
The Prior and the learned pulled a face
And stopped all that in no time. 'How? what's here?
'Quite from the mark of painting, bless us all!
'Faces, arms, legs and bodies like the true
'As much as pea and pea! it 's devil's-game!
'Your business is not to catch men with show,
'With homage to the perishable clay,
'But lift them over it, ignore it all,
'Make them forget there's such a thing as flesh.
'Your business is to paint the souls of men –
'Man's soul, and it's a fire, smoke . . . no, it's not . . .
'It's vapour done up like a new-born babe –
'(In that shape when you die it leaves your mouth)
'It's . . . well, what matters talking, it's the soul!
'Give us no more of body than shows soul!
'Here's Giotto, with his Saint a-praising God,
'That sets us praising, – why not stop with him?
'Why put all thoughts of praise out of our head

'With wonder at lines, colours, and what not?
'Paint the soul, never mind the legs and arms!
'Rub all out, try at it a second time.
'Oh, that white smallish female with the breasts,
'She's just my niece . . . Herodias, I would say, –
'Who went and danced and got men's heads cut off!
'Have it all out!' Now, is this sense, I ask?
A fine way to paint soul, by painting body
So ill, the eye can't stop there, must go further
And can't fare worse! Thus, yellow does for white
When what you put for yellow's simply black,
And any sort of meaning looks intense
When all beside itself means and looks nought.
Why can't a painter lift each foot in turn,
Left foot and right foot, go a double step,
Make his flesh liker and his soul more like,
Both in their order? Take the prettiest face,
The Prior's niece . . . patron-saint – is it so pretty
You can't discover if it means hope, fear,
Sorrow or joy? won't beauty go with these?
Suppose I've made her eyes all right and blue,
Can't I take breath and try to add life's flash,
And then add soul and heighten them threefold?
Or say there's beauty with no soul at all –
(I never saw it – put the case the same – )
If you get simple beauty and nought else,
You get about the best thing God invents:
That's somewhat: and you'll find the soul you have missed,
Within yourself, when you return him thanks.
'Rub all out!' Well, well, there's my life, in short,
And so the thing has gone on ever since.
I'm grown a man no doubt, I've broken bounds:
You should not take a fellow eight years old
And make him swear to never kiss the girls.
I'm my own master, paint now as I please –
Having a friend, you see, in the Corner-house!
Lord, it's fast holding by the rings in front –
Those great rings serve more purposes than just
To plant a flag in, or tie up a horse!

And yet the old schooling sticks, the old grave eyes
Are peeping o'er my shoulder as I work,
The heads shake still – 'It's art's decline, my son!
'You're not of the true painters, great and old;
'Brother Angelico's the man, you'll find;
'Brother Lorenzo stands his single peer:
'Fag on at flesh, you'll never make the third!'
*Flower o' the pine,*
*You keep your mistr ... manners, and I'll stick to mine!*
I'm not the third, then: bless us, they must know!
Don't you think they're the likeliest to know,
They with their Latin? So, I swallow my rage,
Clench my teeth, suck my lips in tight, and paint
To please them – sometimes do and sometimes don't;
For, doing most, there's pretty sure to come
A turn, some warm eve finds me at my saints –
A laugh, a cry, the business of the world –
*(Flower o' the peach,*
*Death for us all, and his own life for each!)*
And my whole soul revolves, the cup runs over,
The world and life's too big to pass for a dream,
And I do these wild things in sheer despite,
And play the fooleries you catch me at,
In pure rage! The old mill-horse, out at grass
After hard years, throws up his stiff heels so,
Although the miller does not preach to him
The only good of grass is to make chaff.
What would men have? Do they like grass or no –
May they or mayn't they? all I want's the thing
Settled for ever one way. As it is,
You tell too many lies and hurt yourself:
You don't like what you only like too much,
You do like what, if given you at your word,
You find abundantly detestable.
For me, I think I speak as I was taught;
I always see the garden and God there
A-making man's wife: and, my lesson learned,
The value and significance of flesh,
I can't unlearn ten minutes afterwards.

You understand me: I'm a beast, I know.
But see, now – why, I see as certainly
As that the morning-star's about to shine,
What will hap some day. We've a youngster here
Comes to our convent, studies what I do,
Slouches and stares and lets no atom drop:
His name is Guidi – he'll not mind the monks –
They call him Hulking Tom, he lets them talk –
He picks my practice up – he'll paint apace,
I hope so – though I never live so long,
I know what's sure to follow. You be judge!
You speak no Latin more than I, belike,
However, you're my man, you've seen the world
– The beauty and the wonder and the power,
The shapes of things, their colours, lights and shades,
Changes, surprises, – and God made it all!
– For what? Do you feel thankful, ay or no,
For this fair town's face, yonder river's line,
The mountain round it and the sky above,
Much more the figures of man, woman, child,
These are the frame to? What's it all about?
To be passed over, despised? or dwelt upon,
Wondered at? oh, this last of course! – you say.
But why not do as well as say, – paint these
Just as they are, careless what comes of it?
God's works – paint anyone, and count it crime
To let a truth slip. Don't object, 'His works
'Are here already; nature is complete:
'Suppose you reproduce her – (which you can't)
'There's no advantage! you must beat her, then.'
For, don't you mark? we're made so that we love
First when we see them painted, things we have passed
Perhaps a hundred times nor cared to see;
And so they are better, painted – better to us,
Which is the same thing. Art was given for that;
God uses us to help each other so,
Lending our minds out. Have you noticed, now,
Your cullion's hanging face? A bit of chalk,
And trust me but you should, though! How much more,

If I drew higher things with the same truth!
That were to take the Prior's pulpit-place,
Interpret God to all of you! Oh, oh,
It makes me mad to see what men shall do
And we in our graves! This world's no blot for us,
Nor blank; it means intensely, and means good:
To find its meaning is my meat and drink.
'Ay, but you don't so instigate to prayer!'
Strikes in the Prior: 'when your meaning's plain
'It does not say to folk – remember matins,
'Or, mind you fast next Friday!' Why, for this
What need of art at all? A skull and bones,
Two bits of stick nailed crosswise, or, what's best,
A bell to chime the hour with, does as well.
I painted a Saint Laurence six months since
At Prato, splashed the fresco in fine style:
'How looks my painting, now the scaffold's down?'
I ask a brother: 'Hugely,' he returns –
'Already not one phiz of your three slaves
'Who turn the Deacon off his toasted side,
'But's scratched and prodded to our heart's content,
'The pious people have so eased their own
'With coming to say prayers there in a rage:
'We get on fast to see the bricks beneath.
'Expect another job this time next year,
'For pity and religion grow i' the crowd –
'Your painting serves its purpose!' Hang the fools!

     – That is – you'll not mistake an idle word
Spoke in a huff by a poor monk, God wot,
Tasting the air this spicy night which turns
The unaccustomed head like Chianti wine!
Oh, the church knows! don't misreport me, now!
It's natural a poor monk out of bounds
Should have his apt word to excuse himself:
And hearken how I plot to make amends.
I have bethought me: I shall paint a piece
. . . There's for you! Give me six months, then go, see
Something in Sant' Ambrogio's! Bless the nuns!

They want a cast o' my office. I shall paint
God in the midst, Madonna and her babe,
Ringed by a bowery flowery angel-brood,
Lilies and vestments and white faces, sweet
As puff on puff of grated orris-root
When ladies crowd to Church at midsummer.
And then i' the front, of course a saint or two –
Saint John, because he saves the Florentines,
Saint Ambrose, who puts down in black and white
The convent's friends and gives them a long day,
And Job, I must have him there past mistake,
The man of Uz (and Us without the z,
Painters who need his patience). Well, all these
Secured at their devotion, up shall come
Out of a corner when you least expect,
As one by a dark stair into a great light,
Music and talking, who but Lippo! I! –
Mazed, motionless and moonstruck – I'm the man!
Back I shrink – what is this I see and hear?
I, caught up with my monk's-things by mistake,
My old serge gown and rope that goes all round,
I, in this presence, this pure company!
Where's a hole, where's a corner for escape?
Then steps a sweet angelic slip of a thing
Forward, puts out a soft palm – 'Not so fast!'
– Addresses the celestial presence, 'nay –
'He made you and devised you, after all,
'Though he's none of you! Could Saint John there draw –
'His camel-hair make up a painting-brush?
'We come to brother Lippo for all that,
'*Iste perfecit opus!*' So, all smile –
I shuffle sideways with my blushing face
Under the cover of a hundred wings
Thrown like a spread of kirtles when you're gay
And play hot cockles, all the doors being shut,
Till, wholly unexpected, in there pops
The hothead husband! Thus I scuttle off

97. *Iste perfecit opus* This man accomplished the work

To some safe bench behind, not letting go
The palm of her, the little lily thing
That spoke the good word for me in the nick,
Like the Prior's niece ... Saint Lucy I would say.
And so all's saved for me, and for the church
A pretty picture gained. Go, six months hence!
Your hand, sir, and good-bye: no lights, no lights!
The street's hushed, and I know my own way back,
Don't fear me! There's the grey beginning. Zooks!

## 98        A Toccata of Galuppi's

### I

Oh Galuppi, Baldassaro, this is very sad to find!
I can hardly misconceive you; it would prove me deaf and blind;
But although I take your meaning, 't is with such a heavy mind!

### II

Here you come with your old music, and here's all the good it brings.
What, they lived once thus at Venice where the merchants were the
    kings,
Where Saint Mark's is, where the Doges used to wed the sea with
    rings?

### III

Ay, because the sea's the street there; and 't is arched by ... what you
    call
... Shylock's bridge with houses on it, where they kept the carnival:
I was never out of England – it's as if I saw it all.

### IV

Did young people take their pleasure when the sea was warm in May?
Balls and masks begun at midnight, burning ever to midday,
When they made up fresh adventures for the morrow, do you say?

V

Was a lady such a lady, cheeks so round and lips so red, –
On her neck the small face buoyant, like a bell-flower on its bed,
O'er the breast's superb abundance where a man might base his head?

VI

Well, and it was graceful of them – they'd break talk off and afford
– She, to bite her mask's black velvet – he, to finger on his sword,
While you sat and played Toccatas, stately at the clavichord?

VII

What? Those lesser thirds so plaintive, sixths diminished, sigh on sigh,
Told them something? Those suspensions, those solutions – 'Must we
     die?'
Those commiserating sevenths – 'Life might last! we can but try!'

VIII

'Were you happy?' – 'Yes.' – 'And are you still as happy?' – 'Yes. And
     you?'
– 'Then, more kisses!' – 'Did I stop them, when a million seemed so
     few?'
Hark, the dominant's persistence till it must be answered to!

IX

So, an octave struck the answer. Oh, they praised you, I dare say!
'Brave Galuppi! that was music! good alike at grave and gay!
'I can always leave off talking when I hear a master play!'

X

Then they left you for their pleasure: till in due time, one by one,
Some with lives that came to nothing, some with deeds as well
     undone,
Death stepped tacitly and took them where they never see the sun.

XI

But when I sit down to reason, think to take my stand nor swerve,
While I triumph o'er a secret wrung from nature's close reserve,
In you come with your cold music till I creep thro' every nerve.

### XII

Yes, you, like a ghostly cricket, creaking where a house was burned:
'Dust and ashes, dead and done with, Venice spent what Venice
    earned.
'The soul, doubtless, is immortal – where a soul can be discerned.

### XIII

'Yours for instance: you know physics, something of geology,
'Mathematics are your pastime; souls shall rise in their degree;
'Butterflies may dread extinction, – you'll not die, it cannot be!

### XIV

'As for Venice and her people, merely born to bloom and drop,
'Here on earth they bore their fruitage, mirth and folly were the crop:
'What of soul was left, I wonder, when the kissing had to stop?

### XV

'Dust and ashes!' So you creak it, and I want the heart to scold.
Dear dead women, with such hair, too – what's become of all the gold
Used to hang and brush their bosoms? I feel chilly and grown old.


## 99    'Childe Roland to the Dark Tower Came'

*(See Edgar's song in* Lear)

### I

My first thought was, he lied in every word,
    That hoary cripple, with malicious eye
    Askance to watch the working of his lie
On mine, and mouth scarce able to afford
Suppression of the glee, that pursed and scored
    Its edge, at one more victim gained thereby.

### II

What else should he be set for, with his staff?
    What, save to waylay with his lies, ensnare
    All travellers who might find him posted there,

And ask the road? I guessed what skull-like laugh
Would break, what crutch 'gin write my epitaph
   For pastime in the dusty thoroughfare,

### III

If at his counsel I should turn aside
   Into that ominous tract which, all agree,
   Hides the Dark Tower. Yet acquiescingly
I did turn as he pointed: neither pride
Nor hope rekindling at the end descried,
   So much as gladness that some end might be.

### IV

For, what with my whole world-wide wandering,
   What with my search drawn out thro' years, my hope
   Dwindled into a ghost not fit to cope
With that obstreperous joy success would bring, –
I hardly tried now to rebuke the spring
   My heart made, finding failure in its scope.

### V

As when a sick man very near to death
   Seems dead indeed, and feels begin and end
   The tears and takes the farewell of each friend,
And hears one bid the other go, draw breath
Freelier outside, ('since all is o'er,' he saith,
   'And the blow fallen no grieving can amend;')

### VI

While some discuss if near the other graves
   Be room enough for this, and when a day
   Suits best for carrying the corpse away,
With care about the banners, scarves and staves:
And still the man hears all, and only craves
   He may not shame such tender love and stay.

### VII

Thus, I had so long suffered in this quest,
   Heard failure prophesied so oft, been writ
   So many times among 'The Band' – to wit,
The knights who to the Dark Tower's search addressed
Their steps – that just to fail as they, seemed best,
   And all the doubt was now – should I be fit?

### VIII

So, quiet as despair, I turned from him,
   That hateful cripple, out of his highway
   Into the path he pointed. All the day
Had been a dreary one at best, and dim
Was settling to its close, yet shot one grim
   Red leer to see the plain catch its estray.

### IX

For mark! no sooner was I fairly found
   Pledged to the plain, after a pace or two,
   Than, pausing to throw backward a last view
O'er the safe road, 't was gone; grey plain all round:
Nothing but plain to the horizon's bound.
   I might go on; nought else remained to do.

### X

So, on I went. I think I never saw
   Such starved ignoble nature; nothing throve:
   For flowers – as well expect a cedar grove!
But cockle, spurge, according to their law
Might propagate their kind, with none to awe,
   You'd think; a burr had been a treasure-trove.

### XI

No! penury, inertness and grimace,
   In some strange sort, were the land's portion. 'See
   'Or shut your eyes,' said Nature peevishly,
'It nothing skills: I cannot help my case:
''T is the Last Judgment's fire must cure this place,
   'Calcine its clods and set my prisoners free.'

### XII

If there pushed any ragged thistle-stalk
  Above its mates, the head was chopped; the bents
    Were jealous else. What made those holes and rents
In the dock's harsh swarth leaves, bruised as to baulk
All hope of greenness? 't is a brute must walk
  Pashing their life out, with a brute's intents.

### XIII

As for the grass, it grew as scant as hair
  In leprosy; thin dry blades pricked the mud
    Which underneath looked kneaded up with blood.
One stiff blind horse, his every bone a-stare,
Stood stupefied, however he came there:
  Thrust out past service from the devil's stud!

### XIV

Alive? he might be dead for aught I know,
  With that red gaunt and colloped neck a-strain,
    And shut eyes underneath the rusty mane;
Seldom went such grotesqueness with such woe;
I never saw a brute I hated so;
  He must be wicked to deserve such pain.

### XV

I shut my eyes and turned them on my heart.
  As a man calls for wine before he fights,
    I asked one draught of earlier, happier sights,
Ere fitly I could hope to play my part.
Think first, fight afterwards – the soldier's art:
  One taste of the old time sets all to rights.

### XVI

Not it! I fancied Cuthbert's reddening face
  Beneath its garniture of curly gold,
    Dear fellow, till I almost felt him fold
An arm in mine to fix me to the place,
That way he used. Alas, one night's disgrace!
  Out went my heart's new fire and left it cold.

### XVII

Giles then, the soul of honour – there he stands
 Frank as ten years ago when knighted first.
 What honest man should dare (he said) he durst.
Good – but the scene shifts – faugh! what hangman-hands
Pin to his breast a parchment? His own bands
 Read it. Poor traitor, spit upon and curst!

### XVIII

Better this present than a past like that;
 Back therefore to my darkening path again!
 No sound, no sight as far as eye could strain.
Will the night send a howlet or a bat?
I asked: when something on the dismal flat
 Came to arrest my thoughts and change their train.

### XIX

A sudden little river crossed my path
 As unexpected as a serpent comes.
 No sluggish tide congenial to the glooms;
This, as it frothed by, might have been a bath
For the fiend's glowing hoof – to see the wrath
 Of its black eddy bespate with flakes and spumes.

### XX

So petty yet so spiteful! All along,
 Low scrubby alders kneeled down over it;
 Drenched willows flung them headlong in a fit
Of mute despair, a suicidal throng:
The river which had done them all the wrong,
 Whate'er that was, rolled by, deterred no whit.

### XXI

Which, while I forded, – good saints, how I feared
 To set my foot upon a dead man's cheek,
 Each step, or feel the spear I thrust to seek
For hollows, tangled in his hair or beard!
– It may have been a water-rat I speared,
 But, ugh! it sounded like a baby's shriek.

### XXII

Glad was I when I reached the other bank.
 Now for a better country. Vain presage!
 Who were the strugglers, what war did they wage,
Whose savage trample thus could pad the dank
Soil to a plash? Toads in a poisoned tank,
 Or wild cats in a red-hot iron cage –

### XXIII

The fight must so have seemed in that fell cirque.
 What penned them there, with all the plain to choose?
 No foot-print leading to that horrid mews,
None out of it. Mad brewage set to work
Their brains, no doubt, like galley-slaves the Turk
 Pits for his pastime, Christians against Jews.

### XXIV

And more than that – a furlong on – why, there!
 What bad use was that engine for, that wheel,
 Or brake, not wheel – that harrow fit to reel
Men's bodies out like silk? with all the air
Of Tophet's tool, on earth left unaware,
 Or brought to sharpen its rusty teeth of steel.

### XXV

Then came a bit of stubbed ground, once a wood,
 Next a marsh, it would seem, and now mere earth
 Desperate and done with; (so a fool finds mirth,
Makes a thing and then mars it, till his mood
Changes and off he goes!) within a rood –
 Bog, clay and rubble, sand and stark black dearth.

### XXVI

Now blotches rankling, coloured gay and grim,
 Now patches where some leanness of the soil's
 Broke into moss or substances like boils;
Then came some palsied oak, a cleft in him
Like a distorted mouth that splits its rim
 Gaping at death, and dies while it recoils.

### XXVII

And just as far as ever from the end!
  Nought in the distance but the evening, nought
  To point my footstep further! At the thought,
A great black bird, Apollyon's bosom-friend,
Sailed past, nor beat his wide wing dragon-penned
  That brushed my cap – perchance the guide I sought.

### XXVIII

For, looking up, aware I somehow grew,
  'Spite of the dusk, the plain had given place
  All round to mountains – with such name to grace
Mere ugly heights and heaps now stolen in view.
How thus they had surprised me, – solve it, you!
  How to get from them was no clearer case.

### XXIX

Yet half I seemed to recognize some trick
  Of mischief happened to me, God knows when –
  In a bad dream perhaps. Here ended, then,
Progress this way. When, in the very nick
Of giving up, one time more, came a click
  As when a trap shuts – you 're inside the den!

### XXX

Burningly it came on me all at once,
  This was the place! those two hills on the right,
  Crouched like two bulls locked horn in horn in fight;
While to the left, a tall scalped mountain . . . Dunce,
Dotard, a-dozing at the very nonce,
  After a life spent training for the sight!

### XXXI

What in the midst lay but the Tower itself?
  The round squat turret, blind as the fool's heart,
  Built of brown stone, without a counterpart
In the whole world. The tempest's mocking elf
Points to the shipman thus the unseen shelf
  He strikes on, only when the timbers start.

### XXXII

Not see? because of night perhaps? – why, day
  Came back again for that! before it left,
  The dying sunset kindled through a cleft:
The hills, like giants at a hunting, lay,
Chin upon hand, to see the game at bay, –
  'Now stab and end the creature – to the heft!'

### XXXIII

Not hear? when noise was everywhere! it tolled
  Increasing like a bell. Names in my ears
  Of all the lost adventurers my peers, –
How such a one was strong, and such was bold,
And such was fortunate, yet each of old
  Lost, lost! one moment knelled the woe of years.

### XXXIV

There they stood, ranged along the hill-sides, met
  To view the last of me, a living frame
  For one more picture! in a sheet of flame
I saw them and I knew them all. And yet
Dauntless the slug-horn to my lips I set,
  And blew. '*Childe Roland to the Dark Tower came.*'

## 100      Andrea del Sarto

### (Called 'The Faultless Painter')

But do not let us quarrel any more,
No, my Lucrezia; bear with me for once:
Sit down and all shall happen as you wish.
You turn your face, but does it bring your heart?
I'll work then for your friend's friend, never fear,
Treat his own subject after his own way,
Fix his own time, accept too his own price,
And shut the money into this small hand
When next it takes mine. Will it? tenderly?

Oh, I'll content him, – but to-morrow, Love!
I often am much wearier than you think,
This evening more than usual, and it seems
As if – forgive now – should you let me sit
Here by the window with your hand in mine
And look a half-hour forth on Fiesole,
Both of one mind, as married people use,
Quietly, quietly the evening through,
I might get up to-morrow to my work
Cheerful and fresh as ever. Let us try.
To-morrow, how you shall be glad for this!
Your soft hand is a woman of itself,
And mine the man's bared breast she curls inside.
Don't count the time lost, neither; you must serve
For each of the five pictures we require:
It saves a model. So! keep looking so –
My serpentining beauty, rounds on rounds!
– How could you ever prick those perfect ears,
Even to put the pearl there! oh, so sweet –
My face, my moon, my everybody's moon,
Which everybody looks on and calls his,
And, I suppose, is looked on by in turn,
While she looks – no one's: very dear, no less.
You smile? why, there's my picture ready made,
There's what we painters call our harmony!
A common greyness silvers everything, –
All in a twilight, you and I alike
– You, at the point of your first pride in me
(That's gone you know), – but I, at every point;
My youth, my hope, my art, being all toned down
To yonder sober pleasant Fiesole.
There's the bell clinking from the chapel-top;
That length of convent-wall across the way
Holds the trees safer, huddled more inside;
The last monk leaves the garden; days decrease,
And autumn grows, autumn in everything.
Eh? the whole seems to fall into a shape
As if I saw alike my work and self
And all that I was born to be and do,

A twilight-piece. Love, we are in God's hand.
How strange now, looks the life he makes us lead;
So free we seem, so fettered fast we are!
I feel he laid the fetter: let it lie!
This chamber for example – turn your head –
All that's behind us! You don't understand
Nor care to understand about my art,
But you can hear at least when people speak:
And that cartoon, the second from the door
– It is the thing, Love! so such things should be –
Behold Madonna! – I am bold to say.
I can do with my pencil what I know,
What I see, what at bottom of my heart
I wish for, if I ever wish so deep –
Do easily, too – when I say, perfectly,
I do not boast, perhaps: yourself are judge,
Who listened to the Legate's talk last week,
And just as much they used to say in France.
At any rate 't is easy, all of it!
No sketches first, no studies, that's long past:
I do what many dream of, all their lives,
– Dream? strive to do, and agonize to do,
And fail in doing. I could count twenty such
On twice your fingers, and not leave this town,
Who strive – you don't know how the others strive
To paint a little thing like that you smeared
Carelessly passing with your robes afloat, –
Yet do much less, so much less, Someone says,
(I know his name, no matter) – so much less!
Well, less is more, Lucrezia: I am judged.
There burns a truer light of God in them,
In their vexed beating stuffed and stopped-up brain,
Heart, or whate'er else, than goes on to prompt
This low-pulsed forthright craftsman's hand of mine.
Their works drop groundward, but themselves, I know,
Reach many a time a heaven that's shut to me,
Enter and take their place there sure enough,
Though they come back and cannot tell the world.
My works are nearer heaven, but I sit here.

The sudden blood of these men! at a word –
Praise them, it boils, or blame them, it boils too.
I, painting from myself and to myself,
Know what I do, am unmoved by men's blame
Or their praise either. Somebody remarks
Morello's outline there is wrongly traced,
His hue mistaken; what of that? or else,
Rightly traced and well ordered; what of that?
Speak as they please, what does the mountain care?
Ah, but a man's reach should exceed his grasp,
Or what's a heaven for? All is silver-grey
Placid and perfect with my art: the worse!
I know both what I want and what might gain,
And yet how profitless to know, to sigh
'Had I been two, another and myself,
'Our head would have o'erlooked the world!' No doubt.
Yonder's a work now, of that famous youth
The Urbinate who died five years ago.
('T is copied, George Vasari sent it me.)
Well, I can fancy how he did it all,
Pouring his soul, with kings and popes to see,
Reaching, that heaven might so replenish him,
Above and through his art – for it gives way;
That arm is wrongly put – and there again –
A fault to pardon in the drawing's lines,
Its body, so to speak: its soul is right,
He means right – that, a child may understand.
Still, what an arm! and I could alter it:
But all the play, the insight and the stretch –
Out of me, out of me! And wherefore out?
Had you enjoined them on me, given me soul,
We might have risen to Rafael, I and you!
Nay, Love, you did give all I asked, I think –
More than I merit, yes, by many times.
But had you – oh, with the same perfect brow,
And perfect eyes, and more than perfect mouth,
And the low voice my soul hears, as a bird
The fowler's pipe, and follows to the snare –
Had you, with these the same, but brought a mind!

Some women do so. Had the mouth there urged
'God and the glory! never care for gain.
'The present by the future, what is that?
'Live for fame, side by side with Agnolo!
'Rafael is waiting: up to God, all three!'
I might have done it for you. So it seems:
Perhaps not. All is as God over-rules.
Beside, incentives come from the soul's self;
The rest avail not. Why do I need you?
What wife had Rafael, or has Agnolo?
In this world, who can do a thing, will not;
And who would do it, cannot, I perceive:
Yet the will's somewhat – somewhat, too, the power –
And thus we half-men struggle. At the end,
God, I conclude, compensates, punishes.
'T is safer for me, if the award be strict,
That I am something underrated here,
Poor this long while, despised, to speak the truth.
I dared not, do you know, leave home all day,
For fear of chancing on the Paris lords.
The best is when they pass and look aside;
But they speak sometimes; I must bear it all.
Well may they speak! That Francis, that first time,
And that long festal year at Fontainebleau!
I surely then could sometimes leave the ground,
Put on the glory, Rafael's daily wear,
In that humane great monarch's golden look, –
One finger in his beard or twisted curl
Over his mouth's good mark that made the smile,
One arm about my shoulder, round my neck,
The jingle of his gold chain in my ear,
I painting proudly with his breath on me,
All his court round him, seeing with his eyes,
Such frank French eyes, and such a fire of souls
Profuse, my hand kept plying by those hearts, –
And, best of all, this, this, this face beyond,
This in the background, waiting on my work,
To crown the issue with a last reward!
A good time, was it not, my kingly days?

And had you not grown restless . . . but I know –
'T is done and past; 't was right, my instinct said;
Too live the life grew, golden and not grey,
And I'm the weak-eyed bat no sun should tempt
Out of the grange whose four walls make his world.
How could it end in any other way?
You called me, and I came home to your heart.
The triumph was – to reach and stay there; since
I reached it ere the triumph, what is lost?
Let my hands frame your face in your hair's gold,
You beautiful Lucrezia that are mine!
'Rafael did this, Andrea painted that;
'The Roman's is the better when you pray,
'But still the other's Virgin was his wife – '
Men will excuse me. I am glad to judge
Both pictures in your presence; clearer grows
My better fortune, I resolve to think.
For, do you know, Lucrezia, as God lives,
Said one day Agnolo, his very self,
To Rafael . . . I have known it all these years . . .
(When the young man was flaming out his thoughts
Upon a palace-wall for Rome to see,
Too lifted up in heart because of it)
'Friend, there's a certain sorry little scrub
'Goes up and down our Florence, none cares how,
'Who, were he set to plan and execute
'As you are, pricked on by your popes and kings,
'Would bring the sweat into that brow of yours!'
To Rafael's! – And indeed the arm is wrong.
I hardly dare . . . yet, only you to see,
Give the chalk here – quick, thus the line should go!
Ay, but the soul! he's Rafael! rub it out!
Still, all I care for, if he spoke the truth,
(What he? why, who but Michel Agnolo?
Do you forget already words like those?)
If really there was such a chance, so lost, –
Is, whether you're – not grateful – but more pleased.
Well, let me think so. And you smile indeed!
This hour has been an hour! Another smile?

If you would sit thus by me every night
I should work better, do you comprehend?
I mean that I should earn more, give you more.
See, it is settled dusk now; there's a star;
Morello's gone, the watch-lights show the wall,
The cue-owls speak the name we call them by.
Come from the window, love, – come in, at last,
Inside the melancholy little house
We built to be so gay with. God is just.
King Francis may forgive me: oft at nights
When I look up from painting, eyes tired out,
The walls become illumined, brick from brick
Distinct, instead of mortar, fierce bright gold,
That gold of his I did cement them with!
Let us but love each other. Must you go?
That Cousin here again? he waits outside?
Must see you – you, and not with me? Those loans?
More gaming debts to pay? you smiled for that?
Well, let smiles buy me! have you more to spend?
While hand and eye and something of a heart
Are left me, work's my ware, and what's it worth?
I'll pay my fancy. Only let me sit
The grey remainder of the evening out,
Idle, you call it, and muse perfectly
How I could paint, were I but back in France,
One picture, just one more – the Virgin's face,
Not yours this time! I want you at my side
To hear them – that is, Michel Agnolo –
Judge all I do and tell you of its worth.
Will you? To-morrow, satisfy your friend.
I take the subjects for his corridor,
Finish the portrait out of hand – there, there,
And throw him in another thing or two
If he demurs; the whole should prove enough
To pay for this same Cousin's freak. Beside,
What's better and what's all I care about,
Get you the thirteen scudi for the ruff!
Love, does that please you? Ah, but what does he,
The Cousin! what does he to please you more?

I am grown peaceful as old age to-night.
I regret little, I would change still less.
Since there my past life lies, why alter it?
The very wrong to Francis! – it is true
I took his coin, was tempted and complied,
And built this house and sinned, and all is said.
My father and my mother died of want.
Well, had I riches of my own? you see
How one gets rich! Let each one bear his lot.
They were born poor, lived poor, and poor they died:
And I have laboured somewhat in my time
And not been paid profusely. Some good son
Paint my two hundred pictures – let him try!
No doubt, there's something strikes a balance. Yes,
You loved me quite enough, it seems to-night.
This must suffice me here. What would one have?
In heaven, perhaps, new chances, one more chance –
Four great walls in the New Jerusalem,
Meted on each side by the angel's reed,
For Leonard, Rafael, Agnolo and me
To cover – the three first without a wife,
While I have mine! So – still they overcome
Because there's still Lucrezia, – as I choose.

Again the Cousin's whistle! Go, my Love.


**101**               A Grammarian's Funeral

*Shortly after the Revival of Learning in Europe*


Let us begin and carry up this corpse,
    Singing together.
Leave we the common crofts, the vulgar thorpes
    Each in its tether

Sleeping safe on the bosom of the plain,
 Cared-for till cock-crow:
Look out if yonder be not day again
 Rimming the rock-row!
That's the appropriate country; there, man's thought,
 Rarer, intenser,
Self-gathered for an outbreak, as it ought,
 Chafes in the censer.
Leave we the unlettered plain its herd and crop;
 Seek we sepulture
On a tall mountain, citied to the top,
 Crowded with culture!
All the peaks soar, but one the rest excels;
 Clouds overcome it;
No! yonder sparkle is the citadel's
 Circling its summit.
Thither our path lies; wind we up the heights:
 Wait ye the warning?
Our low life was the level's and the night's;
 He's for the morning.
Step to a tune, square chests, erect each head,
 'Ware the beholders!
This is our master, famous calm and dead,
 Borne on our shoulders


Sleep, crop and herd! sleep, darkling thorpe and croft,
 Safe from the weather!
He, whom we convoy to his grave aloft,
 Singing together,
He was a man born with thy face and throat,
 Lyric Apollo!
Long he lived nameless: how should spring take note
 Winter would follow?
Till lo, the little touch, and youth was gone!
 Cramped and diminished,
Moaned he, 'New measures, other feet anon!
 'My dance is finished?'

No, that's the world's way: (keep the mountain-side,
    Make for the city!)
He knew the signal, and stepped on with pride
    Over men's pity;
Left play for work, and grappled with the world
    Bent on escaping:
'What's in the scroll,' quoth he, 'thou keepest furled?
    'Show me their shaping,
'Theirs who most studied man, the bard and sage, –
    'Give!' – So, he gowned him,
Straight got by heart that book to its last page:
    Learned, we found him.
Yea, but we found him bald too, eyes like lead,
    Accents uncertain:
'Time to taste life,' another would have said,
    'Up with the curtain!'
This man said rather, 'Actual life comes next?
    'Patience a moment!
'Grant I have mastered learning's crabbed text,
    'Still there's the comment.
'Let me know all! Prate not of most or least,
    'Painful or easy!
'Even to the crumbs I'd fain eat up the feast,
    'Ay, nor feel queasy.'
Oh, such a life as he resolved to live,
    When he had learned it,
When he had gathered all books had to give!
    Sooner, he spurned it.
Image the whole, then execute the parts –
    Fancy the fabric
Quite, ere you build, ere steel strike fire from quartz,
    Ere mortar dab brick!

(Here's the town-gate reached: there's the market-place
    Gaping before us.)
Yea, this in him was the peculiar grace
    (Hearten our chorus!)

That before living he'd learn how to live –
 No end to learning:
Earn the means first – God surely will contrive
 Use for our earning.
Others mistrust and say, 'But time escapes:
 'Live now or never!'
He said, 'What's time? Leave Now for dogs and apes!
 'Man has Forever.'
Back to his book then: deeper drooped his head:
 *Calculus* racked him:
Leaden before, his eyes grew dross of lead:
 *Tussis* attacked him.
'Now, master, take a little rest!' – not he!
 (Caution redoubled,
Step two abreast, the way winds narrowly!)
 Not a whit troubled
Back to his studies, fresher than at first,
 Fierce as a dragon
He (soul-hydroptic with a sacred thirst)
 Sucked at the flagon.
Oh, if we draw a circle premature,
 Heedless of far gain,
Greedy for quick returns of profit, sure
 Bad is our bargain!
Was it not great? did not he throw on God,
 (He loves the burthen) –
God's task to make the heavenly period
 Perfect the earthen?
Did not he magnify the mind, show clear
 Just what it all meant?
He would not discount life, as fools do here,
 Paid by instalment.
He ventured neck or nothing – heaven's success
 Found, or earth's failure:
'Wilt thou trust death or not?' He answered 'Yes:
 'Hence with life's pale lure!'

That low man seeks a little thing to do,
    Sees it and does it:
This high man, with a great thing to pursue,
    Dies ere he knows it.
That low man goes on adding one to one,
    His hundred's soon hit:
This high man, aiming at a million,
    Misses an unit.
That, has the world here – should he need the next,
    Let the world mind him!
This, throws himself on God, and unperplexed
    Seeking shall find him.
So, with the throttling hands of death at strife,
    Ground he at grammar;
Still, thro' the rattle, parts of speech were rife:
    While he could stammer
He settled *Hoti's* business – let it be! –
    Properly based *Oun* –
Gave us the doctrine of the enclitic *De*,
    Dead from the waist down.
Well, here's the platform, here's the proper place:
    Hail to your purlieus,
All ye highfliers of the feathered race,
    Swallows and curlews!
Here's the top-peak; the multitude below
    Live, for they can, there:
This man decided not to Live but Know –
    Bury this man there?
Here – here's his place, where meteors shoot, clouds form,
    Lightnings are loosened,
Stars come and go! Let joy break with the storm,
    Peace let the dew send!
Lofty designs must close in like effects:
    Loftily lying,
Leave him – still loftier than the world suspects,
    Living and dying.

## 102  Two in the Campagna

### I

I wonder do you feel to-day
   As I have felt since, hand in hand,
We sat down on the grass, to stray
   In spirit better through the land,
This morn of Rome and May?

### II

For me, I touched a thought, I know,
   Has tantalized me many times,
(Like turns of thread the spiders throw
   Mocking across our path) for rhymes
To catch at and let go.

### III

Help me to hold it! First it left
   The yellowing fennel, run to seed
There, branching from the brickwork's cleft,
   Some old tomb's ruin: yonder weed
Took up the floating weft,

### IV

Where one small orange cup amassed
   Five beetles, – blind and green they grope
Among the honey-meal: and last,
   Everywhere on the grassy slope
I traced it. Hold it fast!

### V

The champaign with its endless fleece
   Of feathery grasses everywhere!
Silence and passion, joy and peace,
   An everlasting wash of air –
Rome's ghost since her decease.

### VI

Such life here, through such lengths of hours,
　　Such miracles performed in play,
Such primal naked forms of flowers,
　　Such letting nature have her way
While heaven looks from its towers!

### VII

How say you? Let us, O my dove,
　　Let us be unashamed of soul,
As earth lies bare to heaven above!
　　How is it under our control
To love or not to love?

### VIII

I would that you were all to me,
　　You that are just so much, no more.
Nor yours nor mine, nor slave nor free!
　　Where does the fault lie? What the core
O' the wound, since wound must be?

### IX

I would I could adopt your will,
　　See with your eyes, and set my heart
Beating by yours, and drink my fill
　　At your soul's springs, – your part my part
In life, for good and ill.

### X

No. I yearn upward, touch you close,
　　Then stand away. I kiss your cheek,
Catch your soul's warmth, – I pluck the rose
　　And love it more than tongue can speak –
Then the good minute goes.

### XI

Already how am I so far
   Out of that minute? Must I go
Still like the thistle-ball, no bar,
   Onward, whenever light winds blow,
Fixed by no friendly star?

### XII

Just when I seemed about to learn!
   Where is the thread now? Off again!
The old trick! Only I discern –
   Infinite passion, and the pain
Of finite hearts that yearn.

103

# Youth and Art

### I

It once might have been, once only:
   We lodged in a street together,
You, a sparrow on the housetop lonely,
   I, a lone she-bird of his feather.

### II

Your trade was with sticks and clay,
   You thumbed, thrust, patted and polished,
Then laughed 'They will see some day
   'Smith made, and Gibson demolished.'

### III

My business was song, song, song;
   I chirped, cheeped, trilled and twittered,
'Kate Brown's on the boards ere long,
   'And Grisi's existence embittered!'

IV

I earned no more by a warble
　　Than you by a sketch in plaster;
You wanted a piece of marble,
　　I needed a music-master.


V

We studied hard in our styles,
　　Chipped each at a crust like Hindoos,
For air looked out on the tiles,
　　For fun watched each other's windows.


VI

You lounged, like a boy of the South,
　　Cap and blouse – nay, a bit of beard too;
Or you got it, rubbing your mouth
　　With fingers the clay adhered to.


VII

And I – soon managed to find
　　Weak points in the flower-fence facing,
Was forced to put up a blind
　　And be safe in my corset-lacing.


VIII

No harm! It was not my fault
　　If you never turned your eye's tail up
As I shook upon *E in alt*,
　　Or ran the chromatic scale up:


IX

For spring bade the sparrows pair,
　　And the boys and girls gave guesses,
And stalls in our street looked rare
　　With bulrush and watercresses.

X

Why did not you pinch a flower
   In a pellet of clay and fling it?
Why did not I put a power
   Of thanks in a look, or sing it?


XI

I did look, sharp as a lynx,
   (And yet the memory rankles)
When models arrived, some minx
   Tripped up-stairs, she and her ankles.


XII

But I think I gave you as good!
   'That foreign fellow, – who can know
'How she pays, in a playful mood,
   'For his tuning her that piano?'


XIII

Could you say so, and never say
   'Suppose we join hands and fortunes,
'And I fetch her from over the way,
   'Her, piano, and long tunes and short tunes?'


XIV

No, no: you would not be rash,
   Nor I rasher and something over:
You've to settle yet Gibson's hash,
   And Grisi yet lives in clover.


XV

But you meet the Prince at the Board,
   I'm queen myself at *bals-paré*,
I've married a rich old lord,
   And you're dubbed knight and an R.A.

XVI

Each life unfulfilled, you see;
  It hangs still, patchy and scrappy:
We have not sighed deep, laughed free,
  Starved, feasted, despaired, – been happy.

XVII

And nobody calls you a dunce,
  And people suppose me clever:
This could but have happened once,
  And we missed it, lost it for ever.


104

# Caliban upon Setebos; or, Natural Theology in the Island

*'Thou thoughtest that I was altogether such
a one as thyself.'*

['Will sprawl, now that the heat of day is best,
Flat on his belly in the pit's much mire,
With elbows wide, fists clenched to prop his chin.
And, while he kicks both feet in the cool slush,
And feels about his spine small eft-things course,
Run in and out each arm, and make him laugh:
And while above his head a pompion-plant,
Coating the cave-top as a brow its eye,
Creeps down to touch and tickle hair and beard,
And now a flower drops with a bee inside,
And now a fruit to snap at, catch and crunch, –
He looks out o'er yon sea which sunbeams cross
And recross till they weave a spider-web
(Meshes of fire, some great fish breaks at times)
And talks to his own self, howe'er he please,
Touching that other, whom his dam called God.
Because to talk about Him, vexes – ha,
Could He but know! and time to vex is now,
When talk is safer than in winter-time.

Moreover Prosper and Miranda sleep
In confidence he drudges at their task,
And it is good to cheat the pair, and gibe,
Letting the rank tongue blossom into speech.]

Setebos, Setebos, and Setebos!
'Thinketh, He dwelleth i' the cold o' the moon.

'Thinketh He made it, with the sun to match,
But not the stars; the stars came otherwise;
Only made clouds, winds, meteors, such as that:
Also this isle, what lives and grows thereon,
And snaky sea which rounds and ends the same.

'Thinketh, it came of being ill at ease:
He hated that He cannot change His cold,
Nor cure its ache. 'Hath spied an icy fish
That longed to 'scape the rock-stream where she lived,
And thaw herself within the lukewarm brine
O' the lazy sea her stream thrusts far amid,
A crystal spike 'twixt two warm walls of wave;
Only, she ever sickened, found repulse
At the other kind of water, not her life,
(Green-dense and dim-delicious, bred o' the sun)
Flounced back from bliss she was not born to breathe,
And in her old bounds buried her despair,
Hating and loving warmth alike: so He.

'Thinketh, He made thereat the sun, this isle,
Trees and the fowls here, beast and creeping thing.
Yon otter, sleek-wet, black, lithe as a leech;
Yon auk, one fire-eye in a ball of foam,
That floats and feeds; a certain badger brown
He hath watched hunt with that slant white-wedge eye
By moonlight; and the pie with the long tongue
That pricks deep into oakwarts for a worm,
And says a plain word when she finds her prize,
But will not eat the ants; the ants themselves

That build a wall of seeds and settled stalks
About their hole – He made all these and more,
Made all we see, and us, in spite: how else?
He could not, Himself, make a second self
To be His mate; as well have made Himself:
He would not make what he mislikes or slights,
An eyesore to Him, or not worth His pains:
But did, in envy, listlessness or sport,
Make what Himself would fain, in a manner, be –
Weaker in most points, stronger in a few,
Worthy, and yet mere playthings all the while,
Things He admires and mocks too, – that is it.
Because, so brave, so better though they be,
It nothing skills if He begin to plague.
Look now, I melt a gourd-fruit into mash,
Add honeycomb and pods, I have perceived,
Which bite like finches when they bill and kiss, –
Then, when froth rises bladdery, drink up all,
Quick, quick, till maggots scamper through my brain;
Last, throw me on my back i' the seeded thyme,
And wanton, wishing I were born a bird.
Put case, unable to be what I wish,
I yet could make a live bird out of clay:
Would not I take clay, pinch my Caliban
Able to fly? – for, there, see, he hath wings,
And great comb like the hoopoe's to admire,
And there, a sting to do his foes offence,
There, and I will that he begin to live,
Fly to yon rock-top, nip me off the horns
Of grigs high up that make the merry din,
Saucy through their veined wings, and mind me not.
In which feat, if his leg snapped, brittle clay,
And he lay stupid-like, – why, I should laugh;
And if he, spying me, should fall to weep,
Beseech me to be good, repair his wrong,
Bid his poor leg smart less or grow again, –
Well, as the chance were, this might take or else
Not take my fancy: I might hear his cry,
And give the mankin three sound legs for one,

Or pluck the other off, leave him like an egg,
And lessoned he was mine and merely clay.
Were this no pleasure, lying in the thyme,
Drinking the mash, with brain become alive,
Making and marring clay at will? So He.

'Thinketh, such shows nor right nor wrong in Him,
Nor kind, nor cruel: He is strong and Lord.
'Am strong myself compared to yonder crabs
That march now from the mountain to the sea,
'Let twenty pass, and stone the twenty-first,
Loving not, hating not, just choosing so.
'Say, the first straggler that boasts purple spots
Shall join the file, one pincer twisted off;
'Say, this bruised fellow shall receive a worm,
And two worms he whose nippers end in red;
As it likes me each time, I do: so He.

Well then, 'supposeth He is good i' the main,
Placable if His mind and ways were guessed,
But rougher than His handiwork, be sure!
Oh, He hath made things worthier than Himself,
And envieth that, so helped, such things do more
Than He who made them! What consoles but this?
That they, unless through Him, do nought at all,
And must submit: what other use in things?
'Hath cut a pipe of pithless elder-joint
That, blown through, gives exact the scream o' the jay
When from her wing you twitch the feathers blue:
Sound this, and little birds that hate the jay
Flock within stone's throw, glad their foe is hurt:
Put case such pipe could prattle and boast forsooth
'I catch the birds, I am the crafty thing,
'I make the cry my maker cannot make
'With his great round mouth; he must blow through mine!'
Would not I smash it with my foot? So He.

But wherefore rough, why cold and ill at ease?
Aha, that is a question! Ask, for that,
What knows, – the something over Setebos
That made Him, or He, may be, found and fought,
Worsted, drove off and did to nothing, perchance.
There may be something quiet o'er His head,
Out of His reach, that feels nor joy nor grief,
Since both derive from weakness in some way.
I joy because the quails come; would not joy
Could I bring quails here when I have a mind:
This Quiet, all it hath a mind to, doth.
'Esteemeth stars the outposts of its couch,
But never spends much thought nor care that way.
It may look up, work up, – the worse for those
It works on! 'Careth but for Setebos
The many-handed as a cuttle-fish,
Who, making Himself feared through what He does,
Looks up, first, and perceives he cannot soar
To what is quiet and hath happy life;
Next looks down here, and out of very spite
Makes this a bauble-world to ape yon real,
These good things to match those as hips do grapes.
'T is solace making baubles, ay, and sport.
Himself peeped late, eyed Prosper at his books
Careless and lofty, lord now of the isle:
Vexed, 'stitched a book of broad leaves, arrow-shaped,
Wrote thereon, he knows what, prodigious words;
Has peeled a wand and called it by a name;
Weareth at whiles for an enchanter's robe
The eyed skin of a supple oncelot;
And hath an ounce sleeker than youngling mole,
A four-legged serpent he makes cower and couch,
Now snarl, now hold its breath and mind his eye,
And saith she is Miranda and my wife:
'Keeps for his Ariel a tall pouch-bill crane
He bids go wade for fish and straight disgorge;
Also a sea-beast, lumpish, which he snared,
Blinded the eyes of, and brought somewhat tame,

And split its toe-webs, and now pens the drudge
In a hole o' the rock and calls him Caliban;
A bitter heart that bides its time and bites.
'Plays thus at being Prosper in a way,
Taketh his mirth with make-believes: so He.

His dam held that the Quiet made all things
Which Setebos vexed only: 'holds not so.
Who made them weak, meant weakness He might vex.
Had He meant other, while His hand was in,
Why not make horny eyes no thorn could prick,
Or plate my scalp with bone against the snow,
Or overscale my flesh 'neath joint and joint,
Like an orc's armour? Ay, – so spoil His sport!
He is the One now: only He doth all.

'Saith, He may like, perchance, what profits Him.
Ay, himself loves what does him good; but why?
'Gets good no otherwise. This blinded beast
Loves whoso places flesh-meat on his nose,
But, had he eyes, would want no help, but hate
Or love, just as it liked him: He hath eyes.
Also it pleaseth Setebos to work,
Use all His hands, and exercise much craft,
By no means for the love of what is worked.
'Tasteth, himself, no finer good i' the world
When all goes right, in this safe summer-time,
And he wants little, hungers, aches not much,
Than trying what to do with wit and strength.
'Falls to make something: 'piled yon pile of turfs,
And squared and stuck there squares of soft white chalk,
And, with a fish-tooth, scratched a moon on each,
And set up endwise certain spikes of tree,
And crowned the whole with a sloth's skull a-top,
Found dead i' the woods, too hard for one to kill.
No use at all i' the work, for work's sole sake;
'Shall some day knock it down again: so He.

'Saith He is terrible: watch His feats in proof!
One hurricane will spoil six good months' hope.
He hath a spite against me, that I know,
Just as He favours Prosper, who knows why?
So it is, all the same, as well I find.
'Wove wattles half the winter, fenced them firm
With stone and stake to stop she-tortoises
Crawling to lay their eggs here: well, one wave,
Feeling the foot of Him upon its neck,
Gaped as a snake does, lolled out its large tongue,
And licked the whole labour flat: so much for spite.
'Saw a ball flame down late (yonder it lies)
Where, half an hour before, I slept i' the shade:
Often they scatter sparkles: there is force!
'Dug up a newt He may have envied once
And turned to stone, shut up inside a stone.
Please Him and hinder this? – What Prosper does?
Aha, if He would tell me how! Not He!
There is the sport: discover how or die!
All need not die, for of the things o' the isle
Some flee afar, some dive, some run up trees;
Those at His mercy, – why, they please Him most
When ... when ... well, never try the same way twice!
Repeat what act has pleased, He may grow wroth.
You must not know His ways, and play Him off,
Sure of the issue. 'Doth the like himself:
'Spareth a squirrel that it nothing fears
But steals the nut from underneath my thumb,
And when I threat, bites stoutly in defence:
'Spareth an urchin that contrariwise,
Curls up into a ball, pretending death
For fright at my approach: the two ways please.
But what would move my choler more than this,
That either creature counted on its life
To-morrow and next day and all days to come,
Saying, forsooth, in the inmost of its heart,
'Because he did so yesterday with me,

'And otherwise with such another brute,
'So must he do henceforth and always.' – Ay?
Would teach the reasoning couple what 'must' means!
'Doth as he likes, or wherefore Lord? So He.

'Conceiveth all things will continue thus,
And we shall have to live in fear of Him
So long as He lives, keeps His strength: no change,
If He have done His best, make no new world
To please Him more, so leave off watching this, –
If He surprise not even the Quiet's self
Some strange day, – or, suppose, grow into it
As grubs grow butterflies: else, here are we,
And there is He, and nowhere help at all.

'Believeth with the life, the pain shall stop.
His dam held different, that after death
He both plagued enemies and feasted friends:
Idly! He doth His worst in this our life,
Giving just respite lest we die through pain,
Saving last pain for worst, – with which, an end.
Meanwhile, the best way to escape His ire
Is, not to seem too happy. 'Sees, himself,
Yonder two flies, with purple films and pink,
Bask on the pompion-bell above: kills both.
'Sees two black painful beetles roll their ball
On head and tail as if to save their lives:
Moves them the stick away they strive to clear.

Even so, 'would have Him misconceive, suppose
This Caliban strives hard and ails no less,
And always, above all else, envies Him;
Wherefore he mainly dances on dark nights,
Moans in the sun, gets under holes to laugh,
And never speaks his mind save housed as now:
Outside, 'groans, curses. If He caught me here,
O'erheard this speech, and asked 'What chucklest at?'

'Would, to appease Him, cut a finger off,
Or of my three kid yearlings burn the best,
Or let the toothsome apples rot on tree,
Or push my tame beast for the orc to taste:
While myself lit a fire, and made a song
And sung it, '*What I hate, be consecrate*
'*To celebrate Thee and Thy state, no mate*
'*For Thee; what see for envy in poor me?*'
Hoping the while, since evils sometimes mend,
Warts rub away and sores are cured with slime,
That some strange day, will either the Quiet catch
And conquer Setebos, or likelier He
Decrepit may doze, doze, as good as die.

[What, what? A curtain o'er the world at once!
Crickets stop hissing; not a bird – or, yes,
There scuds His raven that has told Him all!
It was fool's play, this prattling! Ha! The wind
Shoulders the pillared dust, death's house o' the move,
And fast invading fires begin! White blaze –
A tree's head snaps – and there, there, there, there, there,
His thunder follows! Fool to gibe at Him!
Lo! 'Lieth flat and loveth Setebos!
'Maketh his teeth meet through his upper lip,
Will let those quails fly, will not eat this month
One little mess of whelks, so he may 'scape!]


105        Never the Time and the Place

Never the time and the place
    And the loved one all together!
This path – how soft to pace!
    This May – what magic weather!
Where is the loved one's face?
In a dream that loved one's face meets mine,
    But the house is narrow, the place is bleak

Where, outside, rain and wind combine
  With a furtive ear, if I strive to speak,
  With a hostile eye at my flushing cheek,
With a malice that marks each word, each sign!
O enemy sly and serpentine,
  Uncoil thee from the waking man!
    Do I hold the Past
    Thus firm and fast
  Yet doubt if the Future hold I can?
This path so soft to pace shall lead
Thro' the magic of May to herself indeed!
Or narrow if needs the house must be,
Outside are the storms and strangers: we –
Oh, close, safe, warm sleep I and she,
– I and she!


106            Pan and Luna

*Si credere dignum est. – Georgic. iii. 390*


O worthy of belief I hold it was,
Virgil, your legend in those strange three lines!
No question, that adventure came to pass
One black night in Arcadia: yes, the pines,
Mountains and valleys mingling made one mass
Of black with void black heaven: the earth's confines,
The sky's embrace, – below, above, around,
All hardened into black without a bound.

Fill up a swart stone chalice to the brim
With fresh-squeezed yet fast-thickening poppy-juice:
See how the sluggish jelly, late a-swim,
Turns marble to the touch of who would loose
The solid smooth, grown jet from rim to rim,

---

106. *Si credere* ... 'If it is worthy of belief', from the third of Virgil's *Georgics*.

By turning round the bowl! So night can fuse
Earth with her all-comprising sky. No less,
Light, the least spark, shows air and emptiness.

And thus it proved when – diving into space,
Stript of all vapour, from each web of mist
Utterly film-free – entered on her race
The naked Moon, full-orbed antagonist
Of night and dark, night's dowry: peak to base,
Upstarted mountains, and each valley, kissed
To sudden life, lay silver-bright: in air
Flew she revealed, Maid-Moon with limbs all bare.

Still as she fled, each depth – where refuge seemed –
Opening a lone pale chamber, left distinct
Those limbs: mid still-retreating blue, she teemed
Herself with whiteness, – virginal, uncinct
By any halo save what finely gleamed
To outline not disguise her: heaven was linked
In one accord with earth to quaff the joy,
Drain beauty to the dregs without alloy.

Whereof she grew aware. What help? When, lo,
A succourable cloud with sleep lay dense:
Some pine-tree-top had caught it sailing slow,
And tethered for a prize: in evidence
Captive lay fleece on fleece of piled-up snow
Drowsily patient: flake-heaped how or whence,
The structure of that succourable cloud,
What matter? Shamed she plunged into its shroud.

Orbed – so the woman-figure poets call
Because of rounds on rounds – that apple-shaped
Head which its hair binds close into a ball
Each side the curving ears – that pure undraped
Pout of the sister paps – that ... Once for all,
Say – her consummate circle thus escaped
With its innumerous circlets, sank absorbed,
Safe in the cloud – O naked Moon full-orbed!

But what means this? The downy swathes combine,
Conglobe, the smothery coy-caressing stuff
Curdles about her! Vain each twist and twine
Those lithe limbs try, encroached on by a fluff
Fitting as close as fits the dented spine
Its flexile ivory outside-flesh: enough!
The plumy drifts contract, condense, constringe,
Till she is swallowed by the feathery springe.

As when a pearl slips lost in the thin foam
Churned on a sea-shore, and, o'er-frothed, conceits
Herself safe-housed in Amphitrite's dome, –
If, through the bladdery wave-worked yeast, she meets
What most she loathes and leaps from, – elf from gnome
No gladlier, – finds that safest of retreats
Bubble about a treacherous hand wide ope
To grasp her – (divers who pick pearls so grope) –

So lay this Maid-Moon clasped around and caught
By rough red Pan, the god of all that tract:
He it was schemed the snare thus subtly wrought
With simulated earth-breath, – wool-tufts packed
Into a billowy wrappage. Sheep far-sought
For spotless shearings yield such: take the fact
As learned Virgil gives it, – how the breed
Whitens itself for ever: yes, indeed!

If one forefather ram, though pure as chalk
From tinge on fleece, should still display a tongue
Black 'neath the beast's moist palate, prompt men baulk
The propagating plague: he gets no young:
They rather slay him, – sell his hide to caulk
Ships with, first steeped in pitch, – nor hands are wrung
In sorrow for his fate: protected thus,
The purity we love is gained for us.

So did Girl-moon, by just her attribute
Of unmatched modesty betrayed, lie trapped,
Bruised to the breast of Pan, half-god half-brute,

Raked by his bristly boar-sward while he lapped
– Never say, kissed her! that were to pollute
Love's language – which moreover proves unapt
To tell how she recoiled – as who finds thorns
Where she sought flowers – when, feeling, she touched –
    horns!

Then – does the legend say? – first moon-eclipse
Happened, first swooning-fit which puzzled sore
The early sages? Is that why she dips
Into the dark, a minute and no more,
Only so long as serves her while she rips
The cloud's womb through and, faultless as before,
Pursues her way? No lesson for a maid
Left she, a maid herself thus trapped, betrayed?

Ha, Virgil? Tell the rest, you! 'To the deep
Of his domain the wildwood, Pan forthwith
Called her, and so she followed' – in her sleep,
Surely? – 'by no means spurning him.' The myth
Explain who may! Let all else go, I keep
– As of a ruin just a monolith –
Thus much, one verse of five words, each a boon:
Arcadia, night, a cloud, Pan, and the moon.

107                    Spring Song

Dance, yellows and whites and reds, –
Lead your gay orgy, leaves, stalks, heads
Astir with the wind in the tulip-beds!

There's sunshine; scarcely a wind at all
Disturbs starved grass and daisies small
On a certain mound by a churchyard wall.

Daisies and grass be my heart's bedfellows
On the mound wind spares and sunshine mellows:
Dance you, reds and whites and yellows!


108                          Prologue

                          [to *Asolando*]


'The Poet's age is sad: for why?
    In youth, the natural world could show
No common object but his eye
    At once involved with alien glow –
His own soul's iris-bow.

'And now a flower is just a flower:
    Man, bird, beast are but beast, bird, man –
Simply themselves, uncinct by dower
    Of dyes which, when life's day began,
Round each in glory ran.'

Friend, did you need an optic glass,
    Which were your choice? A lens to drape
In ruby, emerald, chrysopras,
    Each object – or reveal its shape
Clear outlined, past escape,

The naked very thing? – so clear
    That, when you had the chance to gaze,
You found its inmost self appear
    Through outer seeming – truth ablaze,
Not falsehood's fancy-haze?

How many a year, my Asolo,
    Since – one step just from sea to land –
I found you, loved yet feared you so –
    For natural objects seemed to stand
Palpably fire-clothed! No –

No mastery of mine o'er these!
  Terror with beauty, like the Bush
Burning but unconsumed. Bend knees,
  Drop eyes to earthward! Language? Tush!
Silence 't is awe decrees.

And now? The lambent flame is – where?
  Lost from the naked world: earth, sky,
Hill, vale, tree, flower, – Italia's rare
  O'er-running beauty crowds the eye –
But flame? The Bush is bare.

Hill, vale, tree, flower – they stand distinct,
  Nature to know and name. What then?
A Voice spoke thence which straight unlinked
  Fancy from fact: see, all's in ken:
Has once my eyelid winked?

No, for the purged ear apprehends
  Earth's import, not the eye late dazed:
The Voice said 'Call my works thy friends!
  At Nature dost thou shrink amazed?
God is it who transcends.'

*Asolo: Sept. 6, 1889*


109               Dubiety

I will be happy if but for once:
  Only help me, Autumn weather,
Me and my cares to screen, ensconce
  In luxury's sofa-lap of leather!

Sleep? Nay, comfort – with just a cloud
  Suffusing day too clear and bright:
Eve's essence, the single drop allowed
  To sully, like milk, Noon's water-white.

Let gauziness shade, not shroud, – adjust,
   Dim and not deaden, – somehow sheathe
Aught sharp in the rough world's busy thrust,
   If it reach me through dreaming's vapour-wreath.

Be life so, all things ever the same!
   For, what has disarmed the world? Outside,
Quiet and peace: inside, nor blame
   Nor want, nor wish whate'er betide.

What is it like that has happened before?
   A dream? No dream, more real by much.
A vision? But fanciful days of yore
   Brought many: mere musing seems not such.

Perhaps but a memory, after all!
   – Of what came once when a woman leant
To feel for my brow where her kiss might fall.
   Truth ever, truth only the excellent!

110                    Speculative

Others may need new life in Heaven –
   Man, Nature, Art – made new, assume!
Man with new mind old sense to leaven,
   Nature – new light to clear old gloom,
Art that breaks bounds, gets soaring-room.

I shall pray: 'Fugitive as precious –
   Minutes which passed, – return, remain!
Let earth's old life once more enmesh us,
   You with old pleasure, me – old pain,
So we but meet nor part again!'

# ELIZA COOK

1812–89

111          On Seeing a Bird-Catcher

Health in his rags, Content upon his face,
He goes th' enslaver of a feathered race:
And cunning snares, warm hearts, like warblers, take;
The one to sing for sport, the other, break.

# EDWARD LEAR
## 1812–88

112  There was an Old Man with a beard,
Who said, 'It is just as I feared! –
  Two Owls and a Hen,
  Four Larks and a Wren,
Have all built their nests in my beard!'

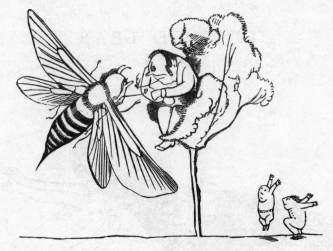

113   There was an Old Man in a tree,
      Who was horribly bored by a bee;
          When they said, 'Does it buzz?'
          He replied, 'Yes, it does!
      It's a regular brute of a bee!'

114   There was a Young Lady of Tyre,
      Who swept the loud chords of a lyre;
          At the sound of each sweep
          She enraptured the deep,
      And enchanted the city of Tyre.

115      There was an Old Man who said, 'Hush!
I perceive a young bird in this bush!'
    When they said, 'Is it small?'
    He replied, 'Not at all!
It is four times as big as the bush!'

116      There was an Old Man of Cape Horn,
Who wished he had never been born;
    So he sat on a chair,
    Till he died of despair,
That dolorous Man of Cape Horn.

117       There was an Old Person of Cromer,
Who stood on one leg to read Homer;
    When he found he grew stiff,
    He jumped over the cliff,
Which concluded that Person of Cromer.

118       There was an Old Person of Troy,
Whose drink was warm brandy and soy,
    Which he took with a spoon,
    By the light of the moon,
In sight of the city of Troy.

119   There was an Old Person of Tring,
Who embellished his nose with a ring;
    He gazed at the moon
    Every evening in June,
That ecstatic Old Person of Tring.

120   There was an Old Man on some rocks,
Who shut his wife up in a box;
    When she said, 'Let me out!'
    He exclaimed, 'Without doubt,
You will pass all your life in that box.'

121 ## The Owl and the Pussy-Cat

### I

The Owl and the Pussy-Cat went to sea
  In a beautiful pea-green boat,
They took some honey, and plenty of money,
  Wrapped up in a five-pound note.
The Owl looked up to the stars above,
  And sang to a small guitar,
'O lovely Pussy! O Pussy, my love,
  'What a beautiful Pussy you are,
      'You are,
      'You are!
  'What a beautiful Pussy you are!'

### II

Pussy said to the Owl, 'You elegant fowl!
  'How charmingly sweet you sing!
'O let us be married! too long we have tarried:
  'But what shall we do for a ring?'
They sailed away for a year and a day,
  To the land where the Bong-tree grows,
And there in a wood a Piggy-wig stood,
  With a ring at the end of his nose,
      His nose,
      His nose,
  With a ring at the end of his nose.

### III

'Dear Pig, are you willing to sell for one shilling
  'Your ring?' Said the Piggy, 'I will.'
So they took it away, and were married next day
  By the Turkey who lives on the hill.
They dined on mince, and slices of quince,
  Which they ate with a runcible spoon;
And hand in hand, on the edge of the sand,
  They danced by the light of the moon,

The moon,
The moon,
They danced by the light of the moon.


122   The Courtship of the Yonghy-Bonghy-Bò

I

On the Coast of Coromandel
    Where the early pumpkins blow,
  In the middle of the woods
  Lived the Yonghy-Bonghy-Bò.
Two old chairs, and half a candle, –
One old jug without a handle, –
    These were all his worldly goods:
    In the middle of the woods,
    These were all the worldly goods,
Of the Yonghy-Bonghy-Bò,
Of the Yonghy-Bonghy-Bò.


II

Once, among the Bong-trees walking
  Where the early pumpkins blow,
    To a little heap of stones
    Came the Yonghy-Bonghy-Bò.
There he heard a Lady talking,
To some milk-white Hens of Dorking, –
    ''Tis the Lady Jingly Jones!
    'On that little heap of stones
    'Sits the Lady Jingly Jones!'
  Said the Yonghy-Bonghy-Bò,
  Said the Yonghy-Bonghy-Bò.


III

'Lady Jingly! Lady Jingly!
  'Sitting where the pumpkins blow,
    'Will you come and be my wife?'
  Said the Yonghy-Bonghy-Bò.

'I am tired of living singly, –
'On this coast so wild and shingly, –
   'I'm a-weary of my life;
   'If you'll come and be my wife,
   'Quite serene would be my life!' –
Said the Yonghy-Bonghy-Bò,
Said the Yonghy-Bonghy-Bò.


IV

'On this Coast of Coromandel,
   'Shrimps and watercresses grow,
     'Prawns are plentiful and cheap,'
Said the Yonghy-Bonghy-Bò.
'You shall have my chairs and candle,
'And my jug without a handle! –
   'Gaze upon the rolling deep
   ('Fish is plentiful and cheap):
   'As the sea, my love is deep!'
Said the Yonghy-Bonghy-Bò,
Said the Yonghy-Bonghy-Bò.


V

Lady Jingly answered sadly,
   And her tears began to flow, –
     'Your proposal comes too late,
   'Mr. Yonghy-Bonghy-Bò!
'I would be your wife most gladly!'
(Here she twirled her fingers madly)
   'But in England I've a mate!
   'Yes! you've asked me far too late,
   'For in England I've a mate,
'Mr. Yonghy-Bonghy-Bò!
'Mr. Yonghy-Bonghy-Bò!


VI

'Mr. Jones – (his name is Handel, –
'Handel Jones, Esquire, & Co.)
   'Dorking fowls delights to send,
'Mr. Yonghy-Bonghy-Bò!

'Keep, oh! keep your chairs and candle,
'And your jug without a handle, –
 'I can merely be your friend!
 ' – Should my Jones more Dorkings send,
 'I will give you three, my friend!
'Mr. Yonghy-Bonghy-Bò!
'Mr. Yonghy-Bonghy-Bò!

### VII

'Though you've such a tiny body,
 'And your head so large doth grow, –
  'Though your hat may blow away,
 'Mr. Yonghy-Bonghy-Bò!
'Though you're such a Hoddy Doddy –
'Yet I wish that I could modi-
  'fy the words I needs must say!
  'Will you please to go away?
  'That is all I have to say –
'Mr. Yonghy-Bonghy-Bò!
'Mr. Yonghy-Bonghy-Bò!'

### VIII

Down the slippery slopes of Myrtle,
 Where the early pumpkins blow,
  To the calm and silent sea
 Fled the Yonghy-Bonghy-Bò.
There, beyond the Bay of Gurtle,
Lay a large and lively Turtle; –
  'You're the Cove,' he said, 'for me;
  'On your back beyond the sea,
  'Turtle, you shall carry me!'
Said the Yonghy-Bonghy-Bò,
Said the Yonghy-Bonghy-Bò.

### IX

Through the silent-roaring ocean
 Did the Turtle swiftly go;
  Holding fast upon his shell
 Rode the Yonghy-Bonghy-Bò.

With a sad primæval motion
Towards the sunset isles of Boshen
    Still the Turtle bore him well.
    Holding fast upon his shell,
    'Lady Jingly Jones, farewell!'
Sang the Yonghy-Bonghy-Bò,
Sang the Yonghy-Bonghy-Bò.


X

From the Coast of Coromandel,
   Did that Lady never go;
     On that heap of stones she mourns
   For the Yonghy-Bonghy-Bò.
On that Coast of Coromandel,
In his jug without a handle,
     Still she weeps, and daily moans;
     On that little heap of stones
     To her Dorking Hens she moans,
For the Yonghy-Bonghy-Bò,
For the Yonghy-Bonghy-Bò.

# W. E. AYTOUN
## 1813–65

La Mort D'Arthur

*Not* by *Alfred Tennyson*

Slowly, as one who bears a mortal hurt,
Through which the fountain of his life runs dry,
Crept good King Arthur down unto the lake.
A roughening wind was bringing in the waves
With cold, dull plash and plunging to the shore,
And a great bank of clouds came sailing up
Athwart the aspect of the gibbous moon,
Leaving no glimpse save starlight, as he sank,
With a short stagger, senseless on the stones.

No man yet knows how long he lay in swound;
But long enough it was to let the rust
Lick half the surface of his polished shield;
For it was made by far inferior hands
Than forged his helm, his breastplate, and his greaves,
Whereon no canker lighted, for they bore
The magic stamp of **Mechi's Silver Steel.**

# CHARLOTTE BRONTË
## 1816–55

124               Diving

Look into thought and say what dost thou see;
  Dive, be not fearful how dark the waves flow;
Sing through the surge, and bring pearls up to me;
  Deeper, ay, deeper; the fairest lie low.

'I have dived, I have sought them, but none have I found;
  In the gloom that closed o'er me no form floated by;
As I sank through the void depths, so black and profound,
  How dim died the sun and how far hung the sky!

'What had I given to hear the soft sweep
  Of a breeze bearing life through that vast realm of death!
Thoughts were untroubled and dreams were asleep:
  The spirit lay dreadless and hopeless beneath.'


125       On the Death of Emily Jane Brontë

My darling, thou wilt never know
The grinding agony of woe
  That we have borne for thee.
Thus may we consolation tear
E'en from the depth of our despair
  And wasting misery.

The nightly anguish thou art spared
When all the crushing truth is bared
  To the awakening mind,

When the galled heart is pierced with grief,
Till wildly it implores relief,
  But small relief can find.

Nor know'st thou what it is to lie
Looking forth with streaming eye
  On life's lone wilderness.
'Weary, weary, dark and drear,
How shall I the journey bear,
  The burden and distress?'

Then since thou art spared such pain
We will not wish thee here again;
  He that lives must mourn.
God help us through our misery
And give us rest and joy with thee
  When we reach our bourne!

                    *December 24, 1848*

# SHIRLEY BROOKS

## 1816–74

126      The Mud-Fish

### BY AN INDIGNANT TORY FOOTMAN

'The Mud-fish at the Crystal Palace escaped from his tank, and
could not be found. The other day he was discovered in the marble
canal, under a fountain, where he had been amusing himself by
eating the gold-fish, and doubling his size.'

> In Sir Joseph's marble dishes
> Cuts about them golden Fishes,
> All their life in splendour passes,
> Them's you see, Us Hupper Classes.
>
> From his tank, while folks is sleeping,
> Comes the nasty Mud-fish leaping,
> With no end of spite to-ward us,
> That's, you see, the Lower Horders.
>
> Up and down our basin scouring,
> All his betters he's devouring,
> Gorging till he gets enormous,
> Just as would them low Reformers.
>
> Moral struck me when I seed 'em:
> Don't give low folks too much freedom:
> Gold fish lives on this here basis,
> *Keep the Mud-fish in their places.*

# EMILY BRONTË
## 1818–48

127              Remembrance

Cold in the earth – and the deep snow piled above thee,
Far, far, removed, cold in the dreary grave!
Have I forgot, my only Love, to love thee,
Severed at last by Time's all-severing wave?

Now, when alone, do my thoughts no longer hover
Over the mountains, on that northern shore,
Resting their wings where heath and fern-leaves cover
Thy noble heart for ever, ever more?

Cold in the earth – and fifteen wild Decembers,
From those brown hills, have melted into spring:
Faithful, indeed, is the spirit that remembers
After such years of change and suffering!

Sweet Love of youth, forgive, if I forget thee,
While the world's tide is bearing me along;
Other desires and other hopes beset me,
Hopes which obscure, but cannot do thee wrong!

No later light has lightened up my heaven,
No second morn has ever shone for me;
All my life's bliss from thy dear life was given,
All my life's bliss is in the grave with thee.

But, when the days of golden dreams had perished,
And even Despair was powerless to destroy;
Then did I learn how existence could be cherished,
Strengthened, and fed without the aid of joy.

Then did I check the tears of useless passion –
Weaned my young soul from yearning after thine;
Sternly denied its burning wish to hasten
Down to that tomb already more than mine.

And, even yet, I dare not let it languish,
Dare not indulge in memory's rapturous pain;
Once drinking deep of that divinest anguish,
How could I seek the empty world again?

128    High waving heather 'neath stormy blasts bending
Midnight and moonlight and bright shining stars
Darkness and glory rejoicingly blending
Earth rising to heaven and heaven descending
Man's spirit away from its drear dungeon sending
Bursting the fetters and breaking the bars

All down the mountain sides wild forests lending
One mighty voice to the life giving wind
Rivers their banks in the jubilee rending
Fast through the valleys a reckless course wending
Wider and deeper their waters extending
Leaving a desolate desert behind

Shining and lowering and swelling and dying
Changing forever from midnight to noon
Roaring like thunder like soft music sighing
Shadows on shadows advancing and flying
Lightning bright flashes the deep gloom defying
Coming as swiftly and fading as soon

129   The night is darkening round me
     The wild winds coldly blow
     But a tyrant spell has bound me
     And I cannot cannot go

     The giant trees are bending
     Their bare boughs weighed with snow
     And the storm is fast descending
     And yet I cannot go

     Clouds beyond clouds above me
     Wastes beyond wastes below
     But nothing drear can move me
     I will not cannot go

130   I'm happiest when most away
     I can bear my soul from its home of clay
     On a windy night when the moon is bright
     And my eye can wander through worlds of light

     When I am not and none beside
     Nor earth nor sea nor cloudless sky
     But only spirit wandering wide
     Through infinite immensity

131   How still, how happy! those are words
     That once would scarce agree together
     I loved the plashing of the surge –
     The changing heaven the breezy weather,

More than smooth seas and cloudless skies
And solemn, soothing, softened airs
That in the forest woke no sighs
And from the green spray shook no tears

How still, how happy! now I feel
Where silence dwells is sweeter far
Than laughing mirth's most joyous swell
However pure its raptures are

Come sit down on this sunny stone
'Tis wintery light o'er flowerless moors –
But sit – for we are all alone
And clear expand heaven's breathless shores

I could think in the withered grass
Spring's budding wreaths we might discern
The violet's eye might shyly flash
And young leaves shoot among the fern

It is but thought – full many a night
The snow shall clothe those hills afar
And storms shall add a drearier blight
And winds shall wage a wilder war

Before the lark may herald in
Fresh foliage twined with blossoms fair
And summer days again begin
Their glory-haloed crown to wear

Yet my heart loves December's smile
As much as July's golden beam
Then let us sit and watch the while
The blue ice curdling on the stream –

132
        Upon her soothing breast
        She lulled her little child
        A winter sunset in the west
        A dreary glory smiled

133
        No coward soul is mine
        No trembler in the world's storm-troubled sphere
        I see Heaven's glories shine
        And Faith shines equal arming me from Fear

        O God within my breast
        Almighty ever-present Deity
        Life, that in me hast rest
        As I Undying Life, have power in thee

        Vain are the thousand creeds
        That move men's hearts, unutterably vain,
        Worthless as withered weeds
        Or idlest froth amid the boundless main

        To waken doubt in one
        Holding so fast by thy infinity
        So surely anchored on
        The steadfast rock of Immortality

        With wide-embracing love
        Thy spirit animates eternal years
        Pervades and broods above,
        Changes, sustains, dissolves, creates and rears

        Though Earth and moon were gone
        And suns and universes ceased to be
        And thou wert left alone
        Every Existence would exist in thee

There is not room for Death
Nor atom that his might could render void
Since thou art Being and Breath
And what thou art may never be destroyed

# EMILY BRONTË *or*
# CHARLOTTE BRONTË

**134**  Often rebuked, yet always back returning
 To those first feelings that were born with me,
And leaving busy chase of wealth and learning
 For idle dreams of things which cannot be:

Today, I will seek not the shadowy region;
 Its unsustaining vastness waxes drear;
And visions rising, legion after legion,
 Bring the unreal world too strangely near.

I'll walk, but not in old heroic traces,
 And not in paths of high morality,
And not among the half-distinguished faces,
 The clouded forms of long-past history.

I'll walk where my own nature would be leading:
 It vexes me to choose another guide:
Where the grey flocks in ferny glens are feeding;
 Where the wild wind blows on the mountain side.

What have those lonely mountains worth revealing?
 More glory and more grief than I can tell:
The earth that wakes *one* human heart to feeling
 Can centre both the worlds of Heaven and Hell.

# ARTHUR HUGH CLOUGH
## 1819–61

135            Amours de Voyage

*Oh, you are sick of self-love, Malvolio,*
*And taste with a distempered appetite!*

                            Shakspeare

*Il doutait de tout, même de l'amour.*

                           French Novel

*Solvitur ambulando.*    Solutio Sophismatum

*Flevit amores*
*Non elaboratum ad pedem.*        Horace

### CANTO I

*Over the great windy waters, and over the clear-crested summits,*
   *Unto the sun and the sky, and unto the perfecter earth,*
*Come, let us go, – to a land wherein gods of the old time wandered,*
   *Where every breath even now changes to ether divine.*
*Come, let us go; though withal a voice whisper, 'The world that we*
      *live in,*
   *Whithersoever we turn, still is the same narrow crib;*
*'Tis but to prove limitation, and measure a cord, that we travel;*
   *Let who would 'scape and be free go to his chamber and think;*
*'Tis but to change idle fancies for memories wilfully falser;*
   *''Tis but to go and have been.' – Come, little bark! let us go.*

---

135. *Epigraphs:* Shakespeare, *Twelfth Night*, I v 85–6; 'French Novel' unidentified – 'He was doubtful about everything, even love'; 'It [the problem] is solved by walking' – *Sophistical Solution*; Horace, *Epodes* xiv 10–11, altering 'amorem' to plural 'amores': 'he lamented his love in simple metres'

### I *Claude to Eustace*

Dear Eustatio, I write that you may write me an answer,
Or at the least to put us again *en rapport* with each other.
Rome disappoints me much, – St. Peter's, perhaps, in especial;
Only the Arch of Titus and view from the Lateran please me:
This, however, perhaps is the weather, which truly is horrid.
Greece must be better, surely; and yet I am feeling so spiteful,
That I could travel to Athens, to Delphi, and Troy, and Mount Sinai,
Though but to see with my eyes that these are vanity also.
   Rome disappoints me much; I hardly as yet understand, but
*Rubbishy* seems the word that most exactly would suit it.
All the foolish destructions, and all the sillier savings,
All the incongruous things of past incompatible ages,
Seem to be treasured up here to make fools of present and future.
Would to Heaven the old Goths had made a cleaner sweep of it!
Would to Heaven some new ones would come and destroy these
     churches!
However, one can live in Rome as also in London.
Rome is better than London, because it is other than London.
It is a blessing, no doubt, to be rid, at least for a time, of
All one's friends and relations, – yourself (forgive me!) included, –
All the *assujettissement* of having been what one has been,
What one thinks one is, or thinks that others suppose one;
Yet, in despite of all, we turn like fools to the English.
Vernon has been my fate; who is here the same that you knew him, –
Making the tour, it seems, with friends of the name of Trevellyn.

### II *Claude to Eustace*

Rome disappoints me still; but I shrink and adapt myself to it.
Somehow a tyrannous sense of a superincumbent oppression
Still, wherever I go, accompanies ever, and makes me
Feel like a tree (shall I say?) buried under a ruin of brickwork.
Rome, believe me, my friend, is like its own Monte Testaceo,
Merely a marvellous mass of broken and castaway wine-pots.

135,I, i. *assujettissement* subjection

Ye gods! what do I want with this rubbish of ages departed,
Things that nature abhors, the experiments that she has failed in?
What do I find in the Forum? An archway and two or three pillars.
Well, but St. Peter's? Alas, Bernini has filled it with sculpture!
No one can cavil, I grant, at the size of the great Coliseum.
Doubtless the notion of grand and capacious and massive amusement,
This the old Romans had; but tell me, is this an idea?
Yet of solidity much, but of splendour little is extant:
'Brickwork I found thee, and marble I left thee!' their Emperor
      vaunted;
'Marble I thought thee, and brickwork I find thee!' the Tourist may
      answer.

### III *Georgina Trevellyn to Louisa ---*

At last, dearest Louisa, I take up my pen to address you.
Here we are, you see, with the seven-and-seventy boxes,
Courier, Papa and Mamma, the children, and Mary and Susan:
Here we all are at Rome, and delighted of course with St. Peter's,
And very pleasantly lodged in the famous Piazza di Spagna.
Rome is a wonderful place, but Mary shall tell you about it;
Not very gay, however; the English are mostly at Naples;
There are the A.'s, we hear, and most of the W. party.
    George, however, is come; did I tell you about his mustachios?
Dear, I must really stop, for the carriage, they tell me, is waiting;
Mary will finish; and Susan is writing, they say, to Sophia.
Adieu, dearest Louise, – evermore your faithful Georgina.
Who can a Mr. Claude be whom George has taken to be with?
Very stupid, I think, but George says so *very* clever.

### IV *Claude to Eustace*

No, the Christian faith, as at any rate I understood it,
With its humiliations and exaltations combining,
Exaltations sublime, and yet diviner abasements,
Aspirations from something most shameful here upon earth and
In our poor selves to something most perfect above in the heavens, –
No, the Christian faith, as I, at least, understood it,
Is not here, O Rome, in any of these thy churches;

Is not here, but in Freiburg, or Rheims, or Westminster Abbey.
What in thy Dome I find, in all thy recenter efforts,
Is a something, I think, more *rational* far, more earthly,
Actual, less ideal, devout not in scorn and refusal,
But in a positive, calm, Stoic-Epicurean acceptance.
This I begin to detect in St. Peter's and some of the churches,
Mostly in all that I see of the sixteenth-century masters;
Overlaid of course with infinite gauds and gewgaws,
Innocent, playful follies, the toys and trinkets of childhood,
Forced on maturer years, as the serious one thing needful,
By the barbarian will of the rigid and ignorant Spaniard.

    Curious work, meantime, re-entering society: how we
Walk a livelong day, great Heaven, and watch our shadows!
What our shadows seem, forsooth, we will ourselves be.
Do I look like that? you think me that: then I *am* that.

## V *Claude to Eustace*

Luther, they say, was unwise; like a half-taught German, he could not
See that old follies were passing most tranquilly out of remembrance;
Leo the Tenth was employing all efforts to clear out abuses;
Jupiter, Juno, and Venus, Fine Arts, and Fine Letters, the Poets,
Scholars, and Sculptors, and Painters, were quietly clearing away the
Martyrs, and Virgins, and Saints, or at any rate Thomas Aquinas:
He must forsooth make a fuss and distend his huge Wittenberg lungs,
    and
Bring back Theology once yet again in a flood upon Europe:
Lo you, for forty days from the windows of heaven it fell; the
Waters prevail on the earth yet more for a hundred and fifty;
Are they abating at last? the doves that are sent to explore are
Wearily fain to return, at the best with a leaflet of promise, –
Fain to return, as they went, to the wandering wave-tost vessel, –
Fain to re-enter the roof which covers the clean and the unclean, –
Luther, they say, was unwise; he didn't see how things were going;
Luther was foolish, – but, O great God! what call you Ignatius?
O my tolerant soul, be still! but you talk of barbarians,
Alaric, Attila, Genseric; – why, they came, they killed, they
Ravaged, and went on their way; but these vile, tyrannous Spaniards,
These are here still, – how long, O ye heavens, in the country of Dante?

These, that fanaticized Europe, which now can forget them, release not
This, their choicest of prey, this Italy; here you see them, –
Here, with emasculate pupils and gimcrack churches of Gesu,
Pseudo-learning and lies, confessional-boxes and postures, –
Here, with metallic beliefs and regimental devotions, –
Here, overcrusting with slime, perverting, defacing, debasing,
Michael Angelo's dome, that had hung the Pantheon in heaven,
Raphael's Joys and Graces, and thy clear stars, Galileo!

## VI *Claude to Eustace*

Which of three Misses Trevellyn it is that Vernon shall marry
Is not a thing to be known; for our friend is one of those natures
Which have their perfect delight in the general tender-domestic;
So that he trifles with Mary's shawl, ties Susan's bonnet,
Dances with all, but at home is most, they say, with Georgina,
Who is, however, *too* silly in my apprehension for Vernon.
I, as before when I wrote, continue to see them a little;
Not that I like them much or care a *bajocco* for Vernon,
But I am slow at Italian, have not many English acquaintance,
And I am asked, in short, and am not good at excuses.
Middle-class people these, bankers very likely, not wholly
Pure of the taint of the shop; will at table d'hôte and restaurant
Have their shilling's worth, their penny's pennyworth even:
Neither man's aristocracy this, nor God's, God knoweth!
Yet they are fairly descended, they give you to know, well connected;
Doubtless somewhere in some neighbourhood have, and are careful to
    keep, some
Threadbare-genteel relations, who in their turn are enchanted
Grandly among county people to introduce at assemblies
To the unpennied cadets our cousins with excellent fortunes.
Neither man's aristocracy this, nor God's, God knoweth!

## VII *Claude to Eustace*

Ah, what a shame, indeed, to abuse these most worthy people!
Ah, what a sin to have sneered at their innocent rustic pretensions!
Is it not laudable really, this reverent worship of station?
Is it not fitting that wealth should tender this homage to culture?

Is it not touching to witness these efforts, if little availing,
Painfully made, to perform the old ritual service of manners?
Shall not devotion atone for the absence of knowledge? and
    fervour
Palliate, cover, the fault of a superstitious observance?
Dear, dear, what do I say? but, alas! just now, like Iago,
I can be nothing at all, if it is not critical wholly;
So in fantastic height, in coxcomb exultation,
Here in the garden I walk, can freely concede to the Maker
That the works of His hand are all very good: His creatures,
Beast of the field and fowl, He brings them before me; I name them;
That which I name them, they are, – the bird, the beast, and the
    cattle.
But for Adam, – alas, poor critical coxcomb Adam!
But for Adam there is not found an help-meet for him.

## VIII *Claude to Eustace*

No, great Dome of Agrippa, thou art not Christian! canst not,
Strip and replaster and daub and do what they will with thee, be so!
Here underneath the great porch of colossal Corinthian columns,
Here as I walk, do I dream of the Christian belfries above them;
Or, on a bench as I sit and abide for long hours, till thy whole vast
Round grows dim as in dreams to my eyes, I repeople thy niches,
Not with the Martyrs, and Saints, and Confessors, and Virgins, and
    children,
But with the mightier forms of an older, austerer worship;
And I recite to myself, how
                  Eager for battle here
    Stood Vulcan, here matronal Juno,
        And with the bow to his shoulder faithful
    He who with pure dew laveth of Castaly
    His flowing locks, who holdeth of Lycia
    The oak forest and the wood that bore him,
        Delos' and Patara's own Apollo.

### IX *Claude to Eustace*

Yet it is pleasant, I own it, to be in their company; pleasant,
Whatever else it may be, to abide in the feminine presence.
Pleasant, but wrong, will you say? But this happy, serene coexistence
Is to some poor soft souls, I fear, a necessity simple,
Meat and drink and life, and music, filling with sweetness,
Thrilling with melody sweet, with harmonies strange overwhelming,
All the long-silent strings of an awkward, meaningless fabric.
Yet as for that, I could live, I believe, with children; to have those
Pure and delicate forms encompassing, moving about you,
This were enough, I could think; and truly with glad resignation
Could from the dream of Romance, from the fever of flushed
   adolescence,
Look to escape and subside into peaceful avuncular functions.
Nephews and nieces! alas, for as yet I have none! and, moreover,
Mothers are jealous, I fear me, too often, too rightfully; fathers
Think they have title exclusive to spoiling their own little darlings;
And by the law of the land, in despite of Malthusian doctrine,
No sort of proper provision is made for that most patriotic,
Most meritorious subject, the childless and bachelor uncle.

### X *Claude to Eustace*

Ye, too, marvellous Twain, that erect on the Monte Cavallo
Stand by your rearing steeds in the grace of your motionless
   movement,
Stand with your upstretched arms and tranquil regardant faces,
Stand as instinct with life in the might of immutable manhood, –
O ye mighty and strange, ye ancient divine ones of Hellas.
Are ye Christian too? to convert and redeem and renew you,
Will the brief form have sufficed, that a Pope has set up on the apex
Of the Egyptian stone that o'ertops you, the Christian symbol?
And ye, silent, supreme in serene and victorious marble,
Ye that encircle the walls of the stately Vatican chambers,
Juno and Ceres, Minerva, Apollo, the Muses and Bacchus,
Ye unto whom far and near come posting the Christian pilgrims,
Ye that are ranged in the halls of the mystic Christian Pontiff,

Are ye also baptized; are ye of the kingdom of Heaven?
Utter, O some one, the word that shall reconcile Ancient and Modern!
Am I to turn me from this unto thee, great Chapel of Sixtus?

### XI *Claude to Eustace*

These are the facts. The uncle, the elder brother, the squire (a
Little embarrassed, I fancy), resides in the family place in
Cornwall, of course; 'Papa is in business,' Mary informs me;
He's a good sensible man, whatever his trade is. The mother
Is – shall I call it fine? – herself she would tell you refined, and
Greatly, I fear me, looks down on my bookish and maladroit manners;
Somewhat affecteth the blue; would talk to me often of poets;
Quotes, which I hate, Childe Harold; but also appreciates
    Wordsworth;
Sometimes adventures on Schiller; and then to religion diverges;
Questions me much about Oxford; and yet, in her loftiest flights still
Grates the fastidious ear with the slightly mercantile accent.

Is it contemptible, Eustace – I'm perfectly ready to think so, –
Is it, – the horrible pleasure of pleasing inferior people?
I am ashamed my own self; and yet true it is, if disgraceful,
That for the first time in life I am living and moving with freedom.
I, who never could talk to the people I meet with my uncle, –
I, who have always failed, – I, trust me, can suit the Trevellyns;
I, believe me, – great conquest, am liked by the country bankers.
And I am glad to be liked, and like in return very kindly.
So it proceeds; *Laissez faire, laissez aller*, – such is the watchword.
Well, I know there are thousands as pretty and hundreds as pleasant,
Girls by the dozen as good, and girls in abundance with polish
Higher and manners more perfect than Susan or Mary Trevellyn.
Well, I know, after all, it is only juxtaposition, –
Juxtaposition, in short; and what is juxtaposition?

### XII *Claude to Eustace*

But I am in for it now, – *laissez faire*, of a truth, *laissez aller*.
Yes, I am going, – I feel it, I feel and cannot recall it, –
Fusing with this thing and that, entering into all sorts of relations,

Tying I know not what ties, which, whatever they are, I know one
    thing,
Will, and must, woe is me, be one day painfully broken, –
Broken with painful remorses, with shrinkings of soul, and relentings,
Foolish delays, more foolish evasions, most foolish renewals.
But I have made the step, have quitted the ship of Ulysses;
Quitted the sea and the shore, passed into the magical island;
Yet on my lips is the *moly*, medicinal, offered of Hermes.
I have come into the precinct, the labyrinth closes around me,
Path into path rounding slyly; I pace slowly on, and the fancy,
Struggling awhile to sustain the long sequences weary, bewildered,
Fain must collapse in despair; I yield, I am lost, and know nothing;
Yet in my bosom unbroken remaineth the clue; I shall use it.
Lo, with the rope on my loins I descend through the fissure; I sink, yet
Inly secure in the strength of invisible arms up above me;
Still, wheresoever I swing, wherever to shore, or to shelf, or
Floor of cavern untrodden, shell sprinkled, enchanting, I know I
Yet shall one time feel the strong cord tighten about me, –
Feel it, relentless, upbear me from spots I would rest in; and though the
Rope sway wildly, I faint, crags wound me, from crag unto crag re-
Bounding, or, wide in the void, I die ten deaths, ere the end I
Yet shall plant firm foot on the broad lofty spaces I quit, shall
Feel underneath me again the great massy strengths of abstraction,
Look yet abroad from the height o'er the sea whose salt wave I have
    tasted.

### XIII *Georgina Trevellyn to Louisa* ---

Dearest Louisa, – Inquire, if you please, about Mr. Claude --- .
He has been once at R., and remembers meeting the H.'s.
Harriet L., perhaps, may be able to tell you about him.
It is an awkward youth, but still with very good manners;
Not without prospects, we hear; and, George says, highly connected.
Georgy declares it absurd, but Mamma is alarmed, and insists he has
Taken up strange opinions, and may be turning a Papist.
Certainly once he spoke of a daily service he went to.
'Where?' we asked, and he laughed and answered, 'At the Pantheon.'
This was a temple, you know, and now is a Catholic church; and

Though it is said that Mazzini has sold it for Protestant service,
Yet I suppose this change can hardly as yet be effected.
Adieu again, – evermore, my dearest, your loving Georgina.

### P.S. by Mary Trevellyn

I am to tell you, you say, what I think of our last new acquaintance.
Well, then, I think that George has a very fair right to be jealous.
I do not like him much, though I do not dislike being with him.
He is what people call, I suppose, a superior man, and
Certainly seems so to me; but I think he is terribly selfish.

*Alba, thou findest me still, and, Alba, thou findest me ever,*
  *Now from the Capitol steps, now over Titus's Arch,*
*Here from the large grassy spaces that spread from the Lateran portal,*
  *Towering o'er aqueduct lines lost in perspective between,*
*Or from a Vatican window, or bridge, or the high Coliseum,*
  *Clear by the garlanded line cut of the Flavian ring.*
*Beautiful can I not call thee, and yet thou hast power to o'ermaster,*
  *Power of mere beauty; in dreams, Alba, thou hauntest me still.*
*Is it religion? I ask me; or is it a vain superstition?*
  *Slavery abject and gross? service, too feeble, of truth?*
*Is it an idol I bow to, or is it a god that I worship?*
  *Do I sink back on the old, or do I soar from the mean?*
*So through the city I wander and question, unsatisfied ever,*
  *Reverent so I accept, doubtful because I revere.*

## CANTO II

*Is it illusion? or does there a spirit from perfecter ages,*
  *Here, even yet, amid loss, change, and corruption, abide?*
*Does there a spirit we know not, though seek, though we find,*
    *comprehend not,*
  *Here to entice and confuse, tempt and evade us, abide?*
*Lives in the exquisite grace of the column disjointed and single,*
  *Haunts the rude masses of brick garlanded gaily with vine,*
*E'en in the turret fantastic surviving that springs from the ruin,*
  *E'en in the people itself? is it illusion or not?*

*Is it illusion or not that attracteth the pilgrim transalpine,*
  *Brings him a dullard and dunce hither to pry and to stare?*
*Is it illusion or not that allures the barbarian stranger,*
  *Brings him with gold to the shrine, brings him in arms to the*
    *gate?*

### I *Claude to Eustace*

What do the people say, and what does the government do? – you
Ask, and I know not at all. Yet fortune will favour your hopes; and
I, who avoided it all, am fated, it seems, to describe it.
I, who nor meddle nor make in politics, – I who sincerely
Put not my trust in leagues nor any suffrage by ballot,
Never predicted Parisian millenniums, never beheld a
New Jerusalem coming down dressed like a bride out of heaven
Right on the Place de la Concorde, – I, nevertheless, let me say it,
Could in my soul of souls, this day, with the Gaul at the gates shed
One true tear for thee, thou poor little Roman Republic;
What, with the German restored, with Sicily safe to the Bourbon,
Not leave one poor corner for native Italian exertion?
France, it is foully done! and you, poor foolish England, –
You, who a twelvemonth ago said nations must choose for themselves,
  you
Could not, of course, interfere, – you, now, when a nation has
  chosen –
Pardon this folly! *The Times* will, of course, have announced the
  occasion,
Told you the news of to-day; and although it was slightly in error
When it proclaimed as a fact the Apollo was sold to a Yankee,
You may believe when it tells you the French are at Civita Vecchia.

### II *Claude to Eustace*

*Dulce* it is, and *decorum*, no doubt, for the country to fall, – to
Offer one's blood an oblation to Freedom, and die for the Cause; yet
Still, individual culture is also something, and no man

---

**135,II, ii.** *Dulce et decorum est pro patria mori* It is sweet and fitting to die for one's country (Horace, *Odes* III ii 13)

Finds quite distinct the assurance that he of all others is called on,
Or would be justified even, in taking away from the world that
Precious creature, himself. Nature sent him here to abide here;
Else why send him at all? Nature wants him still, it is likely;
On the whole, we are meant to look after ourselves; it is certain
Each has to eat for himself, digest for himself, and in general
Care for his own dear life, and see to his own preservation;
Nature's intentions, in most things uncertain, in this are decisive;
Which, on the whole, I conjecture the Romans will follow, and I shall.
　So we cling to our rocks like limpets; Ocean may bluster,
Over and under and round us; we open our shells to imbibe our
Nourishment, close them again, and are safe, fulfilling the purpose
Nature intended, – a wise one, of course, and a noble, we doubt not.
Sweet it may be and decorous, perhaps, for the country to die; but,
On the whole, we conclude the Romans won't do it, and I sha'n't.

### III *Claude to Eustace*

Will they fight? They say so. And will the French? I can hardly,
Hardly think so; and yet – He is come, they say, to Palo,
He is passed from Monterone, at Santa Severa
He hath laid up his guns. But the Virgin, the Daughter of Roma,
She hath despised thee and laughed thee to scorn, – the Daughter of
　　Tiber,
She hath shaken her head and built barricades against thee!
Will they fight? I believe it. Alas! 'tis ephemeral folly,
Vain and ephemeral folly, of course, compared with pictures,
Statues, and antique gems! – Indeed: and yet indeed too,
Yet methought, in broad day did I dream, – tell it not in St. James's,
Whisper it not in thy courts, O Christ Church! – yet did I, waking,
Dream of a cadence that sings, *Si tombent nos jeunes héros, la*
*Terre en produit de nouveaux contre vous tous prêts à se battre*;
Dreamt of great indignations and angers transcendental,
Dreamt of a sword at my side and a battle-horse underneath me.

135,II, iii. *Si tombent* . . . Lines from the *Marseillaise*: If our young heroes fall, the earth
produces new ones, ready to fight against all of you

## IV *Claude to Eustace*

Now supposing the French or the Neapolitan soldier
Should by some evil chance come exploring the Maison Serny
(Where the family English are all to assemble for safety),
Am I prepared to lay down my life for the British female?
Really, who knows? One has bowed and talked, till, little by little,
All the natural heat has escaped of the chivalrous spirit.
Oh, one conformed, of course; but one doesn't die for good
      manners,
Stab or shoot, or be shot, by way of graceful attention.
No, if it should be at all, it should be on the barricades there;
Should I incarnadine ever this inky pacifical finger,
Sooner far should it be for this vapour of Italy's freedom,
Sooner far by the side of the d——d and dirty plebeians.
Ah, for a child in the street I could strike; for the full-blown lady –
Somehow, Eustace, alas! I have not felt the vocation.
Yet these people of course will expect, as of course, my protection,
Vernon in radiant arms stand forth for the lovely Georgina,
And to appear, I suppose, were but common civility. Yes, and
Truly I do not desire they should either be killed or offended.
Oh, and of course, you will say, 'When the time comes, you will be
      ready.'
Ah, but before it comes, am I to presume it will be so?
What I cannot feel now, am I to suppose that I shall feel?
Am I not free to attend for the ripe and indubious instinct?
Am I forbidden to wait for the clear and lawful perception?
Is it the calling of man to surrender his knowledge and insight,
For the mere venture of what may, perhaps, be the virtuous action?
Must we, walking our earth, discern a little, and hoping
Some plain visible task shall yet for our hands be assigned us, –
Must we abandon the future for fear of omitting the present,
Quit our own fireside hopes at the alien call of a neighbour,
To the mere possible shadow of Deity offer the victim?
And is all this, my friend, but a weak and ignoble refining,
Wholly unworthy the head or the heart of Your Own
      Correspondent?

## V *Claude to Eustace*

Yes, we are fighting at last, it appears. This morning, as usual,
*Murray*, as usual, in hand, I enter the Caffè Nuovo;
Seating myself with a sense as it were of a change in the weather,
Not understanding, however, but thinking mostly of Murray,
And, for to-day is their day, of the Campidoglio Marbles;
*Caffè-latte!* I call to the waiter, – and *Non c' è latte*,
This is the answer he makes me, and this is the sign of a battle.
So I sit; and truly they seem to think anyone else more
Worthy than me of attention. I wait for my milkless *nero*,
Free to observe undistracted all sorts and sizes of persons,
Blending civilian and soldier in strangest costume, coming in, and
Gulping in hottest haste, still standing, their coffee, – withdrawing
Eagerly, jangling a sword on the steps, or jogging a musket
Slung to the shoulder behind. They are fewer, moreover, than usual,
Much and silenter far; and so I begin to imagine
Something is really afloat. Ere I leave, the Caffè is empty,
Empty too the streets, in all its length the Corso
Empty, and empty I see to my right and left the Condotti.
  Twelve o'clock, on the Pincian Hill, with lots of English,
Germans, Americans, French, – the Frenchmen, too, are protected, –
So we stand in the sun, but afraid of a probable shower;
So we stand and stare, and see, to the left of St. Peter's,
Smoke, from the cannon, white, – but that is at intervals only, –
Black, from a burning house, we suppose, by the Cavalleggieri;
And we believe we discern some lines of men descending
Down through the vineyard-slopes, and catch a bayonet gleaming.
Every ten minutes, however, – in this there is no misconception, –
Comes a great white puff from behind Michel Angelo's dome,
    and
After a space the report of a real big gun, – not the Frenchman's! –
That must be doing some work. And so we watch and conjecture.
  Shortly, an Englishman comes, who says he has been to St. Peter's,
Seen the Piazza and troops, but that is all he can tell us;
So we watch and sit, and, indeed, it begins to be tiresome. –

135,II, v. *Non c' è latte* There is no milk

All this smoke is outside; when it has come to the inside,
It will be time, perhaps, to descend and retreat to our houses.
  Half-past one, or two. The report of small arms frequent,
Sharp and savage indeed; that cannot all be for nothing:
So we watch and wonder; but guessing is tiresome, very.
Weary of wondering, watching, and guessing, and gossiping idly,
Down I go, and pass through the quiet streets with the knots of
National Guards patrolling, and flags hanging out at the windows,
English, American, Danish, – and, after offering to help an
Irish family moving *en masse* to the Maison Serny,
After endeavouring idly to minister balm to the trembling
Quinquagenarian fears of two lone British spinsters,
Go to make sure of my dinner before the enemy enter.
But by this there are signs of stragglers returning; and voices
Talk, though you don't believe it, of guns and prisoners taken;
And on the walls you read the first bulletin of the morning. –
This is all that I saw, and all I know of the battle.


### VI *Claude to Eustace*


Victory! Victory! – Yes! ah, yes, thou republican Zion,
Truly the kings of the earth are gathered and gone by together;
Doubtless they marvelled to witness such things, were astonished,
        and so forth.
Victory! Victory! Victory! – Ah, but it is, believe me,
Easier, easier far, to intone the chant of the martyr
Than to indite any pæan of any victory. Death may
Sometimes be noble; but life, at the best, will appear an illusion.
While the great pain is upon us, it is great; when it is over,
Why, it is over. The smoke of the sacrifice rises to heaven,
Of a sweet savour, no doubt, to Somebody; but on the altar,
Lo, there is nothing remaining but ashes and dirt and ill odour.
  So it stands, you perceive; the labial muscles that swelled with
Vehement evolution of yesterday Marseillaises,
Articulations sublime of defiance and scorning, to-day col-
Lapse and languidly mumble, while men and women and papers
Scream and re-scream to each other the chorus of Victory. Well, but
I am thankful they fought, and glad that the Frenchmen were
        beaten.

### VII *Claude to Eustace*

So, I have seen a man killed! An experience that, among others!
Yes, I suppose I have; although I can hardly be certain,
And in a court of justice could never declare I had seen it.
But a man was killed, I am told, in a place where I saw
Something; a man was killed, I am told, and I saw something.
    I was returning home from St. Peter's; *Murray*, as usual,
Under my arm, I remember; had crossed the St. Angelo bridge; and
Moving towards the Condotti, had got to the first barricade, when
Gradually, thinking still of St. Peter's, I became conscious
Of a sensation of movement opposing me, – tendency this way
(Such as one fancies may be in a stream when the wave of the tide is
Coming and not yet come, – a sort of noise and retention);
So I turned, and, before I turned, caught sight of stragglers
Heading a crowd, it is plain, that is coming behind that corner.
Looking up, I see windows filled with heads; the Piazza,
Into which you remember the Ponte St. Angelo enters,
Since I passed, has thickened with curious groups; and now the
Crowd is coming, has turned, has crossed that last barricade, is
Here at my side. In the middle they drag at something. What is it?
Ha! bare swords in the air, held up? There seem to be voices
Pleading and hands putting back; official, perhaps; but the swords
    are
Many, and bare in the air. In the air? they descend; they are smiting,
Hewing, chopping – At what? In the air once more upstretched? And –
Is it blood that's on them? Yes, certainly blood! Of whom, then?
Over whom is the cry of this furor of exultation?

While they are skipping and screaming, and dancing their caps on the
    points of
Swords and bayonets, I to the outskirts back, and ask a
Mercantile-seeming bystander, 'What is it?' and he, looking always
That way, makes me answer, 'A Priest, who was trying to fly to
The Neapolitan army,' – and thus explains the proceeding.

You didn't see the dead man? No; – I began to be doubtful;
I was in black myself, and didn't know what mightn't happen, –
But a National Guard close by me, outside of the hubbub,
Broke his sword with slashing a broad hat covered with dust, – and
Passing away from the place with Murray under my arm, and
Stooping, I saw through the legs of the people the legs of a body.

You are the first, do you know, to whom I have mentioned the matter.
Whom should I tell it to else? – these girls? – the Heavens forbid it! –
Quidnuncs at Monaldini's? – idlers upon the Pincian?

If I rightly remember, it happened on that afternoon when
Word of the nearer approach of a new Neapolitan army
First was spread. I began to bethink me of Paris Septembers,
Thought I could fancy the look of that old 'Ninety-two. On that evening
Three or four, or, it may be, five, of these people were slaughtered.
Some declared they had, one of them, fired on a sentinel; others
Say they were only escaping; a Priest, it is currently stated,
Stabbed a National Guard on the very Piazza Colonna:
History, Rumour of Rumours, I leave it to thee to determine!

But I am thankful to say the government seems to have strength to
Put it down; it has vanished, at least; the place is most peaceful.
Through the Trastevere walking last night, at nine of the clock, I
Found no sort of disorder; I crossed by the Island-bridges,
So by the narrow streets to the Ponte Rotto, and onwards
Thence by the Temple of Vesta, away to the great Coliseum,
Which at the full of the moon is an object worthy a visit.

### VIII *Georgina Trevellyn to Louisa* ---

Only think, dearest Louisa, what fearful scenes we have witnessed! –

\* \* \* \* \* \*

George has just seen Garibaldi, dressed up in a long white cloak, on
Horseback, riding by, with his mounted negro behind him:
This is a man, you know, who came from America with him,
Out of the woods, I suppose, and uses a *lasso* in fighting,
Which is, I don't quite know, but a sort of noose, I imagine;

This he throws on the heads of the enemy's men in a battle,
Pulls them into his reach, and then most cruelly kills them:
Mary does not believe, but we heard it from an Italian.
Mary allows she was wrong about Mr. Claude *being selfish*;
He was *most* useful and kind on the terrible thirtieth of April.
Do not write here any more; we are starting directly for Florence:
We should be off to-morrow, if only Papa could get horses;
All have been seized everywhere for the use of this dreadful Mazzini.

*P.S.*

Mary has seen thus far. – I am really so angry, Louisa, –
Quite out of patience, my dearest! What can the man be intending?
I am quite tired; and Mary, who might bring him to in a moment,
Lets him go on as he likes, and neither will help nor dismiss him.

### IX *Claude to Eustace*

It is most curious to see what a power a few calm words (in
Merely a brief proclamation) appear to possess on the people.
Order is perfect, and peace; the city is utterly tranquil;
And one cannot conceive that this easy and *nonchalant* crowd, that
Flows like a quiet stream through street and market-place, entering
Shady recesses and bays of church, *osteria*, and *caffè*,
Could in a moment be changed to a flood as of molten lava,
Boil into deadly wrath and wild homicidal delusion.
   Ah, 'tis an excellent race, – and even in old degradation,
Under a rule that enforces to flattery, lying, and cheating,
E'en under Pope and Priest, a nice and natural people.
Oh, could they but be allowed this chance of redemption! – but clearly
That is not likely to be. Meantime, notwithstanding all journals,
Honour for once to the tongue and the pen of the eloquent writer!
Honour to speech! and all honour to thee, thou noble Mazzini!

135,II, ix. *osteria* inn

## X *Claude to Eustace*

I am in love, meantime, you think; no doubt you would think so.
I am in love, you say; with those letters, of course, you would say so.
I am in love, you declare. I think not so; yet I grant you
It is a pleasure indeed to converse with this girl. Oh, rare gift,
Rare felicity, this! she can talk in a rational way, can
Speak upon subjects that really are matters of mind and of thinking,
Yet in perfection retain her simplicity; never, one moment,
Never, however you urge it, however you tempt her, consents to
Step from ideas and fancies and loving sensations to those vain
Conscious understandings that vex the minds of mankind.
No, though she talk, it is music; her fingers desert not the keys; 'tis
Song, though you hear in the song the articulate vocables sounded,
Syllabled singly and sweetly the words of melodious meaning.
    I am in love, you say; I do not think so, exactly.

## XI *Claude to Eustace*

There are two different kinds, I believe, of human attraction:
One which simply disturbs, unsettles, and makes you uneasy,
And another that poises, retains, and fixes and holds you.
I have no doubt, for myself, in giving my voice for the latter.
I do not wish to be moved, but growing where I was growing,
There more truly to grow, to live where as yet I had languished.
I do not like being moved: for the will is excited; and action
Is a most dangerous thing; I tremble for something factitious,
Some malpractice of heart and illegitimate process;
We are so prone to these things, with our terrible notions of duty.

## XII *Claude to Eustace*

Ah, let me look, let me watch, let me wait, unhurried, unprompted!
Bid me not venture on aught that could alter or end what is present!
Say not, Time flies, and Occasion, that never returns, is departing!
Drive me not out, ye ill angels with fiery swords, from my Eden,
Waiting, and watching, and looking! Let love be its own inspiration!

Shall not a voice, if a voice there must be, from the airs that environ,
Yea, from the conscious heavens, without our knowledge or effort,
Break into audible words? And love be its own inspiration?

### XIII *Claude to Eustace*

Wherefore and how I am certain, I hardly can tell; but it *is* so.
She doesn't like me, Eustace; I think she never will like me.
Is it my fault, as it is my misfortune, my ways are not her ways?
Is it my fault, that my habits and modes are dissimilar wholly?
'Tis not her fault; 'tis her nature, her virtue, to misapprehend them:
'Tis not her fault; 'tis her beautiful nature, not ever to know me.
Hopeless it seems, – yet I cannot, though hopeless, determine to leave it:
She goes – therefore I go; she moves, – I move, not to lose her.

### XIV *Claude to Eustace*

Oh, 'tisn't manly, of course, 'tisn't manly, this method of wooing;
'Tisn't the way very likely to win. For the woman, they tell you,
Ever prefers the audacious, the wilful, the vehement hero;
She has no heart for the timid, the sensitive soul; and for knowledge, –
Knowledge, O ye Gods! – when did they appreciate knowledge?
Wherefore should they, either? I am sure I do not desire it.
   Ah, and I feel too, Eustace, she cares not a tittle about me!
(Care about me, indeed! and do I really expect it?)
But my manner offends; my ways are wholly repugnant;
Every word that I utter estranges, hurts, and repels her;
Every moment of bliss that I gain, in her exquisite presence,
Slowly, surely, withdraws her, removes her, and severs her from me.
Not that I care very much! – any way I escape from the boy's own
Folly, to which I am prone, of loving where it is easy.
Not that I mind very much! Why should I? I am not in love, and
Am prepared, I think, if not by previous habit,
Yet in the spirit beforehand for this and all that is like it;
It is an easier matter for us contemplative creatures,
Us upon whom the pressure of action is laid so lightly;
We, discontented indeed with things in particular, idle,
Sickly, complaining, by faith, in the vision of things in general,
Manage to hold on our way without, like others around us,

Seizing the nearest arm to comfort, help, and support us.
Yet, after all, my Eustace, I know but little about it.
All I can say for myself, for present alike and for past, is,
Mary Trevellyn, Eustace, is certainly worth your acquaintance.
You couldn't come, I suppose, as far as Florence to see her?

### XV  *Georgina Trevellyn to Louisa* ---

...... To-morrow we're starting for Florence,
Truly rejoiced, you may guess, to escape from republican terrors;
Mr. C. and Papa to escort us; we by *vettura*
Through Siena, and Georgy to follow and join us by Leghorn.
Then – Ah, what shall I say, my dearest? I tremble in thinking!
You will imagine my feelings, – the blending of hope and of sorrow!
How can I bear to abandon Papa and Mamma and my Sisters?
Dearest Louise, indeed it is very alarming; but, trust me
Ever, whatever may change, to remain your loving Georgina.

### *P.S. by Mary Trevellyn*

...... 'Do I like Mr. Claude any better?'
I am to tell you, – and, 'Pray, is it Susan or I that attract him?'
This he never has told, but Georgina could certainly ask him.
All I can say for myself is, alas! that he rather repels me.
There! I think him agreeable, but also a little repulsive.
So be content, dear Louisa; for one satisfactory marriage
Surely will do in one year for the family you would establish;
Neither Susan nor I shall afford you the joy of a second.

### *P.S. by Georgina Trevellyn*

Mr. Claude, you must know, is behaving a little bit better;
He and Papa are great friends; but he really is too *shilly-shally*, –
So unlike George! Yet I hope that the matter is going on fairly.
I shall, however, get George, before he goes, to say something.
Dearest Louise, how delightful to bring young people together!

135,II, XV. *vettura* carriage

Is it to Florence we follow, or are we to tarry yet longer,
 E'en amid clamour of arms, here in the city of old,
Seeking from clamour of arms in the Past and the Arts to be hidden,
 Vainly 'mid Arts and the Past seeking one life to forget?
Ah, fair shadow, scarce seen, go forth! for anon he shall follow, –
 He that beheld thee, anon, whither thou leadest must go!
Go, and the wise, loving Muse, she also will follow and find thee!
 She, should she linger in Rome, were not dissevered from thee!

## CANTO III

Yet to the wondrous St. Peter's, and yet to the solemn Rotonda,
 Mingling with heroes and gods, yet to the Vatican Walls,
Yet may we go, and recline, while a whole mighty world seems above us,
 Gathered and fixed to all time into one roofing supreme;
Yet may we, thinking on these things, exclude what is meaner around
   us;
 Yet, at the worst of the worst, books and a chamber remain;
Yet may we think, and forget, and possess our souls in resistance. –
 Ah, but away from the stir, shouting, and gossip of war,
Where, upon Apennine slope, with the chestnut the oak-trees
   immingle,
 Where, amid odorous copse bridle-paths wander and wind,
Where, under mulberry-branches, the diligent rivulet sparkles,
 Or amid cotton and maize peasants their water-works ply,
Where, over fig-tree and orange in tier upon tier still repeated,
 Garden on garden upreared, balconies step to the sky, –
Ah, that I were far away from the crowd and the streets of the city,
 Under the vine-trellis laid, my beloved, with thee!

### I *Mary Trevellyn to Miss Roper, – on the way to Florence*

Why doesn't Mr. Claude come with us? you ask. – We don't know.
You should know better than we. He talked of the Vatican marbles;
But I can't wholly believe that this was the actual reason, –
He was so ready before, when we asked him to come and escort us.
Certainly he is odd, my dear Miss Roper. To change so
Suddenly, just for a whim, was not quite fair to the party, –

Not quite right. I declare, I really almost am offended:
I, his great friend, as you say, have doubtless a title to be so.
Not that I greatly regret it, for dear Georgina distinctly
Wishes for nothing so much as to show her adroitness. But, oh, my
Pen will not write any more; – let us say nothing further about it.

*   *   *   *   *   *

Yes, my dear Miss Roper, I certainly called him repulsive;
So I think him, but cannot be sure I have used the expression
Quite as your pupil should; yet he does most truly repel me.
Was it to you I made use of the word? or who was it told you?
Yes, repulsive; observe, it is but when he talks of ideas
That he is quite unaffected, and free, and expansive, and easy;
I could pronounce him simply a cold intellectual being. –
When does he make advances? – He thinks that women should woo
     him;
Yet, if a girl should do so, would be but alarmed and disgusted.
She that should love him must look for small love in return, – like the ivy
On the stone wall, must expect but a rigid and niggard support, and
E'en to get that must go searching all round with her humble embraces.

II Claude to Eustace, – from Rome

Tell me, my friend, do you think that the grain would sprout in the
     furrow,
Did it not truly accept as its *summum* and *ultimum bonum*
That mere common and may-be indifferent soil it is set in?
Would it have force to develop and open its young cotyledons,
Could it compare, and reflect, and examine one thing with another?
Would it endure to accomplish the round of its natural functions,
Were it endowed with a sense of the general scheme of existence?
     While from Marseilles in the steamer we voyage to Civita Vecchia,
Vexed in the squally seas as we lay by Capraja and Elba,
Standing, uplifted, alone on the heaving poop of the vessel,
Looking around on the waste of the rushing incurious billows,
'This is Nature,' I said: 'we are born as it were from her waters;
Over her billows that buffet and beat us, her offspring uncared-for,

135,III, ii. *Summum et ultimum bonum* Complete and ultimate good

Casting one single regard of a painful victorious knowledge,
Into her billows that buffet and beat us we sink and are swallowed.'
This was the sense in my soul, as I swayed with the poop of the
    steamer;
And as unthinking I sat in the hall of the famed Ariadne,
Lo, it looked at me there from the face of a Triton in marble.
It is the simpler thought, and I can believe it the truer.
Let us not talk of growth; we are still in our Aqueous Ages.

### III *Claude to Eustace*

Farewell, Politics, utterly! What can I do? I cannot
Fight, you know; and to talk I am wholly ashamed. And although I
Gnash my teeth when I look in your French or your English papers,
What is the good of that? Will swearing, I wonder, mend matters?
Cursing and scolding repel the assailants? No, it is idle;
No, whatever befalls, I will hide, will ignore or forget it.
Let the tail shift for itself; I will bury my head. And what's the
Roman Republic to me, or I to the Roman Republic?
   Why not fight? – In the first place, I haven't so much as a musket;
In the next, if I had, I shouldn't know how I should use it;
In the third, just at present I'm studying ancient marbles;
In the fourth, I consider I owe my life to my country;
In the fifth – I forget, but four good reasons are ample.
Meantime, pray let 'em fight, and be killed. I delight in devotion.
So that I 'list not, hurrah for the glorious army of martyrs!
*Sanguis martyrum semen Ecclesiæ*; though it would seem this
Church is indeed of the purely Invisible, Kingdom-come kind:
Militant here on earth! Triumphant, of course, then, elsewhere!
Ah, good Heaven, but I would I were out far away from the pother!

### IV *Claude to Eustace*

Not, as we read in the words of the olden-time inspiration,
Are there two several trees in the place we are set to abide in;
But on the apex most high of the Tree of Life in the Garden,
Budding, unfolding, and falling, decaying and flowering ever,

135,III, iii. *Sanguis martyrum* ... The blood of martyrs is the seed of the Church

Flowering is set and decaying the transient blossom of Knowledge, –
Flowering alone, and decaying, the needless unfruitful blossom.
    Or as the cypress-spires by the fair-flowing stream Helles-pontine,
Which from the mythical tomb of the godlike Protesilaüs
Rose sympathetic in grief to his love-lorn Laodamia,
Evermore growing, and, when in their growth to the prospect
    attaining,
Over the low sea-banks, of the fatal Ilian city,
Withering still at the sight which still they upgrow to encounter.
    Ah, but ye that extrude from the ocean your helpless faces,
Ye over stormy seas leading long and dreary processions,
Ye, too, brood of the wind, whose coming is whence we discern not,
Making your nest on the wave, and your bed on the crested billow,
Skimming rough waters, and crowding wet sands that the tide shall
    return to,
Cormorants, ducks, and gulls, fill ye my imagination!
Let us not talk of growth; we are still in our Aqueous Ages.

### V *Mary Trevellyn to Miss Roper, – from Florence*

Dearest Miss Roper, – Alas! we are all at Florence quite safe, and
You, we hear, are shut up! indeed, it is sadly distressing!
We were most lucky, they say, to get off when we did from the troubles.
Now you are really besieged; they tell us it soon will be over;
Only I hope and trust without any fight in the city.
Do you see Mr. Claude? – I thought he might do something for you.
I am quite sure on occasion he really would wish to be useful.
What is he doing? I wonder; – still studying Vatican marbles?
Letters, I hope, pass through. We trust your brother is better.

### VI *Claude to Eustace*

Juxtaposition, in fine; and what is juxtaposition?
Look you, we travel along in the railway carriage or steamer,
And, *pour passer le temps*, till the tedious journey be ended,
Lay aside paper or book, to talk with the girl that is next one;
And, *pour passer le temps*, with the terminus all but in prospect,
Talk of eternal ties and marriages made in heaven.
    Ah, did we really accept with a perfect heart the illusion!

Ah, did we really believe that the Present indeed is the Only!
Or through all transmutation, all shock and convulsion of passion,
Feel we could carry undimmed, unextinguished, the light of our
    knowledge!
  But for his funeral train which the bridegroom sees in the distance,
Would he so joyfully, think you, fall in with the marriage procession?
But for that final discharge, would he dare to enlist in that service?
But for that certain release, ever sign to that perilous contract?
But for that exit secure, ever bend to that treacherous doorway? –
Ah, but the bride, meantime, – do you think she sees it as he does?
  But for the steady fore-sense of a freer and larger existence,
Think you that man could consent to be circumscribed here into
    action?
But for assurance within of a limitless ocean divine, o'er
Whose great tranquil depths unconscious the wind-tost surface
Breaks into ripples of trouble that come and change and endure not, –
But that in this, of a truth, we have our being, and know it,
Think you we men could submit to live and move as we do here?
Ah, but the women, – God bless them! they don't think at all about it.
Yet we must eat and drink, as you say. And as limited beings
Scarcely can hope to attain upon earth to an Actual Abstract,
Leaving to God contemplation, to His hands knowledge confiding,
Sure that in us if it perish, in Him it abideth and dies not,
Let us in His sight accomplish our petty particular doings, –
Yes, and contented sit down to the victual that He has provided.
Allah is great, no doubt, and Juxtaposition his prophet.
Ah, but the women, alas! they don't look at it in that way.
Juxtaposition is great; – but, my friend, I fear me, the maiden
Hardly would thank or acknowledge the lover that sought to obtain
    her,
Not as the thing he would wish, but the thing he must even put up
    with, –
Hardly would tender her hand to the wooer that candidly told her
That she is but for a space, an *ad-interim* solace and pleasure, –
That in the end she shall yield to a perfect and absolute something,
Which I then for myself shall behold, and not another, –
Which, amid fondest endearments, meantime I forget not, forsake not.
Ah, ye feminine souls, so loving and so exacting,

Since we cannot escape, must we even submit to deceive you?
Since, so cruel is truth, sincerity shocks and revolts you,
Will you have us your slaves to lie to you, flatter and – leave you?

### VII *Claude to Eustace*

Juxtaposition is great, – but, you tell me, affinity greater.
Ah, my friend, there are many affinities, greater and lesser,
Stronger and weaker; and each, by the favour of juxtaposition,
Potent, efficient, in force, – for a time; but none, let me tell you,
Save by the law of the land and the ruinous force of the will, ah,
None, I fear me, at last quite sure to be final and perfect.
Lo, as I pace in the street, from the peasant-girl to the princess,
*Homo sum, nihil humani a me alienum puto*, –
*Vir sum, nihil fæminei*, – and e'en to the uttermost circle,
All that is Nature's is I, and I all things that are Nature's.
Yes, as I walk, I behold, in a luminous, large intuition,
That I can be and become anything that I meet with or look at:
I am the ox in the dray, the ass with the garden stuff panniers;
I am the dog in the doorway, the kitten that plays in the window,
On sunny slab of the ruin the furtive and fugitive lizard,
Swallow above me that twitters, and fly that is buzzing about me;
Yea, and detect, as I go, by a faint, but a faithful assurance,
E'en from the stones of the street, as from rocks or trees of the forest,
Something of kindred, a common, though latent vitality, greets me;
And, to escape from our strivings, mistakings, misgrowths, and
    perversions,
Fain could demand to return to that perfect and primitive silence,
Fain be enfolded and fixed, as of old, in their rigid embraces.

### VIII *Claude to Eustace*

And as I walk on my way, I behold them consorting and coupling;
Faithful it seemeth, and fond, very fond, very probably faithful,
All as I go on my way, with a pleasure sincere and unmingled.
    Life is beautiful, Eustace, entrancing, enchanting to look at;

**135,III, vii.** *Homo sum* ... I am a man; I think nothing human alien to me (from the
Roman playwright Terence) *Vir sum* ... I am male, [I think] nothing female [alien to me]

As are the streets of a city we pace while the carriage is changing,
As a chamber filled-in with harmonious, exquisite pictures,
Even so beautiful Earth; and could we eliminate only
This vile hungering impulse, this demon within us of craving,
Life were beatitude, living a perfect divine satisfaction.

### IX *Claude to Eustace*

*Mild monastic faces in quiet collegiate cloisters:*
So let me offer a single and celibatarian phrase, a
Tribute to those whom perhaps you do not believe I can honour.
But, from the tumult escaping, 'tis pleasant, of drumming and
    shouting,
Hither, oblivious awhile, to withdraw, of the fact or the falsehood,
And amid placid regards and mildly courteous greetings
Yield to the calm and composure and gentle abstraction that reign o'er
*Mild monastic faces in quiet collegiate cloisters:*
  Terrible word, Obligation! You should not, Eustace, you should not,
No, you should not have used it. But, oh, great Heavens, I repel it!
Oh, I cancel, reject, disavow, and repudiate wholly
Every debt in this kind, disclaim every claim, and dishonour,
Yea, my own heart's own writing, my soul's own signature! Ah, no!
I will be free in this; you shall not, none shall, bind me.
No, my friend, if you wish to be told, it was this above all things,
This that charmed me, ah, yes, even this, that she held me to nothing.
No, I could talk as I pleased; come close; fasten ties, as I fancied;
Bind and engage myself deep; – and lo, on the following morning
It was all e'en as before, like losings in games played for nothing.
Yes, when I came, with mean fears in my soul, with a semi-
    performance
At the first step breaking down in its pitiful rôle of evasion,
When to shuffle I came, to compromise, not meet, engagements,
Lo, with her calm eyes there she met me and knew nothing of it, –
Stood unexpecting, unconscious. *She* spoke not of obligations,
Knew not of debt – ah, no, I believe you, for excellent reasons.

### X *Claude to Eustace*

*Hang* this thinking, at last! what good is it? oh, and what evil!
Oh, what mischief and pain! like a clock in a sick man's chamber,
Ticking and ticking, and still through each covert of slumber pursuing.

What shall I do to thee, O thou Preserver of men? Have compassion;
Be favourable, and hear! Take from me this regal knowledge;
Let me, contented and mute, with the beasts of the fields, my brothers,
Tranquilly, happily lie, – and eat grass, like Nebuchadnezzar!

### XI *Claude to Eustace*

Tibur is beautiful, too, and the orchard slopes, and the Anio
Falling, falling yet, to the ancient lyrical cadence;
Tibur and Anio's tide; and cool from Lucretilis ever,
With the Digentian stream, and with the Bandusian fountain,
Folded in Sabine recesses, the valley and villa of Horace: –
So not seeing I sang; so seeing and listening say I,
Here as I sit by the stream, as I gaze at the cell of the Sibyl,
Here with Albunea's home and the grove of Tiburnus beside me;
Tivoli beautiful is, and musical, O Teverone,
Dashing from mountain to plain, thy parted impetuous waters!
Tivoli's waters and rocks; and fair unto Monte Gennaro
(Haunt even yet, I must think, as I wander and gaze, of the shadows,
Faded and pale, yet immortal, of Faunus, the Nymphs, and the
    Graces),
Fair in itself, and yet fairer with human completing creations,
Folded in Sabine recesses the valley and villa of Horace: –
So not seeing I sang, so now – Nor seeing, nor hearing,
Neither by waterfall lulled, nor folded in sylvan embraces,
Neither by cell of the Sibyl, nor stepping the Monte Gennaro,
Seated on Anio's bank, nor sipping Bandusian waters,
But on Montorio's height, looking down on the tile-clad streets, the
Cupolas, crosses, and domes, the bushes and kitchen-gardens,
Which, by the grace of the Tibur, proclaim themselves Rome of the
    Romans, –
But on Montorio's height, looking forth to the vapoury mountains,

Cheating the prisoner Hope with illusions of vision and fancy, –
But on Montorio's height, with these weary soldiers by me,
Waiting till Oudinot enter, to reinstate Pope and Tourist.

### XII *Mary Trevellyn to Miss Roper*

Dear Miss Roper, – It seems, George Vernon, before we left Rome,
    said
Something to Mr. Claude about what they call his attentions.
Susan, two nights ago, for the first time, heard this from Georgina.
It is *so* disagreeable and *so* annoying to think of!
If it could only be known, though we never may meet him again, that
It was all George's doing, and we were entirely unconscious,
It would extremely relieve – Your ever affectionate Mary.

### P.S. (*1*)

Here is your letter arrived this moment, just as I wanted.
So you have seen him, – indeed, – and guessed, – how dreadfully
    clever!
What did he really say? and what was your answer exactly?
Charming! – but wait for a moment, I haven't read through the letter.

### P.S. (2)

Ah, my dearest Miss Roper, do just as you fancy about it.
If you think it sincerer to tell him I know of it, do so.
Though I should most extremely dislike it, I know I could manage.
It is the simplest thing, but surely wholly uncalled for.
Do as you please; you know I trust implicitly to you.
Say whatever is right and needful for ending the matter.
Only don't tell Mr. Claude, what I will tell you as a secret,
That I should like very well to show him myself I forget it.

### P.S. (*3*)

I am to say that the wedding is finally settled for Tuesday.
Ah, my dear Miss Roper, you surely, surely can manage
Not to let it appear that I know of that odious matter.

It would be pleasanter far for myself to treat it exactly
As if it had not occurred; and I do not think he would like it.
I must remember to add, that as soon as the wedding is over
We shall be off, I believe, in a hurry, and travel to Milan;
There to meet friends of Papa's, I am told, at the Croce di Malta;
Then I cannot say whither, but not at present to England.

### XIII *Claude to Eustace*

Yes, on Montorio's height for a last farewell of the city, –
So it appears; though then I was quite uncertain about it.
So, however, it was. And now to explain the proceeding.

I was to go, as I told you, I think, with the people to Florence.
Only the day before, the foolish family Vernon
Made some uneasy remarks, as we walked to our lodging together,
As to intentions, forsooth, and so forth. I was astounded,
Horrified quite; and obtaining just then, as it happened, an offer
(No common favour) of seeing the great Ludovisi collection,
Why, I made this a pretence, and wrote that they must excuse me.
How could I go? Great Heavens! to conduct a permitted flirtation
Under those vulgar eyes, the observed of such observers!
Well, but I now, by a series of fine diplomatic inquiries,
Find from a sort of relation, a good and sensible woman,
Who is remaining at Rome with a brother too ill for removal,
That it was wholly unsanctioned, unknown, – not, I think, by Georgina:
She, however, ere this, – and that is the best of the story, –
She and the Vernon, thank Heaven, are wedded and gone –
    honeymooning.
So – on Montorio's height for a last farewell of the city.
Tibur I have not seen, nor the lakes that of old I had dreamt of;
Tibur I shall not see, nor Anio's waters, nor deep en-
Folded in Sabine recesses the valley and villa of Horace;
Tibur I shall not see; – but something better I shall see.

   Twice I have tried before, and failed in getting the horses;
Twice I have tried and failed: this time it shall not be a failure.

*Therefore farewell, ye hills, and ye, ye envineyarded ruins!*
  *Therefore farewell, ye walls, palaces, pillars, and domes!*
*Therefore farewell, far seen, ye peaks of the mythic Albano,*
  *Seen from Montorio's height, Tibur and Æsula's hills!*
*Ah, could we once, ere we go, could we stand, while, to ocean*
      *descending,*
  *Sinks o'er the yellow dark plain slowly the yellow broad sun,*
*Stand, from the forest emerging at sunset, at once in the champaign,*
  *Open, but studded with trees, chestnuts umbrageous and old,*
*E'en in those fair open fields that incurve to thy beautiful hollow,*
  *Nemi, imbedded in wood, Nemi, inurned in the hill! –*
*Therefore farewell, ye plains, and ye hills, and the City Eternal!*
  *Therefore farewell! We depart, but to behold you again!*


### CANTO IV

*Eastward, or Northward, or West? I wander and ask as I wander,*
  *Weary, yet eager and sure, Where shall I come to my love?*
*Whitherward hasten to seek her? Ye daughters of Italy, tell me,*
  *Graceful and tender and dark, is she consorting with you?*
*Thou that out-climbest the torrent, that tendest thy goats to the summit,*
  *Call to me, child of the Alp, has she been seen on the heights?*
*Italy, farewell I bid thee! for whither she leads me, I follow.*
  *Farewell the vineyard! for I, where I but guess her, must go.*
*Weariness welcome, and labour, wherever it be, if at last it*
  *Bring me in mountain or plain into the sight of my love.*


#### I  *Claude to Eustace, – from Florence*


Gone from Florence; indeed! and that is truly provoking; –
Gone to Milan, it seems; then I go also to Milan.
Five days now departed; but they can travel but slowly; –
I quicker far; and I know, as it happens, the house they will go to. –
Why, what else should I do? Stay here and look at the pictures,
Statues, and churches? Alack, I am sick of the statues and pictures! –
No, to Bologna, Parma, Piacenza, Lodi, and Milan,
Off go we to-night, – and the Venus go to the Devil!

### II *Claude to Eustace, – from Bellaggio*

Gone to Como, they said; and I have posted to Como.
There was a letter left; but the *cameriere* had lost it.
Could it have been for me? They came, however, to Como,
And from Como went by the boat, – perhaps to the Splügen, –
Or to the Stelvio, say, and the Tyrol; also it might be
By Porlezza across to Lugano, and so to the Simplon
Possibly, or the St. Gothard, – or possibly, too, to Baveno,
Orta, Turin, and elsewhere. Indeed, I am greatly bewildered.

### III *Claude to Eustace, – from Bellaggio*

I have been up the Splügen, and on the Stelvio also:
Neither of these can I find they have followed; in no one inn, and
This would be odd, have they written their names. I have been to
    Porlezza;
There they have not been seen, and therefore not at Lugano.
What shall I do? Go on through the Tyrol, Switzerland, Deutschland,
Seeking, an inverse Saul, a kingdom, to find only asses?
   There is a tide, at least, in the *love* affairs of mortals,
Which, when taken at flood, leads on to the happiest fortune, –
Leads to the marriage-morn and the orange-flowers and the altar,
And the long lawful line of crowned joys to crowned joys succeeding. –
Ah, it has ebbed with me! Ye gods, and when it was flowing,
Pitiful fool that I was, to stand fiddle-faddling in that way!

### IV *Claude to Eustace, – from Bellaggio*

I have returned and found their names in the book at Como.
Certain it is I was right, and yet I am also in error.
Added in feminine hand, I read, *By the boat to Bellaggio*. –
So to Bellaggio again, with the words of her writing to aid me.
Yet at Bellaggio I find no trace, no sort of remembrance.
So I am here, and wait, and know every hour will remove them.

V *Claude to Eustace, – from Bellaggio*

I have but one chance left, – and that is going to Florence.
But it is cruel to turn. The mountains seem to demand me, –
Peak and valley from far to beckon and motion me onward.
Somewhere amid their folds she passes whom fain I would follow;
Somewhere among those heights she haply calls me to seek her.
Ah, could I hear her call! could I catch the glimpse of her raiment!
Turn, however, I must, though it seem I turn to desert her;
For the sense of the thing is simply to hurry to Florence,
Where the certainty yet may be learnt, I suppose, from the Ropers.

VI *Mary Trevellyn, from Lucerne, to Miss Roper, at Florence*

Dear Miss Roper, – By this you are safely away, we are hoping,
Many a league from Rome; ere long we trust we shall see you.
How have you travelled? I wonder; – was Mr. Claude your companion?
As for ourselves, we went from Como straight to Lugano;
So by the Mount St. Gothard; we meant to go by Porlezza,
Taking the steamer, and stopping, as you had advised, at Bellaggio,
Two or three days or more; but this was suddenly altered,
After we left the hotel, on the very way to the steamer.
So we have seen, I fear, not one of the lakes in perfection.
Well, he is not come, and now, I suppose, he will not come.
What will you think, meantime? – and yet I must really confess it; –
What will you say? I wrote him a note. We left in a hurry,
Went from Milan to Como, three days before we expected.
But I thought, if he came all the way to Milan, he really
Ought not to be disappointed; and so I wrote three lines to
Say I had heard he was coming, desirous of joining our party; –
If so, then I said, we had started for Como, and meant to
Cross the St. Gothard, and stay, we believed, at Lucerne, for the
        summer.
Was it wrong? and why, if it was, has it failed to bring him?
Did he not think it worth while to come to Milan? He knew (you
Told him) the house we should go to. Or may it, perhaps, have
        miscarried?
Any way, now, I repent, and am heartily vexed that I wrote it.

*There is a home on the shore of the Alpine sea, that upswelling*
  *High up the mountain-sides spreads in the hollow between;*
*Wilderness, mountain, and snow from the land of the olive conceal it;*
  *Under Pilatus's hill low by its river it lies:*
*Italy, utter the word, and the olive and vine will allure not, –*
  *Wilderness, forest, and snow will not the passage impede;*
*Italy, unto thy cities receding, the clue to recover,*
  *Hither, recovered the clue, shall not the traveller haste?*

## CANTO V

*There is a city, upbuilt on the quays of the turbulent Arno,*
  *Under Fiesole's heights, – thither are we to return?*
*There is a city that fringes the curve of the inflowing waters,*
  *Under the perilous hill fringes the beautiful bay, –*
*Parthenope, do they call thee? – the Siren, Neapolis, seated*
  *Under Vesevus's hill, – are we receding to thee? –*
*Sicily, Greece, will invite, and the Orient; – or are we to turn to*
  *England, which may after all be for its children the best?*

### I *Mary Trevellyn, from Lucerne, to Miss Roper, at Florence*

So you are really free, and living in quiet at Florence;
That is delightful news; you travelled slowly and safely;
Mr. Claude got you out; took rooms at Florence before you;
Wrote from Milan to say so; had left directly for Milan,
Hoping to find us soon; – *if he could, he would, you are certain. –*
Dear Miss Roper, your letter has made me exceedingly happy.
    You are quite sure, you say, he asked you about our intentions;
You had not heard as yet of Lucerne, but told him of Como. –
Well, perhaps he will come; – however, I will not expect it.
Though you say you are sure, – *if he can, he will, you are certain.*
O my dear, many thanks from your ever affectionate Mary.

## II *Claude to Eustace*

*Florence*

*Action will furnish belief,* – but will that belief be the true one?
This is the point, you know. However, it doesn't much matter.
What one wants, I suppose, is to predetermine the action,
So as to make it entail, not a chance belief, but the true one.
*Out of the question,* you say; *if a thing isn't wrong, we may do it.*
Ah! but this *wrong,* you see – but I do not know that it matters.
Eustace, the Ropers are gone, and no one can tell me about them.

*Pisa*

Pisa, they say they think; and so I follow to Pisa,
Hither and thither inquiring. I weary of making inquiries.
I am ashamed, I declare, of asking people about it. –
Who are your friends? You said you had friends who would certainly
  know them.

*Florence*

But it is idle, moping, and thinking, and trying to fix her
Image more and more in, to write the old perfect inscription
Over and over again upon every page of remembrance.
I have settled to stay at Florence to wait for your answer.
Who are your friends? Write quickly and tell me. I wait for your
  answer.

## III *Mary Trevellyn to Miss Roper, – at Lucca Baths*

You are at Lucca baths, you tell me, to stay for the summer;
Florence was quite too hot; you can't move further at present.
Will you not come, do you think, before the summer is over?
Mr. C. got you out with very considerable trouble;
And he was useful and kind, and seemed so happy to serve you.
Didn't stay with you long, but talked very openly to you;
Made you almost his confessor, without appearing to know it, –
What about? – and you say you didn't need his confessions.
O my dear Miss Roper, I dare not trust what you tell me!
  Will he come, do you think? I am really so sorry for him.

They didn't give him my letter at Milan, I feel pretty certain.
You had told him Bellagio. We didn't go to Bellagio;
So he would miss our track, and perhaps never come to Lugano,
Where we were written in full, *To Lucerne across the St. Gothard*.
But he could write to you; – you would tell him where you were going.

## IV *Claude to Eustace*

Let me, then, bear to forget her. I will not cling to her falsely;
Nothing factitious or forced shall impair the old happy relation.
I will let myself go, forget, not try to remember;
I will walk on my way, accept the chances that meet me,
Freely encounter the world, imbibe these alien airs, and
Never ask if new feelings and thoughts are of her or of others.
Is she not changing herself? – the old image would only delude me.
I will be bold, too, and change, – if it must be. Yet if in all things,
Yet if I do but aspire evermore to the Absolute only,
I shall be doing, I think, somehow, what she will be doing; –
I shall be thine, O my child, some way, though I know not in what way,
Let me submit to forget her; I must; I already forget her.

## V *Claude to Eustace*

Utterly vain is, alas! this attempt at the Absolute, – wholly!
I, who believed not in her, because I would fain believe nothing,
Have to believe as I may, with a wilful, unmeaning acceptance.
I, who refused to enfasten the roots of my floating existence
In the rich earth, cling now to the hard, naked rock that is left me, –
Ah! she was worthy, Eustace, – and that, indeed, is my comfort, –
Worthy a nobler heart than a fool such as I could have given her.

––––––––––

Yes, it relieves me to write, though I do not send, and the chance
    that
Takes may destroy my fragments. But as men pray, without asking
Whether One really exist to hear or do anything for them, –
Simply impelled by the need of the moment to turn to a Being

In a conception of whom there is freedom from all limitation, –
So in your image I turn to an *ens rationis* of friendship,
Even so write in your name I know not to whom nor in what wise.

---

There was a time, methought it was but lately departed,
When, if a thing was denied me, I felt I was bound to attempt it;
Choice alone should take, and choice alone should surrender.
There was a time, indeed, when I had not retired thus early,
Languidly thus, from pursuit of a purpose I once had adopted.
But it is over, all that! I have slunk from the perilous field in
Whose wild struggle of forces the prizes of life are contested.
It is over, all that! I am a coward, and know it.
Courage in me could be only factitious, unnatural, useless.

---

Comfort has come to me here in the dreary streets of the city,
Comfort – how do you think?– with a barrel-organ to bring it.
Moping along the streets, and cursing my day as I wandered,
All of a sudden my ear met the sound of an English psalm-tune.
Comfort me it did, till indeed I was very near crying.
Ah, there is some great truth, partial, very likely, but needful,
Lodged, I am strangely sure, in the tones of the English psalm-tune:
Comfort it was at least; and I must take without question
Comfort, however it come, in the dreary streets of the city.

---

What with trusting myself, and seeking support from within me,
Almost I could believe I had gained a religious assurance,
Formed in my own poor soul a great moral basis to rest on.
Ah, but indeed I see, I feel it factitious entirely;
I refuse, reject, and put it utterly from me;
I will look straight out, see things, not try to evade them;
Fact shall be fact for me, and the Truth the Truth as ever,
Flexible, changeable, vague, and multiform, and doubtful. –
Off, and depart to the void, thou subtle, fanatical tempter!

---

135,V, v. *ens rationis* a being of the mind (here an imaginary 'type' of friendship)

I shall behold thee again (is it so?) at a new visitation,
O ill genius thou! I shall, at my life's dissolution
(When the pulses are weak, and the feeble light of the reason
Flickers, an unfed flame retiring slow from the socket),
Low on a sick-bed laid, hear one, as it were, at the doorway,
And, looking up, see thee standing by, looking emptily at me;
I shall entreat thee then, though now I dare to refuse thee, –
Pale and pitiful now, but terrible then to the dying. –
Well, I will see thee again, and while I can, will repel thee.

## VI *Claude to Eustace*

Rome is fallen, I hear, the gallant Medici taken,
Noble Manara slain, and Garibaldi has lost *il Moro*; –
Rome is fallen; and fallen, or falling, heroical Venice.
I, meanwhile, for the loss of a single small chit of a girl, sit
Moping and mourning here, – for her, and myself much smaller.
   Whither depart the souls of the brave that die in the battle,
Die in the lost, lost fight, for the cause that perishes with them?
Are they upborne from the field on the slumberous pinions of angels
Unto a far-off home, where the weary rest from their labour,
And the deep wounds are healed, and the bitter and burning moisture
Wiped from the generous eyes? or do they linger, unhappy,
Pining, and haunting the grave of their by-gone hope and endeavour?
   All declamation, alas! though I talk, I care not for Rome nor
Italy; feebly and faintly, and but with the lips, can lament the
Wreck of the Lombard youth, and the victory of the oppressor.
Whither depart the brave? – God knows; I certainly do not.

## VII *Mary Trevellyn to Miss Roper*

He has not come as yet; and now I must not expect it.
You have written, you say, to friends at Florence, to see him,
If he perhaps should return; – but that is surely unlikely.
Has he not written to you? – he did not know your direction.
Oh, how strange never once to have told him where you were going!
Yet if he only wrote to Florence, that would have reached you.
If what you say he said was true, why has he not done so?
Is he gone back to Rome, do you think, to his Vatican marbles? –

O my dear Miss Roper, forgive me! do not be angry! –
You have written to Florence; – your friends would certainly find him.
Might you not write to him? – but yet it is so little likely!
I shall expect nothing more. – Ever yours, your affectionate Mary.

### VIII *Claude to Eustace*

I cannot stay at Florence, not even to wait for a letter.
Galleries only oppress me. Remembrance of hope I had cherished
(Almost more than as hope, when I passed through Florence the first
    time)
Lies like a sword in my soul. I am more a coward than ever,
Chicken-hearted, past thought. The *caffès* and waiters distress me.
All is unkind, and, alas! I am ready for any one's kindness.
Oh, I knew it of old, and knew it, I thought, to perfection,
If there is any one thing in the world to preclude all kindness,
It is the need of it, – it is this sad, self-defeating dependence.
Why is this, Eustace? Myself, were I stronger, I think I could tell you.
But it is odd when it comes. So plumb I the deeps of depression,
Daily in deeper, and find no support, no will, no purpose.
All my old strengths are gone. And yet I shall have to do something.
Ah, the key of our life, that passes all wards, opens all locks,
Is not *I will*, but *I must*. I must, – I must, – and I do it.

––––––––––

After all, do I know that I really cared so about her?
Do whatever I will, I cannot call up her image;
For when I close my eyes, I see, very likely, St. Peter's,
Or the Pantheon façade, or Michel Angelo's figures,
Or, at a wish, when I please, the Alban hills and the Forum, –
But that face, those eyes, – ah, no, never anything like them;
Only, try as I will, a sort of featureless outline,
And a pale blank orb, which no recollection will add to.
After all, perhaps there was something factitious about it;
I have had pain, it is true: I have wept, and so have the actors.

––––––––––

At the last moment I have your letter, for which I was waiting;
I have taken my place, and see no good in inquiries.
Do nothing more, good Eustace, I pray you. It only will vex me.
Take no measures. Indeed, should we meet, I could not be certain;
All might be changed, you know. Or perhaps there was nothing to be
    changed.
It is a curious history, this; and yet I foresaw it;
I could have told it before. The Fates, it is clear, are against us;
For it is certain enough I met with the people you mention;
They were at Florence the day I returned there, and spoke to me even;
Stayed a week, saw me often; departed, and whither I know not.
Great is Fate, and is best. I believe in Providence partly.
What is ordained is right, and all that happens is ordered.
Ah, no, that isn't it. But yet I retain my conclusion.
I will go where I am led, and will not dictate to the chances.
Do nothing more, I beg. If you love me, forbear interfering.

### IX *Claude to Eustace*

Shall we come out of it all, some day, as one does from a tunnel?
Will it be all at once, without our doing or asking,
We shall behold clear day, the trees and meadows about us,
And the faces of friends, and the eyes we loved looking at us?
Who knows? Who can say? It will not do to suppose it.

### X *Claude to Eustace, – from Rome*

Rome will not suit me, Eustace; the priests and soldiers possess it;
Priests and soldiers: – and, ah! which is the worst, the priest or the
    soldier?
    Politics farewell, however! For what could I do? with inquiring,
Talking, collating the journals, go fever my brain about things o'er
Which I can have no control. No, happen whatever may happen,
Time, I suppose, will subsist; the earth will revolve on its axis;
People will travel; the stranger will wander as now in the city;
Rome will be here, and the Pope the *custode* of Vatican marbles.
    I have no heart, however, for any marble or fresco;
I have essayed it in vain; 'tis in vain as yet to essay it:
But I may haply resume some day my studies in this kind;

Not as the Scripture says, is, I think, the fact. Ere our death-day,
Faith, I think, does pass, and Love; but Knowledge abideth.
Let us seek Knowledge; – the rest may come and go as it happens.
Knowledge is hard to seek, and harder yet to adhere to.
Knowledge is painful often; and yet when we know, we are happy.
Seek it, and leave mere Faith and Love to come with the chances.
As for Hope, – to-morrow I hope to be starting for Naples.
Rome will not do, I see, for many very good reasons.
 Eastward, then, I suppose, with the coming of winter, to Egypt.


   XI *Mary Trevellyn to Miss Roper*


You have heard nothing; of course, I know you can have heard
  nothing.
Ah, well, more than once I have broken my purpose, and
  sometimes,
Only too often, have looked for the little lake-steamer to bring him.
But it is only fancy, – I do not really expect it.
Oh, and you see I know so exactly how he would take it:
Finding the chances prevail against meeting again, he would banish
Forthwith every thought of the poor little possible hope, which
I myself could not help, perhaps, thinking only too much of;
He would resign himself, and go. I see it exactly.
So I also submit, although in a different manner.
 Can you not really come? We go very shortly to England.


*So go forth to the world, to the good report and the evil!*
 *Go, little book! thy tale, is it not evil and good?*
*Go, and if strangers revile, pass quietly by without answer.*
 *Go, and if curious friends ask of thy rearing and age,*
*Say, 'I am flitting about many years from brain unto brain of*
 *Feeble and restless youths born to inglorious days:*
*But,' so finish the word, 'I was writ in a Roman chamber,*
*When from Janiculan heights thundered the cannon of France.'*

# GEORGE ELIOT

1819–80

Brother and Sister

## I

I cannot choose but think upon the time
When our two lives grew like two buds that kiss
At lightest thrill from the bee's swinging chime,
Because the one so near the other is.

He was the elder and a little man
Of forty inches, bound to show no dread,
And I the girl that puppy-like now ran,
Now lagged behind my brother's larger tread.

I held him wise, and when he talked to me
Of snakes and birds, and which God loved the best,
I thought his knowledge marked the boundary
Where men grew blind, though angels knew the rest.

If he said 'Hush!' I tried to hold my breath;
Wherever he said 'Come!' I stepped in faith.

## II

Long years have left their writing on my brow,
But yet the freshness and the dew-fed beam
Of those young mornings are about me now,
When we two wandered toward the far-off stream

With rod and line. Our basket held a store
Baked for us only, and I thought with joy
That I should have my share, though he had more,
Because he was the elder and a boy.

The firmaments of daisies since to me
Have had those mornings in their opening eyes,
The bunchèd cowslip's pale transparency
Carries that sunshine of sweet memories,

    And wild-rose branches take their finest scent
    From those blest hours of infantine content.

### III

Our mother bade us keep the trodden ways,
Stroked down my tippet, set my brother's frill,
Then with the benediction of her gaze
Clung to us lessening, and pursued us still

Across the homestead to the rookery elms,
Whose tall old trunks had each a grassy mound,
So rich for us, we counted them as realms
With varied products: here were earth-nuts found,

And here the Lady-fingers in deep shade;
Here sloping toward the Moat the rushes grew,
The large to split for pith, the small to braid;
While over all the dark rooks cawing flew,

    And made a happy strange solemnity,
    A deep-toned chant from life unknown to me.

### IV

Our meadow-path had memorable spots:
One where it bridged a tiny rivulet,
Deep hid by tangled blue Forget-me-nots;
And all along the waving grasses met

My little palm, or nodded to my cheek,
When flowers with upturned faces gazing drew
My wonder downward, seeming all to speak
With eyes of souls that dumbly heard and knew.

Then came the copse, where wild things rushed unseen,
And black-scathed grass betrayed the past abode
Of mystic gypsies, who still lurked between
Me and each hidden distance of the road.

A gypsy once had startled me at play,
Blotting with her dark smile my sunny day.

## V

Thus rambling we were schooled in deepest lore,
And learned the meanings that give words a soul,
The fear, the love, the primal passionate store,
Whose shaping impulses make manhood whole.

Those hours were seed to all my after good;
My infant gladness, through eye, ear, and touch,
Took easily as warmth a various food
To nourish the sweet skill of loving much.

For who in age shall roam the earth and find
Reasons for loving that will strike out love
With sudden rod from the hard year-pressed mind?
Were reasons sown as thick as stars above,

'Tis love must see them, as the eye sees light:
Day is but Number to the darkened sight.

## VI

Our brown canal was endless to my thought;
And on its banks I sat in dreamy peace,
Unknowing how the good I loved was wrought,
Untroubled by the fear that it would cease.

Slowly the barges floated into view
Rounding a grassy hill to me sublime
With some Unknown beyond it, whither flew
The parting cuckoo toward a fresh spring time.

The wide-arched bridge, the scented elder-flowers,
The wondrous watery rings that died too soon,
The echoes of the quarry, the still hours
With white robe sweeping-on the shadeless noon,

   Were but my growing self, are part of me,
   My present Past, my root of piety.

## VII

Those long days measured by my little feet
Had chronicles which yield me many a text;
Where irony still finds an image meet
Of full-grown judgments in this world perplext.

One day my brother left me in high charge,
To mind the rod, while he went seeking bait,
And bade me, when I saw a nearing barge,
Snatch out the line, lest he should come too late.

Proud of the task, I watched with all my might
For one whole minute, till my eyes grew wide,
Till sky and earth took on a strange new light
And seemed a dream-world floating on some tide –

   A fair pavilioned boat for me alone
   Bearing me onward through the vast unknown.

## VIII

But sudden came the barge's pitch-black prow,
Nearer and angrier came my brother's cry,
And all my soul was quivering fear, when lo!
Upon the imperilled line, suspended high,

A silver perch! My guilt that won the prey,
Now turned to merit, had a guerdon rich
Of songs and praises, and made merry play,
Until my triumph reached its highest pitch

When all at home were told the wondrous feat,
And how the little sister had fished well.
In secret, though my fortune tasted sweet,
I wondered why this happiness befell.

  'The little lass had luck,' the gardener said:
  And so I learned, luck was with glory wed.

## IX

We had the self-same world enlarged for each
By loving difference of girl and boy:
The fruit that hung on high beyond my reach
He plucked for me, and oft he must employ

A measuring glance to guide my tiny shoe
Where lay firm stepping-stones, or call to mind
'This thing I like my sister may not do,
For she is little, and I must be kind.'

Thus boyish Will the nobler mastery learned
Where inward vision over impulse reigns,
Widening its life with separate life discerned,
A Like unlike, a Self that self restrains.

  His years with others must the sweeter be
  For those brief days he spent in loving me.

## X

His sorrow was my sorrow, and his joy
Sent little leaps and laughs through all my frame;
My doll seemed lifeless and no girlish toy
Had any reason when my brother came.

I knelt with him at marbles, marked his fling
Cut the ringed stem and make the apple drop,
Or watched him winding close the spiral string
That looped the orbits of the humming top.

Grasped by such fellowship my vagrant thought
Ceased with dream-fruit dream-wishes to fulfil;
My aëry-picturing fantasy was taught
Subjection to the harder, truer skill

That seeks with deeds to grave a thought-tracked line,
And by 'What is,' 'What will be' to define.


## XI


School parted us; we never found again
That childish world where our two spirits mingled
Like scents from varying roses that remain
One sweetness, nor can evermore be singled.

Yet the twin habit of that early time
Lingered for long about the heart and tongue:
We had been natives of one happy clime,
And its dear accent to our utterance clung.

Till the dire years whose awful name is Change
Had grasped our souls still yearning in divorce,
And pitiless shaped them in two forms that range,
Two elements which sever their life's course.

But were another childhood-world my share,
I would be born a little sister there.

*1869*

# ERNEST JONES

1819–68

137          The Factory Town

The night had sunk along the city,
    It was a bleak and cheerless hour;
The wild winds sang their solemn ditty
    To cold grey wall and blackened tower.

The factories gave forth lurid fires
    From pent-up hells within their breast;
E'en Etna's burning wrath expires,
    But *man's* volcanoes never rest.

Women, children, men were toiling,
    Locked in dungeons close and black,
Life's fast-failing thread uncoiling
    Round the wheel, the *modern rack*!

E'en the very stars seemed troubled
    With the mingled fume and roar;
The city like a cauldron bubbled,
    With its poison boiling o'er.

For the reeking walls environ
    Mingled groups of death and life:
Fellow-workmen, flesh and iron,
    Side by side in deadly strife.

There, amid the wheels' dull droning
    And the heavy, choking air,
Strength's repining, labour's groaning,
    And the throttling of despair, –

With the dust around them whirling,
   And the white, cracked, fevered lips,
And the shuttle's ceaseless twirling,
   And the short life's toil eclipse –

Stood half-naked infants shivering
   With heart-frost amid the heat;
Manhood's shrunken sinews quivering
   To the engine's horrid beat!

Woman's aching heart was throbbing
   With her wasting children's pain,
While red Mammon's hand was robbing
   God's thought-treasure from their brain!

Yet their lord bids proudly wander
   Stranger eyes thro' factory scenes;
'Here are men, and engines yonder.'
   'I see nothing but *machines*!'

Hark! amid that bloodless slaughter
   Comes the wailing of despair:
'Oh! for but one drop of water!
   'Oh! for but one breath of air!

'One fresh touch of dewy grasses,
   'Just to cool this shrivelled hand!
'Just to catch one breeze that passes
   'From some shady forest land.'

No! though 'twas a night of summer
   With a scent of new mown hay
From where the moon, the fairies' mummer,
   On distant fields enchanted lay!

On the lealands slept the cattle,
   Freshness through the forest ran –
While, in Mammon's mighty battle,
   Man was immolating man!

While the rich, with power unstable,
  Crushed the pauper's heart of pain,
As though those rich were heirs of *Abel*,
  And the poor the sons of *Cain*.

While the proud from drowsy riot,
  Staggered past his church unknown,
Where his God, in the great quiet,
  Preached the livelong night alone!

While the bloated trader passes,
  Lord of loom and lord of mill;
On his pathway rush the masses,
  Crushed beneath his stubborn will.

Eager slaves, a willing heriot,
  O'er their brethren's living road
Drive him in his golden chariot,
  Quickened by his golden goad.

Young forms – with their pulses stifled,
  Young heads – with the eldered brain,
Young hearts – of their spirit rifled,
  Young lives – sacrificed in vain:

There they lie – the withered corses,
  With not one regretful thought,
Trampled by thy fierce steam-horses,
  England's mighty *Juggernaut*!

Over all the solemn heaven
  Arches, like a God's reproof
At the offerings man has driven
  To Hell's altars, loom and woof!

Hear ye not the secret sighing?
  And the tear drop thro' the night?
See ye not a nation dying
  For want of rest, and air, and light?

Perishing for want of *Nature*!
   Crowded in the stifling town –
Dwarfed in brain and shrunk in stature –
   Generations growing *down*!

Thinner wanes the rural village,
   Smokier lies the fallow plain –
Shrinks the cornfields' pleasant tillage,
   Fades the orchard's rich domain;

And a banished population
   Festers in the fetid street: –
Give us, God, to save our nation,
   Less of *cotton*, more of *wheat*.

Take us back to lea and wild wood,
   Back to nature and to Thee!
To the child restore his childhood –
   To the man his dignity!

Lo! the night hangs o'er the city,
   And the hours in fever fly,
And the wild winds sing their ditty,
   And the generations die.

# CHARLES KINGSLEY
## 1819–75

138        The Poetry of a Root Crop

Underneath their eider-robe
Russet swede and golden globe,
Feathered carrot, burrowing deep,
Steadfast wait in charmèd sleep;
Treasure-houses wherein lie,
Locked by angels' alchemy,
Milk and hair, and blood, and bone,
Children of the barren stone;
Children of the flaming Air,
With his blue eye keen and bare,
Spirit-peopled smiling down
On frozen field and toiling town –
Toiling town that will not heed
God His voice for rage and greed;
Frozen fields that surpliced lie,
Gazing patient at the sky;
Like some marble carven nun,
With folded hands when work is done,
Who mute upon her tomb doth pray,
Till the resurrection day.


139        Airly Beacon

Airly Beacon, Airly Beacon;
  Oh the pleasant sight to see
Shires and towns from Airly Beacon,
  While my love climbed up to me!

Airly Beacon, Airly Beacon;
   Oh the happy hours we lay
Deep in ferns on Airly Beacon,
   Courting through the summer's day!

Airly Beacon, Airly Beacon;
   Oh the weary haunt for me,
All alone on Airly Beacon,
   With his baby on my knee!

140            A Lament

The merry merry lark was up and singing,
   And the hare was out and feeding on the lea;
And the merry merry bells below were ringing,
   When my child's laugh rang through me.

Now the hare is snared and dead beside the snow-yard,
   And the lark beside the dreary winter sea;
And the baby in his cradle in the churchyard
   Sleeps sound till the bell brings me.

141          The Last Buccaneer

Oh England is a pleasant place for them that's rich and high,
But England is a cruel place for such poor folks as I;
And such a port for mariners I ne'er shall see again
As the pleasant Isle of Avès, beside the Spanish main.

There were forty craft in Avès that were both swift and stout,
All furnished well with small arms and cannons round about;
And a thousand men in Avès made laws so fair and free
To choose their valiant captains and obey them loyally.

Thence we sailed against the Spaniard with his hoards of plate
    and gold,
Which he wrung with cruel tortures from Indian folk of old;
Likewise the merchant captains, with hearts as hard as stone,
Who flog men and keel-haul them, and starve them to the bone.

Oh the palms grew high in Avès, and fruits that shone like gold,
And the colibris and parrots they were gorgeous to behold;
And the negro maids to Avès from bondage fast did flee,
To welcome gallant sailors, a-sweeping in from sea.

Oh sweet it was in Avès to hear the landward breeze,
A-swing with good tobacco in a net between the trees,
With a negro lass to fan you, while you listened to the roar
Of the breakers on the reef outside, that never touched the shore.

But Scripture saith, an ending to all fine things must be;
So the King's ships sailed on Avès, and quite put down were we.
All day we fought like bulldogs, but they burst the booms at
    night;
And I fled in a piragua, sore wounded, from the fight.

Nine days I floated starving, and a negro lass beside,
Till for all I tried to cheer her, the poor young thing she died;
But as I lay a gasping, a Bristol sail came by,
And brought me home to England, to beg until I die.

And now I'm old and going – I'm sure I can't tell where;
One comfort is, this world's so hard, I can't be worse off there:
If I might but be a sea-dove, I'd fly across the main,
To the pleasant Isle of Avès, to look at it once again.

# ANNE BRONTË
1820–49

142                    Song

We know where deepest lies the snow,
And where the frost-winds keenest blow,
        O'er every mountain's brow;
We long have known and learnt to bear
The wandering outlaw's toil and care,
But where we late were hunted, there
        Our foes are hunted now.

We have their princely homes, and they
To our wild haunts are chased away,
        Dark woods, and desert caves.
And we can range from hill to hill,
And chase our vanquished victors still;
Small respite will they find until
        They slumber in their graves.

But I would rather be the hare,
That crouching in its sheltered lair
        Must start at every sound;
That forced from cornfields waving wide
Is driven to seek the bare hillside,
Or in the tangled copse to hide,
        Than be the hunter's hound.

# ANNE EVANS

1820–70

143
## Over!

A knight came prancing on his way,
And across the path a lady lay:
'Stoop a little and hear me speak!'
Then, 'You are strong, and I am weak:
  Ride over me now, and kill me.'

He opened wide his gay blue eyes,
Like one o'ermastered by surprise;
His cheek and brow grew burning red,
'Long looked-for, come at last,' she said,
  'Ride over me now, and kill me.'

Then softly spoke the knight, and smiled:
'Fair maiden, whence this mood so wild?'
'Smile on,' said she, 'my reign is o'er,
But do my bidding yet once more:
  Ride over me now, and kill me.'

He smote his steed of dapple-gray,
And lightly cleared her where she lay;
But still, as he sped on amain,
She murmured ever, 'Turn again:
  Ride over me now, and kill me.'

# JEAN INGELOW

## 1820–97

144    'Wake, baillie, wake! the crafts are out;
           Wake!' said the knight, 'be quick!
       For high street, bye street, over the town
           They fight with poker and stick.'
       Said the squire, 'A fight so fell was ne'er
           In all thy bailliewick.'
       What said the old clock in the tower?
           'Tick, tick, tick!'

       'Wake, daughter, wake! the hour draws on;
           Wake!' quoth the dame, 'be quick!
       The meats are set, the guests are coming,
           The fiddler waxing his stick.'
       She said, 'The bridegroom waiting and waiting
           To see thy face is sick.'
       What said the new clock in her bower?
           'Tick, tick, tick!'


145              Loss and Waste

       Up to far Osteroe and Suderoe
         The deep sea-floor lies strewn with Spanish wrecks,
       O'er minted gold the fair-haired fishers go,
         O'er sunken bravery of high carvèd decks.

       In earlier days great Carthage suffered bale
         (All her waste works choke under sandy shoals);
       And reckless hands tore down the temple veil;
         And Omar burned the Alexandrian rolls.

The Old World arts men suffered not to last,
  Flung down they trampled lie and sunk from view,
He lets wild forest for these ages past
  Grow over the lost cities of the New.

O for a life that shall not be refused
To see the lost things found, and waste things used.

# EBENEZER JONES
## 1820–60

146                                   High Summer

> I never wholly feel that summer is high,
> However green the trees, or loud the birds,
> However movelessly eye winking herds,
> Stand in field ponds, or under large trees lie, –
> Till I do climb all cultured pastures by,
> That hedged by hedgerows studiously fretted trim,
> Smile like a lady's face with lace laced prim,
> And on some moor or hill that seeks the sky
> Lonely and nakedly, – utterly lie down,
> And feel the sunshine throbbing on body and limb,
> My drowsy brain in pleasant drunkenness swim,
> Each rising thought sink back, and dreamily drown,
> Smiles creep o'er my face, and smother my lips, and cloy,
> Each muscle sink to itself, and separately enjoy.


147                                 The Poet's Death

Now the Poet's death was certain, and the leech had left the room;
Only those who fondly loved him, waited to receive the doom;
And the sister he loved best, whiter than hemlock did veer;
And she bent, and 'life is going' faintly whispered in his ear.

Though her fingers clasped his fingers, though her cheek by his did lay;
Though she whispered 'I am dying; with thee, death hath no dismay;'
Fiercely sprang the startled Poet, and his eye did fight through space;
While dark agony did thicken his drawn lips, and wrench his face.

Sister arms did wind around him, knelt his sire beside the bed;
And his mother busied round him, love extinguishing her dread;
But the Poet heeded nothing, fixing still his fighting eye,
Gathering, gathering, gathering inward, that he was that hour to die.

Now the sound of smothered sobbings smote upon his distant mind,
And he turned a glance around him, that each gazer's love divined;
The torture in his face did stagger once before his mother's look;
Then came back more whiteningly, while his neck did downward
    crook.

From his crook'd down neck, his visage struggled love back through its
    pain,
First to one, and then to another, and then left them all again;
As the sister wept against him, shudderingly to her he turned;
And his lips did open at her, and his eyes for language yearned.

Quick at her his lips did open, strivingly his eyelids rose,
But no sound, no word, no murmur, their fast gesturings did disclose;
Straightly pointed he his arm then, where his poet-desk was lain;
To his grasp the sister brought it, while the stillness throbbed amain.

From his desk the Poet tore the unformed scriptures of his soul;
And to them he fiercely pointed, while his eyes large tears did roll;
'Perfected, my memory earth to endless time would love and bless;
I must die, and these will live not!' through his lips at last did press.

Whiter grew the gazing faces, as the cliffs that sunshine smites,
When they found no aid could come from earthly loves, or priestly
    rites;
O'er his scriptures he fell forward, and they all did trust and say,
That the last wild pang was on him, for as still as stone he lay.

But than lightning's flash more sudden, he did spurn the abhorred bed;
And a moment he stood tottering, tossed defyingly his head;
Ere one reached him, he was fallen, lifeless, and his wide dulled eye
Rigid with the fierce defiance that had just refused to die.

To the gloomy troop of Atheists, gibberingly the sister ran;
While the praying father kneeling, hurled at her his pious ban;
In the churchyard lies the Poet, and his scent the air depraves;
And ten thousand thousand like him, stuff the earth with such like
    graves.

# MENELLA BUTE SMEDLEY
## 1820–77

148                    A Bird's-Eye View

Quoth the boy, 'I'll climb that tree,
    And bring down a nest I know.'
Quoth the girl, 'I will not see
    Little birds defrauded so.
Cowardly their nests to take,
And their little hearts to break,
And their little eggs to steal.
    Leave them happy for my sake, –
Surely little birds can feel!'

Quoth the boy, 'My senses whirl;
    Until now I never heard
Of the wisdom of a girl,
    Or the feelings of a bird!
Pretty Mrs. Solomon,
Tell me what you reckon on
When you prate in such a strain;
    If I wring their necks anon,
Certainly they *might* feel – pain!'

Quoth the girl, 'I watch them talk,
    Making love and making fun,
In the pretty ash-tree walk,
    When my daily task is done.
In their little eyes I find
They are very fond and kind.
Every change of song or voice,
    Plainly proveth to my mind,
They can suffer and rejoice.'

And the little Robin-bird
  (Nice brown back and crimson breast)
All the conversation heard,
  Sitting trembling in his nest.
'What a world,' he cried, 'of bliss,
Full of birds and girls, were this!
Blithe we'd answer to their call;
  But a great mistake it is
Boys were ever made at all.'

# DORA GREENWELL

1821–82

149            A Scherzo

(*A Shy Person's Wishes*)

With the wasp at the innermost heart of a peach,
On a sunny wall out of tip-toe reach,
With the trout in the darkest summer pool,
With the fern-seed clinging behind its cool
Smooth frond, in the chink of an aged tree,
In the woodbine's horn with the drunken bee,
With the mouse in its nest in a furrow old,
With the chrysalis wrapt in its gauzy fold;
With things that are hidden, and safe, and bold,
With things that are timid, and shy, and free,
Wishing to be;
With the nut in its shell, with the seed in its pod,
With the corn as it sprouts in the kindly clod,
Far down where the secret of beauty shows
In the bulb of the tulip, before it blows;
With things that are rooted, and firm, and deep,
Quiet to lie, and dreamless to sleep;
With things that are chainless, and tameless, and proud,
With the fire in the jagged thunder-cloud,
With the wind in its sleep, with the wind in its waking,
With the drops that go to the rainbow's making,
Wishing to be with the light leaves shaking,
Or stones on some desolate highway breaking;
Far up on the hills, where no foot surprises
The dew as it falls, or the dust as it rises;
To be couched with the beast in its torrid lair,
Or drifting on ice with the polar bear,
With the weaver at work at his quiet loom;
Anywhere, anywhere, out of this room!

150 ## A Valentine

I said to One I loved, 'Why art thou sad?'
  And he made answer, 'There hath been a tune
  Long floating round my brain; morn, night, and
      noon,
With inarticulate cadence making glad,
  Yet vexing me, because I could not find
  Words sweet enough to set to it, and bind
Its music round about my heart for aye.
Till, musing late above an ancient book,
  The window being open, breezes fleet
Lifted the rare old page, and sudden shook
  A loose leaf, writ with song, unto my feet:
In these quaint words methought lies hid the key
  To all those cadences faint struggling round,
Now will I wed them to that melody,
  And set my Life to music by their sound;
E'en so I practised them upon my lute
Early and late, yet found they would not suit
  Together, though so sweet! and all the strain
Broke into discords! still the strain goes on,
But only angers me, its meaning gone;
  Nor will I ever seek to find it words again!'

*February 13*

# FREDERICK LOCKER-LAMPSON
## 1821–95

151                      Beggars

*They eat, and drink, and scheme, and plod, –*
*They go to church on Sunday;*
*And many are afraid of God –*
*And more of Mrs. Grundy.*

I am pacing the Mall in a rapt reverie,
I am thinking if Sophy is thinking of me,
When I'm roused by a ragged and shivering wretch,
Who seems to be well on his way to Jack Ketch.

He has got a bad face, and a shocking bad hat;
A comb in his fist, and he sees I'm a flat,
For he says, 'Buy a comb, it's a fine un to wear;
On'y try it, my Lord, through your whiskers and 'air.'

He eyes my gold chain, as if greedy to crib it;
He looks just as if he'd been blown from a gibbet.
I pause . . .! I pass on, and beside the club fire
I settle that Sophy is all I desire.

As I stroll from the club, and am deep in a strophè
That rolls upon all that's delightful in Sophy,
I'm humbly addressed by an 'object' unnerving,
So tatter'd a wretch must be 'highly deserving.'

She begs, – I am touch'd, but I've great circumspection;
I stifle remorse with the soothing reflection
That cases of vice are by no means a rarity –
The worst vice of all's indiscriminate charity.

Am I right? How I wish that my clerical guide
Would settle this question – and others beside.
For always one's heart to be hardening thus,
If wholesome for Beggars, is hurtful for us.

A few minutes later I'm happy and free
To sip *Its own Sophykins*' five-o'clock tea:
Her table is loaded, for when a girl marries,
What bushels of rubbish they send her from *Barry's*!

'There's a present for *you*, Sir!' Yes, thanks to her thrift,
My Pet has been able to buy me a gift;
And she slips in my hand, the delightfully sly Thing,
A paper-weight form'd of a bronze lizard writhing.

'What a charming *cadeau*! and so truthfully moulded;
But perhaps you don't know, or deserve to be scolded,
That in casting this metal a live, harmless lizard
Was cruelly tortured in ghost and in gizzard?'

'Po-oh!' – says my Lady (she always says 'Pooh'
When she's wilful, and does what she oughtn't to do!)
'Hopgarten protests they've no feeling, and so
It was only their *muscular movement* you know!'

Thinks I (when I've said *au revoir*, and depart –
A Comb in my pocket, a Weight – at my heart),
And when wretched Mendicants writhe, there's a notion
That begging is only their 'muscular motion.'

# MATTHEW ARNOLD
## 1822–88

152        The Sick King in Bokhara

*Hussein*

O most just Vizier, send away
The cloth-merchants, and let them be,
Them and their dues, this day! the King
Is ill at ease, and calls for thee.

*The Vizier*

O merchants, tarry yet a day
Here in Bokhara! but at noon,
To-morrow, come, and ye shall pay
Each fortieth web of cloth to me,
As the law is, and go your way.

O Hussein, lead me to the King!
Thou teller of sweet tales, thine own,
Ferdousi's, and the others', lead!
How is it with my lord?

*Hussein*
                  Alone,
Ever since prayer-time, he doth wait,
O Vizier! without lying down,
In the great window of the gate,
Looking into the Registàn,
Where through the sellers' booths the slaves
Are this way bringing the dead man. –
O Vizier, here is the King's door!

*The King*

O Vizier, I may bury him?

*The Vizier*

O King, thou know'st, I have been sick
These many days, and heard no thing
(For Allah shut my ears and mind),
Not even what thou dost, O King!
Wherefore, that I may counsel thee,
Let Hussein, if thou wilt, make haste
To speak in order what hath chanced.

*The King*

O Vizier, be it as thou say'st!

*Hussein*

Three days since, at the time of prayer,
A certain Moollah, with his robe
All rent, and dust upon his hair,
Watch'd my lord's coming forth, and push'd
The golden mace-bearers aside,
And fell at the King's feet, and cried:

'Justice, O King, and on myself!
On this great sinner, who did break
The law, and by the law must die!
Vengeance, O King!'

               But the King spake:
'What fool is this, that hurts our ears
With folly? or what drunken slave?
My guards, what, prick him with your spears!
Prick me the fellow from the path!'
As the King said, so it was done,
And to the mosque my lord pass'd on.

But on the morrow, when the King
Went forth again, the holy book
Carried before him, as is right,
And through the square his way he took;
My man comes running, fleck'd with blood
From yesterday, and falling down
Cries out most earnestly: 'O King,
My lord, O King, do right, I pray!

'How canst thou, ere thou hear, discern
If I speak folly? but a king,
Whether a thing be great or small,
Like Allah, hears and judges all.

'Wherefore hear thou! Thou know'st, how fierce
In these last days the sun hath burn'd;
That the green water in the tanks
Is to a putrid puddle turn'd;
And the canal, which from the stream
Of Samarcand is brought this way,
Wastes, and runs thinner every day.

'Now I at nightfall had gone forth
Alone, and in a darksome place
Under some mulberry-trees I found
A little pool; and in short space,
With all the water that was there
I fill'd my pitcher, and stole home
Unseen; and having drink to spare,
I hid the can behind the door,
And went up on the roof to sleep.

'But in the night, which was with wind
And burning dust, again I creep
Down, having fever, for a drink.

'Now meanwhile had my brethren found
The water-pitcher, where it stood
Behind the door upon the ground,

And call'd my mother; and they all,
As they were thirsty, and the night
Most sultry, drain'd the pitcher there;
That they sate with it, in my sight,
Their lips still wet, when I came down.

'Now mark! I, being fever'd, sick
(Most unblest also), at that sight
Brake forth, and cursed them – dost thou hear? –
One was my mother – Now, do right!'

But my lord mused a space, and said:
'Send him away, Sirs, and make on!
It is some madman!' the King said.
As the King bade, so was it done.

The morrow, at the self-same hour,
In the King's path, behold, the man,
Not kneeling, sternly fix'd! he stood
Right opposite, and thus began,
Frowning grim down: 'Thou wicked King,
Most deaf where thou shouldst most give ear!
What, must I howl in the next world,
Because thou wilt not listen here?

'What, wilt thou pray, and get thee grace,
And all grace shall to me be grudged?
Nay but, I swear, from this thy path
I will not stir till I be judged!'

Then they who stood about the King
Drew close together and conferr'd;
Till that the King stood forth and said:
'Before the priests thou shalt be heard.'

But when the Ulemas were met,
And the thing heard, they doubted not;
But sentenced him, as the law is,
To die by stoning on the spot.

Now the King charged us secretly:
'Stoned must he be, the law stands so.
Yet, if he seek to fly, give way;
Hinder him not, but let him go.'

So saying, the King took a stone,
And cast it softly; – but the man,
With a great joy upon his face,
Kneel'd down, and cried not, neither ran.

So they, whose lot it was, cast stones,
That they flew thick and bruised him sore.
But he praised Allah with loud voice,
And remain'd kneeling as before.

My lord had cover'd up his face;
But when one told him, 'He is dead,'
Turning him quickly to go in,
'Bring thou to me his corpse,' he said.

And truly, while I speak, O King,
I hear the bearers on the stair;
Wilt thou they straightway bring him in?
– Ho! enter ye who tarry there!

*The Vizier*

O King, in this I praise thee not!
Now must I call thy grief not wise.
Is he thy friend, or of thy blood,
To find such favour in thine eyes?

Nay, were he thine own mother's son,
Still, thou art king, and the law stands.
It were not meet the balance swerved,
The sword were broken in thy hands.

But being nothing, as he is,
Why for no cause make sad thy face? –
Lo, I am old! three kings, ere thee,
Have I seen reigning in this place.

But who, through all this length of time,
Could bear the burden of his years,
If he for strangers pain'd his heart
Not less than those who merit tears?

Fathers we *must* have, wife and child,
And grievous is the grief for these;
This pain alone, which *must* be borne,
Makes the head white, and bows the knees.

But other loads than this his own
One man is not well made to bear.
Besides, to each are his own friends,
To mourn with him, and show him care.

Look, this is but one single place,
Though it be great; all the earth round,
If a man bear to have it so,
Things which might vex him shall be found.

Upon the Russian frontier, where
The watchers of two armies stand
Near one another, many a man,
Seeking a prey unto his hand,

Hath snatch'd a little fair-hair'd slave;
They snatch also, towards Mervè,
The Shiah dogs, who pasture sheep,
And up from thence to Orgunjè.

And these all, labouring for a lord,
Eat not the fruit of their own hands;
Which is the heaviest of all plagues,
To that man's mind, who understands.

The kaffirs also (whom God curse!)
Vex one another, night and day;
There are the lepers, and all sick;
There are the poor, who faint alway.

All these have sorrow, and keep still,
Whilst other men make cheer, and sing.
Wilt thou have pity on all these?
No, nor on this dead dog, O King!

*The King*

O Vizier, thou art old, I young!
Clear in these things I cannot see.
My head is burning, and a heat
Is in my skin which angers me.

But hear ye this, ye sons of men!
They that bear rule, and are obey'd,
Unto a rule more strong than theirs
Are in their turn obedient made.

In vain therefore, with wistful eyes
Gazing up hither, the poor man,
Who loiters by the high-heap'd booths,
Below there, in the Registàn,

Says: 'Happy he, who lodges there!
With silken raiment, store of rice,
And for this drought, all kinds of fruits,
Grape-syrup, squares of colour'd ice,

'With cherries serv'd in drifts of snow.'
In vain hath a king power to build
Houses, arcades, enamell'd mosques;
And to make orchard-closes, fill'd

With curious fruit-trees brought from far;
With cisterns for the winter-rain,
And, in the desert, spacious inns
In divers places – if that pain

Is not more lighten'd, which he feels,
If his will be not satisfied;
And that it be not, from all time
The law is planted, to abide.

Thou wast a sinner, thou poor man!
Thou wast athirst; and didst not see,
That, though we take what we desire,
We must not snatch it eagerly.

And I have meat and drink at will,
And rooms of treasures, not a few.
But I am sick, nor heed I these;
And what I would, I cannot do.

Even the great honour which I have,
When I am dead, will soon grow still;
So have I neither joy, nor fame.
But what I can do, that I will.

I have a fretted brick-work tomb
Upon a hill on the right hand,
Hard by a close of apricots,
Upon the road of Samarcand;

Thither, O Vizier, will I bear
This man my pity could not save,
And, plucking up the marble flags,
There lay his body in my grave.

Bring water, nard, and linen rolls!
Wash off all blood, set smooth each limb!
Then say: 'He was not wholly vile,
Because a king shall bury him.'

153           # To Marguerite – Continued

Yes! in the sea of life enisled,
With echoing straits between us thrown,
Dotting the shoreless watery wild,
We mortal millions live *alone*.
The islands feel the enclasping flow,
And then their endless bounds they know.

But when the moon their hollows lights,
And they are swept by balms of spring,
And in their glens, on starry nights,
The nightingales divinely sing;
And lovely notes, from shore to shore,
Across the sounds and channels pour –

Oh! then a longing like despair
Is to their farthest caverns sent;
For surely once, they feel, we were
Parts of a single continent!
Now round us spreads the watery plain –
Oh might our marges meet again!

Who order'd, that their longing's fire
Should be, as soon as kindled, cool'd?
Who renders vain their deep desire? –
A God, a God their severance ruled!
And bade betwixt their shores to be
The unplumb'd, salt, estranging sea.

154         Resignation

              *To Fausta*

*To die be given us, or attain!*
*Fierce work it were, to do again.*
So pilgrims, bound for Mecca, pray'd
At burning noon; so warriors said,
Scarf'd with the cross, who watch'd the miles
Of dust which wreathed their struggling files
Down Lydian mountains; so, when snows
Round Alpine summits, eddying, rose,
The Goth, bound Rome-wards; so the Hun,
Crouch'd on his saddle, while the sun
Went lurid down o'er flooded plains
Through which the groaning Danube strains
To the drear Euxine; – so pray all,
Whom labours, self-ordain'd, enthrall;
Because they to themselves propose
On this side the all-common close
A goal which, gain'd, may give repose.
So pray they; and to stand again
Where they stood once, to them were pain;
Pain to thread back and to renew
Past straits, and currents long steer'd through.

But milder natures, and more free –
Whom an unblamed serenity
Hath freed from passions, and the state
Of struggle these necessitate;
Whom schooling of the stubborn mind
Hath made, or birth hath found, resign'd –
These mourn not, that their goings pay
Obedience to the passing day.
These claim not every laughing Hour
For handmaid to their striding power;
Each in her turn, with torch uprear'd,
To await their march; and when appear'd,

Through the cold gloom, with measured race,
To usher for a destined space
(Her own sweet errands all forgone)
The too imperious traveller on.
These, Fausta, ask not this; nor thou,
Time's chafing prisoner, ask it now!

We left, just ten years since, you say,
That wayside inn we left to-day.
Our jovial host, as forth we fare,
Shouts greeting from his easy chair.
High on a bank our leader stands,
Reviews and ranks his motley bands,
Makes clear our goal to every eye –
The valley's western boundary.
A gate swings to! our tide hath flow'd
Already from the silent road.
The valley-pastures, one by one,
Are threaded, quiet in the sun;
And now beyond the rude stone bridge
Slopes gracious up the western ridge.
Its woody border, and the last
Of its dark upland farms is past –
Cool farms, with open-lying stores,
Under their burnish'd sycamores;
All past! and through the trees we glide,
Emerging on the green hill-side.
There climbing hangs, a far-seen sign,
Our wavering, many-colour'd line;
There winds, upstreaming slowly still
Over the summit of the hill.
And now, in front, behold outspread
Those upper regions we must tread!
Mild hollows, and clear heathy swells,
The cheerful silence of the fells.
Some two hours' march with serious air,
Through the deep noontide heats we fare;
The red-grouse, springing at our sound,
Skims, now and then, the shining ground;

No life, save his and ours, intrudes
Upon these breathless solitudes.
O joy! again the farms appear.
Cool shade is there, and rustic cheer;
There springs the brook will guide us down,
Bright comrade, to the noisy town.
Lingering, we follow down; we gain
The town, the highway, and the plain.
And many a mile of dusty way,
Parch'd and road-worn, we made that day;
But, Fausta, I remember well,
That as the balmy darkness fell
We bathed our hands with speechless glee,
That night, in the wide-glimmering sea.

Once more we tread this self-same road,
Fausta, which ten years since we trod;
Alone we tread it, you and I,
Ghosts of that boisterous company.
Here, where the brook shines, near its head,
In its clear, shallow, turf-fringed bed;
Here, whence the eye first sees, far down,
Capp'd with faint smoke, the noisy town;
Here sit we, and again unroll,
Though slowly, the familiar whole.
The solemn wastes of heathy hill
Sleep in the July sunshine still;
The self-same shadows now, as then,
Play through this grassy upland glen;
The loose dark stones on the green way
Lie strewn, it seems, where then they lay;
On this mild bank above the stream,
(You crush them!) the blue gentians gleam.
Still this wild brook, the rushes cool,
The sailing foam, the shining pool!
These are not changed; and we, you say,
Are scarce more changed, in truth, than they.

The gipsies, whom we met below,
They, too, have long roam'd to and fro;
They ramble, leaving, where they pass,
Their fragments on the cumber'd grass.
And often to some kindly place
Chance guides the migratory race,
Where, though long wanderings intervene,
They recognise a former scene.
The dingy tents are pitch'd; the fires
Give to the wind their wavering spires;
In dark knots crouch round the wild flame
Their children, as when first they came;
They see their shackled beasts again
Move, browsing, up the grey-wall'd lane.
Signs are not wanting, which might raise
The ghost in them of former days –
Signs are not wanting, if they would;
Suggestions to disquietude.
For them, for all, time's busy touch,
While it mends little, troubles much.
Their joints grow stiffer – but the year
Runs his old round of dubious cheer;
Chilly they grow – yet winds in March,
Still, sharp as ever, freeze and parch;
They must live still – and yet, God knows,
Crowded and keen the country grows;
It seems as if, in their decay,
The law grew stronger every day.
So might they reason, so compare,
Fausta, times past with times that are.
But no! – they rubb'd through yesterday
In their hereditary way,
And they will rub through, if they can,
To-morrow on the self-same plan,
Till death arrive to supersede,
For them, vicissitude and need.

The poet, to whose mighty heart
Heaven doth a quicker pulse impart,
Subdues that energy to scan
Not his own course, but that of man.
Though he move mountains, though his day
Be pass'd on the proud heights of sway,
Though he hath loosed a thousand chains,
Though he hath borne immortal pains,
Action and suffering though he know –
He hath not lived, if he lives so.
He sees, in some great-historied land,
A ruler of the people stand,
Sees his strong thought in fiery flood
Roll through the heaving multitude,
Exults – yet for no moment's space
Envies the all-regarded place.
Beautiful eyes meet his – and he
Bears to admire uncravingly;
They pass – he, mingled with the crowd,
Is in their far-off triumphs proud.
From some high station he looks down,
At sunset, on a populous town;
Surveys each happy group, which fleets,
Toil ended, through the shining streets,
Each with some errand of its own –
And does not say: *I am alone*.
He sees the gentle stir of birth
When morning purifies the earth;
He leans upon a gate and sees
The pastures, and the quiet trees.
Low, woody hill, with gracious bound,
Folds the still valley almost round;
The cuckoo, loud on some high lawn,
Is answer'd from the depth of dawn;
In the hedge straggling to the stream,
Pale, dew-drench'd, half-shut roses gleam;
But, where the farther side slopes down,
He sees the drowsy new-waked clown

In his white quaint-embroider'd frock
Make, whistling, tow'rd his mist-wreathed flock –
Slowly, behind his heavy tread,
The wet, flower'd grass heaves up its head.
Lean'd on his gate, he gazes – tears
Are in his eyes, and in his ears
The murmur of a thousand years.
Before him he sees life unroll,
A placid and continuous whole –
That general life, which does not cease,
Whose secret is not joy, but peace;
That life, whose dumb wish is not miss'd
If birth proceeds, if things subsist;
The life of plants, and stones, and rain,
The life he craves – if not in vain
Fate gave, what chance shall not control,
His sad lucidity of soul.

You listen – but that wandering smile,
Fausta, betrays you cold the while!
Your eyes pursue the bells of foam
Wash'd, eddying, from this bank, their home.
*Those gipsies, so your thoughts I scan,*
*Are less, the poet more, than man.*
*They feel not, though they move and see;*
*Deeper the poet feels; but he*
*Breathes, when he will, immortal air,*
*Where Orpheus and where Homer are.*
*In the day's life, whose iron round*
*Hems us all in, he is not bound;*
*He leaves his kind, o'erleaps their pen,*
*And flees the common life of men.*
*He escapes thence, but we abide –*
*Not deep the poet sees, but wide.*

The world in which we live and move
Outlasts aversion, outlasts love,
Outlasts each effort, interest, hope,
Remorse, grief, joy; – and were the scope

Of these affections wider made,
Man still would see, and see dismay'd,
Beyond his passion's widest range,
Far regions of eternal change.
Nay, and since death, which wipes out man,
Finds him with many an unsolved plan,
With much unknown, and much untried,
Wonder not dead, and thirst not dried,
Still gazing on the ever full
Eternal mundane spectacle –
This world in which we draw our breath,
In some sense, Fausta, outlasts death.

    Blame thou not, therefore, him who dares
Judge vain beforehand human cares;
Whose natural insight can discern
What through experience others learn;
Who needs not love and power, to know
Love transient, power an unreal show;
Who treads at ease life's uncheer'd ways –
Him blame not, Fausta, rather praise!
Rather thyself for some aim pray
Nobler than this, to fill the day;
Rather that heart, which burns in thee,
Ask, not to amuse, but to set free;
Be passionate hopes not ill resign'd
For quiet, and a fearless mind.
And though fate grudge to thee and me
The poet's rapt security,
Yet they, believe me, who await
No gifts from chance, have conquer'd fate.
They, winning room to see and hear,
And to men's business not too near,
Through clouds of individual strife
Draw homeward to the general life.
Like leaves by suns not yet uncurl'd;
To the wise, foolish; to the world,
Weak; – yet not weak, I might reply,
Not foolish, Fausta, in His eye,

To whom each moment in its race,
Crowd as we will its neutral space,
Is but a quiet watershed
Whence, equally, the seas of life and death are fed.

Enough, we live! – and if a life,
With large results so little rife,
Though bearable, seem hardly worth
This pomp of worlds, this pain of birth;
Yet, Fausta, the mute turf we tread,
The solemn hills around us spread,
This stream which falls incessantly,
The strange-scrawl'd rocks, the lonely sky,
If I might lend their life a voice,
Seem to bear rather than rejoice.
And even could the intemperate prayer
Man iterates, while these forbear,
For movement, for an ampler sphere,
Pierce Fate's impenetrable ear;
Not milder is the general lot
Because our spirits have forgot,
In action's dizzying eddy whirl'd,
The something that infects the world.

155                    Dover Beach

The sea is calm to-night.
The tide is full, the moon lies fair
Upon the straits; – on the French coast the light
Gleams and is gone; the cliffs of England stand,
Glimmering and vast, out in the tranquil bay.
Come to the window, sweet is the night-air!
Only, from the long line of spray
Where the sea meets the moon-blanch'd land,
Listen! you hear the grating roar
Of pebbles which the waves draw back, and fling,
At their return, up the high strand,

Begin, and cease, and then again begin,
With tremulous cadence slow, and bring
The eternal note of sadness in.

Sophocles long ago
Heard it on the Ægæan, and it brought
Into his mind the turbid ebb and flow
Of human misery; we
Find also in the sound a thought,
Hearing it by this distant northern sea.

The Sea of Faith
Was once, too, at the full, and round earth's shore
Lay like the folds of a bright girdle furl'd.
But now I only hear
Its melancholy, long, withdrawing roar,
Retreating, to the breath
Of the night-wind, down the vast edges drear
And naked shingles of the world.

Ah, love, let us be true
To one another! for the world, which seems
To lie before us like a land of dreams,
So various, so beautiful, so new,
Hath really neither joy, nor love, nor light,
Nor certitude, nor peace, nor help for pain;
And we are here as on a darkling plain
Swept with confused alarms of struggle and flight,
Where ignorant armies clash by night.

## 156    Lines Written in Kensington Gardens

In this lone, open glade I lie,
Screen'd by deep boughs on either hand;
And at its end, to stay the eye,
Those black-crown'd, red-boled pine-trees stand!

Birds here make song, each bird has his,
Across the girdling city's hum.
How green under the boughs it is!
How thick the tremulous sheep-cries come!

Sometimes a child will cross the glade
To take his nurse his broken toy;
Sometimes a thrush flit overhead
Deep in her unknown day's employ.

Here at my feet what wonders pass,
What endless, active life is here!
What blowing daisies, fragrant grass!
An air-stirr'd forest, fresh and clear.

Scarce fresher is the mountain-sod
Where the tired angler lies, stretch'd out,
And, eased of basket and of rod,
Counts his day's spoil, the spotted trout.

In the huge world, which roars hard by,
Be others happy if they can!
But in my helpless cradle I
Was breathed on by the rural Pan.

I, on men's impious uproar hurl'd,
Think often, as I hear them rave,
That peace has left the upper world
And now keeps only in the grave.

Yet here is peace for ever new!
When I who watch them am away,
Still all things in this glade go through
The changes of their quiet day.

Then to their happy rest they pass!
The flowers upclose, the birds are fed,
The night comes down upon the grass,
The child sleeps warmly in his bed.

Calm soul of all things! make it mine
To feel, amid the city's jar,
That there abides a peace of thine,
Man did not make, and cannot mar.

The will to neither strive nor cry,
The power to feel with others give!
Calm, calm me more! nor let me die
Before I have begun to live.

157                Revolutions

Before man parted for this earthly strand,
While yet upon the verge of heaven he stood,
God put a heap of letters in his hand,
And bade him make with them what word he could.

And man has turn'd them many times; made Greece,
Rome, England, France; – yes, nor in vain essay'd
Way after way, changes that never cease!
The letters have combined, something was made.

But ah! an inextinguishable sense
Haunts him that he has not made what he should;
That he has still, though old, to recommence,
Since he has not yet found the word God would.

And empire after empire, at their height
Of sway, have felt this boding sense come on;
Have felt their huge frames not constructed right,
And droop'd, and slowly died upon their throne.

One day, thou say'st, there will at last appear
The word, the order, which God meant should be.
– Ah! we shall know *that* well when it comes near;
The band will quit man's heart, he will breathe free.

158                           Philomela

Hark! ah, the nightingale –
The tawny-throated!
Hark, from that moonlit cedar what a burst!
What triumph! hark! – what pain!

O wanderer from a Grecian shore,
Still, after many years, in distant lands,
Still nourishing in thy bewilder'd brain
That wild, unquench'd, deep-sunken, old-world pain –
Say, will it never heal?
And can this fragrant lawn
With its cool trees, and night,
And the sweet, tranquil Thames,
And moonshine, and the dew,
To thy rack'd heart and brain
Afford no balm?

Dost thou to-night behold,
Here, through the moonlight on this English grass,
The unfriendly palace in the Thracian wild?
Dost thou again peruse
With hot cheeks and sear'd eyes
The too clear web, and thy dumb sister's shame?
Dost thou once more assay
Thy flight, and feel come over thee,
Poor fugitive, the feathery change
Once more, and once more seem to make resound
With love and hate, triumph and agony,
Lone Daulis, and the high Cephissian vale?
Listen, Eugenia –
How thick the bursts come crowding through the leaves!
Again – thou hearest?
Eternal passion!
Eternal pain!

159   Rugby Chapel

*November, 1857*

Coldly, sadly descends
The autumn-evening. The field
Strewn with its dank yellow drifts
Of wither'd leaves, and the elms,
Fade into dimness apace,
Silent; – hardly a shout
From a few boys late at their play!
The lights come out in the street,
In the school-room windows; – but cold,
Solemn, unlighted, austere,
Through the gathering darkness, arise
The chapel-walls, in whose bound
Thou, my father! art laid.

There thou dost lie, in the gloom
Of the autumn evening. But ah!
That word, *gloom*, to my mind
Brings thee back, in the light
Of thy radiant vigour, again;
In the gloom of November we pass'd
Days not dark at thy side;
Seasons impair'd not the ray
Of thy buoyant cheerfulness clear.
Such thou wast! and I stand
In the autumn evening, and think
Of bygone autumns with thee.

Fifteen years have gone round
Since thou arosest to tread,
In the summer-morning, the road
Of death, at a call unforeseen,
Sudden. For fifteen years,
We who till then in thy shade
Rested as under the boughs

Of a mighty oak, have endured
Sunshine and rain as we might,
Bare, unshaded, alone,
Lacking the shelter of thee.

O strong soul, by what shore
Tarriest thou now? For that force,
Surely, has not been left vain!
Somewhere, surely, afar,
In the sounding labour-house vast
Of being, is practised that strength,
Zealous, beneficent, firm!

Yes, in some far-shining sphere,
Conscious or not of the past,
Still thou performest the word
Of the Spirit in whom thou dost live –
Prompt, unwearied, as here!
Still thou upraisest with zeal
The humble good from the ground,
Sternly repressest the bad!
Still, like a trumpet, dost rouse
Those who with half-open eyes
Tread the border-land dim
’Twixt vice and virtue; reviv’st,
Succourest! – this was thy work,
This was thy life upon earth.

What is the course of the life
Of mortal men on the earth? –
Most men eddy about
Here and there – eat and drink,
Chatter and love and hate,
Gather and squander, are raised
Aloft, are hurl’d in the dust,
Striving blindly, achieving
Nothing; and then they die –
Perish; – and no one asks
Who or what they have been,

More than he asks what waves,
In the moonlit solitudes mild
Of the midmost Ocean, have swell'd,
Foam'd for a moment, and gone.

And there are some, whom a thirst
Ardent, unquenchable, fires,
Not with the crowd to be spent,
Not without aim to go round
In an eddy of purposeless dust,
Effort unmeaning and vain.
Ah yes! some of us strive
Not without action to die
Fruitless, but something to snatch
From dull oblivion, nor all
Glut the devouring grave!
We, we have chosen our path –
Path to a clear-purposed goal,
Path of advance! – but it leads
A long, steep journey, through sunk
Gorges, o'er mountains in snow.
Cheerful, with friends, we set forth –
Then, on the height, comes the storm.
Thunder crashes from rock
To rock, the cataracts reply,
Lightnings dazzle our eyes.
Roaring torrents have breach'd
The track, the stream-bed descends
In the place where the wayfarer once
Planted his footstep – the spray
Boils o'er its borders! aloft
The unseen snow-beds dislodge
Their hanging ruin; alas,
Havoc is made in our train!
Friends, who set forth at our side,
Falter, are lost in the storm.
We, we only are left!
With frowning foreheads, with lips

Sternly compress'd, we strain on,
On – and at nightfall at last
Come to the end of our way,
To the lonely inn 'mid the rocks;
Where the gaunt and taciturn host
Stands on the threshold, the wind
Shaking his thin white hairs –
Holds his lantern to scan
Our storm-beat figures, and asks:
Whom in our party we bring?
Whom we have left in the snow?

Sadly we answer: We bring
Only ourselves! we lost
Sight of the rest in the storm.
Hardly ourselves we fought through,
Stripp'd, without friends, as we are.
Friends, companions, and train,
The avalanche swept from our side.

But thou would'st not *alone*
Be saved, my father! *alone*
Conquer and come to thy goal,
Leaving the rest in the wild.
We were weary, and we
Fearful, and we in our march
Fain to drop down and to die.
Still thou turnedst, and still
Beckonedst the trembler, and still
Gavest the weary thy hand.
If, in the paths of the world,
Stones might have wounded thy feet,
Toil or dejection have tried
Thy spirit, of that we saw
Nothing – to us thou wast still
Cheerful, and helpful, and firm!
Therefore to thee it was given
Many to save with thyself;

And, at the end of thy day,
O faithful shepherd! to come,
Bringing thy sheep in thy hand.

And through thee I believe
In the noble and great who are gone;
Pure souls honour'd and blest
By former ages, who else –
Such, so soulless, so poor,
Is the race of men whom I see –
Seem'd but a dream of the heart,
Seem'd but a cry of desire.
Yes! I believe that there lived
Others like thee in the past,
Not like the men of the crowd
Who all round me to-day
Bluster or cringe, and make life
Hideous, and arid, and vile;
But souls temper'd with fire,
Fervent, heroic, and good,
Helpers and friends of mankind.

Servants of God! – or sons
Shall I not call you? because
Not as servants ye knew
Your Father's innermost mind,
His, who unwillingly sees
One of his little ones lost –
Yours is the praise, if mankind
Hath not as yet in its march
Fainted, and fallen, and died!

See! In the rocks of the world
Marches the host of mankind,
A feeble, wavering line.
Where are they tending? – A God
Marshall'd them, gave them their goal.
Ah, but the way is so long!
Years they have been in the wild!

Sore thirst plagues them, the rocks,
Rising all round, overawe;
Factions divide them, their host
Threatens to break, to dissolve.
– Ah, keep, keep them combined!
Else, of the myriads who fill
That army, not one shall arrive;
Sole they shall stray; in the rocks
Stagger for ever in vain,
Die one by one in the waste.

Then, in such hour of need
Of your fainting, dispirited race,
Ye, like angels, appear,
Radiant with ardour divine!
Beacons of hope, ye appear!
Languor is not in your heart,
Weakness is not in your word,
Weariness not on your brow.
Ye alight in our van! at your voice,
Panic, despair, flee away.
Ye move through the ranks, recall
The stragglers, refresh the outworn,
Praise, re-inspire the brave!
Order, courage, return.
Eyes rekindling, and prayers,
Follow your steps as ye go.
Ye fill up the gaps in our files,
Strengthen the wavering line,
Stablish, continue our march,
On, to the bound of the waste,
On, to the City of God.

160                    Growing Old

What is it to grow old?
Is it to lose the glory of the form,
The lustre of the eye?
Is it for beauty to forgo her wreath?
– Yes, but not this alone.

Is it to feel our strength –
Not our bloom only, but our strength – decay?
Is it to feel each limb
Grow stiffer, every function less exact,
Each nerve more loosely strung?

Yes, this, and more; but not
Ah, 'tis not what in youth we dream'd 'twould be!
'Tis not to have our life
Mellow'd and soften'd as with sunset-glow,
A golden day's decline.

'Tis not to see the world
As from a height, with rapt prophetic eyes,
And heart profoundly stirr'd;
And weep, and feel the fulness of the past,
The years that are no more.

It is to spend long days
And not once feel that we were ever young;
It is to add, immured
In the hot prison of the present, month
To month with weary pain.

It is to suffer this,
And feel but half, and feebly, what we feel.
Deep in our hidden heart
Festers the dull remembrance of a change,
But no emotion – none.

It is – last stage of all –
When we are frozen up within, and quite
The phantom of ourselves,
To hear the world applaud the hollow ghost
Which blamed the living man.

# ROBERT LEIGHTON

1822–69

161               The Bunch of Larks

Portly he was, in carriage somewhat grand;
    Of gentleman he wore the accepted marks:
He thrid the busy street, and in his hand
        He bore a bunch of larks!

There be some things that *may* be carried – yes,
    A gentleman may carry larks – if dead;
Or any slaughter'd game; not fish, still less
        The homely beef or bread.

I met him in the street, and turn'd about,
    And mused long after he had flaunted by.
A bunch of larks! and his intent, no doubt,
        To have them in a pie.

Yes, four-and-twenty larks baked in a pie!
    O, what a feast of melody is there!
The ringing chorus of a summer sky!
        A dish of warbling air!

How many dusty wanderers of the earth
    Have those still'd voices lifted from the dust!
And now to end their almost Heavenly mirth
        Beneath a gourmand's crust!

But as he picks their thin ambrosial throats,
    Will no accusing memories arise,
Of grassy glebes, and heaven-descending notes,
        And soul-engulfing skies?

'Give me,' cries he, 'the *substance* of a thing –
Something that I can eat, or drink, or feel –
A poem for the money it will bring –
Larks for the dainty meal.'

Well, he may have his substance, and I mine.
Deep in my soul the throbbing lark-notes lie.
My substance lasts, and takes a life divine –
His passes with the pie.

# ELIZA OGILVY

1822–1912

162                    A Nightmare

I dreamed that I was sick and sore at heart,
Till weary of its aching, rash I said,
'Come hither fate, and end for me this strife.'
Then fate, in guise of one in armour, came
And laid his mailed hand heavy on my breast,
Crushing as with a vice, whereat I shrieked,
And fain would have my troubles back, and cried,
'Youth's sharpest pangs are blunt compared to fate's.
Unhand me, tyrant, let me be as erst.'
But still the mailed hand pressed upon my heart,
And still the pulse beat stronger for the pain.

# WILLIAM JOHNSON CORY
## 1823–92


163  Εἶπέ τιξ, Ἡράκλειτε, τεὸν μόρον [Heraclitus]

They told me, Heraclitus, they told me you were dead;
They brought me bitter news to hear and bitter tears to shed.
I wept, as I remembered, how often you and I
Had tired the sun with talking and sent him down the sky.

And now that thou art lying, my dear old Carian guest,
A handful of grey ashes, long long ago at rest,
Still are thy pleasant voices, thy nightingales, awake,
For Death, he taketh all away, but them he cannot take.

163. Title as first line, from an epigram by Callimachus.

# COVENTRY PATMORE
## 1823–96

164          The Wife's Tragedy

Man must be pleased; but him to please
Is woman's pleasure; down the gulf
Of his condoled necessities
She casts her best, she flings herself.
How often flings for nought, and yokes
Her heart to an icicle or whim,
Whose each impatient word provokes
Another, not from her, but him;
While she, too gentle even to force
His penitence by kind replies,
Waits by, expecting his remorse,
With pardon in her pitying eyes;
And if he once, by shame oppress'd,
A comfortable word confers,
She leans and weeps against his breast,
And seems to think the sin was hers;
And whilst his love has any life,
Or any eye to see her charms,
At any time, she's still his wife,
Dearly devoted to his arms;
She loves with love that cannot tire;
And when, ah woe, she loves alone,
Through passionate duty love springs higher,
As grass grows taller round a stone.

## 165                    Departure

It was not like your great and gracious ways!
Do you, that have nought other to lament,
Never, my Love, repent
Of how, that July afternoon,
You went,
With sudden, unintelligible phrase,
And frighten'd eye,
Upon your journey of so many days,
Without a single kiss, or a good-bye?
I knew, indeed, that you were parting soon;
And so we sate, within the low sun's rays,
You whispering to me, for your voice was weak,
Your harrowing praise.
Well, it was well,
To hear you such things speak,
And I could tell
What made your eyes a growing gloom of love,
As a warm South-wind sombres a March grove.
And it was like your great and gracious ways
To turn your talk on daily things, my Dear,
Lifting the luminous, pathetic lash
To let the laughter flash,
Whilst I drew near,
Because you spoke so low that I could scarcely hear.
But all at once to leave me at the last,
More at the wonder than the loss aghast,
With huddled, unintelligible phrase,
And frighten'd eye,
And go your journey of all days
With not one kiss, or a good-bye,
And the only loveless look the look with which you pass'd:
'Twas all unlike your great and gracious ways.

166                        The Toys

My little Son, who look'd from thoughtful eyes
And moved and spoke in quiet grown-up wise,
Having my law the seventh time disobey'd,
I struck him, and dismiss'd
With hard words and unkiss'd,
His Mother, who was patient, being dead.
Then, fearing lest his grief should hinder sleep,
I visited his bed,
But found him slumbering deep,
With darken'd eyelids, and their lashes yet
From his late sobbing wet.
And I, with moan,
Kissing away his tears, left others of my own;
For, on a table drawn beside his head,
He had put, within his reach,
A box of counters and a red-vein'd stone,
A piece of glass abraded by the beach
And six or seven shells,
A bottle with bluebells
And two French copper coins, ranged there with
     careful art,
To comfort his sad heart.
So when that night I pray'd
To God, I wept, and said:
Ah, when at last we lie with tranced breath,
Not vexing Thee in death,
And Thou rememberest of what toys
We made our joys,
How weakly understood,
Thy great commanded good,
Then, fatherly not less
Than I whom Thou hast moulded from the clay,
Thou'lt leave Thy wrath, and say,
'I will be sorry for their childishness.'

167          Magna Est Veritas

Here, in this little Bay,
Full of tumultuous life and great repose,
Where, twice a day,
The purposeless, glad ocean comes and goes,
Under high cliffs, and far from the huge town,
I sit me down.
For want of me the world's course will not fail:
When all its work is done, the lie shall rot;
The truth is great, and shall prevail,
When none cares whether it prevail or not.


168          A London Fête

All night fell hammers, shock on shock;
With echoes Newgate's granite clang'd:
The scaffold built, at eight o'clock
They brought the man out to be hang'd.
Then came from all the people there
A single cry, that shook the air;
Mothers held up their babes to see,
Who spread their hands, and crow'd for glee;
Here a girl from her vesture tore
A rag to wave with, and join'd the roar;
There a man, with yelling tired,
Stopp'd, and the culprit's crime inquired;
A sot, below the doom'd man dumb,
Bawl'd his health in the world to come;
These blasphemed and fought for places;
Those, half-crush'd, cast frantic faces,
To windows, where, in freedom sweet,
Others enjoy'd the wicked treat.
At last, the show's black crisis pended;
Struggles for better standings ended;

The rabble's lips no longer curst,
But stood agape with horrid thirst;
Thousands of breasts beat horrid hope;
Thousands of eyeballs, lit with hell,
Burnt one way all, to see the rope
Unslacken as the platform fell.
The rope flew tight; and then the roar
Burst forth afresh; less loud, but more
Confused and affrighting than before.
A few harsh tongues for ever led
The common din, the chaos of noises,
But ear could not catch what they said.
As when the realm of the damn'd rejoices
At winning a soul to its will,
That clatter and clangour of hateful voices
Sicken'd and stunn'd the air, until
The dangling corpse hung straight and still.
The show complete, the pleasure past,
The solid masses loosen'd fast:
A thief slunk off, with ample spoil,
To ply elsewhere his daily toil;
A baby strung its doll to a stick;
A mother praised the pretty trick;
Two children caught and hang'd a cat;
Two friends walk'd on, in lively chat;
And two, who had disputed places,
Went forth to fight, with murderous faces.

# WILLIAM BRIGHTY RANDS
## 1823–82

169          Lilliput Levee

Where does Pinafore Palace stand?
Right in the middle of Lilliput-land!
There the Queen eats bread-and-honey,
There the King counts up his money!

Oh, the Glorious Revolution!
Oh, the Provisional Constitution!
Now that the Children, clever bold folks,
Have turn'd the tables upon the Old Folks!

Easily the thing was done,
For the Children were more than two to one;
Brave as lions, quick as foxes,
With hoards of wealth in their money-boxes!

They seized the keys, they patrolled the street,
They drove the policeman off his beat,
They built barricades, they stationed sentries –
You must give the word, when you come to the entries!

They dress'd themselves in the Riflemen's clothes,
They had pea-shooters, they had arrows and bows,
So as to put resistance down –
Order reigns in Lilliput-town!

They made the baker bake hot rolls,
They made the wharfinger send in coals,
They made the butcher kill the calf,
They cut the telegraph-wires in half.

They went to the chemist's, and with their feet
They kick'd the physic all down the street;
They went to the school-room and burnt the books,
They munched the puffs at the pastrycook's.

They sucked the jam, they lost the spoons,
They sent up several fire-balloons,
They let off crackers, they burnt a guy,
They piled a bonfire ever so high.

They offered a prize for the laziest boy,
And one for the most Magnificent toy,
They split or burnt the canes off-hand,
They made new laws in Lilliput-land.

*Never do to-day what you can*
*Put off till to-morrow*, one of them ran;
*Late to bed and late to rise*,
Was another law which they did devise.

Lilliput-land was a paradise
Of everything you can say that's nice! –
A magic lantern for all to see,
Rabbits to keep, and a Christmas-tree.

A boat, a house that went on wheels,
An organ to grind, and sherry at meals,
Drums and wheelbarrows, Roman candles,
Whips with whistles let into the handles.

A real live giant, a roc to fly,
A goat to tease, a copper to sky,
A garret of apples, a box of paints,
A saw and a hammer, and no complaints.

Nail up the door, slide down the stairs,
Saw off the legs of the parlour-chairs –
That was the way in Lilliput-land,
The Children having the upper hand.

They made the Old Folks come to school,
All in pinafores, – that was the rule, –
Made them say, *Eena-deener-duss,*
*Kattler-wheeler-whiler-wuss;*

They made them learn all sorts of things
That nobody liked. They had catechisings;
They kept them in, they sent them down
In class, in school, in Lilliput-town.

O but they gave them tit-for-tat!
Thick bread-and-butter, and all that;
Stick-jaw pudding that tires your chin
With the marmalade spread ever so thin!

They governed the clock in Lilliput-land,
They altered the hour or the minute-hand,
They made the day fast, they made the day slow,
Just as they wish'd the time to go.

They never waited for king or for cat;
They never wiped their shoes on the mat;
Their joy was great; their joy was greater;
They rode in the baby's perambulator!

There was a Levee in Lilliput-town,
At Pinafore Palace. Smith, and Brown,
Jones, and Robinson had to attend –
All to whom they cards did send.

Every one rode in a cab to the door;
Every one came in a pinafore;
Lady and gentleman, rat-tat-tat,
Loud knock, proud knock, opera hat!

The place was covered with silver and gold,
The place was as full as it ever could hold;
The ladies kissed her Majesty's hand;
Such was the custom in Lilliput-land.

His Majesty knighted eight or ten,
Perhaps a score, of the gentlemen,
Some of them short and some of them tall –
*Arise, Sir What's-a-name What-do-you-call!*

Nuts, and nutmeg (that's in the negus);
The bill of fare would perhaps fatigue us;
Forty-five fiddlers to play the fiddle;
Right foot, left foot, down the middle.

Conjuring tricks with the poker and tongs,
Riddles and Forfeits, singing of songs;
One fat man, too fat by far,
Tried 'Twinkle, twinkle, little star!'

His voice was gruff, his pinafore tight,
His wife said, 'Mind, dear, sing it right,'
But he forgot, and said Fa-la-la!
The Queen of Lilliput's own papa!

She frowned, and ordered him up to bed;
He said he was sorry; she shook her head;
His clean shirt-front with his tears was stained –
But discipline had to be maintained.

The Constitution! The Law! The Crown!
Order reigns in Lilliput-town!
The Queen is Jill, and the King is John;
I trust the Government will get on.

I noticed, being a man of rhymes,
An advertisement in the *Lilliput Times*: –
'PINAFORE PALACE. This is to state
That the Court is in want of a Laureate.

Nothing menial required.
Poets, willing to be hired,
May send in Specimens, at once,
Care of the Chamberlain DOUBLEDUNCE.'

Said I to myself, here's a chance for me,
The Lilliput Laureate for to be!
And these are the Specimens I sent in
To Pinafore Palace. Shall I win?

# WILLIAM CALDWELL ROSCOE
## 1823–59

170         By the Seashore
### (FRAGMENT)

Upon the reedy margin of the shore,
   Shallow and waste, I stand,
And hear far Ocean's low continuous roar
   Over the flats and sand.

The wide gray sky hangs low above the verge,
   No white-winged sea-bird flies;
No sound, save the eternal-sounding surge,
   With equal fall and rise.

While the salt sea-wind whispers in my ears,
   Fitful and desolate,
I seem absolved from the departed years,
   Not grieved and not elate.

# WILLIAM ALLINGHAM
## 1824–89

171     By and by, we shall meet
       Something truly worth our while,
     Shall begin to live at last,
       By and by.

     By and by, days that fleet
       After days, in countless file
     Bring one day, like all the past,
       And we die.


172         Writing

     A man who keeps a diary, pays
     Due toll to many tedious days;
     But life becomes eventful – then
     His busy hand forgets the pen.
     Most books, indeed, are records less
     Of fulness than of emptiness.


173         In Snow

     O English mother, in the ruddy glow
     Hugging your baby closer when outside
     You see the silent, soft, and cruel snow
     Falling again, and think what ills betide
     Unshelter'd creatures, – your sad thoughts may go
     Where War and Winter now, two spectre-wolves,
     Hunt in the freezing vapour that involves
     Those Asian peaks of ice and gulfs below.

Does this young Soldier heed the snow that fills
His mouth and open eyes? or mind, in truth,
To-night, *his* mother's parting syllables?
Ha! is't a red coat? – Merely blood. Keep ruth
For others; this is but an Afghan youth
Shot by the stranger on his native hills.

*1878*

174       The Fairy King

The Fairy King was old.
He met the Witch of the wold.
'Ah ha, King!' quoth she,
'Now thou art old like me.'
'Nay, Witch!' quoth he,
'I am not old like thee.'

The King took off his crown,
It almost bent him down;
His age was too great
To carry such a weight.
'Give it me!' she said,
And clapt it on her head.

Crown sank to ground;
The Witch no more was found.
The sweet spring-songs were sung,
The Fairy King grew young,
His crown was made of flowers,
He lived in woods and bowers.

175      Everything passes and vanishes;
             Everything leaves its trace;
         And often you see in a footstep
             What you could not see in a face.

# SYDNEY THOMPSON DOBELL

## 1824–74

176          The Wounded

'Thou canst not wish to live,' the surgeon said.
He clutched him, as a soul thrust forth from bliss
Clings to the ledge of Heaven! 'Would'st thou keep this
Poor branchless trunk?' 'But she would lean my head
Upon her breast; oh, let me live!' 'Be wise.'
'I could be very happy; both these eyes
Are left me; I should see her; she would kiss
My forehead: only let me live.' – He dies
Even in the passionate prayer. 'Good Doctor, say
If thou canst give more than another day
Of life?' 'I think there may be hope.' 'Pass on.
I will not buy it with some widow's son!'
'Help,' 'help,' 'help,' 'help!' 'God curse thee!' 'Doctor, stay,
Yon Frenchman went down earlier in the day.'


177          The Botanist's Vision

The sun that in Breadalbane's lake doth fall
Was melting to the sea down golden Tay,
When a cry came along the peopled way,
'Sebastopol is ours!' From that wild call
I turned, and leaning on a time-worn wall
Quaint with the touch of many an ancient day,
The mappèd mould and mildewed marquetry
Knew with my focussed soul; which bent down all
Its sense, power, passion, to the sole regard
Of each green minim, as it were but born

To that one use. I strode home stern and hard;
In my hot hands I laid my throbbing head,
And all the living world and all the dead
Began a march which did not end at morn.

# WALTER C. SMITH
## 1824–1908

Found and Lost

I knew him the moment he came
Past the screen by the folding door,
Though I could not remember his name,
Or where I had seen him before:
And me, too, he knew at a glance,
For a light kindled up in his eye
When I stept a short step in advance,
And greeted him as he passed by.

Yet it was not a notable face; –
Just what you may meet any day
At the hunt or the ball or the race,
Or the club or a country-seat;
Somewhat ruddy, high-featured, and full,
With well-chiselled nostrils and chin,
Eye blue, like a clear crystal pool,
And the hair on his temples was thin.

A forgettable face in this land,
Where so many are cast in its mould,
Nothing striking about it, or grand,
Only handsome and manly and cold.
I was over with Soult, and had seen
'The Duke' and 'Sir Peel' and the rest,
At the time when they crowned their young Queen,
Yet this was the face I knew best.

Each feature stood clear in my mind,
And how in his moods it would look,
When troubled or fretful or kind,
Or chastened by pain and rebuke.
'Twas strange how familiar I seemed
With the trick of that face and its truth:
Was he some one of whom I had dreamed?
Or perhaps an old friend of my youth?

But where had I seen him? and when?
And his name, too, what could it be?
I had mixed in the world among men,
I had travelled by land and by sea;
Could I hope, in the vanishing throng
Of memories fast growing dim,
To pick out this one man, among
The crowd, and identify him?

You have felt how a name or a word
At the tip of your tongue shall appear,
And you know it so well, 'tis absurd
That you cannot lay hold of it clear;
So I seemed to be still on the nick
Of finding out who he could be,
When lo! by some cozening trick
He was gone, like that lost word from me.

As I gazed after him, too, I caught
A look 'twas not hard to divine;
It was plain that the very same thought
Was brooding in his head as mine.
For he knit his brows hard as he cast
A swift, searching glance now and then
At the face he had known in the past –
But where had he seen it, and when?

Then he whispered to Soult, and I knew
That my general told him my name;
But my name did not give him the clue
That he wished, and he still looked the same.
I did as he did, too, and heard
His name from the man at the door;
But it was just a strange foreign word,
And I never had heard it before.

So we stood there apart in the throng,
A wonder and puzzle to each,
Nor heeded the harp or the song,
Or the hiss of their sibilant speech,
Though he chatted with Soult of the wars,
While I waited on, silent of course –
He was a milord, and had stars,
And I but a captain of Horse.

But he tired of this puzzling, and soon
Had put it quite out of his head;
For I marked him keep time to a tune,
And laugh when a good thing was said.
These Islanders are not like us;
Quite patient of mystery they;
But a secret that fascinates thus
We must search, till we clear it away.

I could not, then, rid me of it,
But brooded in silence apart,
Nor laughed at their humour and wit,
Nor praised what they showed of their Art.
They thought me a churl, no doubt,
For my answers were not to the point;
And I thought they were talking about
Merest nothings, and all out of joint.

Not once did he cross me again,
I am sure, for a week and a day;
But still in the sun and the rain,
In the season of work and of play,
He haunted me all day and night,
And this way and that way I went,
Ever groping about for the light,
Like a hound that is seeking the scent.

I searched out my memories all,
Went over the Past like a book,
Page by page, even dared to recall
Things that covered my soul with rebuke –
Whom I'd gambled with, drank with, or fought,
Who were rivals in old love affairs,
Who was owing me money, or ought
To be paid what I owed, unawares.

Strange things by that search were revealed,
Old stories not good to recall,
Things that Fate, too, for ever had sealed,
Wrongs that could not be righted at all.
Who shall ope all his cupboards, and find
Nothing there to repent or regret,
No scraps of old writing that blind
With tears the dim eyes that they wet?

Yet 'twas good for me so to review
My former life, scene after scene;
It gave me some thoughts that were new,
And revived better thoughts that had been.
It shamed me no less, here and there,
And it set me to putting things right;
But on this one perplexing affair
It shed not a glimmer of light.

Not a drop of his blood had I shed,
Not a livre was he in my debt,
Not a card with him e'er had I played,
Nor as rivals in love had we met.
I was baffled, and threw myself down
On the close-shaven grass of the Park,
And heard the far hum of the town,
And the clear even-song of the lark.

Then all of a sudden, when I
With long, fruitless searching was spent,
Half-minded no longer to try,
Lo! one unconnected event,
Which, neither before nor behind,
Had linked itself on to my thought,
Broke clear as a star on my mind,
And I knew I had found what I sought.

One moment the curtain concealed
Every hint of the scene and the play;
Then Phew! all the stage was revealed
In the blaze of a bright summer day;
And I knew that I had him at last,
Knew, without any doubt, it was he –
That face, in the far away Past,
That lay so long staring at me.

We had had a brisk skirmish one day
Of outposts, when Soult was in Spain,
And wounded and bleeding I lay,
Thinking ne'er to do battle again;
And the vultures were soaring up high,
And the lean dogs were creeping about,
And the grey-hooded crow, hopping nigh,
Kept watch for the life to ebb out.

I lay on the bank of a stream,
A brooklet some yard or two wide,
That whispered to me like a dream
As it slowly lapsed on by my side –
A dream of our beautiful France,
With its white orchard bloom and its grain,
And the vintages gay in Provence,
I was never to look on again.

And right on the opposite bank
A handsome young English face
Kept gazing at me with a blank,
Vague look from his red resting-place.
'He is plainly dying,' I said,
'But gallant and stout for his years'
For close by his side, and stark dead,
Lay one of our brave cuirassiers.

So hour after hour there we lay,
And looked at each other across
The brook that went trickling away,
Slowly licking our blood from the moss;
Now we heard the loud bugle-calls clear,
Then the noise of the fighting grew weak,
And the lean dogs came snarling up near,
And the hooded crow whetted his beak.

And all those long hours I perused
His features there, line upon line,
Half-conscious and dim and confused,
As he, too, lay reading at mine;
I scanned him again and again,
He was the one thing I could see,
And he printed himself on my brain,
Till he seemed like a portion of me.

If I closed my eyes, still he was there
As plain as he had been before;
If I lifted my eyelids to stare,
He was lying there dabbled in gore.
'He is plainly dying,' I thought,
'And better for me he were dead,
Those pain-stricken features will not
Be e'er blotted out of my head.'

And never a word could we speak;
I was lying half-choked with my blood,
Slow-gasping and fainting and weak,
And grasping a handful of mud;
While he from the opposite brink
Looked across, as if looking his last;
And oh for some water to drink
From the brook that went rippling past!

Then there fell, as it were, a great mist
On my eyes, and I saw him no more,
Nor thought of him even, nor wist
Was he living or dead, till the door
Of the guest-hall opened, and he
Strode stately into the room,
And that face flashed out upon me,
Like a face from the shades of the tomb.

Now it all came back, and I rushed
To his club to remind him again
Of the day when our life-blood had gushed,
And mixed in the brooklet in Spain:
But I found he had gone, as they said
Was his way, whither nobody knew,
Perhaps, where the icebergs are bred,
Perhaps, to Japan or Peru.

A traveller, restless and bold,
He would turn now his wandering feet
To seas that were frozen with cold,
Now to plains that were blasted with heat:
He knew the Red man of the West,
Had rid with the wild Bedaween,
And oft been the African's guest,
Where the spoor of the lion was seen.

Yet would he come back, they averred,
And take his old seat by the fire,
As if nothing meanwhile had occurred
To make foolish people admire.
But I never have seen him again!
And oh to know what it could mean,
That printing of him on my brain
Who was only once more to be seen.

We are tricked by illusory light,
Are we mocked by realities too?
Is our life but a dream of the night
Whose facts have no purpose in view?
So strangely my path he had crossed!
So strongly my mind had impressed!
If he must like a shadow be lost,
Why passed he not light as the rest?

You paint a likeness with care,
Yet smudge it all out the next day,
For you feel that the soul was not there,
And the soul is the man, as you say:
But what if your picture were all
You had hoped e'er to make it, and then
You turned the face back to the wall,
Which was touching the spirits of men?

Do you grudge them the joy they have found?
Do you mean but to mock and to spite?
Why sow the quick seed in the ground
But to trample it next out of sight?
God or Nature, that shapes each event,
Does He labour to quicken desire,
Just to disappoint hopes He has sent,
Just to quench His own fresh-kindled fire?

It is dark to me, dark as the night
That moonless and starless moves on,
With only such glimmer of light,
As to show the clouds brooding thereon.
And I never shall see him again,
Or know what was meant by the look
That was printed so deep on my brain,
As we lay by the slow Spanish brook.

# ADELAIDE ANNE PROCTER

## 1825–64

179             Envy

He was the first always: Fortune
    Shone bright in his face.
I fought for years; with no effort
    He conquered the place:
We ran; my feet were all bleeding,
    But he won the race.

Spite of his many successes,
    Men loved him the same;
My one pale ray of good fortune
    Met scoffing and blame.
When we erred, they gave him pity,
    But me – only shame.

My home was still in the shadow,
    His lay in the sun:
I longed in vain: what he asked for
    It straightway was done.
Once I staked all my heart's treasure,
    We played – and he won.

Yes; and just now I have seen him,
    Cold, smiling, and blest,
Laid in his coffin. God help me!
    While he is at rest,
I am cursed still to live: – even
    Death loved him the best.

# HENRY SEPTIMUS SUTTON

## 1825–1901

180                              Man

Man doth usurp all space,
Stares thee in rock, bush, river, in the face.
Never yet thine eyes beheld a tree;
'Tis no sea thou seest in the sea,
'Tis but a disguised humanity.
To avoid thy fellow, vain thy plan;
All that interests a man is man.


181                     Who Shall Deliver?

He spake; – from vanity, it seem'd to be;
Was silent; still he saw 'twas vanity.
He own'd his vainness; vanity took possession
Of that most sad confession.
He vow'd to kill the weed, and strove to do 't,
And hew'd and hack'd down to the very root:
Alas, rank vanity would still be thriving
And prosp'ring even in that very striving.
Then fell he down and pray'd: – Lord, take my breath,
And save me from the body of this death.


182                      A Love-Letter

No; I cannot thank the care
That my feelings sought to spare.
Not compliment with compliment
Should deal, but man with man. You meant

To save me pain, and therefore bent
The truth aside. This goes, my friend,
Of all true love to make an end.

Do you love me? Come then nigh me;
Prick me, man! Never relent!
Cut and hack and scarify me; –
If the truth can make me sore
Let me be a wound all o'er: –
Do this but with pure intent,
I am
      Yours
         For evermore.

# MORTIMER COLLINS
## 1827–76

183          Hartley Coleridge

Little we know of him whom best we know:
Only the spirit's foam doth overflow
In daily converse. Pure and marvellous deep
Its stronger elements must ever sleep
Within the chalice of the human heart;
Those are the noblest who can dwell apart
In their own royalty.
                    Some few years ago
Helvellyn, shrouded in October snow,
Saw me, a careless student-cottager,
Hiding afar from earth's unending stir
Where a great glen the mighty hills divides.

There, silently, the strong-winged eagle glides;
There many ravens haunt; there dwelt, moreover,
Beside myself, one solitary rover
Of chasm and valley. My small cottage lay
Under great granite barriers which the grey
Hill-Titan planted, by a midnight-hued
Tarn of the mountains: but the turf was strewed
With pine-cones from three Norway giants, tall
Each, as the mast of some high admiral
Around my comrade's dwelling. Down below
The valley widened, and a happy glow
Of brighter sunshine always seemed to break
On the blue bosom of its gemlike lake.

Who was my comrade, knew I not: but we
Over the hills together wandered free;
Our mutton-ham and coffee matutine
Together took; and when the western line

Of sunset amber died o'er mere and wold
Returned together to our haunts of old,
Perspiring, weary, with an appetite
Such as Achilles might have felt at night,
Which made our charr and grouse no common-place delight.

What colloquy we held: of matters human,
Subhuman, superhuman; loving woman;
Old fashioned childhood of its late-left state
Dreaming; stern Death, which keeps inviolate
The coming world; hill-legends that belong
To northern minstrels of barbaric song;
The Erd Gheist, whom our cottage hosts had heard
Uprooting pines above; the royal bird
Whose wide wings seemed a speck in upper air:
Each other's names we knew not – well aware
(Whatever may be due to social claims)
Minds are of higher consequence than names.
Homer we spake of; and his favorite
The sage Odysseus, whose quick eyes were bright
With no mean wisdom both of heaven and earth.
'You might have been Odysseus' in my mirth
Once said I when, with half-poetic glee,
We had improvised a modern Odyssey.
There was a wondrous sadness in his eye,
As from his ready lips came this reply.

'He was a man of action; I of thought.
Born otherwise, my life had still been nought
But a vext vision. Not, alas, for me
Brass prows cut furrows in the purple sea.
Well had I loved to roam for evermore;
Destiny binds me to the weary shore.
Well had I loved war's onset; but this arm
Is nerveless, bound by some magician's charm.
The man of action, who must weakly dwell
Under the influence of so strange a spell.
Becomes a rhymer in the wildwood shade:
Of such material are poets made.

'I have not known, nor ever can I know
The passion which in happier hearts may glow
Hot as the noontide: not to cool my drouth
Comes sweet low music from a ruddy mouth;
No dream of tresses thick, of dim brown eyes,
Haunts me all lonely; perfect beauty dies
Out from the mirror of my soul. I feign
Within me, oft, a somewhat loftier strain:
The moonlight through some palace-oriel streams
On silken vesture; and a maiden seems
To listen shyly to my pleading tones:
She fades ev'n while I clasp her; she disowns
The dreamy fiction of an empty heart.
The angry Parcæ bid me stay apart
High in these huge grey hills, whence foaming rivers start.'

# EMILY PFEIFFER

## 1827–90

184                     Triolet

Warm from the wall she chose a peach,
    She took the wasps for councillors;
She said: 'such little things can teach:'
Warm from the wall she chose a peach;
She waved the fruit within my reach,
    Then passed it to a friend of hers: –
Warm from the wall she chose a peach,
    She took the wasps for councillors.

# ELIZABETH CHARLES
## 1828–96

## FROM THE UNNAMED WOMEN

### I

185

The hand that might have drawn aside
　The veil, which from unloving sight
Those shrinking forms avails to hide,
　With tender care has wrapped it tight.

He would not have the sullied name
　Once fondly spoken in a home,
A mark for strangers' righteous blame,
　Branded through every age to come.

And thus we only speak of them
　As those on whom His mercies meet, –
'She whom the Lord would not condemn,'
　And 'She who bathed with tears His feet.'

Trusted to no evangelist,
　First heard where sins no more defile,
Read from the Book of Life by Christ,
　And consecrated by His smile.

# GEORGE MEREDITH

## 1828–1909

186                    Modern Love

I

By this he knew she wept with waking eyes:
That, at his hand's light quiver by her head,
The strange low sobs that shook their common bed,
Were called into her with a sharp surprise,
And strangled mute, like little gaping snakes,
Dreadfully venomous to him. She lay
Stone-still, and the long darkness flowed away
With muffled pulses. Then, as midnight makes
Her giant heart of Memory and Tears
Drink the pale drug of silence, and so beat
Sleep's heavy measure, they from head to feet
Were moveless, looking through their dead black years,
By vain regret scrawled over the blank wall.
Like sculptured effigies they might be seen
Upon their marriage-tomb, the sword between;
Each wishing for the sword that severs all.

## II

It ended, and the morrow brought the task.
Her eyes were guilty gates, that let him in
By shutting all too zealous for their sin:
Each sucked a secret, and each wore a mask.
But, oh, the bitter taste her beauty had!
He sickened as at breath of poison-flowers:
A languid humour stole among the hours,
And if their smiles encountered, he went mad
And raged deep inward, till the light was brown
Before his vision, and the world forgot,
Looked wicked as some old dull murder-spot.
A star with lurid beams, she seemed to crown
The pit of infamy: and then again
He fainted on his vengefulness, and strove
To ape the magnanimity of love,
And smote himself, a shuddering heap of pain.

## III

This was the woman; what now of the man?
But pass him. If he comes beneath a heel,
He shall be crushed until he cannot feel,
Or, being callous, haply till he can.
But he is nothing: – nothing? Only mark
The rich light striking out from her on him!
Ha! what a sense it is when her eyes swim
Across the man she singles, leaving dark
All else! Lord God, who mad'st the thing so fair,
See that I am drawn to her even now!
It cannot be such harm on her cool brow
To put a kiss? Yet if I meet him there!
But she is mine! Ah, no! I know too well
I claim a star whose light is overcast:
I claim a phantom-woman in the Past.
The hour has struck, though I heard not the bell!

IV

All other joys of life he strove to warm,
And magnify, and catch them to his lip:
But they had suffered shipwreck with the ship,
And gazed upon him sallow from the storm.
Or if Delusion came, 'twas but to show
The coming minute mock the one that went.
Cold as a mountain in its star-pitched tent,
Stood high Philosophy, less friend than foe:
Whom self-caged Passion, from its prison-bars,
Is always watching with a wondering hate.
Not till the fire is dying in the grate,
Look we for any kinship with the stars.
Oh, wisdom never comes when it is gold,
And the great price we pay for it full worth:
We have it only when we are half-earth.
Little avails that coinage to the old!

V

A message from her set his brain aflame.
A world of household matters filled her mind,
Wherein he saw hypocrisy designed:
She treated him as something that is tame,
And but at other provocation bites.
Familiar was her shoulder in the glass,
Through that dark rain: yet it may come to pass
That a changed eye finds such familiar sights
More keenly tempting than new loveliness.
The 'What has been' a moment seemed his own:
The splendours, mysteries, dearer because known,
Nor less divine: Love's inmost sacredness,
Called to him, 'Come!' – In his restraining start,
Eyes nurtured to be looked at, scarce could see
A wave of the great waves of Destiny
Convulsed at a checked impulse of the heart.

## VI

It chanced his lips did meet her forehead cool.
She had no blush, but slanted down her eye.
Shamed nature, then, confesses love can die:
And most she punishes the tender fool
Who will believe what honours her the most!
Dead! is it dead? She has a pulse, and flow
Of tears, the price of blood-drops, as I know,
For whom the midnight sobs around Love's ghost,
Since then I heard her, and so will sob on.
The love is here; it has but changed its aim.
O bitter barren woman! what's the name?
The name, the name, the new name thou hast won?
Behold me striking the world's coward stroke!
That will I not do, though the sting is dire.
– Beneath the surface this, while by the fire
They sat, she laughing at a quiet joke.

## VII

She issues radiant from her dressing-room,
Like one prepared to scale an upper sphere:
– By stirring up a lower, much I fear!
How deftly that oiled barber lays his bloom!
That long-shanked dapper Cupid with frisked curls,
Can make known women torturingly fair;
The gold-eyed serpent dwelling in rich hair,
Awakes beneath his magic whisks and twirls.
His art can take the eyes from out my head,
Until I see with eyes of other men;
While deeper knowledge crouches in its den,
And sends a spark up: – is it true we are wed?
Yea! filthiness of body is most vile,
But faithlessness of heart I do hold worse.
The former, it were not so great a curse
To read on the steel-mirror of her smile.

## VIII

Yet it was plain she struggled, and that salt
Of righteous feeling made her pitiful.
Poor twisting worm, so queenly beautiful!
Where came the cleft between us? whose the fault?
My tears are on thee, that have rarely dropped
As balm for any bitter wound of mine:
My breast will open for thee at a sign!
But, no: we are two reed-pipes, coarsely stopped:
The God once filled them with his mellow breath;
And they were music till he flung them down,
Used! used! Hear now the discord-loving clown
Puff his gross spirit in them, worse than death!
I do not know myself without thee more:
In this unholy battle I grow base:
If the same soul be under the same face,
Speak, and a taste of that old time restore!

## IX

He felt the wild beast in him betweenwhiles
So masterfully rude, that he would grieve
To see the helpless delicate thing receive
His guardianship through certain dark defiles.
Had he not teeth to rend, and hunger too?
But still he spared her. Once: 'Have you no fear?'
He said: 'twas dusk; she in his grasp; none near.
She laughed: 'No, surely; am I not with you?'
And uttering that soft starry 'you,' she leaned
Her gentle body near him, looking up;
And from her eyes, as from a poison-cup,
He drank until the flittering eyelids screened.
Devilish malignant witch! and oh, young beam
Of heaven's circle-glory! Here thy shape
To squeeze like an intoxicating grape –
I might, and yet thou goest safe, supreme.

## X

But where began the change; and what's my crime?
The wretch condemned, who has not been arraigned,
Chafes at his sentence. Shall I, unsustained,
Drag on Love's nerveless body thro' all time?
I must have slept, since now I wake. Prepare,
You lovers, to know Love a thing of moods:
Not like hard life, of laws. In Love's deep woods,
I dreamt of loyal Life: – the offence is there!
Love's jealous woods about the sun are curled;
At least, the sun far brighter there did beam. –
My crime is, that the puppet of a dream,
I plotted to be worthy of the world.
Oh, had I with my darling helped to mince
The facts of life, you still had seen me go
With hindward feather and with forward toe,
Her much-adored delightful Fairy Prince!

## XI

Out in the yellow meadows, where the bee
Hums by us with the honey of the Spring,
And showers of sweet notes from the larks on wing,
Are dropping like a noon-dew, wander we.
Or is it now? or was it then? for now,
As then, the larks from running rings pour showers:
The golden foot of May is on the flowers,
And friendly shadows dance upon her brow.
What's this, when Nature swears there is no change
To challenge eyesight? Now, as then, the grace
Of heaven seems holding earth in its embrace.
Nor eyes, nor heart, has she to feel it strange?
Look, woman, in the West. There wilt thou see
An amber cradle near the sun's decline:
Within it, featured even in death divine,
Is lying a dead infant, slain by thee.

## XII

Not solely that the Future she destroys,
And the fair life which in the distance lies
For all men, beckoning out from dim rich skies:
Nor that the passing hour's supporting joys
Have lost the keen-edged flavour, which begat
Distinction in old times, and still should breed
Sweet Memory, and Hope, – earth's modest seed,
And heaven's high-prompting: not that the world is flat
Since that soft-luring creature I embraced,
Among the children of Illusion went:
Methinks with all this loss I were content,
If the mad Past, on which my foot is based,
Were firm, or might be blotted: but the whole
Of life is mixed: the mocking Past will stay:
And if I drink oblivion of a day,
So shorten I the stature of my soul.

## XIII

'I play for Seasons; not Eternities!'
Says Nature, laughing on her way. 'So must
All those whose stake is nothing more than dust!'
And lo, she wins, and of her harmonies
She is full sure! Upon her dying rose,
She drops a look of fondness, and goes by,
Scarce any retrospection in her eye;
For she the laws of growth most deeply knows,
Whose hands bear, here, a seed-bag – there, an urn.
Pledged she herself to aught, 'twould mark her end!
This lesson of our only visible friend,
Can we not teach our foolish hearts to learn?
Yes! yes! – but, oh, our human rose is fair
Surpassingly! Lose calmly Love's great bliss,
When the renewed for ever of a kiss
Whirls life within the shower of loosened hair!

## XIV

What soul would bargain for a cure that brings
Contempt the nobler agony to kill?
Rather let me bear on the bitter ill,
And strike this rusty bosom with new stings!
It seems there is another veering fit,
Since on a gold-haired lady's eyeballs pure,
I looked with little prospect of a cure,
The while her mouth's red bow loosed shafts of wit.
Just heaven! can it be true that jealousy
Has decked the woman thus? and does her head
Swim somewhat for possessions forfeited?
Madam, you teach me many things that be.
I open an old book, and there I find,
That 'Women still may love whom they deceive.'
Such love I prize not, madam: by your leave,
The game you play at is not to my mind.

## XV

I think she sleeps: it must be sleep, when low
Hangs that abandoned arm toward the floor;
The face turned with it. Now make fast the door.
Sleep on: it is your husband, not your foe!
The Poet's black stage-lion of wronged love,
Frights not our modern dames: – well if he did!
Now will I pour new light upon that lid,
Full-sloping like the breasts beneath. 'Sweet dove,
Your sleep is pure. Nay, pardon: I disturb.
I do not? good!' Her waking infant-stare
Grows woman to the burden my hands bear:
Her own handwriting to me when no curb
Was left on Passion's tongue. She trembles through;
A woman's tremble – the whole instrument: –
I show another letter lately sent.
The words are very like: the name is new.

## XVI

In our old shipwrecked days there was an hour,
When in the firelight steadily aglow,
Joined slackly, we beheld the red chasm grow
Among the clicking coals. Our library-bower
That eve was left to us: and hushed we sat
As lovers to whom Time is whispering.
From sudden-opened doors we heard them sing:
The nodding elders mixed good wine with chat.
Well knew we that Life's greatest treasure lay
With us, and of it was our talk. 'Ah, yes!
Love dies!' I said: I never thought it less.
She yearned to me that sentence to unsay.
Then when the fire domed blackening, I found
Her cheek was salt against my kiss, and swift
Up the sharp scale of sobs her breast did lift: –
Now am I haunted by that taste! that sound!

## XVII

At dinner, she is hostess, I am host.
Went the feast ever cheerfuller? She keeps
The Topic over intellectual deeps
In buoyancy afloat. They see no ghost.
With sparkling surface-eyes we ply the ball:
It is in truth a most contagious game:
HIDING THE SKELETON, shall be its name.
Such play as this, the devils might appal!
But here's the greater wonder; in that we
Enamoured of an acting nought can tire,
Each other, like true hypocrites, admire;
Warm-lighted looks, Love's ephemerioe,
Shoot gaily o'er the dishes and the wine.
We waken envy of our happy lot.
Fast, sweet, and golden, shows the marriage-knot.
Dear guests, you now have seen Love's corpse-light shine.

## XVIII

Here Jack and Tom are paired with Moll and Meg.
Curved open to the river-reach is seen
A country merry-making on the green.
Fair space for signal shakings of the leg.
That little screwy fiddler from his booth,
Whence flows one nut-brown stream, commands the joints
Of all who caper here at various points.
I have known rustic revels in my youth:
The May-fly pleasures of a mind at ease.
An early goddess was a country lass:
A charmed Amphion-oak she tripped the grass.
What life was that I lived? The life of these?
Heaven keep them happy! Nature they seem near.
They must, I think, be wiser than I am;
They have the secret of the bull and lamb.
'Tis true that when we trace its source, 'tis beer.

## XIX

No state is enviable. To the luck alone
Of some few favoured men I would put claim.
I bleed, but her who wounds I will not blame.
Have I not felt her heart as 'twere my own
Beat thro' me? could I hurt her? heaven and hell!
But I could hurt her cruelly! Can I let
My Love's old time-piece to another set,
Swear it can't stop, and must for ever swell?
Sure, that's one way Love drifts into the mart
Where goat-legged buyers throng. I see not plain: –
My meaning is, it must not be again.
Great God! the maddest gambler throws his heart.
If any state be enviable on earth,
'Tis yon born idiot's, who, as days go by,
Still rubs his hands before him, like a fly,
In a queer sort of meditative mirth.

## XX

I am not of those miserable males
Who sniff at vice and, daring not to snap,
Do therefore hope for heaven. I take the hap
Of all my deeds. The wind that fills my sails,
Propels; but I am helmsman. Am I wrecked,
I know the devil has sufficient weight
To bear: I lay it not on him, or fate.
Besides, he's damned. That man I do suspect
A coward, who would burden the poor deuce
With what ensues from his own slipperiness.
I have just found a wanton-scented tress
In an old desk, dusty for lack of use.
Of days and nights it is demonstrative,
That, like some aged star, gleam luridly.
If for those times I must ask charity,
Have I not any charity to give?

## XXI

We three are on the cedar-shadowed lawn;
My friend being third. He who at love once laughed,
Is in the weak rib by a fatal shaft
Struck through, and tells his passion's bashful dawn
And radiant culmination, glorious crown,
When 'this' she said: went 'thus': most wondrous she.
Our eyes grow white, encountering: that we are three,
Forgetful; then together we look down.
But he demands our blessing; is convinced
That words of wedded lovers must bring good.
We question; if we dare! or if we should!
And pat him, with light laugh. We have not winced.
Next, she has fallen. Fainting points the sign
To happy things in wedlock. When she wakes,
She looks the star that thro' the cedar shakes:
Her lost moist hand clings mortally to mine.

## XXII

What may the woman labour to confess?
There is about her mouth a nervous twitch.
'Tis something to be told, or hidden: – which?
I get a glimpse of hell in this mild guess.
She has desires of touch, as if to feel
That all the household things are things she knew.
She stops before the glass. What sight in view?
A face that seems the latest to reveal!
For she turns from it hastily, and tossed
Irresolute, steals shadow-like to where
I stand; and wavering pale before me there,
Her tears fall still as oak-leaves after frost.
She will not speak. I will not ask. We are
League-sundered by the silent gulf between.
You burly lovers on the village green,
Yours is a lower, and a happier star!

## XXIII

'Tis Christmas weather, and a country house
Receives us: rooms are full: we can but get
An attic-crib. Such lovers will not fret
At that, it is half-said. The great carouse
Knocks hard upon the midnight's hollow door,
But when I knock at hers, I see the pit.
Why did I come here in that dullard fit?
I enter, and lie couched upon the floor.
Passing, I caught the coverlet's quick beat: –
Come, Shame, burn to my soul! and Pride, and Pain –
Foul demons that have tortured me, enchain!
Out in the freezing darkness the lambs bleat.
The small bird stiffens in the low starlight.
I know not how, but shuddering as I slept,
I dreamed a banished angel to me crept:
My feet were nourished on her breasts all night.

## XXIV

The misery is greater, as I live!
To know her flesh so pure, so keen her sense,
That she does penance now for no offence,
Save against Love. The less can I forgive!
The less can I forgive, though I adore
That cruel lovely pallor which surrounds
Her footsteps; and the low vibrating sounds
That come on me, as from a magic shore.
Low are they, but most subtle to find out
The shrinking soul. Madam, 'tis understood
When women play upon their womanhood;
It means, a Season gone. And yet I doubt
But I am duped. That nun-like look waylays
My fancy. Oh! I do but wait a sign!
Pluck out the eyes of pride! thy mouth to mine!
Never! though I die thirsting. Go thy ways!

## XXV

You like not that French novel? Tell me why.
You think it quite unnatural. Let us see.
The actors are, it seems, the usual three:
Husband, and wife, and lover. She – but fie!
In England we'll not hear of it. Edmond,
The lover, her devout chagrin doth share;
Blanc-mange and absinthe are his penitent fare,
Till his pale aspect makes her over-fond:
So, to preclude fresh sin, he tries rosbif.
Meantime the husband is no more abused:
Auguste forgives her ere the tear is used.
Then hangeth all on one tremendous IF: –
*If* she will choose between them. She does choose;
And takes her husband, like a proper wife.
Unnatural? My dear, these things are life:
And life, some think, is worthy of the Muse.

## XXVI

Love ere he bleeds, an eagle in high skies,
Has earth beneath his wings: from reddened eve
He views the rosy dawn. In vain they weave
The fatal web below while far he flies.
But when the arrow strikes him, there's a change.
He moves but in the track of his spent pain,
Whose red drops are the links of a harsh chain,
Binding him to the ground, with narrow range.
A subtle serpent then has Love become.
I had the eagle in my bosom erst:
Henceforward with the serpent I am cursed.
I can interpret where the mouth is dumb.
Speak, and I see the side-lie of a truth.
Perchance my heart may pardon you this deed:
But be no coward: – you that made Love bleed,
You must bear all the venom of his tooth!

## XXVII

Distraction is the panacea, Sir!
I hear my oracle of Medicine say.
Doctor! that same specific yesterday
I tried, and the result will not deter
A second trial. Is the devil's line
Of golden hair, or raven black, composed?
And does a cheek, like any sea-shell rosed,
Or clear as widowed sky, seem most divine?
No matter, so I taste forgetfulness.
And if the devil snare me, body and mind,
Here gratefully I score: – he seemèd kind,
When not a soul would comfort my distress!
O sweet new world, in which I rise new made!
O Lady, once I gave love: now I take!
Lady, I must be flattered. Shouldst thou wake
The passion of a demon, be not afraid.

## XXVIII

I must be flattered. The imperious
Desire speaks out. Lady, I am content
To play with you the game of Sentiment,
And with you enter on paths perilous;
But if across your beauty I throw light,
To make it threefold, it must be all mine.
First secret; then avowed. For I must shine
Envied, – I, lessened in my proper sight!
Be watchful of your beauty, Lady dear!
How much hangs on that lamp you cannot tell.
Most earnestly I pray you, tend it well:
And men shall see me as a burning sphere;
And men shall mark you eyeing me, and groan
To be the God of such a grand sunflower!
I feel the promptings of Satanic power,
While you do homage unto me alone.

## XXIX

Am I failing? For no longer can I cast
A glory round about this head of gold.
Glory she wears, but springing from the mould;
Not like the consecration of the Past!
Is my soul beggared? Something more than earth
I cry for still: I cannot be at peace
In having Love upon a mortal lease.
I cannot take the woman at her worth!
Where is the ancient wealth wherewith I clothed
Our human nakedness, and could endow
With spiritual splendour a white brow
That else had grinned at me the fact I loathed?
A kiss is but a kiss now! and no wave
Of a great flood that whirls me to the sea.
But, as you will! we'll sit contentedly,
And eat our pot of honey on the grave.

## XXX

What are we first? First, animals; and next
Intelligences at a leap; on whom
Pale lies the distant shadow of the tomb,
And all that draweth on the tomb for text.
Into which state comes Love, the crowning sun:
Beneath whose light the shadow loses form.
We are the lords of life, and life is warm.
Intelligence and instinct now are one.
But Nature says: 'My children most they seem
When they least know me: therefore I decree
That they shall suffer.' Swift doth young Love flee,
And we stand wakened, shivering from our dream.
Then if we study Nature we are wise.
Thus do the few who live but with the day:
The scientific animals are they. –
Lady, this is my sonnet to your eyes.

## XXXI

This golden head has wit in it. I live
Again, and a far higher life, near her.
Some women like a young philosopher;
Perchance because he is diminutive.
For woman's manly god must not exceed
Proportions of the natural nursing size.
Great poets and great sages draw no prize
With women: but the little lap-dog breed,
Who can be hugged, or on a mantel-piece
Perched up for adoration, these obtain
Her homage. And of this we men are vain?
Of this! 'Tis ordered for the world's increase!
Small flattery! Yet she has that rare gift
To beauty, Common Sense. I am approved.
It is not half so nice as being loved,
And yet I do prefer it. What's my drift?

## XXXII

Full faith I have she holds that rarest gift
To beauty, Common Sense. To see her lie
With her fair visage an inverted sky
Bloom-covered, while the underlids uplift,
Would almost wreck the faith; but when her mouth
(Can it kiss sweetly? sweetly!) would address
The inner me that thirsts for her no less,
And has so long been languishing in drouth,
I feel that I am matched; that I am man!
One restless corner of my heart or head,
That holds a dying something never dead,
Still frets, though Nature giveth all she can.
It means, that woman is not, I opine,
Her sex's antidote. Who seeks the asp
For serpents' bites? 'Twould calm me could I clasp
Shrieking Bacchantes with their souls of wine!

## XXXIII

'In Paris, at the Louvre, there have I seen
The sumptuously-feathered angel pierce
Prone Lucifer, descending. Looked he fierce,
Showing the fight a fair one? Too serene!
The young Pharsalians did not disarray
Less willingly their locks of floating silk:
That suckling mouth of his, upon the milk
Of heaven might still be feasting through the fray.
Oh, Raphael! when men the Fiend do fight,
They conquer not upon such easy terms.
Half serpent in the struggle grow these worms.
And does he grow half human, all is right.'
This to my Lady in a distant spot,
Upon the theme: *While mind is mastering clay,*
*Gross clay invades it.* If the spy you play,
My wife, read this! Strange love talk, is it not?

## XXXIV

Madam would speak with me. So, now it comes:
The Deluge or else Fire! She's well; she thanks
My husbandship. Our chain on silence clanks.
Time leers between, above his twiddling thumbs.
Am I quite well? Most excellent in health!
The journals, too, I diligently peruse.
Vesuvius is expected to give news:
Niagara is no noisier. By stealth
Our eyes dart scrutinizing snakes. She's glad
I'm happy, says her quivering under-lip.
'And are not you?' 'How can I be?' 'Take ship!
For happiness is somewhere to be had.'
'Nowhere for me!' Her voice is barely heard.
I am not melted, and make no pretence.
With commonplace I freeze her, tongue and sense.
Niagara or Vesuvius is deferred.

## XXXV

It is no vulgar nature I have wived.
Secretive, sensitive, she takes a wound
Deep to her soul, as if the sense had swooned,
And not a thought of vengeance had survived.
No confidences has she: but relief
Must come to one whose suffering is acute.
O have a care of natures that are mute!
They punish you in acts: their steps are brief.
What is she doing? What does she demand
From Providence or me? She is not one
Long to endure this torpidly, and shun
The drugs that crowd about a woman's hand.
At Forfeits during snow we played, and I
Must kiss her. 'Well performed!' I said: then she:
''Tis hardly worth the money, you agree?'
Save her? What for? To act this wedded lie!

## XXXVI

My Lady unto Madam makes her bow.
The charm of women is, that even while
You're probed by them for tears, you yet may smile,
Nay, laugh outright, as I have done just now.
The interview was gracious: they anoint
(To me aside) each other with fine praise:
Discriminating compliments they raise,
That hit with wondrous aim on the weak point:
My Lady's nose of Nature might complain.
It is not fashioned aptly to express
Her character of large-browed steadfastness.
But Madam says: Thereof she may be vain!
Now, Madam's faulty feature is a glazed
And inaccessible eye, that has soft fires,
Wide gates, at love-time only. This admires
My Lady. At the two I stand amazed.

## XXXVII

Along the garden terrace, under which
A purple valley (lighted at its edge
By smoky torch-flame on the long cloud-ledge
Whereunder dropped the chariot), glimmers rich,
A quiet company we pace, and wait
The dinner-bell in prae-digestive calm.
So sweet up violet banks the Southern balm
Breathes round, we care not if the bell be late:
Though here and there grey seniors question Time
In irritable coughings. With slow foot
The low rosed moon, the face of Music mute,
Begins among her silent bars to climb.
As in and out, in silvery dusk, we thread,
I hear the laugh of Madam, and discern
My Lady's heel before me at each turn.
Our tragedy, is it alive or dead?

## XXXVIII

Give to imagination some pure light
In human form to fix it, or you shame
The devils with that hideous human game: –
Imagination urging appetite!
Thus fallen have earth's greatest Gogmagogs,
Who dazzle us, whom we can not revere:
Imagination is the charioteer
That, in default of better, drives the hogs.
So, therefore, my dear Lady, let me love!
My soul is arrowy to the light in you.
You know me that I never can renew
The bond that woman broke: what would you have?
'Tis Love, or Vileness! not a choice between,
Save petrifaction! What does Pity here?
She killed a thing, and now it's dead, 'tis dear.
Oh, when you counsel me, think what you mean!

## XXXIX

She yields: my Lady in her noblest mood
Has yielded: she, my golden-crownëd rose!
The bride of every sense! more sweet than those
Who breathe the violet breath of maidenhood.
O visage of still music in the sky!
Soft moon! I feel thy song, my fairest friend!
True harmony within can apprehend
Dumb harmony without. And hark! 'tis nigh!
Belief has struck the note of sound: a gleam
Of living silver shows me where she shook
Her long white fingers down the shadowy brook,
That sings her song, half-waking, half in dream.
What two come here to mar this heavenly tune?
A man is one: the woman bears my name,
And honour. Their hands touch! Am I still tame?
God, what a dancing spectre seems the moon!

## XL

I bade my Lady think what she might mean.
Know I my meaning, I? Can I love one,
And yet be jealous of another? None
Commits such folly. Terrible Love, I ween,
Has might, even dead, half sighing to upheave
The lightless seas of selfishness amain:
Seas that in a man's heart have no rain
To fall and still them. Peace can I achieve,
By turning to this fountain-source of woe,
This woman, who's to Love as fire to wood?
She breathed the violet breath of maidenhood
Against my kisses once! but I say, No!
The thing is mocked at! Helplessly afloat,
I know not what I do, whereto I strive,
The dread that my old love may be alive,
Has seized my nursling new love by the throat.

## XLI

How many a thing which we cast to the ground,
When others pick it up becomes a gem!
We grasp at all the wealth it is to them;
And by reflected light its worth is found.
Yet for us still 'tis nothing! and that zeal
Of false appreciation quickly fades.
This truth is little known to human shades,
How rare from their own instinct 'tis to feel!
They waste the soul with spurious desire,
That is not the ripe flame upon the bough.
We two have taken up a lifeless vow
To rob a living passion: dust for fire!
Madam is grave, and eyes the clock that tells
Approaching midnight. We have struck despair
Into two hearts. O, look we like a pair
Who for fresh nuptials joyfully yield all else?

## XLII

I am to follow her. There is much grace
In women when thus bent on martyrdom.
They think that dignity of soul may come,
Perchance, with dignity of body. Base!
But I was taken by that air of cold
And statuesque sedateness, when she said
'I'm going'; lit a taper, bowed her head,
And went, as with the stride of Pallas bold.
Fleshly indifference horrible! The hands
Of Time now signal: O, she's safe from me!
Within those secret walls what do I see?
Where first she set the taper down she stands:
Not Pallas: Hebe shamed! Thoughts black as death,
Like a stirred pool in sunshine break. Her wrists
I catch: she faltering, as she half resists,
'You love...? love...? love...?' all on an indrawn breath.

## XLIII

Mark where the pressing wind shoots javelin-like,
Its skeleton shadow on the broad-backed wave!
Here is a fitting spot to dig Love's grave;
Here where the ponderous breakers plunge and strike,
And dart their hissing tongues high up the sand:
In hearing of the ocean, and in sight
Of those ribbed wind-streaks running into white.
If I the death of Love had deeply planned,
I never could have made it half so sure,
As by the unblest kisses which upbraid
The full-waked sense; or failing that, degrade!
'Tis morning: but no morning can restore
What we have forfeited. I see no sin:
The wrong is mixed. In tragic life, God wot,
No villain need be! Passions spin the plot:
We are betrayed by what is false within.

## XLIV

They say, that Pity in Love's service dwells,
A porter at the rosy temple's gate.
I missed him going: but it is my fate
To come upon him now beside his wells;
Whereby I know that I Love's temple leave,
And that the purple doors have closed behind.
Poor soul! if in those early days unkind,
Thy power to sting had been but power to grieve,
We now might with an equal spirit meet,
And not be matched like innocence and vice.
She for the Temple's worship has paid price,
And takes the coin of Pity as a cheat.
She sees through simulation to the bone:
What's best in her impels her to the worst:
Never, she cries, shall Pity soothe Love's thirst,
Or foul hypocrisy for truth atone!

## XLV

It is the season of the sweet wild rose,
My Lady's emblem in the heart of me!
So golden-crownèd shines she gloriously,
And with that softest dream of blood she glows:
Mild as an evening heaven round Hesper bright!
I pluck the flower, and smell it, and revive
The time when in her eyes I stood alive.
I seem to look upon it out of Night.
Here's Madam, stepping hastily. Her whims
Bid her demand the flower, which I let drop.
As I proceed, I feel her sharply stop,
And crush it under heel with trembling limbs.
She joins me in a cat-like way, and talks
Of company, and even condescends
To utter laughing scandal of old friends.
These are the summer days, and these our walks.

## XLVI

At last we parley: we so strangely dumb
In such a close communion! It befell
About the sounding of the Matin-bell,
And lo! her place was vacant, and the hum
Of loneliness was round me. Then I rose,
And my disordered brain did guide my foot
To that old wood where our first love-salute
Was interchanged: the source of many throes!
There did I see her, not alone. I moved
Toward her, and made proffer of my arm.
She took it simply, with no rude alarm;
And that disturbing shadow passed reproved.
I felt the pained speech coming, and declared
My firm belief in her, ere she could speak.
A ghastly morning came into her cheek,
While with a widening soul on me she stared.

## XLVII

We saw the swallows gathering in the sky,
And in the osier-isle we heard them noise.
We had not to look back on summer joys,
Or forward to a summer of bright dye:
But in the largeness of the evening earth
Our spirits grew as we went side by side.
The hour became her husband and my bride.
Love that had robbed us so, thus blessed our dearth!
The pilgrims of the year waxed very loud
In multitudinous chatterings, as the flood
Full brown came from the West, and like pale blood
Expanded to the upper crimson cloud.
Love that had robbed us of immortal things,
This little moment mercifully gave,
Where I have seen across the twilight wave
The swan sail with her young beneath her wings.

## XLVIII

Their sense is with their senses all mixed in,
Destroyed by subtleties these women are!
More brain, O Lord, more brain! or we shall mar
Utterly this fair garden we might win.
Behold! I looked for peace, and thought it near.
Our inmost hearts had opened, each to each.
We drank the pure daylight of honest speech.
Alas! that was the fatal draught, I fear.
For when of my lost Lady came the word,
This woman, O this agony of flesh!
Jealous devotion bade her break the mesh,
That I might seek that other like a bird.
I do adore the nobleness! despise
The act! She has gone forth, I know not where.
Will the hard world my sentience of her share?
I feel the truth; so let the world surmise.

## XLIX

He found her by the ocean's moaning verge,
Nor any wicked change in her discerned;
And she believed his old love had returned,
Which was her exultation, and her scourge.
She took his hand, and walked with him, and seemed
The wife he sought, though shadow-like and dry.
She had one terror, lest her heart should sigh,
And tell her loudly she no longer dreamed.
She dared not say, 'This is my breast: look in.'
But there's a strength to help the desperate weak.
That night he learned how silence best can speak
The awful things when Pity pleads for Sin.
About the middle of the night her call
Was heard, and he came wondering to the bed.
'Now kiss me, dear! it may be, now!' she said.
Lethe had passed those lips, and he knew all.

## L

Thus piteously Love closed what he begat:
The union of this ever-diverse pair!
These two were rapid falcons in a snare,
Condemned to do the flitting of the bat.
Lovers beneath the singing sky of May,
They wandered once; clear as the dew on flowers:
But they fed not on the advancing hours:
Their hearts held cravings for the buried day.
Then each applied to each that fatal knife,
Deep questioning, which probes to endless dole.
Ah, what a dusty answer gets the soul
When hot for certainties in this our life! –
In tragic hints here see what evermore
Moves dark as yonder midnight ocean's force,
Thundering like ramping hosts of warrior horse,
To throw that faint thin line upon the shore!

# ARTHUR MUNBY

1828–1910

187            The Serving Maid

When you go out at early morn,
   Your busy hands, sweet drudge, are bare;
   For you must work, and none are there
To see with scorn – to feel with scorn.

And when the weekly wars begin,
   Your arms are naked to the hilt,
   And many a sturdy pail's a-tilt
To sheathe them in – to plunge them in.

For you at least can understand
   That daily work is hard and stern,
   That those who toil for bread must learn
To bare the hand – to spoil the hand.

But in the evening, when they dine,
   And you behind each frequent chair
   Are flitting lightly here and there
To bring them wine – to pour them wine;

Oh then, from every dainty eye
   That may not so be shock'd or grieved,
   Your hands are hid, your arms are sleeved:
We ask not why – we tell not why.

Ah fools! Though you for workday scours,
   And they for show, unveil their charms,
   Love is not bound to snowy arms,
He thinks of yours – he speaks of yours:

To me his weighted shaft has come;
    Though hand and arm are both unseen,
    Your rosy wrist peeps out between
And sends it home – and speeds it home.

188          The Blessed Damozel

The blessed damozel leaned out
    From the gold bar of Heaven;
Her eyes were deeper than the depth
    Of waters stilled at even;
She had three lilies in her hand,
    And the stars in her hair were seven.

Her robe, ungirt from clasp to hem,
    No wrought flowers did adorn,
But a white rose of Mary's gift,
    For service meetly worn;
Her hair that lay along her back
    Was yellow like ripe corn.

Herseemed she scarce had been a day
    One of God's choristers;
The wonder was not yet quite gone
    From that still look of hers;
Albeit, to them she left, her day
    Had counted as ten years.

(To one, it is ten years of years.
    ... Yet now, and in this place,
Surely she leaned o'er me – her hair
    Fell all about my face ...
Nothing: the autumn-fall of leaves.
    The whole year sets apace.)

It was the rampart of God's house
    That she was standing on;
By God built over the sheer depth

The which is Space begun;
So high, that looking downward thence
   She scarce could see the sun.

It lies in Heaven, across the flood
   Of ether, as a bridge.
Beneath, the tides of day and night
   With flame and darkness ridge
The void, as low as where this earth
   Spins like a fretful midge.

Around her, lovers, newly met
   'Mid deathless love's acclaims,
Spoke evermore among themselves
   Their heart-remembered names;
And the souls mounting up to God
   Went by her like thin flames.

And still she bowed herself and stooped
   Out of the circling charm;
Until her bosom must have made
   The bar she leaned on warm,
And the lilies lay as if asleep
   Along her bended arm.

From the fixed place of Heaven she saw
   Time like a pulse shake fierce
Through all the worlds. Her gaze still strove
   Within the gulf to pierce
Its path; and now she spoke as when
   The stars sang in their spheres.

The sun was gone now; the curled moon
   Was like a little feather
Fluttering far down the gulf; and now
   She spoke through the still weather.
Her voice was like the voice the stars
   Had when they sang together.

(Ah sweet! Even now, in that bird's song,
     Strove not her accents there,
Fain to be hearkened? When those bells
     Possessed the mid-day air,
Strove not her steps to reach my side
     Down all the echoing stair?)

'I wish that he were come to me,
     For he will come,' she said.
'Have I not prayed in Heaven? – on earth,
     Lord, Lord, has he not pray'd?
Are not two prayers a perfect strength?
     And shall I feel afraid?

'When round his head the aureole clings,
     And he is clothed in white,
I'll take his hand and go with him
     To the deep wells of light;
As unto a stream we will step down,
     And bathe there in God's sight.

'We two will stand beside that shrine,
     Occult, withheld, untrod,
Whose lamps are stirred continually
     With prayer sent up to God;
And see our old prayers, granted, melt
     Each like a little cloud.

'We two will lie i' the shadow of
     That living mystic tree
Within whose secret growth the Dove
     Is sometimes felt to be,
While every leaf that His plumes touch
     Saith His Name audibly.

'And I myself will teach to him,
     I myself, lying so,
The songs I sing here; which his voice

Shall pause in, hushed and slow,
And find some knowledge at each pause,
   Or some new thing to know.'

(Alas! we two, we two, thou say'st!
   Yea, one wast thou with me
That once of old. But shall God lift
   To endless unity
The soul whose likeness with thy soul
   Was but its love for thee?)

'We two,' she said, 'will seek the groves
   Where the lady Mary is,
With her five handmaidens, whose names
   Are five sweet symphonies,
Cecily, Gertrude, Magdalen,
   Margaret and Rosalys.

'Circlewise sit they, with bound locks
   And foreheads garlanded;
Into the fine cloth white like flame
   Weaving the golden thread,
To fashion the birth-robes for them
   Who are just born, being dead.

'He shall fear, haply, and be dumb:
   Then will I lay my cheek
To his, and tell about our love,
   Not once abashed or weak:
And the dear Mother will approve
   My pride, and let me speak.

'Herself shall bring us, hand in hand,
   To Him round whom all souls
Kneel, the clear-ranged unnumbered heads
   Bowed with their aureoles:
And angels meeting us shall sing
   To their citherns and citoles.

'There will I ask of Christ the Lord
   Thus much for him and me: –
Only to live as once on earth
   With Love, – only to be,
As then awhile, for ever now
   Together, I and he.'

She gazed and listened and then said,
   Less sad of speech than mild, –
'All this is when he comes.' She ceased.
   The light thrilled towards her, fill'd
With angels in strong level flight.
   Her eyes prayed, and she smil'd.

(I saw her smile.) But soon their path
   Was vague in distant spheres:
And then she cast her arms along
   The golden barriers,
And laid her face between her hands,
   And wept. (I heard her tears.)

189                 Nuptial Sleep

At length their long kiss severed, with sweet smart:
   And as the last slow sudden drops are shed
   From sparkling eaves when all the storm has fled,
So singly flagged the pulses of each heart.
Their bosoms sundered, with the opening start
   Of married flowers to either side outspread
   From the knit stem; yet still their mouths, burnt red,
Fawned on each other where they lay apart.

Sleep sank them lower than the tide of dreams,
   And their dreams watched them sink, and slid away.
Slowly their souls swam up again, through gleams

Of watered light and dull drowned waifs of day;
   Till from some wonder of new woods and streams
He woke, and wondered more: for there she lay.

190            A Superscription

Look in my face; my name is Might-have-been;
   I am also called No-more, Too-late, Farewell;
   Unto thine ear I hold the dead-sea shell
Cast up thy Life's foam-fretted feet between;
Unto thine eyes the glass where that is seen
   Which had Life's form and Love's, but by my spell
   Is now a shaken shadow intolerable,
Of ultimate things unuttered the frail screen.

Mark me, how still I am! But should there dart
   One moment through thy soul the soft surprise
   Of that winged Peace which lulls the breath of sighs, –
Then shalt thou see me smile, and turn apart
Thy visage to mine ambush at thy heart
   Sleepless with cold commemorative eyes.

191             He and I

Whence came his feet into my field, and why?
   How is it that he sees it all so drear?
   How do I see his seeing, and how hear
The name his bitter silence knows it by?
This was the little fold of separate sky
   Whose pasturing clouds in the soul's atmosphere
   Drew living light from one continual year:
How should he find it lifeless? He, or I?

Lo! this new Self now wanders round my field,
     With plaints for every flower, and for each tree
     A moan, the sighing wind's auxiliary:
And o'er sweet waters of my life, that yield
Unto his lips no draught but tears unseal'd,
     Even in my place he weeps. Even I, not he.

# ALEXANDER SMITH

1829–67

192                    Glasgow

Sing, Poet, 'tis a merry world;
That cottage smoke is rolled and curled
    In sport, that every moss
Is happy, every inch of soil; –
Before *me* runs a road of toil
    With my grave cut across.
Sing, trailing showers and breezy downs –
*I* know the tragic hearts of towns.

City! I am true son of thine;
Ne'er dwelt I where great mornings shine
    Around the bleating pens;
Ne'er by the rivulets I strayed,
And ne'er upon my childhood weighed
    The silence of the glens.
Instead of shores where ocean beats,
I hear the ebb and flow of streets.

Black Labour draws his weary waves,
Into their secret-moaning caves;
    But with the morning light,
That sea again will overflow
With a long weary sound of woe,
    Again to faint in night.
Wave am I in that sea of woes,
Which, night and morning, ebbs and flows.

I dwelt within a gloomy court,
Wherein did never sunbeam sport;
   Yet there my heart was stirr'd –
My very blood did dance and thrill,
When on my narrow window-sill,
   Spring lighted like a bird.
Poor flowers – I watched them pine for weeks,
With leaves as pale as human cheeks.

Afar, one summer, I was borne;
Through golden vapours of the morn,
   I heard the hills of sheep:
I trod with a wild ecstasy
The bright fringe of the living sea:
   And on a ruined keep
I sat, and watched an endless plain
Blacken beneath the gloom of rain.

O fair the lightly sprinkled waste,
O'er which a laughing shower has raced!
   O fair the April shoots!
O fair the woods on summer days,
While a blue hyacinthine haze
   Is dreaming round the roots!
In thee, O City! I discern
Another beauty, sad and stern.

Draw thy fierce streams of blinding ore,
Smite on a thousand anvils, roar
   Down to the harbour-bars;
Smoulder in smoky sunsets, flare
On rainy nights, with street and square
   Lie empty to the stars.
From terrace proud to alley base
I know thee as my mother's face.

When sunset bathes thee in his gold,
In wreaths of bronze thy sides are rolled,
    Thy smoke is dusky fire;
And, from the glory round thee poured,
A sunbeam like an angel's sword
    Shivers upon a spire.
Thus have I watched thee, Terror! Dream!
While the blue Night crept up the stream.

The wild Train plunges in the hills,
He shrieks across the midnight rills;
    Streams through the shifting glare,
The roar and flap of foundry fires,
That shake with light the sleeping shires;
    And on the moorlands bare,
    He sees afar a crown of light
Hang o'er thee in the hollow night.

At midnight, when thy suburbs lie
As silent as a noonday sky,
    When larks with heat are mute,
I love to linger on thy bridge,
All lonely as a mountain ridge,
    Disturbed but by my foot;
While the black lazy stream beneath,
Steals from its far-off wilds of heath.

And through thy heart, as through a dream,
Flows on that black disdainful stream;
    All scornfully it flows,
Between the huddled gloom of masts,
Silent as pines unvexed by blasts –
    'Tween lamps in streaming rows.
O wondrous sight! O stream of dread!
O long dark river of the dead!

Afar, the banner of the year
Unfurls: but dimly prisoned here,
   'Tis only when I greet
A dropt rose lying in my way,
A butterfly that flutters gay
   Athwart the noisy street,
I know the happy Summer smiles
Around thy suburbs, miles on miles.

'Twere neither pæan now, nor dirge,
The flash and thunder of the surge
   On flat sands wide and bare;
No haunting joy or anguish dwells
In the green light of sunny dells,
   Or in the starry air.
Alike to me the desert flower,
The rainbow laughing o'er the shower.

While o'er thy walls the darkness sails,
I lean against the churchyard rails;
   Up in the midnight towers
The belfried spire, the street is dead,
I hear in silence over head
   The clang of iron hours:
It moves me not – I know her tomb
Is yonder in the shapeless gloom.

All raptures of this mortal breath,
Solemnities of life and death,
   Dwell in thy noise alone:
Of me thou hast become a part –
Some kindred with my human heart
   Lives in thy streets of stone;
For we have been familiar more
Than galley-slave and weary oar.

The beech is dipped in wine; the shower
Is burnished; on the swinging flower
   The latest bee doth sit.
The low sun stares through dust of gold,
And o'er the darkening heath and wold
   The large ghost-moth doth flit.
In every orchard Autumn stands,
With apples in his golden hands.

But all these sights and sounds are strange;
Then wherefore from thee should I range?
   Thou hast my kith and kin:
My childhood, youth, and manhood brave;
Thou hast that unforgotten grave
   Within thy central din.
A sacredness of love and death
Dwells in thy noise and smoky breath.

# T. E. BROWN
## 1830–97

A Sermon at Clevedon

*Good Friday*

Go on! Go on!
Don't wait for me!
*Isaac was Abraham's son –*
Yes, certainly –
*And as they clomb Moriah –*
I know! I know!
*A type of the Messiah –*
Just so! just so!
Perfectly right; and then the ram
Caught in the – *listening?* Why of course I am!
*Wherefore, my brethren, that was counted* – yes –
*To Abraham for righteousness –*
Exactly, so I said –
At least – but go a-head!
*Now mark*
*The conduct of the Patriarch –*
*'Behold the wood!'*
*Isaac exclaimed* – By Jove, an Oxford hood!
*'But where'* –
What long straight hair!
*'Where is the lamb?'*
You mean – the ram:
No, no! I beg your pardon!
There's the Churchwarden,
In the Clerk's pew –
Stick tipped with blue –
*Now Justification –*
*'By Faith?'* I fancy; Aye, the old equation;

Go it, Justice! Go it, Mercy!
Go it, Douglas! Go it, Percy!
I back the winner,
And have a vague conception of the sinner –
Limbs nude,
Horatian attitude,
Nursing his foot in Sublapsarian mood –
More power
To you my friend! you're good for half-an-hour.
Dry bones! dry bones!
But in my ear the long-drawn west wind moans,
Sweet voices seem to murmur from the wave;
And I can sit, and look upon the stones
That cover Hallam's grave.

# SEBASTIAN EVANS

1830–1909

## What the Trumpeter Said

### 1855

At a pot-house bar as I chanced to pass
I saw three men by the flare of the gas:
Soldiers two, with their red-coats gay,
And the third from Chelsea, a pensioner grey,
With three smart hussies as bold as they.
Drunk and swearing and swaggering all,
With their foul songs scaring the quiet Mall,
While the clash of glasses and clink of spurs
Kept time to the roystering quiristers,
And the old man sat and stamped with his stump:
When I heard a trumpeter trumpet a trump: –
'To the wars! – To the wars!
'March, march!
'Quit your petty little tittle-tattle,
'Quit the bottle for the battle,
'And march!
'To the wars, to the wars!
'March, march with a tramp!
'To the wars!
'Up, you toper at your tipple, bottle after bottle at the tap!
'Quit your pretty dirty Betty! Clap her garter in your cap,
'And march!
'To the trench and the sap!
'To the little victual of the camp!
'To the little liquor of the camp!
'To the breach and the storm!
'To the roaring and the glory of the wars!
'To the rattle and the battle and the scars!'
Trumpeter, trumpet it out!

# CHRISTINA G. ROSSETTI
## 1830–94

195                 Goblin Market

Morning and evening
Maids heard the goblins cry:
'Come buy our orchard fruits,
Come buy, come buy:
Apples and quinces,
Lemons and oranges,
Plump unpecked cherries,
Melons and raspberries,
Bloom-down-cheeked peaches,
Swart-headed mulberries,
Wild free-born cranberries,
Crab-apples, dewberries,
Pine-apples, blackberries,
Apricots, strawberries; –
All ripe together
In summer weather, –
Morns that pass by,
Fair eves that fly;
Come buy, come buy:
Our grapes fresh from the vine,
Pomegranates full and fine,
Dates and sharp bullaces,
Rare pears and greengages,
Damsons and bilberries,
Taste them and try:
Currants and gooseberries,
Bright-fire-like barberries,
Figs to fill your mouth,
Citrons from the South,
Sweet to tongue and sound to eye;
Come buy, come buy.'

Evening by evening
Among the brookside rushes,
Laura bowed her head to hear,
Lizzie veiled her blushes:
Crouching close together
In the cooling weather,
With clasping arms and cautioning lips,
With tingling cheeks and finger tips.
'Lie close,' Laura said,
Pricking up her golden head:
'We must not look at goblin men,
We must not buy their fruits:
Who knows upon what soil they fed
Their hungry thirsty roots?'
'Come buy,' call the goblins
Hobbling down the glen.
'Oh,' cried Lizzie, 'Laura, Laura,
You should not peep at goblin men.'
Lizzie covered up her eyes,
Covered close lest they should look;
Laura reared her glossy head,
And whispered like the restless brook:
'Look, Lizzie, look, Lizzie,
Down the glen tramp little men.
One hauls a basket,
One bears a plate,
One lugs a golden dish
Of many pounds' weight.
How fair the vine must grow
Whose grapes are so luscious;
How warm the wind must blow
Through those fruit bushes.'
'No,' said Lizzie: 'No, no, no;
Their offers should not charm us,
Their evil gifts would harm us.'
She thrust a dimpled finger
In each ear, shut eyes and ran:
Curious Laura chose to linger
Wondering at each merchant man.

One had a cat's face,
One whisked a tail,
One tramped at a rat's pace,
One crawled like a snail,
One like a wombat prowled obtuse and furry,
One like a ratel tumbled hurry skurry.
She heard a voice like voice of doves
Cooing all together:
They sounded kind and full of loves
In the pleasant weather.

Laura stretched her gleaming neck
Like a rush-imbedded swan,
Like a lily from the beck,
Like a moonlit poplar branch,
Like a vessel at the launch
When its last restraint is gone.

Backwards up the mossy glen
Turned and trooped the goblin men,
With their shrill repeated cry,
'Come buy, come buy.'
When they reached where Laura was
They stood stock still upon the moss,
Leering at each other,
Brother with queer brother;
Signalling each other,
Brother with sly brother.
One set his basket down,
One reared his plate;
One began to weave a crown
Of tendrils, leaves and rough nuts brown
(Men sell not such in any town);
One heaved the golden weight
Of dish and fruit to offer her:
'Come buy, come buy,' was still their cry.
Laura stared but did not stir,

Longed but had no money:
The whisk-tailed merchant bade her taste
In tones as smooth as honey,
The cat-faced purr'd,
The rat-paced spoke a word
Of welcome, and the snail-paced even was heard;
One parrot-voiced and jolly
Cried 'Pretty Goblin' still for 'Pretty Polly'; –
One whistled like a bird.

But sweet-tooth Laura spoke in haste:
'Good Folk, I have no coin;
To take were to purloin:
I have no copper in my purse,
I have no silver either,
And all my gold is on the furze
That shakes in windy weather
Above the rusty heather.'
'You have much gold upon your head,'
They answered all together:
'Buy from us with a golden curl.'
She clipped a precious golden lock,
She dropped a tear more rare than pearl,
Then sucked their fruit globes fair or red:
Sweeter than honey from the rock,
Stronger than man-rejoicing wine,
Clearer than water flowed that juice;
She never tasted such before,
How should it cloy with length of use?
She sucked and sucked and sucked the more
Fruits which that unknown orchard bore;
She sucked until her lips were sore;
Then flung the emptied rinds away
But gathered up one kernel-stone,
And knew not was it night or day
As she turned home alone.

Lizzie met her at the gate
Full of wise upbraidings:
'Dear, you should not stay so late,
Twilight is not good for maidens;
Should not loiter in the glen
In the haunts of goblin men.
Do you not remember Jeanie,
How she met them in the moonlight,
Took their gifts both choice and many,
Ate their fruits and wore their flowers
Plucked from bowers
Where summer ripens at all hours?
But ever in the noonlight
She pined and pined away;
Sought them by night and day,
Found them no more but dwindled and grew grey;
Then fell with the first snow,
While to this day no grass will grow
Where she lies low:
I planted daisies there a year ago
That never blow.
You should not loiter so.'
'Nay, hush,' said Laura:
'Nay, hush, my sister:
I ate and ate my fill,
Yet my mouth waters still;
To-morrow night I will
Buy more:' and kissed her:
'Have done with sorrow;
I'll bring you plums tomorrow
Fresh on their mother twigs,
Cherries worth getting;
You cannot think what figs
My teeth have met in,
What melons icy-cold
Piled on a dish of gold
Too huge for me to hold,

What peaches with a velvet nap,
Pellucid grapes without one seed:
Odorous indeed must be the mead
Whereon they grow, and pure the wave they drink
With lilies at the brink,
And sugar-sweet their sap.'

Golden head by golden head,
Like two pigeons in one nest
Folded in each other's wings,
They lay down in their curtained bed:
Like two blossoms on one stem,
Like two flakes of new-fall'n snow,
Like two wands of ivory
Tipped with gold for awful kings.
Moon and stars gazed in at them,
Wind sang to them lullaby,
Lumbering owls forbore to fly,
Not a bat flapped to and fro
Round their rest:
Cheek to cheek and breast to breast
Locked together in one nest.

Early in the morning
When the first cock crowed his warning,
Neat like bees, as sweet and busy,
Laura rose with Lizzie:
Fetched in honey, milked the cows,
Aired and set to rights the house,
Kneaded cakes of whitest wheat,
Cakes for dainty mouths to eat,
Next churned butter, whipped up cream,
Fed their poultry, sat and sewed;
Talked as modest maidens should:
Lizzie with an open heart,
Laura in an absent dream,
One content, one sick in part;
One warbling for the mere bright day's delight,
One longing for the night.

At length slow evening came:
They went with pitchers to the reedy brook;
Lizzie most placid in her look,
Laura most like a leaping flame.
They drew the gurgling water from its deep.
Lizzie plucked purple and rich golden flags,
Then turning homeward said: 'The sunset flushes
Those furthest loftiest crags;
Come, Laura, not another maiden lags,
No wilful squirrel wags,
The beasts and birds are fast asleep.'
But Laura loitered still among the rushes
And said the bank was steep.

And said the hour was early still,
The dew not fall'n, the wind not chill;
Listening ever, but not catching
The customary cry,
'Come buy, come buy,'
With its iterated jingle
Of sugar-baited words:
Nor for all her watching
Once discerning even one goblin
Racing, whisking, tumbling, hobbling –
Let alone the herds
That used to tramp along the glen,
In groups or single,
Of brisk fruit-merchant men.

Till Lizzie urged, 'O Laura, come;
I hear the fruit-call, but I dare not look:
You should not loiter longer at this brook:
Come with me home.
The stars rise, the moon bends her arc,
Each glowworm winks her spark,
Let us get home before the night grows dark:

For clouds may gather
Though this is summer weather,
Put out the lights and drench us through;
Then if we lost our way what should we do?'

Laura turned cold as stone
To find her sister heard that cry alone,
That goblin cry,
'Come buy our fruits, come buy.'
Must she then buy no more such dainty fruit?
Must she no more such succous pasture find,
Gone deaf and blind?
Her tree of life drooped from the root:
She said not one word in her heart's sore ache:
But peering thro' the dimness, nought discerning,
Trudged home, her pitcher dripping all the way;
So crept to bed, and lay
Silent till Lizzie slept;
Then sat up in a passionate yearning.
And gnashed her teeth for baulked desire, and wept
As if her heart would break.

Day after day, night after night,
Laura kept watch in vain
In sullen silence of exceeding pain.
She never caught again the goblin cry,
'Come buy, come buy;' –
She never spied the goblin men
Hawking their fruits along the glen:
But when the noon waxed bright
Her hair grew thin and grey;
She dwindled, as the fair full moon doth turn
To swift decay and burn
Her fire away.

One day remembering her kernel-stone
She set it by a wall that faced the south;
Dewed it with tears, hoped for a root,
Watched for a waxing shoot,

But there came none.
It never saw the sun,
It never felt the trickling moisture run:
While with sunk eyes and faded mouth
She dreamed of melons, as a traveller sees
False waves in desert drouth
With shade of leaf-crowned trees,
And burns the thirstier in the sandful breeze.

She no more swept the house,
Tended the fowls or cows,
Fetched honey, kneaded cakes of wheat,
Brought water from the brook:
But sat down listless in the chimney-nook
And would not eat.

Tender Lizzie could not bear
To watch her sister's cankerous care
Yet not to share.
She night and morning
Caught the goblins' cry:
'Come buy our orchard fruits,
Come buy, come buy:' –
Beside the brook, along the glen,
She heard the tramp of goblin men,
The voice and stir
Poor Laura could not hear;
Longed to buy fruit to comfort her,
But feared to pay too dear.
She thought of Jeanie in her grave,
Who should have been a bride;
But who for joys brides hope to have
Fell sick and died
In her gay prime,
In earliest winter time,
With the first glazing rime,
With the first snow-fall of crisp winter time.

Till Laura dwindling
Seemed knocking at Death's door.
Then Lizzie weighed no more
Better and worse;
But put a silver penny in her purse,
Kissed Laura, crossed the heath with clumps of furze
At twilight, halted by the brook:
And for the first time in her life
Began to listen and look.

Laughed every goblin
When they spied her peeping:
Came towards her hobbling,
Flying, running, leaping,
Puffing and blowing,
Chuckling, clapping, crowing,
Clucking and gobbling,
Mopping and mowing,
Full of airs and graces,
Pulling wry faces,
Demure grimaces,
Cat-like and rat-like,
Ratel- and wombat-like,
Snail-paced in a hurry,
Parrot-voiced and whistler,
Helter skelter, hurry skurry,
Chattering like magpies,
Fluttering like pigeons,
Gliding like fishes, –
Hugged her and kissed her:
Squeezed and caressed her:
Stretched up their dishes,
Panniers, and plates:
'Look at our apples
Russet and dun,
Bob at our cherries,
Bite at our peaches,
Citrons and dates,

Grapes for the asking,
Pears red with basking
Out in the sun,
Plums on their twigs;
Pluck them and suck them,
Pomegranates, figs.'

'Good folk,' said Lizzie,
Mindful of Jeanie:
'Give me much and many:'
Held out her apron,
Tossed them her penny.
'Nay, take a seat with us,
Honour and eat with us,'
They answered grinning:
'Our feast is but beginning.
Night yet is early,
Warm and dew-pearly,
Wakeful and starry:
Such fruits as these
No man can carry;
Half their bloom would fly,
Half their dew would dry,
Half their flavour would pass by.
Sit down and feast with us,
Be welcome guest with us,
Cheer you and rest with us.' –
'Thank you,' said Lizzie: 'But one waits
At home alone for me:
So without further parleying,
If you will not sell me any
Of your fruits though much and many,
Give me back my silver penny
I tossed you for a fee.' –
They began to scratch their pates,
No longer wagging, purring,
But visibly demurring,
Grunting and snarling.

One called her proud,
Cross-grained, uncivil;
Their tones waxed loud,
Their looks were evil.
Lashing their tails
They trod and hustled her,
Elbowed and jostled her,
Clawed with their nails,
Barking, mewing, hissing, mocking,
Tore her gown and soiled her stocking,
Twitched her hair out by the roots,
Stamped upon her tender feet,
Held her hands and squeezed their fruits
Against her mouth to make her eat.

White and golden Lizzie stood,
Like a lily in a flood, –
Like a rock of blue-veined stone
Lashed by tides obstreperously, –
Like a beacon left alone
In a hoary roaring sea,
Sending up a golden fire, –
Like a fruit-crowned orange-tree
White with blossoms honey-sweet
Sore beset by wasp and bee, –
Like a royal virgin town
Topped with gilded dome and spire
Close beleaguered by a fleet
Mad to tug her standard down.

One may lead a horse to water,
Twenty cannot make him drink.
Though the goblins cuffed and caught her,
Coaxed and fought her,
Bullied and besought her,
Scratched her, pinched her black as ink,
Kicked and knocked her,
Mauled and mocked her,

Lizzie uttered not a word;
Would not open lip from lip
Lest they should cram a mouthful in:
But laughed in heart to feel the drip
Of juice that syruped all her face,
And lodged in dimples of her chin,
And streaked her neck which quaked like curd.
At last the evil people
Worn out by her resistance
Flung back her penny, kicked their fruit
Along whichever road they took,
Not leaving root or stone or shoot;
Some writhed into the ground,
Some dived into the brook
With ring and ripple,
Some scudded on the gale without a sound,
Some vanished in the distance.

In a smart, ache, tingle,
Lizzie went her way;
Knew not was it night or day;
Sprang up the bank, tore thro' the furze,
Threaded copse and dingle,
And heard her penny jingle
Bouncing in her purse, –
Its bounce was music to her ear.
She ran and ran
As if she feared some goblin man
Dogged her with gibe or curse
Or something worse:
But not one goblin scurried after,
Nor was she pricked by fear;
The kind heart made her windy-paced
That urged her home quite out of breath with haste
And inward laughter.

She cried 'Laura,' up the garden,
'Did you miss me?
Come and kiss me.

Never mind my bruises,
Hug me, kiss me, suck my juices
Squeezed from goblin fruits for you,
Goblin pulp and goblin dew.
Eat me, drink me, love me;
Laura, make much of me;
For your sake I have braved the glen
And had to do with goblin merchant men.'

Laura started from her chair,
Flung her arms up in the air,
Clutched her hair:
'Lizzie, Lizzie, have you tasted
For my sake the fruit forbidden?
Must your light like mine be hidden,
Your young life like mine be wasted,
Undone in mine undoing
And ruined in my ruin,
Thirsty, cankered, goblin-ridden?' –
She clung about her sister,
Kissed and kissed and kissed her:
Tears once again
Refreshed her shrunken eyes,
Dropping like rain
After long sultry drouth;
Shaking with aguish fear, and pain,
She kissed and kissed her with a hungry mouth.

Her lips began to scorch,
That juice was wormwood to her tongue,
She loathed the feast:
Writhing as one possessed she leaped and sung,
Rent all her robe, and wrung
Her hands in lamentable haste,
And beat her breast.
Her locks streamed like the torch
Borne by a racer at full speed,
Or like the mane of horses in their flight,
Or like an eagle when she stems the light

Straight toward the sun,
Or like a caged thing freed,
Or like a flying flag when armies run.

Swift fire spread through her veins, knocked at her
    heart,
Met the fire smouldering there
And overbore its lesser flame;
She gorged on bitterness without a name:
Ah fool, to choose such part
Of soul-consuming care!
Sense failed in the mortal strife:
Like the watch-tower of a town
Which an earthquake shatters down,
Like a lightning-stricken mast,
Like a wind-uprooted tree
Spun about,
Like a foam-topped waterspout
Cast down headlong in the sea,
She fell at last;
Pleasure past and anguish past,
Is it death or is it life?

Life out of death.
That night long Lizzie watched by her,
Counted her pulse's flagging stir,
Felt for her breath,
Held water to her lips, and cooled her face
With tears and fanning leaves.
But when the first birds chirped about their eaves,
And early reapers plodded to the place
Of golden sheaves,
And dew-wet grass
Bowed in the morning winds so brisk to pass,
And new buds with new day
Opened of cup-like lilies on the stream,
Laura awoke as from a dream,
Laughed in the innocent old way,

Hugged Lizzie but not twice or thrice;
Her gleaming locks showed not one thread of grey,
Her breath was sweet as May,
And light danced in her eyes.

Days, weeks, months, years
Afterwards, when both were wives
With children of their own;
Their mother-hearts beset with fears,
Their lives bound up in tender lives;
Laura would call the little ones
And tell them of her early prime,
Those pleasant days long gone
Of not-returning time:
Would talk about the haunted glen,
The wicked, quaint fruit-merchant men,
Their fruits like honey to the throat
But poison in the blood;
(Men sell not such in any town):
Would tell them how her sister stood
In deadly peril to do her good,
And win the fiery antidote:
Then joining hands to little hands
Would bid them cling together, –
'For there is no friend like a sister
In calm or stormy weather;
To cheer one on the tedious way,
To fetch one if one goes astray,
To lift one if one totters down,
To strengthen whilst one stands.'

196            Monna Innominata

A SONNET OF SONNETS

*Beatrice, immortalized by 'altissimo poeta ... cotanto amante' [the greatest poet and lover combined]; Laura, celebrated by a great though an inferior bard, – have alike paid the exceptional penalty of exceptional honour, and have come down to us resplendent with charms, but (at least, to my apprehension) scant of attractiveness.*

*These heroines of world-wide fame were preceded by a bevy of unnamed ladies, 'donne innominate', sung by a school of less conspicuous poets; and in that land and that period which gave simultaneous birth to Catholics, to Albigenses, and to Troubadours, one can imagine many a lady as sharing her lover's poetic aptitude, while the barrier between them might be one held sacred by both, yet not such as to render mutual love incompatible with mutual honour.*

*Had such a lady spoken for herself, the portrait left us might have appeared more tender, if less dignified, than any drawn even by a devoted friend. Or had the Great Poetess of our own day and nation only been unhappy instead of happy, her circumstances would have invited her to bequeath to us, in lieu of the 'Portuguese Sonnets', an inimitable 'donna innominata' drawn not from fancy but from feeling, and worthy to occupy a niche beside Beatrice and Laura.*

I

*'Lo dì che han detto a' dolci amici addio.' – Dante*

*'Amor, con quanto sforzo oggi mi vinci!' – Petrarca*

Come back to me, who wait and watch for you: –
   Or come not yet, for it is over then,
    And long it is before you come again,
So far between my pleasures are and few.

---

**196,1.** *Epigraphs: Purgatorio* 8, 3: 'That day when they have said adieu to their sweet friends'; *Sonnetti* 64, 12: 'Love, with what strength you overcome me today!'

While, when you come not, what I do I do
　　Thinking 'Now when he comes,' my sweetest 'when':
　　For one man is my world of all the men
This wide world holds; O love, my world is you.
Howbeit, to meet you grows almost a pang
　　Because the pang of parting comes so soon;
　　My hope hangs waning, waxing, like a moon
　　　Between the heavenly days on which we meet:
Ah me, but where are now the songs I sang
　　When life was sweet because you called them sweet?

## 2

*'Era già l'ora che volge il desio.' – Dante*

*'Ricorro al tempo ch'io vi vidi prima.' – Petrarca*

I wish I could remember, that first day,
　　First hour, first moment of your meeting me,
　　If bright or dim the season, it might be
Summer or Winter for aught I can say;
So unrecorded did it slip away,
　　So blind was I to see and to foresee,
　　So dull to mark the budding of my tree
That would not blossom yet for many a May.
If only I could recollect it, such
　　A day of days! I let it come and go
　　As traceless as a thaw of bygone snow;
It seemed to mean so little, meant so much;
If only now I could recall that touch,
　　First touch of hand in hand – Did one but know!

196,2. *Epigraphs: Purgatorio* 8, 1: 'It was now the hour that longing turns back';
*Sonnetti* 18, 3: 'I recall the time when I first saw you.'

## 3

*'O ombre vane, fuor che ne l'aspetto!' – Dante*

*'Immaginata guida la conduce.' – Petrarca*

I dream of you, to wake: would that I might
  Dream of you and not wake but slumber on;
  Nor find with dreams the dear companion gone,
As, Summer ended, Summer birds take flight.
In happy dreams I hold you full in sight,
  I blush again who waking look so wan;
  Brighter than sunniest day that ever shone,
In happy dreams your smile makes day of night.
Thus only in a dream we are at one,
    Thus only in a dream we give and take
      The faith that maketh rich who take or give;
  If thus to sleep is sweeter than to wake,
    To die were surely sweeter than to live,
Though there be nothing new beneath the sun.

## 4

*'Poca favilla gran fiamma seconda.' – Dante*

*'Ogni altra cosa, ogni pensier va fore,
E sol ivi con voi rimansi amore.' – Petrarca*

I loved you first: but afterwards your love
  Outsoaring mine, sang such a loftier song
  As drowned the friendly cooings of my dove.
Which owes the other most? My love was long,

---

196,3. *Epigraphs: Purgatorio* 2, 79: 'O shades empty save in outward show!'; *Sonnetti* 236, 9: 'An imagined guide conducts her.'
196,4. *Paradiso* 1, 34: 'A mighty flame follows a tiny spark'; *Canzone* 9, 45–6: 'All other things, all thoughts disappear, and love alone remains there with you.'

And yours one moment seemed to wax more strong;
   I loved and guessed at you, you construed me
   And loved me for what might or might not be –
Nay, weights and measures do us both a wrong.
For verily love knows not 'mine' or 'thine';
   With separate 'I' and 'thou' free love has done,
   For one is both and both are one in love:
Rich love knows nought of 'thine that is not mine';
   Both have the strength and both the length thereof,
   Both of us, of the love which makes us one.


## 5

*'Amor che a nullo amato amar perdona.' – Dante*

*'Amor m'addusse in sì gioiosa spene.' – Petrarca*


O my heart's heart, and you who are to me
   More than myself myself, God be with you,
   Keep you in strong obedience leal and true
To Him whose noble service setteth free;
Give you all good we see or can foresee,
   Make your joys many and your sorrows few,
   Bless you in what you bear and what you do,
Yea, perfect you as He would have you be.
So much for you; but what for me, dear friend?
   To love you without stint and all I can,
To-day, to-morrow, world without an end;
   To love you much and yet to love you more,
   As Jordan at his flood sweeps either shore;
   Since woman is the helpmeet made for man.


196,5. *Epigraphs: Inferno* 5, 103: 'Love, which excuses no beloved from loving';
*Sonnetti* 43, 11: 'Love has led me on in such joyful hope.'

## 6

*'Or puoi la quantitate*
*Comprender de l'amor che a te mi scalda.' – Dante*

*'Non vo' che da tal nodo amor mi scioglia.' – Petrarca*

Trust me, I have not earned your dear rebuke, –
  I love, as you would have me, God the most;
  Would lose not Him, but you, must one be lost,
Nor with Lot's wife cast back a faithless look,
Unready to forego what I forsook;
  This say I, having counted up the cost,
  This, though I be the feeblest of God's host,
The sorriest sheep Christ shepherds with His crook.
Yet while I love my God the most, I deem
  That I can never love you overmuch;
  I love Him more, so let me love you too;
  Yea, as I apprehend it, love is such
I cannot love you if I love not Him,
  I cannot love Him if I love not you.

## 7

*'Qui primavera sempre ed ogni frutto.' – Dante*

*'Ragionando con meco ed io con lui.' – Petrarca*

'Love me, for I love you': and answer me,
  'Love me, for I love you' – so shall we stand
  As happy equals in the flowering land
Of love, that knows not a dividing sea.

196,6. *Epigraphs: Purgatorio* 21, 133: 'Now you can understand the measure of the love for you which burns in me'; *Ballati* 4, 17: 'I do not want love to release me from such bondage.'
196,7. *Purgatorio* 28, 143: 'Here the spring is everlasting, and all fruits'; *Sonnetti* 28, 14: 'Conversing with me and I with him.'

Love builds the house on rock and not on sand,
   Love laughs what while the winds rave desperately;
And who hath found love's citadel unmanned?
   And who hath held in bonds love's liberty? –
My heart's a coward though my words are brave –
   We meet so seldom, yet we surely part
   So often; there's a problem for your art!
     Still I find comfort in his Book who saith,
Though jealousy be cruel as the grave,
   And death be strong, yet love is strong as death.

## 8

*'Come dicesse a Dio, D'altro non calme.'* – Dante

*'Spero trovar pietà non che perdono.'* – Petrarca

'I, if I perish, perish' – Esther spake:
   And bride of life or death she made her fair
   In all the lustre of her perfumed hair
And smiles that kindle longing but to slake.
She put on pomp of loveliness, to take
   Her husband through his eyes at unaware;
   She spread abroad her beauty for a snare,
Harmless as doves and subtle as a snake.
She trapped him with one mesh of silken hair,
   She vanquished him by wisdom of her wit,
     And built her people's house that it should stand: –
     If I might take my life so in my hand,
And for my love to Love put up my prayer,
   And for love's sake by Love be granted it!

196,8. *Epigraphs: Purgatorio* 8, 12: 'As though saying to God, "I care for nothing else"';
*Sonnetti* 1, 8: 'I hope to find not only forgiveness, but pity.'

## 9

*'O dignitosa coscienza e netta!' – Dante*

*'Spirto più acceso di virtuti ardenti.' – Petrarca*

Thinking of you, and all that was, and all
    That might have been and now can never be,
    I feel your honoured excellence, and see
Myself unworthy of the happier call:
For woe is me who walk so apt to fall,
    So apt to shrink afraid, so apt to flee,
    Apt to lie down and die (ah woe is me!)
Faithless and hopeless turning to the wall.
And yet not hopeless quite nor faithless quite,
Because not loveless; love may toil all night,
But take at morning; wrestle till the break
    Of day, but then wield power with God and man: –
    So take I heart of grace as best I can,
Ready to spend and be spent for your sake.

## 10

*'Con miglior corso e con migliore stella.' – Dante*

*'La vita fugge e non s'arresta un' ora.' – Petrarca*

Time flies, hope flags, life plies a wearied wing;
    Death following hard on life gains ground apace;
    Faith runs with each and rears an eager face,
Outruns the rest, makes light of everything,

---

196,9. *Epigraphs: Purgatorio* 3, 8: 'O noble and clear conscience!'; *Sonnetti* 242, 3: 'A spirit all on fire with ardent virtues.'
196,10. *Paradiso* 1, 40: 'With a better course, and a more favourable star'; *Sonnetti* 231, 1: 'Life flees without a moment's pause.'

Spurns earth, and still finds breath to pray and sing;
   While love ahead of all uplifts his praise,
   Still asks for grace and still gives thanks for grace,
Content with all day brings and night will bring.
Life wanes; and when love folds his wings above
   Tired hope, and less we feel his conscious pulse,
      Let us go fall asleep, dear friend, in peace:
      A little while, and age and sorrow cease;
      A little while, and life reborn annuls
Loss and decay and death, and all is love.


## II

'*Vien dietro a me e lascia dir le genti.*' – *Dante*

'*Contando i casi della vita nostra.*' – *Petrarca*


Many in aftertimes will say of you
   'He loved her' – while of me what will they say?
   Not that I loved you more than just in play,
For fashion's sake as idle women do.
Even let them prate; who know not what we knew
   Of love and parting in exceeding pain,
   Of parting hopeless here to meet again,
Hopeless on earth, and heaven is out of view.
But by my heart of love laid bare to you,
   My love that you can make not void nor vain,
Love that foregoes you but to claim anew
      Beyond this passage of the gate of death,
   I charge you at the Judgment make it plain
      My love of you was life and not a breath.


196,II. *Epigraphs: Purgatorio* 5, 13: 'Follow me and let the people talk'; *Sonnetti* 244, 12: 'Reckoning the incidents of our [earthly] life.'

## I 2

*'Amor, che ne la mente mi ragiona.' – Dante*

*'Amor vien nel bel viso di costei.' – Petrarca*

If there be any one can take my place
  And make you happy whom I grieve to grieve,
  Think not that I can grudge it, but believe
I do commend you to that nobler grace,
That readier wit than mine, that sweeter face;
  Yea, since your riches make me rich, conceive
  I too am crowned, while bridal crowns I weave,
And thread the bridal dance with jocund pace.
For if I did not love you, it might be
  That I should grudge you some one dear delight;
    But since the heart is yours that was mine own,
  Your pleasure is my pleasure, right my right,
Your honourable freedom makes me free,
    And you companioned I am not alone.

## I 3

*'E drizzeremo glí occhi al Primo Amore.' – Dante*

*'Ma trovo peso non da le mie braccia.' – Petrarca*

If I could trust mine own self with your fate,
  Shall I not rather trust it in God's hand?
  Without Whose Will one lily doth not stand,
Nor sparrow fall at his appointed date;

---

**196,12.** *Epigraphs: Purgatorio* 2, 112: 'Love, that discourses to me in my mind';
*Sonnetti* 12, 2: 'Love appears in this woman's beautiful face.'
**196,13.** *Paradiso* 32, 142: 'And let us turn our eyes to the Primal Love'; *Sonnetti* 18, 5:
'But I find the burden too heavy for my arms.'

Who numbereth the innumerable sand,
  Who weighs the wind and water with a weight,
  To Whom the world is neither small nor great,
Whose knowledge foreknew every plan we planned.
Searching my heart for all that touches you,
  I find there only love and love's goodwill
Helpless to help and impotent to do,
  Of understanding dull, of sight most dim;
  And therefore I commend you back to Him
Whose love your love's capacity can fill.

## 14

*'E la Sua Volontade è nostra pace.' – Dante*

*'Sol con questi pensier, con altre chiome.' – Petrarca*

Youth gone, and beauty gone if ever there
  Dwelt beauty in so poor a face as this;
  Youth gone and beauty, what remains of bliss?
I will not bind fresh roses in my hair,
To shame a cheek at best but little fair, –
  Leave youth his roses, who can bear a thorn, –
I will not seek for blossoms anywhere,
  Except such common flowers as blow with corn.
Youth gone and beauty gone, what doth remain?
  The longing of a heart pent up forlorn,
    A silent heart whose silence loves and longs;
    The silence of a heart which sang its songs
  While youth and beauty made a summer morn,
Silence of love that cannot sing again.

**196,14.** *Epigraphs: Paradiso* 3, 85: 'And his will is our peace'; *Sestine* 2, 32: 'Alone with these thoughts, and with changed [grey] hair.'

197                    An Old-World Thicket

                    *'Una selva oscura.' – Dante*

    Awake or sleeping (for I know not which)
       I was or was not mazed within a wood
       Where every mother-bird brought up her brood
          Safe in some leafy niche
    Of oak or ash, of cypress or of beech,

    Of silvery aspen trembling delicately,
       Of plane or warmer-tinted sycomore,
       Of elm that dies in secret from the core,
          Of ivy weak and free,
    Of pines, of all green lofty things that be.

    Such birds they seemed as challenged each desire;
       Like spots of azure heaven upon the wing,
       Like downy emeralds that alight and sing,
          Like actual coals on fire,
    Like anything they seemed, and everything.

    Such mirth they made, such warblings and such chat
       With tongue of music in a well-tuned beak,
       They seemed to speak more wisdom than we speak,
          To make our music flat
    And all our subtlest reasonings wild or weak.

    Their meat was nought but flowers like butterflies,
       With berries coral-coloured or like gold;
       Their drink was only dew, which blossoms hold
          Deep where the honey lies;
    Their wings and tails were lit by sparkling eyes.

197. *Una selva oscura* A dark wood (*Inferno*, 1, 2)

The shade wherein they revelled was a shade
   That danced and twinkled to the unseen sun;
   Branches and leaves cast shadows one by one,
     And all their shadows swayed
In breaths of air that rustled and that played.

A sound of waters neither rose nor sank,
   And spread a sense of freshness through the air;
   It seemed not here or there, but everywhere,
     As if the whole earth drank,
Root fathom-deep and strawberry on its bank.

But I who saw such things as I have said
   Was overdone with utter weariness;
   And walked in care, as one whom fears oppress
     Because above his head
Death hangs, or damage, or the dearth of bread.

Each sore defeat of my defeated life
   Faced and outfaced me in that bitter hour;
   And turned to yearning palsy all my power,
     And all my peace to strife,
Self stabbing self with keen lack-pity knife.

Sweetness of beauty moved me to despair,
   Stung me to anger by its mere content,
   Made me all lonely on that way I went,
     Piled care upon my care,
Brimmed full my cup, and stripped me empty and bare:

For all that was but showed what all was not,
   But gave clear proof of what might never be;
   Making more destitute my poverty,
     And yet more blank my lot,
And me much sadder by its jubilee.

Therefore I sat me down: for wherefore walk?
    And closed mine eyes: for wherefore see or hear?
    Alas, I had no shutter to mine ear,
        And could not shun the talk
Of all rejoicing creatures far or near.

Without my will I hearkened and I heard
    (Asleep or waking, for I know not which),
    Till note by note the music changed its pitch;
        Bird ceased to answer bird,
And every wind sighed softly if it stirred.

The drip of widening waters seemed to weep,
    All fountains sobbed and gurgled as they sprang,
    Somewhere a cataract cried out in its leap
        Sheer down a headlong steep;
High over all cloud-thunders gave a clang.

Such universal sound of lamentation
    I heard and felt, fain not to feel or hear;
    Nought else there seemed but anguish far and near;
        Nought else but all creation
Moaning and groaning wrung by pain or fear,

Shuddering in the misery of its doom:
    My heart then rose a rebel against light,
    Scouring all earth and heaven and depth and height,
        Ingathering wrath and gloom,
Ingathering wrath to wrath and night to night.

Ah me, the bitterness of such revolt,
    All impotent, all hateful, and all hate,
    That kicks and breaks itself against the bolt
        Of an imprisoning fate,
And vainly shakes, and cannot shake the gate.

Agony to agony, deep called to deep,
   Out of the deep I called of my desire;
   My strength was weakness and my heart was fire;
     Mine eyes that would not weep
Or sleep, scaled height and depth, and could not sleep;

The eyes, I mean, of my rebellious soul,
   For still my bodily eyes were closed and dark:
   A random thing I seemed without a mark,
     Racing without a goal,
Adrift upon life's sea without an ark.

More leaden than the actual self of lead
   Outer and inner darkness weighed on me.
   The tide of anger ebbed. Then fierce and free
     Surged full above my head
The moaning tide of helpless misery.

Why should I breathe, whose breath was but a sigh?
   Why should I live, who drew such painful breath?
   Oh weary work, the unanswerable why! –
     Yet I, why should I die,
Who had no hope in life, no hope in death?

Grasses and mosses and the fallen leaf
   Make peaceful bed for an indefinite term;
   But underneath the grass there gnaws a worm –
     Haply, there gnaws a grief –
Both, haply always; not, as now, so brief.

The pleasure I remember, it is past;
   The pain I feel, is passing passing by;
   Thus all the world is passing, and thus I:
     All things that cannot last
Have grown familiar, and are born to die.

And being familiar, have so long been borne
   That habit trains us not to break but bend:
   Mourning grows natural to us who mourn
      In foresight of an end,
But that which ends not who shall brave or mend?

Surely the ripe fruits tremble on their bough,
   They cling and linger trembling till they drop:
   I, trembling, cling to dying life; for how
      Face the perpetual Now?
Birthless and deathless, void of start or stop,

Void of repentance, void of hope and fear,
   Of possibility, alternative,
   Of all that ever made us bear to live
      From night to morning here,
Of promise even which has no gift to give.

The wood, and every creature of the wood,
   Seemed mourning with me in an undertone;
   Soft scattered chirpings and a windy moan,
      Trees rustling where they stood
And shivered, showed compassion for my mood.

Rage to despair; and now despair had turned
   Back to self-pity and mere weariness,
   With yearnings like a smouldering fire that burned,
      And might grow more or less,
And might die out or wax to white excess.

Without, within me, music seemed to be;
   Something not music, yet most musical,
   Silence and sound in heavenly harmony;
      At length a pattering fall
Of feet, a bell, and bleatings, broke through all.

Then I looked up. The wood lay in a glow
  From golden sunset and from ruddy sky;
    The sun had stooped to earth though once so high;
    Had stooped to earth, in slow
Warm dying loveliness brought near and low.

Each water drop made answer to the light,
  Lit up a spark and showed the sun his face;
    Soft purple shadows paved the grassy space
    And crept from height to height,
From height to loftier height crept up apace.

While opposite the sun a gazing moon
  Put on his glory for her coronet,
    Kindling her luminous coldness to its noon,
    As his great splendour set;
One only star made up her train as yet.

Each twig was tipped with gold, each leaf was edged
  And veined with gold from the gold-flooded west;
    Each mother-bird, and mate-bird, and unfledged
    Nestling, and curious nest,
Displayed a gilded moss or beak or breast.

And filing peacefully between the trees,
  Having the moon behind them, and the sun
    Full in their meek mild faces, walked at ease
    A homeward flock, at peace
With one another and with every one.

A patriarchal ram with tinkling bell
  Led all his kin; sometimes one browsing sheep
    Hung back a moment, or one lamb would leap
    And frolic in a dell;
Yet still they kept together, journeying well,

And bleating, one or other, many or few,
  Journeying together toward the sunlit west;
  Mild face by face, and woolly breast by breast,
    Patient, sun-brightened too,
Still journeying toward the sunset and their rest.


198                    Forget Me Not

        'Forget me not, forget me not!'
          The maiden once did say,
        When to some far-off battle-field
          Her lover sped away.

        'Forget me not, forget me not!'
          Says now the chamber-maid
        When the traveller on his journey
          No more will be delayed.


199                    Spring Quiet

        Gone were but the Winter,
          Come were but the Spring,
        I would go to a covert
          Where the birds sing;

        Where in the whitethorn
          Singeth a thrush,
        And a robin sings
          In the holly-bush.

        Full of fresh scents
          Are the budding boughs
        Arching high over
          A cool green house:

Full of sweet scents,
    And whispering air
Which sayeth softly:
    'We spread no snare;

'Here dwell in safety,
    Here dwell alone,
With a clear stream
    And a mossy stone.

'Here the sun shineth
    Most shadily;
Here is heard an echo
    Of the far sea,
    Though far off it be.'

200                          Song

When I am dead, my dearest,
    Sing no sad songs for me;
Plant thou no roses at my head,
    Nor shady cypress tree:
Be the green grass above me
    With showers and dewdrops wet:
And if thou wilt, remember,
    And if thou wilt, forget.

I shall not see the shadows,
    I shall not feel the rain;
I shall not hear the nightingale
    Sing on as if in pain:
And dreaming through the twilight
    That doth not rise nor set,
Haply I may remember,
    And haply may forget.

201 ## Song

Oh roses for the flush of youth,
    And laurel for the perfect prime;
But pluck an ivy branch for me
    Grown old before my time.

Oh violets for the grave of youth,
    And bay for those dead in their prime;
Give me the withered leaves I chose
    Before in the old time.

202 ## Remember

Remember me when I am gone away,
    Gone far away into the silent land;
    When you can no more hold me by the hand,
Nor I half turn to go yet turning stay.
Remember me when no more day by day
    You tell me of our future that you plann'd:
    Only remember me; you understand
It will be late to counsel then or pray.
Yet if you should forget me for a while
    And afterwards remember, do not grieve:
    For if the darkness and corruption leave
    A vestige of the thoughts that once I had,
Better by far you should forget and smile
    Than that you should remember and be sad.

203    From the Antique

The wind shall lull us yet,
    The flowers shall spring above us:
And those who hate forget,
    And those forget who love us.

The pulse of hope shall cease,
    Of joy and of regretting:
We twain shall sleep in peace,
    Forgotten and forgetting.

For us no sun shall rise,
    Nor wind rejoice, nor river,
Where we with fast-closed eyes
    Shall sleep and sleep for ever.

204    'These All Wait Upon Thee'

Innocent eyes not ours
Are made to look on flowers,
Eyes of small birds and insects small:
Morn after summer morn
The sweet rose on her thorn
Opens her bosom to them all.
The least and last of things
That soar on quivering wings,
Or crawl among the grass blades out of sight,
Have just as clear a right
To their appointed portion of delight
As Queens or Kings.

205                           A Wish

I wish I were a little bird
    That out of sight doth soar;
I wish I were a song once heard
    But often pondered o'er,
Or shadow of a lily stirred
    By wind upon the floor,
Or echo of a loving word
    Worth all that went before,
Or memory of a hope deferred
    That springs again no more.


206                            May

I cannot tell you how it was;
But this I know: it came to pass –
Upon a bright and breezy day
When May was young, ah pleasant May!
As yet the poppies were not born
Between the blades of tender corn;
The last eggs had not hatched as yet,
Nor any bird forgone its mate.

I cannot tell you what it was;
But this I know: it did but pass.
It passed away with sunny May,
With all sweet things it passed away,
And left me old, and cold, and grey.

207                    In an Artist's Studio

One face looks out from all his canvases,
   One selfsame figure sits or walks or leans:
   We found her hidden just behind those screens,
That mirror gave back all her loveliness.
A queen in opal or in ruby dress,
   A nameless girl in freshest summer-greens,
   A saint, an angel – every canvas means
The same one meaning, neither more nor less.
He feeds upon her face by day and night,
   And she with true kind eyes looks back on him
Fair as the moon and joyful as the light:
   Not wan with waiting, not with sorrow dim;
Not as she is, but was when hope shone bright;
   Not as she is, but as she fills his dream.


208                    Fata Morgana

A blue-eyed phantom far before
   Is laughing, leaping toward the sun:
Like lead I chase it evermore,
   I pant and run.

It breaks the sunlight bound on bound:
   Goes singing as it leaps along
To sheep-bells with a dreamy sound
   A dreamy song.

I laugh, it is so brisk and gay;
   It is so far before, I weep:
I hope I shall lie down some day,
   Lie down and sleep.

209        Introspective

I wish it were over the terrible pain,
Pang after pang again and again:
First the shattering ruining blow,
Then the probing steady and slow.

Did I wince? I did not faint:
My soul broke but was not bent;
Up I stand like a blasted tree
By the shore of the shivering sea.

On my boughs neither leaf nor fruit,
No sap in my uttermost root,
Brooding in an anguish dumb
On the short past and the long to-come.

Dumb I was when the ruin fell,
Dumb I remain and will never tell;
O my soul, I talk with thee
But not another the sight must see.

I did not start when the torture stung,
I did not faint when the torture wrung;
Let it come tenfold if come it must,
But I will not groan when I bite the dust.


210    In the Round Tower at Jhansi, June 8, 1857

A hundred, a thousand to one; even so;
    Not a hope in the world remained:
The swarming howling wretches below
    Gained and gained and gained.

Skene looked at his pale young wife.
  'Is the time come?' – 'The time is come.' –
Young, strong, and so full of life,
  The agony struck them dumb.

Close his arm about her now,
  Close her cheek to his,
Close the pistol to her brow –
  God forgive them this!

'Will it hurt much?' – 'No, mine own:
  I wish I could bear the pang for both.' –
'I wish I could bear the pang alone:
  Courage, dear, I am not loth.'

Kiss and kiss: 'It is not pain
  Thus to kiss and die.
One kiss more.' – 'And yet one again.' –
  'Good-bye.' – 'Good-bye.'

211           A Birthday

My heart is like a singing bird
  Whose nest is in a watered shoot:
My heart is like an apple-tree
  Whose boughs are bent with thickset fruit;
My heart is like a rainbow shell
  That paddles in a halcyon sea;
My heart is gladder than all these
  Because my love is come to me.

Raise me a dais of silk and down;
  Hang it with vair and purple dyes;
Carve it in doves and pomegranates,
  And peacocks with a hundred eyes;

Work it in gold and silver grapes,
        In leaves and silver fleurs-de-lys;
Because the birthday of my life
        Is come, my love is come to me.


212                    Winter: My Secret

        I tell my secret? No indeed, not I:
        Perhaps some day, who knows?
        But not to-day; it froze, and blows, and snows,
        And you're too curious: fie!
        You want to hear it? well:
        Only, my secret's mine, and I won't tell.

        Or, after all, perhaps there's none:
        Suppose there is no secret after all,
        But only just my fun.
        To-day's a nipping day, a biting day;
        In which one wants a shawl,
        A veil, a cloak, and other wraps:
        I cannot ope to every one who taps,
        And let the draughts come whistling through my hall;
        Come bounding and surrounding me,
        Come buffeting, astounding me,
        Nipping and clipping through my wraps and all.
        I wear my mask for warmth: who ever shows
        His nose to Russian snows
        To be pecked at by every wind that blows?
        You would not peck? I thank you for good will,
        Believe, but leave that truth untested still.

        Spring's an expansive time: yet I don't trust
        March with its peck of dust,
        Nor April with its rainbow-crowned brief showers,
        Nor even May, whose flowers
        One frost may wither through the sunless hours.

Perhaps some languid summer day,
When drowsy birds sing less and less,
And golden fruit is ripening to excess,
If there's not too much sun nor too much cloud,
And the warm wind is neither still nor loud,
Perhaps my secret I may say,
Or you may guess.

213    'The Heart Knoweth Its Own Bitterness'

When all the over-work of life
　　Is finished once, and fast asleep
We swerve no more beneath the knife
　　But taste that silence cool and deep;
Forgetful of the highways rough,
　　Forgetful of the thorny scourge,
　　Forgetful of the tossing surge,
Then shall we find it is enough?

How can we say 'enough' on earth –
　　'Enough' with such a craving heart?
I have not found it since my birth,
　　But still have bartered part for part.
I have not held and hugged the whole,
　　But paid the old to gain the new:
　　Much have I paid, yet much is due,
Till I am beggared sense and soul.

I used to labour, used to strive
　　For pleasure with a restless will:
Now if I save my soul alive
　　All else what matters, good or ill?
I used to dream alone, to plan
　　Unspoken hopes and days to come: –
　　Of all my past this is the sum –
I will not lean on child of man.

To give, to give, not to receive!
   I long to pour myself, my soul,
Not to keep back or count or leave,
   But king with king to give the whole.
I long for one to stir my deep –
   I have had enough of help and gift –
   I long for one to search and sift
Myself, to take myself and keep.

You scratch my surface with your pin,
   You stroke me smooth with hushing breath; –
Nay pierce, nay probe, nay dig within,
   Probe my quick core and sound my depth.
You call me with a puny call,
   You talk, you smile, you nothing do;
   How should I spend my heart on you,
My heart that so outweighs you all?

Your vessels are by much too strait:
   Were I to pour, you could not hold.
Bear with me: I must bear to wait
   A fountain sealed thro' heat and cold.
Bear with me days or months or years:
   Deep must call deep until the end
   When friend shall no more envy friend
Nor vex his friend at unawares.

Not in this world of hope deferred,
   This world of perishable stuff: –
Eye hath not seen nor ear hath heard
   Nor heart conceived that full 'enough':
Here moans the separating sea,
   Here harvests fail, here breaks the heart:
   There God shall join and no man part,
I full of Christ and Christ of me.

214                                     Up-Hill

Does the road wind up-hill all the way?
    Yes, to the very end.
Will the day's journey take the whole long day?
    From morn to night, my friend.

But is there for the night a resting-place?
    A roof for when the slow dark hours begin.
May not the darkness hide it from my face?
    You cannot miss that inn.

Shall I meet other wayfarers at night?
    Those who have gone before.
Then must I knock, or call when just in sight?
    They will not keep you standing at that door.

Shall I find comfort, travel-sore and weak?
    Of labour you shall find the sum.
Will there be beds for me and all who seek?
    Yea, beds for all who come.


215                                     Song

Two doves upon the selfsame branch,
    Two lilies on a single stem,
Two butterflies upon one flower: –
    Oh happy they who look on them!

Who look upon them hand in hand
    Flushed in the rosy summer light;
Who look upon them hand in hand,
    And never give a thought to night.

216                          A Dirge

Why were you born when the snow was falling?
You should have come to the cuckoo's calling,
Or when grapes are green in the cluster,
Or at least when lithe swallows muster
    For their far off flying
    From summer dying.

Why did you die when the lambs were cropping?
You should have died at the apples' dropping,
When the grasshopper comes to trouble,
And the wheat-fields are sodden stubble,
    And all winds go sighing
    For sweet things dying.


217                    An 'Immurata' Sister

Life flows down to death; we cannot bind
    That current that it should not flee:
Life flows down to death, as rivers find
    The inevitable sea.

Men work and think, but women feel;
    And so (for I'm a woman, I)
    And so I should be glad to die,
And cease from impotence of zeal,
And cease from hope, and cease from dread,
    And cease from yearnings without gain,
    And cease from all this world of pain,
And be at peace among the dead.

Hearts that die, by death renew their youth,
    Lightened of this life that doubts and dies;
Silent and contented, while the Truth
    Unveiled makes them wise.

Why should I seek and never find
   That something which I have not had?
   Fair and unutterably sad
The world hath sought time out of mind;
The world hath sought and I have sought, –
   Ah empty world and empty I!
For we have spent our strength for nought,
   And soon it will be time to die.

Sparks fly upward toward their fount of fire,
   Kindling, flashing, hovering: –
Kindle, flash, my soul; mount higher and higher,
   Thou whole burnt-offering!

## 218        A Christmas Carol

In the bleak mid-winter
   Frosty wind made moan,
Earth stood hard as iron,
   Water like a stone;
Snow had fallen, snow on snow,
   Snow on snow,
In the bleak mid-winter
   Long ago.

Our God, Heaven cannot hold Him
   Nor earth sustain;
Heaven and earth shall flee away
   When He comes to reign:
In the bleak mid-winter
   A stable-place sufficed
The Lord God Almighty
   Jesus Christ.

Enough for Him, whom cherubim
    Worship night and day,
A breastful of milk
    And a mangerful of hay;
Enough for Him, whom angels,
    Fall down before,
The ox and ass and camel
    Which adore.

Angels and archangels
    May have gathered there,
Cherubim and seraphim
    Throng'd the air,
But only His mother
    In her maiden bliss
Worshipped the Beloved
    With a kiss.

What can I give Him,
    Poor as I am?
If I were a shepherd
    I would bring a lamb,
If I were a Wise Man
    I would do my part, –
Yet what I can I give Him,
    Give my heart.

219             *from* Sing-Song

A NURSERY RHYME BOOK

### I

My baby has a father and a mother,
    Rich little baby!
Fatherless, motherless, I know another
    Forlorn as may be:
    Poor little baby!

### II

'Kookoorookoo! kookoorookoo!'
    Crows the cock before the morn;
'Kikirikee! kikirikee!'
    Roses in the east are born.

'Kookoorookoo! kookoorookoo!'
    Early birds begin their singing;
'Kikirikee! kikirikee!'
    The day, the day, the day is springing.

### III

Dead in the cold, a song-singing thrush,
Dead at the foot of a snowberry bush, –
Weave him a coffin of rush,
Dig him a grave where the soft mosses grow,
Raise him a tombstone of snow.

### IV

Hear what the mournful linnets say:
    'We built our nest compact and warm,
But cruel boys came round our way
    And took our summerhouse by storm.

'They crushed the eggs so neatly laid;
   So now we sit with drooping wing,
And watch the ruin they have made,
   Too late to build, too sad to sing.'

## V

Crying, my little one, footsore and weary?
   Fall asleep, pretty one, warm on my shoulder:
I must tramp on through the winter night dreary,
   While the snow falls on me colder and colder.

You are my one, and I have not another;
   Sleep soft, my darling, my trouble and treasure;
Sleep warm and soft in the arms of your mother,
   Dreaming of pretty things, dreaming of pleasure.

## VI

How many seconds in a minute?
Sixty, and no more in it.

How many minutes in an hour?
Sixty for sun and shower.

How many hours in a day?
Twenty-four for work and play.

How many days in a week?
Seven both to hear and speak.

How many weeks in a month?
Four, as the swift moon runn'th.

How many months in a year?
Twelve the almanack makes clear.

How many years in an age?
One hundred says the sage.

How many ages in time?
No one knows the rhyme.

## VII

What is pink? a rose is pink
By the fountain's brink.
What is red? a poppy's red
In its barley bed.
What is blue? the sky is blue
Where the clouds float through.
What is white? a swan is white
Sailing in the light.
What is yellow? pears are yellow,
Rich and ripe and mellow.
What is green? the grass is green,
With small flowers between.
What is violet? clouds are violet
In the summer twilight.
What is orange? why, an orange,
Just an orange!

## VIII

I planted a hand
    And there came up a palm,
I planted a heart
    And there came up balm.

Then I planted a wish,
    But there sprang a thorn,
While heaven frowned with thunder
    And earth sighed forlorn.

## IX

A frisky lamb
And a frisky child
Playing their pranks
   In a cowslip meadow:
The sky all blue
And the air all mild
And the fields all sun
   And the lanes half shadow.

## X

'Ferry me across the water,
   Do, boatman, do.'
'If you've a penny in your purse
   I'll ferry you.'

'I have a penny in my purse,
   And my eyes are blue;
So ferry me across the water,
   Do, boatman, do.'

'Step into my ferry-boat,
   Be they black or blue,
And for the penny in your purse
   I'll ferry you.'

## XI

O sailor, come ashore,
   What have you brought for me?
Red coral, white coral,
   Coral from the sea.

I did not dig it from the ground,
    Nor pluck it from a tree;
Feeble insects made it
    In the stormy sea.

## XII

An emerald is as green as grass;
    A ruby red as blood;
A sapphire shines as blue as heaven;
    A flint lies in the mud.

A diamond is a brilliant stone,
    To catch the world's desire;
An opal holds a fiery spark;
    But a flint holds fire.

## XIII

What does the bee do?
    Bring home honey.
And what does Father do?
    Bring home money.
And what does Mother do?
    Lay out the money.
And what does baby do?
    Eat up the honey.

## XIV

Baby lies so fast asleep
    That we cannot wake her:
Will the Angels clad in white
    Fly from heaven to take her?

Baby lies so fast asleep
    That no pain can grieve her;
Put a snowdrop in her hand,
    Kiss her once and leave her.

220                     My Mouse

A Venus seems my Mouse
Come safe ashore from foaming seas,
Which in a small way and at ease
        Keeps house.

An Iris seems my Mouse,
Bright bow of that exhausted shower
Which made a world of sweet-herbs flower
        And boughs.

A darling Mouse it is: –
Part hope not likely to take wing,
Part memory, part anything
        You please.

Venus-cum-Iris Mouse
From shifting tides set safe apart,
In no mere bottle, in my heart
        Keep house.

221                  'Summer Is Ended'

To think that this meaningless thing was ever a rose,
        Scentless, colourless, *this!*
    Will it ever be thus (who knows?)
        Thus with our bliss,
    If we wait till the close?

Though we care not to wait for the end, there comes the end,
        Sooner, later, at last,
    Which nothing can mar, nothing mend:
        An end locked fast,
    Bent we cannot re-bend.

222                     Pastime

A boat amid the ripples, drifting, rocking;
Two idle people, without pause or aim;
While in the ominous West there gathers darkness
        Flushed with flame.

A hay-cock in a hay-field backing, lapping,
Two drowsy people pillowed round about;
While in the ominous West across the darkness
        Flame leaps out.

Better a wrecked life than a life so aimless,
Better a wrecked life than a life so soft:
The ominous West glooms thundering, with its fire
        Lit aloft.


223                   A Frog's Fate

Contemptuous of his home beyond
The village and the village pond,
A large-souled Frog who spurned each byeway
Hopped along the imperial highway.

Nor grunting pig nor barking dog
Could disconcert so great a Frog.
The morning dew was lingering yet,
His sides to cool, his tongue to wet:
The night-dew when the night should come
A travelled Frog would send him home.

Not so, alas! The wayside grass
Sees him no more: not so, alas!
A broad-wheeled waggon unawares
Ran him down, his joys, his cares.
From dying choke one feeble croak

The Frog's perpetual silence broke: –
'Ye buoyant Frogs, ye great and small,
Even I am mortal after all!
My road to fame turns out a wry way:
I perish on the hideous highway;
Oh for my old familiar byeway!'

The choking Frog sobbed and was gone;
The Waggoner strode whistling on.
Unconscious of the carnage done,
Whistling that Waggoner strode on –
Whistling (it may have happened so)
'A froggy would a-wooing go.'
A hypothetic frog trolled he
Obtuse to a reality.

O rich and poor, O great and small,
Such oversights beset us all:
The mangled Frog abides incog,
The uninteresting actual frog:
The hypothetic frog alone
Is the one frog we dwell upon.

# ANONYMOUS

224                Johnny Sands

A man whose name was Johnny Sands
    Had married Betty Haigh,
And tho' she brought him gold and lands,
    She proved a terrible plague.
For, oh, she was a scolding wife,
    Full of caprice and whim,
He said that he was tired of life,
    And she was tired of him
    And she was tired of him.

Says he, then I will drown myself –
    The river runs below
Says she, pray do you silly elf,
    I wished it long ago.
Says he, upon the brink I'll stand,
    Do you run down the hill
And push me in with all your might.
    Says she, my love, I will
    Says she, my love, I will.

For fear that I should courage lack
    And try to save my life,
Pray tie my hands behind my back.
    I will, replied his wife.
She tied them fast as you may think,
    And when securely done,
Now stand, she says, upon the brink,
    And I'll prepare to run,
    And I'll prepare to run.

All down the hill his loving bride,
   Now ran with all her force
To push him in – he stepped aside
   And she fell in of course
Now splashing, dashing, like a fish,
   Oh, save me, Johnny Sands,
I can't my dear, tho' much I wish,
   For you have tied my hands
   For you have tied my hands.


225                 The Way to Live

*Chorus.*
*A man and a woman got married one day,*
*And thus unto each other did say,*
*As we the world must now begin,*
*We will deal in every following thing.*

*She.* We will deal in apples, plums and pears,
*He.* We will mend old bellows and bottom old chairs,
*She.* We will buy old metal, rope and bags,
*He.* Yes, and I'll go out a gathering rags.

*She.* We will sell red herrings and ginger pop,
*He.* Hot baked sheep's head and taters hot,
*She.* We'll keep a school of high degree,
*He.* And learn the children A. B. C,
*She.* We'll sell fat bacon, butter and lard,
*He.* And great long songs for a penny a yard,
*She.* I'll sell potash, starch and blues,
*He.* And I'll go sweeping the chimney flues.
*She.* I'll make bustles and lady's frills,
*He.* And I'll sell mussels and pickled eels,
*She.* We'll deal in razors, strops and hones,
*He.* And I'll go out a picking up bones,
*She.* We'll deal in paper, take in the news,
*He.* And I'll go a cobbling ladies' shoes,

*Both*. And we'll learn the ladies all complete,
    To dance the Polka at threepence a week.
*She*. We'll deal in lollipops, sugar and figs,
*He*. We'll buy a donkey, ducks, hens and pigs,
*She*. We'll have a mangle, and buy old clothes,
*He*. And I'll make salve for the ladies' toes.
*She*. We'll deal in pickled cabbage and eggs,
*He*. And make tin dishes and wooden legs.
*She*. We'll deal in sausages, tripe and lard,
*He*. And if we can't live, 'twill be devilish hard.

*She*. We'll deal in Oils, sperm, train and neat,
*He*. And I'll make stockings for children's feet,
*She*. We will sell hot muffins and home baked bread,
*He*. Pins and needles, cotton and thread.
*She*. We'll grind old razors, scissors and knives,
*He*. And keep lodgings for single men and their wives,
*She*. We'll deal in lobsters, shrimps and sprats,
*He*. And I'll sell meat for the ladies' cats.

*She*. We'll deal in fish, fresh, boiled, and fried,
*He*. And let out donkeys a penny a ride,
*She*. I will the ladies' fortune tell,
*He*. And I'll cry, Old umbrellas to sell,
*She*. We will take in the blooming ladies bright,
*He*. And sleep in the garret at threepence a night,
*She*. I'll sing, Come buy my Crockery ware,
*He*. And I'll go dressing the ladies' hair.

*She*. We'll sell ripe Cherries, pea soup and milk,
*He*. Oranges, lemons and pickled wilks,
*She*. Wooden rolling-pins at the Royal Exchange,
*He*. And if we can't get on we may think it strange.

# C. S. CALVERLEY
## 1831–84

## Peace

*A study*

He stood, a worn-out City clerk –
  Who'd toil'd, and seen no holiday,
For forty years from dawn to dark –
  Alone beside Caermarthen Bay.

He felt the salt spray on his lips;
  Heard children's voices on the sands;
Up the sun's path he saw the ships
  Sail on and on to other lands;

And laugh'd aloud. Each sight and sound
  To him was joy too deep for tears;
He sat him on the beach, and bound
  A blue bandana round his ears,

And thought how, posted near his door,
  His own green door on Camden Hill,
Two bands at least, most likely more,
  Were mingling at their own sweet will

Verdi with Vance. And at the thought
  He laugh'd again, and softly drew
That Morning Herald that he'd bought
  Forth from his breast, and read it through.

# EDWARD ROBERT BULWER LYTTON

## 1831–91

227                          Seaward

### 1

The green grows ever greyer as we pass;
   The lean soil sandier; the spacious air
More breezy; raggeder the bristly grass;
   And the few crookèd leafless trees more rare.

### 2

And now nor grass, nor trees! But only stones
   Tufted with patches of wild rosemary
And spurge. Behind them hidden, something moans;
   And large white birds come with a questioning cry.

### 3

What's there, beyond? A thing unsearch'd and strange;
   Not happier, but different. Something vast
And new. Some unimaginable change
   From what has been. Perchance the end at last?

# LEWIS CARROLL
### 1832–98

Jabberwocky

'Twas brillig, and the slithy toves
  Did gyre and gimble in the wabe:
All mimsy were the borogoves,
  And the mome raths outgrabe.

'Beware the Jabberwock, my son!
  The jaws that bite, the claws that catch!
Beware the Jubjub bird, and shun
  The frumious Bandersnatch!'

He took his vorpal sword in hand:
  Long time the manxome foe he sought –
So rested he by the Tumtum tree,
  And stood awhile in thought.

And as in uffish thought he stood,
  The Jabberwock, with eyes of flame,
Came whiffling through the tulgey wood,
  And burbled as it came!

One, two! One, two! And through and through
  The vorpal blade went snicker-snack!
He left it dead, and with its head
  He went galumphing back.

'And hast thou slain the Jabberwock?
  Come to my arms, my beamish boy!
O frabjous day! Callooh! Callay!'
  He chortled in his joy.

'Twas brillig, and the slithy toves
    Did gyre and gimble in the wabe:
All mimsy were the borogoves,
    And the mome raths outgrabe.


229        The Walrus and the Carpenter

The sun was shining on the sea,
    Shining with all his might:
He did his very best to make
    The billows smooth and bright –
And this was odd, because it was
    The middle of the night.

The moon was shining sulkily,
    Because she thought the sun
Had got no business to be there
    After the day was done –
'It's very rude of him,' she said,
    'To come and spoil the fun!'

The sea was wet as wet could be,
    The sands were dry as dry.
You could not see a cloud, because
    No cloud was in the sky:
No birds were flying overhead –
    There were no birds to fly.

The Walrus and the Carpenter
    Were walking close at hand;
They wept like anything to see
    Such quantities of sand:
'If this were only cleared away,'
    They said, 'it *would* be grand!'

'If seven maids with seven mops
   Swept it for half a year,
Do you suppose,' the Walrus said,
   'That they could get it clear?'
'I doubt it,' said the Carpenter,
   And shed a bitter tear.

'O Oysters, come and walk with us!'
   The Walrus did beseech.
'A pleasant walk, a pleasant talk,
   Along the briny beach:
We cannot do with more than four,
   To give a hand to each.'

The eldest Oyster looked at him,
   But never a word he said:
The eldest Oyster winked his eye,
   And shook his heavy head –
Meaning to say he did not choose
   To leave the oyster-bed.

But four young Oysters hurried up,
   All eager for the treat:
Their coats were brushed, their faces washed,
   Their shoes were clean and neat –
And this was odd, because, you know,
   They hadn't any feet.

Four other Oysters followed them,
   And yet another four;
And thick and fast they came at last,
   And more, and more, and more –
All hopping through the frothy waves,
   And scrambling to the shore.

The Walrus and the Carpenter
   Walked on a mile or so,
And then they rested on a rock
   Conveniently low:
And all the little Oysters stood
   And waited in a row.

'The time has come,' the Walrus said,
   'To talk of many things:
Of shoes – and ships – and sealing-wax –
   Of cabbages – and kings –
And why the sea is boiling hot –
   And whether pigs have wings.'

'But wait a bit,' the Oysters cried,
   'Before we have our chat;
For some of us are out of breath,
   And all of us are fat!'
'No hurry!' said the Carpenter.
   They thanked him much for that.

'A loaf of bread,' the Walrus said,
   'Is what we chiefly need:
Pepper and vinegar besides
   Are very good indeed –
Now if you're ready, Oysters dear,
   We can begin to feed.'

'But not on us!' the Oysters cried,
   Turning a little blue.
'After such kindness, that would be
   A dismal thing to do!'
'The night is fine,' the Walrus said.
   'Do you admire the view?

'It was so kind of you to come!
    And you are very nice!'
The Carpenter said nothing but
    'Cut us another slice:
I wish you were not quite so deaf –
    I've had to ask you twice!'

'It seems a shame,' the Walrus said,
    'To play them such a trick,
After we've brought them out so far,
    And made them trot so quick!'
The Carpenter said nothing but
    'The butter's spread too thick!'

'I weep for you,' the Walrus said:
    'I deeply sympathize.'
With sobs and tears he sorted out
    Those of the largest size,
Holding his pocket-handkerchief
    Before his streaming eyes.

'O Oysters,' said the Carpenter,
    'You've had a pleasant run!
Shall we be trotting home again?'
    But answer came there none –
And this was scarcely odd, because
    They'd eaten every one.

# JOSEPH SKIPSEY
## 1832–1903

230                     'Get Up!'

'Get up!' the caller calls, 'Get up!'
    And in the dead of night,
To win the bairns their bite and sup,
    I rise a weary wight.

My flannel dudden donn'd, thrice o'er
    My birds are kiss'd, and then
I with a whistle shut the door,
    I may not ope again.


231             The Stars Are Twinkling

The stars are twinkling in the sky,
    As to the pit I go;
I think not of the sheen on high,
    But of the gloom below.

Not rest or peace, but toil and strife,
    Do there the soul enthral;
And turn the precious cup of life
    Into a cup of gall.

232                          Mother Wept

Mother wept, and father sighed;
    With delight a-glow
Cried the lad, 'To-morrow,' cried,
    'To the pit I go.'

Up and down the place he sped, –
    Greeted old and young;
Far and wide the tidings spread;
    Clapt his hands and sung.

Came his cronies; some to gaze
    Wrapt in wonder; some
Free with counsel; some with praise;
    Some with envy dumb.

'May he,' many a gossip cried,
    'Be from peril kept;'
Father hid his face and sighed,
    Mother turned and wept.


233                          A Golden Lot

In the coal-pit, or the factory,
    I toil by night or day,
And still to the music of labour
    I lilt my heart-felt lay;

I lilt my heart-felt lay –
    And the gloom of the deep, deep mine,
Or the din of the factory dieth away,
    And a Golden Lot is mine.

# RICHARD WATSON DIXON

1833–1900

234                              Dream

I

With camel's hair I clothed my skin,
    I fed my mouth with honey wild;
And set me scarlet wool to spin,
    And all my breast with hyssop filled;
Upon my brow and cheeks and chin
    A bird's blood spilled.

I took a broken reed to hold,
    I took a sponge of gall to press;
I took weak water-weeds to fold
    About my sacrificial dress.

I took the grasses of the field,
    The flax was bolled upon my crine;
And ivy thorn and wild grapes healed
    To make good wine.

I took my scrip of manna sweet,
    My cruse of water did I bless;
I took the white dove by the feet,
    And flew into the wilderness.

## II

The tiger came and played;
Uprose the lion in his mane;
The jackal's tawny nose
And sanguine dripping tongue
Out of the desert rose
And plunged its sands among;
The bear came striding o'er the desert plain.

Uprose the horn and eyes
And quivering flank of the great unicorn,
And galloped round and round;
Uprose the gleaming claw
Of the leviathan, and wound
In steadfast march did draw
Its course away beyond the desert's bourn.

I stood within a maze
Woven round about me by a magic art,
And ordered circle-wise:
The bear more near did tread,
And with two fiery eyes,
And with a wolfish head,
Did close the circle round in every part.

## III

With scarlet corded horn,
With frail wrecked knees and stumbling pace,
The scapegoat came:
His eyes took flesh and spirit dread in flame
At once, and he died looking towards my face.

235        The Mystery of the Body

Smiling with a pliant grace
Rose on me a learned face:
Smiled the soul when smiled the eyes? –
Up when ran the traceries
Of the forehead arching high,
Did the inner faculty
Tempering the hidden nerve
Mould the momentary curve,
Waking motions strange between
Spirit fine and fleshly screen?

May I then a likeness find
In the features of the mind
And the antic of the flesh?
Wherefore should the wrinkled mesh
Of the forehead arching high
Image the soul's pleasantry?

236                Song

The feathers of the willow
Are half of them grown yellow
    Above the swelling stream;
And ragged are the bushes,
And rusty now the rushes,
    And wild the clouded gleam.

The thistle now is older,
His stalk begins to moulder,
    His head is white as snow;
The branches all are barer,
The linnet's song is rarer,
    The robin pipeth now.

# WILLIAM MORRIS
## 1834–96

237        ### The Haystack in the Floods

Had she come all the way for this,
To part at last without a kiss?
Yea, had she borne the dirt and rain
That her own eyes might see him slain
Beside the haystack in the floods?

Along the dripping leafless woods,
The stirrup touching either shoe,
She rode astride as troopers do;
With kirtle kilted to her knee,
To which the mud splash'd wretchedly;
And the wet dripp'd from every tree
Upon her head and heavy hair,
And on her eyelids broad and fair;
The tears and rain ran down her face.
By fits and starts they rode apace,
And very often was his place
Far off from her; he had to ride
Ahead, to see what might betide
When the roads cross'd; and sometimes, when
There rose a murmuring from his men,
Had to turn back with promises;
Ah me! she had but little ease;
And often for pure doubt and dread
She sobb'd, made giddy in the head
By the swift riding; while, for cold,
Her slender fingers scarce could hold
The wet reins; yea, and scarcely, too,
She felt the foot within her shoe

Against the stirrup: all for this,
To part at last without a kiss
Beside the haystack in the floods.

For when they near'd that old soak'd hay,
They saw across the only way
That Judas, Godmar, and the three
Red running lions dismally
Grinn'd from his pennon, under which
In one straight line along the ditch,
They counted thirty heads.

           So then,
While Robert turn'd round to his men,
She saw at once the wretched end,
And, stooping down, tried hard to rend
Her coif the wrong way from her head,
And hid her eyes; while Robert said:
'Nay, love, 'tis scarcely two to one,
At Poictiers where we made them run
So fast – why, sweet my love, good cheer,
The Gascon frontier is so near,
Nought after this.'

           But, 'O!' she said,
'My God! my God! I have to tread
The long way back without you; then
The court at Paris; those six men;
The gratings of the Chatelet;
The swift Seine on some rainy day
Like this, and people standing by
And laughing, while my weak hands try
To recollect how strong men swim.
All this, or else a life with him,
For which I should be damned at last.
Would God that this next hour were past!'

He answer'd not, but cried his cry,
'St. George for Marny!' cheerily;
And laid his hand upon her rein.
Alas! no man of all his train
Gave back that cheery cry again;
And, while for rage his thumb beat fast
Upon his sword-hilts, some one cast
About his neck a kerchief long,
And bound him.

        Then they went along
To Godmar; who said: 'Now, Jehane,
Your lover's life is on the wane
So fast, that, if this very hour
You yield not as my paramour,
He will not see the rain leave off –
Nay, keep your tongue from gibe and scoff,
Sir Robert, or I slay you now.'

She laid her hand upon her brow,
Then gazed upon the palm, as though
She thought her forehead bled, and – 'No!'
She said, and turn'd her head away,
As there were nothing else to say,
And everything were settled: red
Grew Godmar's face from chin to head:
'Jehane, on yonder hill there stands
My castle, guarding well my lands:
What hinders me from taking you,
And doing that I list to do
To your fair wilful body, while
Your knight lies dead?'

        A wicked smile
Wrinkled her face, her lips grew thin,
A long way out she thrust her chin:
'You know that I should strangle you
While you were sleeping; or bite through

Your throat, by God's help – ah!' she said,
'Lord Jesus, pity your poor maid!
For in such wise they hem me in,
I cannot choose but sin and sin,
Whatever happens: yet I think
They could not make me eat or drink,
And so should I just reach my rest.'
'Nay, if you do not my behest,
O Jehane! though I love you well,'
Said Godmar, 'would I fail to tell
All that I know?' 'Foul lies,' she said.
'Eh? lies, my Jehane? by God's head,
At Paris folks would deem them true!
Do you know, Jehane, they cry for you:
"Jehane the brown! Jehane the brown!
Give us Jehane to burn or drown!" –
Eh – gag me Robert! – sweet my friend,
This were indeed a piteous end
For those long fingers, and long feet,
And long neck, and smooth shoulders sweet;
An end that few men would forget
That saw it – So, an hour yet:
Consider, Jehane, which to take
Of life or death!'

        So, scarce awake,
Dismounting, did she leave that place,
And totter some yards: with her face
Turn'd upward to the sky she lay,
Her head on a wet heap of hay,
And fell asleep: and while she slept,
And did not dream, the minutes crept
Round to the twelve again; but she,
Being waked at last, sigh'd quietly,
And strangely childlike came, and said:
'I will not.' Straightway Godmar's head,
As though it hung on strong wires, turn'd
Most sharply round, and his face burn'd.

For Robert – both his eyes were dry,
He could not weep, but gloomily
He seem'd to watch the rain; yea, too,
His lips were firm; he tried once more
To touch her lips; she reach'd out, sore
And vain desire so tortured them,
The poor grey lips, and now the hem
Of his sleeve brush'd them.

                    With a start,
Up Godmar rose, thrust them apart;
From Robert's throat he loosed the bands
Of silk and mail; with empty hands
Held out, she stood and gazed, and saw
The long bright blade without a flaw
Glide out from Godmar's sheath, his hand
In Robert's hair; she saw him bend
Back Robert's head; she saw him send
The thin steel down; the blow told well,
Right backward the knight Robert fell,
And moaned as dogs do, being half dead,
Unwitting, as I deem: so then
Godmar turn'd grinning to his men,
Who ran, some five or six, and beat
His head to pieces at their feet.

Then Godmar turn'd again and said:
'So, Jehane, the first fitte is read!
Take note, my lady, that your way
Lies backward to the Chatelet!'
She shook her head and gazed awhile
At her cold hands with a rueful smile,
As though this thing had made her mad.

This was the parting that they had
Beside the haystack in the floods.

238                   Echoes of Love's House

Love gives every gift whereby we long to live:
'Love takes every gift, and nothing back doth give.'

Love unlocks the lips that else were ever dumb:
'Love locks up the lips whence all things good might come.'

Love makes clear the eyes that else would never see:
'Love makes blind the eyes to all but me and thee.'

Love turns life to joy till nought is left to gain:
'Love turns life to woe till hope is nought and vain.'

Love, who changest all, change me nevermore!
'Love, who changest all, change my sorrow sore!'

Love burns up the world to changeless heaven and blest,
'Love burns up the world to a void of all unrest.'

And there we twain are left, and no more work we need:
'And I am left alone, and who my work shall heed?'

Ah! I praise thee, Love, for utter joyance won!
'And is my praise nought worth for all my life undone?'


239                        Pomona

I am the ancient Apple-Queen,
As once I was so am I now.
For evermore a hope unseen,
Betwixt the blossom and the bough.

Ah, where's the river's hidden Gold!
And where the windy grave of Troy?
Yet come I as I came of old,
From out the heart of Summer's joy.

# JAMES THOMSON
## 1834–82

240                    The City of Dreadful Night

*'Per me si va nella città dolente.'*

*Dante*

*'Poi di tanto adoprar, di tanti moti*
*D'ogni celeste, ogni terrena cosa,*
*Girando senza posa,*
*Per tornar sempre là donde son mosse;*
*Uso alcuno, alcun frutto*
*Indovinar non so.'*

*'Sola nel mondo eterna, a cui si volve*
*Ogni creata cosa,*
*In te, morte, si posa*
*Nostra ignuda natura;*
*Lieta no, ma sicura*
*Dell' antico dolor ...*
*Però ch' esser beato*
*Nega ai mortali e nega a' morti il fato.'*

*Leopardi*

---

240. Epigraphs: *Per me si va* ... 'Through me is the way into the city of sorrow,' *Inferno* III 1. *Poi di tanto adoprar* ... From Giacomo Leopardi's *Canti*, XXIII, 93–8: 'After so much effort, after so many movements of all heavenly and all earthly things, turning without pause in order always to return to their starting point, I cannot discover any use or any gain [in the process]'. *Sola nel mondo eterna* ... From 'Coro di Morti' (Chorus of the Dead), ll. 1–6, 31–2, which appears in Leopardi's essay 'Dialoguo di Federico Ruysch e delle sue Mummie' (*Operette Morali*): 'Alone in the eternal world, towards which all created things move, in you, death, our bare nature comes to rest: not joyful, but safe from the ancient sorrow ... still, fate denies bliss to (living) mortals and to the dead.'

## PROEM

Lo, thus, as prostrate, 'In the dust I write
    My heart's deep languor and my soul's sad tears.'
Yet why evoke the spectres of black night
    To blot the sunshine of exultant years?
Why disinter dead faith from mouldering hidden?
Why break the seals of mute despair unbidden,
    And wail life's discords into careless ears?

Because a cold rage seizes one at whiles
    To show the bitter old and wrinkled truth
Stripped naked of all vesture that beguiles
    False dreams, false hopes, false masks and modes of
                youth;
Because it gives some sense of power and passion
In helpless impotence to try to fashion
    Our woe in living words howe'er uncouth.

Surely I write not for the hopeful young,
    Or those who deem their happiness of worth,
Or such as pasture and grow fat among
    The shows of life and feel nor doubt nor dearth,
Or pious spirits with a God above them
To sanctify and glorify and love them,
    Or sages who foresee a heaven on earth.

For none of these I write, and none of these
    Could read the writing if they deigned to try:
So may they flourish, in their due degrees,
    On our sweet earth and in their unplaced sky.
If any cares for the weak words here written,
It must be some one desolate, Fate-smitten,
    Whose faith and hope are dead, and who would die.

Yes, here and there some weary wanderer
   In that same city of tremendous night,
Will understand the speech, and feel a stir
   Of fellowship in all-disastrous fight;
'I suffer mute and lonely, yet another
Uplifts his voice to let me know a brother
   Travels the same wild paths though out of sight.'

O sad Fraternity, do I unfold
   Your dolorous mysteries shrouded from of yore?
Nay, be assured; no secret can be told
   To any who divined it not before:
None uninitiate by many a presage
Will comprehend the language of the message,
   Although proclaimed aloud for evermore.

I

The City is of Night; perchance of Death,
   But certainly of Night; for never there
Can come the lucid morning's fragrant breath
   After the dewy dawning's cold grey air;
The moon and stars may shine with scorn or pity;
The sun has never visited that city,
   For it dissolveth in the daylight fair.

Dissolveth like a dream of night away;
   Though present in distempered gloom of thought
And deadly weariness of heart all day.
   But when a dream night after night is brought
Throughout a week, and such weeks few or many
Recur each year for several years, can any
   Discern that dream from real life in aught?

For life is but a dream whose shapes return,
   Some frequently, some seldom, some by night
And some by day, some night and day: we learn,
   The while all change and many vanish quite,

In their recurrence with recurrent changes
A certain seeming order; where this ranges
   We count things real; such is memory's might.

A river girds the city west and south,
   The main north channel of a broad lagoon,
Regurging with the salt tides from the mouth;
   Waste marshes shine and glister to the moon
For leagues, then moorland black, then stony ridges;
Great piers and causeways, many noble bridges,
   Connect the town and islet suburbs strewn.

Upon an easy slope it lies at large,
   And scarcely overlaps the long curved crest
Which swells out two leagues from the river marge.
   A trackless wilderness rolls north and west,
Savannahs, savage woods, enormous mountains,
Bleak uplands, black ravines with torrent fountains;
   And eastward rolls the shipless sea's unrest.

The city is not ruinous, although
   Great ruins of an unremembered past,
With others of a few short years ago
   More sad, are found within its precincts vast.
The street-lamps always burn; but scarce a casement
In house or palace front from roof to basement
   Doth glow or gleam athwart the mirk air cast.

The street-lamps burn amidst the baleful glooms,
   Amidst the soundless solitudes immense
Of rangèd mansions dark and still as tombs.
   The silence which benumbs or strains the sense
Fulfils with awe the soul's despair unweeping:
Myriads of habitants are ever sleeping,
   Or dead, or fled from nameless pestilence!

Yet as in some necropolis you find
   Perchance one mourner to a thousand dead,
So there; worn faces that look deaf and blind

Like tragic masks of stone. With weary tread,
Each wrapt in his own doom, they wander, wander,
Or sit foredone and desolately ponder
Through sleepless hours with heavy drooping head.

Mature men chiefly, few in age or youth,
A woman rarely, now and then a child:
A child! If here the heart turns sick with ruth
To see a little one from birth defiled,
Or lame or blind, as preordained to languish
Through youthless life, think how it bleeds with anguish
To meet one erring in that homeless wild.

They often murmur to themselves, they speak
To one another seldom, for their woe
Broods maddening inwardly and scorns to wreak
Itself abroad; and if at whiles it grow
To frenzy which must rave, none heeds the clamour,
Unless there waits some victim of like glamour,
To rave in turn, who lends attentive show.

The City is of Night, but not of Sleep;
There sweet sleep is not for the weary brain;
The pitiless hours like years and ages creep,
A night seems termless hell. This dreadful strain
Of thought and consciousness which never ceases,
Or which some moments' stupor but increases,
This, worse than woe, makes wretches there insane.

They leave all hope behind who enter there:
One certitude while sane they cannot leave,
One anodyne for torture and despair;
The certitude of Death, which no reprieve
Can put off long; and which, divinely tender,
But waits the outstretched hand to promptly render
That draught whose slumber nothing can bereave.*

*Though the Garden of thy Life be wholly waste, the sweet flowers withered, the fruit-trees barren, over its wall hang ever the rich dark clusters of the Vine of Death, within easy reach of thy hand, which may pluck of them when it will. [Thomson's note]

## II

Because he seemed to walk with an intent
   I followed him; who, shadowlike and frail,
Unswervingly though slowly onward went,
   Regardless, wrapt in thought as in a veil:
Thus step for step with lonely sounding feet
We travelled many a long dim silent street.

At length he paused: a black mass in the gloom,
   A tower that merged into the heavy sky;
Around, the huddled stones of grave and tomb:
   Some old God's-acre now corruption's sty:
He murmured to himself with dull despair,
Here Faith died, poisoned by this charnel air.

Then turning to the right went on once more,
   And travelled weary roads without suspense;
And reached at last a low wall's open door,
   Whose villa gleamed beyond the foliage dense:
He gazed, and muttered with a hard despair,
Here Love died, stabbed by its own worshipped pair.

Then turning to the right resumed his march,
   And travelled streets and lanes with wondrous strength,
Until on stooping through a narrow arch
   We stood before a squalid house at length:
He gazed, and whispered with a cold despair,
Here Hope died, starved out in its utmost lair.

When he had spoken thus, before he stirred,
   I spoke, perplexed by something in the signs
Of desolation I had seen and heard
   In this drear pilgrimage to ruined shrines:
When Faith and Love and Hope are dead indeed,
Can Life still live? By what doth it proceed?

As whom his one intense thought overpowers,
　　He answered coldly, Take a watch, erase
The signs and figures of the circling hours,
　　Detach the hands, remove the dial-face;
The works proceed until run down; although
Bereft of purpose, void of use, still go.

Then turning to the right paced on again,
　　And traversed squares and travelled streets whose glooms
Seemed more and more familiar to my ken;
　　And reached that sullen temple of the tombs;
And paused to murmur with the old despair,
Here Faith died, poisoned by this charnel air.

I ceased to follow, for the knot of doubt
　　Was severed sharply with a cruel knife:
He circled thus for ever tracing out
　　The series of the fraction left of Life;
Perpetual recurrence in the scope
Of but three terms, dead Faith, dead Love, dead Hope.*

### III

Although lamps burn along the silent streets;
　　Even when moonlight silvers empty squares
The dark holds countless lanes and close retreats;
　　But when the night its sphereless mantle wears
The open spaces yawn with gloom abysmal,
The sombre mansions loom immense and dismal,
　　The lanes are black as subterranean lairs.

And soon the eye a strange new vision learns:
　　The night remains for it as dark and dense,
Yet clearly in this darkness it discerns
　　As in the daylight with its natural sense;

---

*Life divided by that persistent three = LXX/333 = 210. [Thomson's note]

Perceives a shade in shadow not obscurely,
Pursues a stir of black in blackness surely,
   Sees spectres also in the gloom intense.

The ear, too, with the silence vast and deep
   Becomes familiar though unreconciled;
Hears breathings as of hidden life asleep,
   And muffled throbs as of pent passions wild,
Far murmurs, speech of pity or derision;
But all more dubious than the things of vision,
   So that it knows not when it is beguiled.

No time abates the first despair and awe,
   But wonder ceases soon; the weirdest thing
Is felt least strange beneath the lawless law
   Where Death-in-Life is the eternal king;
Crushed impotent beneath this reign of terror,
Dazed with such mysteries of woe and error,
   The soul is too outworn for wondering.

## IV

He stood alone within the spacious square
   Declaiming from the central grassy mound,
With head uncovered and with streaming hair,
   As if large multitudes were gathered round:
A stalwart shape, the gestures full of might,
The glances burning with unnatural light: –

As I came through the desert thus it was,
As I came through the desert: All was black,
In heaven no single star, on earth no track;
A brooding hush without a stir or note,
The air so thick it clotted in my throat;
And thus for hours; then some enormous things
Swooped past with savage cries and clanking wings:
   But I strode on austere;
   No hope could have no fear.

As I came through the desert thus it was,
As I came through the desert: Eyes of fire
Glared at me throbbing with a starved desire;
The hoarse and heavy and carnivorous breath
Was hot upon me from deep jaws of death;
Sharp claws, swift talons, fleshless fingers cold
Plucked at me from the bushes, tried to hold:
    But I strode on austere;
    No hope could have no fear.

As I came through the desert thus it was,
As I came through the desert: Lo you, there,
That hillock burning with a brazen glare;
Those myriad dusky flames with points a-glow
Which writhed and hissed and darted to and fro;
A Sabbath of the Serpents, heaped pell-mell
For Devil's roll-call and some *fête* of Hell:
    Yet I strode on austere;
    No hope could have no fear.

As I came through the desert thus it was,
As I came through the desert: Meteors ran
And crossed their javelins on the black sky-span;
The zenith opened to a gulf of flame,
The dreadful thunderbolts jarred earth's fixed frame;
The ground all heaved in waves of fire that surged
And weltered round me sole there unsubmerged:
    Yet I strode on austere;
    No hope could have no fear.

As I came through the desert thus it was,
As I came through the desert: Air once more,
And I was close upon a wild sea-shore;
Enormous cliffs arose on either hand,
The deep tide thundered up a league-broad strand;
White foambelts seethed there, wan spray swept and flew;
The sky broke, moon and stars and clouds and blue:
    And I strode on austere;
    No hope could have no fear.

As I came through the desert thus it was,
As I came through the desert: On the left
The sun arose and crowned a broad crag-cleft;
There stopped and burned out black, except a rim,
A bleeding eyeless socket, red and dim;
Whereon the moon fell suddenly south-west,
And stood above the right-hand cliffs at rest:
    Still I strode on austere;
    No hope could have no fear.

As I came through the desert thus it was,
As I came through the desert: From the right
A shape came slowly with a ruddy light;
A woman with a red lamp in her hand,
Bareheaded and barefooted on that strand;
O desolation moving with such grace!
O anguish with such beauty in thy face!
    I fell as on my bier,
    Hope travailed with such fear.

As I came through the desert thus it was,
As I came through the desert: I was twain,
Two selves distinct that cannot join again;
One stood apart and knew but could not stir,
And watched the other stark in swoon and her;
And she came on, and never turned aside,
Between such sun and moon and roaring tide:
    And as she came more near
    My soul grew mad with fear.

As I came through the desert thus it was,
As I came through the desert: Hell is mild
And piteous matched with that accursèd wild;
A large black sign was on her breast that bowed,
A broad black band ran down her snow-white shroud;
That lamp she held was her own burning heart,
Whose blood-drops trickled step by step apart:
    The mystery was clear;
    Mad rage had swallowed fear.

As I came through the desert thus it was,
As I came through the desert: By the sea
She knelt and bent above that senseless me;
Those lamp-drops fell upon my white brow there,
She tried to cleanse them with her tears and hair;
She murmured words of pity, love, and woe,
She heeded not the level rushing flow:
    And mad with rage and fear,
    I stood stonebound so near.

As I came through the desert thus it was,
As I came through the desert: When the tide
Swept up to her there kneeling by my side,
She clasped that corpse-like me, and they were borne
Away, and this vile me was left forlorn;
I know the whole sea cannot quench that heart,
Or cleanse that brow, or wash those two apart:
They love; their doom is drear,
    Yet they nor hope nor fear;
    But I, what do I here?

## V

How he arrives there none can clearly know;
    Athwart the mountains and immense wild tracts,
Or flung a waif upon that vast sea-flow,
    Or down the river's boiling cataracts:
To reach it is as dying fever-stricken;
To leave it, slow faint birth intense pangs quicken;
    And memory swoons in both the tragic acts.

But being there one feels a citizen;
    Escape seems hopeless to the heart forlorn:
Can Death-in-Life be brought to life again?
    And yet release does come; there comes a morn
When he awakes from slumbering so sweetly
That all the world is changed for him completely,
    And he is verily as if new-born.

He scarcely can believe the blissful change,
   He weeps perchance who wept not while accurst;
Never again will he approach the range
   Infected by that evil spell now burst:
Poor wretch! who once hath paced that dolent city
Shall pace it often, doomed beyond all pity,
   With horror ever deepening from the first.

Though he possess sweet babes and loving wife,
   A home of peace by loyal friendships cheered,
And love them more than death or happy life,
   They shall avail not; he must dree his weird;
Renounce all blessings for that imprecation,
Steal forth and haunt that builded desolation,
   Of woe and terrors and thick darkness reared.

## VI

I sat forlornly by the river-side,
   And watched the bridge-lamps glow like golden stars
Above the blackness of the swelling tide,
   Down which they struck rough gold in ruddier bars;
And heard the heave and plashing of the flow
Against the wall a dozen feet below.

Large elm-trees stood along that river-walk;
   And under one, a few steps from my seat,
I heard strange voices join in stranger talk,
   Although I had not heard approaching feet:
These bodiless voices in my waking dream
Flowed dark words blending with the sombre stream: –

And you have after all come back; come back.
I was about to follow on your track.
And you have failed: our spark of hope is black.

That I have failed is proved by my return:
The spark is quenched, nor ever more will burn.
But listen; and the story you shall learn.

I reached the portal common spirits fear,
And read the words above it, dark yet clear,
'Leave hope behind, all ye who enter here:'

And would have passed in, gratified to gain
That positive eternity of pain,
Instead of this insufferable inane.

A demon warder clutched me, Not so fast;
First leave your hopes behind! – But years have passed
Since I left all behind me, to the last:

You cannot count for hope, with all your wit,
This bleak despair that drives me to the Pit:
How could I seek to enter void of it?

He snarled, What thing is this which apes a soul,
And would find entrance to our gulf of dole
Without the payment of the settled toll?

Outside the gate he showed an open chest:
Here pay their entrance fees the souls unblest;
Cast in some hope, you enter with the rest.

This is Pandora's box; whose lid shall shut,
And Hell-gate too, when hopes have filled it; but
They are so thin that it will never glut.

I stood a few steps backwards, desolate;
And watched the spirits pass me to their fate,
And fling off hope, and enter at the gate.

When one casts off a load he springs upright,
Squares back his shoulders, breathes with all his might,
And briskly paces forward strong and light:

But these, as if they took some burden, bowed;
The whole frame sank; however strong and proud
Before, they crept in quite infirm and cowed.

And as they passed me, earnestly from each
A morsel of his hope I did beseech,
To pay my entrance; but all mocked my speech.

Not one would cede a tittle of his store,
Though knowing that in instants three or four
He must resign the whole for evermore.

So I returned. Our destiny is fell;
For in this Limbo we must ever dwell,
Shut out alike from Heaven and Earth and Hell.

The other sighed back, Yea; but if we grope
With care through all this Limbo's dreary scope,
We yet may pick up some minute lost hope;

And, sharing it between us, entrance win,
In spite of fiends so jealous for gross sin:
Let us without delay our search begin.

## VII

Some say that phantoms haunt those shadowy streets,
   And mingle freely there with sparse mankind;
And tell of ancient woes and black defeats,
   And murmur mysteries in the grave enshrined:
But others think them visions of illusion,
Or even men gone far in self-confusion;
   No man there being wholly sane in mind.

And yet a man who raves, however mad,
   Who bares his heart and tells of his own fall,
Reserves some inmost secret good or bad:
   The phantoms have no reticence at all:
The nudity of flesh will blush though tameless,
The extreme nudity of bone grins shameless,
   The unsexed skeleton mocks shroud and pall.

I have seen phantoms there that were as men
    And men that were as phantoms flit and roam;
Marked shapes that were not living to my ken,
    Caught breathings acrid as with Dead Sea foam:
The City rests for man so weird and awful,
That his intrusion there might seem unlawful,
    And phantoms there may have their proper home.

## VIII

While I still lingered on that river-walk,
    And watched the tide as black as our black doom,
I heard another couple join in talk,
    And saw them to the left hand in the gloom
Seated against an elm bole on the ground,
Their eyes intent upon the stream profound.

'I never knew another man on earth
    But had some joy and solace in his life,
    Some chance of triumph in the dreadful strife:
My doom has been unmitigated dearth.'

'We gaze upon the river, and we note
The various vessels large and small that float,
Ignoring every wrecked and sunken boat.'

'And yet I asked no splendid dower, no spoil
    Of sway or fame or rank or even wealth;
    But homely love with common food and health,
And nightly sleep to balance daily toil.'

'This all-too humble soul would arrogate
Unto itself some signalising hate
From the supreme indifference of Fate!'

'Who is most wretched in this dolorous place?
    I think myself; yet I would rather be
    My miserable self than He, than He
Who formed such creatures to His own disgrace.

'The vilest thing must be less vile than Thou
   From whom it had its being, God and Lord!
   Creator of all woe and sin! abhorred,
Malignant and implacable! I vow

'That not for all Thy power furled and unfurled,
   For all the temples to Thy glory built,
   Would I assume the ignominious guilt
Of having made such men in such a world.'

'As if a Being, God or Fiend, could reign,
At once so wicked, foolish, and insane,
As to produce men when He might refrain!

'The world rolls round for ever like a mill;
It grinds out death and life and good and ill;
It has no purpose, heart or mind or will.

'While air of Space and Time's full river flow
The mill must blindly whirl unresting so:
It may be wearing out, but who can know?

'Man might know one thing were his sight less dim;
That it whirls not to suit his petty whim,
That it is quite indifferent to him.

'Nay, does it treat him harshly as he saith?
It grinds him some slow years of bitter breath,
Then grinds him back into eternal death.'

## IX

It is full strange to him who hears and feels,
   When wandering there in some deserted street,
The booming and the jar of ponderous wheels,
   The trampling clash of heavy ironshod feet:
Who in this Venice of the Black Sea rideth?
Who in this city of the stars abideth
   To buy or sell as those in daylight sweet?

The rolling thunder seems to fill the sky
   As it comes on; the horses snort and strain,
The harness jingles, as it passes by;
   The hugeness of an overburthened wain:
A man sits nodding on the shaft or trudges
Three parts asleep beside his fellow-drudges:
   And so it rolls into the night again.

What merchandise? whence, whither, and for whom?
   Perchance it is a Fate-appointed hearse,
Bearing away to some mysterious tomb
   Or Limbo of the scornful universe
The joy, the peace, the life-hope, the abortions
Of all things good which should have been our portions,
   But have been strangled by that City's curse.

## X

The mansion stood apart in its own ground;
   In front thereof a fragrant garden-lawn,
High trees about it, and the whole walled round:
   The massy iron gates were both withdrawn;
And every window of its front shed light,
Portentous in that City of the Night.

But though thus lighted it was deadly still
   As all the countless bulks of solid gloom:
Perchance a congregation to fulfil
   Solemnities of silence in this doom,
Mysterious rites of dolour and despair
Permitting not a breath of chant or prayer?

Broad steps ascended to a terrace broad
   Whereon lay still light from the open door;
The hall was noble, and its aspect awed,
   Hung round with heavy black from dome to floor;
And ample stairways rose to left and right
Whose balustrades were also draped with night.

I paced from room to room, from hall to hall,
   Nor any life throughout the maze discerned;
But each was hung with its funereal pall,
   And held a shrine, around which tapers burned,
With picture or with statue or with bust,
All copied from the same fair form of dust:

A woman very young and very fair;
   Beloved by bounteous life and joy and youth,
And loving these sweet lovers, so that care
   And age and death seemed not for her in sooth:
Alike as stars, all beautiful and bright,
These shapes lit up that mausoléan night.

At length I heard a murmur as of lips,
   And reached an open oratory hung
With heaviest blackness of the whole eclipse;
   Beneath the dome a fuming censer swung;
And one lay there upon a low white bed,
With tapers burning at the foot and head:

The Lady of the images: supine,
   Deathstill, lifesweet, with folded palms she lay:
And kneeling there as at a sacred shrine
   A young man wan and worn who seemed to pray:
A crucifix of dim and ghostly white
Surmounted the large altar left in night: –

The chambers of the mansion of my heart,
In every one whereof thine image dwells,
Are black with grief eternal for thy sake.

The inmost oratory of my soul,
Wherein thou ever dwellest quick or dead,
Is black with grief eternal for thy sake.

I kneel beside thee and I clasp the cross,
With eyes for ever fixed upon that face,
So beautiful and dreadful in its calm.

I kneel here patient as thou liest there;
As patient as a statue carved in stone,
Of adoration and eternal grief.

While thou dost not awake I cannot move;
And something tells me thou wilt never wake,
And I alive feel turning into stone.

Most beautiful were Death to end my grief,
Most hateful to destroy the sight of thee,
Dear vision better than all death or life.

But I renounce all choice of life or death,
For either shall be ever at thy side,
And thus in bliss or woe be ever well. –

He murmured thus and thus in monotone,
    Intent upon that uncorrupted face,
Entranced except his moving lips alone:
    I glided with hushed footsteps from the place.
This was the festival that filled with light
That palace in the City of the Night.

## XI

What men are they who haunt these fatal glooms,
    And fill their living mouths with dust of death,
And make their habitations in the tombs,
    And breathe eternal sighs with mortal breath,
And pierce life's pleasant veil of various error
To reach that void of darkness and old terror
    Wherein expire the lamps of hope and faith?

They have much wisdom yet they are not wise,
    They have much goodness yet they do not well,
(The fools we know have their own Paradise,
    The wicked also have their proper Hell);

They have much strength but still their doom is stronger,
Much patience but their time endureth longer,
   Much valour but life mocks it with some spell.

They are most rational and yet insane:
   An outward madness not to be controlled;
A perfect reason in the central brain,
   Which has no power, but sitteth wan and cold,
And sees the madness, and foresees as plainly
The ruin in its path, and trieth vainly
   To cheat itself refusing to behold.

And some are great in rank and wealth and power,
   And some renowned for genius and for worth;
And some are poor and mean, who brood and cower
   And shrink from notice, and accept all dearth
Of body, heart and soul, and leave to others
All boons of life: yet these and those are brothers,
   The saddest and the weariest men on earth.

## XII

Our isolated units could be brought
   To act together for some common end?
For one by one, each silent with his thought,
   I marked a long loose line approach and wend
Athwart the great cathedral's cloistered square,
And slowly vanish from the moonlit air.

Then I would follow in among the last:
   And in the porch a shrouded figure stood,
Who challenged each one pausing ere he passed,
   With deep eyes burning through a blank white hood:
Whence come you in the world of life and light
To this our City of Tremendous Night? –

From pleading in a senate of rich lords
For some scant justice to our countless hordes
Who toil half-starved with scarce a human right:
I wake from daydreams to this real night.

From wandering through many a solemn scene
Of opium visions, with a heart serene
And intellect miraculously bright:
I wake from daydreams to this real night.

From making hundreds laugh and roar with glee
By my transcendent feats of mimicry,
And humour wanton as an elfish sprite:
I wake from daydreams to this real night.

From prayer and fasting in a lonely cell,
Which brought an ecstasy ineffable
Of love and adoration and delight:
I wake from daydreams to this real night.

From ruling on a splendid kingly throne
A nation which beneath my rule has grown
Year after year in wealth and arts and might:
I wake from daydreams to this real night.

From preaching to an audience fired with faith
The Lamb who died to save our souls from death,
Whose blood hath washed our scarlet sins wool-white:
I wake from daydreams to this real night.

From drinking fiery poison in a den
Crowded with tawdry girls and squalid men,
Who hoarsely laugh and curse and brawl and fight:
I wake from daydreams to this real night.

From picturing with all beauty and all grace
First Eden and the parents of our race,
A luminous rapture unto all men's sight:
I wake from daydreams to this real night.

From writing a great work with patient plan
To justify the ways of God to man,
And show how ill must fade and perish quite:
I wake from daydreams to this real night.

From desperate fighting with a little band
Against the powerful tyrants of our land,
To free our brethren in their own despite:
I wake from daydreams to this real night.

Thus, challenged by that warder sad and stern,
  Each one responded with his countersign,
Then entered the cathedral; and in turn
  I entered also, having given mine;
But lingered near until I heard no more,
And marked the closing of the massive door.

## XIII

Of all things human which are strange and wild
  This is perchance the wildest and most strange,
And showeth man most utterly beguiled,
  To those who haunt that sunless City's range;
That he bemoans himself for aye, repeating
How Time is deadly swift, how life is fleeting,
  How naught is constant on the earth but change.

The hours are heavy on him and the days;
  The burden of the months he scarce can bear;
And often in his secret soul he prays
  To sleep through barren periods unaware,
Arousing at some longed-for date of pleasure;
Which having passed and yielded him small treasure,
  He would outsleep another term of care.

Yet in his marvellous fancy he must make
  Quick wings for Time, and see it fly from us;
This Time which crawleth like a monstrous snake,
  Wounded and slow and very venomous;

Which creeps blindwormlike round the earth and ocean,
Distilling poison at each painful motion,
   And seems condemned to circle ever thus.

And since he cannot spend and use aright
   The little time here given him in trust,
But wasteth it in weary undelight
   Of foolish toil and trouble, strife and lust,
He naturally claimeth to inherit
The everlasting Future, that his merit
   May have full scope; as surely is most just.

O length of the intolerable hours,
   O nights that are as æons of slow pain,
O Time, too ample for our vital powers,
   O Life, whose woeful vanities remain
Immutable for all of all our legions
Through all the centuries and in all the regions,
   Not of your speed and variance *we* complain.

*We* do not ask a longer term of strife,
   Weakness and weariness and nameless woes;
We do not claim renewed and endless life
   When this which is our torment here shall close,
An everlasting conscious inanition!
We yearn for speedy death in full fruition,
   Dateless oblivion and divine repose.

## XIV

Large glooms were gathered in the mighty fane,
   With tinted moongleams slanting here and there;
And all was hush: no swelling organ-strain,
   No chant, no voice or murmuring of prayer;
No priests came forth, no tinkling censers fumed,
And the high altar space was unillumed.

Around the pillars and against the walls
    Leaned men and shadows; others seemed to brood
Bent or recumbent in secluded stalls.
    Perchance they were not a great multitude
Save in that city of so lonely streets
Where one may count up every face he meets.

All patiently awaited the event
    Without a stir or sound, as if no less
Self-occupied, doomstricken, while attent.
    And then we heard a voice of solemn stress
From the dark pulpit, and our gaze there met
Two eyes which burned as never eyes burned yet:

Two steadfast and intolerable eyes
    Burning beneath a broad and rugged brow;
The head behind it of enormous size.
    And as black fir-groves in a large wind bow,
Our rooted congregation, gloom-arrayed,
By that great sad voice deep and full were swayed: –

O melancholy Brothers, dark, dark, dark!
O battling in black floods without an ark!
    O spectral wanderers of unholy Night!
My soul hath bled for you these sunless years,
With bitter blood-drops running down like tears:
    Oh, dark, dark, dark, withdrawn from joy and light!

My heart is sick with anguish for your bale;
Your woe hath been my anguish; yea, I quail
    And perish in your perishing unblest.
And I have searched the highths and depths, the scope
Of all our universe, with desperate hope
    To find some solace for your wild unrest.

And now at last authentic word I bring,
Witnessed by every dead and living thing;
    Good tidings of great joy for you, for all:

There is no God; no Fiend with names divine
Made us and tortures us; if we must pine,
  It is to satiate no Being's gall.

It was the dark delusion of a dream,
That living Person conscious and supreme,
  Whom we must curse for cursing us with life;
Whom we must curse because the life He gave
Could not be buried in the quiet grave,
  Could not be killed by poison or by knife.

This little life is all we must endure,
The grave's most holy peace is ever sure,
  We fall asleep and never wake again;
Nothing is of us but the mouldering flesh,
Whose elements dissolve and merge afresh
  In earth, air, water, plants, and other men.

We finish thus; and all our wretched race
Shall finish with its cycle, and give place
  To other beings, with their own time-doom:
Infinite æons ere our kind began;
Infinite æons after the last man
  Has joined the mammoth in earth's tomb and womb.

We bow down to the universal laws,
Which never had for man a special clause
  Of cruelty or kindness, love or hate:
If toads and vultures are obscene to sight,
If tigers burn with beauty and with might,
  Is it by favour or by wrath of Fate?

All substance lives and struggles evermore
Through countless shapes continually at war,
  By countless interactions interknit:
If one is born a certain day on earth,
All times and forces tended to that birth,
  Not all the world could change or hinder it.

I find no hint throughout the Universe
Of good or ill, of blessing or of curse;
    I find alone Necessity Supreme;
With infinite Mystery, abysmal, dark,
Unlighted ever by the faintest spark
    For us the flitting shadows of a dream.

O Brothers of sad lives! they are so brief;
A few short years must bring us all relief:
    Can we not bear these years of labouring breath?
But if you would not this poor life fulfil,
Lo, you are free to end it when you will,
    Without the fear of waking after death. –

The organ-like vibrations of his voice
    Thrilled through the vaulted aisles and died away;
The yearning of the tones which bade rejoice
    Was sad and tender as a requiem lay:
Our shadowy congregation rested still
As brooding on that 'End it when you will.'

## XV

Wherever men are gathered, all the air
    Is charged with human feeling, human thought;
Each shout and cry and laugh, each curse and prayer,
    Are into its vibrations surely wrought;
Unspoken passion, wordless meditation,
Are breathed into it with our respiration;
    It is with our life fraught and overfraught.

So that no man there breathes earth's simple breath,
    As if alone on mountains or wide seas;
But nourishes warm life or hastens death
    With joys and sorrows, health and foul disease,
Wisdom and folly, good and evil labours,
Incessant of his multitudinous neighbours;
    He in his turn affecting all of these.

That City's atmosphere is dark and dense,
    Although not many exiles wander there,
With many a potent evil influence,
    Each adding poison to the poisoned air;
Infections of unutterable sadness,
Infections of incalculable madness,
    Infections of incurable despair.

## XVI

Our shadowy congregation rested still,
    As musing on that message we had heard
And brooding on that 'End it when you will;'
    Perchance awaiting yet some other word;
When keen as lightning through a muffled sky
Sprang forth a shrill and lamentable cry: –

The man speaks sooth, alas! the man speaks sooth:
    We have no personal life beyond the grave;
There is no God; Fate knows nor wrath nor ruth:
    Can I find here the comfort which I crave?

In all eternity I had one chance,
    One few years' term of gracious human life:
The splendours of the intellect's advance,
    The sweetness of the home with babes and wife;

The social pleasures with their genial wit;
    The fascination of the worlds of art,
The glories of the worlds of nature, lit
    By large imagination's glowing heart;

The rapture of mere being, full of health;
    The careless childhood and the ardent youth,
The strenuous manhood winning various wealth,
    The reverend age serene with life's long truth:

All the sublime prerogatives of Man;
    The storied memories of the times of old,
The patient tracking of the world's great plan
    Through sequences and changes myriadfold.

This chance was never offered me before;
    For me the infinite Past is blank and dumb:
This chance recurreth never, nevermore;
    Blank, blank for me the infinite To-come.

And this sole chance was frustrate from my birth,
    A mockery, a delusion; and my breath
Of noble human life upon this earth
    So racks me that I sigh for senseless death.

My wine of life is poison mixed with gall,
    My noonday passes in a nightmare dream,
I worse than lose the years which are my all:
    What can console me for the loss supreme?

Speak not of comfort where no comfort is,
    Speak not at all: can words make foul things fair?
Our life's a cheat, our death a black abyss:
    Hush and be mute envisaging despair. –

This vehement voice came from the northern aisle
    Rapid and shrill to its abrupt harsh close;
And none gave answer for a certain while,
    For words must shrink from these most wordless woes;
At last the pulpit speaker simply said,
With humid eyes and thoughtful drooping head: –

My Brother, my poor Brothers, it is thus;
This life itself holds nothing good for us,
    But it ends soon and nevermore can be;
And we knew nothing of it ere our birth,
And shall know nothing when consigned to earth:
    I ponder these thoughts and they comfort me.

## XVII

How the moon triumphs through the endless nights!
　How the stars throb and glitter as they wheel
Their thick processions of supernal lights
　Around the blue vault obdurate as steel!
And men regard with passionate awe and yearning
The mighty marching and the golden burning,
　And think the heavens respond to what they feel.

Boats gliding like dark shadows of a dream,
　Are glorified from vision as they pass
The quivering moonbridge on the deep black stream;
　Cold windows kindle their dead glooms of glass
To restless crystals; cornice, dome, and column
Emerge from chaos in the splendour solemn;
　Like faëry lakes gleam lawns of dewy grass.

With such a living light these dead eyes shine,
　These eyes of sightless heaven, that as we gaze
We read a pity, tremulous, divine,
　Or cold majestic scorn in their pure rays:
Fond man! they are not haughty, are not tender;
There is no heart or mind in all their splendour,
　They thread mere puppets all their marvellous maze.

If we could near them with the flight unflown,
　We should but find them worlds as sad as this,
Or suns all self-consuming like our own
　Enringed by planet worlds as much amiss:
They wax and wane through fusion and confusion;
The spheres eternal are a grand illusion,
　The empyréan is a void abyss.

## XVIII

I wandered in a suburb of the north,
    And reached a spot whence three close lanes led down,
Beneath thick trees and hedgerows winding forth
    Like deep brook channels, deep and dark and lown:
The air above was wan with misty light,
The dull grey south showed one vague blur of white.

I took the left-hand lane and slowly trod
    Its earthen footpath, brushing as I went
The humid leafage; and my feet were shod
    With heavy languor, and my frame downbent,
With infinite sleepless weariness outworn,
So many nights I thus had paced forlorn.

After a hundred steps I grew aware
    Of something crawling in the lane below;
It seemed a wounded creature prostrate there
    That sobbed with pangs in making progress slow,
The hind limbs stretched to push, the fore limbs then
To drag; for it would die in its own den.

But coming level with it I discerned
    That it had been a man; for at my tread
It stopped in its sore travail and half-turned,
    Leaning upon its right, and raised its head,
And with the left hand twitched back as in ire
Long grey unreverend locks befouled with mire.

A haggard filthy face with bloodshot eyes,
    An infamy for manhood to behold.
He gasped all trembling, What, you want my prize?
    You leave, to rob me, wine and lust and gold
And all that men go mad upon, since you
Have traced my sacred secret of the clue?

You think that I am weak and must submit;
   Yet I but scratch you with this poisoned blade,
And you are dead as if I clove with it
   That false fierce greedy heart. Betrayed! betrayed!
I fling this phial if you seek to pass,
And you are forthwith shrivelled up like grass.

And then with sudden change, Take thought! take thought!
   Have pity on me! it is mine alone.
If you could find, it would avail you naught;
   Seek elsewhere on the pathway of your own:
For who of mortal or immortal race
The lifetrack of another can retrace?

Did you but know my agony and toil!
   Two lanes diverge up yonder from this lane;
My thin blood marks the long length of their soil;
   Such clue I left, who sought my clue in vain:
My hands and knees are worn both flesh and bone;
I cannot move but with continual moan.

But I am in the very way at last
   To find the long-lost broken golden thread
Which reunites my present with my past,
   If you but go your own way. And I said,
I will retire as soon as you have told
Whereunto leadeth this lost thread of gold.

And so you know it not! he hissed with scorn;
   I feared you, imbecile! It leads me back
From this accursed night without a morn,
   And through the deserts which have else no track,
And through vast wastes of horror-haunted time,
To Eden innocence in Eden's clime:

And I become a nursling soft and pure,
   An infant cradled on its mother's knee,
Without a past, love-cherished and secure;

Which if it saw this loathsome present Me,
Would plunge its face into the pillowing breast,
And scream abhorrence hard to lull to rest.

He turned to grope; and I retiring brushed
   Thin shreds of gossamer from off my face,
And mused, His life would grow, the germ uncrushed;
   He should to antenatal night retrace,
And hide his elements in that large womb
Beyond the reach of man-evolving Doom.

And even thus, what weary way were planned,
   To seek oblivion through the far-off gate
Of birth, when that of death is close at hand!
   For this is law, if law there be in Fate:
What never has been, yet may have its when;
The thing which has been, never is again.

## XIX

The mighty river flowing dark and deep,
   With ebb and flood from the remote sea-tides
Vague-sounding through the City's sleepless sleep,
   Is named the River of the Suicides;
For night by night some lorn wretch overweary,
And shuddering from the future yet more dreary,
   Within its cold secure oblivion hides.

One plunges from a bridge's parapet,
   As by some blind and sudden frenzy hurled;
Another wades in slow with purpose set
   Until the waters are above him furled;
Another in a boat with dreamlike motion
Glides drifting down into the desert ocean,
   To starve or sink from out the desert world.

They perish from their suffering surely thus,
   For none beholding them attempts to save,
The while each thinks how soon, solicitous,

He may seek refuge in the self-same wave;
Some hour when tired of ever-vain endurance
Impatience will forerun the sweet assurance
   Of perfect peace eventual in the grave.

When this poor tragic-farce has palled us long,
   Why actors and spectators do we stay? –
To fill our so-short *rôles* out right or wrong;
   To see what shifts are yet in the dull play
For our illusion; to refrain from grieving
Dear foolish friends by our untimely leaving:
   But those asleep at home, how blest are they!

Yet it is but for one night after all:
   What matters one brief night of dreary pain?
When after it the weary eyelids fall
   Upon the weary eyes and wasted brain;
And all sad scenes and thoughts and feelings vanish
In that sweet sleep no power can ever banish,
   That one best sleep which never wakes again.

## XX

I sat me weary on a pillar's base,
   And leaned against the shaft; for broad moonlight
O'erflowed the peacefulness of cloistered space,
   A shore of shadow slanting from the right:
The great cathedral's western front stood there,
A wave-worn rock in that calm sea of air.

Before it, opposite my place of rest,
   Two figures faced each other, large, austere;
A couchant sphinx in shadow to the breast,
   An angel standing in the moonlight clear;
So mighty by magnificence of form,
They were not dwarfed beneath that mass enorm.

Upon the cross-hilt of a naked sword
   The angel's hands, as prompt to smite, were held;
His vigilant, intense regard was poured
   Upon the creature placidly unquelled,
Whose front was set at level gaze which took
No heed of aught, a solemn trance-like look.

And as I pondered these opposèd shapes
   My eyelids sank in stupor, that dull swoon
Which drugs and with a leaden mantle drapes
   The outworn to worse weariness. But soon
A sharp and clashing noise the stillness broke,
And from the evil lethargy I woke.

The angel's wings had fallen, stone on stone,
   And lay there shattered; hence the sudden sound:
A warrior leaning on his sword alone
   Now watched the sphinx with that regard profound;
The sphinx unchanged looked forthright, as aware
Of nothing in the vast abyss of air.

Again I sank in that repose unsweet,
   Again a clashing noise my slumber rent;
The warrior's sword lay broken at his feet:
   An unarmed man with raised hands impotent
Now stood before the sphinx, which ever kept
Such mien as if with open eyes it slept.

My eyelids sank in spite of wonder grown;
   A louder crash upstartled me in dread:
The man had fallen forward, stone on stone,
   And lay there shattered, with his trunkless head
Between the monster's large quiescent paws,
Beneath its grand front changeless as life's laws.

The moon had circled westward full and bright,
    And made the temple-front a mystic dream,
And bathed the whole enclosure with its light,
    The sworded angel's wrecks, the sphinx supreme:
I pondered long that cold majestic face
Whose vision seemed of infinite void space.


## XXI


Anear the centre of that northern crest
    Stands out a level upland bleak and bare,
From which the city east and south and west
    Sinks gently in long waves; and thronèd there
An Image sits, stupendous, superhuman,
The bronze colossus of a wingèd Woman,
Upon a graded granite base foursquare.

Low-seated she leans forward massively,
    With cheek on clenched left hand, the forearm's might
Erect, its elbow on her rounded knee;
    Across a clasped book in her lap the right
Upholds a pair of compasses; she gazes
With full set eyes, but wandering in thick mazes
    Of sombre thought beholds no outward sight.

Words cannot picture her; but all men know
    That solemn sketch the pure sad artist wrought
Three centuries and threescore years ago,
    With phantasies of his peculiar thought:
The instruments of carpentry and science
Scattered about her feet, in strange alliance
    With the keen wolf-hound sleeping undistraught;

Scales, hour-glass, bell, and magic-square above;
    The grave and solid infant perched beside,
With open winglets that might bear a dove,
    Intent upon its tablets, heavy-eyed;

Her folded wings as of a mighty eagle,
But all too impotent to lift the regal
   Robustness of her earth-born strength and pride;

And with those wings, and that light wreath which seems
   To mock her grand head and the knotted frown
Of forehead charged with baleful thoughts and dreams,
   The household bunch of keys, the housewife's gown
Voluminous, indented, and yet rigid
As if a shell of burnished metal frigid,
   The feet thick-shod to tread all weakness down;

The comet hanging o'er the waste dark seas,
   The massy rainbow curved in front of it,
Beyond the village with the masts and trees;
   The snaky imp, dog-headed, from the Pit,
Bearing upon its batlike leathern pinions
Her name unfolded in the sun's dominions,
   The 'MELENCOLIA' that transcends all wit.

Thus has the artist copied her, and thus
   Surrounded to expound her form sublime,
Her fate heroic and calamitous;
   Fronting the dreadful mysteries of Time,
Unvanquished in defeat and desolation,
Undaunted in the hopeless conflagration
   Of the day setting on her baffled prime.

Baffled and beaten back she works on still,
   Weary and sick of soul she works the more,
Sustained by her indomitable will:
   The hands shall fashion and the brain shall pore,
And all her sorrow shall be turned to labour,
Till Death the friend-foe piercing with his sabre
   That mighty heart of hearts ends bitter war.

But as if blacker night could dawn on night,
   With tenfold gloom on moonless night unstarred,
A sense more tragic than defeat and blight,
   More desperate than strife with hope debarred,
More fatal than the adamantine Never
Encompassing her passionate endeavour,
   Dawns glooming in her tenebrous regard:

The sense that every struggle brings defeat
   Because Fate holds no prize to crown success;
That all the oracles are dumb or cheat
   Because they have no secret to express;
That none can pierce the vast black veil uncertain
Because there is no light beyond the curtain;
   That all is vanity and nothingness.

Titanic from her high throne in the north,
   The City's sombre Patroness and Queen,
In bronze sublimity she gazes forth
   Over her Capital of teen and threne,
Over the river with its isles and bridges,
The marsh and moorland, to the stern rock-ridges,
   Confronting them with a coëval mien.

The moving moon and stars from east to west
   Circle before her in the sea of air;
Shadows and gleams glide round her solemn rest.
   Her subjects often gaze up to her there:
The strong to drink new strength of iron endurance,
The weak new terrors; all, renewed assurance
   And confirmation of the old despair.

# ALFRED AUSTIN

## 1835–1913

241  Give me October's meditative haze,
Its gossamer mornings, dewy-wimpled eves,
Dewy and fragrant, fragrant and secure,
The long slow sound of farmward-wending wains,
When homely Love sups quiet 'mid his sheaves,
Sups 'mid his sheaves, his sickle at his side,
And all is peace, peace and plump fruitfulness.

# SIR ALFRED COMYNS LYALL

1835–1911

242                        Badminton

Hardly a shot from the gate we stormed,
　　Under the Moree battlement's shade;
Close to the glacis our game was formed,
　　There had the fight been, and there we played.

Lightly the demoiselles tittered and leapt,
　　Merrily capered the players all;
North, was the garden where Nicholson slept,
　　South, was the sweep of a battered wall.

Near me a Musalmán, civil and mild,
　　Watched as the shuttlecocks rose and fell;
And he said, as he counted his beads and smiled,
　　'God smite their souls to the depths of hell.'

# JOHN LEICESTER WARREN, LORD DE TABLEY

### 1835–95

243        On a Portrait of Sir John Suckling

Two hundred years, my hero, thou hast lain
Rusting in earth. The world has gone its way
Careless that Death has mown thy golden youth.
Soldiers have fought and died and known not thee.
Maidens have loved, who never heard thy name.
And thou, whom Muses crowned with every gift,
While yet a boy – tho' in achievement man
And monarch – young in years yet ripe in fame,
Art snatched away; while this grim raven, Death,
Feeds on the light and glory of the world.
Heroic heart, long silent in the dust;
Where is the warrior's tomb, what grey church tower
Is honoured by thy rest? Art thou inurned
In some dim Norfolk village, whence thy race
Came of a kindly stock who fed their beeves
And grew their grain? Hast thou an effigy
Armoured in stone, with angels at the base
In alabaster sorrow; as the mode
Ran of sepulchral grief? And overhead
Thy gauntlet and thy banner and thy helm
Nailed to the chancel wall, and covered quite
With cobwebs. While thy wasted banner droops
As if the spiders wove its ragged sides.
And this thy hatchment, azure once and gules,
And three stags golden, emblems of thy race,
Effaced and tarnished, half the tinctures gone.
Oblivion and a hecatomb of dust
Invade the silent precincts of thy rest,
And thro' the lancet window I can hear
The voices of the village, forge and mart,
Harrow and spade, the mill-wheel and the plough.

While in the coppice sole, one nightingale
Sings me reminders of a note as sweet
And tender as her own; and while she sings
Thou art not quite forgot, my soldier bard,
Here in the pastoral village of thy youth.

Tender and great, true poet, dauntless heart,
We cannot see with eyes as clear as thine.
A sordid time dwarfs down the race of men.
They may not touch the lute or draw the sword
As thou didst, half immortal. So we hang
A wreath of homage on our captain's urn.

Farewell, to other scenes we must begone.
The elms are shining in the sun: the roofs
Melt with the mighty rain. The uprolled cloud
Soars in its majesty away through heaven.
The morning breaks in red and lustre. Earth
Is glad because of her. But we bewail
The young glad light of our Apollo gone,
Thy laurel, and thy lyre with broken chords,
And snapt below the hilt, thy gallant sword.

Where is the winsome lady whom he met
In that old spring among the old-world flowers?
Where are her fairy footsteps, where are gone
Aglaura's graceful curls? The tender rose
That lay against her cavalier's soft kiss:
The lordly, the invincible, the king
Of every Muse. Surely, that giant wreath,
Stamped on the opening page of thy renown,
Made out of all the woods, that leaf shedding
Of rathe Castalia's orchards, that green round
Shall wrap thee in with honour, dear and dead,
True gentleman, great type of ages gone,
To shallow natures in the days of smoke:
Radiant Apollo, warrior, Englishman,
To whom the cannon calling or the lute
Came with an equal voice: colleague of gods,

Such as the puny mothers of the world
No longer nourish on degenerate breasts,
The giants of the dawn, that never more
Shall come again. Old England, hear me say,
This man has lain in dust two hundred years,
Hast thou another such, my country, peer
To the great gone-away?

244                    The Study of a Spider

From holy flower to holy flower
Thou weavest thine unhallowed bower.
The harmless dewdrops, beaded thin,
Ripple along thy ropes of sin.
Thy house a grave, a gulf thy throne
Affright the fairies every one.
Thy winding sheets are gray and fell,
Imprisoning with nets of hell
The lovely births that winnow by,
Winged sisters of the rainbow sky:
Elf-darlings, fluffy, bee-bright things,
And owl-white moths with mealy wings,
And tiny flies, as gauzy thin
As e'er were shut electrum in.
These are thy death spoils, insect ghoul,
With their dear life thy fangs are foul.
Thou felon anchorite of pain
Who sittest in a world of slain.
Hermit, who tunest song unsweet
To heaving wing and writhing feet.
A glutton of creation's sighs,
Miser of many miseries.
Toper, whose lonely feasting chair
Sways in inhospitable air.
The board is bare, the bloated host
Drinks to himself toast after toast.

His lip requires no goblet brink,
But like a weasel must he drink.
The vintage is as old as time
And bright as sunset, pressed and prime.

Ah, venom mouth and shaggy things
And paunch grown sleek with sacrifice,
Thy dolphin back and shoulders round
Coarse-hairy, as some goblin hound
Whom a hag rides to sabbath on,
While shuddering stars in fear grow wan.
Thou palace priest of treachery,
Thou type of selfish lechery,
I break the toils around thy head
And from their gibbets take thy dead.


245        The Knight in the Wood

The thing itself was rough and crudely done,
Cut in coarse stone, spitefully placed aside
As merest lumber, where the light was worst
On a back staircase. Overlooked it lay
In a great Roman palace crammed with art.
It had no number in the list of gems,
Weeded away long since, pushed out and banished,
Before insipid Guidos over-sweet
And Dolce's rose sensationalities,
And curly chirping angels spruce as birds.
And yet the motive of this thing ill-hewn
And hardly seen did touch me. O, indeed,
The skill-less hand that carved it had belonged
To a most yearning and bewildered brain:
There was such desolation in the work;
And through its utter failure the thing spoke
With more of human message, heart to heart,
Than all these faultless, smirking, skin-deep saints,
In artificial troubles picturesque,

And martyred sweetly, not one curl awry –
Listen; a clumsy knight, who rode alone
Upon a stumbling jade in a great wood
Belated. The poor beast with head low-bowed
Snuffing the treacherous ground. The rider leant
Forward to sound the marish with his lance.
You saw the place was deadly; that doomed pair,
The wretched rider and the hide-bound steed,
Feared to advance, feared to return – That's all!

246                    The Pilgrim Cranes

The pilgrim cranes are moving to their south,
    The clouds are herded pale and rolling slow.
One flower is withered in the warm wind's mouth,
    Whereby the gentle waters always flow.

The cloud-fire wanes beyond the lighted trees.
    The sudden glory leaves the mountain dome.
Sleep into night, old anguish mine, and cease
    To listen for a step that will not come.

247                 Lines to a Lady-Bird

        Cow-lady, or sweet lady-bird,
        Of thee a song is seldom heard.
        What record of thy humble days
        Almost ignored in poets' lays,
        Salutes thy advent? Oversung
        Is Philomel by many lyres;
        And how the lark to heaven aspires,
        Is rumoured with abundant fame,
        While dim oblivion wraps thy name.
        Hail! then, thou unpresuming thing,
        A bright mosaic of the spring,

Enamelled brooch upon the breast
Of the rich-bosomed rose caressed.
Thy wings the balmy zephyrs bear
When woods unfold in vernal air,
When crumpled buds around expand,
Thou lightest on our very hand.
Red as a robin thou dost come,
Confiding, in entreaty dumb.
Who would impede thy harmless track,
Or crush thy wing or burnished back?
'Tis said, thy lighting and thy stay
Bring luck: and few would brush away
The small unbidden crawling guest,
But let thee sheathe thy wings in rest,
And take thy voluntary flight
Uninjured to some flower's delight.
For there is nothing nature through,
Lovely and curious as you:
A little dome-shaped insect round,
With five black dots on a carmine ground.
What art thou? I can hardly tell.
A little tortoise of the dell
With carapace or vaulted shell
Of shining crimson? Or again,
I picture thee, in fancy plain,
A little spotted elfin cow,
Of whose sweet milk a milkmaid fairy
Makes syllabub in Oberon's dairy.
Thou hast a legend-pedigree
That gives thy race a high degree
From the shed blood of Venus sweet,
Thorn-wounded in her pearly feet,
As thro' the dewy woods she went,
Love-lorn, in utter discontent,
Listening afar the echoing horn
Of coy Adonis, in whose scorn
The Love-queen languished, love-forlorn.
He burned to hunt the boar at bay,
And loathed the lover's idle play;

So Venus followed in the chase
And from her wounded heel a trace
Of blood-drip tinged the dewy mead,
And, from the ichor she did bleed,
From Aphrodite's precious blood,
Arose the lady-birds, a brood
As gentle as the hurt of love,
That gave them birth and parentage
In legends of the golden age.
But, coming to our modern day,
Thee peevish children scare away,
And speed thy flight with evil rhyme,
Waving an idle hand meantime,
To make thee spread thy wings in fear
With rumours of disaster near,
And tidings of thy home in flames,
And all thy burning children's names,
How all are scorched but Ann alone
Who safely crept inside a stone;
With many an old unlettered fable
Of churlish lips inhospitable.
And when these fancies all are past,
I see thee as thou art at last,
A welcome sign of genial spring,
Awaited as a swallow's wing,
The cuckoo's call, the drone of bee,
The small gnat's dancing minstrelsy.
Ere hawthorn buds are sweetly stirred
I bid thee hail, bright lady-bird!

*August 21st, 1895*

# FRANCES RIDLEY HAVERGAL
## 1836–79

Under the Surface

### I

On the surface, foam and roar,
  Restless heave and passionate dash,
Shingle rattle along the shore,
  Gathering boom and thundering crash.

Under the surface, soft green light,
  A hush of peace and an endless calm,
Winds and waves from a choral height,
  Falling sweet as a far-off psalm.

On the surface, swell and swirl,
  Tossing weed and drifting waif,
Broken spars that the mad waves whirl,
  Where wreck-watching rocks they chafe.

Under the surface, loveliest forms,
  Feathery fronds with crimson curl,
Treasures too deep for the raid of storms,
  Delicate coral and hidden pearl.

### II

On the surface, lilies white,
  A painted skiff with a singing crew,
Sky-reflections soft and bright,
  Tremulous crimson, gold and blue.

Under the surface, life in death,
    Slimy tangle and oozy moans,
Creeping things with watery breath,
    Blackening roots and whitening bones.

On the surface, a shining reach,
    A crystal couch for the moonbeams' rest,
Starry ripples along the beach,
    Sunset songs from the breezy west.

Under the surface, glooms and fears,
    Treacherous currents swift and strong,
Deafening rush in the drowning ears:
    Have ye rightly read my song?

# ALGERNON CHARLES SWINBURNE

## 1837–1909

A Match

If love were what the rose is,
    And I were like the leaf,
Our lives would grow together
In sad or singing weather,
Blown fields or flowerful closes,
    Green pleasure or grey grief;
If love were what the rose is,
    And I were like the leaf.

If I were what the words are,
    And love were like the tune,
With double sound and single
Delight our lips would mingle,
With kisses glad as birds are
    That get sweet rain at noon;
If I were what the words are,
    And love were like the tune.

If you were life, my darling,
    And I your love were death,
We'd shine and snow together
Ere March made sweet the weather
With daffodil and starling
    And hours of fruitful breath;
If you were life, my darling,
    And I your love were death.

If you were thrall to sorrow,
　And I were page to joy,
We'd play for lives and seasons
With loving looks and treasons
And tears of night and morrow
　And laughs of maid and boy;
If you were thrall to sorrow,
　And I were page to joy.

If you were April's lady,
　And I were lord in May,
We'd throw with leaves for hours
And draw for days with flowers,
Till day like night were shady
　And night were bright like day;
If you were April's lady,
　And I were lord in May.

If you were queen of pleasure,
　And I were king of pain,
We'd hunt down love together,
Pluck out his flying-feather,
And teach his feet a measure,
　And find his mouth a rein;
If you were queen of pleasure,
　And I were king of pain.

250　　　　　　A Cameo

There was a graven image of Desire
　　Painted with red blood on a ground of gold
　　Passing between the young men and the old,
And by him Pain, whose body shone like fire,
And Pleasure with gaunt hands that grasped their hire.
　　Of his left wrist, with fingers clenched and cold,
　　The insatiable Satiety kept hold,
Walking with feet unshod that pashed the mire.

The senses and the sorrows and the sins,
    And the strange loves that suck the breasts of Hate
Till lips and teeth bite in their sharp indenture,
Followed like beasts with flap of wings and fins.
    Death stood aloof behind a gaping grate,
Upon whose lock was written *Peradventure*.


251             The Sundew

A little marsh-plant, yellow green,
And pricked at lip with tender red.
Tread close, and either way you tread
Some faint black water jets between
Lest you should bruise the curious head.

A live thing maybe; who shall know?
The summer knows and suffers it;
For the cool moss is thick and sweet
Each side, and saves the blossom so
That it lives out the long June heat.

The deep scent of the heather burns
About it; breathless though it be,
Bow down and worship; more than we
Is the least flower whose life returns,
Least weed renascent in the sea.

We are vexed and cumbered in earth's sight
With wants, with many memories;
These see their mother what she is,
Glad-growing, till August leave more bright
The apple-coloured cranberries.

Wind blows and bleaches the strong grass,
Blown all one way to shelter it
From temple of strayed kine, with feet
Felt heavier than the moorhen was,
Strayed up past patches of wild wheat.

You call it sundew: how it grows,
If with its colour it have breath,
If life taste sweet to it, if death
Pain its soft petal, no man knows:
Man has no sight or sense that saith.

My sundew, grown of gentle days,
In these green miles the spring begun
Thy growth ere April had half done
With the soft secret of her ways
Or June made ready for the sun.

O red-lipped mouth of marsh-flower,
I have a secret halved with thee.
The name that is love's name to me
Thou knowest, and the face of her
Who is my festival to see.

The hard sun, as thy petals knew,
Coloured the heavy moss-water:
Thou wert not worth green midsummer
Nor fit to live to August blue,
O sundew, not remembering her.

252     The Garden of Proserpine

Here, where the world is quiet,
   Here, where all trouble seems
Dead winds' and spent waves' riot
   In doubtful dreams of dreams;
I watch the green field growing

For reaping folk and sowing,
For harvest-time and mowing,
    A sleepy world of streams.

I am tired of tears and laughter,
    And men that laugh and weep;
Of what may come hereafter
    For men that sow to reap:
I am weary of days and hours,
Blown buds of barren flowers,
Desires and dreams and powers
    And everything but sleep.

Here life has death for neighbour,
    And far from eye or ear
Wan waves and wet winds labour,
    Weak ships and spirits steer;
They drive adrift, and whither
They wot not who make thither;
But no such winds blow hither,
    And no such things grow here.

No growth of moor or coppice,
    No heather-flower or vine,
But bloomless buds of poppies,
    Green grapes of Proserpine,
Pale beds of blowing rushes
Where no leaf blooms or blushes
Save this whereout she crushes
    For dead men deadly wine.

Pale, without name or number,
    In fruitless fields of corn,
They bow themselves and slumber
    All night till light is born;
And like a soul belated,
In hell and heaven unmated,
By cloud and mist abated
    Comes out of darkness morn.

Though one were strong as seven,
   He too with death shall dwell,
Nor wake with wings in heaven,
   Nor weep for pains in hell;
Though one were fair as roses,
His beauty clouds and closes;
And well though love reposes,
   In the end it is not well.

Pale, beyond porch and portal,
   Crowned with calm leaves, she stands
Who gathers all things mortal
   With cold immortal hands;
Her languid lips are sweeter
Than love's who fears to greet her
To men that mix and meet her
   From many times and lands.

She waits for each and other,
   She waits for all men born;
Forgets the earth her mother,
   The life of fruits and corn;
And spring and seed and swallow
Take wing for her and follow
Where summer song rings hollow
   And flowers are put to scorn.

There go the loves that wither,
   The old loves with wearier wings;
And all dead years draw thither,
   And all disastrous things;
Dead dreams of days forsaken,
Blind buds that snows have shaken,
Wild leaves that winds have taken,
   Red strays of ruined springs.

We are not sure of sorrow,
   And joy was never sure;
To-day will die to-morrow;
   Time stoops to no man's lure;
And love, grown faint and fretful,
With lips but half regretful
Sighs, and with eyes forgetful
   Weeps that no loves endure.

From too much love of living,
   From hope and fear set free,
We thank with brief thanksgiving
   Whatever gods may be
That no life lives for ever;
That dead men rise up never;
That even the weariest river
   Winds somewhere safe to sea.

Then star nor sun shall waken,
   Nor any change of light:
Nor sound of waters shaken,
   Nor any sound or sight:
Nor wintry leaves nor vernal,
Nor days nor things diurnal;
Only the sleep eternal
   In an eternal night.

253             Love and Sleep

Lying asleep between the strokes of night
   I saw my love lean over my sad bed,
   Pale as the duskiest lily's leaf or head,
Smooth-skinned and dark, with bare throat made to bite,
Too wan for blushing and too warm for white,
   But perfect-coloured without white or red.
   And her lips opened amorously, and said –
I wist not what, saving one word – Delight.

And all her face was honey to my mouth,
  And all her body pasture to mine eyes;
    The long lithe arms and hotter hands than fire,
The quivering flanks, hair smelling of the south,
  The bright light feet, the splendid supple thighs
    And glittering eyelids of my soul's desire.


254                Ilicet

    There is an end of joy and sorrow;
    Peace all day long, all night, all morrow,
      But never a time to laugh or weep.
    The end is come of pleasant places,
    The end of tender words and faces,
      The end of all, the poppied sleep.

    No place for sound within their hearing,
    No room to hope, no time for fearing,
      No lips to laugh, no lids for tears.
    The old years have run out all their measure;
    No chance of pain, no chance of pleasure,
      No fragment of the broken years.

    Outside of all the worlds and ages,
    There where the fool is as the sage is,
      There where the slayer is clean of blood,
    No end, no passage, no beginning,
    There where the sinner leaves off sinning,
      There where the good man is not good.

    There is not one thing with another,
    But Evil saith to Good: My brother,
      My brother, I am one with thee:
    They shall not strive nor cry for ever:
    No man shall choose between them: never
      Shall this thing end and that thing be.

Wind wherein seas and stars are shaken
Shall shake them, and they shall not waken;
   None that has lain down shall arise;
The stones are sealed across their places;
One shadow is shed on all their faces,
   One blindness cast on all their eyes.

Sleep, is it sleep perchance that covers
Each face, as each face were his lover's?
   Farewell; as men that sleep fare well.
The grave's mouth laughs unto derision
Desire and dread and dream and vision,
   Delight of heaven and sorrow of hell.

No soul shall tell nor lip shall number
The names and tribes of you that slumber;
   No memory, no memorial.
'Thou knowest' – who shall say thou knowest?
There is none highest and none lowest:
   An end, an end, an end of all.

Good night, good sleep, good rest from sorrow
To these that shall not have good morrow;
   The gods be gentle to all these.
Nay, if death be not, how shall they be?
Nay, is there help in heaven? it may be
   All things and lords of things shall cease.

The stooped urn, filling, dips and flashes;
The bronzèd brims are deep in ashes;
   The pale old lips of death are fed.
Shall this dust gather flesh hereafter?
Shall one shed tears or fall to laughter,
   At sight of all these poor old dead?

Nay, as thou wilt; these know not of it;
Thine eyes' strong weeping shall not profit,
   Thy laughter shall not give thee ease;

Cry aloud, spare not, cease not crying,
Sigh, till thou cleave thy sides with sighing,
   Thou shalt not raise up one of these.

Burnt spices flash, and burnt wine hisses,
The breathing flame's mouth curls and kisses
   The small dried rows of frankincense;
All round the sad red blossoms smoulder,
Flowers coloured like the fire, but colder,
   In sign of sweet things taken hence;

Yea, for their sake and in death's favour
Things of sweet shape and of sweet savour
   We yield them, spice and flower and wine;
Yea, costlier things than wine or spices,
Whereof none knoweth how great the price is,
   And fruit that comes not of the vine.

From boy's pierced throat and girl's pierced bosom
Drips, reddening round the blood-red blossom,
   The slow delicious bright soft blood,
Bathing the spices and the pyre,
Bathing the flowers and fallen fire,
   Bathing the blossom by the bud.

Roses whose lips the flame has deadened
Drink till the lapping leaves are reddened
   And warm wet inner petals weep;
The flower whereof sick sleep gets leisure,
Barren of balm and purple pleasure,
   Fumes with no native steam of sleep.

Why will ye weep? what do ye weeping?
For waking folk and people sleeping,
   And sands that fill and sands that fall,
The days rose-red, the poppied hours,
Blood, wine, and spice and fire and flowers,
   There is one end of one and all.

Shall such an one lend love or borrow?
Shall these be sorry for thy sorrow?
   Shall these give thanks for words or breath?
Their hate is as their loving-kindness;
The frontlet of their brows is blindness,
   The armlet of their arms is death.

Lo, for no noise or light of thunder
Shall these grave-clothes be rent in sunder;
   He that hath taken, shall he give?
He hath rent them: shall he bind together?
He hath bound them: shall he break the tether?
   He hath slain them: shall he bid them live?

A little sorrow, a little pleasure,
Fate metes us from the dusty measure
   That holds the date of all of us;
We are born with travail and strong crying,
And from the birth-day to the dying
   The likeness of our life is thus.

One girds himself to serve another,
Whose father was the dust, whose mother
   The little dead red worm therein;
They find no fruit of things they cherish;
The goodness of a man shall perish,
   It shall be one thing with his sin.

In deep wet ways by grey old gardens
Fed with sharp spring the sweet fruit hardens;
   They know not what fruits wane or grow;
Red summer burns to the utmost ember;
They know not, neither can remember,
   The old years and flowers they used to know.

Ah, for their sakes, so trapped and taken,
For theirs, forgotten and forsaken,
   Watch, sleep not, gird thyself with prayer.

Nay, where the heart of wrath is broken,
Where long love ends as a thing spoken,
    How shall thy crying enter there?

Though the iron sides of the old world falter,
The likeness of them shall not alter
    For all the rumour of periods,
The stars and seasons that come after,
The tears of latter men, the laughter
    Of the old unalterable gods.

Far up above the years and nations,
The high gods, clothed and crowned with patience,
    Endure through days of deathlike date;
They bear the witness of things hidden;
Before their eyes all life stands chidden,
    As they before the eyes of Fate.

Not for their love shall Fate retire,
Nor they relent for our desire,
    Nor the graves open for their call
The end is more than joy and anguish,
Than lives that laugh and lives that languish,
    The poppied sleep, the end of all.

255                     A Rhyme

        Babe, if rhyme be none
            For that sweet small word
        Babe, the sweetest one
            Ever heard,

        Right it is and meet
            Rhyme should keep not true
        Time with such a sweet
            Thing as you.

Meet it is that rhyme
    Should not gain such grace:
What is April's prime
    To your face?

What to yours is May's
    Rosiest smile? what sound
Like your laughter sways
    All hearts round?

None can tell in metre
    Fit for ears on earth
What sweet star grew sweeter
    At your birth.

Wisdom doubts what may be:
    Hope, with smile sublime,
Trusts: but neither, baby,
    Knows the rhyme.

Wisdom lies down lonely;
    Hope keeps watch from far;
None but one seer only
    Sees the star.

Love alone, with yearning
    Heart for astrolabe,
Takes the star's height, burning
    O'er the babe.

# AUGUSTA WEBSTER

## 1837–94

## Mother and Daughter

*An Uncompleted Sonnet-Sequence*

### I

Young laughters, and my music! Aye till now
  The voice can reach no blending minors near;
   'Tis the bird's trill because the spring is here
And spring means trilling on a blossomy bough;
'Tis the spring joy that has no why or how,
  But sees the sun and hopes not nor can fear –
  Spring is so sweet and spring seems all the year.
Dear voice, the first-come birds but trill as thou.

Oh music of my heart, be thus for long:
Too soon the spring bird learns the later song;
  Too soon a sadder sweetness slays content;
Too soon! There comes new light on onward day,
There comes new perfume o'er a rosier way:
  Comes not again the young spring joy that went.

*Rome, November 1881*

## II

That she is beautiful is not delight,
   As some think mothers joy, by pride of her,
   To witness questing eyes caught prisoner
And hear her praised the livelong dancing night;
But the glad impulse that makes painters' sight
   Bids me note her and grow the happier;
   And love that finds me as her worshipper
Reveals me each best loveliness aright.

   Oh goddess head! Oh innocent brave eyes!
Oh curved and parted lips where smiles are rare
And sweetness ever! Oh smooth shadowy hair
Gathered around the silence of her brow!
   Child, I'd needs love thy beauty stranger-wise:
And oh the beauty of it, being thou!

## III

I watch the sweet grave face in timorous thought
   Lest I should see it dawn to some unrest
   And read that in her heart is youth's ill guest,
The querulous young sadness, born of nought,
That wearies of the strife it has not fought,
   And finds the life it has not had unblest,
   And asks it knows not what that should be best,
And till Love come has never what it sought.

But she is still. A full and crystal lake
   So gives its skies their passage to its deeps
In an unruffled morn where no winds wake,
   And, strong and fretless, stirs not, nor yet sleeps.
My darling smiles and 'tis for gladness' sake;
   She hears a woe, 'tis simple tears she weeps.

## IV

'Tis but a child. The quiet Juno gaze
  Breaks at a trifle into mirth and glow,
  Changed as a folded bud bursts into blow,
And she springs, buoyant, on some busy craze,
Or, in the rhythm of her girlish plays,
  Like light upon swift waves floats to and fro,
  And, whatsoe'er's her mirth, needs me to know,
And keeps me young by her young innocent ways.

Just now she and her kitten raced and sprang
  To catch the daisy ball she tossed about;
  Then they grew grave, and found a shady tree,
And kitty tried to see the notes she sang:
  Now she flies hitherward – 'Mother! Quick! Come see!
  Two hyacinths in my garden almost out!'

## V

Last night the broad blue lightnings flamed the sky;
  We watched, our breaths caught as each burst its way,
  And through its fire out-leaped the sharp white ray,
And sudden dark re-closed when it went by:
But she, that where we are will needs be nigh,
  Had tired with hunting orchids half the day.
  Her father thought she called us; he and I,
Half anxious, reached the bedroom where she lay.

Oh lily face upon the whiteness blent!
  How calm she lay in her unconscious grace!
A peal crashed on the silence ere we went;
  She stirred in sleep, a little changed her place,
  'Mother,' she breathed, a smile grew on her face:
'Mother,' my darling breathed, and slept content.

## VI

Sometimes, as young things will, she vexes me,
   Wayward, or too unheeding, or too blind.
   Like aimless birds that, flying on a wind,
Strike slant against their own familiar tree;
Like venturous children pacing with the sea,
   That turn but when the breaker spurts behind
   Outreaching them with spray: she in such kind
Is borne against some fault, or does not flee.

And so, may be, I blame her for her wrong,
   And she will frown and lightly plead her part,
And then I bid her go. But 'tis not long:
   Then comes she lip to ear and heart to heart.
And thus forgiven her love seems newly strong,
   And, oh my penitent, how dear thou art!

## VII

Her father lessons me I at times am hard,
   Chiding a moment's fault as too grave ill,
   And let some little blot my vision fill,
Scanning her with a narrow near regard.
True. Love's unresting gaze is self-debarred
   From all sweet ignorance, and learns a skill,
   Not painless, of such signs as hurt love's will,
That would not have its prize one tittle marred.

Alas! Who rears and loves a dawning rose
   Starts at a speck upon one petal's rim:
Who sees a dusk creep in the shrined pearl's glows,
   Is ruined at once: 'My jewel growing dim!'
I watch one bud that on my bosom blows,
   I watch one treasured pearl for me and him.

## VIII

A little child she, half defiant came
 Reasoning her case – 'twas not so long ago –
 'I cannot mind your scolding, for I know
However bad I were you'd love the same.'
And I, what countering answer could I frame?
 'Twas true, and true, and God's self told her so.
 One does but ask one's child to smile and grow,
And each rebuke has love for its right name.

And yet, methinks, sad mothers who for years,
 Watching the child pass forth that was their boast,
Have counted all the footsteps by new fears
Till even lost fears seem hopes whereof they're reft
And of all mother's good love sole is left –
 Is their Love, Love, or some remembered ghost?

## IX

Oh weary hearts! Poor mothers that look back!
 So outcasts from the vale where they were born
 Turn on their road and, with a joy forlorn,
See the far roofs below their arid track:
So in chill buffets while the sea grows black
 And windy skies, once blue, are tost and torn,
 We are not yet forgetful of the morn,
And praise anew the sunshine that we lack.

Oh, sadder than pale sufferers by a tomb
 That say 'My dead is happier, and is more,'
 Are they who dare no 'is' but tell what's o'er –
 Thus the frank childhood, those the lovable ways –
 Stirring the ashes of remembered days
For yet some sparks to warm the livelong gloom.

## X

### *Love's Counterfeit*

Not Love, not Love, that worn and footsore thrall
   Who, crowned with withered buds and leaves gone dry,
   Plods in his chains to follow one passed by,
Guerdoned with only tears himself lets fall.
Love is asleep and smiling in his pall,
   And this that wears his shape and will not die
   Was once his comrade shadow, Memory –
His shadow that now stands for him in all.

And there are those who, hurrying on past reach,
   See the dim follower and laugh, content,
     'Lo, Love pursues me, go where'er I will!'
Yet, longer gazing, some may half beseech,
     'This *must* be Love that wears his features still:
Or else when was the moment that Love went?'

## XI

### *Love's Mourner*

'Tis men who say that through all hurt and pain
   The woman's love, wife's, mother's, still will hold,
   And breathes the sweeter and will more unfold
For winds that tear it, and the sorrowful rain.
So in a thousand voices has the strain
   Of this dear patient madness been retold,
   That men call woman's love. Ah! they are bold,
Naming for love that grief which *does* remain.

Love faints that looks on baseness face to face:
   Love pardons all; but by the pardonings dies,
   With a fresh wound of each pierced through the breast.
And there stand pityingly in Love's void place
   Kindness of household wont familiar-wise.
   And faith to Love – faith to our dead at rest.

## XII

She has made me wayside posies: here they stand,
  Bringing fresh memories of where they grew.
  As new-come travellers from a world we knew
Wake every while some image of their land,
So these whose buds our woodland breezes fanned
  Bring to my room the meadow where they blew,
  The brook-side cliff, the elms where wood-doves coo –
And every flower is dearer for her hand.

Oh blossoms of the paths she loves to tread,
  Some grace of her is in all thoughts you bear:
  For in my memories of your homes that were
The old sweet loneliness they kept is fled,
And would I think it back I find instead
  A presence of my darling mingling there.

## XIII

My darling scarce thinks music sweet save mine:
  'Tis that she does but love me more than hear.
  She'll not believe my voice to stranger ear
Is merely measure to the note and line;
'Not so,' she says; 'Thou hast a secret thine:
  The others' singing 's only rich, or clear,
  But something in thy tones brings music near;
As though thy song could search me and divine.'

Oh voice of mine that in some day not far
  Time, the strong creditor, will call his debt,
Will dull – and even to her – will rasp and mar,
  Sing Time asleep because of her regret,
Be twice thy life the thing her fancies are,
  Thou echo to the self she knows not yet.

*Caserta, April, 1882*

## XIV

To love her as to-day is so great bliss
   I needs must think of morrows almost loth,
   Morrows wherein the flower's unclosing growth
Shall make my darling other than she is.
The breathing rose excels the bud I wis,
   Yet bud that will be rose is sweet for both;
   And by-and-by seems like some later troth
Named in the moment of a lover's kiss.

Yes, I am jealous, as of one now strange
   That shall instead of her possess my thought,
Of her own self made new by any change,
   Of her to be by ripening morrows brought.
My rose of women under later skies!
Yet, ah! my child with the child's trustful eyes!

*Cernobbio*

## XV

That some day Death who has us all for jest
   Shall hide me in the dark and voiceless mould,
   And him whose living hand has mine in hold,
Where loving comes not nor the looks that rest,
Shall make us nought where we are known the best,
   Forgotten things that leave their track untold
   As in the August night the sky's dropped gold –
This seems no strangeness, but Death's natural hest.

But looking on the dawn that is her face
   To know she too is Death's seems misbelief;
She should not find decay, but, as the sun
Moves mightier from the veil that hides his place,
Keep ceaseless radiance. Life is Death begun:
   But Death and her! That's strangeness passing grief.

## XVI

She will not have it that my day wanes low,
   Poor of the fire its drooping sun denies,
   That on my brow the thin lines write good-byes
Which soon may be read plain for all to know,
Telling that I have done with youth's brave show;
   Alas! and done with youth in heart and eyes,
   With wonder and with far expectancies,
Save but to say 'I knew such long ago.'

She will not have it. Loverlike to me,
   She with her happy gaze finds all that's best,
She sees this fair and that unfretted still,
   And her own sunshine over all the rest:
So she half keeps me as she'd have me be,
And I forget to age, through her sweet will.

## XVII

And how could I grow old while she's so young?
   Methinks her heart sets time for mine to beat,
   We are so near; her new thoughts, incomplete,
Find their shaped wording happen on my tongue;
Like bloom on last year's winterings newly sprung
   My youth upflowers with hers, and must repeat
   Old joyaunces in me nigh obsolete.
Could I grow older while my child's so young?

And there are tales how youthful blood instilled
   Thawing frore Age's veins gave life new course,
And quavering limbs and eyes made indolent
   Grew freshly eager with beginning force:
She so breathes impulse. Were my years twice spent,
Not burdening Age, with her, could make me chilled.

## XVIII

'Tis hard that the full summer of our round
   Is but the turn where winter's sign-post's writ;
   That to have reached the best is leaving it;
The final loss bears date from having found.
So some proud vessel in a narrow sound
   Sails at high water with the fair wind fit,
   And lo! the ebb along the sandy spit,
Lower and lower till she jars, aground.

'Tis hard. We are young still but more content;
   'Tis our ripe flush, the heyday of our prime;
We learn full breath, how rich of the air we are!
   But suddenly we note a touch of time,
A little fleck that scarcely seems to mar;
And we know then that some time since youth went.

## XIX

Life on the wane: yes, sudden that news breaks.
   And yet I would 'twere suddenly and less soon;
   Since no forewarning makes loss opportune.
And now I watch that slow advance Time makes:
Watch as, while silent flow spreads broad the lakes
   Mid the land levels of a smooth lagoon,
   One waiting, pitiful, on a tidal dune,
Aware too long before it overtakes.

Ah! there's so quick a joy in hues and sun,
   And will my eyes see dim? Will vacant sense
Forget the lark, the surges on the beach?
   Shall I step wearily and wish 'twere done?
   Well, if it be love will not too go hence,
Love will have new glad secrets yet to teach.

## XX

There's one I miss. A little questioning maid
  That held my finger, trotting by my side,
  And smiled out of her pleased eyes open wide,
Wondering and wiser at each word I said.
And I must help her frolics if she played,
  And I must feel her trouble if she cried;
  My lap was hers past right to be denied;
She did my bidding, but I more obeyed.

Dearer she is to-day, dearer and more;
  Closer to me, since sister womanhoods meet;
Yet, like poor mothers some long while bereft,
I dwell on toward ways, quaint memories left,
  I miss the approaching sound of pit-pat feet,
The eager baby voice outside my door.

## XXI

Hardly in any common tender wise,
  With petting talk, light lips on her dear cheek,
  The love I mean my child will bear to speak,
Loth of its own less image for disguise;
But liefer will it floutingly devise,
  Using a favourite jester's mimic pique,
  Prompt, idle, by-names with their sense to seek,
And takes for language laughing ironies.

But she, as when some foreign tongue is heard,
  Familiar on our lips and closely known,
We feel the every purport of each word
  When ignorant ears reach empty sound alone,
So knows the core within each merry gird,
  So gives back such a meaning in her own.

## XXII

The brook leaps riotous with its life just found,
  That freshets from the mountain rains have fed,
Beats at the boulders in its hindered bed,
And fills the valley with its triumphing sound.
The strong unthirsty tarn sunk in deep ground
  Has never a sigh wherewith its wealth is said,
  Has no more ripples than the May-flies tread:
Silence of waters is where they abound.

And love, whatever love, sure, makes small boast:
'Tis the new lovers tell, in wonder yet.
Oh happy need! Enriched stream's jubilant gush!
But who being spouses well have learned love's most,
  Being child and mother learned not nor forget,
These in their joyfulness feel the tarn's strong hush.

## XXIII

Birds sing 'I love you, love' the whole day through,
  And not another song can they sing right;
  But, singing done with, loving's done with quite,
The autumn sunders every twittering two.
And I'd not have love make too much ado
  With sweet parades of fondness and delight,
  Lest iterant wont should make caresses trite,
Love-names mere cuckoo ousters of the true.

Oh heart can hear heart's sense in senseless nought,
  And heart that's sure of heart has little speech.
What shall it tell? The other knows its thought.
  What shall one doubt or question or beseech
Who is assured and knows and, unbesought,
  Possesses the dear trust that each gives each.

## XXIV

'You scarcely are a mother, at that rate.
   Only one child!' The blithe soul pitied loud.
   And doubtless she, amid her household crowd,
When one brings care in another's fortunate;
When one fares forth another's at her gate.
   Yea, were her first-born folded in his shroud,
   Not with a whole despair would she be bowed,
She has more sons to make her heart elate.

Many to love her singly, mother theirs,
   To give her the dear love of being their need,
   To storm her lap by turns and claim their kiss,
To kneel around her at their bed-time prayers;
   Many to grow her comrades! Some have this.
   Yet I, I do not envy them indeed.

*Ramsgate, 1886*

## XXV

You think that you love each as much as one,
   Mothers with many nestlings 'neath your wings.
   Nay, but you know not. Love's most priceless things
Have unity that cannot be undone.
You give the rays, I the englobed full sun;
   I give the river, you the separate springs:
   My motherhood's all my child's with all it brings –
None takes the strong entireness from her: none.

You know not. You love yours with various stress;
   This with a graver trust, this with more pride;
This maybe with more needed tenderness:
I by each uttermost passion of my soul
Am turned to mine; she is one, she has the whole:
   How should you know who appraise love and divide?

## XXVI

Of my one pearl so much more joy I gain
   As he that to his sole desire is sworn,
   Indifferent what women more were born,
And if she loved him not all love were vain,
Gains more, because of her – yea, through all pain,
   All love and sorrows, were they two forlorn –
   Than whoso happiest in the lands of morn
Mingles his heart amid a wifely train.

Oh! Child and mother, darling! Mother and child!
   And who but we? We, darling, paired alone?
   Thou hast all thy mother; thou art all my own.
   That passion of maternity which sweeps
Tideless 'neath where the heaven of thee hath smiled
   Has but one channel, therefore infinite deeps.

## XXVII

Since first my little one lay on my breast
   I never needed such a second good,
   Nor felt a void left in my motherhood
She filled not always to the utterest.
The summer linnet, by glad yearnings pressed,
   Builds room enough to house a callow brood:
   I prayed not for another child – nor could;
My solitary bird had my heart's nest.

But she is cause that any baby thing
   If it but smile, is one of mine in truth,
   And every child becomes my natural joy:
And, if my heart gives all youth fostering,
   Her sister, brother, seems the girl or boy:
   My darling makes me mother to their youth.

# DAVID GRAY
## 1838–61

257          The Brooklet

O deep unlovely brooklet, moaning slow
   Thro' moorish fen in utter loneliness!
The partridge cowers beside thy loamy flow
   In pulseful tremor, when with sudden press
The huntsman fluskers thro' the rustled heather.    *beats*
   In March thy sallow-buds from vermeil shells   *(to startle*
Break, satin-tinted, downy as the feather       *the game)*
   Of moss-chat that among the purplish bells
Breasts into fresh new life her three unborn.
   The plover hovers o'er thee, uttering clear
And mournful-strange, his human cry forlorn:
   While wearily, alone, and void of cheer
Thou guid'st thy nameless waters from the fen,
To sleep unsunned in an untrampled glen.

# JOHN TODHUNTER
## 1839–1916

258                              Rain

The kindled clouds loom bright as burning smoke
  O'er the vast conflagration of the sky,
  Rain in their folds, and inland heavily
  Roll o'er the sodden fallows, all a-soak
Under the glowing sunset. Since I woke,
  Till now with skirts updrawn sullenly fly
  The hosts of gloom, has rain, rain rushing by,
  Battered the woodlands with his watery stroke.
In baffled rage, tempestuous melancholy,
  Throbs my oppress'd heart, as of one afar
  From some last field of death and victory;
Who waits to hear his comrades' onset-volley,
  Swordless and sick. What means this ghostly war?
  What cause, what cloudy banner summons me?

# THOMAS HARDY
## 1840–1928

259            Friends Beyond

William Dewy, Tranter Reuben, Farmer Ledlow late at plough,
     Robert's kin, and John's, and Ned's,
And the Squire, and Lady Susan, lie in Mellstock churchyard now!

'Gone,' I call them, gone for good, that group of local hearts and heads;
     Yet at mothy curfew-tide,
And at midnight when the noon-heat breathes it back from walls and
         leads,

They've a way of whispering to me – fellow-wight who yet abide –
     In the muted, measured note
Of a ripple under archways, or a lone cave's stillicide:

'We have triumphed: this achievement turns the bane to antidote,
     Unsuccesses to success,
Many thought-worn eves and morrows to a morrow free of thought.

'No more need we corn and clothing, feel of old terrestrial stress;
     Chill detraction stirs no sigh;
Fear of death has even bygone us: death gave all that we possess.'

W. D. – 'Ye mid burn the wold bass-viol that I set such vallie by.'
     *Squire.* – 'You may hold the manse in fee,
You may wed my spouse, my children's memory of me may decry.'

*Lady.* – 'You may have my rich brocades, my laces; take each household
         key;
     Ransack coffer, desk, bureau;
Quiz the few poor treasures hid there, con the letters kept by me.'

*Far.* – 'Ye mid zell my favourite heifer, ye mid let the charlock grow,
    Foul the grinterns, give up thrift.'          *granary bins*
*Wife.* – 'If ye break my best blue china, children, I shan't care or ho.'
                                                         *be anxious*


*All.* – 'We've no wish to hear the tidings, how the people's fortunes
       shift;
    What your daily doings are;
Who are wedded, born, divided; if your lives beat slow or swift.


'Curious not the least are we if our intents you make or mar,
    If you quire to our old tune,
If the City stage still passes, if the weirs still roar afar.'


– Thus, with very gods' composure, freed those crosses late and soon
    Which, in life, the Trine allow
(Why, none witteth), and ignoring all that haps beneath the moon,


William Dewy, Tranter Reuben, Farmer Ledlow late at plough,
    Robert's kin, and John's, and Ned's,
And the Squire, and Lady Susan, murmur mildly to me now.


  **260**                        Neutral Tones

        We stood by a pond that winter day,
        And the sun was white, as though chidden of God,
        And a few leaves lay on the starving sod;
           – They had fallen from an ash, and were gray.

        Your eyes on me were as eyes that rove
        Over tedious riddles solved years ago;
        And some words played between us to and fro
           On which lost the more by our love.

The smile on your mouth was the deadest thing
Alive enough to have strength to die;
And a grin of bitterness swept thereby
    Like an ominous bird a-wing . . .

Since then, keen lessons that love deceives,
And wrings with wrong, have shaped to me
Your face, and the God-curst sun, and a tree,
    And a pond edged with grayish leaves.

*1867*

261              Her Dilemma

(IN — CHURCH)

The two were silent in a sunless church,
Whose mildewed walls, uneven paving-stones,
And wasted carvings passed antique research;
And nothing broke the clock's dull monotones.

Leaning against a wormy poppy-head,
So wan and worn that he could scarcely stand,
– For he was soon to die, – he softly said,
'Tell me you love me!' – holding long her hand.

She would have given a world to breathe 'yes' truly,
So much his life seemed hanging on her mind,
And hence she lied, her heart persuaded throughly,
'Twas worth her soul to be a moment kind.

But the sad need thereof, his nearing death,
So mocked humanity that she shamed to prize
A world conditioned thus, or care for breath
Where Nature such dilemmas could devise.

*1866*

262

I look into my glass,
And view my wasting skin,
And say, 'Would God it came to pass
My heart had shrunk as thin!'

For then, I, undistrest
By hearts grown cold to me,
Could lonely wait my endless rest
With equanimity.

But Time, to make me grieve,
Part steals, lets part abide;
And shakes this fragile frame at eve
With throbbings of noontide.

263     The Dead Drummer [Drummer Hodge]

I

They throw in Drummer Hodge, to rest
    Uncoffined – just as found:
His landmark is a kopje-crest
    That breaks the veldt around;
And foreign constellations west
    Each night above his mound.

II

Young Hodge the Drummer never knew –
    Fresh from his Wessex home –
The meaning of the broad Karoo,
    The Bush, the dusty loam,
And why uprose to nightly view
    Strange stars amid the gloam.

### III

Yet portion of that unknown plain
  Will Hodge for ever be;
His homely Northern breast and brain
  Grow up a Southern tree,
And strange-eyed constellations reign
  His stars eternally.

264         In the Old Theatre, Fiesole

*(April 1887)*

I traced the Circus whose gray stones incline
Where Rome and dim Etruria interjoin,
Till came a child who showed an ancient coin
That bore the image of a Constantine.

She lightly passed; nor did she once opine
How, better than all books, she had raised for me
In swift perspective Europe's history
Through the vast years of Cæsar's sceptred line.

For in my distant plot of English loam
'Twas but to delve, and straightway there to find
Coins of like gravure. As with one half blind
Whom common simples cure, her act flashed home
In that mute moment to my opened mind
The world-imprinting power of perished Rome.

265      Rome: At the Pyramid of Cestius near
           the Graves of Shelley and Keats

*(1887)*

Who, then, was Cestius,
  And what is he to me? –
Amid thick thoughts and memories multitudinous
  One thought alone brings he.

I can recall no word
  Of anything he did;
For me he is a man who died and was interred
  To leave a pyramid

Whose purpose was exprest
  Not with its first design,
Nor till, far down in Time, beside it found their rest
  Two countrymen of mine.

Cestius in life, maybe,
  Slew, breathed out threatening;
I know not. This I know: in death all silently
  He does a kindlier thing,

In beckoning pilgrim feet
  With marble finger high
To where, by shadowy wall and history-haunted street,
  Those matchless singers lie ...

– Say, then, he lived and died
  That stones which bear his name
Should mark, through Time, where two immortal Shades abide;
  It is an ample fame.

## 266 Lausanne: In Gibbon's Old Garden: 11–12 p.m.

### *June 27, 1897*

*The 110th anniversary of the completion of the 'Decline
and Fall' at the same hour and place.*

A spirit seems to pass,
Formal in pose, but grave and grand withal:
He contemplates a volume stout and tall,
And far lamps fleck him through the thin acacias.

Anon the book is closed,
With 'It is finished!' And at the alley's end
He turns, and soon on me his glances bend;
And, as from earth, comes speech – small, muted, yet composed.

'How fares the Truth now? – Ill?
– Do pens but slily further her advance?
May one not speed her but in phrase askance?
Do scribes aver the Comic to be Reverend still?

'Still rule those minds on earth
At whom sage Milton's wormwood words were hurled:
*"Truth like a bastard comes into the world
Never without ill-fame to him who gives her birth"*?'

## 267                An August Midnight

### I

A shaded lamp and a waving blind,
And the beat of a clock from a distant floor:
On this scene enter – winged, horned, and spined –
A longlegs, a moth, and a dumbledore;
While 'mid my page there idly stands
A sleepy fly, that rubs its hands ...

II

Thus meet we five, in this still place,
At this point of time, at this point in space.
– My guests parade my new-penned ink,
Or bang at the lamp-glass, whirl, and sink.
'God's humblest, they!' I muse. Yet why?
They know Earth-secrets that know not I.

*Max Gate, 1899*

268        The Darkling Thrush

I leant upon a coppice gate
        When Frost was spectre-gray,
And Winter's dregs made desolate
        The weakening eye of day.
The tangled bine-stems scored the sky
        Like strings from broken lyres,
And all mankind that haunted nigh
        Had sought their household fires.

The land's sharp features seemed to be
        The Century's corpse outleant,
His crypt the cloudy canopy,
        The wind his death-lament.
The ancient pulse of germ and birth
        Was shrunken hard and dry,
And every spirit upon earth
        Seemed fervourless as I.

At once a voice outburst among
        The bleak twigs overhead
In a full-hearted evensong
        Of joy illimited;

An aged thrush, frail, gaunt, and small,
    In blast-beruffled plume,
Had chosen thus to fling his soul
    Upon the growing gloom.

So little cause for carollings
    Of such ecstatic sound
Was written on terrestrial things
    Afar or nigh around,
That I could think there trembled through
    His happy good-night air
Some blessed Hope, whereof he knew
    And I was unaware.

*December 1900*

269        The Ruined Maid

'O 'melia, my dear, this does everything crown!
Who could have supposed I should meet you in Town?
And whence such fair garments, such prosperi-ty?' –
'O didn't you know I'd been ruined?' said she.

– 'You left us in tatters, without shoes or socks,
Tired of digging potatoes, and spudding up docks;
And now you've gay bracelets and bright feathers three!' –
'Yes: that's how we dress when we're ruined,' said she.

– 'At home in the barton you said "thee" and "thou,"
And "thik oon," and "theäs oon," and "t'other"; but now
Your talking quite fits 'ee for high compa-ny!' –
'Some polish is gained with one's ruin,' said she.

– 'Your hands were like paws then, your face blue and bleak
But now I'm bewitched by your delicate cheek,
And your little gloves fit as on any la-dy!'–
'We never do work when we're ruined,' said she.

– 'You used to call home-life a hag-ridden dream,
And you'd sigh, and you'd sock; but at present you seem
To know not of megrims or melancho-ly!' –
'True. There's an advantage in ruin,' said she.

– 'I wish I had feathers, a fine sweeping gown,
And a delicate face, and could strut about Town!' –
'My dear – a raw country girl, such as you be,
Isn't equal to that. You ain't ruined,' said she.

*Westbourne Park Villas, 1866*

270            The Respectable Burgher

ON 'THE HIGHER CRITICISM'

Since Reverend Doctors now declare
That clerks and people must prepare
To doubt if Adam ever were;
To hold the flood a local scare;
To argue, though the stolid stare,
That everything had happened ere
The prophets to its happening sware;
That David was no giant-slayer,
Nor one to call a God-obeyer
In certain details we could spare,
But rather was a debonair
Shrewd bandit, skilled as banjo-player:
That Solomon sang the fleshly Fair,
And gave the Church no thought whate'er:
That Esther with her royal wear,
And Mordecai, the son of Jair,
And Joshua's triumphs, Job's despair,
And Balaam's ass's bitter blare;
Nebuchadnezzar's furnace-flare,
And Daniel and the den affair,
And other stories rich and rare,

Were writ to make old doctrine wear
Something of a romantic air:
That the Nain widow's only heir,
And Lazarus with cadaverous glare
(As done in oils by Piombo's care)
Did not return from Sheol's lair:
That Jael set a fiendish snare,
That Pontius Pilate acted square,
That never a sword cut Malchus' ear;
And (but for shame I must forbear)
That — — did not reappear! . . .
– Since thus they hint, nor turn a hair,
All churchgoing will I forswear,
And sit on Sundays in my chair,
And read that moderate man Voltaire.

271              The Self-Unseeing

        Here is the ancient floor,
        Footworn and hollowed and thin,
        Here was the former door
        Where the dead feet walked in.

        She sat here in her chair,
        Smiling into the fire;
        He who played stood there,
        Bowing it higher and higher.

        Childlike, I danced in a dream;
        Blessings emblazoned that day;
        Everything glowed with a gleam;
        Yet we were looking away!

272    De Profundis I [In Tenebris I]

*'Percussus sum sicut foenum, et aruit cor meum.' – Ps. ci.*

Wintertime nighs;
But my bereavement-pain
It cannot bring again:
      Twice no one dies.

Flower-petals flee;
But, since it once hath been,
No more that severing scene
      Can harrow me.

Birds faint in dread:
I shall not lose old strength
In the lone frost's black length:
      Strength long since fled!

Leaves freeze to dun;
But friends can not turn cold
This season as of old
      For him with none.

Tempests may scath;
But love can not make smart
Again this year his heart
      Who no heart hath.

Black is night's cope;
But death will not appal
One who, past doubtings all,
      Waits in unhope.

272. *Title:* 'Out of the depths' (Psalm 130); later title 'In the shadows' *Epigraph:* 'My heart is smitten, and withered like grass' (Psalm 102: 4; Hardy's number, 101, is from the Latin (Vulgate) bible)

# HARRIET ELEANOR HAMILTON KING

## 1840–1920

## 273

A Dream Maiden

My baby is sleeping overhead,
    My husband is in the town;
In my large white bed uncurtained,
    All alone I lay me down.

And dreamily I have said my prayers,
    And dreamily closed my eyes,
And the youth in my blood moves sweetly
    As my pulses fall and rise.

I lie so peaceful and lonely,
    A maiden in spirit-land,
With the moonbeams in at the window,
    And hand laid close to hand.

I wander forth in the moonbeams,
    All free of heart alone,
Neither awake nor dreaming,
    To-night it is all one.

Light of step across the carpet
    Of the flower-entangled spring,
Light of spirit through the haunted
    Wood pathways murmuring.

The earth is telling her secrets,
    Never shy or strange to me;
My heart beating only silence,
    One with her mystery.

All over the beautiful distance
   The air is so fresh and pure,
The night is so cool and silvery,
   The calm is so secure.

And afar, down into the sunrise,
   The glittering dream-worlds shine;
And by this free heart triumphant
   I pass on to make them mine.

O elfin maiden, turn homeward,
   And dream not so cold and wild! –
Have I not turned a woman?
   Have I not husband and child?

# COSMO MONKHOUSE
## 1840–1901

## 274

## A Ballad of a Shield

It was all of a shield on a tree,
Hung high so that passers might see;
  From the South it shone forth
  Like gold; from the North
It was silver as silver could be.

And this is the tale that it told
Of a fight that was foughten of old
  By Sir Hugh, who had seen
  But its silvery sheen,
And Sir Arthur, who swore it was gold.

They met with their lances in rest,
And a shock that had shaken the best.
  Sir Arthur was sound
  As he leapt from the ground,
But Sir Hugh had a dint in the breast.

Then neither spake ever a word,
But out from the scabbard the sword;
  And the blade of Sir Hugh
  Found a little way through,
And Sir Arthur was down on the sward.

Sir Arthur declared it was well,
But a pang, like a torture of hell,
  Smit Sir Hugh at the sight
  Of the blood-dappled knight,
And then he, too, staggered and fell.

But now, in the fight they had crost,
And they looked through the boughs as they tost,
   When gold on the blue
   Was the shield to Sir Hugh,
To Sir Arthur as silver as frost.

Then neither could speak if he tried,
But each stretched an arm from his side, –
   With a smile on the lip,
   And the ghost of a grip,
They loved one another and died.

# MATHILDE BLIND

## 1841–96

275    On Reading the 'Rubáiyat' of Omar Khayyam

IN A KENTISH ROSE GARDEN

Beside a Dial in the leafy close,
Where every bush was burning with the Rose.
With million roses falling flake by flake
Upon the lawn in fading summer snows:

I read the Persian Poet's rhyme of old,
Each thought a ruby in a ring of gold –
Old thoughts so young, that, after all these years,
They're writ on every rose-leaf yet unrolled.

You may not know the secret tongue aright
The Sunbeams on their rosy tablets write;
Only a poet may perchance translate
Those ruby-tinted hieroglyphs of light.

# GEORGE AUGUSTUS SIMCOX

## 1841–1905

276                                  In the Jacquerie

Anstice and Amalie, watching late,
Sate over Sir Raoul's castle-gate,
And saw the rabble foam up in hate:
Raoul would fight and Amalie fly,
But Anstice sate quietly waiting to die.

Raoul was beaten down to his knee,
They tore from his girdle the silver key
Of the postern where Amalie meant to flee;
He cast to the tower a warning cry
Where Anstice sate quietly waiting to die.

They bound his hands and they bound his feet,
They left him his shirt for winding-sheet,
They hung up Sir Raoul against the sky;
But Anstice sate quietly waiting to die.

Amalie covered her golden head,
Hid her face from the noble dead;
But, looking out with a tearless eye,
Anstice sate quietly waiting to die.

Amalie slank through the gate to flee,
She stumbled over the caitiff's knee
Who had taken Sir Raoul's silver key:
She swooned to earth and no help was nigh;
But Anstice sate quietly waiting to die.

The rabble sate drinking the wine and mead,
And Amalie served them in beggar's weed;
But she cast up a torch to avenge her shame,
And the roof fell down on their heads in flame,
And the beams of the tower fell down from high
Where Anstice sate quietly waiting to die.

The tower lies sunk in the castle moat,
And the cushat warbles her one clear note
In the elms that grow into the brooding sky,
Where Anstice sate long ago waiting to die.

# EDWARD DOWDEN

1843–1913

277             The Pool

A wood obscure in this man's haunt of love,
    And midmost in the wood where leaves fall sere,
A pool unplumbed; no winds these waters move,
    Gathered as in a vase from year to year.

And he has thought that he himself lies drowned,
    Wan-faced where the pale water glimmereth,
And that the voiceless man who paces round
    The brink, nor sheds a tear now, is his wraith.

# MARY MONTGOMERIE LAMB

## 1843–1905

278          'For One Man's Pleasure'

Two magpies sought my garden-glade,
   (It brings good luck to look at *two*!)
   Tho' not as billing ring-doves woo
Do pies discourse of love! They made
A grievous chatter in the shade:
   But, by-and-by, with much ado,
   They built a nest, and then I knew
I should be lucky whilst they stay'd!
I ween two blither fowl than these,
   You had not seen beneath the sun!
   Wherefore, the gard'ner took a gun
And shot one near the early peas, –
The sad mate lingers, ill at ease;
   (It bodes bad luck to look at *one*!)

# ROBERT BRIDGES

## 1844–1930

On a Dead Child

Perfect little body, without fault or stain on thee,
  With promise of strength and manhood full and fair!
    Though cold and stark and bare,
The bloom and the charm of life doth awhile remain on thee.

Thy mother's treasure wert thou; – alas! no longer
  To visit her heart with wondrous joy; to be
    Thy father's pride; – ah, he
Must gather his faith together, and his strength make stronger.

To me, as I move thee now in the last duty,
  Dost thou with a turn or gesture anon respond;
    Startling my fancy fond
With a chance attitude of the head, a freak of beauty.

Thy hand clasps, as 'twas wont, my finger, and holds it:
  But the grasp is the clasp of Death, heartbreaking and stiff;
    Yet feels to my hand as if
'Twas still thy will, thy pleasure and trust that enfolds it.

So I lay thee there, thy sunken eyelids closing, –
  Go lie thou there in thy coffin, thy last little bed! –
    Propping thy wise, sad head,
Thy firm, pale hands across thy chest disposing.

So quiet! doth the change content thee? – Death, whither hath
      he taken thee?
  To a world, do I think, that rights the disaster of this?
    The vision of which I miss,
Who weep for the body, and wish but to warm thee and awaken
      thee?

Ah! little at best can all our hopes avail us
  To lift this sorrow, or cheer us, when in the dark,
      Unwilling, alone we embark,
And the things we have seen and have known and have heard of,
      fail us.

# GERARD MANLEY HOPKINS
## 1844–89

280              Heaven-Haven

*(A nun takes the veil )*

I have desired to go
    Where springs not fail,
To fields where flies no sharp and sided hail
    And a few lilies blow.

And I have asked to be
    Where no storms come,
Where the green swell is in the havens dumb,
    And out of the swing of the sea.

281              Spring and Fall

*To a young child*

Margaret, are you gríeving
Over Goldengrove unleaving?
Leáves, líke the things of man, you
With your fresh thoughts care for, can you?
Ah! as the heart grows older
It will come to such sights colder
By and by, nor spare a sigh
Though worlds of wanwood leafmeal lie;
And yet you *will* weep and know why.
Now no matter, child, the name:
Sorrow's springs are the same.

Nor mouth had, no nor mind, expressed
What héart héard of, ghóst guéssed:
It is the blight man was born for,
It is Margaret you mourn for.


282                    The Windhover

                   *To Christ our Lord*

I caught this morning morning's minion, king-
    dom of daylight's dauphin, dapple-dáwn-drawn Falcon, in his riding
    Of the rólling level úndernéath him steady áir, and stríding
High there, how he rung upon the rein of a wimpling wing
In his ecstacy! then off, off forth on swing,
    As a skate's heel sweeps smooth on a bow-bend: the hurl and gliding
    Rebuffed the big wind. My heart in hiding
Stirred for a bird, – the achieve of, the mastery of the thing!

Brute beauty and valour and act, oh, air, pride, plume, here
    Buckle! A N D the fire that breaks from thee then, a billion
Times told lovelier, more dangerous, O my chevalier!

    No wonder of it: shéer plód makes plóugh down síllion
Shine, and blue-bleak embers, ah my dear,
    Fall, gáll themsélves, and gásh góld-vermilion.


283                    Pied Beauty

    Glory be to God for dappled things –
        For skies of couple-colour as a brinded cow;
            For rose-moles all in stipple upon trout that swim;
    Fresh-firecoal chestnut-falls; finches' wings;
        Landscape plotted and pieced – fold, fallow, and plough;
            And áll trades, their gear and tackle and trim.

All things counter, original, spáre, strange;
　Whatever is fickle, frecklèd (who knows how?)
　　With swíft, slów; sweet, sóur; adázzle, dím;
　He fathers-forth whose beauty is pást change:
　　　　　　　Práise hím.


284　　　　　　Spelt from Sibyl's Leaves

Earnest, earthless, equal, attuneable, | vaulty, voluminous, . . .
　Stupendous
Evening strains to be tíme's vást, | womb-of-all, home-of-all, hearse-
　of-all night.
Her fond yellow hornlight wound to the west, | her wild hollow
　hoarlight hung to the height
Waste; her earliest stars, earl-stars, | stárs principal, overbend us,
Fíre-féaturing heaven. For earth | her being has unbound, her dapple is
　at an end, as -
Tray or aswarm, all throughther, in throngs; | self in self steepèd and
　páshed – qúite
Disremembering, dísmémbering | áll now. Heart, you round me right
With: óur évening is over us; óur night | whélms, whélms, ánd will end
　us.
Only the beak-leaved boughs dragonish | damask the tool-smooth
　bleak light; black,
Ever so black on it. Óur tale, o óur oracle! | lét life, wáned, ah lét life
　wind
Off hér once skéined stained véined varíety | upon, áll on twó spools;
　párt, pen, páck
Now her áll in twó flocks, twó folds, – black, white; | right, wrong;
　reckon but, reck but, mind
But thése two; wáre of a wórld where bút these | twó tell, each off the
　óther; of a rack
Where, selfwrung, selfstrung, sheathe- and shelterless, | thóughts
　agaínst thoughts ín groans grínd.

285    As kingfishers catch fire, dragonflies dráw fláme;
        As tumbled over rim in roundy wells
        Stones ring; like each tucked string tells, each hung bell's
    Bow swung finds tongue to fling out broad its name;
    Each mortal thing does one thing and the same:
        Deals out that being indoors each one dwells;
        Selves – goes itself; *myself* it speaks and spells,
    Crying *Whát I do is me: for that I came.*

    Í say móre: the just man justices;
        Kéeps gráce: thát keeps all his goings graces;
    Acts in God's eye what in God's eye he is –
        Chríst – for Christ plays in ten thousand places,
    Lovely in limbs, and lovely in eyes not his
        To the Father through the features of men's faces.

286    ## That Nature Is a Heraclitean Fire and of the Comfort of the Resurrection

Cloud-puffball, torn tufts, tossed pillows | flaunt forth, then chevy on
    an air –
Built thoroughfare: heaven-roysterers, in gay-gangs | they throng; they
    glitter in marches.
Down roughcast, down dazzling whitewash, | wherever an elm arches,
Shivelights and shadowtackle in long | lashes lace, lance, and pair.
Delightfully the bright wind boisterous | ropes, wrestles, beats earth
    bare
Of yestertempest's creases; in pool and rut peel parches
Squandering ooze to squeezed | dough, crust, dust; stanches, starches
Squadroned masks and manmarks | treadmire toil there
Footfretted in it. Million-fuelèd, | nature's bonfire burns on.
But quench her bonniest, dearest | to her, her clearest-selvèd spark
Man, how fast his firedint, | his mark on mind, is gone!
Both are in an unfathomable, all is in an enormous dark
Drowned. O pity and indig | nation! Manshape, that shone

Sheer off, disseveral, a star, | death blots black out; nor mark
　　　　　Is any of him at all so stark
But vastness blurs and time | beats level. Enough! The resurrection,
A heart's-clarion! Away grief's gasping, | joyless days, dejection.
　　　　　Across my foundering deck shone
A beacon, an eternal beam. | Flesh fade, and mortal trash
Fall to the residuary worm; | world's wildfire, leave but ash:
　　　　　In a flash, at a trumpet crash,
I am all at once what Christ is, | since he was what I am, and
This jack, joke, poor potsherd, | patch, matchwood, immortal diamond,
　　　　　Is immortal diamond.

287　No worst, there is none. Pitched past pitch of grief,
　　　More pangs will, schooled at forepangs, wilder wring.
　　　Comforter, where, where is your comforting?
　　　Mary, mother of us, where is your relief?
　　　My cries heave, herds-long; huddle in a main, a chief
　　　Woe, world-sorrow; on an age-old anvil wince and sing –
　　　Then lull, then leave off. Fury had shrieked 'No ling-
　　　ering ! Let me be fell: force I must be brief'.

　　　O the mind, mind has mountains; cliffs of fall
　　　Frightful, sheer, no-man-fathomed. Hold them cheap
　　　May who ne'er hung there. Nor does long our small
　　　Durance deal with that steep or deep. Here! creep,
　　　Wretch, under a comfort serves in a whirlwind: all
　　　Life death does end and each day dies with sleep.

288    Repeat that, repeat,
      Cuckoo, bird, and open ear wells, heart-springs, delightfully
          sweet,
      With a ballad, with a ballad, a rebound
      Off trundled timber and scoops of the hillside ground, hollow
          hollow hollow ground:
      The whole landscape flushes on a sudden at a sound.


289      It was a hard thing to undo this knot.
        The rainbow shines, but only in the thought
        Of him that looks. Yet not in that alone,
        For who makes rainbows by invention?
        And many standing round a waterfall
        See one bow each, yet not the same to all,
        But each a hand's breadth further than the next.
        The sun on falling waters writes the text
        Which yet is in the eye or in the thought.
        It was a hard thing to undo this knot.

# CAROLINE, LADY LINDSAY
### 1844–1912

290          Of a Bird-Cage

*One of those made in Germany by convicts*
*sentenced to penal servitude*

A tiny prison built by prisoned hands
To coop some bright-wing'd thing; a mimic cell,
Wrought amid sighs by one who knew full well
The smart and pressure of enforcèd bands,
When high-soul'd courage failed him to assuage
The close-laid torture of a life-locked cage.

Perchance he wept his own deep grief and pain.
Alas, each day the sun rose high to set
In clouds of golden hope! And yet, and yet,
Time mattered naught. Him freedom called in vain,
As in the future she might beckon it –
That bird now free – who captive here should sit.

Thus with vague sympathy was each space barr'd,
Yet none less sure. Here shall the creature eat,
Here drink, here restless perch in cold or heat,
Setting to melody the sentence hard
Fate spells the words of. Plane the cramping floor,
Bend down the latch, and firmly bolt the door!

# ALEXANDER ANDERSON
## 1845–1909

291          Railway Dreamings

I work upon the line to-day,
    The rails on either side of me,
But all my fancies wing their way,
    Like swallows flying out to sea.

And ever as they speed, I dream
    Of all the coming thousand things
That time will herald with a beam
    Of light from off his windless wings:

What changes in the great to Be
    Evolving broad, and far, and grand,
What faiths by which our kind shall see
    That spinning creeds is spinning sand:

What worlds we dare not dream of now,
    When Science with her eagle ken
Holds a white hand above her brow
    To bring them nearer unto men:

When all the canker and the pride
    Shall sink, and all the good in store
Will work and toil with us, and glide
    Like Christ, among the lowly poor:

When war, a red and sulky hell
    Upbursting through the green of earth,
Shall sink for ever, but to dwell
    In chaos where it first had birth:

When all the lower man is sunk,
   To leave him as of old again,
Ere that one taint had made him drunk
   With the wild wine that devils drain:

What songs whose melody shall start
   The higher music pure and free,
In poets hymning strong of heart
   The labour Epics that will be.

Then the great brotherhood of man
   Will sing its universal psalm,
And Peace from paradise again
   Come smiling underneath the palm.

Ay, speed the time when, strong of breath
   And heart that not a fear can quail,
We keep to all the higher faith
   As the wild engine keeps the rail:

When, brain and heart no longer twain,
   We work – God's sky above us blue –
'Stand clear, man, for that Pullman train,
   Not twenty lengths of rail from you!'

I leap aside, the train roars past,
   And all my fancies, worn and sick,
Come slowly back, to die at last
   In the sharp raspings of the pick.

# L. S. BEVINGTON

1845–95

'Egoisme à Deux'

When the great universe hung nebulous
   Betwixt the unprevented and the need,
Was it foreseen that you and I should be? –
      Was it decreed?

While time leaned onward through eternities,
   Unrippled by a breath and undistraught,
Lay there at leisure Will that we should breathe? –
      Waited a Thought?

When the warm swirl of chaos-elements
   Fashioned the chance that woke to sentient strife,
Did there a Longing seek, and hasten on
      Our mutual life?

That flux of many accidents but now
   That brought you near and linked your hand in mine, –
That fused our souls in love's most final faith, –
      Was it divine?

293                    One More Bruised Heart!

One more bruised heart laid bare! one victim more!
   One more wail heard! Oh, is there never end
   Of all these passionate agonies, that rend
Young hopes to tatters through enslavements sore?
So long, pale child, your patient spirit bore
   Its wrong in secret, ere you sought a friend;
   And yet, what love of mine can ever mend
Again for you the veil your tyrant tore?

Oh, there are woes too bitter to be shown!
   Oh, there are tears too burning to be seen!
   Yet purest sympathy, select and clean,
May feel the agony its very own.
Sweet slave-child, whom your voiceless griefs oppress,
I cannot cure; I may in part express.

# WILLIAM CANTON

## 1845–1926

294 The Haunted Bridge

With high-pitched arch, low parapet,
　　And narrow thoroughfare, it stands
As strong as when the mortar set
　　Beneath the Roman mason's hands.

An ancient ivy grips its walls,
　　Tall grasses tuft its coping-stones;
Beneath, through citron shadow, falls
　　The stream in drowsy undertones.

No road leads hence. The stonechat flits
　　Along green fallow grey with stone;
But here a dark-eyed urchin sits,
　　To whom the Painted Men were known.

Hush! do not move, but only look.
　　When sunny days are long and fine
This Roman truant baits a hook,
　　Drops o'er the keystone here a line,

And, dangling sandalled feet, looks down
　　To see the swift trout dart and gleam –
Or scarcely see them, hanging brown
　　With heads against the clear brown stream.

295           The Crow

With rakish eye and plenished crop,
    Oblivious of the farmer's gun,
Upon the naked ash-tree top
    The Crow sits basking in the sun.

An old ungodly rogue, I wot!
    For, perched in black against the blue,
His feathers, torn with beak and shot,
    Let woful glints of April through.

The year's new grass, and, golden-eyed,
    The daisies sparkle underneath,
And chestnut trees on either side
    Have opened every ruddy sheath.

But doubtful still of frost and snow,
    The ash alone stands stark and bare,
And on its topmost twig the Crow
    Takes the glad morning's sun and air.

# EUGENE LEE-HAMILTON
## 1845–1907

A Snails' Derby

Once, in this Tuscan garden, Noon's huge ball
   So slowly crossed the sky above my head,
   As I lay idle on my dull wheeled bed,
That, sick of Day's inexorable crawl,

I set some snails a-racing on the wall –
   With their striped shells upon their backs, instead
   Of motley jockeys – black, white, yellow, red;
And watched them till the twilight's tardy fall.

And such my life, as years go one by one:
   A garden where I lie beyond the flowers,
And where the snails outrace the creeping sun.

For me there are no pinions to the hours;
   Compared with them, the snails like racers run:
Wait but Death's night; and, lo, the great ball lowers.

# 'MICHAEL FIELD'

## KATHERINE HARRIS BRADLEY, 1846–1914
### *and* EDITH EMMA COOPER, 1862–1913

297         L'Indifférent

WATTEAU

*The Louvre*

He dances on a toe
As light as Mercury's:
*Sweet herald, give thy message!* No,
He dances on; the world is his,
The sunshine and his wingy hat;
    His eyes are round
    Beneath the brim:
To merely dance where he is found
    Is fate to him
And he was born for that.

He dances in a cloak
Of vermeil and of blue:
*Gay youngster, underneath the oak,*
*Come, laugh and love!* In vain we woo;
He is a human butterfly; –
    No soul, no kiss,
    No glance nor joy!
Though old enough for manhood's bliss,
    He is a boy,
Who dances and must die.

298
A curling thread
Uncoils overhead –
From the chimney-stack
A replenished track
Of vapour, in haste
To increase and waste,
Growing wings as it grows
Of amber and rose,
With an upward flight
To the frosty light.
Puff on puff
Of the soft breath-stuff,
Till the cloudy fleece
Thickens its feathers; its rounds increase,
Mingle and widen, and lose the line
Of their dull confine,
Thinning mote by mote
As they upward float,
And by-and-bye
Are effaced on the sky.


299                     Cyclamens

They are terribly white:
There is snow on the ground,
And a moon on the snow at night;
The sky is cut by the winter light;
Yet I, who have all these things in ken,
Am struck to the heart by the chiselled white
Of this handful of cyclamen.

300                              Irises

        In a vase of gold
        And scarlet, how cold
      The flicker of wrinkled grays
In this iris-sheaf! My eyes fill with wonder
At the tossed, moist light, at the withered scales under
      And among the uncertain sprays.

        The wavings of white
        On the cloudy light,
      And the finger-marks of pearl;
The facets of crystal, the golden feather,
The way that the petals fold over together,
      The way that the buds unfurl!


301          It was deep April, and the morn
       Shakspere was born;
  The world was on us, pressing sore;
  My Love and I took hands and swore,
     Against the world, to be
  Poets and lovers evermore,
  To laugh and dream on Lethe's shore,
  To sing to Charon in his boat,
  Heartening the timid souls afloat;
  Of judgment never to take heed,
  But to those fast-locked souls to speed,
  Who never from Apollo fled,
  Who spent no hour among the dead;
     Continually
     With them to dwell,
  Indifferent to heaven and hell.

# JAMES LOGIE ROBERTSON
## 1846–1922

302         The White Winter – Hughie Snawed Up

> '*Jam satis terris nivis atque diræ*
> *Grandinis misit Pater.*'
> – *Car. i. 2.*

Man, but it's vexin'! There's the Law
For five months noo been white wi' snaw;
An', when we lookit for a thaw,
    An' lowser weather,
It's gaitherin' for anither fa',
    As black as ever!

It's no' alane that fother's dear,
Yowes stervin', an' the lambin' near,
An' Winter owre the Ochils drear
    Drivin' unstintit, –
But, Lordsake! what's come owre the year?
    An' what's ahint it?

Wha kens but what oor aixle tree
'S been slew'd aboot, or dung ajee,          *dashed aside*
An' aff thro' space awa' we flee
    In a daft orbit?
Whilk mak's the seasons, as we see,
    Be sair disturbit.

Wha kens but what we've seen the heel
O' Simmer in a last fareweel?
Nae mair green gowany braes to speel     *flowery hillsides*
                                              *to climb*

---

302. *Epigraph*: The opening lines of Horace, *Carmina* [Odes] I, 2: 'Enough already of
dire snow and hail has the Father [of the gods] sent upon the earth'

Wi' joyfu' crook,
Nor dip in Devon, whaur a wiel                    *pool*
    Invites to dook!

What aince has been may be aince mair,
An' aince – as learnèd clerks declare –
This planet's fortune was to fare,
    In ages auld,
Thro' regions o' the frigid air,
    Past kennin' cauld.

Nae doot but this was centuries gane,
When human cretur' there was nane,
An' this auld warld, her liefu' lane,          *rightful course*
    Bowl'd thro' the nicht,
Wi' tangles hingin' fra a mune                      *icicles*
    That was her licht.

An eldritch scene that licht display'd!
There lay the continents array'd,
Like corpses o' the lately dead,
    In a cauld sheet,
Wi' icebergs sittin' at their head
    An' at their feet!

What aince has been may happen twice, –
It's weel kenn'd *we* hae little ch'ice;
An' if it be the Age o' Ice
    Return'd aince mair –
Faith, tak' this present for a spice,
    It offers fair!

The snaw a' owre lies sax feet deep;
Ae half oor time we're howkin' sheep;              *hooking*
We haena haen a blanket sleep                   *(out of drifts)*
    Sin' the New Year;
An' here we're at oor hin'most neep,                *turnip*
    An' term-time near!

It's juist as bad wi' ither folk:
A shepherd's missin' wi' his flock;
An eagle's ravagin' the Knock;
　An' nearer hame,
A dearth o' whisky's at the Crook,
　An' aumries toom.  *store-cupboards*
*empty*

The gates are blockit up a' roun' 's,
Silent are a' the seas an' soun's,
An' at the very trons in toons,  *market-places*
　It's hoch deep lyin':  *in towns*
In fac', the Winter's broken boun's,
　There's nae denyin'.

It may be – for we're grown sae wice,
We're no' juist to be smoor'd like mice,  *smothered*
It may be that by some device
　We'll fricht the snaw,  *frighten off*
An' gie this threaten'd Age o' Ice
　The ca' awa'!

Some braw electrical machine
Amang the cluds may intervene,
Send licht an' heat, an' change the scene
　The warld throughoot;
An' burn oor skins, an' blind oor een,
　Wi't a', nae doot!

Come back, come back, oor ain auld sun,
Thy auld-appointed path to run;
An' a' the freits that were begun  *omens*
　To shore us ill  *threaten*
Shall, in the crackin' of a gun,
　Flee owre the hill.

Then, as of auld, when skies are clear,
An' springin' corn begins to breer,
Those joys your shepherd's heart shall cheer
　　That charm'd of yore;
An' life on Devon be as dear
　　As heretofore!


303　　　　　　A Back-Lying Farm

A back-lying farm but lately taken in;
　　Forlorn hill-slopes and grey, without a tree;
　　And at their base a waste of stony lea
Through which there creeps, too small to make a din,
Even where it slides over a rocky linn,
　　A stream, unvisited of bird or bee,
　　Its flowerless banks a bare sad sight to see.
All round, with ceaseless plaint, though spent and thin,
　　Like a lost child far-wandered from its home,
　　A querulous wind all day doth coldly roam.
Yet here, with sweet calm face, tending a cow,
　　Upon a rock a girl bareheaded sat,
Singing unheard, while with unlifted brow
　　She twined the long wan grasses in her hat.

# ALICE MEYNELL
## 1847–1922

The Modern Mother

Oh what a kiss
With filial passion overcharged is this!
    To this misgiving breast
This child runs, as a child ne'er ran to rest
Upon the light heart and the unoppressed.

Unhoped, unsought!
A little tenderness, this mother thought
    The utmost of her meed.
She looked for gratitude; content indeed
With thus much that her nine years' love had bought.

Nay, even with less.
This mother, giver of life, death, peace, distress,
    Desired ah! not so much
Thanks as forgiveness; and the passing touch
Expected, and the slight, the brief caress.

O filial light
Strong in these childish eyes, these new, these bright
    Intelligible stars! Their rays
Are near the constant earth, guides in the maze,
Natural, true, keen in this dusk of days.

305         A Dead Harvest

*In Kensington Gardens*

Along the graceless grass of town
They rake the rows of red and brown,
Dead leaves, unlike the rows of hay,
Delicate, neither gold nor grey,
Raked long ago and far away.

A narrow silence in the park;
Between the lights a narrow dark.
One street rolls on the north, and one,
Muffled, upon the south doth run.
Amid the mist the work is done.

A futile crop; – for it the fire
Smoulders, and, for a stack, a pyre.
So go the town's lives on the breeze,
Even as the sheddings of the trees;
Bosom nor barn is filled with these.


306                Parentage

*'When Augustus Cæsar legislated against the unmarried citizens of
Rome, he declared them to be, in some sort, slayers of the people.'*

Ah no, not these!
These, who were childless, are not they who gave
So many dead unto the journeying wave,
The helpless nurslings of the cradling seas;
Not they who doomed by infallible decrees
Unnumbered man to the innumerable grave.

But those who slay
Are fathers. Theirs are armies. Death is theirs,
The death of innocences and despairs;

The dying of the golden and the grey.
The sentence, when these speak it, has no Nay.
And she who slays is she who bears, who bears.

307               Renouncement

I must not think of thee; and, tired yet strong,
    I shun the thought that lurks in all delight –
    The thought of thee – and in the blue Heaven's height,
And in the sweetest passage of a song.

O just beyond the fairest thoughts that throng
    This breast, the thought of thee waits, hidden yet bright;
    But it must never, never come in sight;
I must stop short of thee the whole day long.

But when sleep comes to close each difficult day,
    When night gives pause to the long watch I keep,
        And all my bonds I needs must loose apart,

Must doff my will as raiment laid away, –
    With the first dream that comes with the first sleep
        I run, I run, I am gathered to thy heart.

308               Cradle-Song at Twilight

The child not yet is lulled to rest.
    Too young a nurse, the slender Night
So laxly holds him to her breast
    That throbs with flight.

He plays with her and will not sleep.
    For other playfellows she sighs;
An unmaternal fondness keep
    Her alien eyes.

# DIGBY MACKWORTH DOLBEN
## 1848–67

309              Sister Death

My sister Death! I pray thee come to me
  Of thy sweet charity,
And be my nurse but for a little while;
  I will indeed lie still,
And not detain thee long, when once is spread,
  Beneath the yew, my bed:
I will not ask for lilies or for roses;
  But when the evening closes,
Just take from any brook a single knot
  Of pale Forget-me-not,
And lay them in my hand, until I wake,
  For his dear sake;
(For should he ever pass and by me stand,
  He yet might understand – )
Then heal the passion and the fever
  With one cool kiss, for ever.

# W. E. HENLEY
## 1849–1903

## *FROM* IN HOSPITAL

310                               Waiting

A square, squat room (a cellar on promotion),
   Drab to the soul, drab to the very daylight,
   Plasters astray in unnatural-looking tinware;
   Scissors and lint and apothecary's jars.

Here, on a bench a skeleton would writhe from,
   Angry and sore, I wait to be admitted:
   Wait till my heart is lead upon my stomach,
   While at their ease two dressers do their chores.

One has a probe – it feels to me a crowbar.
   A small boy sniffs and shudders after bluestone.
   A poor old tramp explains his poor old ulcers.
   Life is (I think) a blunder and a shame.


311                               Interior

   The gaunt brown walls
Look infinite in their decent meanness.
There is nothing of home in the noisy kettle,
   The fulsome fire.

   The atmosphere
Suggests the trail of a ghostly druggist.
Dressings and lint on the long, lean table –
   Whom are they for?

The patients yawn,
Or lie as in training for shroud and coffin.
A nurse in the corridor scolds and wrangles.
    It's grim and strange.

Far footfalls clank.
The bad burn waits with his head unbandaged.
My neighbour chokes in the clutch of chloral ...
    O, a gruesome world!

312                             Music

Down the quiet eve,
Thro' my window with the sunset
Pipes to me a distant organ
Foolish ditties;

And, as when you change
Pictures in a magic lantern,
Books, beds, bottles, floor, and ceiling
Fade and vanish,

And I 'm well once more ...
August flares adust and torrid,
But my heart is full of April
Sap and sweetness.

In the quiet eve
I am loitering, longing, dreaming ...
Dreaming, and a distant organ
Pipes me ditties.

I can see the shop,
I can smell the sprinkled pavement,
Where she serves – her chestnut chignon
Thrills my senses!

O, the sight and scent,
Wistful eve and perfumed pavement!
In the distance pipes an organ ...
The sensation

Comes to me anew,
And my spirit for a moment
Thro' the music breathes the blessèd
Airs of London.

313            Discharged

Carry me out
Into the wind and the sunshine,
Into the beautiful world.

O, the wonder, the spell of the streets!
The stature and strength of the horses,
The rustle and echo of footfalls,
The flat roar and rattle of wheels!
A swift tram floats huge on us ...
It's a dream?
The smell of the mud in my nostrils
Blows brave – like a breath of the sea!

As of old,
Ambulant, undulant drapery,
Vaguely and strangely provocative,
Flutters and beckons. O, yonder –
Is it? – the gleam of a stocking!
Sudden, a spire
Wedged in the mist! O, the houses,
The long lines of lofty, grey houses,
Cross-hatched with shadow and light!
These are the streets ...
Each is an avenue leading
Whither I will!

Free ...!
Dizzy, hysterical, faint,
I sit, and the carriage rolls on with me
Into the wonderful world.

*The Old Infirmary. Edinburgh, 1873–75*

---

314                     Back-View

                        *To D. F.*

I watched you saunter down the sand:
Serene and large, the golden weather
Flowed radiant round your peacock feather,
And glistered from your jewelled hand.
Your tawny hair, turned strand on strand
And bound with blue ribands together,
Streaked the rough tartan, green like heather,
That round your lissome shoulder spanned.
Your grace was quick my sense to seize:
The quaint looped hat, the twisted tresses,
The close-drawn scarf, and under these
The flowing, flapping draperies –
My thought an outline still caresses,
Enchanting, comic, Japanese!

315                     To W. R.

Madam Life's a piece in bloom
    Death goes dogging everywhere:
She's the tenant of the room,
    He's the ruffian on the stair.

You shall see her as a friend,
   You shall bilk him once and twice;
But he'll trap you in the end,
   And he'll stick you for her price.

With his kneebones at your chest,
   And his knuckles in your throat,
You would reason – plead – protest!
   Clutching at her petticoat;

But she's heard it all before,
   Well she knows you've had your fun,
Gingerly she gains the door,
   And your little job is done.

316        On the way to Kew,
           By the river old and gray,
           Where in the Long Ago
           We laughed and loitered so,
           I met a ghost to-day,
           A ghost that told of you –
           A ghost of low replies
           And sweet, inscrutable eyes
           Coming up from Richmond
           As you used to do.

           By the river old and gray,
           The enchanted Long Ago
           Murmured and smiled anew.
           On the way to Kew,
           March had the laugh of May,
           The bare boughs looked aglow,
           And old, immortal words
           Sang in my breast like birds,
           Coming up from Richmond
           As I used with you.

With the life of Long Ago
Lived my thought of you.
By the river old and gray
Flowing his appointed way
As I watched I knew
What is so good to know –
Not in vain, not in vain,
Shall I look for you again
Coming up from Richmond
On the way to Kew.

# WILLIAM LARMINIE

1849–1900

317                    The Nameless Doon

Who were the builders? Question not the silence
That settles on the lake for evermore,
Save when the sea-bird screams and to the islands
The echo answers from the steep-cliffed shore.
O half-remaining ruin, in the lore
Of human life a gap shall all deplore
Beholding thee; since thou art like the dead
Found slain, no token to reveal the why,
The name, the story. Some one murderèd
We know, we guess; and gazing upon thee,
And, filled by thy long silence of reply,
We guess some garnered sheaf of tragedy; –
Of tribe or nation slain so utterly
That even their ghosts are dead, and on their grave
Springeth no bloom of legend in its wildness;
And age by age weak washing round the islands
No faintest sigh of story lisps the wave.

# PHILIP BOURKE MARSTON
## 1850–87

318                          Speechless

### UPON THE MARRIAGE OF TWO DEAF
### AND DUMB PERSONS

Their lips upon each other's lips are laid;
　　Strong moans of joy, wild laughter, and short cries
　　Seem uttered in the passion of their eyes.
He sees her body fair, and fallen head,
And she the face whereon her soul is fed;
　　And by the way her white breasts sink and rise,
　　He knows she must be shaken by sweet sighs;
Though all delight of sound for them be dead.

They dance a strange, weird measure, who know not
　　The tune to which their dancing feet are led;
Their breath in kissing is made doubly hot
　　With flame of pent-up speech; strange light is shed
　　　About their spirits, as they mix and meet
　　　In passion-lighted silence, 'tranced and sweet.


319                          Grief's Aspects

Grief does not come alike to all, I know.
　　To some, grief cometh like an armèd man,
　　Crying, 'Arise, and strive with me who can!'
And some are brought to heavenly peace through woe,
And watch a new life from the old life grow;
　　And some there be who strive beneath the ban,
　　And, having struggled hotly for a span,
Tread on the fallen body of their foe.

My grief has taken hold of me, and led
   My feet to lands of any spring unknown.
There has he bound me in strong chains, and said,
   'Behold, we are forevermore alone!
Drink from my hand thy wine, and eat my bread
   At last, I have thee solely for my own.'

320              After

    A little time for laughter,
      A little time to sing,
      A little time to kiss and cling,
    And no more kissing after.

    A little while for scheming
      Love's unperfected schemes;
      A little time for golden dreams,
    Then no more any dreaming.

    A little while 't was given
      To me to have thy love;
      Now, like a ghost, alone I move
    About a ruined heaven.

    A little time for speaking,
      Things sweet to say and hear;
      A time to seek, and find thee near,
    Then no more any seeking.

    A little time for saying
      Words the heart breaks to say;
      A short, sharp time wherein to pray,
    Then no more need for praying;

But long, long years to weep in,
  And comprehend the whole
  Great grief that desolates the soul;
And eternity to sleep in.

# ROBERT LOUIS STEVENSON
## 1850–94

The Light-Keeper

### I

The brilliant kernel of the night,
The flaming lightroom circles me:
I sit within a blaze of light
Held high above the dusky sea.
Far off the surf doth break and roar
Along bleak miles of moonlit shore,
Where through the tides the tumbling wave
Falls in an avalanche of foam
And drives its churnèd waters home
Up many an undercliff and cave.

The clear bell chimes: the clockworks strain:
The turning lenses flash and pass,
Frame turning within glittering frame
With frosty gleam of moving glass:
Unseen by me, each dusky hour
The sea-waves welter up the tower
Or in the ebb subside again;
And ever and anon all night,
Drawn from afar by charm of light,
A sea-bird beats against the pane.

And lastly when dawn ends the night
And belts the semi-orb of sea,
The tall, pale pharos in the light
Looks white and spectral as may be.
The early ebb is out: the green
Straight belt of seaweed now is seen,

That round the basement of the tower
Marks out the interspace of tide;
And watching men are heavy-eyed,
And sleepless lips are dry and sour.

The night is over like a dream:
The sea-birds cry and dip themselves;
And in the early sunlight, steam
The newly-bared and dripping shelves,
Around whose verge the glassy wave
With lisping wash is heard to lave;
While, on the white tower lifted high,
With yellow light in faded glass
The circling lenses flash and pass
And sickly shine against the sky.

## II

As the steady lenses circle
With a frosty gleam of glass;
And the clear bell chimes,
And the oil brims over the lip of the burner,
Quiet and still at his desk,
The lonely Light-Keeper
Holds his vigil.

Lured from afar,
The bewildered seagull beats
Dully against the lantern;
Yet he stirs not, lifts not his head
From the desk where he reads,
Lifts not his eyes to see
The chill blind circle of night
Watching him through the panes.
This is his country's guardian,
The outmost sentry of peace.
This is the man,
Who gives up all that is lovely in living
For the means to live.

Poetry cunningly gilds
The life of the Light-Keeper,
Held on high in the blackness
In the burning kernel of night:
The seaman sees and blesses him;
The Poet, deep in a sonnet,
Numbers his inky fingers
Fitly to praise him;
Only we behold him,
Sitting, patient and stolid,
Martyr to a salary.

322       Love – what is love? A great and aching heart;
Wrung hands; and silence; and a long despair.
Life – what is life? Upon a moorland bare
To see love coming and see love depart.

## *FROM* A CHILD'S GARDEN OF VERSES

323                Bed in Summer

In winter I get up at night
And dress by yellow candle-light.
In summer, quite the other way,
I have to go to bed by day.

I have to go to bed and see
The birds still hopping on the tree,
Or hear the grown-up people's feet
Still going past me in the street.

And does it not seem hard to you,
When all the sky is clear and blue,
And I should like so much to play
To have to go to bed by day?

324                    At the Seaside

When I was down beside the sea
A wooden spade they gave to me
    To dig the sandy shore.
My holes were empty like a cup,
In every hole the sea came up,
    Till it could come no more.

325             Whole Duty of Children

A child should always say what's true
And speak when he is spoken to,
And behave mannerly at table:
At least as far as he is able.

326                        Rain

The rain is raining all around,
    It falls on field and tree,
It rains on the umbrellas here,
    And on the ships at sea.

327 ## Singing

Of speckled eggs the birdie sings
  And nests among the trees;
The sailor sings of ropes and things
  In ships upon the seas.

The children sing in far Japan,
  The children sing in Spain;
The organ with the organ man
  Is singing in the rain.

328 ## The Land of Nod

From breakfast on through all the day
At home among my friends I stay;
But every night I go abroad
Afar into the Land of Nod.

All by myself I have to go,
With none to tell me what to do –
All alone beside the streams
And up the mountain-sides of dreams.

The strangest things are there for me,
Both things to eat and things to see,
And many frightening sights abroad
Till morning in the Land of Nod.

Try as I like to find the way,
I never can get back by day,
Nor can remember plain and clear
The curious music that I hear.

# 'CAERLEON'

*fl.* 1876–?

329     Aeschylus Homer and Shakespeare, souls
        Vast, sublime –
    Apennine Alp and Andes, covered
        With eternal rime –

    Inland waters and waters at sea –
        Grass of the field –
    Vain to compass you, vain to number,
        The soul must yield!

    Ye press, overcome, and destroy:
        All thoughts fly:
    I am crushed, I breathe not, live not,
        I that was I.

# F. B. MONEY-COUTTS

## 1852–1923

330                    The Commonest Lot

The beam that drifts about the sea,
Nosed by the dog-fish, slimed by sea-snails, draws
Into itself through seams and flaws
    The ocean imperceptibly.

Quick currents sift it through and through;
With jelly creatures feeding on its sides;
The sea-flower round it glooms and slides
    With languid motion, to and fro.

The wave within weighs more and more
Down, till the burden over-balance it;
Down, till the flat-fish o'er it flit,
    The sand-worm burrow to its core.


## EPITAPHS


331                      A Fair Woman

In this green chest is laid away
    The fairest frock she ever wore;
It clothed her both by night and day,
    And none shall wear it evermore.

## 332                    An Infant

This sweet infant never knew
What a woman's lips can do!
Yet a woman's lips no less
Brought him to this loneliness.

# WILLIAM RENTON

### 1852–?[after 1905]

333                              The Foal

The mouse-brown foal that fain had fed
From off the green his mother crops
So quietly in her own place.
Craning in vain and bending, stops,
Intent upon his match with space,
And rises beaten by half a head.
And last he sets himself to slide
His spidery-slender limbs aside,
If so be now to reach the mead. –
He must stride
Ere he can feed.

334                            Peat Cutting

There are no shadows on this shaggy moor,
But breaks darker than shadow where the peat
Glooms unresisting from the level heath.
For while no rampart rises from the plain,
Dark fosses show; and slenderer crannies lurk,
Refrains of these dark steeps, and give the tone
To those dusk patches and the heather brown.
Blue-shirted in the midst one delver toils,
Or seems to toil, with that uncertain port
The toiler feigns luxuriously to wear
To one who watches in repose from far.
Women white-hooded trundle to and fro,
One coming and one going, soundless barrows,
Now empty and now laden with the clods
Yon delver seems to cut or seems to lift

Athwart the bank; and stow the sodden peats
In rank, beside the ranks of peats abake
That stand like bricks upon a brickfield ranged.
A cart hard by the road-way stretches prone:
And points to where his yokefellow afar –
So far he seems a part of yon far fell –
Grazes at will – the solitary bond
Between the silent toilers moving there
And all the busy life unheard below.
Nor he through them but they through him may breathe
As through a lung communion with their kind.


335            The Fork of the Road

An utter moorland, high, and wide, and flat;
A beaten roadway, branching out in grave distaste
And weather-beaten and defaced,
Pricking its ears along the solitary waste –
A signpost; pointing this way, pointing that.


336              Spring Floods

                (IN NORMANDY)

A power is in the floods awake,
Whose wind-swept waters shirk and cringe,
And rally, breaking to a fringe;
The river lost in its own lake;
The old year's crows' nests, and the pollards drowned,
Like creels adrift, a floating commonweal.
The mill is flooded to the wheel.
The farms are flooded, mound by mound;
Like rafts they seem to us (who pass and flee),
And tided out from land, and drifting down
To towers and a town –
A city by a sea.

# MAY PROBYN
## (*fl.* 1878–?)

337         A Mésalliance

(TRIOLET)

Is she mine, – and for life, –
    And drinks tea from her saucer!
She eats with her knife –
Is she mine – and for life?
When I asked her to wife
    All her answer was 'Lor', sir!'
Is she mine? and for life?
    And drinks tea from her saucer!

# OSCAR WILDE
## 1854–1900

338                    Les Ballons

Against these turbid turquoise skies
    The light and luminous balloons
    Dip and drift like satin moons,
Drift like silken butterflies;

Reel with every windy gust,
    Rise and reel like dancing girls,
    Float like strange transparent pearls,
Fall and float like silver dust.

Now to the low leaves they cling,
    Each with coy fantastic pose,
    Each a petal of a rose
Straining at a gossamer string.

Then to the tall trees they climb,
    Like thin globes of amethyst,
    Wandering opals keeping tryst
With the rubies of the lime.

339                  Symphony in Yellow

An omnibus across the bridge
    Crawls like a yellow butterfly,
    And, here and there, a passer-by
Shows like a little restless midge.

Big barges full of yellow hay
   Are moved against the shadowy wharf,
   And, like a yellow silken scarf,
The thick fog hangs along the quay.

The yellow leaves begin to fade
   And flutter from the Temple elms,
   And at my feet the pale green Thames
Lies like a rod of rippled jade.


340          The Harlot's House

We caught the tread of dancing feet,
We loitered down the moonlit street,
And stopped beneath the harlot's house.

Inside, above the din and fray,
We heard the loud musicians play
The 'Treues Liebes Herz' of Strauss.

Like strange mechanical grotesques,
Making fantastic arabesques,
The shadows raced across the blind.

We watched the ghostly dancers spin
To sound of horn and violin,
Like black leaves wheeling in the wind.

Like wire-pulled automatons,
Slim silhouetted skeletons
Went sidling through the slow quadrille.

They took each other by the hand,
And danced a stately saraband;
Their laughter echoed thin and shrill.

Sometimes a clockwork puppet pressed
A phantom lover to her breast,
Sometimes they seemed to try to sing.

Sometimes a horrible marionette
Came out, and smoked its cigarette
Upon the steps like a live thing.

Then, turning to my love, I said,
'The dead are dancing with the dead,
The dust is whirling with the dust.'

But she – she heard the violin,
And left my side, and entered in:
Love passed into the house of lust.

Then suddenly the tune went false,
The dancers wearied of the waltz,
The shadows ceased to wheel and whirl.

And down the long and silent street,
The dawn, with silver-sandalled feet,
Crept like a frightened girl.

# JAMES CHAPMAN WOODS

*fl.* 1879–1931

341                                Fate

High up above all cross and change,
   And war of wind and storm of sea,
In sunless space where no gods range,
   Or life is, dwell the sisters three.
High up above the highest star, –
   Above all suns and moons of time,
Whose hush no murmur mounts to mar,
   Whose height no tireless wing can climb, –
In a drear land, where light is lost
   In wreaths and folds of ashen cloud,
And lurid flame of torches tossed
   Flares blood-red through the leaden shroud, –
Where gaunt rocks gleam in depths of gloom
   And mountain walls shut in the dark,
Blackened with many a misty plume,
   Crowning the pine-trunks close and stark,
Sit three weird women, worn and grey,
   With faces whiter than the dead; –
Hard eyes that seem the same alway, –
   Cold eyes that never tears have shed;
And broad brows frozen in a frown,
   And vexed with counsel grave and wise
     Of love and death, desire and hate.
O cruel, sleepless lids, drop down; –
   Drop down and hide them, lest our eyes
     Freeze at the eyes of Fate!

\* \* \*

My love lifts wondering eyes: – 'What songs for June!'
  I should have laughed at Fate, –
A phantom whom some prank of the mad moon
  Sent from her ivory gate
To frighten fools! We women grow the men, –
  Must we grow poets too,
Or lose all lightning out of song? Say then
  If a girl's songs ring true!'

# JANE BARLOW

## 1857–1917

342          Honey-Harvest

Μη φθινοπωριζ ανεμων
χειμερια κατα πνοα δαμαλιζοι χρονον.

Setting of summer all golden and sun's setting
Glory kindle in a garden where flower-knots glow
Like a pane of jewelled stain from the lattice fallen low,
High that was holden in the wide west's fiery fretting.

Hummeth around it unceasing the land, hummeth
Loud with drone of the wheels that whir gathering rich gain,
Field by field bereft must yield, with each amber-beaded grain
Man's hoard increasing ere the wintry dearth-day cometh.

Guerdon of toil 'mid the blossoms, a rare guerdon,
Filmy wings quiver questing and murmurous make
Fragrant air round bud-lips fair, for the dew-pure nectar's sake
Hid in their bosoms, now the honey-bee's sweet burden.

Golden the granary's harvest, the hive's golden,
Rapt from troubling of storm-blast, from frost-blight's despair;
So be wise 'neath smiling skies, so, ere all thy world lie bare,
Store – else thou starvest – store memories dear and olden.

---

**342.** *Epigraph*: Pindar, *Pythian Odes* v 120–21: '[Let] not some wintry gust of autumn's winds destroy his days.' (I am grateful to Dr Adam Roberts for this reference and translation.)

# JOHN DAVIDSON

1857–1909

343                    Thirty Bob a Week

I couldn't touch a stop and turn a screw,
    And set the blooming world a-work for me,
Like such as cut their teeth – I hope, like you –
    On the handle of a skeleton gold key;
I cut mine on a leek, which I eat it every week:
    I'm a clerk at thirty bob as you can see.

But I don't allow it's luck and all a toss;
    There's no such thing as being starred and crossed;
It's just the power of some to be a boss,
    And the bally power of others to be bossed:
I face the music, sir; you bet I ain't a cur;
    Strike me lucky if I don't believe I'm lost!

For like a mole I journey in the dark,
    A-travelling along the underground
From my Pillar'd Halls and broad Suburbean Park,
    To come the daily dull official round;
And home again at night with my pipe all alight,
    A-scheming how to count ten bob a pound.

And it's often very cold and very wet,
    And my missis stitches towels for a hunks;
And the Pillar'd Halls is half of it to let –
    Three rooms about the size of travelling trunks.
And we cough, my wife and I, to dislocate a sigh,
    When the noisy little kids are in their bunks.

But you never hear her do a growl or whine,
    For she's made of flint and roses, very odd;
And I've got to cut my meaning rather fine,

Or I'd blubber, for I'm made of greens and sod:
So p'r'aps we are in Hell for all that I can tell,
   And lost and damn'd and served up hot to God.

I ain't blaspheming, Mr Silver-tongue;
   I'm saying things a bit beyond your art:
Of all the rummy starts you ever sprung,
   Thirty bob a week's the rummiest start!
With your science and your books and your the'ries about
      spooks,
   Did you ever hear of looking in your heart?

I didn't mean your pocket, Mr, no:
   I mean that having children and a wife,
With thirty bob on which to come and go,
   Isn't dancing to the tabor and the fife:
When it doesn't make you drink, by Heaven! it makes you
      think,
   And notice curious items about life.

I step into my heart and there I meet
   A god-almighty devil singing small,
Who would like to shout and whistle in the street,
   And squelch the passers flat against the wall;
If the whole world was a cake he had the power to take,
   He would take it, ask for more, and eat it all.

And I meet a sort of simpleton beside,
   The kind that life is always giving beans;
With thirty bob a week to keep a bride
   He fell in love and married in his teens:
At thirty bob he stuck; but he knows it isn't luck:
   He knows the seas are deeper than tureens.

And the god-almighty devil and the fool
   That meet me in the High Street on the strike,
When I walk about my heart a-gathering wool,

Are my good and evil angels if you like.
And both of them together in every kind of weather
    Ride me like a double-seated bike.

That's rough a bit and needs its meaning curled.
    But I have a high old hot un in my mind –
A most engrugious notion of the world,
    That leaves your lightning 'rithmetic behind:
I give it at a glance when I say 'There ain't no chance,
    Nor nothing of the lucky-lottery kind.'

And it's this way that I make it out to be:
    No fathers, mothers, countries, climates – none;
Not Adam was responsible for me,
    Nor society, nor systems, nary one:
A little sleeping seed, I woke – I did, indeed –
    A million years before the blooming sun.

I woke because I thought the time had come;
    Beyond my will there was no other cause;
And everywhere I found myself at home,
    Because I chose to be the thing I was;
And in whatever shape of mollusc or of ape
    I always went according to the laws.

I was the love that chose my mother out;
    I joined two lives and from the union burst;
My weakness and my strength without a doubt
    Are mine alone for ever from the first:
It's just the very same with a difference in the name
    As 'Thy will be done.' You say it if you durst!

They say it daily up and down the land
    As easy as you take a drink, it's true;
But the difficultest go to understand,
    And the difficultest job a man can do,
Is to come it brave and meek with thirty bob a week,
    And feel that that's the proper thing for you.

It's a naked child against a hungry wolf;
   It's playing bowls upon a splitting wreck;
It's walking on a string across a gulf
   With millstones fore-and-aft about your neck;
But the thing is daily done by many and many a one;
   And we fall, face forward, fighting, on the deck.

344            A Labourer's Wife

*Tune – Ta-ra-ra-boom-de-ay*

All the day I worked and played
When I was a little maid,
Soft and nimble as a mouse,
Living in my father's house.
If I lacked my liberty,
All my thoughts were free as free;
Though my hands were hacked all o'er,
Ah! my heart was never sore.

Oh! once I had my fling!
I romped at ging-go-ring;
I used to dance and sing,
And play at everything.
I never feared the light;
I shrank from no one's sight;
I saw the world was right;
I always slept at night.

What a simpleton was I
To go and marry on the sly!
Now I work and never play:
Three pale children all the day
Fight and whine; and Dick, my man,
Is drunk as often as he can.
Ah! my head and bones are sore,
And my heart is hacked all o'er.

Yet, once I had my fling;
I romped at ging-go-ring;
I used to dance and sing,
And play at everything.
Now I fear the light;
I shrink from every sight;
I see there's nothing right;
I hope to die to-night.


345                    New Year's Day

BASIL SANDY BRIAN

*Brian*
This trade that we ply with the pen,
Unworthy of heroes or men,
Assorts ever less with my humour:
Mere tongues in the raiment of rumour,
We review and report and invent:
In drivel our virtue is spent.

*Basil*
From the muted tread of the feet,
And the slackening wheels, I know
The air is hung with snow,
And carpeted the street.

*Brian*
Ambition, and passion, and power
Come out of the north and the west,
Every year, every day, every hour,
Into Fleet Street to fashion their best;
They would shape what is noble and wise;
They must live by a traffic in lies.

*Basil*

Sweet rivers of living blood
Poured into an ocean of mud.

*Brian*

Newspapers flap o'er the land,
And darken the face of the sky;
A covey of dragons, wide-vanned,
Circle-wise clanging, they fly.
No nightingale sings; overhead
The lark never mounts to the sun;
Beauty and truth are dead,
And the end of the world begun.

*Basil*

Far away in a valley of peace,
Swaddled in emerald,
The snow-happed primroses
Tarry till spring has called.

*Sandy*

And here where the Fleet once tripped
In its ditch to the drumlie Thames,
We journalists, haughty though hipped,
Are calling our calling names.

*Brian*

But you know, as I know, that our craft
Is the meanest in act and intention;
You know that the Time-spirit laughed
In his sleeve at the Dutchman's invention:
Old Coster of Haarlem, I mean,
Whose print was the first ever seen.

*Basil*

I can hear in that valley of mine,
Loud-voiced on a leafless spray,
How the robin sings, flushed with his holly wine,
Of the moonlight blossoms of May.

*Brian*

These dragons that hide the sun!
The serpents, flying and fiery,
That knotted a nation in one
Writhen mass; the scaley and wirey,
And flame-breathing terror the saint
Still manfully slays on our coins;
The reptile hedge-artists paint
On creaking tavern-signs;
Gargouille, famous in France
That entered Rouen to his sorrow;
The dragon, Petrarca's lance
Overthrew in defence of his Laura;
The sea-beast Perseus killed;
Proserpine's triple team;
Tarasque whose blood was spilled
In Rhone's empurpled stream;
For far-flying strength and ire
And venom might never withstand
The least of the flourishing quire
In Fleet Street stalled and the Strand.

*Basil*

Through the opening gate of the year
Sunbeams and snowdrops peer.

*Brian*

Fed by us here and groomed
In this pestilent reeking stye,
These dragons I say have doomed
Religion and poetry.

*Sandy*

They may doom till the moon forsakes
Her dark, star-daisied lawn;
They may doom till doomsday breaks
With angels to trumpet the dawn;
While love enchants the young,

And the old have sorrow and care,
No song shall be unsung,
Unprayed no prayer.

*Brian*
Leaving the dragons alone –
I say what the prophet says –
The tyrant on the throne
Is the morning and evening press.
In all the land his spies,
A little folk but strong,
A second plague of flies,
Buzz of the right and the wrong;
Swarm in our ears and our eyes –
News and scandal and lies.
Men stand upon the brink
Of a precipice every day;
A drop of printer's ink
Their poise may overweigh;
So they think what the papers think,
And do as the papers say.
Who reads the daily press,
His soul's lost here and now;
Who writes for it is less
Than the beast that tugs a plough.

*Basil*
Round happy household fires
I hear sweet voices sing;
And the lamb's-wool of our sires,
Spiced ale, is a draught for a king.

*Sandy*
Now, journalist, perpend.
You soil your bread and butter:
Shall guttersnipes pretend
To satirise the gutter?
Are parsons ever seen
To butt against the steeple?

Brian, I fear you've been
With very superior people.
We, the valour and brains of the age,
The brilliant, adventurous souls,
No longer in berserkir rage –

*Brian*
Spare us the berserkir rage!

*Sandy*
Not I; the phrase outrolls
As freshly to me this hour,
As when on my boyish sense
It struck like a trumpet-blare.
You may cringe and cower
To critical pretence;
If people will go bare
They may count on bloody backs;
Cold are the hearts that care
If a girl be blue-eyed or black-eyed;
Only to souls of hacks
Are phrases hackneyed. –
When the damsel had her bower,
And the lady kept her state,
The splendour and the power
That made adventure great,
Were not more strong and splendid
Than the subtle might we wield;
Though chivalry be ended,
There are champions in the field.
Nor are we warriors giftless:
Deep magic's in our stroke;
Ours are the shoes of swiftness:
And ours the darkling cloak;
We fear no golden charmer;
We dread no form of words;
We wear enchanted armour,
We wield enchanted swords.
To us the hour belongs;

Our daily victory is
O'er hydras, giant wrongs,
And dwarf iniquities.
We also may behold,
Before our boys are old,
When time shall have unfurled
His heavy-hanging mists,
How the future of the world
Was shaped by journalists.

*Basil*
Sing hey for the journalist!
He is your true soldado;
Both time and chance he'll lead a dance,
And find out Eldorado.

*Brian*
Sing hey for Eldorado!

*Basil*
A catch, a catch, we'll trowl!

*Brian*
Sing hey for Eldorado!

*Sandy*
And bring a mazer-bowl,
With ale a-frothing brimmed.

*Brian*
We may not rest without it.

*Sandy*
With dainty ribbons trimmed,
And love-birds carved about it.

*Basil*
With roasted apples scented
And spiced with cloves and mace.

*Brian*
Praise him who ale invented!

*Sandy*
In heaven he has a place!

*Basil*
Such a camarado
Heaven's hostel never missed!

*Brian*
Sing hey for Eldorado!

*Sandy*
Sing ho for the journalist!

*Basil*
We drink them and we sing them
In mighty humming ale.

*Brian*
May fate together bring them!

*Sandy*
Amen!

*Basil*
   Wass hael!

*Brian*
     Drinc hael!

# A. MARY F. ROBINSON
## 1857–1944

346                     Neurasthenia

I watch the happier people of the house
    Come in and out, and talk, and go their ways;
I sit and gaze at them; I cannot rouse
    My heavy mind to share their busy days.

I watch them glide, like skaters on a stream,
    Across the brilliant surface of the world.
But I am underneath: they do not dream
    How deep below the eddying flood is whirl'd.

They cannot come to me, nor I to them;
    But, if a mightier arm could reach and save,
Should I forget the tide I had to stem?
    Should I, like these, ignore the abysmal wave?

Yes! in the radiant air how could I know
How black it is, how fast it is, below?


347                     Twilight

When I was young the twilight seemed too long.

How often on the western window seat
    I leaned my book against the misty pane
    And spelled the last enchanting lines again,
The while my mother hummed an ancient song,
Or sighed a little and said: 'The hour is sweet!'
When I, rebellious, clamoured for the light.

But now I love the soft approach of night,
  And now with folded hands I sit and dream
  While all too fleet the hours of twilight seem;
And thus I know that I am growing old.

O granaries of Age! O manifold
And royal harvest of the common years!
There are in all thy treasure-house no ways
But lead by soft descent and gradual slope
To memories more exquisite than Hope.
Thine is the Iris born of olden tears,
And thrice more happy are the happy days
That live divinely in thy lingering rays.

So autumn roses bear a lovelier flower;
So in the emerald after-sunset hour
The orchard wall and trembling aspen trees
Appear an infinite Hesperides.
Ay, as at dusk we sit with folded hands,
Who knows, who cares in what enchanted lands
We wander while the undying memories throng?

When I was young the twilight seemed too long.

# CONSTANCE NADEN
## 1858–89

348              Christ, the Nazarene

The copyist group was gathered round
A time-worn fresco, world-renowned,
Whose central glory once had been
The face of Christ, the Nazarene.

And every copyist of the crowd
With his own soul that face endowed,
Gentle, severe, majestic, mean;
But which was Christ, the Nazarene?

Then one who watched them made complaint,
And marvelled, saying, 'Wherefore paint
Till ye be sure your eyes have seen
The face of Christ, the Nazarene?'

# EDITH NESBIT

1858–1924

349　　　　　　　　　On Dit

Cold is the wind – the flowers below,
　　Fearful of winter's hand, lie curled;
But Spring will come again you know,
　　And glorify the world.

Dark is the night – no stars or moon;
　　But at its blackest, night is done,
All after hastens to the noon,
　　The triumph of the sun.

And life is sad, and love is brief.
　　Be patient; there will be, they say,
New life, divine beyond belief,
　　Somehow, somewhere, some day.

# DOLLIE RADFORD
## 1858–1920

## From the Suburbs

It rushes home, our own express,
So cheerfully, no one would guess
    The weight it carries

Of tired husbands, back from town,
For each of whom, in festal gown,
    A fond wife tarries.

For each of whom a better half,
At even, serves the fatted calf,
    In strange disguises,

At anxious boards of all degree,
Down to the simple 'egg at tea,'
    Which love devises.

For whom all day, disconsolate,
Deserted villas have to wait,
    Detached and Semi –

Barred by their own affairs, which are
As hard to pass through as the far
    Famed Alpine Gemmi.

Sometimes as I at leisure roam,
Admiring my suburban home,
    I wonder sadly

If men will always come and go
In these vast numbers, to and fro,
    So fast and madly.

I muse on what the spell can be,
Which causes this activity:
   Who of our Sages

The potent charm has meted out
To tall and thin, to short and stout,
    Of varying ages.

I think, when other fancy flags,
The magic lies within the bags
    Which journey ever

In silent, black mysterious ways,
With punctual owners, all their days
    And fail them never.

In some perhaps sweet flowers lie,
Sweet flowers which shape a destiny
    To pain or pleasure,

Or lady's glove, or ringlet bright,
Or many another keepsake light,
   Which true knights treasure.

May be – may be – Romance is rife,
Despite our busy bustling life,
    And rules us gaily,

And shows no sign of weariness,
But in our very own express,
    Does travel daily.

# SIR WILLIAM WATSON

## 1858–1935

351            The Play of 'King Lear'

Here Love the slain with Love the slayer lies;
    Deep drown'd are both in the same sunless pool.
Up from its depths that mirror thundering skies
    Bubbles the wan mirth of the mirthless Fool.


352            Byron the Voluptuary

Too avid of earth's bliss, he was of those
    Whom Delight flies because they give her chase.
Only the odour of her wild hair blows
    Back in their faces hungering for her face.


353    The Metropolitan Underground Railway

Here were a goodly place wherein to die; –
    Grown latterly to sudden change averse,
All violent contrasts fain avoid would I
    On passing from this world into a worse.

# A. E. HOUSMAN

1859–1936

354

Loveliest of trees, the cherry now
Is hung with bloom along the bough,
And stands about the woodland ride
Wearing white for Eastertide.

Now, of my threescore years and ten,
Twenty will not come again,
And take from seventy springs a score,
It only leaves me fifty more.

And since to look at things in bloom
Fifty springs are little room,
About the woodlands I will go
To see the cherry hung with snow.

355

When I was one-and-twenty
    I heard a wise man say,
'Give crowns and pounds and guineas
    But not your heart away;
Give pearls away and rubies
    But keep your fancy free.'
But I was one-and-twenty,
    No use to talk to me.

When I was one-and-twenty
    I heard him say again,
'The heart out of the bosom
    Was never given in vain;

'Tis paid with sighs a plenty
   And sold for endless rue.'
And I am two-and-twenty,
   And oh, 'tis true, 'tis true.

356      It nods and curtseys and recovers
   When the wind blows above,
The nettle on the grave of lovers
   That hanged themselves for love.

The nettle nods, the wind blows over,
   The man, he does not move,
The lover of the grave, the lover
   That hanged himself for love.

357      Others, I am not the first,
Have willed more mischief than they durst:
If in the breathless night I too
Shiver now, 'tis nothing new.

More than I, if truth were told,
Have stood and sweated hot and cold,
And through their reins in ice and fire
Fear contended with desire.

Agued once like me were they,
But I like them shall win my way
Lastly to the bed of mould
Where there's neither heat nor cold.

But from my grave across my brow
Plays no wind of healing now,
And fire and ice within me fight
Beneath the suffocating night.


358

Into my heart an air that kills
From yon far country blows:
What are those blue remembered hills,
What spires, what farms are those?

This is the land of lost content,
I see it shining plain,
The happy highways where I went
And cannot come again.


359

Far in a western brookland
That bred me long ago
The poplars stand and tremble
By pools I used to know.

There, in the windless night-time,
The wanderer, marvelling why,
Halts on the bridge to hearken
How soft the poplars sigh.

He hears: long since forgotten
In fields where I was known,
Here I lie down in London
And turn to rest alone.

There, by the starlit fences,
    The wanderer halts and hears
My soul that lingers sighing
    About the glimmering weirs.


360               I hoed and trenched and weeded,
    And took the flowers to fair:
I brought them home unheeded;
    The hue was not the wear.

So up and down I sow them
    For lads like me to find,
When I shall lie below them,
    A dead man out of mind.

Some seed the birds devour,
    And some the season mars,
But here and there will flower
    The solitary stars,

And fields will yearly bear them
    As light-leaved spring comes on,
And luckless lads will wear them
    When I am dead and gone.

# J. K. STEPHEN
## 1859–92

361    Poetic Lamentation on the Insufficiency of
       Steam Locomotion in the Lake District

Bright Summer spreads his various hue
    O'er nestling vales and mountains steep,
Glad birds are singing in the blue,
    In joyous chorus bleat the sheep.
But men are walking to and fro,
    Are riding, driving far and near,
And nobody as yet can go
    By train to Buttermere.

The sunny lake, the mountain track,
    The leafy groves are little gain,
While Rydal's pleasant pathways lack
    The rattle of the passing train.
But oh! what poet would not sing
    That heaven-kissing rocky cone,
On whose steep side the railway king
    Shall set his smoky throne?

Helvellyn in those happy days
    With tunnelled base and grimy peak
Will mark the lamp's approaching rays,
    Will hear the whistle's warning shriek:
Will note the coming of the mails,
    And watch with unremitting stare
The dusky grove of iron rails
    Which leads to Euston-square.

Wake, England, wake! 'tis now the hour
    To sweep away this black disgrace –
The want of locomotive power

In so enjoyable a place.
Nature has done her part, and why
  Is mightier man in his to fail?
I want to hear the porters cry,
  'Change here for Ennerdale!'

Man! nature must be sought and found
  In lonely pools, on verdant banks;
Go, fight her on her chosen ground,
  Turn shapely Thirlmere into tanks:
Pursue her to her last retreats,
  And if perchance a garden plot
Is found among the London streets,
  Smoke, steam and spare it not.

Presumptuous nature! do not rate
  Unduly high thy humble lot,
Nor vainly strive to emulate
  The fame of Stephenson and Watt.
The beauties which thy lavish pride
  Has scattered through the smiling land
Are little worth till sanctified
  By man's completing hand.

362        England and America

*1  On a Rhine Steamer*

Republic of the West,
  Enlightened, free, sublime,
Unquestionably best
  Production of our time.

The telephone is thine,
  And thine the Pullman Car,
The caucus, the divine
  Intense electric star.

To thee we likewise owe
    The venerable names
Of Edgar Allan Poe,
    And Mr Henry James.

In short it's due to thee,
    Thou kind of Western star,
That we have come to be
    Precisely what we are.

But every now and then,
    It cannot be denied,
You breed a kind of men
    Who are not dignified,

Or courteous or refined,
    Benevolent or wise,
Or gifted with a mind
    Beyond the common size,

Or notable for tact,
    Agreeable to me,
Or anything, in fact,
    That people ought to be.

   2   *On a Parisian Boulevard*

Britannia rules the waves,
    As I have heard her say;
She frees whatever slaves
    She meets upon her way.

A teeming mother she
    Of Parliaments and Laws;
Majestic, mighty, free:
    Devoid of common flaws.

For her did Shakspere write
  His admirable plays:
For her did Nelson fight
  And Wolseley win his bays.

Her sturdy common sense
  Is based on solid grounds:
By saving numerous pence
  She spends effective pounds.

The Saxon and the Celt
  She equitably rules;
Her iron rod is felt
  By countless knaves and fools.

In fact, mankind at large,
  Black, yellow, white and red,
Is given to her in charge,
  And owns her as a head.

But every here and there –
  Deny it if you can –
She breeds a vacant stare
  Unworthy of a man:

A look of dull surprise;
  A nerveless idle hand:
An eye which never tries
  To threaten or command:

In short, a kind of man,
  If man indeed he be,
As worthy of our ban
  As any that we see:

Unspeakably obtuse,
  Abominably vain,
Of very little use,
  And execrably plain.

# FRANCIS THOMPSON
## 1859–1907

363            At Lord's

It is little I repair to the matches of the Southron folk,
Though my own red roses there may blow;
It is little I repair to the matches of the Southron folk,
    Though the red roses crest the caps, I know.
For the field is full of shades as I near the shadowy coast,
And a ghostly batsman plays to the bowling of a ghost,
And I look through my tears on a soundless-clapping host
    As the run-stealers flicker to and fro,
      To and fro: –
O my Hornby and my Barlow long ago!

364            The End of It

She did not love to love; but hated him
For making her to love, and so her whim
    From passion taught misprision to begin;
    And all this sin
Was because love to cast out had no skill
Self, which was regent still.
Her own self-will made void her own self's will.

365    ## Daphne

The river-god's daughter, – the sun-god sought her,
   Sleeping with never a zephyr by her.
Under the noon he made his prey sure,
Woofed in weeds of a woven azure,
   As down he shot in a whistle of fire.

Slid off, fair daughter! her vesturing water;
   Like a cloud from the scourge of the winds fled she:
With the breath in her hair of the keen Apollo,
And feet less fleet than the feet that follow,
   She throes in his arms to a laurel-tree.

Risen out of birth's waters the soul distraught errs,
   Nor whom nor whither she flieth knows she:
With the breath in her hair of the keen Apollo,
And fleet the beat of the feet that follow,
   She throes in his arms to a poet, woe's me!

You plucked the boughed verse the poet bears –
   It shudders and bleeds as it snaps from the tree.
A love-banning love, did the god but know it,
Which barks the man about with the poet,
   And muffles his heart of mortality!

Yet I translate – ward of song's gate! –
   Perchance all ill this mystery.
We both are struck with the self-same quarrel;
We grasp the maiden, and clasp the laurel –
   Do we weep or we laugh more, *Phoebe mi?*

'His own green lays, unwithering bays,
   Gird Keats' unwithering brow,' say ye?
O fools, that is only the empty crown!
The sacred head has laid it down
   With Hob, Dick, Marian, and Margery.

# ROSAMUND MARRIOTT WATSON
## 1860–1911

366                                    Aubade

The lights are out in the street, and a cool wind swings
Loose poplar plumes on the sky;
Deep in the gloom of the garden the first bird sings:
Curt, hurried steps go by
Loud in the hush of the dawn past the linden screen,
Lost in a jar and a rattle of wheels unseen
Beyond on the wide highway: —
Night lingers dusky and dim in the pear-tree boughs,
Hangs in the hollows of leaves, though the thrushes rouse,
And the glimmering lawn grows grey.
Yours, my heart knoweth, yours only, the jewelled gloom,
Splendours of opal and amber, the scent, the bloom,
Yours all, and your own demesne —
Scent of the dark, of the dawning, of leaves and dew;
Nothing that was but hath changed — 'tis a world made new —
A lost world risen again.

The lamps are out in the street, and the air grows bright —
Come — lest the miracle fade in the broad, bare light,
The new world wither away:
Clear is your voice in my heart, and you call me — whence?
Come — for I listen, I wait, — bid me rise, go hence,
Or ever the dawn turn day.

# MARY E. COLERIDGE
## 1861–1907

367            Winged Words

As darting swallows skim across a pool,
    Whose tranquil depths reflect a tranquil sky,
So, o'er the depths of silence, dark and cool,
    Our winged words dart playfully,
       And seldom break
      The quiet surface of the lake,
       As they flit by.


368            L'Oiseau Bleu

   The lake lay blue below the hill.
     O'er it, as I looked, there flew
Across the waters, cold and still,
     A bird whose wings were palest blue.

   The sky above was blue at last,
     The sky beneath me blue in blue.
A moment, ere the bird had passed,
     It caught his image as he flew.


369            Marriage

No more alone sleeping, no more alone waking,
    Thy dreams divided, thy prayers in twain;
Thy merry sisters to-night forsaking,
    Never shall we see thee, maiden, again.

Never shall we see thee, thine eyes glancing,
  Flashing with laughter and wild in glee,
Under the mistletoe kissing and dancing,
  Wantonly free.

There shall come a matron walking sedately,
  Low-voiced, gentle, wise in reply.
Tell me, O tell me, can I love her greatly?
  All for her sake must the maiden die!

370        Night is fallen within, without,
          Come, Love, soon!
        I am weary of my doubt.
        The golden fire of the Sun is out,
          The silver fire of the Moon.

        Love shall be
        A child in me
          When they are cinders gray,
        With the earth and with the sea,
        With the star that shines on thee,
          And the night and day.

371          The White Women*

Where dwell the lovely, wild white women folk,
  Mortal to man?
They never bowed their necks beneath the yoke,
They dwelt alone when the first morning broke
  And Time began.

* From a legend of Malory, told by Hugh Clifford [author's note].

Taller are they than man, and very fair,
    Their cheeks are pale,
At sight of them the tiger in his lair,
The falcon hanging in the azure air,
    The eagles quail.

The deadly shafts their nervous hands let fly
    Are stronger than our strongest – in their form
Larger, more beauteous, carved amazingly,
And when they fight, the wild white women cry
    The war-cry of the storm.

Their words are not as ours. If man might go
    Among the waves of Ocean when they break
And hear them – hear the language of the snow
Falling on torrents – he might also know
    The tongue they speak.

Pure are they as the light; they never sinned,
    But when the rays of the eternal fire
Kindle the West, their tresses they unbind
And fling their girdles to the Western wind,
    Swept by desire.

Lo, maidens to the maidens then are born,
    Strong children of the maidens and the breeze,
Dreams are not – in the glory of the morn,
Seen through the gates of ivory and horn –
    More fair than these.

And none may find their dwelling. In the shade
    Primeval of the forest oaks they hide.
One of our race, lost in an awful glade,
Saw with his human eyes a wild white maid,
    And gazing, died.

# MAY KENDALL

1861–c. 1931

## 372

Lay of the Trilobite

A mountain's giddy height I sought,
　　Because I could not find
Sufficient vague and mighty thought
　　To fill my mighty mind;
And as I wandered ill at ease,
　　There chanced upon my sight
A native of Silurian seas,
　　An ancient Trilobite.

So calm, so peacefully he lay,
　　I watched him even with tears:
I thought of Monads far away
　　In the forgotten years.
How wonderful it seemed and right,
　　The providential plan,
That he should be a Trilobite,
　　And I should be a Man!

And then, quite natural and free
　　Out of his rocky bed,
That Trilobite he spoke to me
　　And this is what he said:
'I don't know how the thing was done,
　　Although I cannot doubt it;'
But Huxley – he if anyone
　　Can tell you all about it;

'How all your faiths are ghosts and dreams,
　　How in the silent sea
Your ancestors were Monotremes –
　　Whatever these may be;

How you evolved your shining lights
  Of wisdom and perfection
From Jelly-fish and Trilobites
  By Natural Selection.

'You've Kant to make your brains go round,
  Hegel you have to clear them,
You've Mr. Browning to confound,
  And Mr. Punch to cheer them!
The native of an alien land
  You call a man and brother,
And greet with hymn-book in one hand
  And pistol in the other!

'You've Politics to make you fight
  As if you were possessed:
You've cannon and you've dynamite
  To give the nations rest:
The side that makes the loudest din
  Is surest to be right,
And oh, a pretty fix you're in!'
  Remarked the Trilobite.

'But gentle, stupid, free from woe
  I lived among my nation,
I didn't care – I didn't know
  That I was a Crustacean.*
I didn't grumble, didn't steal,
  I *never* took to rhyme:
Salt water was my frugal meal,
  And carbonate of lime.'

Reluctantly I turned away,
  No other word he said;
An ancient Trilobite, he lay

---

*He was not a Crustacean. He has since discovered that he was an Arachnid, or something similar. But he says it does not matter. He says they told him wrong once, and they may again (Kendall's note).

Within his rocky bed.
I did not answer him, for that
    Would have annoyed my pride:
I merely bowed, and raised my hat,
    But in my heart I cried: –

'I wish our brains were not so good,
    I wish our skulls were thicker,
I wish that Evolution could
    Have stopped a little quicker;
For oh, it was a happy plight,
    Of liberty and ease,
To be a simple Trilobite
    In the Silurian seas!'

# AMY LEVY

1861–89

## 373

## Epitaph

### (ON A COMMONPLACE PERSON
### WHO DIED IN BED)

This is the end of him, here he lies:
The dust in his throat, the worm in his eyes,
The mould in his mouth, the turf on his breast;
This is the end of him, this is best.
He will never lie on his couch awake,
Wide-eyed, tearless, till dim daybreak.
Never again will he smile and smile
When his heart is breaking all the while.
He will never stretch out his hands in vain
Groping and groping – never again.
Never ask for bread, get a stone instead,
Never pretend that the stone is bread.
Never sway and sway 'twixt the false and true,
Weighing and noting the long hours through.
Never ache and ache with the chok'd up sighs;
This is the end of him, here he lies.

# A. C. BENSON

1862–1925

374                          Thomas Gray

Singer most melancholy, most austere,
  So overcharged with greatness, that thy frame
  Was all too frail to feed the aspiring flame,
And sank in chill disdain and secret fear,

Save that thy idle fingers now and then
  Touched unawares a slender chord divine;
  Oh if but half the silence that was thine
Were shared to-day by clamorous minstrel men!

I thread the woodland where thy feet have strayed;
  The gnarled trunks dreaming out their ancient tale
    Are fair as then; the same sad chime I hear
  That floats at eve across the purple vale;
    The music of thy speech is in my ear,
And I am glad because thou wast afraid.

*Burnham, 1892*


375                          The Ant-Heap

High in the woodland, on the mountain side,
  I ponder, half a golden afternoon,
Storing deep strength to battle with the tide
  I must encounter soon.

Absorbed, inquisitive, alert, irate,
  The wiry wood-ants run beneath the pines,
And bristle if a careless footfall grate
  Among their travelled lines.

With prey unwieldy, slain in alien lands,
  When shadows fall aslant, laden they come,
Where, piled of red fir-needles, guarded stands
  Their dry and rustling dome.

They toil for what they know not; rest they shun;
  They nip the soft intruder; when they die,
They grapple pain and fate, and ask from none
  The pity they deny.

# SIR HENRY NEWBOLT

1862–1938

376          Gillespie

Riding at dawn, riding alone,
　　Gillespie left the town behind;
Before he turned by the Westward road
　　A horseman crossed him, staggering blind.

'The Devil's abroad in false Vellore,
　　The Devil that stabs by night,' he said,
'Women and children, rank and file,
　　Dying and dead, dying and dead.'

Without a word, without a groan,
　　Sudden and swift Gillespie turned,
The blood roared in his ears like fire,
　　Like fire the road beneath him burned.

He thundered back to Arcot gate,
　　He thundered up through Arcot town,
Before he thought a second thought
　　In the barrack yard he lighted down.

'Trumpeter, sound for the Light Dragoons,
　　Sound to saddle and spur,' he said;
'He that is ready may ride with me,
　　And he that can may ride ahead.'

Fierce and fain, fierce and fain,
　　Behind him went the troopers grim,
They rode as ride the Light Dragoons,
　　But never a man could ride with him.

Their rowels ripped their horses' sides,
   Their hearts were red with a deeper goad,
But ever alone before them all
   Gillespie rode, Gillespie rode.

Alone he came to false Vellore,
   The walls were lined, the gates were barred;
Alone he walked where the bullets bit,
   And called above to the Sergeant's Guard.

'Sergeant, Sergeant, over the gate,
   Where are your officers all?' he said;
Heavily came the Sergeant's voice,
   'There are two living, and forty dead.'

'A rope, a rope,' Gillespie cried:
   They bound their belts to serve his need;
There was not a rebel behind the wall
   But laid his barrel and drew his bead.

There was not a rebel among them all
   But pulled his trigger and cursed his aim,
For lightly swung and rightly swung
   Over the gate Gillespie came.

He dressed the line, he led the charge,
   They swept the wall like a stream in spate,
And roaring over the roar they heard
   The galloper guns that burst the gate.

Fierce and fain, fierce and fain,
   The troopers rode the reeking flight:
The very stones remember still
   The end of them that stab by night.

They've kept the tale a hundred years,
   They'll keep the tale a hundred more:
Riding at dawn, riding alone,
   Gillespie came to false Vellore.

# ROBERT FULLER MURRAY
## 1863–94

377         A Ballad of Refreshment

The lady stood at the station bar,
   (Three currants in a bun)
And oh she was proud, as ladies are.
   (And the bun was baked a week ago.)

For a weekly wage she was standing there,
   (Three currants in a bun)
With a prominent bust and light gold hair.
   (And the bun was baked a week ago.)

The express came in at half-past two,
   (Three currants in a bun)
And there lighted a man in the navy blue.
   (And the bun was baked a week ago.)

A stout sea-captain he was, I ween.
   (Three currants in a bun)
Much travel had made him very keen.
   (And the bun was baked a week ago.)

A sober man and steady was he.
   (Three currants in a bun)
He called not for brandy, but called for tea.
   (And the bun was baked a week ago.)

'Now something to eat, for the train is late.'
   (Three currants in a bun)
She brought him a bun on a greasy plate.
   (And the bun was baked a week ago.)

He left the bun, and he left the tea,
   (Three currants in a bun)
She charged him a shilling and let him be,
And the train went on at a quarter to three.
   (And the bun is old and weary.)


378           Βρεκεκεκεζ Κοαζ Κοαζ

I love the inoffensive frog,
   'A little child, a limber elf,'
With health and spirits all agog,
He does the long jump in a bog
Or teaches men to swim and dive.
If he should be cut up alive,
   Should I not be cut up myself?

So I intend to be straightway
   An Anti-Vivisectionist;
I'll read Miss Cobbe five hours a day
And watch the little frogs at play,
With no desire to see their hearts
At work, or other inward parts,
   If other inward parts exist.

**378.** *Title*: 'Brekekekex Koax Koax', the onomatopoeic refrain of the chorus in Aristophanes' *The Frogs*

# VICTOR PLARR

## 1863–1929

379                    The Solitaries

*(On the Anniversary of the Death of John Hampden, June 24, 1643)*

> Hampden, when charge on charge o'er Chalgrove Field
>   Was broken, and thou took'st thy desolate way
> Forth from the battle, ere the clarions pealed
>   To tell thee thy old cause had lost the day,
>
> Thou wounded unto death, thou quite fordone,
>   Thou riding with droopt head and hands declined
> Upon the saddle, hadst indeed begun
>   To be the symbol of the Lonely Mind.
>
> For some there be who dwell in solitude,
>   Though honours brighten and though friends acclaim,
> And hourly fame and faith repel the rude
>   Onset of thickening years and Death's last shame;
>
> Ay, some, great Rebel, though exceeding strait
>   Their little walk in life, more than obscure,
> Like thee have still foretasted the lone fate
>   Which at the close of all thou didst endure.
>
> To live alone – that is their doom: to die
>   Unhelpt by earthly aids, lover or friend,
> Reason, a bird along the lonely sky,
>   Guiding their desolate footsteps unto the end;
>
> Reason, a golden angel climbing still
>   In uttermost heav'n above their painful road,
> A strong compelling spirit, whose stern will
>   Is their prime glory and their heavy load.

Thou hadst a mighty king wherewith to cope:
　　They but oppressors small, who, day by day,
Pettily sap their every faith and hope:
　　Yet are ye one in sorrows, thou and they!

Hampden, on this June morn, when every air
　　Is sweet with rose-bloom and the summer's breath,
Some solitaries know thy last despair
　　Through Reason and old ever-beckoning Death.


380　　　　　　The Imperial Prayers

*Suggested by a passage in Mr. Valentine Chirol's the
'Far Eastern Question'*

Silenced the streets with sand of holy hue,
Shrouded the curious houses with faint sheen
Of silk and broid'ry, which for months between
These awful feasts none but the moth dare view;
The Son of Heaven, the Unutterable Kwang Hsu,
Borne in his lofty-looming palanquin,
By slaves who, if they stumble, die unseen,
Flits like a ghost through midnight – what to do?

The West stands clamouring outside his door:
We plan division of his lands and fame,
Yet hold Heredity for proven Truth.
To pray to his great Fathers gone before,
– Might not Marc Brutus once have done the same? –
Goes that spoiled, wretched, and mysterious youth.

381  On Change of Opinions

As you advance in years you long
    For what you scorned when but a boy:
Then 'twas the town, now the birds' song
    Is your obsession and your joy.

And, as you lie and die, maybe
    You will look back, unreconciled
To that dark hour, and clearly see
    Yourself a little wistful child.

Into the jaws of death you'll bring
    No virile triumph, wrought with pain;
But only to the monster fling
    The daydream and the daisy-chain,

The lispéd word, the gentle touch,
    The wonder, and the mystic thought,
For old gray Death upon his crutch
    To rake into his Bag of Nought.

382  Twilight-Piece

The golden river-reach afar
    Kisses the golden skies of even,
And there's the first faint lover's star
    Alight along the walls of heaven.

The river murmurs to the boughs,
    The boughs make music each to each,
And still an amorous west wind soughs
    And loiters down the lonesome reach.

And here on the slim arch that spans
  The rippling stream, in dark outline,
You see the poor old fisherman's
  Bowed form and patient rod and line.

A picture better than all art,
  Since none could catch that sunset stain,
Or set in the soft twilight's heart
  This small strange touch of human pain!

383        Epitaphium Citharistriæ

Stand not uttering sedately
  Trite oblivious praise above her!
Rather say you saw her lately
  Lightly kissing her last lover.

Whisper not, 'There is a reason
  Why we bring her no white blossom:'
Since the snowy bloom's in season
  Strow it on her sleeping bosom:

Oh, for it would be a pity
  To o'erpraise her or to flout her:
She was wild, and sweet, and witty –
  Let's not say dull things about her.

383. *Title*: Epitaph of a devotee of Venus

384                              Shadows

A song of shadows: never glory was
    But it had some soft shadow that would lie
On wall, on quiet water, on smooth grass,
    Or in the vistas of the phantasy:

The shadow of the house upon the lawn,
    Upon the house the shadow of the tree,
And through the moon-steeped hours unto the dawn
    The shadow of thy beauty over me.


385                    At Citoyenne Tussaud's

The place is full of whispers – 'Mark you, sirs,
This one is he who struck our moralists mute
Before the crime which proved him wholly brute!
Mark well his face!' The gaping sight-seers
Nudge one another, and no tongue but stirs
In awe-struck comment on hat, coat, and boot,
Mean smirking smile, base air of smug repute,
Worn by some prince of viler murderers!

Nay, I like most these lank-tressed doctrinaires
Who cluster round their powerless guillotine;
Aquiline, delicate, dark, their thin cheeks mired
By their own blood – these Carriers and Héberts:
They only look so proud and so serene:
They only look so infinitely tired!

# STEPHEN PHILLIPS
## 1864–1915

386      O thou art put to many uses, sweet!
Thy blood will urge the rose, and surge in Spring;
But yet! ...

And all the blue of thee will go to the sky,
And all thy laughter to the rivers run;
But yet! ...

Thy tumbling hair will in the West be seen,
And all thy trembling bosom in the dawn;
But yet! ...

Thy briefness in the dewdrop shall be hung,
And all the frailness of thee on the foam;
But yet! ...

Thy soul shall be upon the moonlight spent,
Thy mystery spread upon the evening mere.
And yet! ...

# RUDYARD KIPLING

## 1865–1936

Danny Deever

'What are the bugles blowin' for?' said Files-on-Parade.
'To turn you out, to turn you out,' the Colour-Sergeant said.
'What makes you look so white, so white?' said Files-on-Parade.
'I'm dreadin' what I've got to watch,' the Colour-Sergeant said.
   For they're hangin' Danny Deever, you can hear the Dead March
      play,
   The Regiment's in 'ollow square – they're hangin' him to-day;
   They've taken of his buttons off an' cut his stripes away,
   An' they're hangin' Danny Deever in the mornin'.

'What makes the rear-rank breathe so 'ard?' said Files-on-Parade.
'It's bitter cold, it's bitter cold,' the Colour-Sergeant said.
'What makes that front-rank man fall down?' said Files-on-Parade.
'A touch o' sun, a touch o' sun,' the Colour-Sergeant said.
   They are hangin' Danny Deever, they are marchin' of 'im round,
   They 'ave 'alted Danny Deever by 'is coffin on the ground;
   An' 'e'll swing in 'arf a minute for a sneakin' shootin' hound –
   O they're hangin' Danny Deever in the mornin'!

''Is cot was right-'and cot to mine,' said Files-on-Parade.
''E's sleepin' out an' far to-night,' the Colour-Sergeant said.
'I've drunk 'is beer a score o' times,' said Files-on-Parade.
''E's drinkin' bitter beer alone,' the Colour-Sergeant said.
   They are hangin' Danny Deever, you must mark 'im to 'is place,
   For 'e shot a comrade sleepin' – you must look 'im in the face;
   Nine 'undred of 'is county an' the regiment's disgrace,
   While they're hangin' Danny Deever in the mornin'.

'What's that so black agin the sun?' said Files-on-Parade.
'It's Danny fightin' 'ard for life,' the Colour-Sergeant said.
'What's that that whimpers over'ead?' said Files-on-Parade.

'It's Danny's soul that's passin' now,' the Colour-Sergeant said.
>     For they're done with Danny Deever, you can 'ear the quickstep
>         play,
>     The regiment's in column, an' they're marchin' us away;
>     Ho! the young recruits are shakin', an' they'll want their beer
>         to-day,
>     After hangin' Danny Deever in the mornin'.

388                        Tommy

I went into a public-'ouse to get a pint o' beer,
The publican 'e up an' sez, 'We serve no red-coats here.'
The girls be'ind the bar they laughed an' giggled fit to die,
I outs into the street again an' to myself sez I:
>     O it's Tommy this, an' Tommy that, an' 'Tommy, go away;'
>     But it's 'Thank you, Mister Atkins,' when the band begins to play,
>     The band begins to play, my boys, the band begins to play,
>     O it's 'Thank you, Mister Atkins,' when the band begins to play.

I went into a theatre as sober as could be,
They gave a drunk civilian room, but 'adn't none for me;
They sent me to the gallery or round the music-'alls,
But when it comes to fightin', Lord! they'll shove me in the stalls!
>     For it's Tommy this, an' Tommy that, an' 'Tommy, wait outside';
>     But it's 'Special train for Atkins' when the trooper's on the tide,
>     The troopship's on the tide, my boys, the troopship's on the tide,
>     O it's 'Special train for Atkins' when the trooper's on the tide.

Yes, makin' mock o' uniforms that guard you while you sleep
Is cheaper than them uniforms, an' they're starvation cheap;
An' hustlin' drunken soldiers when they're goin' large a bit
Is five times better business than paradin' in full kit.
>     Then it's Tommy this, an' Tommy that, an' 'Tommy, 'ow's yer
>         soul?'
>     But it's 'Thin red line of 'eroes' when the drums begin to roll,
>     The drums begin to roll, my boys, the drums begin to roll,
>     O it's 'Thin red line of 'eroes' when the drums begin to roll.

We aren't no thin red 'eroes, nor we aren't no blackguards too,
But single men in barricks, most remarkable like you;
An' if sometimes our conduck isn't all your fancy paints,
Why, single men in barricks don't grow into plaster saints;
    While it's Tommy this, an' Tommy that, an' 'Tommy, fall be'ind,'
    But it's 'Please to walk in front, sir,' when there's trouble in the
        wind,
    There's trouble in the wind, my boys, there's trouble in the wind,
    O it's 'Please to walk in front, sir,' when there's trouble in the
        wind.

You talk o' better food for us, an' schools, an' fires, an' all:
We'll wait for extry rations if you treat us rational.
Don't mess about the cook-room slops, but prove it to our face
The Widow's Uniform is not the soldier man's disgrace.
    For it's Tommy this, an' Tommy that, an' 'Chuck him out, the
        brute!'
    But it's 'Saviour of 'is country' when the guns begin to shoot;
    An' it's Tommy this, an' Tommy that, an' anything you please;
    An' Tommy ain't a bloomin' fool – you bet that Tommy sees!

### 389          The Widow at Windsor

    'Ave you 'eard o' the Widow at Windsor
      With a hairy gold crown on 'er 'ead?
    She 'as ships on the foam – she 'as millions at 'ome,
      An' she pays us poor beggars in red.
      (Ow, poor beggars in red!)
    There's 'er nick on the cavalry 'orses,
      There's 'er mark on the medical stores –
    An' 'er troopers you'll find with a fair wind be'ind
      That takes us to various wars.
      (Poor beggars! – barbarious wars!)
      Then 'ere's to the Widow at Windsor,
        An' 'ere's to the stores an' the guns,

The men an' the 'orses what makes up the forces
   O' Missis Victorier's sons.
   (Poor beggars! Victorier's sons!)


Walk wide o' the Widow at Windsor,
  For 'alf o' Creation she owns:
We 'ave bought 'er the same with the sword an' the flame,
  An' we've salted it down with our bones.
    (Poor beggars! – it's blue with our bones!)
Hands off o' the sons o' the Widow,
  Hands off o' the goods in 'er shop,
For the Kings must come down an' the Emperors frown
  When the Widow at Windsor says 'Stop!'
    (Poor beggars! – we're sent to say 'Stop!')
      Then 'ere's to the Lodge o' the Widow,
        From the Pole to the Tropics it runs –
      To the Lodge that we tile with the rank an' the file,
        An' open in form with the guns.
      (Poor beggars! – it's always they guns!)


We 'ave 'eard o' the Widow at Windsor,
  It's safest to let 'er alone:
For 'er sentries we stand by the sea an' the land
  Wherever the bugles are blown.
    (Poor beggars! – an' don't we get blown!)
Take 'old o' the Wings o' the Mornin',
  An' flop round the earth till you're dead;
But you won't get away from the tune that they play
  To the bloomin' old rag over'ead.
    (Poor beggars! – it's 'ot over'ead!)
      Then 'ere's to the sons o' the Widow,
        Wherever, 'owever they roam.
      'Ere's all they desire, an' if they require
        A speedy return to their 'ome.
      (Poor beggars! – they'll never see 'ome!)

390            Mandalay

By the old Moulmein Pagoda, lookin' eastward at the sea,
There's a Burma girl a-settin', and I know she thinks o' me;
For the wind is in the palm-trees, and the temple-bells they say:
'Come you back, you British soldier; come you back to Mandalay!'
     Come you back to Mandalay,
     Where the old Flotilla lay:
     Can't you 'ear their paddles chunkin' from Rangoon to
         Mandalay?
     On the road to Mandalay,
     Where the flyin'-fishes play,
     An' the dawn comes up like thunder outer China 'crost the Bay!

'Er petticoat was yaller an' 'er little cap was green,
An' 'er name was Supi-yaw-lat – jes' the same as Theebaw's Queen,
An' I seed her first a-smokin' of a whackin' white cheroot,
An' a-wastin' Christian kisses on an 'eathen idol's foot:
     Bloomin' idol made o' mud –
     Wot they called the Great Gawd Budd –
     Plucky lot she cared for idols when I kissed 'er where she stud!
     On the road to Mandalay ...

When the mist was on the rice-fields an' the sun was droppin' slow,
She'd git 'er little banjo an' she'd sing '*Kulla-lo-lo!*'
With 'er arm upon my shoulder an' 'er cheek agin my cheek
We useter watch the steamers an' the *hathis* pilin' teak.
     Elephints a-pilin' teak
     In the sludgy, squdgy creek,
     Where the silence 'ung that 'eavy you was 'arf afraid to speak!
     On the road to Mandalay ...

But that's all shove be'ind me – long ago an' fur away,
An' there ain't no 'buses runnin' from the Bank to Mandalay;
An' I'm learnin' 'ere in London what the ten-year soldier tells:
'If you've 'eard the East a-callin', you won't never 'eed naught else.'

No! you won't 'eed nothin' else
But them spicy garlic smells,
An' the sunshine an' the palm-trees an' the tinkly temple-bells;
On the road to Mandalay ...

I am sick o' wastin' leather on these gritty pavin'-stones,
An' the blasted Henglish drizzle wakes the fever in my bones;
Tho' I walks with fifty 'ousemaids outer Chelsea to the Strand,
An' they talks a lot o' lovin', but wot do they understand?
Beefy face an' grubby 'and –
Law! wot do they understand?
I've a neater, sweeter maiden in a cleaner, greener land!
On the road to Mandalay ...

Ship me somewheres east of Suez, where the best is like the worst,
Where there aren't no Ten Commandments an' a man can raise a
thirst;
For the temple-bells are callin', an' it's there that I would be –
By the old Moulmein Pagoda, looking lazy at the sea;
On the road to Mandalay,
Where the old Flotilla lay,
With our sick beneath the awnings when we went to Mandalay!
O the road to Mandalay,
Where the flyin'-fishes play,
An' the dawn comes up like thunder outer China 'crost the Bay!

# W. B. YEATS
## 1865–1939

391             An Old Song Re-Sung
[Down by the Salley Gardens]

Down by the salley gardens my love and I did meet;
She passed the salley gardens with little snow-white feet.
She bid me take love easy as the leaves grow on the tree;
But I, being young and foolish, with her would not agree.

In a field by the river my love and I did stand,
And on my leaning shoulder she laid her snow-white hand.
She bid me take life easy as the grass grows on the weirs;
But I was young and foolish and now am full of tears.

392             The Lake Isle of Innisfree

I will arise and go now, and go to Innisfree,
And a small cabin build there, of clay and wattles made;
Nine bean rows will I have there, a hive for the honey bee,
And live alone in the bee-loud glade.

And I shall have some peace there, for peace comes dropping slow,
Dropping from the veils of the morning to where the cricket sings;
There midnight's all a glimmer, and noon a purple glow,
And evening full of the linnet's wings.

I will arise and go now, for always night and day
I hear lake water lapping with low sounds by the shore;
While I stand on the roadway or on the pavements gray,
I hear it in the deep heart's core.

393           The Sorrow of Love

The quarrel of the sparrows in the eaves,
The full round moon and the star-laden sky,
And the loud song of the ever-singing leaves
Had hid away earth's old and weary cry.

And then you came with those red mournful lips,
And with you came the whole of the world's tears,
And all the sorrows of her labouring ships,
And all the burden of her myriad years.

And now the sparrows warring in the eaves,
The crumbling moon, the white stars in the sky,
And the loud chanting of the unquiet leaves,
Are shaken with earth's old and weary cry.

394           Breasal the Fisherman [The Fish]

Although you hide in the ebb and flow
Of the pale tide when the moon has set,
The people of coming days will know
About the casting out of my net,
And how you have leaped times out of mind
Over the little silver cords,
And think that you were hard and unkind,
And blame you with many bitter words.

395           The Song of Wandering Aengus

I went out to the hazel wood,
Because a fire was in my head,
And cut and peeled a hazel wand,
And hooked a berry to a thread;

And when white moths were on the wing,
And moth-like stars were flickering out,
I dropped the berry in a stream
And caught a little silver trout.

When I had laid it on the floor
I went to blow the fire a-flame,
But something rustled on the floor,
And someone called me by my name:
It had become a glimmering girl
With apple blossom in her hair
Who called me by my name and ran
And faded through the brightening air.

Though I am old with wandering
Through hollow lands and hilly lands,
I will find out where she has gone,
And kiss her lips and take her hands;
And walk among long dappled grass,
And pluck till time and times are done,
The silver apples of the moon,
The golden apples of the sun.

396         Aedh Laments the Loss of Love
       [The Lover Mourns for the Loss of Love]

Pale brows, still hands and dim hair,
I had a beautiful friend
And dreamed that the old despair
Would end in love in the end:
She looked in my heart one day
And saw your image was there;
She has gone weeping away.

397           The Valley of the Black Pig

The dews drop slowly and dreams gather: unknown spears
Suddenly hurtle before my dream-awakened eyes,
And then the clash of fallen horsemen and the cries
Of unknown perishing armies beat about my ears.
We who still labour by the cromlec on the shore,
The grey cairn on the hill, when day sinks drowned in dew,
Being weary of the world's empires, bow down to you
Master of the still stars and of the flaming door.


398           Aedh Wishes for the Cloths of Heaven
              [He Wishes for the Cloths of Heaven]

Had I the heavens' embroidered cloths,
Enwrought with golden and silver light,
The blue and the dim and the dark cloths
Of night and light and the half light,
I would spread the cloths under your feet:
But I, being poor, have only my dreams;
I have spread my dreams under your feet;
Tread softly because you tread on my dreams.


399              The Fiddler of Dooney

When I play on my fiddle in Dooney,
Folk dance like a wave of the sea;
My cousin is priest in Kilvarnet,
My brother in Moharabuiee.

I passed my brother and cousin:
They read in their books of prayer;
I read in my book of songs
I bought at the Sligo fair.

When we come at the end of time,
To Peter sitting in state,
He will smile on the three old spirits,
But call me first through the gate;

For the good are always the merry,
Save by an evil chance,
And the merry love the fiddle
And the merry love to dance:

And when the folk there spy me,
They will all come up to me,
With 'Here is the fiddler of Dooney!'
And dance like a wave of the sea.

# ARTHUR SYMONS
## 1865–1945

## The Absinthe Drinker

Gently I wave the visible world away.
　　Far off, I hear a roar, afar yet near,
　　Far off and strange, a voice is in my ear,
And is the voice my own? the words I say
Fall strangely, like a dream, across the day;
　　And the dim sunshine is a dream. How clear,
　　New as the world to lovers' eyes, appear
The men and women passing on their way!

The world is very fair. The hours are all
　　Linked in a dance of mere forgetfulness.
　　　　I am at peace with God and man. O glide,
Sands of the hour-glass that I count not, fall
　　Serenely: scarce I feel your soft caress,
　　　　Rocked on this dreamy and indifferent tide.

# JOHN GRAY
## 1866–1934

401          Song of the Seedling

*To Arthur Sewell Butt*

Tell, little seedling, murmuring germ,
Why are you joyful? What do you sing?
Have you no fear of that crawling thing,
Him that has so many legs? and the worm?

Rain drops patter above my head –
   Drip, drip, drip.
To moisten the mould where my roots are fed –
   Sip, sip, sip.
No thoughts have I of the legged thing,
   Of the worm no fear,
     When the goal is so near;
Every moment my life has run,
The livelong day I've not ceased to sing:
   I must reach the sun, the sun.

402           The Vines

*To André Chevrillon*

'Have you seen the listening snake?'
Bramble clutches for his bride,
Lately she was by his side,
Woodbine, with her gummy hands.

In the ground the mottled snake
Listens for the dawn of day;
Listens, listening death away,
Till the day burst winter's bands.

Painted ivy is asleep,
Stretched upon the bank, all torn,
Sinewy though she be; love-lorn
Convolvuluses cease to creep.

Bramble clutches for his bride,
Woodbine, with her gummy hands,
All his horny claws expands;
She has withered in his grasp.

'Till the day dawn, till the tide
Of the winter's afternoon.'
'Who tells dawning?' – 'Listen, soon.'
Half-born tendrils, grasping, gasp.


403            Spleen

The roses every one were red,
And all the ivy leaves were black.

Sweet, do not even stir your head,
Or all of my despairs come back.

The sky is too blue, too delicate:
Too soft the air, too green the sea.

I fear – how long had I to wait! –
That you will tear yourself from me.

The shining box-leaves weary me,
The varnished holly's glistening,

The stretch of infinite country;
So, saving you, does everything.

# ERNEST DOWSON

## 1867–1900

404      Vitae Summa Brevis Spem Nos Vetat
Incohare Longam

They are not long, the weeping and the laughter,
    Love and desire and hate:
I think they have no portion in us after
    We pass the gate.

They are not long, the days of wine and roses:
    Out of a misty dream
Our path emerges for a while, then closes
    Within a dream.

405      Non Sum Qualis Eram Bonae Sub
Regno Cynarae

Last night, ah, yesternight, betwixt her lips and mine
    There fell thy shadow, Cynara! thy breath was shed
Upon my soul between the kisses and the wine;
    And I was desolate and sick of an old passion,
    Yea, I was desolate and bowed my head:
    I have been faithful to thee, Cynara! in my fashion.

All night upon mine heart I felt her warm heart beat,
    Night-long within mine arms in love and sleep she lay;
Surely the kisses of her bought red mouth were sweet;

404. *Title*: Horace, *Carmina* I iv 15: 'Life's short span forbids us to enter on far-
reaching hopes'
405. *Title*: Horace, *Carmina* IV i 3–4: 'I am not now as I was in the reign of the good
Cynara'

But I was desolate and sick of an old passion,
When I awoke and found the dawn was gray:
   I have been faithful to thee, Cynara! in my fashion.

I have forgot much, Cynara! gone with the wind,
   Flung roses, roses riotously with the throng,
Dancing, to put thy pale, lost lilies out of mind;
   But I was desolate and sick of an old passion,
   Yea, all the time, because the dance was long:
      I have been faithful to thee, Cynara! in my fashion.

I cried for madder music and for stronger wine,
   But when the feast is finished and the lamps expire,
Then falls thy shadow, Cynara! the night is thine;
   And I am desolate and sick of an old passion,
   Yea hungry for the lips of my desire:
      I have been faithful to thee, Cynara! in my fashion.


406                    Spleen

                  *For Arthur Symons*

I was not sorrowful, I could not weep,
And all my memories were put to sleep.

I watched the river grow more white and strange,
All day till evening I watched it change.

All day till evening I watched the rain
Beat wearily upon the window pane.

I was not sorrowful, but only tired
Of everything that ever I desired.

Her lips, her eyes, all day became to me
The shadow of a shadow utterly.

All day mine hunger for her heart became
Oblivion, until the evening came,

And left me sorrowful, inclined to weep,
With all my memories that could not sleep.

407            To William Theodore Peters on
                 His Renaissance Cloak

The cherry-coloured velvet of your cloak
    Time hath not soiled: its fair embroideries
Gleam as when centuries ago they spoke
    To what bright gallant of Her Daintiness,
    Whose slender fingers, long since dust and dead,
    For love or courtesy embroidered
The cherry-coloured velvet of this cloak.

Ah! cunning flowers of silk and silver thread,
    That mock mortality! the broidering dame,
The page they decked, the kings and courts are dead:
    Gone the age beautiful; Lorenzo's name,
    The Borgia's pride are but an empty sound;
    But lustrous still upon their velvet ground,
Time spares these flowers of silk and silver thread.

Gone is that age of pageant and of pride:
    Yet don your cloak, and haply it shall seem,
The curtain of old time is set aside;
    As through the sadder coloured throng you gleam;
    We see once more fair dame and gallant gay,
    The glamour and the grace of yesterday:
The elder, brighter age of pomp and pride.

# LIONEL JOHNSON

1867–1902

408

### By the Statue of King Charles
### at Charing Cross

*To William Watson*

Sombre and rich, the skies;
Great glooms, and starry plains.
Gently the night wind sighs;
Else a vast silence reigns.

The splendid silence clings
Around me: and around
The saddest of all kings
Crowned, and again discrowned.

Comely and calm, he rides
Hard by his own Whitehall:
Only the night wind glides:
No crowds, nor rebels, brawl.

Gone, too, his Court: and yet,
The stars his courtiers are:
Stars in their stations set;
And every wandering star.

Alone he rides, alone,
The fair and fatal king:
Dark night is all his own,
That strange and solemn thing.

Which are more full of fate:
The stars; or those sad eyes?
Which are more still and great:
Those brows; or the dark skies?

Although his whole heart yearn
In passionate tragedy:
Never was face so stern
With sweet austerity.

Vanquished in life, his death
By beauty made amends:
The passing of his breath
Won his defeated ends.

Brief life, and hapless? Nay:
Through death, life grew sublime.
*Speak after sentence?* Yea:
And to the end of time.

Armoured he rides, his head
Bare to the stars of doom:
He triumphs now, the dead,
Beholding London's gloom.

Our wearier spirit faints,
Vexed in the world's employ:
His soul was of the saints;
And art to him was joy.

King, tried in fires of woe!
Men hunger for thy grace:
And through the night I go,
Loving thy mournful face.

Yet, when the city sleeps;
When all the cries are still:
The stars and heavenly deeps
Work out a perfect will.

409                        The Dark Angel

Dark Angel, with thine aching lust
To rid the world of penitence:
Malicious Angel, who still dost
My soul such subtile violence!

Because of thee, no thought, no thing,
Abides for me undesecrate:
Dark Angel, ever on the wing,
Who never reachest me too late!

When music sounds, then changest thou
Its silvery to a sultry fire:
Nor will thine envious heart allow
Delight untortured by desire.

Through thee, the gracious Muses turn
To Furies, O mine Enemy!
And all the things of beauty burn
With flames of evil ecstasy.

Because of thee, the land of dreams
Becomes a gathering place of fears:
Until tormented slumber seems
One vehemence of useless tears.

When sunlight glows upon the flowers,
Or ripples down the dancing sea:
Thou, with thy troop of passionate powers,
Beleaguerest, bewilderest, me.

Within the breath of autumn woods,
Within the winter silences:
Thy venomous spirit stirs and broods,
O Master of impieties!

The ardour of red flame is thine,
And thine the steely soul of ice:
Thou poisonest the fair design
Of nature, with unfair device.

Apples of ashes, golden bright;
Waters of bitterness, how sweet!
O banquet of a foul delight,
Prepared by thee, dark Paraclete!

Thou art the whisper in the gloom,
The hinting tone, the haunting laugh:
Thou art the adorner of my tomb,
The minstrel of mine epitaph.

I fight thee, in the Holy Name!
Yet, what thou dost, is what God saith:
Tempter! should I escape thy flame,
Thou wilt have helped my soul from Death:

The second Death, that never dies,
That cannot die, when time is dead:
Live Death, wherein the lost soul cries,
Eternally uncomforted.

Dark Angel, with thine aching lust!
Of two defeats, of two despairs:
Less dread, a change to drifting dust,
Than thine eternity of cares.

Do what thou wilt, thou shalt not so,
Dark Angel! triumph over me:
*Lonely, unto the Lone I go;*
*Divine, to the Divinity.*

410                     Love's Ways

     You were not cruel always! Nay,
         When I said *Come!* one year ago:
     Could you have lingered by the way?
         Did not the very wind seem slow?

     Then, had you tarried, I had known
         Nor love's delight, nor lost love's pain:
     Then, always had I lived alone.
         Now, you need never come again.

# GEORGE WILLIAM RUSSELL

### 1867–1935

411          ## The Mid-World

This is the red, red region
Your heart must journey through:
Your pains will here be legion
And joy be death for you.

Rejoice to-day: to-morrow
A turning tide shall flow
Through infinite tones of sorrow
To reach an equal woe.

You pass by love unheeding
To gain the goal you long –
But my heart, my heart is bleeding:
I cannot sing this song.

# LAURENCE BINYON
## 1869–1943

412          As I Walked Through London

As I walked through London,
The fresh wound burning in my breast,
As I walked through London,
Longing to have forgotten, to harden my heart, and to rest,
A sudden consolation, a softening light
Touched me: the streets alive and bright,
With hundreds each way thronging, on their tide
Received me, a drop in the stream, unmarked, unknown.
And to my heart I cried:
*Here can thy trouble find shelter, thy wound be eased!*
*For see, not thou alone,*
*But thousands, each with his smart,*
*Deep-hidden, perchance, but felt in the core of the heart!*
And as to a sick man's feverish veins
The full sponge warmly pressed,
Relieves with its burning the burning of forehead and hands,
So, I, to my aching breast,
Gathered the griefs of those thousands, and made them my own;
My bitterest pains
Merged in a tenderer sorrow, assuaged and appeased.

# HILAIRE BELLOC
## 1870–1953

413             The Dodo

The Dodo used to walk around,
   And take the sun and air.
The sun yet warms his native ground –
   The Dodo is not there!

The voice which used to squawk and squeak
   Is now for ever dumb –
Yet may you see his bones and beak
   All in the Mu-se-um.


414             The Marmozet

The species Man and Marmozet
   Are intimately linked;
The Marmozet survives as yet,
   But Men are all extinct.


415             The Camelopard

The Camelopard, it is said
   By travellers (who never lie),
He cannot stretch out straight in bed
   Because he is so high.
The clouds surround his lofty head,
   His hornlets touch the sky.

How shall I hunt this quadruped?
  I cannot tell! Not I!
I'll buy a little parachute
  (A common parachute with wings),
I'll fill it full of arrowroot
  And other necessary things,

And I will slay this fearful brute
With stones and sticks and guns and slings.


416      The Llama

The Llama is a woolly sort of fleecy hairy goat,
With an indolent expression and an undulating throat
  Like an unsuccessful literary man.
And I know the place he lives in (or at least – I think I do)
It is Ecuador, Brazil or Chile – possibly Peru;
  You must find it in the Atlas if you can.
The Llama of the Pampasses you never should confound
(In spite of a deceptive similarity of sound)
  With the Lama who is Lord of Turkestan.
For the former is a beautiful and valuable beast,
But the latter is not lovable nor useful in the least;
And the Ruminant is preferable surely to the Priest
Who battens on the woful superstitions of the East,
  The Mongol of the Monastery of Shan.

# Biographical and Textual Notes

The information given here has been taken from standard works of reference such as the *New Cambridge Bibliography*, the *Oxford Companions* (to English and Irish Literature), the *Dictionary of Literary Biography*, and the *Dictionary of National Biography*. Two more specialized works have greatly assisted me: Angela Leighton and Margaret Reynolds's anthology *Victorian Women Poets* (1995), and John Sutherland's *Longman Companion to Victorian Fiction* (1988) – the latter illustrating the number of Victorian poets who wrote fiction, and vice versa. A list of publications is given for a few major authors: it is complete for individual volumes of verse published in the period, and otherwise selective.

**'A. E.'** (also 'Æ', 'AE') *see entry for* George William Russell.

## WILLIAM ALLINGHAM (1824–89)

Anglo-Irish poet and journalist; born in Ballyshannon, Donegal; worked as a customs official; contributed to *Leigh Hunt's Journal*; publ. first volume of verse, 1850; settled in England 1863; friend of Browning, Carlyle, Leigh Hunt, D. G. Rossetti, and Tennyson; edited *Fraser's Magazine*, 1874–9.

Text: 'In Snow', 'Writing', 'By and by, we shall meet': *Blackberries* [etc.], 1884; 'The Fairy King': *Irish Songs and Poems*, 1887; 'Everything passes and vanishes': *Life and Phantasy*, 1889.

## ALEXANDER ANDERSON (1845–1909)

Scottish poet; born in Kirkconnel, Dumfriesshire, where he worked as a railway platelayer; began publishing verses in 1870 under pseudonym 'Surfaceman' in the journal *The People's Friend*, collected in *A Song of Labour and other poems*, 1873; later assistant librarian at Edinburgh University.

Text: *Songs of the Rail*, 1878.

## ANONYMOUS

Text: 'Victoria', 'The Way to Live': J. Ashton (ed.), *Modern Street Ballads*, 1888; 'Johnny Sands': V. de Sola Pinto and A. E. Rodway (eds.), *The Common Muse*, 1957.

## MATTHEW ARNOLD (1822–88)

Son of Thomas Arnold, reforming headmaster of Rugby School; born in Laleham (near Staines), Middlesex; educ. at Rugby, Winchester, and Balliol College, Oxford, where he won Newdigate Prize for poetry and became close friend of Arthur Hugh Clough; secretary to the Whig statesman Lord Lansdowne, 1847; publ. first volume of verse, 1849; government inspector of schools, 1851–83, and advocate of educational reform; Professor of Poetry at Oxford, 1857–67; turned increasingly to prose (literary, social, and cultural criticism) in his later years.

Publications: *The Strayed Reveller, and other poems*, 1849; *Empedocles on Etna, and other poems*, 1852; *Poems, a New Edition*, 1853 (incl. Preface); *Poems, Second Series*, 1855; *Merope. A Tragedy*, 1858; *On Translating Homer*, 1861; *Essays in Criticism*, 1865; *On the Study of Celtic Literature*, 1867; *Poems* (collected ed.), 1869; *Culture and Anarchy: an Essay in Political and Social Criticism*, 1869; *Literature and Dogma*, 1873; *Poems* (final collected edn), 1885; *Essays in Criticism, Second Series*, 1888.

Text: *Poems*, 1885.

## ALFRED AUSTIN (1835–1913)

Poet, author (novels, essays, etc.), and journalist; born in Leeds; ardent imperialist and follower of Disraeli; joint-editor of *National Review*, 1883–7, then sole editor, 1887–95; Poet Laureate in succession to Tennyson, 1896.

Text: *In Veronica's Garden*, 1895.

## W(illiam) E(dmonstoune) AYTOUN (1813–65)

Scottish lawyer, poet and humorist; Professor of Belles-Lettres at Edinburgh, 1845; Sheriff of Orkney, 1852; satirized the 'Spasmodic School' of poetry in *Firmilian, or the Student of Badajoz*, 1854.

Text: *The Book of Ballads. Edited by Bon Gaultier* [joint pseudonym of Aytoun and Theodore Martin], *A New Edition*, 1849.

## 'B. V.' *see entry for* James Thomson.

## JANE BARLOW (1857–1917)

Irish novelist and poet; born in Clontarf, near Dublin; her father became Vice-Provost of Trinity College; educ. at home; publ. first volume of verse, 1892; her poetry and fiction on Irish subjects were popular in Britain and America.

Text: *Bog-land Studies*, 3rd edn, 1894.

## WILLIAM BARNES (1801–86)

Poet, philologist, and local historian of his native Dorset; born in Bagber, near Sturminster Newton; began as a schoolmaster; publ. first volume of verse, *Poems of Rural Life in the Dorset Dialect*, 1844 (other volumes 1859, 1862); entered priesthood, 1848; held livings at Whitcombe (1848–62) and Cambe, where he was Rector until his death.

Text: *Poems of Rural Life* [collected edn], 1879.

## THOMAS LOVELL BEDDOES (1803–49)

Poet and physiologist; born in Clifton; son of the physician Thomas Beddoes, who had been friend and doctor of Wordsworth and Coleridge; educ. at Charterhouse School and Pembroke College, Oxford; publ. first volume of verse, 1821; studied medicine in Germany and eventually settled at Zurich, 1835; began work on his long dramatic poem *Death's Jest-Book*, 1825, repeatedly revised in subsequent years and not publ. in his lifetime; influenced Browning, and later Swinburne and other poets; forced to flee to Berlin in 1841 because of his liberal political sympathies; committed suicide at Basle.

Text: *Poems Posthumous and Collected*, 1851.

## (Joseph) HILAIRE (Pierre René) BELLOC (1870–1953)

Poet, author (novels, travel-books, history, biography, etc.) and journalist; born in France and educ. in England after his father's death, at the Oratory School and Balliol College, Oxford; publ. first volume of verse, 1896; close friend and collaborator of G. K. Chesterton; Liberal MP for South Salford, 1906–1910; literary editor of the *Morning Post* in the same period; founded the *Eye-Witness*, later the *New Witness*, 1911–23; lifelong Roman Catholic polemicist.

Text: *The Bad Child's Book of Beasts*, 1896, except 'The Llama': *More Beasts for Worse Children*, 1897.

## A[rthur] C[hristopher] BENSON (1862–1925)

Author (biography, criticism, essays) and poet; born at Wellington College, London, where his father was the first headmaster; educ. Eton and Trinity College, Cambridge; housemaster at Eton, and subsequently Master of Magdalene College, Cambridge; author of 'Land of Hope and Glory' (set by Elgar) and other public odes and verses; suffered from profound depression revealed in the diary he kept from 1897.

Text: 'Thomas Gray': *Le Cahier Jaune*, 1892; 'The Ant-Heap': *Lyrics*, 1895.

## L[ouisa] S[arah] BEVINGTON (1845–95)

Born in London; from a Quaker family; became interested in radical social and political ideas; published first book of verse under pseudonym 'Arbor Leigh', 1876; married German artist Ignatz Guggenberger (1883), afterwards separated; by early 1890s was active as journalist and poet in the Anarchist movement.

Text: *Poems, Lyrics, and Sonnets*, 1882.

## (Robert) LAURENCE BINYON (1869–1943)

Poet, art-historian and critic; born in Lancaster; educ. St Paul's School and Trinity College, Oxford; worked at British Museum where he became keeper of oriental prints and drawings.

Text: *Poems*, 1895.

## SAMUEL LAMAN BLANCHARD (1804–45)

Poet, essayist and journalist; born in Great Yarmouth; employed as a clerk in Doctors' Commons; began contributing to literary journals; briefly joined troop of travelling actors; secretary to Zoological Society, 1827; publ. first volume of verse, 1828; editor of several Liberal journals in 1830s; connected with the *Examiner* from 1841; friendships incl. Browning, Dickens, Leigh Hunt and Letitia Landon; publ. Landon's *Life and Literary Remains*, 1841; committed suicide in fit of depression after his wife's death.

Text: *George Cruikshank's Omnibus* (ed. Blanchard), 1842.

## MATHILDE BLIND (1841–96)

Born in Germany; father a Jewish banker; after his death, mother married Karl Blind; family came to England after suppression of Baden insurrection of 1848–9, in which Blind took a leading part; studied in Zurich; publ. first volume of poems in 1867 under the pseudonym 'Claude Lake'; friendships incl. Ford Madox Brown, W. M. Rossetti, the Italian nationalist leader Mazzini, Emma Marx; wrote biographies of Shelley (1881) and George Eliot (1883); freethinker and supporter of women's suffrage.

Text: *Poetical Works*, 1900.

## KATHERINE BRADLEY *see entry for* 'Michael Field'.

## ROBERT (Seymour) BRIDGES (1844–1930)

Poet and critic; born in Walmer, Kent; educ. at Eton and Corpus Christi College, Oxford, where he became a close friend of Hopkins; studied medicine at St Bartholomew's Hospital, London, and practised for seven years; publ. first volume of verse, 1873, but later suppressed it; travelled extensively in Europe and Middle East; retired from medicine on grounds of health, 1881; settled at Boar's Hill, near Oxford; founded Society for Pure English; Poet Laureate, 1913; publ. first collection of Hopkins's poems, 1918; publ. his *magnum opus, The Testament of Beauty*, 1929.

Text: *Shorter Poems*, 1890.

## ANNE BRONTË (1820–49)

Youngest of the Brontë children; born in Haworth, Yorkshire, in the year her Irish father, Patrick Brontë, became perpetual curate; close to Emily with whom she invented the imaginary world of Gondal; at Roe Head school with Charlotte; became governess; adopted pseudonym 'Acton Bell' for publ. of her and her sisters' verse (*Poems by Currer, Ellis, and Acton Bell*, 1846) and two novels, *Agnes Grey*, 1847, and *The Tenant of Wildfell Hall*, 1848; died of consumption at Scarborough, where she is buried.

Text: *The Poems of Anne Brontë*, ed. E. Chitham (Macmillan, 1979); written 1845, first publ. 1902.

## CHARLOTTE BRONTË (1816–55)

Eldest of three surviving sisters; born in Thornton, near Bradford, in Yorkshire, four years before family moved to parsonage in Haworth; educ. at Cowan Bridge School (model for Lowood in *Jane Eyre*) and Roe Head, where she later returned as teacher; created imaginary kingdom of Angria with her brother Branwell; became a governess, 1839–41; studied languages at Brussels with Emily, 1842, and returned in 1843; her love for her teacher, M. Heger, unreciprocated; 'discovered' Emily's poems in 1845 and persuaded her to allow joint publication with her and Anne; maintained her pseudonym, 'Currer Bell', though her real identity became widely known after success of *Jane Eyre* (1847); friend of Mrs Gaskell, who later wrote her biography; publ. memorial edns of *Agnes Grey* and *Wuthering Heights*, 1850, the latter incl. biographical notes on Anne and Emily and unpubl. poems; in 1854 married her father's curate, Arthur Nicholls, but died a few months later, probably from illness associated with pregnancy; buried in Haworth churchyard.

Text: *The Poems of Charlotte Brontë*, ed. T. Winnifrith (Blackwell, 1984).

## EMILY (Jane) BRONTË (1818–48)

Born in Thornton, near Bradford, in Yorkshire, two years before family moved to parsonage in Haworth; educ. mainly at home in Haworth (left school at Roe Head after a few months in 1835 because of homesickness); wrote Gondal stories and poems with Anne; worked briefly as governess in 1837; in 1842 visited Charlotte in Brussels; her poems 'discovered' by Charlotte in 1845; publ. with those of her sisters in 1846 under pseudonym 'Ellis Bell'; *Wuthering Heights* publ. 1847; died of consumption in 1848; buried in Haworth churchyard.

Text: *Complete Poems*, ed. J. Gezari (Penguin, 1992); 'Remembrance' written 1845, part of the Gondal poems and originally entitled 'R. Alcona to J. Brenzaida' (see Gezari, pp. 228–9), first publ. 1846; 'High waving heather' written 1836, first publ. 1902; 'The night is darkening round me' written 1837, first publ. 1902; 'I'm happiest when most away' written ?1838, first publ. 1910; 'How still, how happy' written 1838, first publ. 1902; 'Upon her soothing breast' written ?1839, first publ. 1910; 'No coward soul is mine' written 1846, first publ. 1850. 'The night is darkening round me' is printed in Gezari along with two other manuscript items ('I'll come when thou art saddest' and 'I would have touched the heavenly key') as a 'single poetic utterance' (see editor's note, p. 246), but is here given as a separate item. 'Often rebuked, yet always back returning' is undated, and attrib. to Emily in Charlotte's volume of 1850 (see prec. entry); for the debate over its authorship, see Gezari, pp. 284–5.

## (Charles William) SHIRLEY BROOKS (1816–74)

Journalist and author; born in London, the son of an architect; studied law; after working for *Morning Chronicle, Illustrated London News* and *Literary Gazette*, joined *Punch* in 1851; became editor, 1870.

Text: *Wit and Humour: poems from 'Punch'*, 1875.

T[homas] E[dward] **B R O W N** (1830–97)
Poet and teacher; born in the Isle of Man; educ. King William's College and Christ Church, Oxford; fellow of Oriel College, 1854–8; headmaster of Crypt School, Gloucester, 1861–4 (where one of his pupils was W. E. Henley); second master at Clifton, 1864–93; author of verse tales in Manx dialect (*Fo'c'sle Yarns*, 1881) as well as poems in standard English.

Text: *Collected Poems*, 1900.

## ELIZABETH BARRETT BROWNING (1806–61)

Born at Coxhoe Hall, Durham; her father, from a family of wealthy Jamaican sugar-planters, dominated her life and that of his other (ten surviving) children, forbidding any of them to marry; in 1809 family moved to Hope End, near Ledbury, in Herefordshire, where she grew up and was privately educ. until 1832, when financial difficulties caused family to move to Sidmouth and eventually London; read widely from childhood and became accomplished classical scholar; her juvenile poem *The Battle of Marathon* privately printed, 1820; publ. first volume of verse, 1826; contributed to literary journals and annuals, and gained recognition as poet in 1830s; suffered from illness (probably a form of consumption with spinal complications) and became recluse after death by drowning of favourite brother in 1840; conducted many friendships by correspondence, esp. with Mary Russell Mitford; married Robert Browning in 1846, after clandestine courtship, and travelled with him to Italy; her father broke with her and refused all gestures of reconciliation; eventually settled at Casa Guidi, Florence; her health improved, and she bore a son, 1849; her reputation secured by popular and critical success of *Aurora Leigh*, 1857; passionate supporter of Italian independence from Austria; her strong belief in spiritualist phenomena not shared by her husband; in later years her health declined again; died in Florence and was buried there.

Publications: *An Essay on Mind, with other poems*, 1826; *The Seraphim, and other poems*, 1838; *Poems*, 1844; *Casa Guidi Windows*, 1851; *Aurora Leigh*, 1857; *Poems Before Congress*, 1860; *Last Poems*, 1862.

Text: *Poetical Works*, 1897.

## ROBERT BROWNING (1812–89)

Born in Camberwell, south London; father a clerk in Bank of England and bibliophile; educ. in local schools and at home, apart from a year at University College London, 1827–8; after initial doubts, parents supported his choice of poetry as career; his first poem, *Pauline*, publ. anonymously, 1833, and not acknowledged by him until 1868; established himself critically with *Paracelsus* (1835) but was ridiculed for 'obscurity' of *Sordello* (1840) and failed as playwright; travelled to Italy in 1838 and 1844; publ. plays and poems in cheap format under series title *Bells and Pomegranates*, 1841–6; literary friendships in this period incl. Carlyle, Dickens, Leigh Hunt, Tennyson, B. W. Procter ('Barry Cornwall') and Landor; married Elizabeth Barrett (see above), 1846, and lived with her in Italy; after wife's death returned to England with their son; achieved critical and popular success in 1860s, and became a literary and social celebrity; later friendships incl. Arnold, George Eliot, Benjamin Jowett (Master of Balliol College, which awarded him an honorary fellowship in 1867), F. J. Furnivall (founder, with Emily Hickey, of the Browning Society in 1881) and 'Michael Field'; died in Venice and was buried in Westminster Abbey.

Publications: *Pauline*, 1833; *Paracelsus*, 1835; *Strafford* (play), 1837; *Sordello*, 1840; *Pippa Passes*, 1841; *King Victor and King Charles* (play), 1842; *Dramatic Lyrics*, 1842; *The Return of the Druses* (play), 1843; *A Blot in the 'Scutcheon* (play), 1843; *Colombe's Birthday* (play), 1844; *Dramatic Romances and Lyrics*, 1845; *Luria* and *A Soul's Tragedy* (plays), 1846; *Men and Women*, 1855; *Dramatis Personae*, 1864; *The Ring and the Book*, 1868–9; *Balaustion's Adventure*, 1871; *Prince Hohenstiel-Schwangau*, 1871; *Fifine at the Fair*, 1872; *Red Cotton Night-Cap Country*, 1873; *Aristophanes' Apology*, 1875; *The Inn Album*, 1875; *Pacchiarotto ... with other poems*, 1876; *The Agamemnon of Aeschylus*, 1877; *La Saisiaz* and *The Two Poets of Croisic*, 1878; *Dramatic Idyls*, 1879; *Dramatic Idyls, Second Series*, 1880; *Jocoseria*, 1883; *Ferishtah's Fancies*, 1884; *Parleyings with Certain People of Importance in their Day*, 1887; *Asolando*, 1889.

Text: *Poetical Works*, 1888–9, except the last three poems: *Asolando*, 1889.

## 'CAERLEON' (*fl.* 1876–?)
Unidentified pseudonym.

Text: *Waifs and Strays*, 1876.

## C[harles] S[tuart] CALVERLEY (1831–84)
Poet and translator; born in Martley, Worcestershire; father changed his name from Blayds, 1852; educ. at Harrow; scholar of Balliol College, Oxford, 1850–52, then moved to Christ's College, Cambridge, where he became a fellow, 1857; publ. first volume of verse, 1862; barrister of Inner Temple, 1865; publ. light verse, parodies and translations under initials 'C.S.C.'

Text: *Complete Works*, 1901.

## WILLIAM CANTON (1845–1926)
Poet and journalist; father a colonial civil servant; born in China; educ. in France and studied for priesthood, but subsequently became a protestant; worked as a journalist in London and Glasgow, eventually becoming editor of the *Sunday Magazine*; publ. first volume of verse, 1887; his 'W. V.' books, dedicated to his daughter Winifred Veda, were popular; granted Civil List pension, 1912.

Text: *The Comrades: Poems Old and New*, 1902.

## 'LEWIS CARROLL' (Charles Lutwidge Dodgson) (1832–98)
Born in Daresbury, near Warrington; educ. at Rugby and Christ Church, Oxford, where he became lecturer in mathematics, 1855; adopted pseudonym 'Lewis

Carroll', 1856, for contributions to the light journal *Train*, at the suggestion of its editor, Edmund Yates; lived most of his life in Oxford; besides the famous 'Alice' stories (*Alice's Adventures in Wonderland*, 1865; *Through the Looking-Glass and What Alice Found There*, 1871) wrote other works for children and 'nonsense' poetry (*The Hunting of the Snark*, 1876), mathematical treatises, and occasional essays; passionate amateur photographer, esp. of young girls.

Text: *Through the Looking-Glass* ('Jabberwocky': ch. 1; 'The Walrus and the Carpenter': ch. 4).

## ELIZABETH CHARLES *née* Rundle (1828–96)
Novelist, mainly on subjects of religious history; born in Tavistock, where her father was MP; educ. at home; married 1851; her verse publ. in magazines but not collected until 1882; her best known work, *Chronicles of the Schönberg-Cotta Family*, publ. 1862; friends included leaders of the Clapham sect of Anglican Evangelicalism; supported herself by her writing after husband's death in 1868; wrote many pamphlets for the Society for Promoting Christian Knowledge; founded the Swiss Cottage hospice for the dying in 1885.

Text: *Songs Old and New*, 1882.

## JOHN CLARE (1793–1864)
Born in Helpstone, Northamptonshire, the son of a labourer; worked as hedge-setter and day-labourer; parted from his first love, Mary Joyce, and married Martha Turner, 1820, the year his first volume of poems publ.; his initial success marred by financial difficulties and troubled relations with patrons; in 1837 admitted as insane to High Beech asylum in Epping; escaped 1841 and walked home under delusion that he was married to Mary; re-admitted to Northampton General Asylum where he remained until his death.

Publications: *Poems Descriptive of Rural Life and Scenery*, 1820; *The Village Minstrel and other poems*, 1821; *The Shepherd's Calendar*, 1827; *The Rural Muse*, 1835.

Text: *The Later Poems of John Clare, 1837–1864*, ed. E. Robinson, D. Powell and M. Grainger, Oxford University Press, 1984.

## ARTHUR HUGH CLOUGH (1819–61)
Born in Liverpool, the son of a cotton merchant; educ. at Rugby and Balliol College, Oxford, where he was a close friend of Matthew Arnold; fellow of Oriel College, 1841–8; became friend of Ralph Waldo Emerson, with whom he visited Paris during revolutionary period, May–June 1848; resigned fellowship, Oct. 1848, a month before publ. of his first work, *The Bothie of Toper-na-Fuosich*; in Rome, 1849, during French siege and occupation; held university appointments in London, 1849–52; travelled to America and visited Emerson, then lived in Boston, 1852–3; on his return, took up appointment as Examiner in the Education Office; died in Florence.

Publications: *The Bothie of Toper-na-Fuosich*, 1848; *Ambarvalia*, 1849 (with some poems by Thomas Burbidge); *Amours de Voyage*, 1858 (written 1849); *Poems* (1862) and *Dipsychus* (1865, now known as *Dipsychus and the Spirit*) posthumously publ.

Text: *Poems and Prose Remains*, 1869.

## HARTLEY COLERIDGE (1796–1849)

Eldest son of Samuel Taylor Coleridge; born in Clevedon, Somerset; brought up in Lake District by Robert Southey; educ. at Ambleside School and Merton College, Oxford; probationer fellow of Oriel College, Oxford, 1819, but dismissed for drunkenness, 1820; failed in literary work in London; schoolteacher at Ambleside (1830) and Sedbergh (1837–8); lived for the latter part of his life in Lake District.

Text: *Poems*, 1851.

## MARY E. COLERIDGE (1861–1907)

Poet, novelist and essayist, great-great-niece of Samuel Taylor Coleridge; born in London, and lived at home with her sister all her life; tutored by William Cory; publ. her first novel, 1893; influenced by Christian-Anarchist writings of Tolstoy, and taught at Working Women's College; encouraged to publish poems by Robert Bridges, and publ. first volume under pseudonym 'Anodos', 1896, but most of her verse not collected until after her death.

Text: *Poems*, 1908.

## MORTIMER COLLINS (1827–76)

Author (humorous novels, essays, political satire) and poet; born in Plymouth; taught mathematics in Guernsey, 1850–56; publ. first volume of verse, 1855; left Guernsey, 1856, and worked as a journalist; contributed to *Punch* and many other journals; settled in Berkshire, 1862.

Text: *Idyls and Rhymes*, 1855.

## ELIZA COOK (1812–89)

Born in London, of working-class origin; self-educ.; publ. first volume of verse, 1835; contributed regularly to periodicals; founded *Eliza Cook's Journal*, 1849, closed in 1854 because of her ill-health; awarded Civil List pension, 1864.

Text: *Poetical Works*, 1870.

## EDITH COOPER *see entry for* 'Michael Field'.

## THOMAS COOPER (1805–92)

Born in Gainsborough, where he was apprenticed as shoemaker; self-educ.; opened school in 1827; worked as journalist in Lincoln and London; joined Chartist movement; imprisoned for sedition and conspiracy, 1843–5, and wrote *The Purgatory of Suicides* in Stafford gaol; gave up political activism and in later life wrote and lectured on religious and social subjects.

Text: *Poetical Works*, 1877.

'BARRY CORNWALL' *see entry for* Bryan Waller Procter.

## WILLIAM JOHNSON CORY (1823–92)

Poet, scholar, and author of various educational works; born William Johnson in Torrington, Devon; educ. at Eton and King's College, Cambridge, where he won the Chancellor's Medal for poetry, 1843; assistant master at Eton, and fellow of King's College, 1845–72; publ. first volume of verse, 1858; wrote the Eton Boating Song, 1865; changed name to Cory when he retired.

Text: *Ionica*, 1858.

## F. B. T. COUTTS-NEVILL *see entry for* F. B. Money-Coutts.

## LADY CURRIE *see entry for* Mary Montgomerie Lamb.

## JOHN DAVIDSON (1857–1909)

Scottish poet, born in Barrhead, Renfrewshire; worked as schoolmaster and wrote several plays and a dramatic poem, *Diabolus Amans* (1885), before settling in London, 1889; contributed to *Yellow Book*; gained recognition with *Fleet Street Eclogues*, 1893, and *Ballads and Songs*, 1894; after 1901 wrote blank verse 'Testaments' expounding philosophy of materialism; awarded Civil List pension, 1906; committed suicide by drowning.

Text: *Ballads and Songs*, except 'New Year's Day': *Fleet Street Eclogues*.

## RICHARD WATSON DIXON (1833–1900)

Poet, historian and clergyman; born in London; friend of William Morris, Edward Burne-Jones, and other Pre-Raphaelites; ordained 1858 and held various Church appointments, mainly in north of England; publ. his first volume of poetry, 1861; his long poem, *Mano*, publ. 1883; corresponded with Hopkins, 1878–88; his multi-volume *History of the Church of England* publ. 1877–1900.

Text: 'Dream': *Christ's Company and other poems*, 1861; 'Song': *Historical odes and other poems*, 1864; 'The Mystery of the Body': *Lyrical Poems*, 1887.

## SYDNEY THOMPSON DOBELL (1824–74)

Poet and critic; born in Cranbrook, Kent; educ. at home; his long dramatic poem *Balder* (1854) epitomized the 'Spasmodic School' of poetry ridiculed by Aytoun; collaborated with Alexander Smith on volume of Crimean War sonnets, 1855; became an invalid after a fall among the ruins of Pozzuoli, 1866.

Text: *Poetical Works*, 1875.

## CHARLES LUTWIDGE DODGSON *see entry for* 'Lewis Carroll'.

## DIGBY MACKWORTH DOLBEN (1848–67)

Born in Guernsey; educ. at Eton, where he became a friend of Robert Bridges, a distant cousin, and the passionate admirer of another schoolfellow, Archie Manning; had strong leanings to Roman Catholicism, and on occasions adopted the habit of a Benedictine monk, but had not completed his conversion before his death; drowned while swimming in the River Welland in Northamptonshire.

Text: *Poems*, ed. Bridges, 1911.

## ALFRED DOMETT (1811–87)

Born in Camberwell, south London, the son of a ship-owner; educ. at St John's College, Cambridge; trained as barrister; publ. first volume of verse, 1833; close friend of Robert Browning before emigrating to New Zealand, 1842 (subject of Browning's *Waring*); active in New Zealand politics (prime minister, 1862–3) and cultural life; returned to England, 1871; publ. long poem on Maori life, *Ranolf and Amohia*, 1872.

Text: *Flotsam and Jetsam*, 1877.

## EDWARD DOWDEN (1843–1913)

Irish scholar and critic, born in Cork; educ. at Trinity College, Dublin, where he became professor of English literature, 1867; author of influential study of Shakespeare (1875) and other critical works, incl. biography of Browning; publ. only two volumes of verse, in 1876 and 1913.

Text: *Poems*, ed. Elisabeth Dowden, 1914.

## ERNEST (Christopher) DOWSON (1867–1900)

Born in London, the son of a dry-dock owner in Limehouse; educ. at home by his father, and at Queen's College, Oxford, where he became friends with Lionel Johnson; worked for his father's business in London, and frequented literary and bohemian society in London; contributed to *Yellow Book*, the *Savoy*, and publications of the Rhymers Club; other friendships incl. Aubrey Beardsley and Victor Plarr; converted to Roman Catholicism, 1891–2; in 1891 met Adelaide Foltinowicz, a girl of twelve, who became his mistress; befriended Wilde in France after his trial, 1894; publ. his only volume of verse, 1896; Adelaide broke with him, 1897; died of alcoholism.

Text: *Verses*, 1896, except 'To William Theodore Peters': *Decorations in Verse and Prose*, 1899.

## R(owland) E(yles) EGERTON-WARBURTON (1804–91)

Born in Cheshire; educ. at Eton and Christ Church, Oxford; high sheriff of Cheshire, 1833; his popular *Hunting Songs* first publ. in 1846.

Text: *Poems, Epigrams, and Sonnets*, 1877.

**GEORGE ELIOT** (Mary Ann, *afterwards* Marian, Evans) (1819–80)
Born in Chilvers Coton, Warwickshire, the daughter of a land agent; convert to Evangelicalism in her girlhood, then embraced rational and free-thinking philosophy; transl. Strauss's *Life of Jesus*, 1846; contributed to *Westminster Review* and became assistant editor, 1851; gradually surmounted scandal of unmarried liaison with G. H. Lewes, though remained estranged from her beloved brother Isaac until, after Lewes's death, and a few months before her own, she married John Walter Cross. Her fame as novelist established by *Adam Bede* (1858); her first work of poetry, *The Spanish Gypsy*, publ. 1868.
    Text: *The Legend of Jubal and other poems*, 1874.

**EBENEZER ELLIOTT** (1781–1849)
Self-taught radical poet, from Sheffield, where he became a master-founder; known as the 'Corn Law Rhymer' after the title of *Corn Law Rhymes* (1834), which voiced protest at the 'Bread Tax' and made him famous.
    Text: *Poetical Works*, 1876.

**ANNE EVANS** (1820–70)
Poet and musical composer; born in Market Bosworth, Leicestershire, daughter of the scholar Arthur Benoni Evans, headmaster of Market Bosworth school; sister of Sebastian Evans (see next entry).
    Text: *Poems and Music*, 1880.

**SEBASTIAN EVANS** (1830–1909)
For family, see prec. entry. Journalist and barrister; also worked as a window designer for a Birmingham glass factory, and exhibited paintings at Royal Academy; edited *Birmingham Daily Gazette*, 1867–70, and *People* (which he part-founded), 1878–81; a strong Conservative in politics; transl. *The High History of the Holy Graal*, 1878.
    Text: *Brother Fabian's Manuscript, and other poems*, 1865.

**'VIOLET FANE'** *see entry for* Mary Montgomerie Lamb.

**'MICHAEL FIELD'** (Katherine Harris Bradley, 1846–1914, and Edith Emma Cooper, 1862–1913)
Katherine Bradley educ. Newnham College, Cambridge; publ. first volume of verse under pseudonym 'Arran Leigh', 1875; brought up her niece, Edith Cooper, from childhood; the two became lovers, *c.* 1878; publ. first joint volume under pseudonym, 1889; knew Wilde and many of the literary and artistic figures of the *fin de siècle* but rejected the 'decadent' movement; both converted to Roman Catholicism, 1906.
    Text: *Underneath the Bough*, 1893, except 'L'Indifférent': *Sight and Song*, 1892.

## EDWARD FITZGERALD (1809–83)

Poet and translator; born at Bredfield House, near Woodbridge, Suffolk, the son of wealthy landowners in England and Ireland; educ. Trinity College, Cambridge, where he formed lifelong friendship with Tennyson; other friends incl. Carlyle and Thackeray; publ. 'Rubáiyát of Omar Khayyám' anonymously, 1859; lived reclusively in Suffolk; among other works transl. plays by Calderón, Aeschylus and Sophocles.

Text: *Rubáiyát of Omar Khayyám*, 1859.

## DAVID GRAY (1838–61)

Scottish poet; born in Merkland, Kirkintilloch, in Dumbartonshire; son of a hand-loom weaver; pupil-teacher in Glasgow; contributed verse to *Glasgow Citizen*; travelled to London, 1860, where he obtained some literary work but suffered great hardship; returned briefly to Scotland but came south for reasons of health; in hospital in Torquay, but finally determined to return home; spent last year in Merkland, composing a series of sonnets entitled 'In the Shadows'; his friend Sydney Dobell arranged for posthumous publ. of his poems, 1862.

Text: *The Luggie and other poems*, 1862.

## JOHN (Henry) GRAY (1866–1934)

Born in Bethnal Green, London; his father, a Scot, employed at Royal Naval Dockyard, Woolwich (later Inspector of Stores at Woolwich Arsenal); taught himself languages, music, and painting; worked as an apprentice at the Arsenal; passed civil service examination, 1882, and worked first in the Post Office and then, after passing the London University matriculation examination, the Foreign Office, 1888; converted to Roman Catholicism, 1890; began to frequent literary and bohemian circles, and to contribute verse and translations to *The Dial*; a close friend of Oscar Wilde, 1891–3, and a possible model for Wilde's Dorian Gray; began to turn away from his 'decadent' way of life, 1897; resigned from the Foreign Office, 1898, to study for the priesthood; ordained, 1901; appointed to a parish in Edinburgh, and spent the remainder of his life there, eventually becoming rector of St Peter's, Morningside.

Text: *Silverpoints*, 1893.

## DORA GREENWELL (1821–82)

Poet and essayist; born on the family's estate in County Durham; educ. at home, where she lived until her mother's death in 1871; publ. first volume of poems, 1848; devoutly religious, but a liberal in politics and supporter of progressive causes incl. women's suffrage and educational reform; met and corresponded with other leading women poets (Barrett Browning, Ingelow, Rossetti).

Text: 'A Scherzo': *Poems*, 1867; 'A Valentine': *Poems*, 1861.

**LOUISA SARAH GUGGENBERGER** *see entry for* L. S. Bevington.

**THOMAS GORDON HAKE** (1809–95)
Physician and poet, born in Leeds; educ. Christ's Hospital; studied medicine at St George's Hospital and at Glasgow and Edinburgh; publ. first volume of verse, 1839; friend of D. G. Rossetti, whom he attended in his final illness.
   Text: *Legends of the Morrow*, 1879.

**SIR JOHN HANMER** (afterwards Baron Hanmer) (1809–81)
Whig (Liberal) politician; educ. Eton and Christ Church, Oxford; succeeded to baronetcy, 1828; publ. first volume of verse, 1839; acquaintance of Browning, who praised his sonnets and his opposition to the Corn Laws; MP successively for Shrewsbury, Hull and Flint; created a peer, 1872.
   Text: 'To an Eagle': *Fra Cipolla and other poems*, 1839; 'Poetry by the Way-Side': *Sonnets*, 1840.

**THOMAS HARDY** (1840–1928)
Born near Dorchester, the son of a stonemason; trained as architect and practised in London and Dorchester; wrote poetry from an early age and considered himself as much a poet as a novelist, though his first volume, *Wessex Poems*, not publ. until 1898, three years after his last novel, *Jude the Obscure*; continued to publish volumes of verse, some containing material from earlier periods, until his death; buried in Westminster Abbey.
   Text: 'Friends Beyond', 'Neutral Tones', 'Her Dilemma', 'I look into my glass': *Wessex Poems*, 1896; others: *Poems of the Past and the Present*, 1901 (post-dated 1902).

**FRANCES RIDLEY HAVERGAL** (1836–79)
Born in Astley, Worcestershire, the daughter of William Henry Havergal, a clergyman and composer of sacred music; herself a popular and successful composer of hymns and musical settings of psalms and other religious verse; donated most of her earnings to Christian charities and causes.
   Text: *Poetical Works*, 1884.

**ROBERT STEPHEN HAWKER** (1803–75)
Poet, clergyman and antiquary; born in Stoke Damerel, Devon; educ. Pembroke College, Oxford; won Newdigate Prize for poetry, 1827; from 1834 vicar of Morwenstow in Cornwall, the inspiration and setting of much of his work; addicted to opium; in 1864 publ. *The Quest of the Sangraal*, part of a projected Arthurian epic; in later life converted to Roman Catholicism.
   Text: *Poetical Works*, 1879.

## W(illiam) E(rnest) HENLEY (1849–1903)

Poet, dramatist, and journalist; born in Gloucester, where he was a pupil of T. E. Brown; suffered from tubercular arthritis and had to have a foot amputated; his hospital poems first publ. 1875 in *Cornhill Magazine*; Leslie Stephen, the editor, visited him in Edinburgh Infirmary and introduced him to R. L. Stevenson, who became a close friend and with whom he collaborated on several plays; influential editor of (among others) the *Magazine of Art*, the imperialist *National Observer*, and the *New Review*.

Text: *Poems*, 1898.

## JAMES HENRY (1798–1876)

Irish physician, poet and classical scholar; born in Dublin, and educ. at Trinity College, where he won the gold medal; practised medicine in Dublin until 1845, then devoted himself to study of Virgil in libraries across Europe; besides his poetry and scholarly works, also wrote pamphlets on controversial topics (e.g. attacks on fashions in modern medicine).

Text: *A Half Year's Poems*, 1854, except 'The son's a poor, wretched, unfortunate creature': *Poems, chiefly Philosophical*, 1856. The diacritical marks are Henry's own.

## THOMAS HOOD (1799–1845)

Poet and journalist, born in London; assistant editor of *London Magazine*, 1821–3; friend of Lamb, Hazlitt, De Quincey, and others; edited various journals and annuals, incl. the *Gem* and *New Monthly Magazine*, and became a popular writer of comic and sentimental verse; lived for a time in Germany; received Civil List pension shortly before his death.

Text: *Punch*, Christmas Number, 1843.

## GERARD MANLEY HOPKINS (1844–89)

Born in Stratford, Essex; educ. at Highgate School, where he was briefly taught by Richard Watson Dixon, and Balliol College, Oxford, where he became friends with Robert Bridges; converted to Roman Catholicism, 1866; studied for Jesuit order, 1868–77; worked in several urban and industrial parishes in Liverpool and elsewhere; appointed to chair of Greek and Latin at University College, Dublin, 1884; with few exceptions, his poetry not publ. in his lifetime; his papers passed to Bridges after his death; Bridges withheld poems because of their 'oddity' until 1918.

Text: *Gerard Manley Hopkins*, ed. C. Phillips, Oxford University Press [Oxford Authors], 1986.

## A(lfred) E(dward) HOUSMAN (1859–1936)

Born in Fockbury, Worcestershire; educ. at Bromsgrove School and St John's College, Oxford; failed in final examinations and worked in Patent Office, 1882–92; gradually established reputation as classical scholar; professor of

Latin at University College London, 1892–1911, then at Cambridge until his death.

Text: *A Shropshire Lad*, 1896.

## MARY HOWITT, *née* Botham (1799–1888)

Poet and miscellaneous author (biography, essays, translations, history etc.); born in Coleford, Gloucestershire, from a Quaker family; married William Howitt, also a Quaker, 1821, and collaborated with him in numerous works; early literary friendships included Felicia Hemans and Mary Russell Mitford; her ballads were popular and admired by Elizabeth Barrett Browning; wrote in support of many progressive causes; received Civil List pension after William's death, 1879; lived in Italy; converted to Roman Catholicism, 1882; buried (by special dispensation) in Protestant Cemetery at Rome next to her husband.

Text: *Birds and Flowers*, 1838.

## (James Henry) LEIGH HUNT (1784–1859)

Poet, essayist, and journalist; born in Southgate, Middlesex, and educ. as charity boy at Christ's Hospital; with his brother John, founded in 1808 the leading liberal journal of the period, the *Examiner*; associated personally and professionally with most of the 'second generation' of Romantic writers (Byron, Keats, Shelley, Lamb, Hazlitt, etc.), whose work he published and supported; imprisoned for libelling the Prince Regent, 1813; lampooned, with Keats and Hazlitt, as member of the 'Cockney School' of poetry; edited several other journals in subsequent years, besides continuing to write essays and poems, and became the friend of Browning, Carlyle and Dickens, among other Victorian writers; awarded Civil List pension, 1847.

Text: *Poetical Works*, 1860.

## JEAN INGELOW (1820–97)

Poet and author of children's books; born in Boston, Lincolnshire; settled with family in London in 1860s; member of Portfolio Society of women writers and artists (others incl. Dora Greenwell, Adelaide Procter, Christina Rossetti); her poems were extremely popular and commercially successful, both in Britain and America.

Text: 'Wake, baillie, wake!': *Mopsa the Fairy*, 1869; 'Loss and Waste': *Poems*, 1885.

## LIONEL (Pigot) JOHNSON (1867–1902)

Poet and critic, associated with the 'aesthetic' or 'decadent' movement; born in Broadstairs, Kent; educ. at Winchester and New College, Oxford; member of the Rhymers Club and friend of Yeats; converted to Roman Catholicism, 1891; admired Hardy and wrote a full-length study of his work, 1894; publ. first volume of poems, 1895; died of alcoholism.

Text: 'By the Statue of King Charles' and 'The Dark Angel': *Poems*, 1895; 'Love's Ways': *Ireland, with other poems*, 1897.

## WILLIAM JOHNSON *see entry for* William Cory.

## EBENEZER JONES (1820–60)

Born in London; raised in strict Calvinist family; worked as a clerk, and paid for publ. of his only volume, *Studies of Sensation and Event*, 1843; crushed by its failure, and destroyed his unpubl. poems; worked as an accountant; sympathized with Chartists, and collaborated with his friend, the radical journalist and poet W. J. Linton; began writing poetry again shortly before his death from consumption; his reputation revived in 1870s with praise from D. G. Rossetti, William Bell Scott and others.

   Text: *Studies of Sensation and Event*, 1843.

## ERNEST (Charles) JONES (1819–68)

Chartist activist, novelist and poet; born in Berlin and educ. in Germany; family returned to England, 1838; called to Bar, 1844, but did not practise; joined Chartists in 1846 and espoused Feargus O'Connor's 'physical force' doctrine against Thomas Cooper's advocacy of non-violence; edited the *Northern Star* and the *People's Paper*; imprisoned for sedition, 1848–50; contested Parliamentary seats in several elections.

   Text: *The Battle-Day and other poems*, 1855.

## MAY KENDALL (Emma Goldworth Kendall) (1861–*c.* 1931)

Poet, social critic and novelist; daughter of a Wesleyan minister in Bridlington, Yorkshire; publ. first book, *That Very Mab*, with Andrew Lang, 1885; after 1898 devoted herself to causes of social reform.

   Text: *Dreams to Sell*, 1887. The title of this volume comes from the poem by Beddoes (no. 48).

## HARRIET ELEANOR HAMILTON KING, *née* Hamilton (1840–1920)

Place of birth not found; in youth a passionate advocate of Italian independence and unification, and from 1862 conducted important correspondence with Mazzini (publ. 1912); married Henry King, a banker, 1863; in later life converted to Roman Catholicism.

   Text: *A Book of Dreams*, 1883.

## CHARLES KINGSLEY (1819–75)

Born in Holme, Devon; educ. at Helston Grammar School (where Derwent Coleridge was headmaster), King's College, London, and Magdalene College, Cambridge; ordained 1842 and became curate, then rector, of Eversley in Hampshire; active in Christian Socialist movement with F. D. Maurice, and was a friend of Carlyle and Froude; his first work of poetry, *The Saint's Tragedy*, a verse drama, publ. 1848, the same year as his first novel, *Yeast*; publ. another 'social problem' novel, *Alton Locke*, 1850; turned to patriotic history and legend (*Westward Ho!*, 1855; *Hereward the Wake*, 1866); his best-known children's book, *The Water Babies*, publ. 1863; his controversy with Newman inspired Newman's *Apologia*, 1864; professor of modern history at Cambridge, 1860–69; canon of Chester, 1869, and of Westminster, 1873.

Text: *Collected Poems*, 1872.

## (Joseph) RUDYARD KIPLING (1865–1936)

Born in Bombay; educ. United Services College at Westward Ho!; journalist in India, 1882–9, where he also became a Freemason; stories and poems about India helped him to achieve fame on return to England; in 1892 married Caroline Balestier, an American, and lived in Vermont until 1896; eventually settled in Sussex; refused offer of Laureateship, 1895; spent much time in travel, esp. South Africa; strong but critical supporter of imperialism and unionism; first British writer to be awarded Nobel Prize, 1907.

Text: *Barrack-Room Ballads and other verses*, 1892.

## MARY MONTGOMERIE LAMB ('Violet Fane'; Mrs Singleton, *afterwards* Lady Currie) (1843–1905)

Poet and novelist; born in Littlehampton, Sussex, into wealthy family and educ. privately; began to write in her youth and adopted pseudonym (from Disraeli's novel *Vivian Grey*) to avoid parental disapproval; married Henry Singleton, an Irish landowner, 1864; after his death married the diplomat Sir Philip Henry Wodehouse Currie, 1894, and accompanied him to Constantinople and Rome; portrayed as 'Mrs Sinclair' in W. H. Mallock's satire *The New Republic*, which he dedicated to her.

Text: *Betwixt Two Seas: Poems and Ballads*, 1900.

## LETITIA ELIZABETH LANDON ('L.E.L.') (1802–38)

Born in Chelsea, the daughter of an army agent; began writing in youth and publ. first poem in 1820; enjoyed phenomenal popular and commercial success but was dogged by financial difficulties and gossip about her private life; in 1838 married George Maclean, governor of Cape Coast Castle in West Africa, and accompanied him there; after three months, died of prussic acid poison (whether by accident or suicide is not certain).

Text: Samuel Laman Blanchard, *Life and Literary Remains of L. E. L.*, 1841.

## WALTER SAVAGE LANDOR (1775–1864)

Born in Warwick; educ. at Rugby and Trinity College, Oxford (rusticated 1794); fought in Spain as a volunteer against French occupation, and espoused radical and republican causes throughout his life; publ. first volume of verse, 1795; *Gebir*, an epic romance, publ. 1798; lived in Italy, 1815–35, when he separated from his wife and returned to England; publ. first series of *Imaginary Conversations of Literary Men and Statesmen*, 1824; returned to Italy, 1858; cared for in his last years by Browning, who greatly admired his work.

Text: *Works*, 1846, except 'The Duke of York's Statue' and 'I strove with none': *Last Fruit off an Old Tree*, 1853; 'Plays': *Dry Sticks*, 1858. 'I strove with none' was first published in the *Examiner* with the title 'Dying Speech of an Old Philosopher' and signed 'W. S. L., 30 January 1849' (Landor's birthday).

## WILLIAM LARMINIE (1849–1900)
Irish poet and folklorist; born in Castlebar, County Mayo; educ. Trinity College, Dublin; civil servant in India Office; publ. first of his two volumes of verse, 1889; also publ. *West Irish Folk Tales and Romances*, 1898, based in part on material gathered from Gaelic-speaking storytellers.

Text: *Fand and other poems*, 1892.

## EDWARD LEAR (1812–88)
Born in Holloway, the youngest of twenty children; worked as a zoological draughtsman; invited by Earl of Derby to draw birds in the aviary at Knowsley House; wrote and illustrated limericks to amuse the Earl's grandchildren, publ. as *The Book of Nonsense*, 1846; travelled widely in the Mediterranean and Middle East; gained increasing recognition as landscape artist; suffered from epilepsy and depression; died at San Remo, where he had settled in 1871.

Text: Limericks: *The Book of Nonsense*, 1846; others: *Nonsense Songs*, 1894.

## EUGENE (Jacob) LEE-HAMILTON (1845–1907)
Born in London; educ. at Oriel College, Oxford, and entered diplomatic service; in 1873 disabled by nervous disease and confined to a wheeled bed; lived at Florence; publ. first volume of verse, 1888; restored to health, 1897.

Text: *Sonnets of the Wingless Hours*, 1894.

## ROBERT LEIGHTON (1822–69)
Scottish poet; born in Dundee; worked in the office of his brother, a ship-owner, and completed a circumnavigation of the world, 1842–3; managed a seed-merchant's business, 1854–67.

Text: *Poems*, 1869.

## AMY LEVY (1861–89)
Born in Clapham; first Jewish student of Newnham College, Cambridge, but left after four terms; publ. first volume of poems, 1881; formed close friendships with Olive Schreiner, Clementina Black, and other women writers and thinkers; suffered from lifelong depression; her novel *Reuben Sachs* (1888) caused outcry for its hostile portrayal of Jewish community; committed suicide by inhaling charcoal fumes.

Text: *A Minor Poet and other verse*, 1884.

**CAROLINE** (Blanche Elizabeth), **LADY LINDSAY**, *née* Fitzroy
(1844–1912)
Born in London to wealthy upper-class family; married Sir Henry Coutts Lindsay,
1864, but separated from him in early 1880s; literary friends incl. Browning and
Ruskin; publ. first volume of poems, 1889.
Text: *The Flower-Seller and other poems*, 1896.

**FREDERICK LOCKER-LAMPSON** (1821–95)
Poet and civil servant; born Frederick Locker in Greenwich Hospital, where his
father, Edward Hawke Locker, was civil commissioner; entered civil service as
clerk in Somerset House, 1841; became deputy-reader at Admiralty; left service,
*c.* 1850; publ. his first volume of verse, *London Lyrics*, 1857; adopted name of
Lampson after that of his second wife, 1885.
Text: *London Lyrics*, 1885.

**SIR ALFRED COMYNS LYALL** (1835–1911)
Civil servant and writer, son of the philosopher Alfred Lyall; born in Coulsdon,
Surrey; joined Indian Civil Service, 1856, and was active during Mutiny, 1857–8;
held many high offices incl. lieutenant-governorship of Northwest Provinces and
Oudh; knighted 1881; returned to England, 1887; Rede lecturer at Cambridge,
1891; besides his one volume of poems, wrote historical and biographical studies
of British rule in India.
Text: *Verses written in India*, 1889. The poem is the second of two 'Studies at
Delhi, 1876'; originally publ. in India in 1882, when the last line was not in
quotation marks.

**HENRY FRANCIS LYTE** (1793–1847)
Poet and hymn-writer; born near Kelso, Roxburghshire; educ. Trinity College,
Dublin; ordained 1815; rector of Lower Brixham, Devon, from 1822 until his
death; publ. first volume of verse, 1833; travelled frequently for reasons of health,
and died at Nice, where he is buried.
Text: *Remains*, 1850.

**EDWARD ROBERT BULWER LYTTON**, First Earl of Lytton
(1831–91)
Son of the novelist and statesman Edward Bulwer-Lytton; born in London;
his childhood affected by scandal surrounding his parents' marriage; educ.
Harrow and Bonn; entered diplomatic service and rose to high office in Europe
and India, becoming Viceroy in 1876; publ. first volume of verse under
pseudonym 'Owen Meredith', 1855; in 1877 proclaimed Queen Victoria
Empress of India.
Text: *Marah [and other poems]*, 1892.

## JAMES CLARENCE MANGAN (1803–49)

Irish poet, born in Dublin; worked as a lawyer's clerk; employed in library of Trinity College, Dublin, and contributed to several Irish journals, but constantly in financial difficulties and plagued by alcoholism; died in extreme poverty.

Text: *Poems*, 1859.

## PHILIP BOURKE MARSTON (1850–87)

Son of the dramatist John Westland Marston; born in London; partially blind from the age of three; his precocious literary gifts encouraged by his father and the literary circle in which he grew up; publ. his first volume of verse, 1871; in the same year Mary Nesbit (sister of E. Nesbit), to whom he was betrothed, died of consumption; his life blighted by successive bereavements, incl. his two sisters and his friend James Thomson, and also by the complete loss of his sight; other friends incl. D. G. Rossetti and Swinburne, whose elegy on him was publ. 1891.

Text: *Collected Poems*, 1892.

## GEORGE MEREDITH (1828–1909)

Born in Portsmouth, the son of a tailor and naval outfitter; educ. partly at the progressive Moravian school in Neuwied, Germany; articled to a solicitor in London but soon turned to writing (poetry and journalism, then the novels for which he is best known); married Mary Ellen Nicholls, the widowed daughter of Thomas Love Peacock, 1849; publ. first volume of verse, 1851; his wife deserted him for the painter Henry Wallis, 1858, and died 1861; remarried, 1864; after early hardship and struggle for critical and popular recognition, gradually gained fame and prosperity from his novels and other writings; President of Society of Authors, 1892, and received the Order of Merit, 1905.

Text: *Works*, 1898.

## 'OWEN MEREDITH' *see entry for* Edward Robert Bulwer Lytton.

## ALICE (Christiana Gertrude) MEYNELL, *née* Thompson (1847–1922)

Poet, essayist, and journalist; sister of the painter Elizabeth Butler; born and brought up in Italy, and educ. mainly by her father; family returned to England, 1864; converted to Roman Catholicism, *c.* 1868; publ. first volume of poems, 1875; married Wilfred Meynell, 1877, and collaborated with him in editorship of several journals; literary friendships incl. Francis Thompson, Coventry Patmore and George Meredith; in her last years a strong supporter of women's suffrage.

Text: 'Renouncement': *Poems*, 1893; others: 'Later Poems', 1902.

## THOMAS MILLER (1807–74)

Poet, novelist, and miscellaneous writer (tales, sketches, children's books); born in Gainsborough, the son of a wharfinger; apprenticed at early age to a basket-maker; became acquainted with Thomas Cooper; encouraged by the Nottingham writer and journalist Thomas Bailey, publ. first volume of verse, 1832; moved to London, 1835, where he attracted the patronage of Lady Blessington; set up as bookseller, 1841; wrote tales for the popular *London Journal*; awarded pension by Disraeli, 1874, but died in destitution.

Text: *Birds, Bees and Blossoms: Original Poems for Children*, 1864.

F(rancis) B(urdett) **MONEY-COUTTS** (F. B. T. Coutts-Nevill, 5th Baron Latymer) (1852–1923)
Son of Rev. James Drummond Money and Clara Maria, daughter of Sir Francis Burdett and sister of Lady Burdett-Coutts; educ. Eton and Trinity College, Cambridge; changed name to 'Money-Coutts', 1880, in order to inherit Lady Burdett-Coutts's shares in the banking house of Coutts & Co.; publ. first volume of verse, 1896; in 1912 successfully laid claim to barony of Latymer, in abeyance since 1577; in 1914 made his final change of name, to Coutts-Nevill (the Latymer title having descended to him through the Nevill line).

Text: 'The Commonest Lot': *Poems*, 1896; 'Epitaphs': *The Alhambra and other poems*, 1898.

(William) **COSMO MONKHOUSE** (1840–1901)
Civil servant, art critic and poet; born in London, and educ. St Paul's School; clerk in Board of Trade, 1856; became assistant secretary to Finance Department; publ. first volume of verse, 1865; wrote on painting for several journals incl. the *Academy* and *Saturday Review*; publ. life of Turner, 1879, and study of English water-colourists, 1890.

Text: *Pasiteles the Elder and other poems*, 1901.

**WILLIAM MORRIS** (1834–96)
Born in Walthamstow, the son of a businessman; educ. Marlborough School and Exeter College, Oxford, where he became friends with Edward Burne-Jones; helped found the *Oxford and Cambridge Magazine*, 1856; articled as architect, 1856; studied as a painter, 1857–62, and assisted D. G. Rossetti in Oxford Union frescos; publ. first volume of verse, 1858; married Jane Burden, the model for many Pre-Raphaelite paintings, 1859; she became Rossetti's mistress, with Morris's knowledge and perhaps consent; his long career of combined business and artistic enterprise (beginning with the manufacturing and decorating firm of Morris, Marshall, Faulkener and Co., and ending with the Kelmscott Press) the epitome of the 'arts and crafts' movement; founded Society for the Protection of Ancient Buildings, 1877; in later life a passionate socialist.

Publications: *The Defence of Guinevere and other poems*, 1858; *The Life and Death of Jason*, 1867; *The Earthly Paradise*, 1868–70; *Love is Enough, or The Freeing of Pharamond*, 1873; *Sigurd the Volsing* and *The Fall of the Niblungs*, 1876; *The Pilgrims of Hope* (publ. in the journal *The Commonweal*), 1885; *A Dream of John Ball* (prose), 1888; *Poems by the Way*, 1891; *News from Nowhere* (prose), 1891.

Text: 'The Haystack in the Floods': *The Defence of Guinevere*; others: *Poems by the Way*.

## ARTHUR (Joseph) MUNBY (1828–1910)

Poet and civil servant; born in Clifton Holme, Yorkshire; educ. Trinity College, Cambridge; publ. first volume of verse, 1852; called to Bar, 1855; worked in ecclesiastical commissioners' office, 1858–88; kept his marriage to a maidservant secret.

Text: *Verses New and Old*, 1865.

## ROBERT FULLER MURRAY (1863–94)

Born in Roxbury, Massachusetts, of Scottish-American parentage; father a Unitarian minister; family returned to Britain, 1869; educ. St Andrews University; publ. verse in college magazine, later collected in a volume, 1891; left in 1894 and attempted to earn living as journalist in Edinburgh, but without success; returned to St Andrews; contributed to *Punch*, *Saturday Review*, and other journals; died of consumption.

Text: *The Scarlet Gown: being verses by a St. Andrews Man*, 1891.

## CONSTANCE (Caroline Woodhill) NADEN (1858–89)

Poet and scientific thinker; born in Birmingham; attended botany classes at Birmingham Medical Institute, 1879; studied at Mason College, Birmingham, 1881–7; influenced by Herbert Spencer in development of freethinking and humanist beliefs, which she termed 'Hylo-Idealism'; publ. first volume of verse, 1881; wrote articles for *Journal of Science* and *Agnostic Annual*; in 1887 visited Palestine, Egypt, and India, possibly contracting the infection from which she died.

Text: *Complete Poetical Works*, 1894.

## EDITH NESBIT (Mrs Bland, Mrs Tucker) (1858–1924)

Born in London, daughter of the head of an agricultural college; her sister betrothed to Philip Bourke Marston before her death; married Hubert Bland, later a founder member of Fabian Society, 1880; her marriage marked by complicated sexual liaisons and living arrangements on both sides; publ. first volume of verse, 1886; became supporter of socialist and other radical causes; friendships incl. Eleanor Marx, Annie Besant and G. B. Shaw; began writing the children's stories for which she is famous in 1890s; after husband's death, married Thomas Tucker, 1917.

Text: *Leaves of Life*, 1888.

## SIR HENRY (John) NEWBOLT (1862–1938)

Poet and novelist; born in Bilston, Staffordshire; educ. Clifton and Corpus Christi College, Oxford; called to Bar, 1887, and practised until 1899; publ. first volume of verse, 1896; his patriotic and pro-imperialist writings achieved great popularity;

active in public service; knighted 1915; contributed to official naval history of First World War.

Text: *The Island Race*, 1898.

### ELIZA (Anne Harris) OGILVY, *née* Dick (1822–1912)

Scottish poet, born in Perth; spent three years in India, 1838–41; married David Ogilvy, 1843; publ. first volume of verse, 1846; moved to Italy, 1848; became friends with the Brownings in Florence; returned to Britain, 1852; later friendships incl. the actress Helen Faucit and Sir Arthur Sullivan.

Text: *Poems of Ten Years*, 1856.

### GEORGE OUTRAM (1805–56)

Scottish poet and journalist, best known for humorous verse; born at the Clyde ironworks, near Glasgow, where his father was manager; educ. at University of Edinburgh; called to Scottish Bar, 1827, but unsuccessful as advocate; became editor of *Glasgow Herald*, 1837; collaborated with 'Christopher North' (John Wilson) on 'Dies Boreales', the successor to the dialogues of 'Noctes Ambrosianae'.

Text: *Legal Lyrics and Metrical Illustrations of the Scotch Forms of Process*, 1851.

### COVENTRY (Kersey Dighton) PATMORE (1823–96)

Son of the journalist P. G. Patmore, editor of *New Monthly Magazine*; born in Woodford, Essex; privately educ.; publ. first volume of verse, 1844; assistant in printed books department of British Museum, 1846; contributed to Pre-Raphaelite magazine *The Germ*; married first wife, Emily, 1847, who inspired sequence of poems on married love, collectively titled *The Angel in the House*, 1854–63; friendships in this period incl. the Brownings, Ruskin and Tennyson; Emily died, 1862; travelled to Rome, 1864, and met his second wife, Marianne, who influenced his conversion to Roman Catholicism; after her death, 1880, married Harriet, the governess of his children; in later life formed friendships with Hopkins, Francis Thompson, and Alice Meynell.

Text: *Poems*, 1897.

### EMILY (Jane) PFEIFFER, *née* Davis (1827–90)

Poet and supporter of social causes, esp. women's education; publ. first volume of verse, 1843; married Jurgen Edward Pfeiffer, a wealthy merchant, 1853; among other donations, contributed to building of Aberdare Hall at Cardiff for women students of University of Wales.

Text: *Gerard's Monument and other poems* (2nd edn), 1878; the poem is the first of 'Six Studies in Exotic Forms of Verse'.

### STEPHEN PHILLIPS (1864–1915)

Born in Summertown, near Oxford; educ. at Oundle; cousin of Laurence Binyon; became an actor; publ. first volume of verse, 1884; devoted himself to revival of verse drama, and had considerable success with *Paolo and Francesca* (1900) and other plays, but later works failed.

Text: *Poems*, 1897.

## VICTOR (Gustave) PLARR (1863–1929)

Born near Strasbourg, son of French-Alsatian father and English mother; family moved to Britain after losing home in Franco-Prussian war, 1870; educ. Tonbridge School and Worcester College, Oxford; worked as literary journalist and translator in London; librarian of King's College, London, 1890; member of Rhymers Club, and a close friend of Lionel Johnson and Ernest Dowson; publ. first volume of verse, 1896; became librarian of Royal College of Surgeons, 1897, a post he held until his death.

Text: 'Twilight-Piece', 'Shadows', 'Epitaphium Citharistriæ', 'At Citoyenne Tussaud's': *In the Dorian Mood*, 1896; others: *The Garland of New Poetry by Various Writers*, 1899.

## MAY PROBYN (*fl*. 1878–?)

Poet and novelist; dates of birth and death unknown; lived in Weybridge; publ. first novel, 1878, and first book of verse, 1881; converted to Roman Catholicism before 1895, when she publ. her last volume.

Text: *Pansies*, 1895.

## ADELAIDE ANNE PROCTER (1825–64)

Daughter of the poet B. W. Procter ('Barry Cornwall'); born in London; privately educ.; converted to Roman Catholicism, *c*. 1850; began contributing to Dickens's magazine *Household Words* under pseudonym 'Mary Berwick', 1853; publ. first volume of verse, 1858; dedicated to social causes, esp. employment of women; died of consumption.

Text: *Legends and Lyrics*, 1858.

## BRYAN WALLER PROCTER ('Barry Cornwall') (1787–1874)

Poet, dramatist and essayist; born in London, where he practised as solicitor, then as barrister; publ. first volume of verse, 1819; became metropolitan commissioner in lunacy, 1832; contributed to several journals incl. *Literary Gazette* and *Edinburgh Review*; friendships incl. Lamb, Hazlitt, Leigh Hunt, Dickens, and Browning.

Text: *Dramatic Scenes, with other poems*, 1857.

## DOLLIE RADFORD (*née* Maitland) (1858–1920)

No biographical information found for her early life; married the poet Ernest Radford (a member of the Rhymers Club); publ. her first volume of verse 1891; helped Helen, William Allingham's widow, edit his diary, 1907; her last recorded publ. in 1910, where a preface mentions poems appearing in the *English Review* and other journals; later a friend of D. H. Lawrence.

Text: *A Light Load*, 1891.

## WILLIAM BRIGHTY RANDS (1823–82)

Children's writer (in prose and verse), hymn-writer and journalist; born in London; wrote under pseudonyms 'Henry Holbeach' and 'Matthew Browne' as well as his own name; worked as reporter in House of Commons; publ. first volume of verse, 1857; became known as the 'laureate of the nursery'.

Text: *Lilliput Levee*, 1864.

## WILLIAM RENTON (1852–? [*after* 1905])

No biographical information found apart from date of birth; publ. first volume of verse, 1876, and revised versions in 1905.

Text: *Oils and Water-Colours*, 1876.

## JAMES LOGIE ROBERTSON (1846–1922)

Scottish poet, teacher and essayist; born in Milnathort, a village at the foot of the Ochil hills; trained as a teacher in Edinburgh, and attended the university, where he met Robert Louis Stevenson and contributed to the University Magazine; taught at the Ladies' College in Edinburgh, 1876–1913; publ. first volume of verse, 1878; wrote dialect poems in guise of an Ochil shepherd, 'Hugh Haliburton'; contributed articles to the *Scotsman*, esp. on Scottish literary history, and edited the works of Burns and other Scottish poets.

Text: 'A Back-Lying Farm': *Poems*, 1878; 'The White Winter': *Ochil Idyls and other poems by Hugh Haliburton*, 1891.

## A(gnes) MARY F(rances) ROBINSON (Mme Darmesteter, Mme Duclaux) (1857–1944)

Born in Leamington, Warwickshire; educ. in Brussels, and later studied at University College London; her first volume of verse privately printed, 1878; close friend of the novelist Violet Paget ('Vernon Lee'); married James Darmesteter, a French scholar, 1888, and lived in Paris; after his death married Emile Duclaux, 1901.

Text: *Collected Poems*, 1902.

## WILLIAM CALDWELL ROSCOE (1823–59)

Born in Liverpool, grandson of the Liverpool banker, scholar, and poet William Roscoe (1753–1831); his father, William Stanley Roscoe, also wrote poetry; educ. University College London; his first publ. a verse tragedy, 1846; called to Bar, 1850, but relinquished practice after two years; after his marriage, 1855, lived mainly in Wales; contributed to *National Review*, of which his brother-in-law, the critic R. H. Hutton, was editor, and other journals; his verse not collected until after his death.

Text: *Poems and Essays*, ed. R. H. Hutton, 1860.

## WILLIAM STEWART ROSE (1775–1843)

Poet and translator, son of the Tory treasury minister George Rose; educ. at Eton; MP for Christchurch, 1796; reading clerk of House of Lords, 1800; friend of Walter Scott.

Text: *Rhymes*, 1837.

## CHRISTINA (Georgina) ROSSETTI (1830–94)

Born in London, daughter of Italian poet and scholar Gabriele Rossetti, a political exile who became professor of Italian at King's College, London; her mother, Frances Polidori, was the sister of Byron's physician and companion John Polidori; younger sister of D. G. Rossetti; educ. at home; volume of verse privately printed, 1847; contributed to the Pre-Raphaelite magazine *The Germ* under pseudonym 'Ellen Alleyn'; a devout High Anglican, author of devotional works in prose as well as verse; also wrote short fiction; broke off engagement to the painter James Collinson because of his return to Roman Catholicism, 1850, and later refused the scholar Charles Cayley, also on religious grounds, though they remained friends; lived at home with her mother, travelling to France (1861) and Italy (1865); publ. first commercial volume, *Goblin Market and other poems*, 1862; friendships incl. other women poets (Greenwell, Ingelow, Procter); admired Elizabeth Barrett Browning and Augusta Webster, though she argued against the latter's advocacy of female suffrage; suffered from Graves' disease and lived quietly despite her growing fame; nursed her brother through his last illness, 1882; died of breast cancer.

Publications: *Verses* (privately printed), 1847; *Goblin Market and other poems*, 1862; *The Prince's Progress and other poems*, 1866; *Commonplace and Other Short Stories* (1870); *Sing-Song: A Nursery Rhyme Book*, 1872; *Speaking Likenesses* (short fiction), 1874; *Annus Domini: a Prayer for each Day of the Year*, 1874; *A Pageant and other poems*, 1881; *Called to be Saints: the Minor Festivals Devotionally Studied*, 1881; *Time Flies: A Reading Diary*, 1885; *The Face of the Deep: A Devotional Commentary on the Apocalypse*, 1892.

Text: *Poetical Works*, ed. W. M. Rossetti, 1904.

## DANTE GABRIEL ROSSETTI (Gabriel Charles Dante Rossetti) (1828–82)

For family, see prec. entry; studied painting with Millais and Holman Hunt, with whom, and others, he formed the Pre-Raphaelite Brotherhood, 1848; publ. poems in *The Germ*, incl. 'The Blessed Damozel', 1850; in the same year met Elizabeth Siddal, whom he married, 1860; admired Browning at a time when his poetry had little popularity; other friendships incl. Tennyson and Ruskin, who supported his painting; in 1856 met William Morris, whose wife Jane became his favourite model, and his mistress; after Elizabeth Siddal's death (possibly suicide), 1862, buried some of his manuscripts with her; exhumed these in 1869 and publ. them with others, 1870; attacked by R. Buchanan as leader of 'The Fleshly School of Poetry', 1871; replied with 'The Stealthy School of Criticism', 1872; in his last years suffered from ill health, mental instability and addiction to chloral.

Publications: *The Early Italian Poets* [transl.], 1861; *Poems*, 1870 (incl. first part of the sonnet-sequence *The House of Life*); *Ballads and Sonnets*, 1881 (incl. final part of *The House of Life*); *Poems* (new edition), 1881.

Text: *Poems*, 1882 except 'Nuptial Sleep': *Poems*, 1870.

## GEORGE WILLIAM RUSSELL ('A. E.') (1867–1935)

Irish poet, painter and journalist, a leading figure in the Irish literary revival; born in Lurgan, Armagh; studied art in Dublin but gave up painting for writing, encouraged by Yeats, who also introduced him to theosophy; publ. first volume of verse, 1894; his pseudonym a contraction of 'æon'; helped to found the Abbey Theatre; edited *The Irish Homestead*, 1906–23, and *The Irish Statesman*, 1923–30.

Text: *The Earth Breath*, 1897.

## RICHARD HILL SANDYS (1801–92)

Place of birth unknown; educ. Trinity College, Cambridge; called to Bar, 1826; publ. one volume of verse only; also wrote on legal and religious subjects.

Text: *Waifs and Strays*, 1847.

## WILLIAM BELL SCOTT (1811–90)

Scottish poet and painter; born in Edinburgh; studied art in Edinburgh and London; publ. first volume of verse, 1838; became a friend of D. G. Rossetti and associate of the Pre-Raphaelites; taught in government schools of design in Newcastle upon Tyne, 1843–64; later literary friendships incl. Swinburne.

Text: The Witch's Ballad': *Poems*, 1875; 'Silence': *A Poet's Harvest Home*, 1882.

## GEORGE AUGUSTUS SIMCOX (1841–1905)

Poet and classical scholar, born in London; educ. Corpus Christi College, Oxford; contributed to several journals, incl. *North British Review* and *Nineteenth Century*; his first publ. a verse tragedy, *Prometheus Unbound*, 1867; his only other volume of verse publ. 1869; classical studies incl. a history of Latin literature, 1883; disappeared while staying at Ballycastle, near Belfast; his death possibly the result of a fall from the cliffs.

Text: *Poems and Romances*, 1869.

## JOSEPH SKIPSEY (1832–1903)

Born in Tynemouth, and worked in Northumberland coalpits from age of seven; self-taught; worked in mines and other employment until 1882; publ. first volume of verse, 1859; awarded Civil List pension, 1880; custodian of Shakespeare's birthplace at Stratford, 1889–91.

Text: *Songs and Lyrics*, 1892.

## MENELLA BUTE SMEDLEY (1820–77)

Born in London, and educ. at home by her father, a curate; publ. first volume of verse, 1856; also wrote novels and shorter fiction; for many years acted as housekeeper and amanuensis for her cousin, the novelist Frank Smedley; undertook charitable work and edited a report on pauper schools for girls for the Blue Book, 1873–4.

Text: *Poems Written for a Child: by Two Friends* [Smedley and E. A. Hart], 1868.

## ALEXANDER SMITH (1829–67)

Scottish poet and essayist, born in Kilmarnock; worked as a lace-pattern designer in Glasgow; publ. first volume of verse, 1853; associated with Sydney Dobell in Aytoun's satire on the 'Spasmodic School'; collaborated with Dobell on volume of Crimean War sonnets, 1855; secretary, and later registrar, of Edinburgh University.

Text: *City Poems*, 1857.

## WALTER C(halmers) SMITH (1824–1908)

Scottish poet and clergyman; born in Aberdeen, and educ. at Marischal College; studied at New College, Edinburgh, for ministry of Free Church; ordained 1850 and held appointments in London, at Milnathort (birthplace of James Logie Robertson), Glasgow and Edinburgh, where he was minister of the Free High Church, 1876–94, and moderator of General Assembly, 1893; publ. first volume of verse under pseudonym 'Orwell', 1861.

Text: *Poetical Works*, 1902.

## J(ames) K(enneth) STEPHEN (1859–92)

Son of the judge and controversialist Sir James Fitzjames Stephen, and cousin of Virginia Woolf; born in London; educ. Eton and King's College, Cambridge, where he belonged to the 'Apostles'; called to Bar, but devoted himself to writing and journalism; began a weekly paper, *The Reflector*, 1888; publ. his only two volumes of verse, *Lapsus Calami* and *Quo Musa Tendis?*, 1891; gradually incapacitated from an accident suffered in 1886 and died insane.

Text: *Lapsus Calami*.

## ROBERT LOUIS (Balfour) STEVENSON (1850–94)

Born in Edinburgh, the son of the engineer and meteorologist Thomas Stevenson, engineer to Board of Northern Lighthouses; studied engineering, then law, at Edinburgh University, but decided to become a writer; collaborated with W. E. Henley on a series of plays, 1880–85; achieved fame with *Treasure Island* (1883); publ. his first volume of verse, *A Child's Garden of Verses*, 1885; suffered from chronic bronchial illness for most of his life, and travelled widely in search of health, eventually settling in Samoa, where he died.

Text: selections from *A Child's Garden of Verses*, 1885; 'The Light-Keeper': *Works* (Edinburgh Edition), 1898; 'Love – what is love?': *Poems ... hitherto unpublished*, 1916.

'SURFACEMAN' *see entry for* Alexander Anderson.

## HENRY SEPTIMUS SUTTON (1825–1901)

Poet and journalist; born in Nottingham; a friend of Philip Bailey (author of the long mystic poem *Festus*) and Coventry Patmore; publ. first volume of verse, 1848; chief of *Manchester Examiner and Times* reporting staff, 1853; convert to Swedenborgianism, 1857.

Text: *Poems*, 1886.

## ALGERNON CHARLES SWINBURNE (1837–1909)

Born in London; educ. at Eton and Balliol College, Oxford, where he was a friend of D. G. Rossetti and associated with Pre-Raphaelites; other friendships incl. George Meredith and Richard Monckton Milnes, and the explorer and translator of the *Arabian Nights*, Sir Richard Burton; gained fame with publ. of verse drama in Greek form, *Atalanta in Calydon*, 1865; publ. first volume of verse, *Poems and Ballads*, 1866, attacked by R. Buchanan and others for its atheism and sado-masochistic eroticism; replied in *Notes on Poems and Reviews*; a strong supporter of Italian independence and unification; his physical and mental health undermined by alcoholic and sexual excess; restored by his friend, the critic and author Theodore Watts-Dunton, in whose house he lived from 1879; besides poetry and verse drama, wrote a considerable amount of literary criticism, incl. influential studies of Elizabethan and Jacobean dramatists, Blake, and the Brontës.

Publications: *Atalanta in Calydon*, 1865; *Poems and Ballads*, 1866; *A Song of Italy*, 1867; *Songs before Sunrise*, 1871; *Bothwell* (drama), 1874; *Songs of Two Nations*, 1875; *Erectheus* (drama), 1876; *Poems and Ballads, second series*, 1878; *Songs of the Spring Tides*, 1880; *Studies in Song*, 1880; *Mary Stuart* (drama), 1881; *Tristram of Lyonesse and other poems*, 1882; *A Century of Roundels*, 1883; *A Midsummer Holiday and other poems*, 1884; *Marino Faliero* (drama), 1885; *Poems and Ballads, third series*, 1889; *Astrophel and other poems*, 1894; *The Tale of Balen*, 1896; *A Channel Passage and other poems*, 1904.

Text: *Poems* (6 vols.), 1905.

## ARTHUR (William) SYMONS (1865–1945)

Poet, critic, translator, and journalist; born in Milford Haven; member of the Rhymers Club and friend of Yeats, George Moore, and other writers and artists of the 'aesthetic' or 'decadent' movement; publ. first volume of verse, 1889; editor of the *Savoy*, 1896; publ. work by Aubrey Beardsley, Ernest Dowson, Lionel Johnson, and others; publ. his best-known work, *The Symbolist Movement in Literature*, 1899; suffered severe nervous breakdown, 1908–9; recovered and resumed his career with help from friends incl. Edmund Gosse, and with assistance from Royal Literary Fund.

Text: *Silhouettes* (2nd edn), 1896.

**LORD DE TABLEY** *see entry for* John Byrne Leicester Warren.

**SIR HENRY TAYLOR** (1800–1886)
Verse dramatist and civil servant; born in Bishop-Middleham, Durham; employed in the Colonial Office, 1824–72, when he was knighted; friend of Wordsworth and Southey, and Southey's literary executor; gained recognition with his historical drama *Philip van Artevelde*, 1834; publ. *The Statesman*, an ironic exposition of the art of succeeding in government service, 1836; publ. only one volume of non-dramatic poems, 1847; his autobiography privately printed, 1877.
　Text: *Works*, 1877–8.

**ALFRED TENNYSON** (Lord Tennyson) (1809–92)
Born in Somersby, Lincolnshire, where his father was rector; educ. at home; publ. first volume of verse with his brothers Charles (Turner; see entry) and Frederick, 1827; at Trinity College, Cambridge, joined the 'Apostles' and formed his life's closest friendship with Arthur Hallam; other close friends incl. Edward FitzGerald, who later helped him financially; won the Chancellor's Gold Medal for poetry, 1829; his early poems (1830, 1832) ridiculed by critics; shattered by Hallam's death, 1833; almost immediately began composing poems which were to form *In Memoriam*; engaged to Emily Sellwood, 1837, but engagement broken off 1840; lost his fortune in wood-carving scheme, 1840–43; his critical reputation restored by publ. of *Poems*, 1842, which incl. revised versions of early verse as well as new work; treated in a hydropathic hospital near Cheltenham, 1843–4; granted Civil List pension, 1845; renewed engagement to Emily, 1849; had bumper year in 1850: *In Memoriam* (May), marriage (June), Poet Laureate in succession to Wordsworth (November); his fame now established and steadily increased; settled in Farringford, Isle of Wight, 1853; friends incl. Allingham, Browning (at warm distance), Lear, Patmore; began publ. of Arthurian epic, *Idylls of the King*, 1859; helped Palgrave with selection of *Golden Treasury*, 1860; built second residence, Aldworth, near Haslemere, 1868; refused knighthood, 1873 (also 1874, 1880); accepted peerage, 1883; died at Aldworth; buried in Westminster Abbey.
　Publications: *Poems by Two Brothers*, 1827; *Poems, Chiefly Lyrical*, 1830; *Poems*, 1832; *Poems*, 1842; *The Princess*, 1847; *In Memoriam*, 1850; *Maud, and other poems*, 1855; *Idylls of the King* ('Enid' [subsequently 'The Marriage of Geraint' and 'Geraint and Enid'], 'Vivien' [subsequently 'Merlin and Vivien'], 'Elaine' [subsequently 'Lancelot and Elaine'], and 'Guinevere'), 1859; *Enoch Arden and other poems*, 1864; *The Holy Grail and other poems* (four further *Idylls*: the title poem and 'The Coming of Arthur', 'Pelleas and Ettarre', and 'The Passing of Arthur'), 1869; *Gareth and Lynette* (two further *Idylls*: the title poem and 'The Last Tournament'), 1872; *Queen Mary* (play), 1875; *Harold* (play), 1876; *Ballads and other poems*, 1880; *The Cup and The Falcon* (plays), 1884; *Becket* (play), 1884; *Tiresias and other poems* (incl. 'Balin and Balan', the last of

the *Idylls* to be publ.), 1885; *Locksley Hall Sixty Years After* [and other poems], 1886; *Demeter and other poems*, 1889; *The Foresters* (play), 1892; *The Death of Oenone, Akbar's Dream, and other poems*, 1892.

Text: *Works*, ed. Hallam Tennyson, 1907–8 [Eversley edition].

## CHARLES TENNYSON *see entry for* Charles Tennyson Turner.

## WILLIAM MAKEPEACE THACKERAY (1811–63)
Born in Calcutta, the son of a Collector in the East India Company; educ. at Charterhouse School and Trinity College, Cambridge, where he became a friend of Edward FitzGerald; met Goethe in Weimar, 1830–31; called to Bar, 1831, but never practised; studied drawing in Paris; purchased a struggling weekly newspaper, the *National Standard*, 1833; after its failure, lived in Paris, 1834–7; married in 1836; his wife became insane, 1840, and was confined in an asylum; began to establish reputation as a writer, at first of humorous stories and sketches (*The Yellowplush Papers*, 1837–8; *A Shabby Genteel Story*, 1840; *The FitzBoodle Papers*, 1842–3; *The Book of Snobs*, 1846–7), later of novels (*Vanity Fair*, 1848; *Pendennis*, 1850; *Henry Esmond*, 1852); began association with *Punch*, 1842, and wrote for it until 1854; first editor of *Cornhill Magazine*, 1860; as well as fiction, light verse, and parodies, wrote miscellaneous essays and literary criticism, notably on eighteenth-century writers.

Text: *Ballads and Songs*, 1896.

## WILLIAM THOM (?1798–1848)
Scottish poet; born in Aberdeen; apprenticed as a hand-loom weaver, 1810; subsequently worked in factories in Aberdeen and Inverury; self-taught; during the economic depression of 1837, became a hawker and pedlar, and played the flute in the streets for a living; publ. his first poem in the *Aberdeen Herald*, 1841, and gained recognition and patronage; publ. *Rhymes and Recollections of a Hand-Loom Weaver*, 1844, and enjoyed brief period of critical and commercial success in London; friends incl. Eliza Cook and Mary Howitt; spent his earnings on drink and 'neglected business for unprofitable company' (*DNB*); died in poverty in Dundee.

Text: *Rhymes and Recollections of a Hand-Loom Weaver*, 3rd edn, 1847.

## FRANCIS THOMPSON (1859–1907)
Born in Preston; educ. at Ushaw College; studied medicine in Manchester but failed to qualify; became addicted to opium and lived on the streets in London, 1885–8; rescued by Alice and Wilfrid Meynell, who fostered his career as poet and literary critic; publ. first volume of verse, 1893; died of tuberculosis.

Text: *Works*, ed. W. Meynell, 1913.

## JAMES THOMSON ('B. V.') (1834–82)

Scottish poet, born in Glasgow, the son of a poor merchant seaman; educ. at Royal Caledonian Asylum School in London and trained as army schoolmaster; in Ireland, 1851–2, where he met the reformer and freethinker Charles Bradlaugh, in whose *National Reformer* many of his early poems appeared under the pseudonym 'B. V.' (from Shelley's middle name 'Bysshe' and 'Vonalis', an anagram of the name of the German poet Novalis); discharged from the army, probably for drunkenness, 1862; worked as journalist in London; travelled to Spain as war reporter, 1873; died of illness aggravated by poverty and alcoholic depression.

Text: *The City of Dreadful Night*, 1880.

## JOHN TODHUNTER (1839–1916)

Irish poet and playwright; born in Dublin; educ. Trinity College; practised medicine, 1871–4; moved to London where he was a friend of Yeats and member of the Rhymers Club; publ. first volume of verse, 1876.

Text: *The Banshee and other poems*, 1888.

## 'GRAHAM R. TOMSON' *see entry for* Rosamund Marriott Watson.

## CHARLES (Tennyson) TURNER (1808–79)

Elder brother of Alfred Tennyson (see entry); educ. Trinity College, Cambridge; publ. first volume of verse (after *Poems by Two Brothers*), 1830; ordained 1832; vicar of Grasby, Lincolnshire; changed name to Turner after inheriting a great-uncle's estate, 1835.

Text: 'Wind on the Corn': *Sonnets*, 1864; 'A Brilliant Day', 'A Photograph on the Red Gold', 'Joy Came from Heaven': *Small Tableaux*, 1868; 'Welsh Lucy': *Sonnets, Lyrics, and Translations*, 1873.

## JOHN (Byrne) LEICESTER WARREN, Lord de Tabley (1835–95)

Born at Tabley House, in Cheshire; educ. at Eton and Christ Church, Oxford; called to Bar, 1860; publ. first volume of verse, 1859; a botanist, who compiled a flora of Cheshire; succeeded to the peerage as third baron, 1887; left no descendants.

Text: *Poems, Dramatic and Lyrical*, 1893 except 'Lines to a Lady-Bird': *Collected Poems*, 1903.

## ROSAMUND MARRIOTT WATSON, *née* Ball ('Graham R. Tomson') (1860–1911)

Born in London; married George Armytage, 1878; publ. first volume of verse anonymously, 1883; divorced after her liaison with the painter Arthur Graham Tomson, whom she married, 1887; adopted pseudonym of 'Graham R. Tomson' and enjoyed considerable success; friendships incl. Edith Nesbit, Alice Meynell, and Thomas Hardy (with whom she subsequently quarrelled); contributed to journals incl. the *Yellow Book*; divorced again after liaison with the journalist H. B. Marriott Watson, with whom she lived unmarried; poetry editor of the *Athenaeum*, 1904–11.

Text: *Poems*, 1912.

### SIR (John) WILLIAM WATSON (1858–1935)

Born in Burley-in-Wharfedale, Yorkshire; father a master grocer, afterwards a merchant at Liverpool; publ. first volume of verse, 1880; gained recognition with his third volume, *Wordsworth's Grave, and other poems*, 1890; his verse admired by Gladstone; a candidate for the Laureateship in 1913 (awarded to Bridges); knighted 1917.

Text: *Epigrams of art, life, and nature*, 1884.

### (Julia) AUGUSTA WEBSTER, *née* Davies (1837–94)

Poet, essayist and translator; born in Dorset; father a vice-admiral, later chief constable of Cambridgeshire; studied at Cambridge School of Art; married Thomas Webster, a law lecturer at Trinity College, 1863; publ. first volume of verse under pseudonym 'Cecil Home', 1866; active in feminist causes, esp. education and suffrage, about which she corresponded with Christina Rossetti; member of London School Board, 1879–82.

Text: *Mother and Daughter: An Uncompleted Sonnet-Sequence*, ed. W. M. Rossetti, 1895.

### CHARLES WHITEHEAD (1804–62)

Poet, novelist and dramatist; born in London, the son of a wine-merchant; worked as a clerk; publ. first poem, *The Solitary*, 1831; recommended his friend Charles Dickens to the publishers Chapman and Hall after refusing to take part himself in project which became *Pickwick Papers*; ruined by alcoholism; emigrated to Australia, 1857; died a pauper.

Text: *The Solitary and other poems*, 1849.

### OSCAR (Fingal O'Flahertie Wills) WILDE (1854–1900)

Born in Dublin; father a noted eye surgeon; mother Jane Francesca Elgee, who wrote nationalist poetry under the pseudonym 'Speranza'; educ. at Trinity College, Dublin, then Magdalen College, Oxford, where he won the Newdigate prize for poetry, 1878; influenced at Oxford by Pater's aesthetic philosophy; publ. first volume of verse, 1881; in the same year satirized by Gilbert and Sullivan in *Patience*; cultivated the image of dandy and launched an immensely successful career as dramatist, writer of fiction, journalist and critic, which came to an end with his trial and imprisonment for homosexual offences in 1895; released 1897, and lived in France; died in Paris.

Text: *Works*, 1909.

## JAMES CHAPMAN WOODS (*fl.* 1879–1931)

No biographical information found; publ. first volume of verse, 1879, and another in 1931, incl. poems on the First World War.

Text: *A Child of the People and other poems*, 1879.

## WILLIAM WORDSWORTH (1770–1850)

Born in Cockermouth, Cumberland, the son of an attorney; educ. at Hawkshead School and St John's College, Cambridge; in France, 1791–2; supported French Revolution until advent of Terror; his affair at Blois with Annette Vallon, and the birth of an illegitimate daughter, did not become public knowledge until this century; publ. first poems, 1793; met Coleridge, *c.* 1795; settled with his sister Dorothy at Alfoxden, Somerset, near Coleridge's residence at Nether Stowey; lived at Goslar, 1798–9; publ. *Lyrical Ballads* with Coleridge, 1798; settled at Grasmere, in the Lake District, 1799; married Mary Hutchinson, 1802; his reputation gradually established after publ. of *Poems in two volumes*, 1807, though he continued to attract critical hostility; appointed distributor of stamps for Westmoreland, 1813; attacked by 'second generation' of Romantic writers (Byron, Keats, Hazlitt), and later by Browning, as political turncoat; received Civil List pension, 1842; succeeded Southey as Poet Laureate, 1843.

Text: *Poems*, 1849–50, except 'Upon the Sight of the Portrait of a Female Friend' (written 1840; first publ. 1946): *Poems*, ed. J. O. Hayden, Penguin, 1977.

## W(illiam) B(utler) YEATS (1865–1939)

Born in London of Irish Protestant family; father and brother both painters; educ. at Godolphin School in London and High School, Dublin; studied at School of Art, Dublin, with George William Russell ('A. E.'), with whom he shared an interest in mystical religion; a leading figure in the Irish literary revival, writing both critically and creatively on Irish historical myth and legend (*The Wanderings of Oisin and other poems*, 1889; *The Celtic Twilight*, 1893) and instrumental in founding a national theatre; his work also influenced by unrequited love for nationalist agitator Maud Gonne; his commitment to nationalist cause waned in early years of century, but renewed after Easter Rising, 1916; married Georgie Lee-Hyde, 1917; her experiments with 'automatic writing' influenced his development of the symbolic system which became the framework of his later writing; senator, Irish Free State, 1922–8; awarded Nobel Prize, 1923; with Russell and G. B. Shaw, founded Irish Academy of Letters, 1932; died in France, but re-interred at his childhood home, Drumcliff in Sligo, 1948.

Text: 'An Old Song Re-Sung': *The Wanderings of Oisin and other poems*, 1889; 'The Lake Isle of Innisfree', 'The Sorrow of Love': *The Countess Kathleen and Various Legends and Lyrics*, 1892; 'Breasal the Fisherman', 'The Song of Wandering Aengus', 'Aedh Laments the Loss of Love', 'The Valley of the Black Pig', 'Aedh Wishes for the Cloths of Heaven', 'The Fiddler of Dooney': *The Wind Among the Reeds*, 1899.

# Subject Index

The numbers shown are the poem numbers in the main body of the anthology (not counting the Prelude). The poems which form the Prelude are referred to by the letter 'P' and a roman numeral, e.g. P (iv) refers to the fourth poem in the Prelude, Tennyson's 'To the Queen'. Stanzas or sections of poems are indicated by roman numerals, e.g. 82 (xxx) refers to poem no. 82, section xxx. In only one case, that of Clough's Amours de Voyage, has it been necessary to complicate this scheme by using capitals for the canto numbers and lower-case for the sections: so, 135 (I v) refers to canto I, letter v of the poem.

A poem is included under one or more headings only when that heading corresponds to the main subject of the poem, or to one of its most prominent aspects, or when the poem has a definite form (sonnet, ballad, etc.). Horses, for example, appear in several poems but are the main subject of only one, no. 333 (William Renton's 'The Foal').

# Index of Proper Names

*Reference is to page number. Names of fictional people and places have not been indexed, with the exception of characters from Shakespeare. Legendary and mythological figures (e.g. Greek gods and goddesses, Arthurian knights) have been indexed. Some allusions and descriptive paraphrases in longer poems have been omitted.*

# Index of Poets

*Reference is to page number. Names are given as in the table of contents; pseudonyms (or real names) are recorded, and separately listed for the purpose of cross-reference, in the biographical notes.*

# Index of Titles

Reference is to page number. The index includes alternative titles (e.g. 'Drummer Hodge' for 'The Dead Drummer') and general titles (e.g. A Child's Garden of Verses).

# Index of First Lines

# Permissions

For permission to reprint copyright material in this anthology, the editor and publishers gratefully acknowledge as follows: for 'The Mid-World' from *The Earth Breath* (John Lane/Bodley Head, 1897) by George William Russell ('A.E.') to Colin Smythe Ltd on behalf of the Estate of Diarmuid Russell; for 'The Dodo', 'The Marmozet', 'The Camelopard' and 'The Llama' by Hilaire Belloc from *Cautionary Verses* (Random House) to the Peters Fraser & Dunlop Group Ltd on behalf of the Estate of Hilaire Belloc; for 'As I Walked Through London' by Laurence Binyon from *Poems* (Macmillan, 1895) to the Society of Authors on behalf of the Estate of Laurence Binyon; for 'On a Dead Child' by Robert Bridges from *Poetical Works of Robert Bridges* (1936) to Oxford University Press; for 'We know where deepest lies the snow' by Anne Brontë from *The Poems of Anne Brontë* (Macmillan, 1979), ed. E. Chitham, to Macmillan Ltd; for 'The Gipsy Camp', 'The red bagged bee on never weary wing', 'The thunder mutters louder and more loud', 'Look through the naked bramble and black thorn', 'I am – yet what I am, none cares or knows', 'An invite to Eternity' and 'The Shepherd Boy' from *The Later Poems of John Clare 1837–1864,* ed. Eric Robinson and David Powell (Oxford University Press, 1984) to the Curtis Brown Group Ltd; for 'Song of the Seedling', 'The Vines' and 'Spleen' by John Gray from *Silverpoints* (Elkin Mathews/John Lane, 1893) to the Dominican Order as trustees of the Gray Trust; for 'In the Old Theatre, Fiesole', 'Drummer Hodge', 'Rome: At the Pyramid', 'Lausanne', 'An August Midnight', 'The Darkling Thrush', 'The Ruined Maid', 'The Respectable Burgher', 'The Self-Unseeing', 'In Tenebris I', 'V.R. 1819–1901', 'Friends Beyond', 'Neutral Tones', 'Her Dilemma' and 'I look into my glass' by Thomas Hardy from *Thomas Hardy : The Complete Poems* (Papermac), ed. James Gibson, to Macmillan Ltd; for 'It was a hard thing to undo this knot' from *The Poems of Gerard Manley Hopkins* (Fourth Edition, 1967), ed. W. H. Gardner and N. H. MacKenzie, to Oxford University Press on behalf of the Society of Jesus; for 'Loveliest of trees, the cherry now', 'When I was one-and-twenty', 'It nods and curtseys and recovers', 'Others, I am not the first', 'Into my heart an air that kills', 'Far in a western brookland', 'I hoed and trenched and weeded', and '1887' by A. E. Housman from *A Shropshire Lad* (Kegan Paul, 1896) to the Society of Authors as the literary representative of the Estate of

A. E. Housman; for 'Danny Deever', 'Tommy', 'The Widow at Windsor' and 'Mandalay' from *Rudyard Kipling's Verse: Definitive Edition* (Hodder & Stoughton, 1940) to A. P. Watt Ltd on behalf of the National Trust; for 'Gillespie' by Sir Henry Newbolt from *Poems: Old and New* (John Murray, 1921) to Peter Newbolt; for 'Neurasthenia' and 'Twilight' by Agnes Mary Frances Robinson from *Collected Poems* (A. & C. Black, 1902) to A. & C. Black; for 'The Absinthe Drinker' by Arthur Symons from *Silhouettes* (Elkin Mathews/John Lane, 1896) to Mrs Diana P. Read; for 'Down by the Salley Gardens', 'The Lake Isle of Innisfree', 'The Sorrow of Love', 'The Fish', 'The Song of Wandering Aengus', 'The Lover Mourns for the Loss of Love', 'The Valley of the Black Pig', 'He Wishes for the Cloths of Heaven' and 'The Fiddler of Dooney' by W. B. Yeats from *The Collected Works of W. B. Yeats, Volume 1: The Poems* (Macmillan, 1989), rev. and ed. Richard J. Finneran, to A. P. Watt Ltd on behalf of Michael Yeats and Simon & Schuster.

Every effort has been made to contact or trace copyright holders. The publishers would be grateful to be notified of any additions that should be incorporated in the next edition of this volume.